The Life and Work of Pauline Viardot Garcia, Vol. I: The Years of Fame, 1836-1863

To Carol
with many thanks for being
such a good friend.
Much love, Barbara.

The Life and Work of Pauline Viardot Garcia

Vol. I: The Years of Fame, 1836-1863

by

Barbara Kendall-Davies

Cambridge Scholars Press Ltd.
London

The Life and Work of Pauline Viardot Garcia, Vol. I: The Years of Fame, 1836-1863
by Barbara Kendall-Davies

This book first published 2003 by

Cambridge Scholars Press

119 Station Road, Amersham, Buckinghamshire, HP7 0AH UK

British Library Cataloguing in Publication Data
A catalogue record for this book is available from the British Library

ISBN 1-904303-27-7

To Chris Davies,
my fellow traveller

CONTENTS

ILLUSTRATIONS

ACKNOWLEDGEMENTS

I am indebted to many people in the research and writing of this book, namely Professor Alexandre Zviguilsky, the Tourgueniev scholar and writer who first encouraged me to write about Pauline Viardot, and published my monograph in Cahiers No. 22 (1998), 'Association d'Amis d'Ivan Tourgueniev, Pauline Viardot et Maria Malibran'; the late April Fitzlyon, author of the first English biography of Viardot, 'The Price of Genius'; Professor Patrick Waddington, for his chronology of Viardot Songs, for permission to use his unpublished Ph.D thesis 'Courtavenel - The History of an Artist's Nest and its Role in the Life of Turgenev', and for supplying the illustrations 'Night-time ablutions at Courtavenel' and a sketch of Tourgueniev by Pauline Viardot; Carole Russell Law, founder of the Malibran Society; Joan Boytim of the Voice Studio, Pennsylvania, and Mme Veronique Ayroles of the Musee de la Vie Romantique, Paris, who all supplied me with Viardot songs; Professor Nicolas Zekulin of Calgary university for his thesis on Tourgueniev's life in Baden Baden; Dr. Robert Ignatius Letellier, the Meyerbeer scholar, who was instrumental in getting this book published; Gillian Margolis, B.A., who introduced me to Dr. Letellier; Dr. Celine Peslerbes for allowing me to read her unpublished thesis 'french Musicians in London in the 19th Century'; the music critic Andrew Porter for information on Viardot's preparation for Lady Macbeth; Brian Thompson, author of 'A Monkey Among Crocodiles' for his comments regarding Gounod's sexuality; my publisher, Dr. Andy Nercessian, for his faith in this book; the librarian Tom Gillmor, for his patience and courtesy in leading me through the labyrinth of Mary Evans Picture Library'; to my singing teachers, Mary Parsons, L. R. A. M., A. R. C. M, (who is still teaching at the age of ninety-six): the late Professor Walter Gruner, of the Guildhall School Music and Drama, both of whom informed me about the Garcia family; Mme Mohini Singh, my French teacher; the mezzo Jean Hornbuckle, M. A., and Pat Turner, B. A., for reading early drafts of the work; to the Association of Teachers of Singing who invited me to talk about Viardot and sing her songs at their 2001 Conference; my pianist, jillian Skerry, who drove me around France in search of Viardot, and recorded the CD with me; my husband, baritone Christopher Davies, M.A. (Cantab) for his unfailing love and support and his fine singing of the Viardot songs; to my son, baritone Giles Davies, who prepared the illustrations; to my nephew, the conductor Steven Lloyd, Ray Ricchiardi and Alex Vella for their helpful advice, and finally to my sisters, Mary and Suzy Kendall, and my many friends and students who have been a source of encouragement. I have endeavoured to produce an authentic document, and any errors which may have inadvertently crept in are purely my own responsibility.

NOTES ON THE TRANSLITERATION

With regard to the spelling of Russian names, where these are familiar to English readers, I have used the accepted spelling, but in the case of Tourgueniev, I have adopted the French form as it is closer to its true pronunciation than the anglicized 'Turgenev'.

PROLOGUE

The famous, wealthy, beautiful, charismatic, opera singer, Maria Malibran, the elder sister of Pauline Garcia, was dead, the victim of a riding accident at the age of twenty eight, mourned not only by her husband and family, but by a devoted public across the whole of Europe.

During May and June, 1836, she had been singing in London, but in July she visited the Surrey home of her friend, Lord Lennox. She was pregnant and her second husband, the young Belgian violinist, Charles de Beriot, had forbidden her to ride, but when a group of friends asked her to join them, she was too tempted to refuse. Although she was a fine horsewoman, her borrowed mount was mettlesome, and difficult to control. Suddenly he took to his heels, she was unseated, her foot caught in a stirrup and she was dragged several hundred yards before the horse was finally brought to a halt by one of her companions. Badly shocked and bruised, particularly about the face and head, she swore her friends to secrecy. Back at home, she told Charles that she had fallen down stairs, and he believed her. Despite her severe injuries, she insisted on fulfilling all her engagements during the next few weeks, performing roles that would have taxed a woman in the best of health.

When their engagements in London ended, the de Beriots returned to their home at Ixelles near Brussels. As Maria's bruises were now fading, her mother Joaquina Garcia and fifteen year old Pauline, who lived with her and Charles, were unaware of how badly she had been hurt. She could not deceive herself, however, and realized that there was something terribly wrong. The only person she confided in was Pauline, who was sworn to secrecy. Maria was a volatile creature and had always experienced sudden mood swings but now her behaviour became totally unpredictable. Everyone blamed this on the effects of pregnancy, not realizing the extent of the devastating internal injuries she had so recently sustained.

Pauline Garcia was also a talented musician, whose ambition was to become a concert pianist. On the 14th August, at Liege, she gave her first public concert with Maria, and de Beriot, who was well known in the region, having first performed there in 1825. Maria was extremely proud of Pauline, who accompanied her at the piano, and played a duet with Charles. The King of Prussia was on holiday at Aix la Chapelle, 40 km from Liege, and he requested Maria, Pauline and de Beriot to give a concert, and for Maria to perform the role of Amina in two performances of 'La Sonnambula'. Maria was treated like royalty herself, as the King sent the band of the Royal Guard to greet her arrival.

The de Beriots had a country house at Roissy-en-Brie in France, which they had intended to visit, but leaving Aix, they made a detour in order to give a concert in Lille in northern France on the 27th August. This had been announced in the 'L'Echo du Nord' on the 20th, and it was more convenient to spend a couple of days resting at Ixelles before setting out for Lille.

The concert took place at the Academie royale de musique, and despite Maria's indisposition was an enormous success. Of course no one knew that this would be the last time she would appear in France, and indeed, she sang the Cavatina from 'Ines de Castro' by Persiani, and the closing scene of 'La Sonnambula', with all her customary elan and brilliance, and Pauline and de Beriot played the duet he had composed on themes from the same opera. The second part of the concert began with the overture 'Les Francs Juges' by Berlioz, and ended with French romances sung by Maria. At the finale of such a delightful evening of music, no one could possibly have suspected that her career was drawing to its premature close.

At the beginning of September, the de Beriots were at last able to go to Roissy, where they enjoyed a few days of well earned rest, then, on the 14th September, they left for England where they were engaged to take part in a music festival in the northern city of Manchester. Another singer who had been engaged for the festival was the seventeen year old soprano Clara Novello, a member of the famous publishing family, who was chaperoned by her mother, Sybilla. Mrs. Novello had not seen Maria for a while and was shocked by her appearance; she looked so dreadfully ill that the older woman insisted that she should see a doctor. His diagnosis was that Maria had suffered internal injury, but he couldn't confirm if the baby was still alive, and asked for a second opinion.

In the meantime, Maria carried on with her concerts, and on the 23rd September, she sang a duet with Mme Caradori-Allan which was encored, but she turned to the conductor, Sir George Smart, and whispered: "If I sing again it will kill me," thoroughly alarmed, Sir George exclaimed: "then dear madame, please do not". Assured that she could not disappoint her audience, he took up his baton, and the orchestra began the opening bars of the duet, but all her strength had finally drained away, and she collapsed.

Charles was backstage, waiting to play his next solo, unaware that his unconcious wife was being carried out of the hall. Never was the term 'the show must go on' more fully realized, and the performance continued as Maria was taken to the Mosley Arms Hotel where she and her husband were staying. Mrs. Novello accompanied her and sent for the doctor. The singer had no maid with her, but her friend prevailed upon the landlady to act as nurse, and when the doctor arrived he was accompanied by a colleague. Both men examined the patient and ascertained that the baby was dead, and that, in their considered opinion, the young mother was beyond help. By the time Charles arrived all was over; Maria had died at five minutes to midnight, without regaining consciousness.

The young man's reaction to his wife's death was desperate, driven almost mad with shock and grief, he went completely to pieces. The doctors, concerned for his state of mind, advised him to go home immediately, and within a very short time, he was well clear of Manchester, leaving the authorities to make plans for the funeral. This precipitous behaviour, when it became known, caused a great deal of gossip in the city; some people declared that it showed a guilty conscience, particularly as he had left orders that no death mask was to be made, and rumours spread that Charles had poisoned Maria for her fortune.

When her mother learned what had happened, she realised that despite her grief, she would have to go to England to sort out the mess that Charles had left behind. His sister agreed to look after the household, and Joaquina prepared for the long journey, only pausing to write a letter informing her son, Manuel Garcia, who lived in Paris, of his sister's death.

Once the news was made public, there was a palpable outpouring of grief by Maria's loyal admirers. Everyone had taken this rare spirit to their hearts; she had charmed them, made them laugh or weep with equal skill, excited them, uplifted them, transported them, and they worshipped her. Even the people who knew nothing about opera knew about Mme Malibran, of her concern for the poor, and her generous charitable gifts.

By the time Joaquina Garcia arrived in Manchester, Maria's funeral had already taken place. The weather had been dismal and wet, but it had not deterred several thousand people from lining the streets to see the sad cortege pass on its way to the cemetery. The burial took place, and the authorities considered that they had done their best for Maria; when Joaquina told them that she desired to take her daughter's body back to Belgium, they were extremely reluctant to allow an exhumation, and she had a difficult time trying to persuade them. At last her persistence paid off and she was allowed to take Maria to her last resting place in the cemetery of Laeken near Brussels. Charles, as a way of assuaging his grief, carved a marble bust of his young wife with a laurel wreath on her head. This was placed on a plinth, at the base of which sat an angel playing a lyre, within a monument decorated with classical motifs – his last gift to the remarkable woman he had loved.

CHAPTER ONE

Maria Malibran's death was not the first time Pauline had lost someone close to her. Four years previously, in 1832, her beloved father Manuel del Popolo Vicente Garcia, had died suddenly from a pulmonary infection at the age of fifty-seven. He had been a powerful personality, virile and strong, a man who had carved fame from the harsh rock of life, and his sudden death had been unexpected and devastating.

His had been the proverbial rags to riches story: born into a poor gypsy family in Seville, orphaned at an early age, he had, by his good looks, remarkable personal charm, and outstanding musical talent, become a famous tenor and reputable composer at an age when many young men are just beginning their studies. From his birth he had been surrounded by Spanish gypsy music, rich in Moorish influences, and at the age of seven, his singing won him a place in the choir of Seville Cathedral: by the age of seventeen, he was already making a name for himself in his native Spain, and the portrait of him by Goya, painted when he was in his early twenties, shows a well-built, handsome, confident young man at the height of his powers.

The Garcia children's mother, Joaquina Sitches, met Manuel when as an aspiring young soprano of twenty-two she was engaged to sing in the Madrid opera company where he was under contract as a principal tenor. His history is somewhat mysterious, but it appears that at that time, he was married to another member of the company, Manuela de Morales, who sang indifferently but danced well. Manuel had a young daughter, Josepha, and it is presumed that Manuela was her mother, although this is by no means certain, and the girl could have been his illegitimate child.

Soon the tenor and the new soprano were playing their love scenes offstage, as well as on, and despite his married state, and the sense of guilt, which Joaquina experienced, as a 'good' Catholic, they embarked on a passionate affair. The young singer was attracted by the tenor's good looks and dynamic personality, but in addition he intrigued her because he was evasive about his past. No doubt Joaquina puzzled Manuel, as much as he did her, because she was not completely honest about her background either, and in later years her children wove some interesting myths around their parents.

It was alleged that she came from a noble family, and had been about to take her vows as a nun when Manuel had rescued her from the convent. Whatever the truth of the matter, like the tenor, Joaquina covered her tracks well and little is known about her early life, although the story about Manuel rescuing her sounds plausible enough, considering his fearless character. For example, if she had been an illegitimate child from a noble family, she might well have been placed in a convent, where it would have been convenient to have left her to avoid explanations and embarrassment, particularly if it had been her mother who had transgressed. Many illegitimate girls of 'noble' parentage were 'dumped' in convents, and very few of them professed to a religious vocation. As the writings of Casanova, the eighteenth century philanderer show, convents were meeting places, where daring young men tried their luck with the youthful inmates.

Convent services need singers, and it is possible that Joaquina received her musical training in such a place. Nuns are often good singers and teachers, and this could explain why she was able to join an operatic company as a principal soprano at the age of twenty-two. However, this is mere speculation.

Garcia had a passionate nature and violent temper, and it was whispered that he had once killed a man, although this was never proved. He was someone who found it easy to lead a double life, and caused tongues to wag furiously when he, his wife, and his mistress appeared on stage together. He was accused of being 'like a sultan in his harem', and the theatre management received complaints from the public calling for his dismissal, when scandalous articles appeared in the newspapers. Such was his fierce reputation, however, that his employers decided discretion was the better part of valour and left him alone.

On March 17th, 1805, Joaquina gave birth to Garcia's son, whom they called Manuel Patrizio. His baptismal certificate stated that he was the legitimate son of Manuel Rodriguez Garcia and Joaquina Sitches, but this was not true because it appeared that Manuel was already married, and divorce was not allowed in Spain at that time. On the other hand, Garcia might have been living with Manuela without benefit of clergy, although it is unlikely. For Joaquina's peace of mind, Garcia agreed to a church ceremony, but it was only possible because the priest who officiated was unaware of Garcia's true marital status.

Many years later, Pauline told a friend that her father believed in neither God nor Devil, so it is unlikely that he was bothered by the fact that his 'marriage' was not authentic in the eyes of the Church. But Joaquina, who had been indoctrinated in Catholicism from early childhood, was very perturbed by this state of affairs, and she sacrificed her good name by playing the part of Manuel's mistress, rather than openly posing as his wife because she feared that he would be arrested for bigamy, if the true facts were discovered.

On stage, Garcia's presence was electrifying, and with his dark good looks, brilliant eyes, fine figure and dark curly hair, he made a great impression on the public. His energy was prodigious, and he was nothing if not enterprising: a fine actor, he was also a prolific composer, concocting tonadillas and operettas by the score. His fame continued to grow in Madrid, and other parts of Spain, but his ambition was to shine in the Parisian musical firmament, then considered the mecca for musicians. In 1807, when he was thirty-two, he left Spain in the company of his two 'wives' and two children to try his luck in the French capital, where, on March 24th, 1808, Joaquina gave birth to her second child, Maria Felicite, at 3 rue de Conde.

It seems pretty certain that Garcia's niece found it difficult to endure the unorthodox life-style into which she had been plunged, because she left Paris in April, 1808, and returned to Spain where she was engaged for a season at the Coliseo de la Cruz. After this, she lost contact with her husband, and Joaquina, and young Josepha remained in Paris with Manuel, who, from the time he settled in France, passed her off as his 'niece'. This child later became a professional singer, and sang in Italy under the name of Giuseppina Garcia Ruez, appearing in operas with Maria, and Manuel Patrizio's wife Eugenie Mayer, on many occasions. Her parental status caused her some difficulty because she had been brought up as Garcia's neice, and nobody was quite sure if she was Maria's cousin or really her sister.

Through the good offices of the well-known Italian composer Ferdinando Paer, Garcia had his first big success in France, singing for the first time in Italian, in Paer's 'Griselda', after which he soon became established as one of the most popular singers in Paris.

In 1811, Garcia was engaged as Principal Tenor to the Court Chapel in Naples, where Joachim Murat reigned supreme, having been placed on the Neopolitan throne by the Emperor Napoleon in 1808.. Manuel and Joaquina, together with Josepha, six year old Manuel, and three year old Maria, enjoyed a comfortable life in the southern Italian city, and it was here that Garcia laid the foundations for his vocal dynasty.

Naples was famous for its singing tradition, which had been promulgated by Niccola Porpora, who was born in the city in 1686, becoming the most eminent teacher of his day, and was responsible for the training of two of the most famous singers of their epoch, the castrati Farinelli, and Caffarelli, the vocal superstars of their day.

Garcia met several elderly castrati who had been trained in this bel canto tradition, and they were pleased to share their vocal and musical knowledge with the enthusiastic, clever young tenor. In the seventeenth and eighteenth centuries, the Roman Catholic Church would not allow women to sing in church services, but musical compositions needed soprano voices. Those of boy trebles are short-lived, as the high voice is lost at puberty, therefore, the authorities had to find a way to stop the onset of puberty in order to extend the high childhood voice into adulthood. This was achieved by an operation, whereby young boys were castrated before the advent of puberty, retained their high voices, and the needs of church music were served, without recourse to the use of female voices!

The boys who survived the operation grew very large bodies, which gave them an incredible power and strength, not available to female soprani. The best of them made a truly amazing sound, their voices having the brilliance trumpets, with superb carrying power, ideal for the enormous Baroque buildings, such as St. Peters in Rome, in which they sang.

Of course, by the time Garcia arrived in Naples, the practice of castration was frowned upon, and gradually a more humane attitude prevailed and the barbarism ceased, although in some places it took a long time to eradicate it completely, due to the recalcitrance of certain hard line clerics who still refused to allow women to take part in services.

There is a recording from the beginning of the twentieth century, of a castrato by the name of Moreschi, who although not one of the best examples of this genre, is the only indication we have of how they would have sounded. The enormity of the abuse done to the bodies of these boys is not to be minimised, but their vocal training was second to none, and it was this knowledge that the old singers passed on to Garcia.

Singers were taught as exhaustively and intensively as instrumentalists, because the voice was looked upon as an instrument, and they learned to do the most fantastic vocal gymnastics, as well as becoming first rate musicians and capable composers, who devised their own musical ornamentation, known as 'point d'orgue'. This style of improvisation was extremely fashionable throughout the whole of the eighteenth century, but finally, performers went too far and towards the middle of the nineteenth century, composers decided that excessive decoration imposed on their original compositions made them unrecognisable, so they began to write exactly what they wanted to hear, thereby limiting the singers' high flights of musical fancy.

The years, Garcia spent in Naples were invaluable to him, and later to his children, who all benefited from their father's knowledge as singer and teacher.

It was here that he met and became a great friend of the Italian composer Giaocchino Rossini, himself an expert on voice, who wrote the role of Count Almaviva in 'The Barber of Seville' for him. As the 'Barber' was written for Rome, Rossini took into account the fact that musical pitch there was low, and wrote all the parts higher, which caused difficulties when performed in other cities where pitch was tuned higher than in Rome.

After a while the Garcias returned to France and Manuel was engaged at the Paris Opera, then considered the foremost opera house in Europe. He divided his time between the French capital and London where he became the leading tenor, singing in concerts and opera seasons at Drury Lane with the famous soprano Eliza Vestris, who also managed the theatre.

In 1820, twelve years after the birth of Maria, Joaquina conceived her last child, and on July18th, 1821, Michelle Ferdinande Pauline made her appearance. Her god-parents were Ferdinando Paer, who represented the world of music, and Princess Pauline Galitzine, a member of the Russian aristocracy, who was a leading figure in high society, two elements which would play an increasingly important part in the future life of Pauline, as she was called.

The baby grew up surrounded by adults, with few companions of her own age, in an environment full of music. Her parents were not in their first youth when she was born, and her brother and sister were already in their teens, which probably accounted for the fast progress she made as a child. Her intelligence showed itself early, as did her musical talents, and to her father she came as an unexpected gift, and he treated her far more fondly and tenderly than he had ever done to her siblings.

Garcia was an exciting, complicated man, very creative, but also very erratic, with violence never far beneath the surface, making him a difficult man with whom to live. In the early days of their marriage, Joaquina often suffered at his hands, being brutally treated when he lost control of his temper, but she was always loyal to him, although she shed many tears in private, and found it especially hard to bear when he was physically harsh with the children.

From childhood, both the younger Manuel and Maria were extraordinarily musically gifted, but neither of them had a voice of naturally outstanding quality. Garcia decided that by dint of hard work they could develop into first-rate singers, and put them through a gruelling apprenticeship. As a teacher he had little patience, and treated them with great severity.

Maria was often in tears at her lessons, and there is a story that one day two passers-by heard cries and screams coming from the Garcia house. When one of the men showed alarm and said they must go and see what they could do to help the victim, the other replied laconically, 'Oh, it's only Garcia giving a singing lesson to his daughter."

Although he was usually kinder in his dealings with Pauline because she always seemed to know things without having to be taught, she later remembered a time when he had given her a lesson, and she had failed to read correctly, a phrase he had written. He shouted 'pay attention' so loudly that the little child became distraught. He told her to do it again, but once more she got it wrong. He became even more angry, and cried, 'will you pay attention?'. Pauline tried again, and shaken to the core, actually got it right. Her father turned on her and said, "why didn't you do it the first time with the same care you applied at the last?" Years later she said that this had been a profound lesson to her, and accounted for her life long search for excellence and her great capacity for taking pains in whatever she attempted.

In 1825, Garcia decided to conquer 'the new world', and formed an Italian Opera Company, which he took to New York The nucleus of this team consisted of his own family, with himself as principal tenor, his twenty-year-old son as principal baritone, Maria, who was now seventeen, as the prima donna and Joaquina as the seconda donna, together with other singers for the comprimario roles. He intended to recruit orchestra and chorus when he arrived in New York, where they would be the first company to perform fully staged performances of Italian opera.

Pauline, who was now four years old, accompanied her family. When they disembarked on the 7th November, Garcia was surprised to be met by an elderly Italian gentleman who introduced himself as Lorenzo da Ponte. This was the man who had been Court Poet to Joseph II of Austria, and Wolfgang Amadeus Mozart's librettist He was delighted when he learned that the Garcias were to perform 'his' 'Don Giovanni', and took a proprietary interest in the proceedings. Pauline soon knew this work by heart, because she was always in the theatre during rehearsals and performances.

Although written for a bass baritone, Garcia sang the title role, and was thought to be an ideal interpreter, although musically, he must have made a lot of changes and transpositions in order to sing it comfortably; a practice that would never be countenanced today, when it is strictly baritone or bass territory.

From Pauline's earliest years her father realized that she showed exceptional musical talent, and although she was still so young, he engaged Marcos Vega to give her piano lessons. He had already taught her the rudiments of music and she knew her notes, and could play little pieces that he had written specially for her. Her progress with Vega was extraordinarily speedy, and some years later, she said that she couldn't remember a time when she had not known music.

The New Yorkers, many of whom were Italian immigrants, came to the Park Theatre in droves in order to enjoy such novel, exotic fare, and the company went from strength to strength, artistically and financially rewarded. Rossini's 'Barber of Seville' was a particular favourite with audiences, especially with Maria as the young heroine, Rosina, who is courted by Count Almaviva (played by her father). When Rossini was composing the opera, he had asked Garcia to write a serenade for the Count to sing at the beginning of the first act, as he was too busy to do so himself!

Maria had developed into a fine actress, full of fire, and spirit, and her voice had become a warm, fluid mezzo soprano of extensive range, sustained by a superb vocal technique, but it was her extraordinary personal magnetism which truly captivated her audiences. She had that charisma which cannot be acquired, as it is, seemingly, a gift from God, and constitutes what is perceived as 'star quality', something which cannot be defined, but which is immediately apparent to the public.

Manuel sang Figaro, with ease and aplomb, but his heart wasn't in performing, and he intended to follow some other career when he eventually returned to France. Joaquina played the servant, Bertha, gaining warm applause for her fine singing in her one aria, and for the humour she extracted from the relatively small character role.

All went splendidly for several months, and Garcia had few complaints, except, perhaps, that his own operas were not as popular as those of Rossini and Mozart. However, his world was turned upside down when Maria suddenly declared that she was getting married and retiring from operatic life. Her prospective husband, Eugene Malibran, a French banker, resident in New York, was only five years younger than her father. But he was reputed to be wealthy, and despite parental opposition, Maria married him in a civil ceremony conducted by the French Consul on March 22nd, 1826, two days before her eighteenth birthday, and followed this with a blessing at a Catholic church the next day.

For a short time, she continued to perform her roles while her father strove to find someone to replace her, but then retired from the stage to concentrate on being a wife. It was a double blow to Garcia who had not only lost a daughter, but had forfeited his exceptionally popular prima donna. With Maria gone, audiences began to decline, and soon the New Yorkers decided that they were tired of Italian Opera and looked for further novelties. Garcia decided to move on, heading for Mexico, where he looked forward to speaking Spanish, and mixing with descendants of his own people.

The company performed en route, but conditions were not easy with such large distances to cover before the establishment of railways, nor were artistic requirements easily come by. On one occasion, it was discovered that the orchestral parts for 'The Barber' had been left behind at the last port of call, and it was too far to go back to fetch them. Making the best of things, Garcia wrote them all out from memory! At each new town he had to enrol choristers, teach them their parts and direct rehearsals, as well as recruit instrumentalists. By present day standards it must have been a very hit and miss affair, but Garcia over-flowed with energy and enthusiasm, and he and his wife and son held everything together by their talent, expertise, experience and determination.

Fortunately, they profited financially, and all went well until they reached Vera Cruz, where they were set upon by bandits who robbed them of all their belongings and $6,000 in gold. Pauline remembered this experience vividly until her dying day, and often spoke of it. She recalled how her mother had held her tightly and told her to keep quiet, and how the grown ups had jumped and danced with delight as the men rode away, leaving them without possessions, but alive and unhurt. Little Pauline, however, cried over the loss of her tiny red jacket, which the robber chief had taken, riding off with it draped over his shoulder.

Somehow, the Garcias were able to borrow sufficient funds to get their company back to France, arriving in Paris in 1829. To their surprise, Maria was already in the city, enjoying her celebrity as an up and coming prima donna, thanks to Rossini, who, having heard her sing at a soiree, used his considerable influence to promote her career. Shortly after her marriage, she had discovered that her husband was not rich, but actually, deeply in debt. She decided that the only way to help him was to resume her career in order to make substantial sums of money, and set sail for France without further ado. Although it has usually been assumed that this was a marriage of convenience, a letter which Eugene wrote to friends when he first met Maria, makes it clear that he was really in love with her, and those she wrote to him, when she first arrived in France, were friendly and affectionate and gave the impression that she intended to return to America when she had earned sufficient funds. But in the event, she did not go back, the marriage was over in·all but name, and they never lived together again.

When she discovered that her family had returned to France, she was alarmed and dreaded coming under her father's dictatorship again. She volunteered to pay him a regular sum each month if he promised not to interfere in her life, but he was highly insulted and told her to keep her money. Maria was in a state of panic, and it is clear that she really feared her father, not only for what he might do to her, but for the almost supernatural power he exercised over her.

In 'Otello' and 'The Barber', which they had often sung together, Maria and Garcia had been cast as lovers, and this must have been psychologically difficult for the young girl. In her biography of Maria, April Fitzlyon goes further and hints that there was something dark and incestuous about their relationship. There are certainly disturbing aspects of Maria's character and behaviour, which point to a tormented and restless soul. Despite her natural high spirits and generous nature, she often indulged in frenetic activity, followed by bouts of deep depression and melancholy, and suffered dreadfully from insomnia. These symptoms, indicative of manic depression in the light of modern research, could imply sexual abuse in her childhood and youth.

In 1829, she met and fell in love with Charles de Beriot, who, at that time, was in love with the famous German soprano Henrietta Sontag. This lady was not interested in Charles and later married an Italian diplomat, the Count di Rossi. Maria, although still officially married to Malibran, was determined to win Charles's affection. She listened to his love-sick moans of unrequited love, and consoled him so well that he out-grew his infatuation for Henrietta and fell in love with her instead.

Pauline was at an impressionable age, and it is likely that the bourgeois aspect of her character stemmed from her memories of the fuss the family made over Maria's illicit affair. When she became pregnant they were horrified, and their paranoid fear of scandal was something that had a great effect on Pauline's adult moral attitude. Even when she became a member of the theatrical profession herself, she valued respectability to an inordinate extent. To her, social acceptance was essential, and she held herself aloof from colleagues with loose morals. All her life, she had a strong sense of self preservation, and a resolute will power, and there is little doubt that these were inculcated by Maria's fall from grace, and the reactions of her parents.

The Garcia's attitude is easy to understand, despite appearing hypocritical, because they had done exactly the same as Maria was now doing, and the experience had hardened their resolve to do nothing to cause their own social standing to be examined too closely. They had assiduously striven for an honorable reputation in Parisian society, and were not prepared to throw it away. Manuel was gradually retiring from public performances and concentrating on establishing himself as a fashionable teacher of singing, attracting pupils from the higher echelons of society, who paid him substantial fees. His success depended on his reputation, not only as a famous tenor, but as a gentleman.

Of course, many people in French society had affairs, and as long as everything was kept discreet, there was tacit acceptance, but illegitimacy caused grave disquiet, as it was relatively easy for a woman to pass off another man's child as that of her husband.

Maria endeavoured to keep her condition secret for as long as possible and in the meantime, her professional life continued to prosper. As it happened, her baby only survived for two days after its birth, and she quickly returned to her glittering career. Her fame grew increasingly, particularly in Italy and England, and she became known ever more widely, with numerous articles about her in the newspapers, and prints of her portraits, and figurines selling in their thousands.

Much to her family's chagrin, just as they were breathing a sigh of relief that all had settled down, Maria became pregnant again, but suffered a miscarriage, and it was only with her third pregnancy in 1833 that a healthy child was born. This was her son, Charles Wilfred, another member of the family who was destined to become a musician. Despite her private troubles, Maria could do little wrong as far as her career was concerned and her operatic progress continued triumphantly, but her over-riding ambition was to have her marriage to Malibran annulled so she could marry Charles. In this she was assisted by two family friends, the statesman General de Lafayette, and a lawyer, Louis Viardot, who undertook to investigate the legal possibilities for her.

It took some time, but at last, in 1836, the annulment was granted and she and Charles became man and wife. This was opportune because Maria was pregnant again, but six months after her marriage to Charles, she and the child were dead. Ironically, Eugene Malibran died six weeks later.

With Maria's death, Pauline's life changed irrevocably, and she matured quickly. It had always been assumed by her family that she was destined to be a pianist because that was what she wished for herself.

She was almost eight when the Garcias returned from America. Her studies with Marcos Vega had turned her into a competent pianist, and her father considered that she was advanced enough to play for some of his lessons. She loved working with him and his students, and learned a great deal about his method by listening to what he said to them.

As Joaquina and Charles began to accept the fact that Maria had gone for ever, they turned their attention to Pauline, and came to the conclusion that she should forget her ambition to become a concert pianist, and begin to study singing seriously. Their aspiration was that she should aim to take her sister's place as a prima donna of renown, and they began to map out a career for her. No sooner had this idea taken hold, than Joaquina took charge, as Pauline's vocal teacher. The girl was given no choice in the matter, and at first was not happy at being told to forget her dreams of being a female Franz Liszt. She no longer had any leisure for her own pleasures or interests, because her mother and Charles scheduled her time, making the study of singing her priority.

Of course, Pauline had always sung, having been surrounded by singers since babyhood, and to her, it was as natural as breathing. Her mother proved to be a fine teacher, possessing more patience than her husband, as she was less volatile, and had a calmer disposition. Pauline, although young, made swift progress as she was already a good musician, and was able to concentrate wholly on vocal technique. As her voice developed, she began to enjoy herself, and worked hard at her studies. She was a girl with a great capacity for work, and was so diligent that her family nicknamed her 'the ant'.

After her return to France, Pauline studied the piano with Meysenberg for a while, but her next teacher was the fascinating Franz Liszt, who, although only ten years her senior, was already a celebrity. She had a schoolgirl crush on him, and later said that it was a 'veritable amour', and that she trembled from head to foot at the thought of her lessons with him. He was tall, fair and handsome, with sharply defined good looks, always set off by the most elegant clothes, and he possessed a hypnotic personality. Women fell at his feet in droves and he was one of the very first of the 'superstars'. As well as attracting musicians and music lovers, his concerts were full to overflowing with impressionable young women, who would go to any lengths to obtain souvenirs of his presence, such as cutting pieces of upholstery from his piano stool, and tearing his gloves into ribbons, then fighting to obtain the pieces to keep as mementoes.

He was the lover of the Countess Marie d'Agoult, a wealthy woman from an aristocratic Frankfurt family, six years his senior, who had given up everything for him, her reputation, her husband and her two children. They had run away to Switzerland together, where Marie soon became pregnant.

Pauline's vocal training was very intensive and soon she was advanced enough to consider a public appearance. Although everyone has a voice, that of the professional classical singer has to be painstakingly built-up stage by stage. It is usually taken for granted that some people are simply born with better voices than others, and to a certain extent that is true, but even those most naturally gifted have to form their instrument and develop vocal stamina through strengthening the muscles of the larynx, as well as those of the body, before they can learn to 'play' the voice. The development of a beautiful, true tone is also of paramount importance.

Pauline's mother had received a fine grounding in the vocal arts, not least from her husband, who had benefited tremendously from the period he spent in Naples, and Pauline gained from her parents' vocal knowledge and experience, first when she played for her father's classes, of which she said 'I think I profited by the lessons even more than the pupils did'.and then through her mother's expertise. She later told the German conductor, Julius Rietz that she still possessed pages of exercises and vocal pieces, which her father had written for her when she was a small child, and that they were as difficult as anything she encountered in her adult life. She said that she believed she had sung them almost as well then, as she did when she was a more experienced singer. Her mother also composed pieces for her to sing in her lessons in order to illustrate and develop certain technical points.

After a year, Pauline had progressed so well that Joaquina and de Beriot decided that she was ready to spread her wings. Of course, she had already performed in public in 1836, but as a pianist, now she was to appear with Charles as a singer at an important charity concert in Brussels on the December13[th] 1837, in front of the King and Queen of Belgium, the Prince de Ligne, the diplomatic corps, and members of the aristocracy, in a large hall at the magnificent, Gothic, Hotel de Ville, situated in a great square in the heart of the city. De Beriot was already a celebrity in his native land, and later virtually founded the Belgian School of violin playing, which became world famous, but Pauline was an unknown quantity, and there was much curiosity about the sister of the 'Divine Malibran'.

The young singer took great trouble with her appearance; she loved clothes and was blessed with style and elegance. She was intelligent enough to know that she was no beauty, and that, in fact, many people considered her ugly with her pale, olive skin and exotic looks, but she knew that her figure was trim and that if she took trouble with her toilette and was stylish, she could look her best, feeling comfortable and happy with herself; but what to wear? Her choice fell on a gown of ivory silk, very plain but extremely elegant. The bodice was tightly fitted with a boat shaped neckline, trimmed with fine blonde lace; the skirt was long and full, gathered into tiny pleats at the waist, and balloon sleeves and elbow length gloves. Her deep jet hair was parted in the middle, and simply dressed with silk ribbons and cream flowers pinned to the back of her head. Her only jewellery was a simple gold chain with a cross.

The audience was moved at the sight of this slender girl, with her lustrous eyes and sparkling smile, who looked so youthful and vulnerable, but who, although by no means as beautiful as her sister, had her own fascination and charm. This concert was a test to see how well she could control her considerable nervousness before such a distinguished audience, but she need not have worried because as soon as she began to sing, she was immersed in the music and had no time to think of herself. The beautiful, rich, dark quality of her middle voice began to reveal itself and sent a shiver of remembrance through her audience – the timbre of her voice was so like that of La Malibran, and if they closed their eyes, they could imagine that she had returned to them.

She sang 'The Diavolessa' a rather strange, very demanding and brilliant aria from an opera buffa by Galuppi, triumphing over its difficulties with prodigious facility, improvising a multitude of turns, gruppetti and ornaments, making them sound so spontaneous, despite the fact that she had studied and perfected them in the privacy of her own practice room. She concluded the bravura piece with a crescendo di forza, which brought forth a storm of applause.

Everyone was amazed to hear so much promise in such a young girl, whose technique was already formidable, allowing her to sing with a seamless legato, soaring effortlessly, with a voice extremely flexible and agile. This sound had the warmth of the summer sun in it, and was of a timbre, which went straight to the heart. It was not a creamy voice, but had a distinct tang to it, rather like the bitter sweet taste of Seville oranges. What struck her audience most forcibly, however, was the intensity with which she sang.

She finished with two exotic Spanish folk songs arranged by her father, which brought forth instant applause, approbation and floral tributes. The audience would not let her go and she had to return to the platform for an encore. She was so happy; she had succeeded, she had mastered her nerves and expressed herself to the best of her ability and, above all, had pleased her audience. The faces of Mme Garcia and de Beriot fully expressed their delight, and both felt intuitively that Pauline had the potential to become a first rate artist.

She was a very sensible young girl, and did not let this first flush of success go to her head, indeed her mother would never have allowed such a thing. There was still a great deal of studying to do, and for the next few months Pauline continued her training, building her repertoire, and polishing her technique. Contrary to what her audience might have thought, her voice was not an easy one to control because it was dark and heavy in the middle and it was only by the utmost application and dedication to her daily practice that she was able to tame and develop it.

In the spring of 1838, another concert was arranged by de Beriot, this time in Louvain, about twenty five miles from Brussels, and again, the young singer made an impressive appearance, enchanting a large audience with her exquisite performance. Her mentors were so assured by their protégé's progress, that they decided to expand their horizons outside Belgium. They began planning a six months tour, which would take them to important cities in Germany, Austria and Italy where they would find musicians of the first rank, and audiences of discrimination.

By the middle of April, everything was ready, and Pauline was all eagerness and anticipation at the prospect of visiting so many new places. Their journey took them to Louvain, where she had already sung, then through a flat landscape to St. Trond, Tongres, Maastricht and on to Aachen (Aix la Chapelle), on the German border, where she had played before the King of Prussia in 1836.

She looked forward to seeing the chapel attached to the royal residence, for which the town was famous, having been built in the early ninth century by the great Emperor Charlemagne, but which there had not been time to visit on her previous trip. The imposing edifice is based on the octagonal ground plan of St.Vitale, the early Christian church at Ravenna in Italy, and Pauline felt very small standing in the centre of this unusual church surrounded by majestic columns and arches, sweeping high above her head, as if straining to soar away from the earth. She saw the relics of the powerful emperor, his skull contained in a silver and gold reliquary, decorated with imperial black eagles, encrusted with large precious stones, in the shape of his head and shoulders, with his thigh bone and arm encased in ornately wrought golden casing.

After exploring the chapel, the visitors began to feel chilly in the old stone building, and made their way back to their hotel as the sun was setting. Here they mingled with other guests in one of the public rooms, in which a large log fire burned in the massive stone fireplace, throwing out a welcome warmth and casting an orange/pink glow around the old room, as outside the sky turned to indigo. They conversed for a while with fellow travellers, but soon the evening meal was served – first a clear soup with tiny pieces of meat, vegetables, and pasta, and large freshly baked loaves with home-made butter. After the sightseeing, all the visitors were ravenous, and the smell of the hot soup was as heaven to their nostrils. This was followed by mutton with savoury dumplings, and a fruit torte with lashings of whipped cream, all washed down by either a light beer, cool and fragrant, or fine Rhenish or Moselle wines. For those who still had some appetite left there were strong cheeses, and coffee to complete the meal.

Having eaten well, the family did not linger long in the parlour, but aware of the taxing journey ahead of them next day and their need for an early start, they took their candles, climbed the old curved staircase to their rooms, and sought relief for their aching feet in comfortable feather beds. None of them needed rocking and soon they were sleeping soundly, awoken all too soon by the crow of a cock, and the gentle tapping on each bedroom door by maids bearing pitchers of hot water. The Garcia ladies dressed quickly, and were soon joined at breakfast by Charles. They were just finishing their meal of fresh bread, ham and cheese, when sounds of activity in the yard told them that the coach had arrived, the occupants of which rushed into the inn to grab some food and a welcome drink while the horses were being changed, attempting to digest a hurried breakfast before the signal was given that the equipage was about to resume its journey. With the luggage hoisted onto the back of the vehicle, the travellers clambered aboard, and the heavily laden coach was soon bowling along at a comfortable speed of eight miles an hour. Many of the male passengers had to travel on the roof, as there was not enough room for everyone, and inside it was very cramped and bumpy, but all took it in good spirit.

Charles de Beriot was well known in Germany, and considered to be one of the finest violinists of his generation. His standing in the musical world helped to open doors for his young sister-in-law, who, as the sister of the famous Mme Malibran, was always an object of curiosity. In Germany, she considered herself on neutral ground , and thought that she would find it easier to establish her own genius here. In all the places she sang, large or small, she made a unique impression, although all who had heard her sister recognised the similarity of vocal timbre. Her confidence grew, and it became obvious that she was not, nor ever would be, Malibran's clone. Despite her youth, her individuality was evident, and her listeners enjoyed her performance for its own sake. Here was a serious artiste, whose musicality and dramatic flair were amazing, not least because she was not yet seventeen years old.

She and de Beriot always brought the house down with 'Le Songe de Tartini' by Panseron, a bravura duo for violin and voice, full of trills, roulades and gruppetti. Audiences were swept along by the sheer brilliance of the musicians and the dash and swirl of the piece itself, and they were called back onto the platform every time, eliciting several encores. The arrangements of Pauline's Spanish songs were as joyously received as they had been in Brussels, audiences finding them unusual and exotic, appreciating the rhythmic vitality and brio which Pauline commanded.

Joaquina Garcia, pleased as she was with Pauline's progress, thought that there was still work to be done on the voice itself. Potentially it had a range of three and a half octaves, but only two octaves and a fifth were really usable at present, as the highest register did not equal the quality of the middle and lower range. It was an extraordinary instrument, the lower notes of which sounded like a young tenor, the middle range that of a mezzo, but the high soprano notes, although they came easily, were of a thinner, weaker character. It remained to be seen if this was something inherent in the voice itself or if it could be developed to produce beautiful ringing high notes of luscious quality. Only time and work would tell.

The concerts in Berlin would present the next big challenge because audiences there were known to be musically sophisticated and highly critical. Moving northwards, through the valley of the Spree, with its lakes and verdant swathes of forest where the Electors of Brandenburg had built their capital city, Pauline was naturally apprehensive of what lay ahead of her, but in the meantime, she enjoyed the new sights and sounds through which she travelled.

Stone age nomadic peoples had moved through this area and so had the Romans, but they chose to establish themselves further south on the borders of what became Bavaria and Austria, and Berlin was not founded until the 13th century. It was first mentioned in 1230 AD, and grew from two small fishing settlements on either side of the River Spree. At that time, although its inhabitants were nominally Christians, their beliefs and practises owed a great deal to forest magic, which Richard Wagner later incorporated into his operas.

On May 20th, the 'Gazette Musicale' announced the arrival of Charles de Beriot and Pauline Garcia after 'the brilliant success in all the German towns where they have given concerts'. Pauline was astonished and delighted by the beauty of the Prussian capital, and the spaciousness of its thoroughfares, situated as they were in and around the enormous park of the Tiergarten, where the inhabitants hunted and enjoyed rural pursuits. The coach passed through the park to the Brandenburg Gate, a great neo-classical edifice built in 1791, and topped by a huge sculptured chariot drawn with four horses driven by the Goddess of Peace. The Emperor Napoleon had been greatly attracted to this sculpture and had ordered it to be taken down and despatched to Paris after his victory at Jena, but when he was defeated at Waterloo it was restored to its original site.

The Brandenburg Gate leads into the Avenue Unter den Linden, a straight two mile route which Pauline thought must surely be the most beautiful boulevard in Europe. It takes its name from the double row of linden trees with which it is lined along its entire length, and had many fine buildings, both private and civic, including the opera house and the old town palace of the Prussian royal family.

Intersecting the avenue was the equally long Friedrichstrasse, where all the most fashionable shops, hotels and restaurants were situated. The Garcia's hotel was stylish and comfortable, in contrast to some of the smaller inns en route, where food and cleanliness sometimes left a great deal to be desired.

Pauline was to sing at Court. The King, of course, had heard her in 1836 in Aachen, but she had then been a pianist, and he was curious to hear her sing. Charles had a great many arrangements to make and soon left Pauline and her mother, to go in search of Leopold Ganz, the conductor who would work with them.

The young singer was keen to see the shops and wanted to discover the new Berlin fashions. She was not at all tired, but her mother begged for a little rest and a cup of restorative coffee before venturing out into the metropolis. Pauline thought the shops quite wonderful, and was very tempted by all the lovely things on display. There were bales of embroidered muslins, exquisite silks and brocades of every hue from the Orient, long silk gloves and stockings, garlanded head-dresses, stoles and shawls, and large, superbly decorated bonnets piled high with articial flowers and ribbons. There were dainty, square toed evening slippers and little pull-on boots made of the softest kid dyed in many lovely shades as well as the more serviceable black.

She could not resist the temptation of making some purchases herself, an Indian shawl, in a Paisley design with long fringing, some long cream satin gloves, a pair of evening slippers and a quantity of ribbons and lace. Looking through the bales of materials, she discovered some beautiful shot moire silk, and decided that it would make a wonderfully sumptuous evening gown. She also bought some sprigged muslin for summer day dresses, and deeply satisfied with her purchases, she and Joaquina returned to their hotel for dinner.

The next day, Pauline and Charles rehearsed with the excellent orchestra, and the young singer relished hearing her voice floating over a full body of buoyant sound when she sang the arias of Handel and Gluck which had been requested by the King. When she finished, she was extremely gratified to receive an accolade from the orchestra, who tapped their bows on their music stands to show their appreciation, (not something that happened to every singer), and it gave her courage and confidence for her coming appearance in front of the whole royal family of Prussia, their court, and an audience of 'glitterati'.

The musicians were pleased to see the notice of their arrival in the 'Allgemeine Zeitung' and the advertisement for their concerts on the 21st and 28th of May, which they acknowledged was very welcome publicity, but they were not so pleased at a future date when the same newspaper announced that they were to be married.

On the evening of the 21st, they gave their concert before a splendidly attired audience, the ladies in colourful sik and satin gowns, and a king's ransom in jewellery, shimmering like a collection of exotic butterflys underneath the enormous crystal chandeliers. The men were not less splendid, as most of them were in strikingly colourful uniforms, adorned with gold braid and military orders. One did not have to be in Prussia long to observe the all pervading influence of militarism, and members of the Civil Service wore uniforms, even off duty. If anyone, regardless of their station, from humble clerk to minor royal, failed to comply with this custom, they were fined, or sentenced to periods of imprisonment.

Prussia was the realm of an absolute monarch, with the most formal court in Europe, where democracy was only whispered by dissidents: the death penalty was in operation, the official form of execution on the statute book was breaking on the wheel.

Pauline, of course, was not yet aware of the darker aspects of Prussian life, she only saw the surface glamour and the pre-occupation with culture. On May 23rd, a letter appeared in the 'Gazette musicale' from the eminent music critic, poet and writer, Ludwig Rellstab, friend of Weber, adversary of Gasparo Spontini, composer of 'La Vestale' and director general of the Opera. Rellstab was celebrated for his satirical comments, and severe criticisms, but he liked Pauline

Garcia and admitted that she had conquered him. He said that her voice was a mixture of soprano and tenor, the lower part reminiscent of a cello, and the higher that of a piano', and that no other human voice had struck him in this way. He praised the piece by Panseron, which had been executed with true virtuosity, and frankly declared that he had enjoyed the performance immensely, but above all, he fell in love with Pauline's Spanish songs and her exquisite rendering of them. In his opinion, with her natural vivacity, she conveyed the sense of each word so perfectly, that every member of the audience could be excused for believing that they really understood Spanish.

Although Prussian audiences were considered cold, Pauline's listeners received her ravishing performance with real enthusiasm, and on this occasion, even the Royal Family, who were a very disparate group, constantly quarrelling among themselves and rarely agreeing on anything, found themselves in full accord.

The King was moved by her singing of 'Lascia ch'io pianga', an aria from Handel's 'Rinaldo' which was a great favourite of his, and presented her with an emerald necklace, which absolutely delighted her because it would match beautifully with the emerald silk she had bought, when it came back from the dressmaker. She was introduced to all the family members after the concert, two of whom were destined to become personal friends, Crown Prince William, and his wife, Princess Augusta. William was a handsome man, tall, with dark wavy hair, whose fine figure was superbly set off by his smart cream and gold uniform. He was forty-one years old, but still carried a torch for his dead love, Elisa Radziwill, whom he had not been allowed to marry. His thirty-four year old consort, a princess of the house of Saxe Weimar, was a cultured lady who adored music, and played the piano well. She and William were ill suited, and in her husband's eyes nothing she did was right, and they quarrelled constantly, quite impervious to whoever might be listening. They had a daughter, Princess Louise, named after William's beautiful beloved mother, who had died too young, and she became the Grand Duchess of Baden. Twenty years later, in 1858, their son, Prince Frederick William, was to marry Queen Victoria's eldest daughter, the Princess Royal.

Although he appointed Mendelssohn to found the Berlin Hochschule fur Musik, Prince William was not musical, and admitted that he could hardly tell one tune from another, although he enjoyed listening to military bands. Nevertheless, he liked Pauline,'s singing and thought her personally enchanting. In future years, whenever she came to Berlin, he always seized the opportunity to hear her, and to meet her socially.

Princess Augusta was no less charmed by this talented young woman, and invited her to take tea with her the following day. Pauline was astonished at the affability of the royal couple, having been led to believe that the Hohenzollens were the most stiff-necked family in Europe, with a chillingly cold and formal court.

Pauline played piano duets with the Princess and sang some of her Spanish songs, and one of her own compositions, 'Die Kapelle von Uhland,' which was published in the 'Neue Zeitscrift fur Musik' later that year. Despite her busy schedule, she had never stopped writing songs, having composed from an early age, like her father and sister, and during that summer she also wrote 'Etoile, belle etoile', which she signed 'Francfort, le 18 Aout 1838', but it does not appear to have been published.

At the crack of dawn the ladies and Charles left Berlin for Leipzig, one of the foremost cities in Europe for the training of professional musicians. It was here that the great Johann Sebastian Bach had been the Kapellmeister of the St. Thomas Kirche, where many of his works were first performed at Sunday services. His industry was prodigious but, during his lifetime, he knew little fame, and his music had long been neglected, but the Musical Director of the Gewandhaus Orchestra, the famous Felix Mendelssohn, and other aficionados, such as the cellist, Julius Rietz, were changing all that; under Mendelssohn's direction, the great St. Matthew Passion had been performed to real acclaim, and they were gradually editing and publishing Bach's other works.

As the Garcias and de Beriot travelled south over the verdant plain, covered by many forests, the foothills of the Erz Gebirge, the Saxon alps, rose in the distance. The one hundred and eleven-mile journey necessitated staying in inns along the way. At each staging post, they were served with such substantial nourishment as hot sausages flavoured with herbs and eaten with a spicy mustard sauce, crusty bread, dumplings, pickled white cabbage, a selection of meats, smoked or un-smoked, broth, eggs, cheese and fruit, washed down with fresh milk, or a stein of frothy, light beer.

Nevertheless, it was delightful to see the distant spires of Leipzig on the horizon, and within an hour or so, the coach rumbled through the narrow old streets into the inn courtyard, ostlers ran out, and visitors and luggage were unloaded.

The travellers were naturally, rather tired and dishevelled as they reached their lodgings, the rooms of which were modest, yet clean, and contained large, soft feather beds. Pitchers of hot water were brought and the ravages of the journey repaired, the ladies dressed their hair and changed into freshly ironed clothes in time for dinner. Pauline gazed through the little window that overlooked the main street, and thought the scene very 'gemutlich' as the lamps were lit in the houses opposite, before the shutters were closed for the night.

Each of them slept well, and awoke to a clear bright day, and after breakfast of bread, unsalted butter, strawberry compote and steaming hot, milky coffee, they set out to meet Felix Mendelssohn. Although only thirty-one, Mendelssohn's first compositions had been written when he was eleven years old. His family were rich Jews who had converted to the Lutheran religion. They were cultured, musical people and soon ascertained that young Felix was extraordinarily gifted. They engaged the best teachers available and every musical opportunity was given to him, so that at the tender age of nine he was conducting small groups of instrumentalists in his parents' home. One of those with whom he studied was the father of his intimate friend, Julius Rietz, who was later to play a significant role in Pauline's life. Felix's sister Fanny was a few years older than himself, and was already an accomplished pianist and composer, and the two of them shared a profound affinity, which remained firm throughout their lives.

At seventeen Mendelssohn composed the incidental music to Shakespeare's 'A Midsummer Night's Dream' that includes the wedding march, played at innumerable weddings ever since. Indeed, if he had written nothing other than the music of 'The Dream', he would still have proved himself a master.

Despite his youth, he was famous all over Europe, and to aspiring musicians studying in Leipzig, his work was an essential part of their education. In England, he was the doyen of contemporary composers, and Queen Victoria and Prince Albert were absolutely devoted to him, inviting him to Buckingham Palace or Windsor Castle, so that they could all make music together. On one occasion, the Queen, admitting that she was very nervous, sang him what she believed to be one of his songs, but he had to confess that it was really by his sister, Fanny, although published under his name. At that time, in upper class German families, it was not considered respectable for a woman to publish music under her own name.

Felix was married to the exceptionally beautiful Cecile, and he considered himself the luckiest of men. His young wife had suffered greatly during and after the birth of their first child, Karl, born in the previous February, but Felix had taken her to convalesce at his parent's house in Berlin, and resting in congenial surroundings her customary good health was soon restored.

The small, slim, dark, wiry composer had boundless energy, and the ability to cat nap anywhere, at anytime. During his tenure, the Gewandhaus orchestra had gone from strength to strength and become one of the finest in Germany, thanks to his unflagging enthusiasm, and that of its leader, Felicien David, for whom he wrote his violin concerto.

De Beriot and Mendelssohn were already acquainted and he and the Garcia ladies were warmly greeted, and introduced to the shyly reserved Cecile. Pauline, always susceptible to beauty, considered Cecile one of the loveliest women she had ever seen, with her trim figure, perfect, pearl-like complexion, large, exquisite hazel eyes, and mass of deep brown ringlets, and thought their plump, jolly baby was simply delightful. Details of the concerts were discussed, and rehearsals scheduled. The visitors then took their leave, and indulged in a little sight-seeing on the way back to their lodgings. They passed the old University, established in 1409, ensuring Leipzig's place as a centre of culture and learning; the Auerbach Hof, and Rathaus were admired for their splendid sixteenth century architecture, as well as the picturesque houses along the narrow streets, many of which dated from the 16th and 17th century.

The next day, Pauline worked in earnest, vocalising and singing through her pieces before going with Charles to the rehearsal with Mendelssohn and the orchestra. The maestro was delighted with the young singer; Charles's playing he knew and admired, but he was astonished by the degree of skill already attained by Malibran's sister. Later, over a meal, he described some of Maria's performances, and made Pauline laugh about a production of 'Don Giovanni' at the Paris Opera, when Pellegrini, as Leporello, had over-acted shamelessly, and the mischievous Maria had really 'gone over the top' as Zerlina. However, he said that this was merely high spirits to make up for Pellegrini's awful performance and usually she was 'sublime'. When Pellegrini sang a long and complicated point d'orgue really badly, young Felix cried 'encore' and the wretched bass had to start the whole thing over again, much to the consternation of the audience! Pauline spent many convivial evenings with Felix and his friends while she was in Leipzig, and he taught her to play billiards. She discovered that she had a natural ability for the game, and over the years she developed into a very competent player.

One of Felix's friends was the composer Robert Schumann, who had started his musical life as a promising pianist. However, being impatient to make faster progress, he had invented a wooden splint to strengthen his fourth finger that actually damaged it irreparably, and precluded him from pursuing the career he had envisaged. Fortunately, he was a gifted composer, and also had a sure literary talent, but for some time, he was undecided which path to take. It was notoriously difficult to make money as a composer, but journalism might bring in an income, so he founded the 'Neue Zeitschrift fur Musik', which became a highly respected musical periodical for the advancement of new composers and new music. When Schumann first heard the Polish pianist Frederic Chopin's variations on the duet 'La ci darem la mano' from Mozart's 'Don Giovanni', he famously exclaimed: 'Hats off gentlemen, here is a genius'!

He was now twenty-nine, and in love with the eighteen-year-old pianist Clara Wieck, who had recently returned from giving concerts in Vienna where she had met and been mesmerised by the playing of Franz Liszt. She had made her debut in Leipzig as a very young girl, in fact, Robert had first heard her play when she was nine. Her ambitious father, Friedrich Wieck, was her teacher, and believed that she would have a brilliant career. He was emphatic that nothing should stand in its way, certainly not young Robert Schumann, and did all he could to keep the couple apart.

Schumann sought out Herr Wieck in order to plead his case, but the old man was adamant and Robert told Clara: "My interview with your father was terrible. He was frigid, hostile, confused and contradictory at one and the same time. I felt so lifeless, so humiliated, and am incapable of a single fine thought. I am not so reduced in spirit as to think of giving you up, but embittered by this outrage to my sacred feelings by being treated like one of the common herd. You must be prepared for anything, for if he cannot succeed by force he will employ cunning".

Many people, including Liszt, were against Wieck for his attitude towards Robert. The older musician had real cause for concern however, because it was well known that Clara was by no means the first young lady to take the composer's fancy. It was obvious from his youth, and as he confided in his diary, he had a strong libido and wasted no time in sowing his wild oats.

Another young composer, Heinrich Dorn, was infatuated by Clara, and said that she had 'a graceful figure, with a blooming complexion, delicate white hands, a profusion of black hair, and wise, glowing eyes'. He thought her a lovely creature and found her definitely 'appetising'!

Despite the injury to his hand, which robbed him of his pianistic skills, Robert was now a prolific composer, although all his life he suffered frustration through not being sufficiently able to express his musical ideas at the keyboard. Fortunately, he had the talented Clara to perform his works for him, and as her career developed, she not only became his ideal interpreter, but made his music known to a very wide audience.

Another composer Pauline met was the Englishman, William Sterndale Bennett, who was five years her senior. His musical abilities had also revealed themselves at an early age, and he had been sponsored by Broadwood, the piano making firm to complete his studies in Leipzig. He had already given some Gewandhaus concerts, notably conducting his overture 'Naides', which was considered an interesting work and won general acclaim. It was no doubt due to the influence of Mendelssohn that Bennett became immersed in the music of J.S.Bach, and in London in 1849, he founded the Bach Society, to promote the study and performance of his works. Bennett was also responsible for the first performance in England of the 'St., Matthew Passion' in 1854, and in 1856 became permanent conductor of the Philharmonic Society, an organisation with which Pauline was later to appear on many occasions in London.

On June 25th, she sang at the Gewandhaus for the first time, in the same hall where Clara had made her debut in 1830, at the age of twelve. The programme consisted of an overture by Mozart, an air and variations on a Russian Rondo by de Beriot, an aria and cavatina which Michael Costa had written for Malibran that Pauline sang ; a French song, 'Ouvrez'; a Spanish song, 'Ay, ay, ay', by her father; an overture by Fesco; de Beriot played his 'Caprice'; Pauline sang the final aria and variations devised by de Beriot for Malibran from Donizetti's 'L'Elisir d'Amore' and she and de Beriot ended with their usual 'tour de force', Panserons's 'Le songe de Tartini'. It was a typical programme of the time; soloists performing their own compositions, a mixture of solo vocal pieces, virtuoso instrumental items, and orchestral music.

The critic of the 'Allegemeine Musikalische Zeitung' wrote: 'Mademoiselle Pauline Garcia obtained in her first concert a remarkable success, and was greeted with acclaim on her second appearance. Her ability is already very obvious (she is 17 years old), and her intonation is true and pure. We have not heard her sing any of her own songs yet, but we believe that she is a talented composer'. The critic was not entirely accurate about her age, as she was not actually seventeen untilJuly 18th.

On June 26th, Robert Schumann wrote anonymously in the 'Neue Zeitschrift fur Musik': 'Yesterday evening, Monsieur de Beriot, and Mlle. P. Garcia in the hall of the Gewandhaus, gave one of the more interesting concerts this year, which contributed much to the realm of musical art.

'M. de Beriot is already known as one of the foremost violinists of our time, and his playing upheld his reputation. The name of Garcia is known and respected on two continents but was further enhanced by Mlle. Garcia, who showed a true artistic nature in the opening measures of a song to her own accompaniment. Mlle. Garcia is not a virtuoso of song, she is a singer!'

Later that evening he wrote in his diary: 'Concert this evening of de Beriot and Garcia. I was as dead as a stone, but in the first minutes of her singing, my eyes filled with tears. I saw Clara from a distance; at the end of the performance I spoke a few words to her, and greeted her father with a deadly coolness', and on June 30th he wrote: 'In the afternoon I went to visit de Beriot. He is a pleasant fellow. The house was quiet, and Pauline Garcia was relaxing. She is sensitive, artistic, and lively. Her mother is a nice lady with a beautiful voice. This evening, their second concert. Clara was there with Nanni. Wednesday morning, en route to de Beriot, bumped into Clara who was also paying a visit. I was embarrassed by my efforts to speak French. La Garcia plays the piano very well. She intends to leave for Dresden on Tuesday.'

Clara was a reserved and shy young woman, but she found Pauline's joie de vivre infectious, and envied the French girl's carefree attitude to life. Clara's parents had divorced when she was four years old and she had been brought up by her stern, eccentric father, who, realising that she was a child prodigy had emphasized the musical side of her education to the exclusion of practically everything else. She was amazed by Pauline's wide knowledge of European literature, poetry, history, the classical world and her ability to speak several languages with great fluency, if not always total accuracy.

Despite Robert's complimentary comments regarding Pauline's musical abilities, he did not think that she had yet mastered the measure and style of the German lied. Schubert was one of her favourite composers, and she had possibly sung some of his songs to her friends in private. Nevertheless, Robert believed that she would grow into them in time, and when he published the nine Heine songs of his Liederkreis Op.24 in 1840, he dedicated them to her. It was the first time she had received such an accolade and was overwhelmed by this display of friendship and admiration.

Schumann was a tall, dignified, well built man with a kindly expression, a very short nose, medium length, brown hair, who had a great liking for cigarettes. Where other composers were concerned, he was generous to a fault (Meyerbeer excluded), but as a personality, he was very withdrawn and silent, and often lost in his own inner world. He confessed: 'People are often at a loss to understand me, and no wonder! I meet affectionate advances with icy reserve, and often wound and repel those who wish to help me… It is not that I fail to appreciate the very smallest attention, or to distinguish every subtle change in expression and attitude; it is a fatal something in my words and manner which belies me'.

Pauline quickly became aware of Robert's transparent honesty, his lack of ostentation and conceit, but realised that he would find it difficult to establish himself in the wider musical world because he had no gift for self publicity. When he and Clara were first married, and he accompanied her on her tours, he was often daunted by the fact that he was frequently asked if he was also musical!

All too soon, it was time to leave Leipzig, where Pauline's performances had been acclaimed by a discerning and knowledgeable public, which included many professional musicians and students. It had been wonderful to be in the midst of a group of creative, kindred spirits, who had welcomed her as one of themselves, and she looked forward to her return.

CHAPTER FOUR

1838/39

The following morning the three musicians set off for Dresden, the beautiful
Saxon city on the River Elbe. In 1270, the Margrave of Meissen had chosen it
for his capital because of its prime strategic position, and during the reign of
the Elector, Augustus II, the Strong, it grew into one of the most exquisite and
cultural cities of the German states. Pauline had already heard much about its
charming rococo buildings and the superb Dresden china produced in the
Meisson porcelain factory, about fifteen miles from the city, and was looking
forward to buying something beautiful as a souvenir.

On their arrival, Charles went off to a coffee house to meet some friends and
Pauline and Joaquina unpacked and attended to the restoration of their clothes.
While in the Saxon capital, Pauline and her guardians explored its architectural
gems, including the fine Gothic cathedral, the lovely Bruhl palace, the enchanting Zwinger Pavilion, and several museums exhibiting archaeological remains
and collections of German art, both ancient and modern.

On the day of her first concert, Pauline woke up with a peppery feeling at the
back of her nose, and a slight soreness in her throat. Naturally alarmed, her
mother made her stay in bed until lunch time, plying her with hot drinks and
inhalations of steam. The girl tried to keep calm, but it was very worrying,
something that singers have to live with, being as prone to colds, coughs and
sore throats as any other mortal. The Panseron duo concerned her because it
required brio and freedom of execution, and she was worried that her voice
would not stand up to its demands. Her throat felt very dry and uncomfortable,
and her mother plied her with honey dissolved in hot water to stimulate lubrica-
tion, but Charles said that they must include this piece in the programme as it
was looked for, and would cause great disappointment if they did not perform
it. They debated whether an announcement should be made, but finally, decided against it.

Mme Garcia gave her daughter sage advice, telling her to rely on her technique and to treat the breath lightly, putting over her songs with as much
expression and elan as she could. In the event, as a result of this counsel,

Pauline sang very well, which taught her something valuable: as long as the vocal chords are not infected or inflamed as with laryngitis, and the breath control is good, a singer can perform adequately even with a mild sore throat and stuffy nose. It is not ideal of course, but it is possible to get by in the short term.

Even if Pauline did not feel in great vocal form, she believed that she looked attractive in her gown of apricot silk, with its deep neckline, trimmed with cream lace, revealing her handsome shoulders. A gold filigree brooch was pinned on the tightly fitting bodice that had tiny pin tucks all the way down to a deep point at the waist, and the sleeves had two narrow puffs at the shoulder, then ballooned from the elbow, ending in a tight band at the wrist. The full skirt had bands of lace above the hem and reached to her ankles, revealing a glimpse of white silk stockings, and she had slippers made of the same material as her dress, adorned with tiny, silver buckles. Her hair was plainly dressed, with a head-dress of cream lace with lappets over her ears.

The concert was given at the Conservatoire, and consisted of the same pieces performed in Leipzig. Before the days of recordings, musicians could exist on a small repertoire, singing or playing the same pieces in different towns. Pauline enjoyed learning new music and always sought to increase her repertoire, but being on tour is not conducive to studying and perfecting new works, so she kept to songs that were well prepared and rehearsed.

Her audience consisted of the most cultured and distinguished people in Dresden; the ladies finely dressed, displaying their jewels and elaborate hair styles, and the gentlemen, dignified in evening attire, with jewels in their cravats. Even more than Pauline's obvious musical talent, these people were aware that young as she was, she had nobility, charm, and a charisma which fascinated them. When meeting her socially, they were surprised to encounter a young person who was able to talk knowledgeably on many subjects other than music, and who had a ready sense of humour, a flashing smile, and infectious laugh.

Early in July, Robert Schumann wrote to both Clara and Pauline asking each of them to contribute one of their own compositions for inclusion in a special supplement of the 'Neue Zeitscrift fur Musik'; Pauline's piece was 'Die Kapelle von Uhland'. Clara had hoped to become engaged to Robert on her 18th birthday, but her father still refused to contemplate their union, and Clara was forbidden to see or correspond with the composer. Clara had confided her problems to Pauline, and naturally, the young singer was sympathetic to their plight, comforting her friend with thoughts of a happier future. However, she was totally unaware of Robert's previous romantic entanglements, or the fact that he was most probably enjoying the sexual favours of a servant girl at the same time as he was longing for marriage with Clara.

On July 9th, Clara wrote telling Robert that she was working hard at her composition, and asked him to let her know the deadline for his publication. She said she had written to Pauline, who was in Karlsbad, but thought her letter must have been lost. She told him how much she liked 'this nice girl', who was a fine artist, unaffected and modest, despite her great gifts.

Pauline returned to Leipzig, and Clara told Robert that they played the piano together from early morning till evening. She said that Pauline had copied out her song and would let him have it when they next met. Despite the fact that Clara enjoyed Pauline's friendship, unintentionally, the French girl made her feel inferior because she was well educated and multi-talented, and in comparing herself, Clara lost some of her confidence and was tempted to abandon her music. She lamented the fact that her father was doing all he could to keep her from the man she loved, whose music was her only consolation, and she also resented the fact the Wieck had prevented her from enjoying a balanced education. She told Robert that she intended to spend the following winter with the Garcias.

OnAugust 11th, Robert noted in his diary that Clara had returned to Leipzig on Wednesday morning, and during the afternoon, they had met at the house of Therese Schumann, where for a while they were alone and secure, happier than they had been for years. Later, they were joined by de Beriot and Pauline, who was 'charming'.

Soon after, Pauline spent several days in Weimar where she sang to the Grand Duchess, who gave her a pretty Italian decoration for her hair, and presented Charles with a splendid ring. On August 22nd, she wrote to Clara from Wiesbaden saying that it seemed a hundred years since she had seen her, and hoped she hadn't forgotten her. She wanted to know if she had composed anything new, and said that her piano looked forward to being played upon by Clara, and that she would announce Clara's arrival in M. Fetis's journal.

She told the pianist that she and de Beriot had given a 'lovely' concert on Friday in Frankfurt, and one in Wiesbaden the day before, where "we saw the celebrated Meyerbeer who came over from Schalbach to hear me. He was enormously pleased, and absolutely wants to compose an opera for me". It is surprising that one of Europe's most successful composers should have considered such a project for a girl who had yet to make her operatic debut. If he meant what he said, the wily Meyerbeer must have seen something truly amazing in the youthful singer's dramatic potential.

Early in September, the Garcias and de Beriot left for Austria en route to Italy. For as long as she could remember, Pauline's family had revered the name of the Austrian composer Wolfgang Amadeus Mozart, and she looked forward to visiting Salzburg, his birthplace. Poor Mozart had experienced a difficult life in the principality and grew to loathe Salzburg, where he was treated like a lackey at the Court of Archbishop Colloredo. He could not wait to get away to Vienna, but his sufferings did not make the city any less beautiful.

Pauline was excited when she caught sight of the great, solid form of the Hohensalzburg fortress, set atop the high Monchsberg hill, which dominates Salzburg, and is visible for miles around. The coach passed through the wide valley of the river Salzach, hemmed in with a curtain of foothills, and set against the majestic panorama of the towering alps which lie to the south. It is one of the most breath-taking views in the whole of Europe. Little by little, the vast castle drew nearer, and they entered the town from the north, finding the city spread out on both sides of the river. The view of the baroque domes and towers lying beneath the great fortress was stunning and soon they were in the hustle and bustle of the old city, where stalls full of fresh produce from sur-rounding farms were plentiful, and townspeople exchanged gossip. The smell of horses was overpowering; many of them tethered close by, with urine soaked hay scattered around them. Some of the streets leading from the market place were very narrow, reflecting their medieval past, but elsewhere there were fine open squares and an extraordinarily imposing baroque cathedral.

Despite the concerts she was to give during her stay in the province, Pauline had high hopes of doing a great deal of sight-seeing. She soon discovered that a large part of the medieval city had been destroyed by the Prince Archbishop Wolf Dietrich von Raitenau, at the end of the sixteenth century, in a fever of demolition caused by his obsessive desire to create a Rome of the North, based on classical architectural styles. His father came from an aristocratic Austrian family, and his mother was a member of the fabulously rich Medici clan. Born in 1559, he grew up in Rome, where, from early boyhood, he developed an over-whelming interest in architecture and art.

In 1587, at the age of twenty-eight, he was appointed Prince Archbishop to the wealthy province of Salzburg. The revenue of the region came from the abundant salt deposits and their exportation across Europe. Before the days of refrigeration, salt was as necessary as oil is in the modern world, and with large sums of money available to him, he was now able to indulge his visions of baroque grandeur, and set about transforming the ramshackle medieval city into a classical architectural gem. However, he went too far too quickly, and demolished a large number of buildings, upsetting the worthy burghers of the city. He was deposed in 1612 by Marcus Sitticus von Hohenems, who imprisoned him in the fortress until his death in 1617. It was left to others to make good the devastation he had caused and to transform the medieval city into a baroque paradise.

During the horrific Thirty Years War, which ravaged so much of Western Europe in the seventeenth century, Salzburg was protected by the wisdom and foresight of Archbishop Paris Lodron, who built massive fortifications around the city to ensure its safety.

In Roman times Salzburg, then called Juvavum, had developed on the right bank of the Salzach, where the narrow winding Linzergasse runs uphill to Schallmoos, a pretty village where Mozart and his father, Leopold, used to visit their friends, the Robinig family, who lived in a charming, rococco house with everything under one roof, including the animals.

After unpacking and settling into their lodgings, Charles and his ladies sauntered forth to explore. The sky was the clearest azure, and the whole alpine range was in view – a truly magnificent panorama. Perhaps tomorrow or the next day, the hazy mists would close in and the mountains would retreat so completely that one would doubt that they had ever been there. The little party turned into the long, narrow Getreidegasse to look for Mozart's birthplace. This is one of the few medieval lanes that escaped Wolf Dietrich's demolition gangs and is a repository of fine old Guild signs made of wrought iron, painted and gilded, advertising a multitude of wares for sale, hanging high above splendid, large Renaissance, Baroque or Rococco doorways.

The travellers found the Mozart house, a tall, plain building on several floors, at the far end of the street, near the Rathaus. At street level the entrance is imposing, with huge iron double doors decorated with curlicues, surrounded by an embossed arch, topped with a stone relief of a woman's head. The building backs onto the Universitats Platz where the vast, domed Kollegiankirche stands. When Mozart was born, his father, Leopold, a violinist in the service of the Archbishop, played in the court orchestra, as Wolfgang was to do later. The Garcias and Charles were making a pilgrimage to the birthplace of a man they revered above all other composers, because like all true musicians, they believed that he had been divinely inspired and had reached sublime heights in every form of music, from the humblest piano sonata written in early childhood, to the operas conceived when he was at the height of his powers.

Soon, the late afternoon sun turned the Alps into a glowing pink gateau against the hastening mauve of the sky and quickly sank, leaving no twilight but a deep indigo star lit sky, and they hurried back to their inn, in preparation for their evening meal.

The dining room was very large, and the candles in the wall sconces and on the tables could hardly provide sufficient light in the cavernous old place, where strange shadows played over the walls, as the serving girls moved around. The smell of cooking was strongly Hungarian, and dishes of goulash and veal were served by waitresses wearing the traditional costume of the region, comprising long dirndl dresses in shades of deep red, dark blue or green spattered with tiny alpine flowers, black bodices laced over pewter buttons, white blouses with bulbous sleeves and fringed scarves.

During the meal a group of gypsies entertained the guests with dancing and music played on a zither and violin. Their costumes were very bright and colourful, to match their strange, exotic music. Pauline was fascinated, believing as she did that gypsy blood flowed in her veins. Now, something elemental stirred within her, something she could not deny, despite the fact that in many parts of the world, these people were treated like vagrants and vagabonds.

Next day Pauline and her relatives visited the splendid baroque cathedral in the Dom Platz, its vast interior high domed, with Corinthian pilasters and rounded arches, an enormous cavern decorated in white and gold. The sound of the great organ filled the extensive space with a torrent of vibrant tone, reminding them that Joseph Haydn's brother, Michael, had once been the official organist here.

Afterwards, they walked through the square to the medieval church of the Franziskaner, gaunt, with its dark grey stonework, steeply pitched slate roof and tall spire. Inside, the long nave was very dark, but Pauline loved the effect of the light streaming through the windows in the lofty fifteenth century apse, above a baroque altar, gleaming with gold leaf, behind which stood a tall, slender pillar sprouting branches to formthe Gothic vaulting. The total effect was symbolic of the soul's journey from darkness to light.

They crossed the bridge over the Salzach into the delightful Mirabelle Gardens, where the young Wolf Dietrich built a palace for his mistress Salome Alt, the lady who bore him fifteen children. Hardly anything of the original edifice remains, and the neo classical palace which replaced it, was built in the eighteenth century by Johann Lucas von Hildebrandt.

When Meyerbeer first visited Salzburg in 1812 it was in a sorry state, after the depradations of Napoleon's occupation, and the ending of the centuries old reign of the archbishops. It was little better when Franz Schubert visited in 1825, as he said that he found the city very neglected, with grass growing in the streets, and decaying buildings, but now, two decades later, reconstruction was taking place, and gardens were being tended again.

The visitors took lunch in the garden of St. Peter's Abbey, where monks served their own home made beer and wine and appetising meals of thinly sliced ham, cold meats, pickles, cheeses, fresh bread, and for dessert, a concoction of halved apples and apricots dried in the oven served with butter and cinnamon, and scenting the air with the most delicious, aromatic smell.

Naturally, they could not let their stay in Salzburg pass without visiting the castle and although they found the climb very steep, they were rewarded by a truly magnificent view when they reached the summit of the Festungsberg. Below, the river swivelled swiftly like a demented, silvery snake, whipping itself into a frothy substance, as it careened over boulders and rocks, and on a distant hill, they could see the baroque church of the Maria Plain, its bleached, white stone walls dazzling in the sunshine, and its two massive, onion topped towers glowing golden against the deep blue of the sky.

Under the walls of the castle, huddled the ancient buildings of the Nonnberg Convent from where the hymns of the nuns drifted up on the still, clear air. The Garcias were moved by the pure, sacred sounds, so ethereal and true, and perhaps Joaquina's memories of her own convent days so long ago were stirred.

Pauline did not often go to church services, but she had a deep spiritual quality, and a profound belief in God. Music was her religion because she believed that the voice of God spoke in its harmonies. She disliked dogma, which in extreme cases could breed fanaticism and wondered why the true teachings were so often overlooked. To her it was significant that the great teachers came to teach the people the realities of the spiritual life rather than to found a religion. whichwas usually done by their followers, who organised an establishment, created the dogma, declaring it to be the literal word of God, forming traditions, concocting regimes and dressing up in elaborate vestments. She believed that many of the teachings were misunderstood or misapplied through lack of understanding, errors in translations, or because they became corrupted by those who desired power, sought to control the people, and declared heresies against anybody who disagreed with them. Later in her career, when she sang the roles of Rachel in 'La Juive' and Fides in 'Le Prophete', operas that deal with religious persecution, it was her underlying philosophy which made her interpretation of these characters so powerful.

Years later she confided in Julius Rietz that she was saddened by her mother's apparent lack of real faith. "My mother, as you know, is Spanish, and (which is of greater significance,) was brought up in Spain. It suffices to tell you that she unites a great deal of 'Catholic superstition' to a total lack of religion. She is not quite sure that God exists, but she 'would not swear' that there is no Devil, and I grieve to say that from what I can see, this latter gentleman terribly engrosses her attention." She adds that the Jesuit priest plays on Joaquina's terrors rather than alleviating them, and says that her father believed in neither God nor Devil; his religionbeing life, art, love and that he cared passionately for all that was beautiful. She goes on: "I was too young when my father died to have been influenced in any way by his purely material ideas, that is true. But how did I come by that innate faith which I have borne within me since earliest childhood – a faith that nothing has ever been able to shake, neither the most sceptical of books nor the ethics of the philosophers? I cannot propound any formula for my faith, but I have the firm conviction that the soul is immortal and that all loves shall one day be united – the 'great loves', whatever be their nature, provided that they have made themselves worthy of it. Perhaps in order to reach the goal, one must be put to the test, of several existences in the spheres, in worlds ever lovelier and better. Do not laugh at me, dearest friend, I know no more about it than anybody else, and, above all, I cannot give a definite shape to my thoughts on a subject so difficult, so impossible to explain. But all that I do know is this – that there is within us a divine spark which does not perish, and which will end in becoming a part of the great light."

Coming out of her reverie she and Joaquina made their way across a courtyard and through a doorway into a dark interior. On an upper floor they were shown into the Goldener Stube and Goldener Saal, medieval rooms decorated lavishly with mythical beasts painted in bright jewel colours and intricate gilded carving. In contrast, they saw the large, plain room where the unfortunate Wolf Dietrich had languished for five years. From his window, he had looked down the escarpment to the little track that leads to the Nonnberg Covent. This spot represented freedom to him, and no doubt he longed to be able to sit there in the sun, overlooking the south facing plain and the great bulk of the mighty Untersberg.

The musicians took a carriage to the pretty yellow ochre summer palace of Hellbrunn, built by Marcus Sitticus. Here, he entertained frequently and showed off his notorious water toys, which were activated at the throw of a switch, sending fountains and sprays of water into the air, providing him with much mirth and hilarity at the expense of his guests.

Despite the infantile sense of humour of its creator, it is a beautiful place, with luxuriant gardens and a variety of classical statues in a superb setting. Some way from the house, the Garcias climbed a hill to see the Stone Theatre cut from rock, where in 1618 'The Peri', the first opera to be presented on Austrian soil was performed. Pauline could not resist standing in the centre of the stage, filling her lungs with air, and launching into an aria, in which her mother joined, both ending up falling about with laughter, letting their hair down, alone and unobserved, singing for the sheer joy of living.

When Wolf Dietrich had first discovered that Marcus Sitticus was planning to overthrow him by staging a coup, he fled to the Tyrol with Salome Alt. It was midwinter, and the journey was slow and difficult, due to heavy snow. They were pursued and caught, and the Prince Archbishop was taken back to Salzburg as a prisoner. For the last five years of his life, he could only dream of what might have been, as he gazed hopelessly through his prison window.

Pauline and her mother found another memento of Wolf Dietrich when they visited the church of St. Sebastion in the long, narrowly winding Linzergasse. They had come to see the Mozart family grave, where the composer's parents and sister are buried. Mozart himself was buried in a pauper's grave somewhere on the outskirts of Vienna. Unexpectedly, the Garcias discovered the St. Gabriel's Chapel, the archbishop's mausoleum. The large oak double doors were slightly ajar, and the ladies peeped inside and gasped at the opulence of the chapel, decorated with tiny green and white tiles and stucco work. The cupula was lined with gilded tiles into which were set four round windows, and along the walls were four highly decorated niches with larger than life size statues of the four Evangelists. The altar stood in a rectangular barrel-vaulted recess and in a deep well, covered over by a wrought iron grill, lay the coffin. They discovered that the chapel was built between 1597 and 1603, so Wolf Dietrich must have planned it himself, as it was finished nine years before his imprisonment. Even in death, the man who was dedicated to the art of architecture ensured that he would be surrounded by beauty.

The letters cut in stone on the front of the mausoleum read – RENOVATUM – and although Pauline was not a Latin scholar, she guessed that it meant 'to make new' and found it comforting. There was such peace in the campo santo, and she and her mother sat down for a while, each deep in her own thoughts, reflecting on their own dear ones who were no longer with them.

Soon, they resumed their travels and the next stage of their journey took them through some very isolated, extensive forests, where wolves and other wild animals dwelled. Despite the early autumn days, the weather remained fine, which was a blessing because they had to cross the Hohe Tauern Alps at the Gross Glockner Pass, never an easy task at the best of times. Pauline was in her element, as she travelled through a countryside full of lakes and mountains with picturesque farms and villages, and air so clear they could see for miles. At present all was idyllic, but the travellers realised how hard life must be in the winter when deep snow imprisoned the inhabitants of the farmhouses, isolating them for several months.

The visitors were anxious to get over the alps to the Italian border as soon as possible, and the coach rocked and rolled, as it climbed higher and higher and they had to get out and walk to lighten the load, and to allow the horses time for rest. As the path grew ever steeper and narrower their hearts were often in their mouths as they saw how close the wheels of the vehicle were to the edge of the path, and how deep was the drop below.

After several days of travelling and much buffeting, the coach began to descend, and as they arrived at the Italian frontier, feeling somewhat bruised, they were thankful to find themselves in one piece.

In Padua, they feasted their eyes on the frescos by the thirteenth century painter, sculptor and architect, Giotto di Bondone at the church of St. Justina, which John Evelyn called one of the finest pieces of architecture in Italy. Giotto had brought new life to Italian art, developing a naturalistic style, depicting sacred characters as real people, rather than symbols, and handling perspective in a totally new way. He is often called the 'Father of the Renaissance' because he challenged the old concepts and let in new light, which stemmed from a renewed knowledge of the classical world, and was taken up by his follower Masaccio, who benefited from Giotto's research into perspective and human anatomy that showed in the skilful way he posed his figures.

For Pauline this trip was invaluable in developing her knowledge and appreciation of the visual arts without the trouble of attending an art school. She saw the thirteenth century Palazzo della Raggione, the Basilica of St. Anthony and the famous, ancient university, which made Padua a respected centre of learning. However, one of the most memorable aspects of her visit was when she and her family unexpectedly bumped into Franz Liszt at the Caffe Pedrocchi.

The shock of seeing him so unexpectedly, brought colour to her face and she found herself blushing to the roots of her hair, hoping that it would not be noticed in the rush of greetings, as Liszt gallantly bent down to kiss her mother's hand, then shook Charles's hand heartily. Seeing her standing shyly in the background with her heart beating wildly, he smiled at her, his look tinged with admiration, as he took her hand and kissed it. To him, she had always been a plain, though sweet, talented child, but now he saw a young woman, well dressed and elegant, and as he lifted his head, their eyes met, and such a spasm passed through Pauline's heart that she thought she must faint, though thankfully, she remained on her feet, and strove to appear outwardly calm.

Liszt joined them for a meal and was soon entertaining them with his sparkling repartee. Pauline was full of curiosity to know what had been happening to him since they last met, and listened intently. Occasionally, Franz would look across at her in an interested way, attempting to include her in the conversation. Although she tried to talk naturally to him, her shyness overwhelmed her, and she could only reply laconically to his questions. He was the first man in her life who had made her feel like this and in her youthful heart, she thought she must be in love, and that it would last forever. Apart from his extraordinary charisma, she was drawn to him by his versatility, his understanding, and rich, wide-ranging imagination.

He was a man of the world, experienced, well travelled, sophisticated, and the lover of another woman, the aristocratic Countess Marie d'Agoult, who had been his mistress since 1834, and was presently in Venice, having recently given birth to their second child, Cosima. In a depressed, miserable state, unwell and disillusioned, Marie awaited Liszt's return. She had abandoned husband, home and children, and a high position in society for this man, but he was absent most of the time, and she agonised about the temptations offered to him by adoring females. In March, he had gone to Vienna to give concerts in order to raise money for the victims of a disastrous flood that had practically obliterated Budapest, and it was at that time that Clara Wieck had first heard him play. He had given eight public concerts and raised large sums of money, making himself a hero to the Hungarian people.

Of course, he made light of this charitable act, and of the assistance he had given to the poor of Raiding, the place where he was born. Now he was in Padua on a concert tour that included Bologna, Pisa, and Florence, where he was to settle for the winter months with Marie. Soon she would be pregnant again, and it was during this time that the lovers read the ' Divine Comedy' together, and Liszt began work on the Dante symphony, which he dedicated to Richard Wagner. The couple's third and last child was a son, Daniel.

Liszt's concert in Padua was a glittering affair in an opulent auditorium, his audience mainly consisting of beautifully gowned young ladies, over whom glowed a brilliant chandelier. As the pianist approached the piano, he looked so handsome and striking that Pauline succumbed once more to the excessive feelings of youthful adoration. For the whole time he played she was in ecstasy, not only with the man himself, but with his wonderful pianism, and not even the sudden cessation of the music caused by the breaking of a piano string, brought her completely to earth again. The concert resumed and her hero was called to give encore after encore, at the end of which, he was feted like a gladiator, with women gushing all around him.

Shortly after breakfast, the following morning he called to say goodbye, as he was setting out for Pisa, the next stage of his tour. He took Pauline's hands and squeezed them, his brilliant eyes looking deeply into hers, as he told her how sorry he was not to have been able to spend more time with her, adding 'never mind, when I am next in Brussels, I will give you some piano lessons'. The girl thanked him, but added that shortly she and her mother would be leaving the Belgian capital, as they were planning to make their home in Paris, where Mme Garcia hoped that her daughter would be engaged to sing at the Opera. 'Then I will have to see you there' Liszt responded, and with a few words of farewell and a wave of the hand, he was gone, leaving Pauline feeling distinctly bereft, genuinely pitying poor Marie d'Agoult who was impatiently awaiting him in Venice.

Deeply infatuated, and young as Pauline was, she was intelligent enough not to envy her rival, and acknowledged that she would not change places with her. Liszt was an ideal, and Pauline realised that reality with him would not be so perfect. Having an active imagination, she could indulge all her fantasies about him in a dream world orchestrated by herself, and this adolescent attitude set a precedent for the rest of her life, because Pauline was always more inclined towards an idealistic, spiritual type of love, rather than a purely physical one.

Soon, it was time to return to Brussels, where the Garcias only stayed long enough to put their affairs in order and pack their belongings. They then set out for the French capital, where, on October 28th, their arrival was announced in 'La Revue Musicale'.

Manuel Garcia met his mother and sister, and took them to the apartment he had chosen on the rue de la Michodiere, off the Avenue de l'Opera on the right bank of the Seine. Despite the sixteen-year age gap which separated them, he and Pauline were the best of friends; she enjoyed his naughty sense of humour, appreciated his liveliness of mind and marvelled at his encyclopaedic knowledge of singing.

He was a highly intelligent man who, early in his career, realized that he preferred teaching to performing, and subsequently became Professor of Voice at the Paris Conservatoire, and later at the Royal Academy of Music in London.

Like him, Pauline had an endless curiosity about anything and everything, and she was amazed at the way he always found an answer to her questions, however obscure they might be. To posterity, his main claim to fame, in addition to his reputation as a teacher, was the invention of the laryngoscope, which not only earned him the gratitude of singers, but of the medical profession. Like many discoveries, the basic premise was simple, and it was surprising that no one had thought of it before.

The idea came to him one day when he was looking in the window of a dental supplies shop in the rue de Rivoli, near the Tuilleries Gardens, and he happened to notice a long handled mirror. He bought it, took it home, and began to experiment with it. Using one of his students as a guinea pig, he placed a large mirror on a band around his forehead, then angled the dentist's mirror and peered down the student's throat, while he sang. When Manuel saw the vocal chords in action for the very first time, his heart almost missed a beat, as he realized that he had devised a most useful tool for both physicians and for teachers of singing.

He was married to Eugenie Mayer, who had previously been one of his students. She was a mezzo soprano, thirteen years his junior, with a successful career at the Opera Comique. Although they produced four children, the couple were so ill-matched that Manuel later chose to live in England rather than stay in the same city with her, and they finally separated in 1848.

In November, Pauline sang at the house of Caroline Jaubert, one of the leading Parisian hostesses, who soon realized that the young singer had a very special talent. She took her under her wing, introduced her to influential friends and acquaintances, who in turn, invited Pauline to sing in their fashionable salons. Caroline was a very distinguished woman in her mid-thirties, petite, attractive, intelligent, witty, calculating and extremely elegant. Her salon was noted for the quality of the company it drew, both men and women, although men greatly outnumbered females on most occasions.

One of her most frequent guests was the young poet, playwright and novelist, Alfred de Musset, who adored her. She invited him to hear Pauline, and introduced him to her after the concert. Apparently, it was Pauline's conversation, as much as her musical abilities, which captivated him and he told his brother, Paul: 'she talked like an artist and a Princess'. Alfred expressed the view that genius was a charming thing and he was glad to be alive to see it.

The poet was twenty-eight, and might once have been good looking, but he frequented some of the most disreputable, notorious dens in Paris, where prostitutes and opium were commonplace and his health reflected his dissolute life style. His clothes were so casually worn, as to be practically slovenly, and his fingers, lips and teeth were decidedly yellow, due to his heavy smoking. His figure was tall and he had fair hair, brown eyes, a pouting mouth, long nose and ruddy complexion. Despite his failings, he had masses of charm, and many women were attracted to him because he was amusing, articulate and lively and he relished the company of women. Everything about them fascinated him and he was interested in all that interested them. Although he was a great raconteur, unlike the average man, he did not enjoy discussing politics or serious matters, but loved gossiping with the ladies, making them laugh with his impersonations and caricatures of his friends and acquaintances.

Even when he was a very young man, there was always a great deal of gossip about his womanising and high living. In 1835, he and Caroline Jaubert became lovers, but their passion was short-lived, and they replaced it with a deep and abiding friendship. She was his loyal and discreet friend, the 'godmother' to whom he confided everything because he believed that he could trust her implicitly.

Two years before his liaison with Caroline began, he had embarked on an infamous affair with Aurora, Baroness Dudevant, who had settled in Paris in 1831 when she was twenty seven. She had left her husband, Casimir, with whom she had nothing in common and had never been in love, and her two children, Maurice and Solange, at Nohant, her country chateau in Berry. She dressed as a man, changed her name to George Sand, and escaped to Paris with her twenty-year-old lover, the journalist Jules Sandeau,

Here they set up home together, and George began her career as a writer, shocking society by her habit of wearing men's clothes, and smoking cigars. She was not detered by disaproval because she believed that she had a true literary talent, and dressed as a man in order to break into the masculine world, inhabiting all the bars, cafes and restaurants they frequented, but which were out of bounds to females of quality, most of whom were chaperoned and under parental control while single, and under the jurisdiction of their husbands when married. They were unenfranchised, with no rights to their own property, and naturally, it was only the bravest women who broke with convention, risking alienation from polite society.

George was nothing if not courageous although she was tiny in stature. Her hair was dark and luxuriant, her eyes were large, black, and slightly protruding, and her sex appeal was immense. She had a strong personality, unbounded energy, and was generous to a fault. Her social conscience was second to none, and through her writing she intended to ameliorate the condition of those less fortunate than herself by raising public consciousness, just as the English novelist, Charles Dickens, was doing on the other side of the Channel.

She had an antipathy to the married state, where men subjugated women, and deplored the fact that many females bore child after child, year in and year out whether they belonged to higher, middle, or working class families. Death in childbirth was a real possiblity, but few women had any option but marriage, and spinsters were considered the most unfortunate of creatures, ridiculed andset upon. The genteel poor thought themselves lucky to obtain posts as governesses, and the women of the lower classes turned their hands to whatever work they could find in order to survive. In France, as in England, prostitution was rife, and disease was endemic. Infant mortality was high, and children born from infected parents entered the world in distress, malformed, crippled or mentally handicapped, without hope of a cure.

For women, a glimmer of light appeared in 1840 when an early form of birth control was introduced in the form of the 'Dutch Cap', but it took time for it to become generally available because it was expensive, and needed to be fitted by a gynaecologist, which meant that it was beyond the reach of poor women.

George Sand thrived in Paris, where she felt alive and vital, doing what she was born to do, unimpeded by domestic responsibilities. At first she and Jules Sandeau collaborated, but her success soon outstripped his and strained their relationship, then in 1833, just as their affaire was waning, she met Alfred de

Musset, a man six years her junior, who swept her off her feet. She left Sandeau and set off for a 'honeymoon' in Italy with the poet.

More than most women of her class, George was aware of the double standards between 'men of the world' and their womenfolk.. Despite her own unorthodox behaviour, she had ideals and did not care for what she observed, upset by the flippant attitude of her male friends and acquaintances who had scant regard for women of the lower classes, considering them 'easy game'. The men who frequented brothels literally 'diced with death' because venereal disease was common and highly contagious. Mercury was used as a cure, but its side effects were almost worse than the disease itself. Desiring to experience life to the full, even into the depths of depravity, Alfred paid no heed to the risks he took.

In the same year that he and George became lovers, the novel 'Gamiani ou une nuit d'exces' was published. It is considered by many to be one of the most important erotic French novels, and is often reprinted. Publication was reported to have taken place in Belgium, but it was actually printed clandestinely in Paris. It deals with every kind of sexual license and perversion, including bestiality, and is illustrated with twelve lithographed plates, which have been ascribed to Achille Deveria and Henri Grevedon. By the time the second edition appeared, Alfred de Musset was credited with its authorship. The title-page bears the name 'Alcide, baron de M***', and readers seized upon the initials A.D.M. as representing Alfred de Musset, who, since that time has been acknowledged as the author. In later editions, only these initials appear in place of the author's name.

Shortly after the lovers arrived in Venice, Alfred was taken ill and George sought medical advice from a very handsome young Italian, Dr.Pietro Pagello, to whom she was immediately attracted. By this time, she had become thoroughly bored and disillusioned with Alfred, and it was not long before she seduced Pagello: Alfred took himself off as soon as he was well, and George decamped to France with her new lover.

When she appeared in Paris minus Alfred but with the handsome Pagello in tow, tongues wagged furiously and rumours flew around the salons of the capital like wild fire, the flames of which were fanned considerably when George published a diary revealing all. Informed of this publication, Alfred was furious and deeply hurt, not only because she revealed details of their intimate life together, but because she made him a laughing stock. He was desperately unhappy, yet in spite of all that she had done, he was still in love with her, and said that he was willing to forgive and forget, if she still wanted him. To the relief of all his friends, she did not, because within a short time of her return,

Franz Liszt had introduced her to the Polish pianist, Frederick Chopin. Pagello was homesick and without occupation, and soon decided to return to Italy, leaving George to explore new pastures.

Whatever she thought of Chopin on first meeting him, he declared that he had found her repulsive. He was used to feminine, well bred, aristocratic women, and disliked both George's bohemian appearance and behaviour and decried her habit of smoking Havana cigars. However, he hadn't reckoned with her tenacity and powerful sexual attraction. She pursued him relentlessly, and he was powerless to resist. Despite his fastidiousness, he soon forgot that he had ever found her repugnant and allowed himself to be seduced.

Alfred began to hate his former mistress, and took his revenge by publishing 'Confession d'un enfant du siecle' in 1835, giving his side of the story, causing further titillation and gossip in the 'dovecots', especially as he was rumoured to be the author of 'Gamiani', whose heroine, a woman with Lesbian tendencies, was thought to represent George Sand.

De Musset, Sand and Chopin were destined to play an important part in Pauline's life, and after the concert at Mme Jaubert's house, Alfred de Musset wrote a glowing tribute to the singer in the 'Revue des Deux Mondes'. This highly favourable publicity brought her to the attention of the fashionable world, and in Caroline's elegant salon, she met Alfred and his brother Paul frequently. She also met eminent painters, musicians, politicians, and writers, such as the literary lion, Victor Hugo, and a swarm of aristocrats, one of whom, Prince Belgiojoso, was a fine amateur singer and friend of Rossini, who took a great interest in her.

Caroline preferred not to have too many musicians at her concerts because they were more interested in making their own music. She considered that writers and artists were far better listeners, but she kept the number of politicians to a minimum, as they preferred to talk rather than listen to anybody else. She herself was a fine musician, and was very well informed on musical matters.

Pauline soon grew in confidence, sensing that she was among friends and admirers, who were interested in her for herself, not just as Malibran's sister. Alfred and Paul's mother, Mme de Musset invited the girl to perform at her house and she sang 'Felice Donzella' by Dessauer, some showy arias by Costa and De Beriot, and delighted her attentive listeners with exotic Spanish boleros and ariettes by her father. She sang item after item, and in the end, her mother had to discreetly draw her away, fearful that she would over-tire her voice.

Alfred was ecstatic about her singing, and found her personality alluring. She intrigued him, and he told friends that he considered her as 'au fait with everything as a learned professor.' Naturally, she was flattered by the attention bestowed on her by such a famous young poet, whom she knew to be the former lover of the notorious George Sand. Most girls of Pauline's age and milieu were not long out of the schoolroom, had led sheltered lives, and were kept in blissful ignorance of the scandals of the fashionable world, but the young singer, for all her air of innocence, had been surrounded by adults all her life and heard the current gossip circulating in the fashionable salons in which she now found herself.

She was fully aware of de Musset's eminence as a poet and writer, and was grateful for the professional interest he took in her career, but she was wary of the man himself, and was not attracted to his person at all. Nevertheless, she owed him a debt of gratitude because it was principally through him that she came to be known to the general public as a rising star of the first magnitude.

Alfred made himself agreeable to Mme Garcia and was often invited to the family home. Pauline assumed a reserved attitude towards him because she was never really comfortable in his presence, however, she was pleased with the pencil sketch he drew of her, which catches her personality and expression beautifully, nor was she at all displeased by the fact that he made her look much prettier than she really was.

Through Caroline Jaubert and de Musset's championship, Pauline met many influential people who became her devoted admirers. Alfred de Musset had dreams of a glorious renaissance of the arts and theatre in France, which his friend the Duke of Orleans, heir to the Bourbon throne, shared, and in Pauline they believed that they had discovered a young artist who could help them to realise that dream.

Another young woman, born the same year as Pauline, who had also made a great impression on the poet, was the actress, Eliza Felix, whom Alfred believed to be a genius. She came from a poor Jewish family, and as a child had earned her bread by singing in the streets with her elder sister Sarah. When she became an actress, she relinquished her own name, and called herself Rachel. Her relationship with Alfred was an intimate one, and as she had no family influence to assist her climb to fame, her native cunning helped her to survive and prosper. All her life she used whatever means it took to please men who could further her ambitions, but she was paranoid in her endeavours to avoid scandal, and posed as a virtuous young woman, swearing her lovers to secrecy. She was so successful in covering her tracks that when she performed for the first time in London, she was accepted as a young woman of the highest virtue and taken up by Queen Victoria, the Duchess of Kent, the dowager Queen Adelaide, and ladies of the court.

On 1838, Pauline made her first public appearance in Paris, at the Theatre de la Renaissance. Many of her loyal admirers were there, including Caroline Jaubert, Prince Belgiojoso, and Auguste Barre. Unfortunately for him, Alfred de Musset had omitted to book a stall when the seat in the box he was hoping to occupy did not materialise. That evening he stayed at home and wrote to Caroline telling her what he would have written had he been present. Pauline sang music chosen by her mother and Charles de Beriot, which included arias by the violinist himself and Michael Costa, played badly by a second-rate orchestra. Nevertheless, before she even sang a note, Pauline's charismatic presence commanded attention, and the individuality of her voice and unique ability to stir the emotions of her audience enabled her to overcome all the disadvantages of a poor orchestra and indifferent songs; in addition, she impressed her fashionable audience by her dignified, distinguished bearing, and some of her listeners declared that she had the air of a princess.

Her white, unadorned gown was of Duchesse satin, almost off the shoulder, with large, puffed sleeves decorated with fine lace, and a long full skirt; draped over her arms was a white organza stole; her only jewellery was a black jet necklace, and a black velvet band with a small diamond in the centre, that once belonged to Malibran, was worn on her forehead.

The German poet, Heinrich Heine, who had settled in Paris in 1831, was present and left his impressions of the young singer: "She is not merely a nightingale who delights in trilling and sobbing her songs of spring. Nor is she a rose, being ugly, but in a way that is noble – one might say beautiful – and which transported the lion-painter Lacroix into ecstasies. She reminds us more of the terrible magnificence of a jungle rather than the civilized beauty and tame grace of the European world in which we live. In moments of her passionate performance – particularly when she opens that great mouth with its dazzlingly white teeth and smiles in such a cruelly sweet and gracefully snarling way, one would not be surprised if all of a sudden a giraffe, leopard or even a herd of elephant calves crossed the scene."

Alfred de Musset called on Pauline the day after her concert and asked her to sing everything she had performed the previous evening. His review, which appeared on January 1st, 1839, in the extremely influential government sponsored 'La Revue des Deux Mondes', was one of the most extraordinary pieces of publicity of an untried singer, ever penned. Not only did he praise Pauline, but he linked her genius to a perceptive analysis of the state of the French operatic theatre of the day, and added that a young English girl had practically fainted when she heard Pauline for the first time, thinking it was Malibran's ghost. He also admitted that shivers had gone up and down his spine when he first heard Pauline, as the timbre of her voice was so similar to that of her sister. He declared that anyone who had heard and loved Malibran could not fail to be moved by Pauline, although he admitted added that the likeness was in their sound rather than in their physical features. He acknowledged that Pauline's voice was resonant and clear, at once both bitter and sweet, but said that it was more than a voice, it was a soul, singing, the same soul and genius that Malibran had possessed in such abundance, He further observed; "She abandons herself to inspiration with an easy simplicity which lends everything an air of grandeur....She sings as she breathes". Impressed by her expressive quality, which varied with every phrase, he said: "She possesses that great secret of artists: before she expresses anything, she feels it. She does not listen to her voice, but to her heart"!

He predicted an extraordinary career for her, and prophesied that she would succeed in changing the low theatrical standards then prevailing. Of her other talents, he stated: "She knows five languages, accompanies herself on the piano with the ease and self-assurance of a master, is full of fire and vivacity, and talks like an artist and a princess, draws like Grandville, and sings like her sister..." The Garcias must have been immensely pleased by this flattering review in which he declared: 'Pauline was born a flower, and music is her scent', but would have preferred him to have left out the codicil: 'Rachel, who knows nothing, except how to read and understand, simple, withdrawn, silent, born in poverty.'

In his estimation, both of these girls were touched by genius, and he believed that they would bring about a return of the serenity and sanity of classical conventions after the wild excesses of Romanticism on the French stage. He was determined that artistic truth should reign once more, pure, unclouded, and free from the exaggerated licence that had been allowed to predominate for too long.

There was another journalistic voice, however, which was more down to earth. This belonged to the composer, Hector Berlioz, whose music Pauline had first heard at her concert in Lille in 1836, when his overture 'Les Francs Juges' was played, and which became one of her favourite orchestral pieces. She first met him in 1839, and in time an artistic collaboration and great friendship developed between them. Like Schumann, he had a decided literary gift and wrote music criticism in order to earn a living. However, he loathed journalism, but had to accept what he regarded as 'hack work', because his musical compositions rarely paid the bills, being so avant garde that most people, even other composers, failed to understand them, saying they were too loud, discordant and unintelligible. Some even declared that he was mad, and Chopin maintained that he did not compose music, but merely splattered his pen on the page. Another problem was that his works demanded very large orchestral forces, which was too risky and expensive a venture for impressarios who had to fill their halls with the paying public. On the rare occasions when his music was performed in France, rehearsals were few, with insufficient instruments for all the parts, and too many deputies. His genius was original and revolutionary, and like all pioneers he was frequently misunderstood. In Germany, however, where orchestral music of a profound nature has always been highly valued, his works were enthusiastically received.

He was an ardent admirer of the German eighteenth century composer Christoph Willibald Gluck, who was the operatic reformer of his day. In order to go forward, Gluck had looked back to the days of Classical Greece and Rome, and to the beginnings of Italian opera in the sixteenth century, when the text had been of paramount importance, declaimed on a sustained, legato line with ornamentation kept to a minimum, so that the words were not obscured.

Berlioz took Pauline to task in an article in the 'Journal des Debats', declaring that she had 'ruined' a duet from 'Orfeo' by Gluck. He said her rendering was 'showy and shallow', and blamed her training in the 'debased' Italian tradition, which she had received from her father. Gluck had endeavoured to outlaw the excesses of his day, but old traditions die hard. No doubt Pauline had upset Berlioz by adding her own ornamentation and decoration to the vocal line, something that even when the fashion for it had long declined, she still employed, because she obviously liked it, and considered that it enhanced, rather than detracted, from the emotional content of the music. He appreciated the extensive range of her voice, but considered that its tessitura was too low for the part of Euridice. He also expressed the view that she had a great deal to learn about antique poetry.

As Berlioz became better acquainted with her, he began to realize that she was a serious, dedicated woman, who, given the right guidance, would develop into a fine artist, and he inspired her with a desire to learn more about Gluck's music, with the result that she began to study his works and precepts. Due to Berlioz's influence she usually included Gluck's arias in her concerts, and in time became an acknowledged expert of his style.

However, to many, Berlioz was a pedantic voice crying in the wilderness, and Alfred's article about Pauline carried far more weight with the general public. She was fast becoming a celebrity, and the poet continued to court her, paying frequent visits to the Garcia home. Although Pauline was undoubtedly grateful for the publicity he had given her, she was not anxious for their relationship to assume a more personal aspect; she was fastidious and found him increasingly repulsive with his sexually suggestive, double entente comments. In all fairness, she did try to overcome her aversion, but his lack of eyelashes and red-rimmed eyes, and the shameless way he flirted with Joaquina, who was obviously flattered by his attentions, caused Pauline to retreat from him.

She knew about his visits to Rachel's dressing room after performances at the Comedie Francaise because there was always a good deal of gossip surrounding Alfred and his affairs, but as she did not care about him romantically, she was indifferent to the other ladies in his life. His erotic insinuations were distasteful to her, making her feel tarnished, and intimidated. Her instinct was to keep him at arm's length, and he found her very elusive, quite the opposite to Rachel, who was always ready to receive him with open arms.

Another regular visitor to the Garcia household was Louis Viardot, a long-standing friend who had played an important part in the annulment of Malibran's first marriage. He was thirty eight years old, of medium height and slim build, with dark hair and eyes, a small, shapely moustache and trim beard. This serious, fastidious man, was deeply intellectual, but possessed a certain dry wit, and had a great capacity for kindness. He was always neatly dressed and elegant, although he was no dandy. He was a Burgundian, born in Dijon, whose father was the local Prefect, a civic post that carried a great deal of influence. Louis Viardot was now the director of the Theatre Italien, having taken up the position due to the death of the previous director in a recent disastrous fire at the theatre.

He and Manuel Garcia were friends of long standing, and Pauline enjoyed his company because he was sensitive and could converse about the thingsthat interested her. He was a lawyer, journalist, writer, translator, political philosopher, and an expert on Spanish literature, art, history and culture, whose main claim to fame is as the first French translator of Cervantes' 'Don Quixote'. He had no personal political ambitions, but he was a keen observer and writer of the political scene, a Republican with liberal views, and many left-wing friends, including George Sand. His knowledge of painting was prodigious, and he owned a fine collection of old masters, which he frequently augmented at auction rooms.

Although he was twenty-one years older than Pauline, having been born in 1800, she was hardly aware of the difference in their ages because she had been surrounded by adults from childhood. When she was born, her father was already forty-six, and her brother and sister were much older than herself, so age was not an issue. From her earliest childhood she had behaved like an adult and, in fact, she was more shy with her contemporaries, especially young men of her own age, than with older people. Louis, like herself and Manuel, was full of curiosity about the world, and easily accepted new technological ideas, but in music he was a reactionary and his tastes remained firmly entrenched in the eighteenth century. To him, a great deal of contemporary music was distasteful; he even found much of Rossini's music too modern, but he adored and revered Mozart.

When his visits to the Garcias and those of Alfred coincided, the two men were polite to each other, but Alfred eyed the older man warily, like an animal whose territory is threatened. The poet was beginning to care deeply for Pauline; her reserve piqued him, and her mysterious quality continued to fascinate him. He was spoiled because so many women succumbed easily to his charm and fame, and he resented being cold shouldered by the singer. The fact that he was now pursuing Princess Belgiojoso and enjoying Rachel's favours, did not weigh with him. He boasted that he knew Rachel 'pretty well' and admitted that he would love to 'cross swords with little Pauline for a quarter of an hour'. When this morsel of gossip reached her ears, she was disgusted and resented being publicly discussed in such a way.

Soon, Alfred changed the sobriquet 'little Pauline' into 'cruel Pauline.' Whether he actually went as far as asking her to marry him, or if his proposal was less honourable, is not known, but he was perplexed to find that Pauline was not such an easy conquest as Rachel, and he received a rebuff, which certainly dented his amour propre. It is probable that there were two occasions about which he wrote to Caroline Jaubert, but it may well have been one and the same, although it has never been discovered why he was so upset.

It appears that one day in early January, he visited the Garcias wearing a fur coat, and suffering from a heavy cold and temperature. The apartment was hot and airless, and he found Pauline entertaining the Irish pianist, George Alexander Osborne. Apparently, Alfred overheard Pauline say something to Osborne that greatly agitated the sensitive poet, and upset him so much that he confessed he could not reveal it even to his best friend. On January 11th, he sent a letter to Caroline enclosing a poem, which stemmed from his 'outburst of rage' brought on by the singer's words. After quoting the poem, he wrote; 'There! And I'm madly in love with Rachel!'. 'What do you make of that? I'm not joking....'

His poem was published in the 'Revue des Deux Mondes,' addressed to Mademoiselle X, and was probably read by Pauline, although he did not send her the original. At that time he visited Caroline twice in one day, but she was out; beset by a raging toothache, and annoyed by her absence, he was impatient to pour out his grievances.

He alleged that Pauline and Osborne had exchanged some words in English, (which he called a 'devilish language'), while he was talking to Joaquina, and said that he thought he heard Pauline say two 'horrid words' about him as a joke. He was so offended that he could not bring himself to repeat them. Maybe she simply said 'he's drunk,' due to the redness of his complexion, and his light-headedness that he states was the result of a high temperature, but which, as far as she was concerned, could just as easily have been due to the effects of alcohol. It might also have been 'he smells', which would have been even more offensive, but at that time the general standard of hygiene left a lot to be desired due to the lack of bathrooms, running hot water, washing machines and dry cleaning.

Whatever it was, Alfred was devastated, disillusioned by the girl, yet always holding the singer in high esteem, and she never let him down in his initial appraisal of her genius. All her life, she strove for the highest ideals in music and art, and played a significant part in bringing about the changes of which he dreamed. Despite the hurt she had caused him, Alfred was aroused by Pauline, and against his will, was obsessed by thoughts of her. What he found difficult to bear was the fact that his goddess had fallen off her pedestal, and he now called her 'ungrateful and absurd', although he was never able to deny her entirely.

When she was an old lady, someone asked her to tell them about Alfred de Musset, but she was very dismissive, saying that she had never liked him. She showed no gratitude for the part he had played in bringing her to public attention at the outset of her career, and obviously chose to ignore how much she was in his debt.

CHAPTER SIX

1839

Early in 1839, Pauline received a letter from her Leipzig friend, Clara Wieck, saying that she was coming to Paris in the hope of establishing herself as a concert pianist in the French capital. Naturally, she was sad to leave Robert Schumann behind, but she needed to get away from her dictatorial father, who was still making life impossible for them.

Clara was determined to concentrate on her career, and hoped that the singer would introduce her into influential circles. Pauline wrote suggesting that she should come to live in the rue Michodiere, as it was conveniently situated, and it would be pleasant for her to be with friends.

When the pianist arrived in Paris, accompanied by her chaperone, Henriette Reichmann, she was amazed at the size, noise, and unbelievable volume of traffic and crowds in the metropolis. As the two German girls stepped down from the coach, Clara was relieved to see Pauline and her mother waving at them. The Garcias greeted them warmly, led them to a waiting cab, and off they went to their lodgings where a meal was awaiting them.

Clara delivered her letters of introduction from Felix Mendelssohn, and played in several private houses, but she did not find it easy to break into the upper echelons of Parisian musical circles because there were already so many excellent pianists in the city. Her abilities were never in doubt, but she was reserved and very serious. Small and slight, with an elfin face and soft, dark brown hair, she was a shy, intensely Teutonic young lady, quite out of her depth in the sophisticated social whirl of the French capital. She felt provincial, even though Leipzig was one of the foremost musical centres in Europe where music was thought so important that it drew musicians and students like a magnet. If the Parisians hardly noticed Clara, she considered them very frivolous, with poor musical taste, and more interested in food than art. Nevertheless she envied Pauline's sang froid, and her ability to take everything in her stride, accepting the status quo, confident, carefree, happy and always optimistic. In addition, the French girl had the advantage of a loving, supportive family, and enviable connections in high places.

Clara had few relatives, and had never seen much of her mother because she lived in Berlin. Her dour father had forced his wife to give up any claims to her daughter, and Clara's welfare had been totally in the hands of Herr Wieck. Pauline did her best to bring her friend out in society and introduced her to people who, she thought, might be useful to her, but despite her obvious talent as a pianist, Clara made little impression. Had she been able to lighten up and find some of the elan that her Gallic friend had in abundance, things might have been different.

Finding the city expensive and fast running short of money, Clara left the Garcias, and moved to Bougival, a pretty suburb on the Seine, west of Paris, because the cost of living was cheaper and advertised for pupils as a means of immediate income.

No doubt, on her trip to Leipzig, Pauline had encouraged Clara to envisage a career beyond her native land, and felt responsible for her lonely friend. She liked her very much, appreciated her fine talent, and considered it a waste if Clara failed to gain the opportunity to appear in public before audiences of discrimination. Performers had to set up and finance their own concerts, and sponsor their own publicity, their reputations being made and advertised, not only in the newspapers, but by word of mouth. If they happened to be good at self promotion, like Paganini, they were fortunate indeed, and could make a fortune. If they had patronage, so much the better, but it was a very hard road for those starting out without family connections, finances, or skill in promoting themselves.

Pauline visited Clara at Bougival and entertained her with news and gossip from the metropolis. The girls loved the sleepy little place, with its scattering of houses spread over the hillsthat rise up from the Seine, took delightful walks and enjoyed picnics along its tree lined banks. Often, they climbed up to the old church, its high steeple standing out sharply against the sky, and cut their way through verdant fields covered with wild flowers and mighty, ancient cypress and ash trees. From this highpoint, they had magnificent, undisturbed views over a wide landscape stretching to Paris and its environs in the east, and St. Germaine en Laye and beyond in the west. Those who could afford to do so were building villas and garden pavilions in Italianate style along the river banks, where they spent weekends and holidays in the country, away from the tumult of Paris, yet within easy reach of the city.

A little later, artists such as Manet, Monet, Pissarro, Sisley and Berthe Morisot, the only woman painter of their original group, fell in love with Bougival and its picturesque beauties, and even today, this part of the path along the Seine is called the 'Chemin des Impressionists.'

It was during these excursions that the two young musicians confided their youthful dreams to each other; both of them having visions of life stretching endlessly into a future full of possibility. Pauline was naturally optimistic, but Clara was already finding life difficult. She did not wish to appeal to her father for money, but it was not easy to make ends meet. Pauline did what she could for her, and tried to cheer her up, helping her to look forward to better times; little by little Clara attracted some young pupils, and with her earnings her situation improved. She had peaceful surroundings and used her leisure hours wisely, developing her piano technique and composing songs and piano pieces. When two of her Leipzig friends, Emilie and Elise List, came to stay in Paris with their father, the eminent political economist, Frederick List, Clara sometimes stayed at their house, and they visited her in Bougival. Through her friendships, and her musical activities, her homesickness lessened, but she still missed Robert dreadfully and lived for his letters.

About a mile or so east of Bougival, at Rueil, lies the estate of Malmaison where the Emperor Napoleon and his wife Josephine lived when he was First Consul. The gardens had been Josephine's paradise, with magnificent displays of roses, sent to her from all parts of the world, but since her death in 1814, it had been sadly neglected. The girls sometimes trespassed and enjoyed rambling through the woods that circled the main house, with its plain, elegant, white stucco exterior, long windows, and large canopied wrought-iron porch. They also visited the other side of the park where the elegant chateau of Bois-Preau is situated. Napoleon made a gift of this lovely house to Josephine for her own use, when, despite having children from her first marriage, she failed to produce one with Napoleon. In 1809, although still in love with his wife, he divorced her for dynastic reasons and married Princess Marie Louise, the daughter of the Austrian Emperor, in the hope that she would provide him with the necessary son and heir. She did, but fate was waiting in the wings and decreed that Napoleon's son, who bore the title Duke of Reichstadt, would never succeed his father, who was finally defeated by Wellington at the Battle of Waterloo, and exiled to the island of St. Helena, where he died in imprisonment in 1821. His son died ten years, later at the age of twenty-one.

Napoleon had spent a great deal of his time at Malmaison when he was a vigorous young man, but he rarely visited it after 1804. Josephine, on the other hand, adored the place, which was her permanent home until her death. The romantic young girls were fascinated by the thought of these two Imperial figures having lived, and loved there, and it brought French history wonderfully to life for them. Imaginative as they were, they could easily conjure up the ghosts of the famous couple, and despite the risks of being found and expelled by the caretaker, they considered their visits worth the gamble.

For some time, the two delightful houses had been more or less deserted, the beautiful furnishings, paintings and works of art shrouded in loose covers, and shutters closed at the many long, elegant windows. The estate was inherited by Prince Eugene de Beauharnais, Josephine's son from her first marriage, but in 1824, he was exiled to Bavaria, and died without visiting Malmaison again. Now, Josephine's wonderful gardens were overgrown, a haven for wildlife, where abundant weeds strangled what was left of the roses and exotic plants which Josephine had cherished. Some time later, part of the estate was bought by a businessman named Bourbonne, who built a perfume factory and some houses on the land. Little did Pauline imagine that in 1874, she would buy the estate of 'Les Frenes' and live in a house built on a parcel of land from the Malmaison estate.

Back in Paris, Charles de Beriot was bursting with the news that Pauline had been invited to sing at Her Majesty's Theatre in London, the centre of operatic life in England, and the next best thing to appearing at the Paris Opera. Her debut was scheduled for May, and she would sing Desdemona in Rossini's 'Otello', (a role much associated with her sister), Angiolina in 'La Cenerentola', and Nina in 'La Gazza Ladra', all by Rossini.

The usually calm Mme Garcia was highly excited at the possibilities she foresaw from this engagement, and soon Pauline was hard at work learning the music and Italian text for her roles. There was not much time, but she learned quickly and soon had them memorised. Next came the real work of developing the various characters into three dimensional young women. Joaquina was experienced in stage craft, and was an ideal coach for her daughter, who soon revealed a real gift for acting.

Pauline was fortunate in being blessed with a vivid imagination, an indispensable attribute for an interpretive artist; this enabled her to get under the skin of a character, and she readily accepted her mother's instructions: on movement, deportment and the business of the theatre. Joaquina told her how she must always find her light, but not obstruct the light of her colleagues, how not to upstage, and which foot to use when stepping up or downstage, with which hand to lead, and so forth, all very basic, but necessary for the inexperienced young performer. She also instructed her in the skilful art of stage make-up. At that time the predominance of the footlights (called 'floats', as originally candles were placed in a trough of water along the edge of the stage), cast strange shadows on faces, so heavy make-up was required. Gas lights had recently been introduced at all the major theatres, but candles were also used, and in most places there was a combination of both types of lighting. It was not until the end of the nineteenth century that electricity began to be installed, the Savoy Theatre in London, being the first to use it.

The theatre also has its own etiquette and traditions, which performers must observe. Actors are known to be very superstitious: whistling in the dressing room or quoting from the 'Scottish play' (Macbeth), can make the perpetrators very unpopular with their fellow performers and anyone guilty of such a faux pas is sent out of the room and told to turn around three times before being re-admitted.

Manuel Garcia and de Beriot helped Joaquina to coach Pauline. de Beriot was going to London as Pauline's impressario, and no stone was left unturned to make sure that she was as ready as she could be for this, the biggest challenge of her career to date. The Italian Opera in London took place during the brilliant social season, where to be seen at the opera was the pinnacle of fashion.

In London, all operas were sung in Italian, no matter where they originated. Many of the aristocracy understood Italian, having made the grand tour to that country as part of their education, but at the Paris Opera, everything was performed in French, despite the origin of each particular composer. This made life difficult for the singers, who had to re-learn their parts in different translations, and led eventually to the modern system of performing works in their original language: thus a singer who already knows a work in French will sing the role in French whether in Paris, Vienna, London, Munich or Buenos Aires. Some of the provincial companies perform in the vernacular, but the major houses function with guest singers who travel from place to place for individual productions, and sing in the original language.

The London engagement came Pauline's way due to the unavailability of the twenty-eight-year old Italian prima donna, Giulia Grisi. She was a woman of tremendous popularity in England, especially with the young Queen Victoria, who was a great opera enthusiast. Having achieved her celebrity upon the operatic stage, she kept a ruthless hold upon her position, as Pauline was later to find to her cost. She was a most beautiful woman of Junoesque proportions, a pale, creamy skin and sparkling dark eyes and hair. Her voice was large, smooth and luscious, with a wonderful ability to soar effortlessly. She came from a theatrical family, and had received a fine vocal training in Italy. However, although her technique was impeccable, she learned slowly, and was almost musically illiterate, relying upon her good ear rather than an ability to read music efficiently. Some of the more discerning opera goers thought she lacked refinement and taste, but despite this, she was a great favourite with audiences.

The French poet and critic, Theophile Gautier, wrote 'As to Mademoiselle Grisi, her beauty, her acting, and her voice leave nothing more to be desired; a magnificent trinity not often observed in one person'.

She had not long recovered from a scandal thatoccurred in 1838, the subject of much gossip and rumour at the time. Her husband, Count de Melcy, discovered a letter addressed to her from the young Viscount Castlereagh, to which he took exception, and challenged Castlereagh to a duel, which was fought on June 16th. Before the men raised their pistols to fire, the Viscount handed a piece of paper to M. de Cottreau, de Melcy's second, which declared that Madame Grisi had by no means encouraged his attentions and that the letter that had caused so much harm was the first that he had written to her. Both men fired at the same time, de Melcy's ball hit the Viscount in the right wrist, and the latter's pistol discharged into the air. De Melcy then read the letter, and as his lordship was wounded, he considered his honour satisfied.

In England, by this time, duels were a thing of the past and on the rare occasions that they occurred, were very much frowned upon. It seemed that the Viscount was following in his father's footsteps, because in 1809, he had challenged and fought George Canning, who was then Foreign Secretary in the Tory government, the result being that both men had to resign their posts. Of course, the Grisi affair was a cause celebre because it involved two noblemen and a prima donna, which titillated the curiosity of the populace. As Castlereagh's letter appeared to exonerate Grisi, she was given the benefit of the doubt, and when she next appeared at the opera, the duration of the applause held up the proceedings for several minutes. She was singing in Donizetti's 'Parasina' and Queen Victoria, seeing it for the second time wrote: 'we came in just after Grisi had appeared and before she sang. I never saw Grisi so splendid, or sing so well. The scene with (Antonio) Tamburini is really the finest scene I ever saw. Both acted so beautifully.' Ironically, in this scene Parisina is accused of adultery by her husband! Strangely, this affair did not diminish Grisi's popularity, if anything it increased it, and made her known to a wider audience.

After the duel, the singer left de Melcy whom she had married in 1836 when he was twenty, and she twenty-five. He was an impoverished aristocrat with nothing to offer but his name, and for her this union was an absolute disaster. She was already an established prima donna, earning high fees, and public adulation and now her fortune belonged legally to her dissolute husband. She had only been married for a short time when she realised what a terrible mistake she had made in allying herself with such an undesirable man.

Even if she had been innocent at the time of the duel, or whether it had the effect of pushing her into the arms of the Viscount, she soon became his mistress. When Pauline made her debut, Grisi was already two months pregnant with his child. A boy, who was named George Frederick Ormsby, was born in November of that year. Despite his illegitimacy, he was brought up and educated by Castlereagh who, when it was obvious that his marriage was likely to remain childless, made the boy his heir. The Viscount never allowed him to forget his mother, even when their affair was over, and whenever she was in London, he was brought to visit her.

Grisi was in a privileged, powerful position, with friends in high places, and she was strong minded, determined and ambitious to a fault. She kept a wary eye on Pauline as a possible rival, and two years later when she and Pauline were appearing at Her Majesty's Theatre together, she became obsessively jealous of her, fearing her superior musicianship and dramatic gifts.For many years, she was a thorn in Pauline's flesh, both in London and Paris, making her life a misery as often as she could.

Towards the end of April, Pauline, her mother and Charles left Paris and travelled by coach to the coast, where they caught a packet steamer to Dover. The weather was cool, and the voyage rough and stormy, causing them all to be unwell, and it was a great relief to see the white cliffs and the gaunt, grey castle, as the ship sailed into the busy harbour. Soon they were on their way to London, bowling along through the picturesque Kent countryside in a stage coach at the amazing speed of fourteen miles an hour.

The Old Kent Road led them into the district of Lambeth, south of the Thames, a place of artisans, and craftsmen, as well as rogues and vagabonds. Their destination was the Elephant and Castle Inn, where there was such a melee of people, carriages, coaches, horses, and all manner of detritus that they felt dizzy with the noise and bustle. Here they ate a light meal, and then Charles hailed a Hackney carriage to take them into the City of London sohe could visit his bank. They bowled along the south bank of the Thames and having crossed the river at London Bridge, were immediately caught up in a great traffic jam which seemed to last for an eternity. Carriages and horse drawn vehicles were absolutely chock–a-block, without any leeway in which to turn and go back to find another route, yet it was not only the heavy weight of traffic which caused the huge problem, but the tolls that operated throughout the capital, slowing down the rate of progress to a snail's pace. These taxes were particularly unpopular, as corruption prevailed and people were frequently overcharged. With around a hundred toll gates in London, the populace felt it was being held to ransom, and there was 'the grand total of hurry and worry, vexation and molestation suffered by the travelling public'. Many considered it 'legalised robbery'. All horses and vehicles were charged varying sums to pass through a toll gate, and only royalty, the military, mail coaches, funerals, prison carts and clergymen on official duty were exempt.

At the time of Pauline's debut, England was already entrenched in the Industrial Revolution, being the leader in the field, with France and the rest of Europe still to catch up. Due to high deposits of coal and iron in the north and midlands, industrialisation was rushing along at a furious pace. Railways were installed for the porterage of these commodities, but it was not long before the enterprising 'movers and shakers' realised that they could also be 'people carriers'. Vast investments were under way, and many stood to make huge fortunes.

Agricultural workers left their villages and fields in droves because they believed they could earn better wages in the towns, and in order to cope with the onslaught, cheap houses were thrown up almost overnight, back to back, airless dwellings, with communal yards containing a wash house and solitary privy for dozens of people to share. Factories and mills literally 'ate up', men, women, and children as young as five years old, all of whom worked twelve-hour shifts in grime, dirt and the endless noise of machinery, so loud that they could no longer talk to their fellow workers, but had to develop lip reading skills, and employ gestures in order to be understood. Many became profoundly deaf after a few years exposed to such conditions.

Charles's business completed, the Hackney cab left the city behind, and rolled into the West End, presenting its occupants with a great contrast to the scenes through which they had so recently passed. Here, they were to stay at 184 Regent Street, one of the finest, most elegant thorough-fares in Europe, with splendid hotels and shops. It had been planned by the Prince Regent at the beginning of the nineteenth century, and was intended to lead all the way to Regents Park, a large expanse of verdure and lakes, surrounded by the homes of the seriously rich, designed by the famous architect, John Nash. Charles de Beriot had chosen the lodging, as it was only a five minute walk to Her Majesty's Theatre, which was situated at the lower end of Regent Street, in the ancient Haymarket. It was a busy and noisy area that contained several brothels but was very convenient for rehearsals and performances.

In the early 1800's, the opera had begun at 6.30 pm, but now performances started at 8pm, and rarely ended before midnight, because a ballet was always played after the opera. The high price of tickets, London's enormous distances and the difficulties of getting home late at night, deterred many people from going to the theatre, but was popular with those who lived in or near the centre.

Pauline would have preferred to stay in the suburbs, but it was more convenient to live close to the theatre. Surprisingly, although she had yet to prove
herself as an opera singer, Pauline's contract assured her of a fee of 40,000
francs for a handful of performances.

Money attracted artists to England because London theatres paid more for
talent than anywhere in the world, and although the cost of living was high,
artists considered it worthwhile to appear in Britain.

CHAPTER SEVEN

1839

The lodgings in Regent Street were comfortable, with fine, well proportioned rooms, large windows, festooned with heavy brocade curtains, tied back with fringed tassels, gracious fireplaces, and attractively furnished bedrooms, with pretty floral or striped wallpapers, and furniture that had been the height of fashion in the early years of the century. Pauline immediately fell in love with this out-dated Regency style, and several years later, when she acquired a chateau in the French countryside, she chose furniture of this period, imported from England.

Despite a comfortable bed, she only slept fitfully, because she was excited and agitated at the thought of what lay ahead of her in this strange, teeming, unfamiliar city. After a typically substantial English breakfast of kedgeree, bacon, eggs, sausage, grilled kidneys, bread, butter and tea, Pauline and her companions sauntered forth to visit Her Majesty's Theatre in the Haymarket.

It was an area of ill-repute and prostitution was rife, so much so that 'Haymarket ware' was a euphemism for a loose woman. However, as its name suggests, the Haymarket was a place for the buying and selling of hay, an important commodity at that time, as London was packed with horses, stabled all over the metropolis, and involved in every kind of commercial work, as well as pulling the ubiquitous Hackney cabs and the carriages of the professional and wealthy classes. The quantities of hay needed to feed and nourishthese vast numbers of hard working animals was prodigious, and at dawn, carts began arriving at the market from out-lying farms, with their heavy loads of hay and farm produce, pulled by large, sturdy Shires and Clydesdales.

Many of London's roads were still made of beaten earth, but some were cobbled, and horses hooves striking the stones made a great deal of noise. When it rained, the beaten earth turned to a sea of mud, much to the consternation of the ladies whose hems and shoes were quickly blackened. Crossing sweepers were necessary to clear the horse manure and dirt so that pedestrians could cross the road unimpeded. Most of the sweepers were very young boys, who existed on tips handed to them as they swept the way clear. Pauline was moved by the sight of these poor little urchins, who often had their younger brothers and sisters in tow, as many of them were orphans, or had parents who worked long hours. They rarely had enough to eat, and usually looked pinched and cold, dressed in their flimsy rags. Pauline was to see them each day, and always found a coin for them. She had a kind heart and it affected her greatly to perceive the plight of children in such circumstances. Many of them slept rough under London's bridges and tuberculosis was common among them.

Thin and ill-clothed young girls sold matches, and Pauline wished that there was more she could do for them than simply buying their goods, or giving them a few coins for a warm meal. London was full of such poverty-stricken individuals, both adults and children, and however much one gave, it was a mere drop in the ocean, so great was the need.

Having picked their way along the street, narrowly avoiding carriages and carts, the musicians found themselves at the stage door of Her Majesty's Theatre, a large, elegant, classically designed building with colonnades, and three upper storeys, each of which had balustraded balconies at the long, pedimented windows.

De Beriot gave Pauline's name to the stage door keeper, who showed them the way to the manager's office through a warren of dark, cramped corridors. The lack of backstage space was a serious deficiency of the building, with a number of small dressing rooms and the costume store situated underneath the stage. The area between the ceiling and the roof was used for the painting and storing of scenery, and the passages leading from different parts of the house to the backstage area were labyrinthine. The problem of space was compounded by the fact that the ballet, which took place after an opera performance, had also to be accommodated, and dressing room space was at a premium with opera and ballet principals, fifteen dancers of the corps de ballet and thirty-six choristers to be accommodated, not to mention the number of supernumaries required for most productions.

Pauline and her family were pushed and jostled by people running past them, carrying props, wigs, bits of scenery and all manner of artifacts in their efforts to assist the next production. Eventually, they were led into the inner sanctum of the manager, Pierre Francois Laporte. This gentleman had come to London in 1824, as an actor, but had soon decided that theatrical management would suit him better. Whether others would have agreed with him is debatable, because he was hopelessly ineffectual at administration and man management and for some time had been held to ransom by a group of recalcitrant singers, known as 'The Old Guard', led by the redoubtable Giulia Grisi, which included Fanny Persiani, Antonio Tamburini, Marietta Alboni, Mariani and sundry others, as well as the latest recruit, the young tenor Giovanni Mario.

Laporte greeted Pauline and her mother warmly; Charles he already knew, of course. They talked for sometime of the illustrious Maria, and he said how much she was still missed. This conversation made Pauline nervous because it reminded her that she would be compared with her sister by all who had heard her, especially as she was making her debut in the role of Desdemona with which Maria had been particularly associated in England. Laporte asked her to make herself available for a music rehearsal the following day, then took the group on a tour of his theatre. Pauline noted with approval that the auditorium was the shape of a horse-shoe and lined with wood, ensuring fine acoustic properties. There were several tiers of boxes and in the centre of the ground floor, a wide area was left clear between the pit seats and the boxes on the pit tier for the more 'exquisite and fashionable of the male operatic patrons to quit their boxes or their scanty stalls during the various portions of the performance, and to fill the vacant spaces in the centre and sides of the pit, where they could laugh, lounge, chatter, eye the boxes from convenient vantage points, and likewise criticise and applaud as they wished.' No manager would dare do away with this 'promenade' because for most of the young men in the audience, the activities which took place in the pit were an indispensable feature of the evening's entertainment.

To Pauline, the theatre was a place of magic, like some ancient temple of art. Its smell was indescribably pungent, but she relished it, with its mixture of paint, gas lamps, cigar, cigarette and candle smoke, polish, dirt, dust, greasepaint and the all pervading perfume of human beings. Minus an audience, with only a few working lights on-stage, and the distant banging of carpenters, calls of painters and scene shifters, the dark auditorium was like a primal womb from which great emotions and excitement gushed forth from the hearts of performers and audiences, night after night. The mystery of it all appealed to something deep and profound within the young singer. She wanted so urgently to be a part of this life, and in order to become a member of a rarified world, she was willing and happy to sacrifice much.

The following morning she arrived early for rehearsal, finding the theatre as busy as ever. She was shown to a sparsely furnished room with a small, square piano, music stands, and an assortment of chairs. In a little while, the door flew open and a dark haired man with high forehead, receding hairline, and a thick black beard, entered hurriedly, followed by the repetiteur. This was the conductor, Michael Costa, an Italian who had settled in England many years before, and had made himself indispensable in the concert and operatic world. He perpetually wore a worried frown, his brows knitted together over narrow, wily black eyes, placed rather close together, but when he saw Pauline, his face relaxed into a smile, and he greeted her warmly and kissed her hand. He had been a colleague and personal friend of her sister, and was very happy to have the youngest member of the illustrious Garcia family in his company. Soon, the other principals arrived, the celebrated tenor Giovanni Battista Rubini, who was to sing Otello to Pauline's Desdemona, baritone Antonio Tamburini, with both of whom she would sing frequently during her long career, and the popular bass, Luigi Lablache, a physically enormous creature with a huge talent and heart to match, who was Queen Victoria's beloved singing teacher.

Costa was a hard task-master, but even he couldn't fault the musicianship of his young prima donna. She was excellently prepared, and as all the other singers had performed their roles many times, the rehearsal ran smoothly, and was soon concluded. It was agreed that Pauline should substitute one of the arias written by Rossini for one by Costa, because the Rossini aria was too similar to a piece in 'La Donna del Lago'. Before the days of recordings, composers often re-used items of music from their other works, and Rossini was notorious for doing so. There was a great appetite for new works, and with tight schedules it was very convenient to lift music from one work to another, and an audience hearing a new opera in Bologna was not to know what was heard in Rome, Milan, Paris or London, at the same time.

On May 3rd, Mme Garcia received news of the death of Ferdinando Paer, Pauline's godfather. Her husband had first met the composer in 1808, when he sang in Paer's 'Griselda', and received his first Parisian triumph. It was the first time the Spaniard had sung in Italian and within a month he was established as one of the leading singers in the French capital. Paer's Italianate melodies were a singer's delight, and Garcia relished them. In 1812 Paer succeeded Spontini as director of the Theatre Italien, and some years later, when Manuel Garcia became disgruntled with the directorship of Angelica Catalani at the Paris Opera, he joined Paer's company where several of his own operas were produced, including 'Fazzoletto', which enjoyed considerable success. Ferdinando Paer was four years older than Garcia but survived him by seven years.

Despite the melancholy news from home, Joaquina was delighted to hear from Pierre Laporte that Costa was very pleased with Pauline's progress, and that the girl's readiness meant they could schedule early stage and orchestral rehearsals. The Frenchman, who had many failings as a director, being dilatory, unbusinesslike, and so poor at keeping order amongst his singers that the theatre was often in a state of uproar and anarchy, had, nevertheless, a sure ear for a winning opera. During his tenure at Her Majesty's he introduced a wealth of new works, including 'Le Comte Ory', 'Il Pirata', La Sonnambula', 'Norma', 'I Puritani' and 'Anna Bolena', all of which became tremendously popular and held their place in the repertory.

News soon passed around the theatre, spread by members of the chorus and orchestra, that a new talent in the form of a very young French singer was burgeoning . Theatre staff began to creep into the auditorium from various parts of the building whenever they had a free moment in order to see and hear for themselves. They saw a young girl, inexperienced in stage craft, but with a theatrical intelligence, natural deportment and dignity, and a masterly command of her, admittedly, individual voice, which augured well for her portrayal of Desdemona. Soon, the public were able to judge for themselves, because on May 9th, she made her debut in Rossini's popular opera.

She was naturally nervous, as there would be many people in the audience who would remember Maria's exquisite performances as Desdemona, and of Manuel Garcia's matchless Otello. It was a tremendous challenge for an inexperienced opera singer who was still two months short of her eighteenth birthday, but she was a Garcia and rose nobly to the occasion.

The theatre held a glittering array of the great and the good, which, besides the Queen and Prince Albert, included the Duke of Wellington, (the victor of Waterloo) whose box faced that of Prince Louis Napoleon, (the nephew of his old enemy, who in turn, would become Emperor of France one day), and Lady Blessington, the mistress of Comte d'Orsay. There had been much talk and speculation about Malibran's sister, and everybody was full of expectation, as they anticipated the entrance of the new young singer. The gentlemen of the press were also well represented, and one of them, Henry Fothergill Chorley of the influential journal, 'The Athenaeum' was very prescient in his summing up of Pauline's first performance. Foreseeing what she would become in time, he wrote: 'The death of Maria Malibran enhanced a reputation which had been already in itself formidable enough. Her younger sister, Pauline, had to face the world of art alone and without having natural attractions equal to those of her sister. Her voice was hardly settled, even within its own after-condition and yet, paradoxical as it may seem, she was at ease on the stage, because she brought there instinct for acting, experience of music, knowledge of how to sing, and consummate intelligence. There can be no doubt with anyone who saw that Desdemona on that night, that another great career was begun.

'In the second act, her treatment of the agitated movement in the finale, which precedes the startling and terrible entrance of Desdemona's father, was astounding in its passion and the brilliancy of its musical display, if considered as forming part of a first performance of one so young. All the Malibran fire, courage, and accomplishment without limit, but there was something else besides, and (some of us fancied) beyond these'.

Everybody agreed that Pauline had risen to the occasion splendidly in her first operatic role, and that her youth had contributed to the vulnerability of the young heroine, engendering a deeply moving experience for all those who were present. However, Chorley noticed something, which to some extent, even in her later career held true; she was more appreciated by musicians and cognoscenti than by the general public, for, as he observed: 'To be real, to be serious, to be thoroughly armed and prepared, to be at once young and old, new and experienced, is not enough. Particular qualities are not to be dispensed with in England when the public mind is in a certain state. The absence of regular beauty can sometimes, but not always, be forgiven. Then, this young girl had another drawback in the very completeness of her talent. It was hard to believe that she could be so young, if capable of singing with such perfect execution and such enthusiasm; nor had the voice from the first ever a young sound'.

Queen Victoria was a great admirer of Grisi, and perhaps the comments she made in her journal that evening reflect the opinion of the general public because she stated that although in Pauline Garcia she recognised a remarkable voice, she considered that her looks were against her. "I must say I was delighted and astonished at Garcia's Desdemona – it went to one's heart, and those low notes would make one cry. She is an extraordinary creature, but is, oh, so sadly ugly".

Regarding the voice of the debutante, Chorley was of the opinion that it was a limited mezzo soprano, which, by sheer exercise of will she extended into soprano territory, and which had the effect of weakening her real voice. He felt that she had been given 'a rebel to subdue, not a vassal to command'. Here and there were tones of an engaging tenderness, but also some of a less winning quality. Of course, at this time she was extremely young but the natural timbre of a voice and its characteristics are inborn. Vocal technique can develop and enhance its beauties, and, to a certain extent, overcome defects, but where these are very pronounced they cannot be entirely eliminated even with the finest training.

Nevertheless, Pauline did herself a great deal of good that evening, and was taken up by the influential Marguerite, Lady Blessington, who invited her to sing at Gore House, her elegant Mayfair home. Her ladyship, who was born in 1789, had been literally sold by her father into marriage with a Captain Farmer in Ireland when she was only fifteen. She was a great beauty, but her first husband treated her brutally, 'permanently diverting her sexual impulses into another channel', and while other beautiful women devoted their energies to coquetry, she used hers for intellectual pursuits. Despite her sufferings, she retained her beauty and charming, graceful personality, which was captured by Thomas Lawrence's portrait of her that caused a sensation at the Royal Exhibition of 1821.

After escaping from Ireland and her marriage, Marguerite Blessington took up residence in London. Hers was a detached, but not impersonal view of life, and she fully understood that she needed the good will of influential men in order to gain a place in society. Some time later, she admitted that for a number of years she had been a 'kept mistress'. After the death of her first husband, she married the Earl of Blessington, a wealthy dilettante.

During the time Lord Byron was living in Genoa writing 'Don Juan', he was visited by the Blessingtons, together with Marguerite's sister, Mary Ann Power, and a handsome young travelling companion, Count Alfred D'Orsay. At that time, the poet was suffering from lethargy and avoided visitors as much as possible, but he was entranced by the 'gorgeous Lady Blessington'. Her bearing was aristocratic, without a trace of self-consciousness, something Byron himself never managed to achieve. He also appreciated her husband's qualities, considering him not just a dilettante but a man of taste, sensitivity and judgement.

The poet was equally impressed by Count d'Orsay, a beautiful boy with 'the air of a Cupidon dechaine', who was something of a dandy, but an unaffected one. Despite appearances of a menage a trois, Byron judged the friendship between Marguerite and the Frenchman to be a Platonic one, and did not think that Lord Blessington was a cuckold.

Marguerite noted in her diary: 'Byron is witty, sarcastic, and lively enough… but he does not look like my preconceived notion of the melancholy poet… His hair has already much of silver among its dark brown curls; its texture is very silky, and although it retreats from his temples, leaving his forehead very bare, its growth at the sides and back of his head is abundant… He is so exceedingly thin, that his figure has an almost boyish air; and yet there is something so striking in his whole appearance, that I should not have observed his lameness, had my attention not been called to it by his own visible consciousness of this infirmity… His voice and accent are particularly clear and harmonious, but somewhat effeminate… His laugh is musical…' When he called on her at her hotel the next day, she was utterly amazed by the intimicy and absolute candour of his conversation, 'which even friends would consider too personal for discussion'.

She considered that Byron was at his best in a 'tete a tete' in which he could think aloud, and he told her: "An animated conversation has much the same effect on me as champaigne (sic) – it elevates and makes me giddy". When her ladyship made a deprecating remark regarding scandal, Byron chided her, saying, "scandal has something so piquant – it is a sort of cayenne to the mind — that I confess I like it, particularly if the objects are one's particular friends".

Marguerite found the poet charming, kind and charitable, and was impressed by the gentleness of his manners to people he met when out walking. She observed 'they all seem to know his face, and to like him; and many recount their affairs, as if they were sure of his sympathy'.

Pauline, like many other young females of her day saw Byron in the light of a hero, and was fascinated to be in the presence of a woman who had not only met him, but had been one of his personal friends and she encouraged her hostess to reminisce about him. Lady Blessington's drawing room could boast many influential men of rank, and in addition to Count d'Orsay, the young singer met Prince Louis Napoleon, now an exile in England, after his miraculous escape from imprisonment in the wretched Chateau d'Ham in northern France, and the Lords Chesterfield and Castlereagh; Henry Reeve, the well known actor Charles Macready, Rubini and Richard Monckton Milnes, later Lord Houghton, one of the first English biographers of the poet John Keats. Thanks to the patronage of Lady Blessington, Pauline was soon receiving invitations from other ladies of rank, and became a familiar figure in the drawing rooms of the higher echelons of London society.

Chorley comments: "The impression made on our London world by the new singer was, at first, greater in the concert room than on the stage; and yet, there she had to measure herself against a no less accomplished mistress of the subtlest art of vocal finish than Madame Persiani. Among the most perfect things of their kind ever heard were the duet cadences in the duets from 'Tancredi' which they used to present, and these were mostly combined and composed by the girl – higher in taste than the similar ornaments which Malibran and Sontag had executed, though sometimes, like those, a little far-fetched."

From the start of her career in England, Pauline always had many concert engagements in addition to her work in the opera house. She did not always enjoy these, and one can understand why, from Henri Castil-Blaze's descriptions of conditions imposed on performers at that time. "One knows what the life of a singer is like in the capital of England, the life of a dramatic singer of talent. Three or four afternoon concerts awaiting him after rehearsal and when the curtain falls, and he is able to escape from the theatre, the soirees begin, lasting until dawn. The virtuoso climbs into his coach to go from one to the other" Faced with this situation, Pauline said 'Good gracious, how can one call that 'faire de l'art? I call it 'faire de l'argent!"

She was fortunate to be well connected and financially comfortable, but for many girls from the lower classes, the theatre was synonymous with prostitution, and certainly there were large groups of the population who considered it to be a wicked place, a by-word for promiscuity and loose morals, and they firmly refused to let their own daughters contemplate a stage career, however talented they might be.

Numerous young dancers, actresses and singers were, to term it euphemistically, 'under distinguished patronage', a polite way of saying they were kept women, mistresses of fathers and sons from wealthy, aristocratic families, generating questions of artistic precedence that could be complicated by diplomatic or social influence, adding further stress to a manager's lot.

Queen Victoria's journal contains a conversation with her first Prime Minister, Lord Melbourne: "He was very merry about theatres and has peculiar tastes of his own about actors. In fact, these tastes seem wholly concerned with actresses". Lord Melbourne gave her a rather different impression of the theatre from that conveyed by the discreet Luigi Lablache, who as well as being her singing teacher, was one of the most famous operatic basses of the age. Melbourne thought little of theatrical morals; 'The first actresses' he said ' were all women of bad character'. There was even an uncharacteristic cynicism in some of his comments on the actress and her temptations. When Pauline was hailed as a new discovery, Lord Melbourne proved less than chivalrous; "He talked of Garcia wishing to bring her mother with her, as she was so young. Lord Melbourne said that formerly that was not allowed in the Green Room, and that they said 'if a girl can't take care of herself without her Mother, she can't do so with her'".

These observations throw light on the difficulties experienced by women without means or protection. When they succumb to the blandishments of men, they are considered of 'bad character', but no comment is made about the men who entice them with their riches.

Lord Melbourne also had a poor opinion of the Englishman's taste in music, stating: "The English tolerate music rather than feel it. The Englishman lacks the sensuality, the passion; he is, to a certain extent, salted by his proximity to the sea, which addresses itself to his eyes but not his ears". Pauline would have agreed with him, having little regard for English taste in general.

As the Czech pianist, Wilhelm Kuhe, who settled in England in 1845 comments, musical taste at that time was terribly low, with trifles presented for public consumption which twenty years later would have been booed off the platform.

It was through the work of such serious artists as Pauline that higher standards gradually prevailed, and public taste improved. In 1859, in a letter to the German conductor, Julius Rietz, she said of Costa, the conductor with whom she worked most frequently in England, in opera, oratorio and concert: "He is a good musician, but one who offers sacrifice (though he may never imagine it) to the golden calf, that is to say, to English taste – he knows that in order to make certain things penetrate the ears of the English public, one has to speak very loud. They require Cayenne pepper in all sorts of aliments, moral as well as physical. That is the reason why Costa has been obliged to add military band instruments to his orchestra for oratorios in the Crystal Palace. Costa, transported to Germany, would be a mediocre person; in England he is a man to whom all the public and the musicians ought to feel profoundly obliged. In this world everything is relative, and one should be able to assume the point of view of countries, of epochs, and of peoples".

Indeed orchestral musicians owed a debt of gratitude to Costa who improved their working conditions and pay considerably. Until he took up the cudgels to better their lives, they were ill regarded and ill paid. He was a martinet with a severe demeanour, but his heart was in the right place, and his musicians loved him for his battles on their behalf.

He was a stickler for punctuality, and one day at rehearsal everyone was seated except for an oboist. Costa waited and waited and after something like half an hour had gone bywithno sign of the player, the rehearsal eventually commenced. Finally, the poor, harassed man arrived, full of apologies for his absence. His wife had been in labour and he had not thought it prudent to leave until after the birth of the baby. Costa was impassive throughout this narration, but after the man had finished and the orchestra had stopped laughing, calmly said 'very well, but don't let it happen again".

For all his dour exterior, he had a wry sense of humour, and on another occasion, when one of his violinists asked for time off to attend his brother's wedding, answered: "I'm sorry, I cannot let you off for anything less than a funeral", then added, "Wait! It may prove to be the same thing; you may go!"

Louis Viardot paid a visit to England especially to hear Pauline in her first opera season, and was immensely impressed by her performances. Her second role was that of Angiolina in 'La Cenerentola' which is the Cinderella story, and one of the most charming and delightful of operas, with tremendous opportunity for the heroine to shine, as well as for the ugly sisters, the Prince Ramiro and his valet, Dandini, and Don Magnifico, the father. Unlike the traditional story, there is no fairy godmother. The Prince's tutor, Alidoro, pretends to be a beggar who calls at Magnifico's house asking for food. He is rudely turned away by Clorinda and Thisbe, the sisters, but receives a kind welcome from Angiolina. Returning to the palace, he tells the Prince about this charming, kind young girl, and the Prince arranges a ball in the hope that she will accept his invitation so that he can meet her and decide if she is as lovely as Alidoro says she is.

Chorley thought that in her first ballad, a simple piece in the style of a folk-song, 'C'era un re', Pauline had too much 'malice francais', but notwithstanding this, he considered that she achieved a charming simplicity, which she showed in the tasteful use of the ornaments she devised. He also noticed how much ease and assurance she showed on stage, despite this being only her fourth performance, and she brought the house down with the virtuosity of her brilliant final aria, 'Non piu mesto', complete with her own original point d'orgue, which were copied by other singers. Particularly, Marietta Alboni, one of whose most successful roles was that of Cinderella, until she became too grossly fat to perform it any longer.

As Director of the Theatre Italien, Louis Viardot was becoming influential in the operatic world as, at that time, the French capital was its mecca with the Theatre Italien running a close second to the prestigious Paris Opera. Viardot immediately engaged Pauline to sing Desdemona and Angiolina for him during the autumn season, but due to the rebuilding taking place after the disastrous fire at the Salle Favart, the home of the Theatre Italien, performances would take place at the Odeon.

In addition to the impression made on him by Pauline, Louis Viardot was also enthusiastic about Giovanni Mario, the fine young tenor who was making his debut at Her Majesty's that season. His parents were Italian aristocrats who did not approve of their son's operatic ambitions, so he had promised his father that he would never use their noble name of di Candia on the stage, nor would he ever sing in Italy. He kept to that promise all his life, restricting his performances to England, France, and St. Petersburg, and laying aside his name and title, Count Giovanni di Candia, he simply called himself 'Mario'.

He was extraordinarily handsome, and had the most exquisite natural instrument, which developed into the perfect example of the pure lyric tenor voice. It had compass, volume, richness, grace and flexibility, through which he was able to produce a variety of gradations of colour with great ease, and many people, including Chorley expressed the view that Mario was the heir apparent to Rubini, whose hold upon the public showed little signs of abating, although he was now in his forties. The older singer had long been the pre-eminent tenor, whose singing touched the heart of all his listeners, yet it was more his way of singing than the beauty of the voice itselfthat had such a powerful effect. Chopin said of him: "He sings true notes, never falsetto, and sometimes his ornamental runs go on for hours". He was not a great actor, but he captured his audience by feats of pure vocalism, and his command of his voice was second to none. Now, however, time was taking its toll; his marvellous voice was weakening and showing signs of wear, making it necessary for the management to seek a singer of sufficient calibre to succeed him in the not too distant future.

Mario had amazing potential, but was untried as an actor, and his musical literacy was rather primitive, yet he had an innate, natural talentthat could be cultivated, as he was eager to learn. This fact was soon noted by the celebrated Austrian dancer, Fanny Elssler, who was a great star and soloist of the opera ballet, and many years later, Mario told his daughter that he owed all his stage craft to this woman because she had taken the trouble to direct him on deportment and posture, and coached him in acting. He said that he even learned how to apply his stage make-up from her and was eternally grateful for her tuition. Fanny was delighted to learn that Louis Viardot had engaged Mario to sing Nemorino in Donizetti's 'L'Elisir d'Amore' at the Theatre Italien, and thought that it would be an ideal role for him.

From their first meeting, Pauline and Fanny struck up a friendship, the singer finding excellent qualities in the dancer, who was an intelligent, well bred young woman, of great talent and charisma. She told the singer that she was helping Mario, and said how pleased she was with his progress. Having been impressed by his voice, and the fact that Fanny had taken an artistic interest in him, Pauline also paid attention to the tenor, and having a soft spot for handsome, gifted young men, she must have found him attractive, and vocally interesting. However, within a year or two, and for many years afterwards, she was to be sorely tried by his Machiavelian tendencies, especially when he fell into the clutches of the manipulative Giulia Grisi.

On May 11th, two days after her debut, Pauline wrote to tell Clara Wieck about her London performances: 'My good Clara, I must just write two words to let you know that the day before yesterday, I made my great opera debut here. The English said that it was a real triumph; after the second act I had to appear before the curtain, and at the end of the opera, when I appeared with Rubini, we were greeted with cries and clamours. We will present 'Otello' four or five times, then 'La Cenerentola' and finally, Nina. I would like to tell you more, but have so little time to spare. Send me good news of yourself and your friends, and receive a cordial kiss from your friend, Pauline Garcia.' In a postscript she sends her best wishes to Clara's chaperone, Henriette Reichmann, and her friends the List Sisters who were on a visit to Paris. She says that she has carried out a 'commission' for Felicien David, who had played a concerto for the Philharmonic Society, and sent her mother's best wishes. At this time, the girls corresponded in German, because although Clara had learned French she was not at ease writing it. Later, she became very proficient and both languages were used alternately.

The season ended with the general consensus that it had been a successful one for Pauline, and that she would be welcomed back to London any time she wished to return. She had been accepted into the homes of the aristocracy, and had begun to make acquaintances within their ranks, but in spite of that, for many years she felt an antipathy towards the English and to England itself. She hated the climate, declaring that not one of God's creatures should be expected to live without sunshine, and she loathed the smoke and grime of the capital. The Thames was filthy and foul smelling, full of sewage and refuse of all kinds, periodically generating epidemics of cholera and typhoid. As Charles Dickens remarked: 'Everybody knew that something must be done, but nobody had any idea what it should be, beyond endeavouring to see what effect throwing in quantities of lime would achieve'. Of course, it simply resulted in more toxicity, rather than less.

Pauline, although reserved in her manner, was a friendly girl, and spoke the language well, but she found that the English were suspicious of foreigners, whom they mistrusted, or at best, ignored. Spies were ubiquitous because there was a general fear that the 'goings on' of the French, their traditional enemy who were only a short distance across the Channel, might result in trouble at home. After the 1830 revolution, which had placed Louis Philippe on the French throne, the British government was on its guard and kept a close watch on foreign nationals, many of whom were thought to be potential agents provocateurs, republicans, socialists, or even worse, communists, who might stir up dissidents at home and foment revolution.

Of the population as a whole, only a relatively small number of people travelled widely, and they tended to be members of the intelligentsia and aristocracy. Many of the populace lived and died within a small radius of their homes with little knowledge of what went on in the wider world and this tended to make them very insular.

Even more than the grey skies and inclement, rainy, weather, Pauline dreaded the English Sunday. People simply disappeared, leaving the streets deserted; all shops, pubs, clubs and restaurants closed, and she and her family felt isolated. Large numbers of people in this nominally Christian country were obsessive in their observance of the Sabbath; Protestant ethics were strong, and even if they did not go to church, in their own homes all fun was forbidden. It was not just a day of rest, it was a day of paralysis. No music or dancing was allowed, no games, no singing except that of psalms or hymns, no reading except from the Bible, sermons and dry, religious texts. Many people went to church twice a day, and their children were expected to attend Sunday School in the afternoon as well. On the other hand, for those who worked long hours all week, the day of rest was necessary, and the church provided a measure of social life. They would don their Sunday best and meet friends after the services, but foreign visitors loudly lamented such excess. A few years later when Pauline's colleague, the French tenor Gustave Roger was in London, he expressed the same attitude to Sundays in England, and said they made him feel quite suicidal.

One Englishwoman, with whom Pauline was very much at ease, was her old friend, Clara Novello, but she was not a typical English girl, as her antecedents were Italian and she had spent a great deal of time on the Continent. The Garcias always had a fondness for Clara and her mother because they had been so kind to Maria in her last days.

As soon as the season ended, Pauline and Mme Garcia, accompanied by Charles, lost no time in crossing to the other side of the Channel for a short holiday at Boulogne sur mer, after which they returned to Paris, and Pauline began to prepare for her performances at the Theatre Italien where she would appear in opera for the first time before her compatriots. She had already begun to prove herself on the stage and her name had gone before her with some first rate newspaper reports to attest to her recent success. Parisians wondered if, despite the London reviews, she would succeed in eclipsing her sister's memory.

Pauline Viardot's mentor, the painter Ary Sheffer

Left: A young Giulia Grisi, the Italian
   opera star and rival of Viardot
Above: The legendary Maria
   Malibran, Pauline's elder sister

The execution scene from 'La Juive' with Pauline, as Rachel, about to be boiled alive

The garden at Nohant with two cypresses planted by George Sand on the birth of her children

A box at the opera

Pauline Viardot's confidant, the
German conductor, Julius Rietz

A pencil sketch of Tourgueniev by Pauline

A view of Duns Castle where the Viardots stayed for three months

CHAPTER EIGHT

1839/40

Well rested after her short but relaxing holiday by the sea, Pauline was soon deep in rehearsals at the Odeon. The casts in the operas in which she was to appear were largely as they had been in London. She could wear the costumes designed by herself that she had worn at Her Majesty's and had only to fit into a new production.

During the nineteenth and early twentieth century there was little concern about historical authenticity in the design of stage costumes and Pauline was ahead of her time in endeavouring to be true to the period of the operas in which she sang. She was following in her sister's footsteps because Malibran had designed her own costumes, and at the Tourgueniev, Viardot and Malibran Museum at Bougival there is a watercolour sketch by Maria of a costume she designed for 'Maria Stuarda', and a pencil drawing by Pauline of herself as Zerlina.

At that time, singers were required to supply their own wardrobe, and as this was a costly business, they transported the clothes from place to place for different productions, regardless of what colours or in which periods the other singers appeared. Pauline took great trouble to make sure that everything she wore was true to the period, visiting art galleries, studying portraits and prints to make sure her costume designs were accurate.

The scene designers and painters were highly skilled and the décor was usually authentic, but the overall stage picture was easily spoilt by the ridiculous, motley collection of costumes, and it is amusing that, in the middle of the twentieth century, the stage designer Margaret Harris and her two colleagues, chose the name 'Motley' for their firm, perhaps as a humorous recollection of the days of theatrical 'mix and miss-match'?!

Louis Viardot welcomed Pauline at her first rehearsal, making her feel at home in the new environment, and soon all was underway, the theatre, as usual, a hive of industry. There were some new choristers who had to be taught their parts by rote. Their repetiteur was a violinist who played a section of each vocal line over and over again until they had memorised it accurately, and then moved on to another passage until it finally came together like a jigsaw and they knew all the choruses of the opera by heart. Only the violinist had a copy of the music, placed on a stand in front of him, and the singers had to look over his shoulder to follow the dots on the page, while another man beat time for them. It was all rather chaotic, but gradually they picked up their parts, mostly by ear. Copies were always in short supply, because the process of copying by hand from the manuscript or printed score was costly and laborious.

There was no director as such, and the production was overseen by a 'stage manager'. He was a kind of 'traffic cop', making sure that the singers knew all the right entrances and exits, did not fall over each other, or bump into the scenery or furniture. Before the days of Freud, little attention was paid to the psychology of the characters; that was left to the singer's own imagination and feelings, but gesture was all important, as it is in classical ballet, and there were standard movements to represent different emotions, these being passed down from one generation to another. However, in 1854 Ermanno Morelli produced a written manual of stage gestures, which was published in several languages.

From the beginning, Pauline possessed a subtlety that was uncommon on the stage of her day, and she surprised the public by her 'sobriety' and the smallness of her gestures. She expressed herself through her thoughts, without the excessive exaggeration then accepted as stage acting, but audiences were confused by the fact that she refused to come out of character if they applauded in inappropriate places, and she would not give encores in the middle of a scene, as she believed that it broke the dramatic flow. Most singers were only too happy to acknowledge the applause and sing an encore, but Pauline would not do so because she considered it ridiculous, and she offended and puzzled many people at her English debut, by refusing to comply with this custom.

A Russian aristocrat, visiting the French capital, saw Rosina Stolz, the reigning prima donna of the Paris Opera, and wrote: "Mme Stoltz's singing, or rather her shouting, and her vocal and bodily contortions are in the typically French style, a melodramatic genre in which passion is represented by a kind of anger or rage, and love by something whose name cannot yet be found, as far as I know, in any dictionary."

It was creative interpreters such as Pauline and the notable young French actress, Rachel, who broke through this artificial strait-jacket, and brought about a much more naturalistic approach, although even their performances would probably appear exaggerated by modern standards, but they pioneered the change. In viewing silent films from the beginning of the film era, it is still possible to catch a flavour of what nineteenth century acting in the theatre must have been like when gesture and facial expressions were excessive. With dim, mellow lighting, gestures needed to be slower and larger to register throughout the auditorium.

In addition to the roles she had already sung, Pauline now added two more Rossini characters to her repertoire, Rosina in 'Il Barbiere di Siviglia' and Tancredi, a travesti role. Rosina was an ideal part for such a youthful singer, as she is a skittish, fifteen-year-old,kept a virtual prisoner in the house by her unscrupulous old guardian, Dr. Bartolo, who is hoping to marry her for her money. Each day when he goes out, she sits on her balcony, and one day, she is seen by the Count Almaviva, (the role created by Pauline's father). He falls in love with her, meets his old friend, the barber Figaro, and together they plan to get into the house and rescue her. The Count pretends to be a poor student, in order to see if she will love him for himself alone, and after many adventures and set-backs, they out-wit Bartolo and marry, to live happily ever after – at least until they appear again in the sequel 'The Marriage of Figaro', by Mozart. Both operas are based on plays by the French eighteenth century adventurer, courtier, and dramatist, Pierre Caron de Beaumarchais.

George Sand and Frederick Chopin, who had first met Pauline in the salon of their mutual friend Countess Charlotte Marliani, had not yet returned to Paris from Nohant, George's country home, when Pauline made her debut at the Theatre Italien, and were both very sorry to have missed it. But they read de Musset's article, and were determined to be at her next performance.

Seeing Pauline on the operatic stage, the disgruntled Alfred de Musset was tremendously moved by her powerful portrayals, and wrote a further glowing article about her, which appeared in the 'Revue des Deux Mondes' on the 1st of November, 1839. Her Desdemona had moved him profoundly and he said that 'even the severest critics recognised Mlle Garcia's magnificent voice with its extraordinary range, perfect method, charming ease of emission, powerful dramatic gift, and her truthful imagination'. With his deep knowledge of Shakespeare, his article was not purely adulatory, but contained some useful, constructive criticism. He compared the tempestuous way in which Malibran had played Desdemona, with Pauline's 'overwhelmingly gentle and resigned' interpretation. He said she played the Venetian girl not as a beautiful Amazon, as her sister had done, but as a naïve girl, deeply in love, guiltily aware of how much pain she is giving to her family by her actions, and only brave at the moment of her death. He asked why Desdemona had fainted onto the floor, and not into the armchairthat was near her; Pauline took the hint and did as he suggested.

However, in our virtues lie our vices, and as far as most audiences were concerned, a flamboyant, extrovert creature, such as Malibran, was preferred to Pauline with all her subtlety. They wanted their operatic heroines drawn on a large canvas, not in exquisite miniatures, and this is one of the reasons why Pauline often performed to greater effect in the salon or concert hall than on the opera stage in her early career. Many people remarked that to observe her at close range with the wide variety of expression at her command was to see her at her best. She was criticised for her portrayal of Rosina, who was traditionally played as a brazen coquette, wilful and cheeky, but Pauline gave a more studied, original reading of the role, and Theophile Gautier was perceptive in appreciating the way she played the heroine as an innocent young girl, mischievous but not malicious, and more in keeping with the character she would become as the Countess Almaviva in 'The Marriage of Figaro'. He also appreciated her Tancredi, stating that her slim figure, lack of female voluptuousness and ambiguous sexuality contrived to present a very authentic picture of the young man.

Alfred de Musset, as well as praising Pauline's performances in public, was once more pursuing her in private, but this time he had competition. Louis Viardot was very much in evidence; ever since his visit to see Pauline in London, he had realised that he was falling in love. He could not stop thinking about her, and seized every opportunity to be with her when she was rehearsing or performing in his theatre. As a family friend he was always welcomed by Joaquina, and was often invited to meals at her house, where he met Manuel and other friends and acquaintances. Because he was so much older and more experienced than Pauline, he was able to dissemble the true state of his feelings for her. Unlike de Musset, he did not intimidate her, and she always enjoyed his visits. He was not a garrulous man, but he had a well-stocked mind which appealed to her, and she relished their conversations, pleased when they were able to sit apart from the rest of the company and chat undisturbed together.

So far in her life, the only man who had stirred her youthful passions had been Franz Liszt, and she realised that that was an idealistic love which would never come to anything, but it did set a pattern for the future. Her loves were always more of mind than body, and she was tremendously attracted to brilliant, talented, intelligent men.

As she grew older, the fine blending and balance of the feminine and masculine principles in her nature caused Theophile Gautier and others to speculate on the gender of Pauline and George Sand whom they suspected were really hermaphrodites. Gautier may have been speaking metaphorically, but the Goncourt brothers went further, wagering that when the two women died, if autopsies was carried out, it would be discovered that the clitoris of each woman was like a small penis. Of course, George went to bed with many men, and if her anatomy included such a feature, it would have become common knowledge, but Pauline was not promiscuous and the Goncourt's remarks were probably just tittle-tattle, showing a lack of understanding regarding independent, talented women who followed their own path. On the other hand, women with tremendous drive and capability may possess a larger measure of testosterone than the majority of their sex.

Despite de Musset's continued infatuation with Pauline, she gave him a wide berth. She had always felt uncomfortable in his presence, but since she had known George Sand her distaste for him had increased. George knew many of his secrets and these, no doubt, only confirmed Pauline's instinctive suspicion and dislike. Although there was a difference of seventeen years between them, the two women were immediately attracted to each other, and an intimate friendship developed that lasted all their lives.

Mme Garcia was already beginning to realise that she would not always be able to accompany her daughter on her tours, and began to look around for a husband for Pauline. Joaquina was no longer young and had other family commitments, and Charles de Beriot had his own career to fulfil. He was also contemplating a second marriage, so he would no longer be available to promote and protect Pauline. Alfred de Musset was always fluttering around like a butterfly, and Joaquina began to pick up hints from him that caused her to consider him as a possible husband for her daughter. No doubt she revealed her thoughts to George Sand when she came to visit; after all, he was from a 'tres bonne famille', a very necessary requisite, and he was famous. George stopped Joaquina in her tracks, horrified at her train of thought, and set out to disabuse the older woman's insane ideas about Alfred's suitability. She, more than anyone else, knew all about his unsavoury way of life, and did all she could to dissuade Joaquina from seriously considering his advances.

Knowing of his interest in Pauline as a singer, though not yet the extent to which his personal feelings had become involved, George confided Mme Garcia's plans to Louis Viardot, expressing her disgust at the thought of her dear young friend being married off to such a degenerate. Louis was as dismayed as George, and resolved to ask Mme Garcia for permission to pay his addresses to Pauline. He confessed his true feelings to George, who was overjoyed, and saw immediately all the advantages that this match could bring. She encouraged him, and buoyed him up to such an extent that he agreed to seek an immediate interview with Joaquina.

The Garcias were now living at 5, rue des Champs-Elysees, and George paid them a visit in order to pave the way for Louis. She needed to ascertain Pauline's feelings about her friend, and in a very diplomatic way, without committing Louis, she drew the girl into conversation and soon realised that Pauline did indeed like him very much. When Pauline left the room, George spoke seriously to Joaquina, who being a sensible woman, listened to her intently, weighing up all the pros and cons, as she saw them. Louis was also from a good family, he was financially secure, making money as an investor in railways, and other commercial ventures, as well as his salary as theatre director. He was experienced in the ways of the world, had influence in the theatre, and on a personal level, he and Pauline had a great deal in common. Seen from a worldly point of view, there was no doubt that if he chose, Louis could advance Pauline's career considerably, but Joaquina was not happy about the twenty-one year age gap that separated them. Nevertheless, he was hale and hearty, energetic, and barely forty, hardly in his dotage.

George stressed that she had the girl's best interests at heart, and said how much she and Chopin were devoted to her. A short time previously, she had written to Pauline saying: 'I can truly say that you are the most perfect being I know or have ever known', and she agreed with the composer Adolphe Adam, who, writing to a friend about Pauline, stated: "She sings in, and speaks, five languages, plays the piano like an angel, is as good a harmonist as anyone, sings like her sister, and composes things we would have been proud to have written". High praise indeed, from such a celebrated man. George had few friendships with women, and those had not always been satisfactory, but Pauline, an artist in the truest, deepest sense of the word, and totally unspoilt, she took to her heart. Till the day of her death, George kept her early opinion of Pauline, loving her genius because it was allied to goodness, intelligence and nobility of character.

After the two women had discussed the situation for some time, Joaquina asked Pauline to come and join them, and delicately informed her of M. Viardot's intentions. As might be expected, she was taken by surprise and could not collect her thoughts immediately. It was all so sudden: yes, she knew Alfred was pursuing her, but she did not take him seriously. But Louis, who had always behaved most properly towards her, she had seen only as a family friend, and recently, as her employer at the theatre, having no idea that his feelings towards her had developed into something warmer than friendship.

She asked for time to think over all they had told her. George left, and later that evening, Joaquina sent a message to Manuel, asking him to come and see her because she had something important to discuss with him. Manuel liked

Louis very much, appreciating his upright principles, honesty and sense of humour, and had already been taken into his confidence. He had assured his friend that if his mother and sister were in agreement, he would certainly give his blessing to the marriage, and hoped that Louis would be happier with Pauline than he had ever been with Eugenie.

Garcia had originally been extremely attracted to Eugenie, which was understandable, as she was young, pretty, vivacious and talented; but after they married his infatuation had waned, and he realised that he had made a dreadful mistake. He blamed himself for allowing physical attraction to blind him to the fact that they were totally unsuited to eachother. If only he had he been more cautious he could have avoided much misery for Eugenie as well as himself, but who, in the throes of passion can keep a cool head? He was not even sure that his wife was faithful to him. She was surrounded at the theatre by attractive, talented men, and it would not have been surprising, accepting the state of their marriage, if she had found consolation in the arms of another man. Manuel judged it a 'fait accompli', and strove to make the best of his ill-judged marriage, but finally he had to admit that a separation could not be avoided.

Pauline knew that it was imperative to have a protector in the world of the theatre, but she was not sure that she was ready for marriage yet. George Sand thought that Louis Viardot would be the ideal solution to a problemthat would loom larger as time passed, and she assured Pauline that he really cared for her. Although Pauline respected him immensely, she was not in love with him, and like most young girls, she dreamed of a romantic young lover. Her heart still fluttered at the thought of the dashing Franz Liszt, although she knew that was moonshine, and she had to consider her future in the real world. She asked for more time to think about her answer, and consulted George. Her mature friend persuaded her that she would have to look far and wide to find a more honourable, true and suitable husband than Louis Viardot, and gradually Pauline began to see that the advantages out-weighed the disadvantages. Finally, she signalled to her family that she was willing to see M. Viardot.

George Sand acted as intermediary, and told Louis that she had informed Mme Garcia of his wish to pay his addresses to Pauline, and Joaquina was willing to discuss the matter. He lost no time in presenting himself at the Garcia apartment, and was warmly greeted by Joaquina, who quickly sent for Pauline. The girl entered the room looking pale and shy; it was not often that she was lost for words, but her stomach was full of butterflies, and her mouth was dry with nerves. Her mother pressed her hand, and smiled at them both as she left the room.

In his forty years, Louis had never been married, but two years before, he had come close to it, having been engaged for a short time; however, as he got to know his fiancee better, he realised, to his dismay, that her political affiliations were diametrically opposed to his own. His republican philosophy was the core of his life, and he thought it madness to marry someone with whom he could never be in accord on such a serious issue. It was courting disaster, and he considered that there would be little hope of happiness in such a marriage. Regretting his ungentlemanly behaviour, he asked the lady to release him. To his great relief, she agreed to do so. He was shocked at how close he had come to ruining his life, after all, society was full of such ill-matched marriages that brought great unhappiness and distress, and from that time on, he was extremely circumspect, and had not wished to marry until he found someone with whom he believed he had a real affinity. At first, he had been concerned about the difference in age between himself and Pauline, but had begun to realize that it was not as important as being truly in accord with the other person. He and Pauline saw 'eye to eye' on so many aspects of life, and that was what really mattered.

The girl came slowly into the centre of the room, and the prospective bridegroom beckoned to her to sit down, and then he knelt before her chair. Her hands were clasped in her lap, and her eyes were lowered, as he began to tell her how much she meant to him. She looked up and their eyes met - she smiled at him, and he took her hand and asked her if she would do him the honour of becoming his wife. She blushed a deep rosy pink, which became her greatly, and without a moment's hesitation she thanked him for his offer, and declared that she would be most happy to marry him.

She called her mother into the room, and announced that she had accepted M. Viardot's offer of marriage. Joaquina was relieved and delighted, and she congratulated and embraced them both. Soon the news was all over Paris, and most people thought it a good match, except for one dissenting voice, that of Alfred de Musset, who, vain as ever, was insulted that Louis Viardot had succeeded where he had failed. Now, more than ever, he called her 'cruel Pauline', and became quite spiteful in his remarks about her, her fiance, the loathed George Sand (who was blamed for her involvement), and the whole Garcia clan.

Much amusement and gossip was generated in Parisian salons and cafes, because Alfred assumed the attitude of the spurned lover, despite the fact that he had never had the least encouragement from Pauline. In his chagrin he produced a series of cartoons that are very cruel, but very funny. He depicts poor Louis as a hideous grotesque, whose nose keeps changing its size and shape, and he represents himself as a lover made ill by disappointment, which brings on pneumonia; he takes to his bed and dies forthwith. The sketches also include the sculptor Auguste Barre, one of Pauline's clan of admirers, who is in the middle of modelling a statue of the diva when he hears the news; it has such a devastating effect on him that he pushes his masterpiece aside, and emotionally overcome, climbs onto his trestle table and sits with his head in his hands, a picture of despair.

There is also an illustration of a distraught 'Baron D', who has fallen in love with Pauline at the theatre after having seen her play Tancredi. On receiving the news of her forthcoming marriage, he bursts into tears, then rushes to the theatre to inform all her other admirers of the dire news. De Musset alleged that at one point the betrothal was broken off, but whether this is true, or simply the result of his over-active imagination and wishful thinking, is not known.

He wrote a poem to Pauline entitled 'Adieu', in which he confessed that he only realized how much he loved her when it was too late. After his death, his brother Paul, writing to Caroline Jaubert said how great his appeal had been for many women, but the three exceptions were those who had inspired him the most, and whom he had really loved, George Sand, 'ungrateful Pauline', and Rachel.

Pauline now looked at Louis in a new light. The very fact that he cared for her so much made him attractive to her. She had always appreciated his kindness and thoughtfulness, which were appealing in themselves, and not common attributes in men generally. As for his appearance, he was a very pleasing looking man, and always well dressed in clothes of the best quality, presenting a handsome figure to the world. His general demeanour was serious, but he had an appealing smile.

He invited the Garcia ladies and Manuel to a dinner in his apartment in the rue Favart, and other guests included his younger brother, Leon, an artist who had once painted a fine portrait of Maria Malibran, and his three sisters, forty-five- year old Nanine Guillon, the only married one, Jenny, and thirty-seven-year old Philiberthe, who was always called Berthe. They had long been confident that their brother would remain a confirmed bachelor, and Jenny and Berthe expected to keep house for him for the rest of their lives. When he had announced that he was to marry it was a great shock , and when they learned that he was marrying a mere chit of a girl, they were convinced that he had taken leave of his senses. Pauline on her side was less than overjoyed at the prospect of having to make her home with these women, and Berthe was a real thorn in her flesh, as long as she lived, because they had no affinity whatsoever. Louis's 'too many sisters' haunted her, and even when Jenny died in 1849, Pauline still had to contend with Berthe who lived permanently with the Viardots, and is even buried with them in the cemetery of Montmartre. The forthright George Sand once refused to have Berthe to stay at Nohant because she considered her a 'crushing bore'.

Pauline was now beginning to be courted by people who thought that her celebrity status might help them in their careers. One of these was the German composer, Richard Wagner, who was in Paris in the hope of gaining recognition and performances of his music. In a letter to M. Eduard Avenarius, he wrote: "Tired and done up as hardly ever before, I have this instant come home after knocking around at the Garcia's, Joly's, Dumersan's, Meyerbeer's etc., since 10 o'clock. I must heartily thank you for your offer to take me to the Italian Opera tonight, but hoard it for another time, for which matter, in the Garcia I have made the acquaintance today of a most amiable and obliging creature, who has volunteered to assist me in everything I ask of her, - consequently I'm hoping she'll also be able to procure me tickets for the Opera, etc., from time to time."

Unfortunately for him, the notoriously demanding Wagner did not find Pauline as amenable as he prophesied, and years later, in 1878, he discussed this visit to Paris with his second wife, Cosima, the daughter of Franz Liszt and Marie d'Agoult, who had been brought up in the city by her paternal grandmother, Anna Liszt. In her diary for October 31st she wrote: "Wagner settled down in the evening, and played all sorts of things to the five children, including the songs 'Mignonne' and 'Dors'. When I express my continued pleasure in them, particularly 'Mignonne' he asks me whether I think they would make the same impression in a Paris salon; people there were too heartless to appreciate such idealised images. I told him that I saw in them that quality of tender, smiling resignation which is also characteristic of the French. Then he recalls Pauline Viardot who had discerned enough in the songs to remark on them, but did not sing them; 'that shows what she was like', he says". Pauline also set Ronsard's 'Mignonne' to music, but it is not certain whether she wrote it before or after Wagner's composition.

On January 23rd, 1840, Pauline sang at a soiree at the house of Alfred de Musset's friend, Prince Ferdinand, the Duke of Orleans, the heir to the throne. This young man was a former pupil of Louis's great friend, the painter Ary Scheffer, and it may have been at Scheffer's prompting that the Duke invited Pauline to take part, although it might equally have been on the recommendation of Alfred de Musset.

Ary Scheffer had recently invited Louis and Pauline to dinner at his house in the rue Chaptal, where he had lived since 1830. Pauline liked the attractive, Italian style villa, with its cream stuccoed, classical façade, and arched windows with light green shutters. A driveway led through tall gates into a courtyard, on each side of which Ary had built a studio, one was spacious, with a high ceiling, where he created his largest pictures, and the other was where he entertained and relaxed. He was passionately fond of music, and friends such as Franz Liszt and Charles Halle came to play to him while he painted, or even model for him, as Liszt had done for the central figure in his picture of the Three Kings.

Scheffer came from a family of artists; his father, Johann-Bernard had been employed as Court Painter to the Dutch Royal House, and his mother, Cornelie Lamme-Scheffer, was a highly skilled miniaturist.On being widowed, she moved to Paris, where Ary became a student in the atelier of Pierre Guerin, where two of his fellow students were Eugene Delacroix and Theodore Gericault. His brother Henri was a painter, but his youngest brother, Arnold, was a political columnist who had first met Louis Viardot when they were journalists at 'The Globe'.

In 1822, when he was twenty-seven, Ary had been engaged as drawing master to the Orleans children, his favourites being Princess Marie, Prince Ferdinand, and Princess Louise, who married Queen Victoria's beloved Uncle Leopold, the King of the Belgians. All the children were devoted to their tutor, whom Prince Ferdinand called his 'best friend', declaring that he relied on him totally because he was honest, frank and fair.

Scheffer's talent as a painter was soon recognised, but it was the Salon of 1828, when he presented his 'Les Femmes Souliotes', that brought him to public attention as one of the leading painters of the Romantic School, and his reputation was consolidated at the Salon of 1831, with his paintings based on Goethe's 'Faust', 'Marguerite au rouet' and 'Faust dans son cabinet'.

From around 1818, Ary and his brother Arnold had frequented the circle of General Lafayette to which Louis Viardot belonged, and Ary's studio became a meeting place for Liberals who wished to bring Louis Philippe to power. The revolution of 1830 gave them their opportunity, and Ary, together with Louis-Adolph Thiers, Louis Viardot and a handful of others, seized their moment. Ary rode post haste to Louis Philippe at St. Cloud, and prevailed upon him to accept the throne. In gratitude, the King made Ary his Court Painter, and many royal commissions came his way, including the painting of frescoes at the Palace of Versailles.

Scheffer was tall and slim, with an olive complexion, very dark, curly hair, now flecked with grey, and a small, well-trimmed beard. When he was working he wore a pair of small, steel-rimmed spectacles, which gave him the appearance of a wise, old owl, and a capacious russet linen smock, tied with a wide sash, a cream shirt with the collar turned up, under which was a large, loosely tied cravat. His working area was surprisingly well organised and clean, and there were few, if any paint stains on his smock or hands, as he kept himself well supplied with pieces of cloth dipped in turpentine with which he frequently cleaned his hands. He was five years older than Louis, and Pauline considered him very much a man of the world, knowledgeable and sophisticated. She was a little shy with him at first, but he welcomed her warmly and smiled at her with twinkling eyes, putting her immediately at her ease, and soon she was chatting away, as if she had known him all her life.

He lived with his illegitimate daughter, Cornelie, who was born in 1830, and his mother Cornelie Lamme. In January 1839, Ary's former student, the young Princess Marie d'Orleans died, and in July he lost his mother. For a while he lacked the desire to paint and instead took up sculpture in the form of a large, reclining statue of Cornelie Lamme, which can still be seen in his smaller atelier.

The rue Chaptal, known in the area as 'la Nouvelle Athenes and St. George', lies on the lower slopes of Montmartre, and by the time Ary moved there it had become a mecca for artists, musicians and writers. Although it was still very rural, there were many dance halls and cabarets nearby, as well as a growing number of private mansions and follies, set in spacious gardens full of trees and verdure. The secluded nature of Ary's home was important to him because he was particularly active in the cause of Polish nationalism, and often gave refuge to exiles and escaped political prisoners.

After dinner Pauline accompanied herself at the piano and sang some of her own compositions and Spanish folksongs. Ary Scheffer quietly observed Pauline; his artist's eye appreciated the trimness of her figure, her poise and elegance, and his heart and ear were captivated by her singing. A glow spread over her features, and her lustrous, dark eyes shone with an inner fire, as her unequalled voice rang out in the lofty studio. Louis looked at her lovingly, feeling quite sure that all the world must envy him. Later, having taken her home, he returned for a night-cap with his friend, and asked him what he thought of her. The painter was a good judge of character, and announced that Mlle Garcia was a charming young woman, highly cultured, as everyone knew, with a fine intellect and good heart, but he declared that she was very ugly. Louis was dismayed by his friend's bluntness, but before he could say anything, Ary qualified his remark by stating that if he saw Pauline again, he would fall in love with her.

Scheffer was present at the soiree in the spacious home of his old pupil, Prince Ferdinand, where Pauline sang two of her favourite Schubert songs, 'Gretchen am Spinnrade' a setting from Goethe's 'Faust', and the spine chilling 'Erlkonig', an unusual song for a woman to sing, as it is more suited to a male voice, but Pauline's interpretation was mesmerising and remembered by her listeners years later. She also sang a Melodie by Lachner to a poem by Heinrich Heine.

Seeing her again, in the splendid apartments of the ducal home, surrounded by superb works of art, dressed, as usual, simply, but elegantly, in a dress of dove grey taffeta, with pearl jewellery, singing like a goddess, he was irresistibly drawn to her, and as he had prophesied, he began to fall deeply in love with the woman who was to become his best friend's wife.

On January 30th, he saw her as Desdemona at the Paris Opera when she performed in the third act of 'Otello' with the tenor Gilbert Duprez, at the Benefit of her friend, the dancer Fanny Elssler. Seeing her on stage, Ary became even more aware of the dramatic power she possessed in such abundance. Offstage she was affable and natural, giving no sign of the passions that burned within her, but which, in performance she could unleash at will. Despite her ugliness, Pauline possessed a mysterious power to charm and fascinate men, with an ability to magnetise them that conventionally beautiful women often lack.

She sang with Rubini on February 10th, in another benefit, this time at the Comedie Francaise for the famous Mlle Mars, and onApril 6th 1839 she gave a concert with her friend George Alexander Osborne, the Irish pianist, to whom she had been speaking earlier when Alfred de Musset had become so offended by what he thought he heard her say.

The opera season ended on April 5th, and two weeks later she and Louis were married in a civil ceremony at the Mairie in the Second Arrondissement, surrounded by their families and closest friends. Louis, being rabidly anti-clerical, had been totally opposed to a church wedding, and as his bride was far from orthodox in her religious beliefs, she was perfectly happy to comply with his wishes. Their families were disappointed, of course, especially Joaquina who was sorry it was not to be a large, fashionable, society wedding in one of the great Catholic churches of the metropolis, but Louis was adamant that the marriage ceremony should be a civic one and nothing more.

Despite this hiccup, it was a happy occasion, and the bride's dress of white Chantilly lace became her charmingly, as did the circlet of tiny roses over a short, white veil, the gauzy effect of which gave her usually pale face an unaccustomed glow. Manuel gave the bride away, Ary Scheffer and Leon Viardot were witnesses, and Pauline's cousin, Antonia Sitches was her bridesmaid. As the couple were pronounced man and wife, Joaquina and Aunt Mariquita shed a few happy tears, and the newly wed smiled fondly on them all.

After a short reception, the guests gathered around the departing couple and Pauline threw her small bridal posy, which was caught by Antonia, and then they climbed into their open carriage, waved goodbye to their well-wishers and set off upon their first journey as a married couple.

CHAPTER NINE

1840

Italy was chosen for the honeymoon destination because Louis had been engaged by the Minister of the Interior to research the current state of Italian art galleries and theatres, and as the appointment carried a substantial fee and expenses, business and pleasure could be combined.

Much to the surprise and dismay of Mme Garcia and George Sand, Louis had already proffered his resignation to the Board of the Theatre Italien, taking effect from 1st October, 1840. Pauline had no engagements in Paris for the foreseeable future, and as they would be spending several months in Italy they intended to contact theatre directors in the hope that she would be offered engagements. Since Louis would be acting as her impressario, he needed to be free from commitments in Paris.

At their first staging post, the newly weds enjoyed a leisurely dinner, recalling the events of the day, and even laughed about the hapless Alfred and his cartoons. Despite being annoyed with him for the gossip he had caused, they both had a ready sense of humour and realised that no one took the cruel but hilarious sketches seriously.

At the end of their leisurely meal, they bade goodnight to the maitre d'hote, and made their way to their apartment. Suddenly both of them realised that they were truly alone for the very first time. Louis had always been punctilious in his behaviour towards Pauline and, even now that they were married, apart from holding his wife's hand in the carriage, he had made no move to press his attentions upon her, being aware of the proximity of the postillions.

Now, alone in their room, they both felt an awkward shyness, and their voices took on an artificiality as they made polite conversation, which gradually petered out, leaving each wondering what the other was thinking. Louis removed his tightly fitting coat, and sat on the sofa, loosening his silk cravat, he leant across to Pauline and pulled her towards him, she, caught off balance, toppled, and was suddenly sitting at his feet. Laughter broke the silencethat had enveloped them, and to balance herself from a kneeling position, Pauline put her hands on his shoulders. They seemed to stay sculpted in this position for an age, just looking into each other's eyes, then Louis put his hands under her elbows, raised her up and kissed her. Pauline responded to him, letting out a huge sigh, and then she shyly began to return his embraces.

At breakfast, next morning, she found it hard to meet Louis's eyes: in the light of day, she felt embarrassed, recalling her first sensual encounter with this man whom she had known for most of her life, but who was now her husband.

After a long, and not always comfortable journey, and a mixed bag of inns and hotels, the Viardots finally reached Italy, and made a visit to their first important port of call, the opera house of 'La Scala' in Milan. Here they made the acquaintance of Bartolomeo Merrelli, its director, and discussed possible engagements for Pauline. This gentleman was very agreeable and amenable, and suggested that she should return to sing for his establishment during the Carnival. However, no engagements materialised, due to the usual chaotic situation in Italian opera houses, and Pauline went away empty-handed.

Nevertheless, they enjoyed their stay in Milan, where they were spoilt by the immense amount of beautiful art and architecture, including the famous cathedral, a great edifice composed of a strange mixture of styles, its basic Gothic structure allied to a façade featuring classical elements. The art gallery was a cornucopia of delight that they visited frequently, revelling in the sublime pictures and sculptures on view, providing Louis with an abundance of material for his articles.

As they wandered at leisure through the ancient streets, they were concerned about all the fine architecture that was falling into decay through neglect, and wondered how the civic authorities could allow such a state of affairs to continue.

In Bologna they visited dear old Rossini, who greeted them warmly, and his seraphic, kindly face, under one of his atrociously ill-fitting wigs, beamed at them. He talked of by-gone days when he and Manuel Garcia had been young men, and of the fun they had had, as well as the stresses and strains of putting on operas with the ink still wet on the manuscript. As audiences were always demanding new works, few operas actually reached the printers and publishers. The performers and members of the orchestra had to learn their parts from a single, hand copied line. Later in the century, if a work held its place in the repertoire, a vocal or orchestral score was prepared and published, but many of the individual bits of paper on which the music was originally written disappeared, making it difficult for the compilers and editors to arrive at a definitive version.

Pauline sang to the maestro and he was gratified to learn that the first five roles she had performed had been in his operas. He proffered vocal advice, and coached her in some of his music, showing her exactly how he wished it to be phrased and articulated. She knew that he was a wonderful teacher, knowledgeable about all aspects of the voice, and she gladly accepted his kindly counsel. One of the endearing things about Pauline was that however experienced she became, she was always ready to learn, and like all true artists, she was humble before someone superior in knowledge or skill to herself.

Rossini expressed his discontent with composers of the younger generation who did not have enough respect for the voice, and with conductors intent on changing the diapason, raising pitch in order to flatter the brass section of the orchestra with a brilliant sound, but making it more difficult for singers, particularly sopranos and tenors, who were now 'expected to sing words in regions where previously they were content to warble.' He prophesied that if this practice continued unabated it could only lead to the demise of what he considered to be good singing and cause needless wear and tear on voices.

Unfortunately, it did not abate, and some years later, the English tenor John Sims Reeves was constantly at war with Michael Costa, due to the continuing rise in pitch. This was a matter which caused concern for several decades, as can be seen by a letter in the London 'Daily Telegraph' from a physician, William H. Stone, dated January 7th, 1869: "It is in the last degree scientific to allow instruments, the fabric of men's ingenuity, and subject to whatever modifications he may impress upon them., but good voices are extremely rare, and the compass within which they can exhibit themselves to the greatest advantage is very limited. Surely it is in the interest of all who love music as an art, as an expression of the most intense poetical feeling, to give singers the fullest, freest scope quite unhampered by petty considerations of trifling expense and individual convenience"

Pitch had always varied from place to place but eventually it was standardised, although at what many people considered too high a frequency. At the time Pauline made her debut, French diapason was lower than in England, and English singers expressed the wish to be in line with their French counterparts, as even a slight difference in pitch can be detrimental to a voice when the music already has a high tessitura, but their views were ignored.

When it was time to leave Bologna, the Viardots were sorry to say goodbye to Rossini, who was always such delightful company. A continuous stream of friends and acquaintances filed through his house, often having to sit on the staircase because the reception rooms were full to overflowing, but even physical discomfort was deemed worth it because everybody relished the hospitality of a man who, like his music, was sparkling and amusing, with a wry, sardonic sense of humour.

In Naples, thanks to a warm letter of recommendation from the composer, the Viardots met the Duke of Casarano, and were escorted on many excursions by the influential nobleman. He took them to the ruins of Pompei and Herculaneum, that had been buried under lava and ash during the eruption of Vesuvius in 79 A.D., and had lain undisturbed until found and excavated in the 18th century. These amazing remains drew large numbers of tourists, although women were precluded from seeing all the exhibits, due to a sense of modesty on behalf of the authorities. Louis was fascinated by such a wealth of undisturbed archaeology and wrote a substantial article for the 'Revue des Deux Mondes'.

One of the places that appealed to Pauline most was Venice, which she considered the most romantic of cities, despite the less than sweet smelling canals. She was eager to see the Palazzo Mocenigo, a huge, grey building, only a few hundred yards from the Piazza San Marco, where her hero, the brilliant and flamboyant poet Lord Byron had once lived. Many people remembered him personally, and there were anecdotes still circulating about him twelve years after his death at Missolonghi during the Greek Civil War.

As a fearless youth, his original style of writing, daring adventures in the Levant, his extraordinary personality and dark, good looks had taken all of England, Europe and Russia by storm. He had stirred Pauline's youthful imagination, and she thrived on his work, and longed to hear more about him. Much as she admired his poetry, it was the character of the poet that enthralled her even more, and when she had first sung for Lady Blessington, during the 1839 season, Pauline had encouraged her to talk about him, which Her Ladyship was only too willing to do. The singer's favourite work was 'Don Juan', which she equated with Byron himself, and she found it fascinating to retrace his steps in Venice. It was wonderful to know that he had seen and experienced the same scenes that she was now enjoying, and had lived his life to the full during his short span of thirty-six years.

Visiting Florence, Louis almost fainted from artistic indigestion, so varied were the treasures set before him, and he hardly knew what to write about being so spoilt for choice. He and Pauline took a boat on the River Arno, and sailing at leisure, marvelled at the extraordinarily beautiful skyline and characterful buildings, which the hands of men had wrought along its banks during the Renaissance. They stared in awe at the cathedral that dwarfed the whole area with its magnificent Brunelleschi dome, and the delicate campanile of Giotto. The surrounding Tuscan hills, bathed pink by the evening sun as it sank behind them, framed the superb medieval city to perfection.

On July 12th, Pauline wrote to George Sand from Rome: "Dear, good Madame Sand, In Paris we named you our 'good angel' is that not so? Well, not a day passes without us giving you a prayer of thanks. If our happiness is complete, more, perfect, it is because your predictions have been so well realised. Pardon me, good angel, for making you wait so long to hear of the happiness that is so much a part of your doing, and I hope that this news will not find you indifferent to it. May you be a thousand times blessed".

While staying in the capital, the Viardots were guests at the splendid Villa di Medici, where the twenty-two winners of the ' Prix de Rome' the most prestigious award in France, lived for a term of three years, in order to study the wonders of art and music in the Papal city. The students took meals together twice a day in the palatial dining room hung with portraits of former winners of the prize, but otherwise they were left to their own devices, either studying in their rooms or exploring the city's libraries and galleries.

The Director of the Villa di Medici was the eminent French artist, Jean Dominique Auguste Ingres, who was now sixty. He was an old friend of Louis Viardot, and the foremost defender of Classical principles against the forces of Romanticism, whose leader was the forty-two year old Eugene Delacroix. Ingres could be violent and bad tempered in argument, but he delighted in living in Rome, where he was able to direct his students in their classical studies. He told them: "Drawing is the probity of art", and: " there is no grace without strength".

In addition, he was besotted by music, and was a great enthusiast of the violin, taking his instrument everywhere with him in the hope of being asked to play. The term 'Ingres and his violin' has passed into colloquial French meaning 'a hobby'. The pianist and conductor, Charles Halle, destined to be the founder of the Halle Orchestra in Manchester, said: 'Great artist as he was, with an immense reputation, he thought less of his painting than of his violin playing, which, to say the least of it, was vile. He was generally so moved by any Andante we played together, that he shed copious tears of delight. His immense superiority as an artist made this little weakness very interesting".

At first the Viardots had been disappointed with Rome, seeing only the squalor, the dirt and the vulgarity, with all the confusion and hassle of a seemingly provincial town, but gradually it cast its spell over them, and made them aware of the beauties concealed within—of the wealth of glorious, ancient architecture, the ruins of the classical world, the Baroque splendours of Bernini and Michaelangelo, and the great pictures of Raphael and Da Vinci. Pauline also discovered a residence in the Piazza di Spagna, where her favourite English poet had lodged in 1817, near the famous Spanish Steps and the spectacular Bernini Fountain.

The couple heard Palestrina in the magnificent Sistine Chapel, with its multicoloured ceiling depicting Michaelangelo's stupendous portrayal of God creating Adam. Charles Gounod, at that time a twenty-two year old musician and Prix de Rome winner, said that 'to hear that music in that place was truly sublime', and added "Palestrina's music seems like a translation in song of Michaelangelo" and 'music and painting in the Chapel appear to come from one imagination – a complete synthesis – both artists having no interest in mere effects.'

Naturally, the Viardots went to the opera where they heard the works of Bellini, Donizetti and Mercadante, but they were disappointed at the low standard, finding the singers inferior to those in Paris or London, and thought the productions quite grotesque, with inappropriate, historically ridiculous costumes, such as Roman soldiers dressed in yellow nankeen breeches with red stripes, a sight so funny, they had to stuff their handkerchiefs in their mouths to stifle their laughter.

On Sunday evenings the students at the Villa Medici gathered in Ingres' drawing room to discuss art and make music. The artist was delighted to welcome Pauline to their gathering and, eager to hear her sing, he asked the good looking, fair haired Charles Gounod to play for her.

First, Pauline sang 'La fiancee du brigand' to her own accompaniment, a song that always went down well, no doubt bringing back childhood memories,when she had experienced real bandits in Mexico, and maybe she told that story to her listeners. Ingres then asked for the great scena, 'Wie nahte mir den Schlummer' from Weber's 'Der Freischutz', a particular favourite of his, but Pauline said that she didn't have a copy of the music with her. Gounod told her not to worry, as he believed he could play the aria from memory. She began the long, slow recitative, and immediately everyone was spellbound as her magnetism and the sweetness and purity of her tones seduced them; then came the beautiful, lyrical adagio section, 'Leise, leise fromme weise', and the scene ended with the sparkling Allegro, 'All meine pulse schlagen', a brilliant coloratura section with a rising scale to a top B natural at the close of the piece. It is a virtuoso aria, but Pauline sang it effortlessly, encompassing the long phrases with marvellous lung capacity, and tackling the cabaletta with fire and passion. Her listeners were vociferously enthusiastic and clamoured for more, and she expressed her heartfelt admiration for Gounod who had accompanied her beautifully and sensitively from memory. His musical skill alone would have recommended him to her, but in addition, he was extremely personable and charming, with a most engaging manner. As an encore for the young men who were stamping their feet enthusiastically, she sang 'Una voce poco fa' Rosina's opening aria in 'Il Barbiere', another favourite of her host.

Afterwards, Pauline talked with the young musician who told her that he had seen Maria Malibran as Desdemona in 'Otello' when he was twelve years old, and she had inspired him with the desire to write an opera for her. The Viardots learned from Ingres that in addition to being a fine musician, Gounod was an excellent draughtsman, as his father, a professional artist, had been. The director had set the musician to work on copies and engravings for him, and when Ingres was painting a portrait of the eminent composer and director of the Paris Conservatoire, Cherubini, the young man was a model for the hands.

Despite his musical and artistic talents, Gounod was a man filled with a divine discontent, which expressed itself in a great spiritual yearning. For several years he had lived in a state of confusion and indecision, wondering which career to choose, that of composer or priest. Later, recalling his youth, he said, "I had great need of advice, for I must admit wisdom has never been my strong point. Weakness is very strong when reason isn't there to balance it. Alas! I profited little from it all".

He was under the influence of Charles Gay, a friend who was about to take holy orders in Rome. One day they went to mass together, and Gounod was 'seized in a profound religious experience, the like of which he had never known – believing that he was in communion with angels, the Christ, and God.' In his letters to Gay he discussed in detail the extraordinary moment of divine reunion. To serious musicians, music is a kind of religion, and Charles lived and breathed it.

Unknown to the Viardots, Fanny Hensel, Felix Mendelssohn's sister, whom Pauline had met in Berlin, was also in Rome at that time. During her visit, Fanny met Gounod and despite the thirteen-year difference in age, she and the composer found that they had much in common. In his memoirs he wrote that he was eternally grateful to Fanny for introducing him to the music of Bach, which overwhelmed him in its profundity.

All too quickly the Italian sojourn came to an end and the Viardots embarked on the long journey back to Paris, arriving in the capital at the beginning of August, to begin their new life together at No.12 rue Favart, close to the burnt out shell of the Theatre Italien.

Pauline enjoyed their leisurely journey back to France because it gave them time to talk undisturbed, and she learned a great deal about her husband's past. She was aware of his abiding love for Spain, and of his great interest in Iberian art and culture. With a twinkle in his eye, he mischievously declared that he could never have fallen in love with her had her heritage been other than Spanish: this made her laugh, but reminded her of the fact that she had never visited her parents' homeland and she envied his knowledge of a country about which she had heard much, but had never seen.

After qualifying as a lawyer at the age of twenty-one, Louis had been called to military service, and sent on an expedition to Spain. Being an ardent liberal, he feared that he might be called upon to act adversely against the Spanish people, but fortunately he was assigned to the Commissariat in Seville, under the command of General Ouvrard, where his duties merely involved guarding the wine stores, a 'natural function' for a Burgundian.

During his time in the Iberian Peninsula, he began research on the national school of Spanish painting, with masterpieces by such artists as El Greco, Ribera, Zurbaran, Murillo, Valasqez, and Goya. This study formed the basis of his formidable knowledge of the subject, of which he became an acknowledged expert. He also had the opportunity to indulge his great passion for shooting on numerous hunting expeditions in the countryside around Seville. He described to Pauline the wondrous thrill of the chase, and the fascination of pitting one's wits against those of an animal. She loathed all forms of cruelty and was not wholly convinced by Louis's explanations, but he certainly made it sound very exciting, and he assured her that it was the thrill of the chase, rather than slaughter that attracted him. For a sophisticated man who enjoyed cosmopolitan life and spent a large part of his time visiting art galleries, theatres, salons and cafes, where he met other political philosophers and intellectuals, his love for the countryside appeared in marked contrast, but he successfully balanced both aspects of his life.

On his return to France as a twenty-four year old bachelor, he became a journalist, joining the staff of the 'Globe'. Here he met Arnold Scheffer, a member of the Carbonari, who introduced him to his brother, Ary, the well known painter and political activist, who became his greatest friend. After a time, Viardot left to join the 'National', where he stayed until 1830. He, Ary Scheffer and Louis-Adolphe Thiers were active during the July Revolution, and were largely responsible for persuading Louis Philippe, Duke of Orleans, to accept the French throne. In the same year, he took up an appointment with 'Le Siecle' where he remained until 1836.

During this time, he published a number of books on Spanish subjects, most notably 'Lettres d'un Espagnol' in 1826. This is a rather serious novel full of details about the lives of the Moors in Spain, a subject which always fascinated him, and led to several other books on this theme. However, it was as the first French translator of Cervantes 'Don Quihote' in 1836 that his name reached a wider public. All the critics agreed that it was an excellent piece of work, which

kept faithfully to the original text, and was completely in accord with its Spanish character.

Soon after his return to Paris, Louis became acquainted with Spanish emigrees
who had settled in the capital, forming a substantial colony. Many of them were
artists, musicians and political dissidents who had left Spain because they
were opposed to the regime of Ferdinand VII. Viardot was naturally drawn to
this group, which is where he met and became an intimate friend of the Garcia
family.

In 1834, he returned to Spain to help administer a new government, but he
spent many of his leisure hours in the newly opened art gallery in Madrid,
known as the 'King's Museum'. One of his acquaintances was the extremely
influential banker Alexandre Aguado, Marquis de Las Marismas, who had chosen to support the French during the occupation of Spain, and had taken
French nationality in 1828. He was a noted art collector, for whom Louis wrote
a preface, 'Notices sur les principaux peintres de l'Espagne'. Despite the Spaniard's great enthusiasm for painting, he was even more obsessed by the theatre, paid for the restoration of the Theatre Italien, and appointed Louis Viardot
as its Director.

Aguado was extremely rich, and acted as banker to the Spanish Government,
who ennobled him in gratitude for services rendered, and between 1831 and
1835 he was an associate of Louis Veron, the wealthy newspaper owner and
director of the Paris Opera. The banker was also Rossini's best friend, commis-
sioning a cantata from him on the birth of his son, and putting his splendid
Chateau de Petit-Bourg with its extensive grounds and lake at Rossini's disposal so that he could compose 'William Tell' in peace and quiet. When Aguado
received Louis Viardot's letter of resignation from the Theatre Italien, he regretted losing a man of integrity and principle, (not always easy to find in the
theatrical world), but Louis insisted that he did not want a full time job, preferring to be free to accompany his wife on her tours, and follow the path of a
freelance journalist.

The banker owned a huge amount of property and land, and he exported and
imported in countries as far away as Mexico, thereby creating one of the foremost fortunes in Europe. Louis Viardot took the financial advice offered by this
successful man, who had laid the foundations of Rossini's fortune, and made
some sound investments, particularly in railway stock.

Pauline must have been disappointed by Louis's resignation, and the fact
that she had returned from Italy without an operatic contract was noted in the
Parisian press. No doubt Mesdammes Grisi and Stolz crowed happily at this
news, but it disconcerted Pauline's friends who wondered where she would

find operatic engagements in Paris. Although she had made a fine impression at the Odeon during the previous season, she was now without a stage, while her rivals were well ensconced in the available theatres.

The 'Revue et Gazette Musicale' for August 9th declared bluntly: 'Madame Viardot-Garcia has returned from Italy without contracting any engagements, nor has she done so with the directors of the Theatre Italien, who fear rivalry between Mme Grisi and herself. It is doubtful if Mme Viardot-Garcia will be heard in Paris this winter unless she should join the Opera, which we hope she will'. In spite of any private considerations where Pauline was concerned, Alfred de Musset valued the artiste, and was very upset at this state of affairs, writing in the 'Revue des Deux Mondes' "What is to happen to Pauline Garcia? Her talent is obvious, her success is certain, and established, but will we be able to keep her, or will her glory be gained elsewhere? What is a reputation and who is to make it?"

Giulia Grisi, who had a far finer natural voice than Pauline, as well as being better looking, actually became quite paranoid about the younger woman. There was something feline about the Italian, and like a cat, she mapped out her territory, put up her defences, and was ready to fight a battle with anyone who tried to displace her. It was Pauline's intelligence, scholarship, wide knowledge and superior musicianship that frightened her, because she realized that she could not compete with her rival on an equal footing, and made a determined effort to ensure that Pauline was denied any opportunity to outshine her. This was not difficult for her to do as she had many friends in high places, and as she held great power at the Theatre Italien, the new director of that august institution preferred not to challenge her. She had made life a misery for M. Laporte at Her Majesty's in London, where she acted as the singers' 'shop steward' (before such a post existed), and the Parisian directors, knowing how troublesome she could be, appeased her and allowed her to have her head in order that they might enjoy at least a modicum of peace.

George Sand deeply regretted Louis' decision to leave the 'Italien', because this was not what she had planned for her young friend, and she took him to task, telling him that he must busy himself on Pauline's behalf. He was enjoying his domestic life, and after all the recent travelling was happy to be in his own home again, where he had a great deal of work to do collating the material he had brought back from Italy. He wrote with erudition, and covered a wide area from paintings to mosaics, miniatures and manuscripts, as well as detailing the state of the theatres he had visited and expressing his opinions of the performances he had seen.

In the summer of 1840, George and Chopin did not go to Nohant, but, unlike most of their friends, remained in the city during the hottest part of the year, Chopin in his apartment at 5 rue Tronchet, and George nearby at 16 rue Pigalle, near the Place de Clichy. The writer had been overseeing the production of her drama 'Cosima' at the Comedie Francaise, but in performance, it had not been as enthusiastically received as she had hoped. When she learned that the Viardots were back in Paris, she was highly delighted, and she and Chopin gave the newly-weds a warm welcome. They had dinner and talked into the early hours; the Viardots were keen to hear all about George's play and Chopin's new compositions, and their friends were interested to hear about Italy and all the people they had met and the places they had visited. George was naturally disappointed that Pauline had not acquired a bundle of opera contracts, reluctantly accepting the fact that the Italian opera scene was chaotic and disorganised, and it was unrealistic to expect everything to be arranged immediately. On a personal level, she was gratified to observe that the 'honeymooners' radiated contentment, bringing out the best in each other.

Pauline was due to sing two concerts in Cambrai in a 'grand fete locale' and it suddenly struck her that it would be fun for George to accompany her and Louis on the trip. Chopin did not wish to leave Paris, but the writer was perfectly willing to wipe the dust of the theatre from her feet in the company of congenial friends.

In the event, George thoroughly enjoyed herself and in a letter to her brother, Hippolyte Chatiron, she said: 'My dear friend, In the past few days I have been on a little trip to Cambrai with Pauline Garcia and her husband, Viardot, the ex-director of the 'Italiens'. She has been singing at a musical fete, which was given in this region, and we have travelled in their own carriage, and have stayed at a beautiful hotel in the town. I have been able to enjoy myself without the worry of opening my purse or of ruining myself'.

Although they were only provincial concerts, Pauline was encouraged at her enthusiastic reception by the good people of Cambrai, who applauded heartily and encored her performances. She sang her father's arrangements of Spanish folksongs and 'Consuelo, di mi alma', a song her mother had taught her when she was a little girl. The latter became a great favourite with George Sand, and she even mentioned it in her next book. In Cambrai, Pauline could do no wrong and the local newspapers gave her glowing reviews. George was, naturally, delighted with her protégé's success, and relished Pauline's company. There had always been an affinity between them, despite the large age gap, but now their friendship reached a far deeper level, and they began to use first names with each other, leaving aside the formal Mme Viardot and Mme

Sand, and soon their correspondence included nicknames, Pauline calling George, 'Ninounne' or 'Mignounne', and George referring to Pauline as 'Fifille'.

Both women were interested in mysticism, and this forged a strong bond of friendship and deep understanding between them. There is evidence suggesting that Pauline was a visionary, and George was interested in supernatural experiences. Possibly, they discussed re-incarnation and life after death, because George used these two themes in the novel 'Consuelo' which she was already planning, and began publishing in a serialised form in 1842.

The more George saw of Pauline, the more she was enchanted by her, and confided to her 'Intimate Journal' that she had not loved another woman for ten years as much as she did Pauline, but she was aware that fond as Pauline was of her, the girl's capacity for deep emotion was not as great as that of George herself. From the beginning the writer sensed that the singer would always put her art before everything; that was her passion, but as far as human emotions were concerned, George feared that although she was kind, affectionate and friendly, ultimately, Pauline lacked the courage to love passionately.

George's tragedy was that she loved too passionately, and suffered for it, but she suspected that Pauline would never allow herself to tolerate such distress, and believed that ultimately, her control over her emotions would always triumph. The girl's will-power was of a very high order, which enabled her to keep her passionate nature in check, only releasing it on stage. The adrenaline that passionate emotion engenders can so easily be dissipated and wasted, tearing a person apart, when it is out of control. The fact that Pauline kept this energy in check in her everyday life meant that she had reserves in plenty on which to draw for the characters she portrayed in opera, enabling her to develop into a great dramatic actress.

Observing Pauline's happiness with Louis, George prayed that it would always be so. At present, the young wife was secure and comfortable with a husband who loved and cared for her, but who, George feared, did not unleash the depths of passion that lay buried in Pauline's nature. All was well at the moment, but her friend was young, and Louis was the first man she had known intimately. For the time being, at least, he satisfied her needs, but who knew what temptations life would threaten her with, as she grew older, and if her will power would be strong enough to protect her if she fell passionately in love with another man.

George had known many men intimately, from Baron Dudevant, the man she had married at the age of eighteen and had left eight years later, for Jules Sandeau. Their affair only lasted a short time, then came Alfred de Musset, Dr. Pagello and Chopin, but there were also many other lesser affairs, and throughout her life she continued to have sexual adventures, finding it very easy to fall into bed with most of the men she met.

When she considered the relationship between Pauline and Louis, she felt a chill creep over her, as she thought seriously of her own involvement in this match. She fervently hoped that Pauline would never experience anything to mar the even tenor of her life with her husband, and that she, George, would never have cause to reproach herself for having played the marriage broker.

George was a prolific writer who drew largely on her own experiences for her literary material, and her emotions were the bedrock of her work, whether on purely romantic lines, or those of a political nature. Her output was astonishing, and although by nature idealistic, in the work-place she could be very mercenary, as her life-style required large sums of money, not only for herself, her family, and her dependants, but because she gave away substantial sums to friends and their families when they were in need.

Her political affiliations were indisputably Republican, which was what linked her with Louis Viardot and Ary Scheffer. But Chopin, like many creative artists, was apolitical, except where emotionally involved because of the plight of his own country, which was under the yoke of Imperial Russia. Among exiles, his music became a symbol of Polish Nationalism, yet, he had no party affiliations, and placed no label upon himself. Far from being in the Republican camp, he had many friends and pupils from royal and aristocratic circles: he played his cards very cleverly, and managed to keep a foot in all camps throughout his life.

George and Louis, on the other hand, were strongly under the influence of Pierre Leroux, a rather bizarre journalist with whom Louis had first worked at 'The Globe', and had written articles on Spanish art when Leroux was co-director of the 'Encyclopedie Nouvelle'. Pierre Leroux was a mystical idealist with very unorthodox ideas, whose books George had been reading since 1835, on the recommendation of the celebrated French critic, Charles Augustin Sainte-Beuve, whose circle she frequented. She found Leroux's books pretty unintelligible, but they whetted her curiosity, so she invited the writer to dinner, and asked him to explain his theories, but after two or three hours of conversation, she was none the wiser, merely more confused, not knowing if Leroux was propounding a new religion, a new philosophy. a new political system, or all three. .

Louis, who was very influential at 'Le Siecle', wrote enthusiastic articles about Leroux's work that brought the two writers closer, but Leroux, like other idealists and political strategists, such as Karl Marx, although continuously rich in ideas and theories for the world at large, was hopeless at managing his own affairs. He had a large family, and despite being continuously employed, he was always in need of money.

After their delightful, though short vacation, the Viardots and George returned to Paris, where the writer and Chopin were reunited. On August 31st, Pauline invited them to dinner, adding that 'the good papa Lablache' would be joining them, and she said that depending on their answer, she would either cry or laugh! On November 17th , she wrote to remind her friend of another dinner engagement, and told George to be certain to arrive in good time as they dined at 5.30 pm at the latest, because they were joining a group of thirty friends at the Funambules Theatre in the Boulevard du Temple, to see the 'greatest actor of the age', Paillasse Debureau.

The following day, Pauline wrote again saying that there were more seats available, and could George bring her friend the Italian painter Luigi Calamatta, a former pupil of Ingres, who had painted a notable portrait of the violinist Paganini, and Chopin's great friend Albert Grzymala, (whose name, Pauline admitted, she could not spell, writing it 'XXXXimala').

Thus passed the autumn of 1840, with Louis writing his articles and books, and Pauline entertaining and visiting their friends, as well as giving several concerts, including one which Louis helped to organise in aid of the victims of the disastrous floods at Lyons. This took place onNovember 28th at the Theatre de la Renaissance, where a distinguished audience that included the aged, but still fascinating Mme Recamier, who was said to be the only woman who had dared to disagree with the Emperor Napoleon, and her equally elderly lover, the Viscomte de Chateaubriand, eminent writer and survivor of the French Revolution, and Francois Guizot, a future Prime Minister.

Rachel was one of the performers, and Pauline and the soprano Julie Dorus-Gras sang the duet from 'Andronico' by Mercadante, which was the last piece Malibran had ever sung. One of Pauline's solos was 'Nina' by Coppola, and she had a great success with the exquisite Eighth Psalm 'I cieli immensi narrano' by the largely forgotten, eighteenth century Italian composer, Marcello, which she sang with chorus and orchestra, and which became one of the most important pieces in her concert repertoire.

In her novel 'Consuelo', George Sand describes the young heroine singing this piece, and it is obvious that she was remembering Pauline's performance when she wrote: 'Consuelo knew Marcello's magnificent 'I cieli immensi narrano' by heart. Nothing could be better adapted to the religious glow that now animated the heart of this noble girl. As soon as the first words of this lofty and brilliant production shone before her eyes, she felt as if wafted into another sphere. She thought only of God and of Marcello'. A divine glow overspread her features, and the sacred fire of genius darted from her large black eyes, as the vaulted roof rang with that unequalled voice, and with those lofty accents, which could only proceed from an elevated intellect, joined to a good heart.'

At the beginning of December, George reminded Pauline to make sure that she and Chopin received the tickets that they had been promised for the general rehearsal of the Mozart Requiem in which she was to be one of the contraltos, and asked her when it would take place. This was in preparation for a grand State occasion on December 15th in the Church of Les Invalides when the Emperor Napoleon's remains were to be interred with great ceremony in that illustrious building. The rehearsal actually took place at the Paris Opera on the 12th, but on the 10th Pauline wrote to George expressing her regret that when George and Chopin had called, she and Louis had been at the house of the composer, Joseph Dessauer. She said how difficult it was to obtain tickets for the rehearsal but she would do her best for her friends. Although she was doubtful if she would succeed, she assured George that even if only one ticket materialised, she should have it.

In effect, the rehearsal was one of the most fashionable events of the winter, with a large crowd braving the violently cold weather, all turned out in their best finery, getting crushed and dishevelled for their pains. Despite the discomforts, Adolphe Adam, for one, said that he had never heard Mozart's great work presented with such brilliance. And small wonder, for the soloists taking part were the great international stars of the day, the sopranos, Giulia Grisi, Laure Cinti Damoreau, Fanny Persiani and Julie Dorus–Gras: mezzos Pauline Viardot Garcia, Emma Albertazzi, Eugenie Garcia, and Rosine Stoltz: tenors Gilbert Duprez, Giovanni Battiste Rubini, Alexis Dupont and Ponchard: basses Luigi Lablache, Antonio Tamburini, Nicolas-Prosper Levasseur, and Barroilhet.

The ceremony at Les Invalides was a panoply of State, attended by Royalty, ministers of the Crown, courtiers, statesmen, politicians, and nobility. Despite operatic rivalries, Pauline was in her element, taking her rightful place amongst the elite of her profession, gaining some deserved kudos.

Concerts were not enough for her, however, she wanted to be on the operatic stage where she knew she belonged. She needed the challenge of creating new roles, that was her life blood, and she could not pretend that her home life was fulfilling because in truth, she found the constant presence of Louis' sisters difficult to tolerate, aware that they resented her, and denigrated her for her lack of domestic skills. However, when she tried to help in the house, they castigated her for interfering. George was furious when, calling on Pauline one day, she found her up to her eyes sorting out laundry under the supervision of the 'two old maids'. How could they be so insensitive, surely there were others who could do such routine domestic tasks without involving a genius, who should be given encouragement and space to enable her to practice, compose, or learn scores undisturbed?

Years later, Pauline told Julius Rietz that she could be a good housekeeper when she chose, but that she was hopeless at dealing with servants because she was no good at giving orders. She longed to be free from Louis's sisters, and told George that she was beset by 'les pas trop belles soeurs' – (too many sisters-in-law!)

In addition, she was becoming very disillusioned because of the plots and cabals with which theatrical life abounded. Very often, success had less to do with talent and more with intrigue. Her opening season had been a remarkable victory, but she soon discovered that the Parisian public had little interest in artistry, dedication, musicianship and high ideals, and only appreciated frivolity and novelty.

Despite her disappointment, at least her empty diary gave her time to form and enjoy friendships, and keep up with correspondence. She and Louis were surrounded by interesting people in their neighbourhood, such as Adolphe Adam, composer of the popular opera 'Le Postillon de Longjumeau' and the ballets 'Le Corsair' and 'Giselle', as well as Heinrich Heine, from whose poem the latter was taken, and Theophile Gautier, who had supplied the setting for Adam's music. Hector Berlioz lived nearby and had now heard Pauline several times, causing him to change his first opinion of her. He was very enthusiastic about her performances, stating that she was the last of a dying breed, and that she was one of the few modern singers who understood and was capable of depicting the 'chant large'. He was aware that her musical taste was continually developing, and that the music she sang at her concerts was of a higher order than that chosen for her at the beginning of her career.

Pauline also saw a good deal of Ary Scheffer whom she and Louis often visited in the rue Chaptal, where he entertained them in his studio, and they encountered other musicians, painters and writers who called to see him. Sometimes, she sang to Ary while he worked and he expressed a wish to paint her. She was delighted, spent many happy hours sitting for him, and enjoyed their discussions. As he observed her, she, in turn observed him, with her artist's eye. Despite his technical skill as a painter, he found it very difficult to denote a true resemblance of his sitters, whereas Pauline had a great gift for catching a likeness, even in a hastily drawn sketch. Scheffer was immensely impressed by her natural talent for drawing and painting, although she herself made light of something that came so easily to her.

She watched Ary with fascination, as his long elegant hand with its tapering fingers moved with a deftness and speed across the canvas, and she became aware of his qualities as a human being, appreciating his fine intelligence, and commitment to his liberal principles. Through him and Chopin she met many Polish exiles and heard tragic stories of man's inhumanity to man.

He told Pauline how his political conscience had been stirred through his brother Arnold's involvement with the 'Carbonari' (charcoal burners). This group was first founded by Italian patriots, and Arnold introduced Ary to their leader, General Lafayette, the man who, with Louis Viardot, had been responsible for the annulment of Maria Malibran's first marriage. This secret, political, revolutionary society had originated in southern Italy, in order to overthrow Joachim Murat, the Bonapartist King of Naples, who had employed Manuel Garcia in 1811.

Although forced underground by a repressive government, the organisation had spread northwards and beyond the borders of Italy, winning support in France, and playing a part in Mazzini's 'Young Italy' movement. The composer Giuseppe Verdi was in sympathy with this group, as were many others who were opposed to all forms of absolutism, and the composer became a figure-head and rallying point, because his very name was a call to arms, as the letters VERDI were synonymous with Victor Emmanuele, ('Viva, Emmanuele, Rei d'Italia'), the King of Piedmont whom they hoped to install as king of a United Italy. Eventually they did so, but it is one of life's ironies that he was personally a coarse, vulgar, and unsavoury character.

Ary Scheffer had been drawn more and more into radical politics, which is how he came to play such a prominent role in the July Revolution of 1830. To show his gratitude, Louis Philippe appointed him to paint a series of frescos at Versailles, to celebrate the new reign. Ary's star was in the ascendant, and through his royal connections, he became very influential in the art world. His work was acclaimed at the Salon, that essential venue for any ambitious artist, and the subjects he chose were usually of epic proportions on classical or religious themes, although his early success owed a great deal to Goethe, as it was based on pictures illustrating scenes from 'Faust'. His work contained few examples of contemporary life, other than portraits of the 'great and the good'.

Like Louis, he was fiercely anti-clerical and full of religious doubt, although he had a strong spiritual sense and continually searched for philosophical answers. Pauline too was a seeker by nature, and they had some interesting debates about the meaning of life and death, and the eternal verities. In the picture he painted of her, she has almost the appearance of a nun, and the serious side of her nature is predominant. Her expression is forthright, and somewhat quizzical, but her neck, which is at an awkward angle, is rather too long. Her hair has a central parting and is unadorned, drawn into a knot behind her head. The dress she is wearing is of dark velvet, extremely plain, with long sleeves that have a band of lace at the wrist, and an almost off the shoulder neckline; her only jewellery is a fine gold chain with a cross.

Ary was very much in love with Pauline, but knew that he must always keep this fact a secret because his love could never be fulfilled. As an honorable man, he stuck to his determination to prevent her from discovering the truth; after all, he was more than twice her age, and she was the wife of his dearest friend. Because she was now so comfortable with him, she began to trust him implicitly and accepted him as her mentor and father figure. As he could not be her lover, he accepted the role she had created for him, and became her confidant. Louis trusted his friend, and was pleased to know that Pauline was happily occupied while he was busy writing.

Even when the painting was finished, Pauline still spent a great deal of time with Ary; apart from the fact that she liked being at his house, it kept her out of the way of the 'old dears', and she began the habit of practicing in the studio while Ary worked. She pored over operatic scores, learned new roles, increased her song repertoire, and worked on her own compositions. Whenever her sisters-in-law commented on the time she spent away from her own apartment, she made the excuse that she did not wish to disturb their peace, and said thatin her absence, they and Louis could attend to their own activities without distractions.

Of course, there was gossip when it became known that Pauline visited Ary while Louis was working, and there were many people who assumed that there must be more to this relationship than met the eye, but if any of the spiteful talk came to Louis' ears, he pushed it aside, having complete confidence and trust in his wife and his friend.

Young Cornelie, who missed her grandmother very much, enjoyed Pauline's visits immensely. Only nine years separated them in age and Pauline made up stories for her and taught her songs, as well as helping her to make dresses for her dolls. She also helped Ary to arrange his Friday soirees that were frequented by an array of eminent people from the worlds of art, literature, music and politics.

In his studio students were busily occupied grinding colours, sketching from life, or assisting on the master's canvases. Ary's brother, Henri, enjoyed the convivial atmosphere, and considered that he painted better at his brother's house than in his own. Their other brother, Arnold, was also a frequent visitor, as Ary was a sought after portrait painter and many eminent personalities came to the rue Chaptal, providing the journalist with useful copy.

In the autumn, Pauline was thrilled to receive a letter from her friend Clara Wieck telling her that at last she was Frau Robert Schumann. She had now reached her majority, and Robert had successfully applied to the Court for permission to marry her. Unfortunately, her father was still vehemently against the match. Despite this, the wedding ceremony had taken place in Schonefeld on September 12th, and she told Pauline that she was as happy as she could be in the circumstances, and had not lost hope that it would not be long before her father accepted the fait accompli and was reconciled with them both.

Delighted to be united with Clara at last, Robert was experiencing a spell of prolific creativity such as he had never known before. From the beginning of 1840, while still courting Clara, and full of hope that the time of waiting was coming to an end, he burst into song, and wrote over a hundred lieder in a matter of months, many of which were the finest of his output, including the song cycles, 'Frauenliebe und Leben' to poems by Chamisso; 'Dichterliebe', a setting of twenty-six Heine texts, 'Mit Myrten und Rosen', and 'Liederkreis' Op. 24, a group of nine songs also set to Heine, which he dedicated to Pauline, a sign of friendship that moved her greatly.

By the beginning of 1841, Pauline was still in Paris, where on January 31st she sang at Chez Erard, the elegant town house of the famous piano manufacturer, where concerts were held regularly, with musicians such as Liszt, Thalberg, Kalkbrenner, Moscheles, and on rare occasions, Chopin, performing on the famous pianos. Pauline performed Zerlina's two arias from 'Don Giovanni', 'Parmi les pleurs' from 'Les Huguenots' and the scena from 'Der Freischutz'. She was happy to be invited to perform at such prestigious events, where the most distinguished citizens vied for seats, but unfortunately, there was still no sign of an operatic engagement.

Nevertheless, she was kept occupied, and February was a very busy month for her: on the 3rd she appeared in the Salle Marechaux at the Louvre Palace before King Louis Philippe and his court, again singing the Eighth Psalm of Marcello with choir and orchestra, moving her aristocratic audience to tears with the nobility and pure emotion of her performance. On the 7th she sang at the Paris Conservatoire, performing several pieces by Handel, a composer then considered old fashioned by many smart people, but whom she truly admired, and Fiordiligi's great aria, 'Per pieta' from Mozart's 'Cosi fan Tutte', a piece that requires a dramatic sense in the opening recitative, a seamless legato with depth of feeling in the slow section, and the brilliance of a virtuoso for the finale.

Within a few weeks, however, the picture changed considerably because Pauline was invited to return to England for the forthcoming opera season at Her Majesty's Theatre. Suddenly life looked more rosy; she found fresh energy, and set out with Louis with new hope in her heart. She would have preferred the engagement to be at the Paris Opera, of course, but she did not complain, as London was the next best thing, although she dreaded the weather, and the phlegmatic populace.

Louis would also have preferred to stay in France or at least on the Continent, but he saw advantages in visiting 'perfidious Albion', not least because of the advances being made there in the development of the railways in which he had a financial interest, having had the foresight to ascertain the various benefits which this invention would bring. Fortunately he would not have to waste time hanging around at rehearsals in a draughty auditorium, killing time, as so many husbands of prime donne usually did, because he had been commissioned to write several articles on different aspects of life in Britain for 'Le Siecle'.

As for Pauline, she was preparing to go into battle with the dreaded Giulia Grisi on her own territory, where they would appear in the same operas, and it remained to be seen how well the young Frenchwoman would cope with her ruthless Italian rival.

On their arrival in London, the Viardots lodged at 184 Regent Street, where Pauline had stayed in 1839, and on April 8th, she wrote to George Sand saying that London was still very sad and boring, but that after Easter it would wake up and become as brilliant as it was dull at present. Her mother had been with them but had recently returned to Paris, as her brother Paolo Sitches was ill. The Viardots lived very much to themselves and Pauline confessed that she was homesick for her family and friends. She was uncomplimentary about the English, maintaining that they were as unsympathetic as their dismal weather. In her estimation, they had little liking for foreigners, and went about their own affairs with perfect indifference. However, she told George that she and Louis had been invited to dinner at the house of a 'Monsieur Mills', who had said that he knew the writer well.

This gentleman was Richard Monckton Milnes (later Lord Houghton) politician, writer and traveller, whom the Viardots probably first met in Lady Blessington's salon. He had spent a great deal of time on the Continent, and numbered amongst his friends Rachel, Prosper Merimee, the author of 'Carmen', a former lover of George Sand; also, the reactionary Francois Guizot, and the poet Alphonse de Lamartine, both of whom found themselves on opposite sides during the revolution of 1848.

Pauline's comments about English indifference illustrates the dichotomy between the long tradition of offering asylum to foreigners who were persecuted in their own countries, and a certain amount of xenophobia and lack of interest in foreigners in general. Most people were insular and parochial because they knew very little of what was happening in the rest of the world. Some members of the upper classes travelled widely, and read newspapers and periodicals, but they were in the minority, and most of the population lived and died within a small radius of their homes, which accounted for the insularity for which the English were famous.

It is interesting that even Jane Austen, one of England's foremost writers, who lived through the rise of Napoleon and had relatives serving in the navy during the Penninsular War, hardly makes any mention of such significant events in her novels.

The French, as the traditional enemy, were viewed with suspicion and many people declared that they didn't like them, whether or not they had met any of them personally. The government was extremely wary of the French and their unpredictable politics, and had a real fear of revolution due to the 'goings on' over the Channel.

In England, a radical democratic movement, known as Chartism, taking its name from the 'People's Charter' had begun to make headway among the working classes. It called for universal manhood suffrage, equal electoral districts, vote by ballot, abolition of the property qualification for members of parliament, as well as salaries for them.

The movement had started in Birmingham, when a William Lovett instigated a petition in 1837, which contained 1,280,000 signatures, and was formally adopted at a huge mass meeting in the city in 1838. But it was rejected by Parliament that dreaded an uprising like the one that had taken place in France in 1830. This refusal caused great anger and a large demonstration took place in Newport, Wales, which the authorities dealt with severely, its ringleaders being sentenced to deportation. After this, the Chartists quietened down; however, they did not go away, they merely went underground. The government may have been lulled into a false sense of security for a while, but they feared the working classes, and were extremely nervous of anything that might inflame them.

Although England was ostensibly at peace, there was a ubiquitous network of spies that kept a close check on anyone who might be likely to cause trouble. Vast numbers of Englishmen considered that their nearest neighbours were unreliable, political 'damp squibs' ready to go off at a moment's notice, and it is very possible that Pauline and her husband were watched because Louis made no secret of his republicanism, and it was known that he had many associates of a political shade of pink, if not red, one of whom was that 'dangerous socialist,' George Sand, whose credo was feared in many countries besides England.

Louis, George and the journalist and mystical philosopher, Pierre Leroux, were in the process of planning a new left-wing newspaper, 'La Revue Independente.' Originally, the writer Honore de Balzac, who had known and collaborated with George for years, had suggested founding an 'independent revue' set up by her, himself and Victor Hugo. Through lack of funds, nothing came of this, but George revived the idea, recruiting Louis Viardot as a founder member, with Pierre Leroux as editor-in-chief, and they set about raising 50,000 francs in order to finance the first year of publication.

Many of George's works had first seen the light of day as serialisations in the government backed 'La Revue des Deux Mondes', with whose editor, Francois Buloz, she had had an amicable professional relationship for eight years, but which was now deteriorating. The regime of Louis Philippe had not fulfilled the hopes of the liberals who had placed him upon the throne of France, and they were disgruntled because the monarch had shown himself to be weak, was surrounded by sycophants, and had a corrupt government

Buloz considered 'Horace', George's new novel, to be highly controversial and demanded that she make changes because he foresaw that if she did not, it could lead to political and social unrest. She was incensed and refused to make any changes at all. In answer, he wrote: "You are not a communist, I hope; at least, until you wrote 'Horace' I have never seen any trace of it in your writing". He considered that she was being unduly influenced by the communist philosophy of Pierre Leroux, which is highly probable, taking into account her exaggerated adulation, and the fact that she called him ' a new Plato, a new Christ'.

As she would not make any changes to 'Horace', Buloz had no choice but to refuse to publish the work. She broke with him and his paper referring to him as 'that Shylock who would sell my hide if it were suitable for making a pair of shoes'. It was this falling out that persuaded her that the time had come to set up her own mouthpiece, and brought about the founding of the independent review, and the serialisation of 'Horace'.

This work did nothing to sweeten George's relationship with Marie d'Agoult, once so friendly, but now full of bitterness and rancour. The writer created a cruel portrait of her former friend in the person of the Vicomtesse de Chailly, which was so thinly disguised that everyone in Paris was acutely aware of the origin of the character. George had no interest in simply telling a story; she intended that the plot should promote a proletarian ideal, making her hero a plain working man, chivalrous and kind, as opposed to the weak, unfaithful, bourgeois Horace, and the despicable aristocratic Vicomtesse. She asserted that the aspirations and sentiments of the lower classes could be equally as poetic and sublime, as those of the spoiled and cosseted aristocracy.

Bernard Falk (biographer of Rachel) states that: "probably in no period in history were so many cads loose in Paris society", and interestingly, many young men saw themselves in the character of the indolent, clever, hedonistic Horace, who turns his back on the study of medicine, wastes his parents' money, and throws over his working class girlfriend for the aristocratic viscountess. The portrait of Mme d'Agoult is so transparent that it is quite likely that Liszt assumed that he was Horace. Thus, the shadows between the writer and her two former friends lengthened.

Pauline was peripheral to all this, but there is no doubt that the politics of those close to her reflected on her, because although apolitical herself, she was tarred with the same brush as her radical friends, and it affected her career adversely. At that time, the word 'socialist' filled many people with dread because it was allied with the even more fearsome name of 'communist.' The majority of the aristocracy and bourgeoisie preferred the status quo, however unpleasant, and abhorred dissidents and trouble makers.

Despite the activities of her husband and his friends, Pauline had work to do, and a busier season lay ahead of her in 1841, than in her debut year, with more roles to perform and her own battles to fight. As well as singing Desdemona and Cenerentola, as she had previously done, she was to sing Romeo to Grisi's Giulietta in Bellini's 'I Capuletti e Montecchi', (which she told George Sand was a 'real duel'), and the travesti role of Arsace to her rival's Semiramide, the title role in 'Tancredi', Fidalma in Cimarosa's 'Il Matrimonio Segreto' and Orazia in 'Gli Orazi e Curiazi'. Twelve years previously, Sontag and Malibran had sung in 'Semiramide' together, generating a great deal of excitement due to their supposed rivalry, and now the public were agog to see how Pauline would fare with 'La Grisi'.

She did her best to resist rising to the bait, but the Italian never lost an opportunity to disconcert her, making barbed comments coated in sugar, but which had the venom of a snake behind them. At rehearsal, she took real delight in trying to make Pauline look small, taking advantage of the girl's relative lack of familiarity with the prevailing customs of Her Majesty's Theatre. The older woman had a powerful, authoritative personality, which ensured that she was never without followers, those weaker than herself, who were drawn into her sticky spiders web, doing her bidding in order to keep on good terms with her.

Another string to her bow had appeared in the form of the tenor, Mario, who was putty in her hands.

Her affair with the Viscount Castlereagh had cooled since the advent of this divinely handsome young man with the exquisite voice, who had become besotted with her. In a very short time, they had embarked upon a full-blown love affair that was common knowledge in theatrical circles, but which they endeavoured to keep secret, as Grisi was still officially married to the vindictive Count de Melcy.

An amusing sketch by Pauline illustrates a scene from 'Semiramide' with Grisi as the Queen standing at the top of a flight of steps, looking very grand and imperious, but top heavy, surrounded by courtiers, with Pauline as the youth, Arsace, wearing a short skirt and Phrygian cap, pointing at the mighty one in disdain; Antonio Tamburini stands next to her, his expression impassive, with Puig, the tenor, attempting to restrain the youth.

Chorley thought that the musical standard in the 1841 season was very mixed and regretted that the management had bothered to mount 'Gli Orazi' at all, declaring that it had only been executed 'after a fashion' and observed the change that had taken place in musical drama since Cimarosa had set Corneille's play. "The music – the final duet excepted – seemed, on its revival, pleasing but feeble beyond the power of acting to animate; telling of a time when the pleasure of the ear was cared for on the opera stage, without any close reference to dramatic truth or dignity. Even Malibran's sister, full of young dramatic fervour could do nothing for the heroine, as draped by Cimarosa. 'Gli Orazi' is a weak opera, let it be taken how it will".

Pauline obviously enjoyed singing the role of Tancredi, which she had first performed at the Theatre Italien in 1839 and told George Sand that her success grew daily. She drew another sketch for her friend, this time of herself and Fanny Persiani in costume. It showed the soprano as a tiny figure with a huge nose, and herself as a chivalrous knight towering over her. Chorley records: "A criticism somewhat analogous could be passed on the once-famed 'Tancredi' of Cimarosa's successor (Rossini), which was also revived this year, and with singers no less able than Mme Persiani and Mme Viardot. The latter, it is true, had to fight up against recollections of Mme Pasta as Tancredi; but the music, in spite of Signor Rossini's vivacity and melodic fluency (how superior both to Cimarosa's), in spite of the vocal magnificence and charm of the duets, came over the ear as something behind our time, because it had never been wholly consistent with its purpose. 'Il Tancredi' is already old, without being ancient. Gluck's operas are ancient, without being old."

It was common knowledge that Pauline's relations with Grisi were always highly volatile, and the 'Morning Post' appeared to be mischievously stirring the pot when it stated: "The following Thursday, in contrast (to the house for Grisi's 'Norma'), 'Otello' was played to about the thinnest and coldest house we have seen at this period of the season. "Perhaps some contention between the prime donne may have like-wise contributed to the triste aspect of the house. 'Otello' had been announced for Tuesday, and Grisi (if we mistake not) was to have been Desdemona, whereas it was Mme Viardot who was in possession of the part last night".

This report elicited a reply to the paper from Grisi herself: "Sir, as the public might be led to infer from the article in your journal of this day Friday, 30th April, with reference to the Italian Opera, that some contention between the prime donne may have contributed to the triste aspect of the house, there having been some dispute as to the part of Desdemona, I have to assure you that I have not had any misunderstanding or dispute with either Mme Viardot or the management, M. Laporte having informed me at Paris, previous to my engagement that I was not expected to appear in the opera of 'Otello'. I am sure, Sir, that having inflicted an unjust censure, you will repair the mistake by inserting this letter and oblige. Your obedient servant, Giulia Grisi".

Malicious gossip was to do much to make bad feeling between Viardot and Grisi over the years. Fuel was added to fire by unfortunate remarks made by George Sand, Pauline's most devoted admirer. The singer had written to Sand that she would not flatter the bad taste of the London audiences in the way that Grisi did, just to win applause. George wrote "I hope you will wring the neck of that fat goose who competes beside you, I don't say with you, that would do her too much honour'.

Bad taste or not, the London audiences continued to prefer Grisi to Viardot. After a performance of 'Semiramide' in which both singers appeared, Queen Victoria made a note in her diary that "Grisi sang beautifully, so did Tamburini. Pauline Viardot sang very well, but her voice was so small, one could hardly hear it at times". This is enough to confirm that Pauline suffered nervous tension due to Grisi's attitude to the extent that it affected her performance.

The whispering campaign, and things Pauline suspected were being said behind her back would all have affected a sensitive artist like herself. There are those in the theatre, thankfully, in a minority, whose raison d'etre seems to be to undermine and drain their colleagues in order to bolster their own amour propre, and outshine those they perceive as rivals. Usually they appear as over confident and full of themselves, but underneath they are vulnerable creatures, fearful of being 'found out' because they suspect that they are not as talented as they should be. No doubt Mme Grisi was of this ilk.

From Pauline's point of view the season cannot have been entirely satisfying. 'Gli Orazi' was considered to have been a poorly prepared production, and even Bellini's 'I Capuletti' was judged weak 'in spite of Mme Viardot's picturesqueness and power as Romeo (especially displayed in the second act), and produced no effect".

Nevertheless, she must have been heartened by Henry Chorley's support and his appreciative comments: "Even so early in her career, her singing in 'La Cenerentola' could not be exceeded for invention and brilliancy of style. When she appeared with Rubini she had to subdue her voice so as to match his musical whisper; but for the final rondo she had already invented that reading and those admirably ingenious changes (changes not so much allowed, as demanded by Signor Rossini's music) most of which have since been quietly appropriated by less imaginative singers – to name but one, Madame Alboni."

In addition to her operatic performances, Pauline was invited to sing at some important concerts, one of which was a matinee onMay 17th, for the eminent German conductor, Julius Benedict, in the Concert Hall at Her Majesty's Theatre. Benedict was a small, unprepossessing figure with a charming smile, who had been resident in London for several years, and together with Michael Costa, commanded musical life in England. He had met Maria Malibran in Paris in 1834, and like many others had been immensely impressed by her charm and talent; now, he was interested in her equally talented younger sister. His concerts were very prestigious affairs in which the most illustrious artists performed, but they tended to be very long, sometimes beginning at one pm and finishing at 7pm.

Liszt was now in England, the star celebrity at the concert that boasted a wide array of talent, including Grisi, Mario, Lablache, Mlle Loewe, (a German soprano making her debut in London that season), Viardot, Dorus-Gras, and the English bass John Parry, a great favourite, who sang comic songs and was considered second to none in his chosen genre. By a weird co-incidence, Liszt had recently stayed in the very same room at the Mosley Arms Hotel in Manchester, where Maria had died, and, a typical musician, he had written to a friend from there: 'Poor Malibran....She was an abundant woman (as Victor Hugo said to me one day) who was, perhaps, right to die young. Who knows? She might very well have finished up by going to St. Petersburg and singing out of tune like la Pasta'.

Pauline was delighted to see her teacher again, and he kept her amused with his descriptions of the horrors of his journey from Dublin to London, by way of Scotland, where he had been caught in blizzards, had experienced coaches breaking down and getting stuck in snow-drifts, had missed trains, gone without food, and been so delayed that missed concerts had had to be re-scheduled. It had been an awful time, but fortunately, his colleagues were an entertaining group who had all done their best to make light of their difficulties, and now safe and comfortable in London, he could laugh heartily at all the terrors and discomforts of winter travel in a northern clime.

He considered that marriage suited Pauline, giving her a new-found confidence, which added to her allure. She had always been an interesting girl, but now he saw her in a new light, as a desirable young woman, whose laughter rang out, as he related his adventures. At the concert, her singing impressed him even more than when he had last heard her; and he began to refer to her as 'Illustrissima' (most illustrious one). He was all admiration for her own composition, 'L'Hirondelle', which she began to sing in 1841. It is a sad little song, about a prisoner who makes friends with a swallow that alights on the window sill of his cell each day: the man is envious of the bird's freedom to fly wherever it pleases, and it may be that Pauline was attracted to this text because it reminded her of the imprisonment of poor Wolf Dietrich, whose story had so moved her in Salzburg.

Liszt said that he found her songs 'delicate, gracious and elegant' which gratified her immensely, as she valued his opinion. He still attracted her, and she had to chide herself, because, although she was a married woman, he had the power to enthral her. She cared deeply for Louis, but despite their intimacy, he did not affect her in the way that Maestro Liszt did. Feeling like a silly schoolgirl, she promised herself that she would succeed in getting over this infatuation by an exercise of will. Having enjoyed her 'crush' in the past, it now made her feel guilty, and unfaithful, if only in thought, to her husband.

Of the pianist, Chorley wrote: "His performance roused up the most crowded and coldest audience of the season to something nearer a furore than English men and women often indulge in". Another chronicler comments: "Liszt had a certain majesty of bearing, a commanding sway; he carried his audience by his strong personal magnetism. He would come on the concert stage with the step of a conqueror. Tearing his gloves from his hands, he would seat himself at the piano, run his fingers through his hair, and then attack the instrument with the mien of a commanding general. Whether it was because of his magnificent playing, or whether the surrounding excitement reacted on their sensitive natures, the feminine part of his audience would go mad with excitement."

Charles Halle, himself an excellent pianist, had first met Liszt in Paris in 1836 and stated: 'Liszt was all sunshine and dazzling splendour, subjugating his hearers with a power that none could withstand. For him, there were no difficulties of execution, the most incredible seeming child's play under his fingers. One of the transcendent merits of his playing was the crystal-like clearness, which never failed for a moment even in the most complicated and, to anybody else, impossible passages; it was as if he had etched them in their minutest detail upon the ear of his listener. The power he drew from his instrument was such, as I have never heard since, but never harsh, never suggesting 'thumping'.

However, like some others, he questioned the musical taste of the virtuoso, and added: " If, before his marvellous execution, one had only to bow in admiration, there were some peculiarities of style, or rather of musicianship, which could not be approved. I was very young and impressionable, but still his tacking on the finale of the C sharp minor sonata (Beethoven's) to the variations of the one in A flat, Op. 26, gave me a shock, in spite of the perfection with which both movements were played."

In addition to performing together, Pauline and Liszt met socially at a dinner at Julius Benedict's house at 2, Manchester Square, on Sunday, 10th May, where the other guests included Michael Costa, and Luigi Lablache. Benedict lived in a large, late Georgian town house, where he and his Italian wife, who was a marvellous hostess, entertained lavishly. The conductor's family were wealthy, ensuring him a private income so that he was not reliant solely on his earnings as a musician. Although, as he was always in demand, not only as a conductor, but as an indispensable accompanist, and was a popular composer, those were not negligible.

Pauline was on her own in London at this time, as Louis had gone back to Paris in order to facilitate the setting up of the new journal, 'La Revue Independente'. In a letter to her husband describing the evening at the Benedict's house, she said that Liszt had kept them amused for some six hours, with silly stories and jokes, making them all rock with laughter, and putting poor Lablache almost into a state of suffocation because he laughed so much, he could hardly draw breath. She thoroughly enjoyed Franz's company, and the only barrier between them was the vexed question of George Sand.

Liszt suspected that Pauline, now that she was married to Louis Viardot, must be firmly in her camp. The pianist regretted that his friendship with the writer, which had once been so warm, was now arctic. Being honest, he had to admit that to a large extent the animosity could be laid at the door of his mistress, who was highly strung, temperamental, vindictive, jealous and downright difficult. But, she was the mother of his children, and had sacrificed everything for him, so the least he could do was to remain loyal to her.

George deeply regretted losing Liszt's friendship, which had always meant a great deal to her, and she acknowledged the debt of gratitude she owed him for introducing her to the Abbe de Lammenais, an unorthodox Catholic priest, whose mystical philosophy played a great role in moulding the thought of artists and writers at that time. Liszt also brought the ideas of Saint-Simon to her attention, many of which found their way into her novels. Before she met Chopin, Liszt was already expanding her musical horizons, which had been formed by her grandmother who was steeped in the music of the eighteenth century. Mme Dupin de Francueil had ensured that George received a sound musical education, and the girl became a proficient pianist, but Liszt stirred her imagination and enabled her to understand the inner life of musicians and artists, which always held a fascination for her. In turn, she expanded his views of the world by introducing him to French and European literature, and to

advanced political ideas. Born in a German speaking part of Hungary, he had
never learned Hungarian, and as a child prodigy, touring extensively from the
age of ten, his general education had been very scanty. But he was highly
intelligent, an auto-didact with a great curiosity about life, who was grateful to
George for opening up a wider vista than he had previously encountered.

Like Pauline and George, Liszt was strongly drawn to things mystical and
spiritual, and they all felt safe discussing esoteric matters together without fear
of being laughed at, misunderstood, or thought mad. Liszt had an abiding belief
in God, which he expressed by drawing closer to the Roman Catholic Church,
but for Pauline and George, spirituality had little to do with formalised religion.
Liszt's statement that 'Nothing and nobody has ever been able to shake my
faith in immortality and eternal salvation', was echoed by Pauline.

On a lighter note, the guests at Benedict's dinner party enjoyed much humour at Chopin's expense, because he had given a concert at the Salle Pleyel on
April 26th, after having sufferedextreme agonies of nerves at the thought of the
ordeal to come. He had hoped that Pauline would take part, but when he realised that she would still be in England, he had tried to back out, but it was too
late. He had not appeared in public for nine years, and unlike Liszt, who relished
performance, Chopin dreaded it and was only happy playing for a few friends in
familiar surroundings.

As soon as the proposed event was announced, the box office was besieged, all the tickets were sold immediately, and the Chopinesque nightmare
began. George wrote to Pauline on April 18th: "He does not want any posters,
nor does he want a large audience. He does not wish anyone to mention it, and
he is frightened of so many things that I have suggested he should play on a
dumb piano, without candles, and without an audience." It was ironic that a
musician of his eminence should dread appearing in public, when he had the
ability to transport audiences into a 'seventh heaven' with his exquisite compositions and miraculous playing.

Liszt wrote to Marie informing her that he and Pauline had been fellow guests
at Benedict's house: "After dinner I spoke very categorically to Pauline about
Mme Sand's love of intrigue and gossip, and deplorable lack of sincerity: those
were my two points. Pauline listened, while trying, at first, to defend her friend.
I interrupted her, and she finished by saying: "In any case, I am not very
intimate with Mme Sand". Was Liszt telling the truth, or could Pauline, under
his spell, have proved disloyal to her friend? This could, of course, have been
a diplomatic manoeuvre in order to close a subject that was distasteful to her,
without incurring the rancour of a valued friend with whom she had no wish to
quarrel.

On the other hand, perhaps Liszt, not wanting to excite Marie's jealousy, under-played his relationship with Pauline. The former replied to her lover in a bitchy letter a month later: "How do you get on with Pauline? Badly, I suppose. Has she any success? None, I imagine'. He replied: "I get on so-so with Pauline, but not badly. When it suits me, we will get on better." What was Marie to make of that?

Much of the trouble between George and Marie had originated with a letter that Marie had written from Pisa to their mutual friend, the Countess Charlotte Marliani, in November, 1838. This missive was very indiscreet and spiteful, due to her jealousy of George whose relationship with Chopin was flourishing, while that of Marie and Liszt was falling apart. She wrote: 'The journey to the Balearic islands I find amusing. (George and Chopin's ill-fated trip to Majorca in 1838). It is a pity it didn't take place a year earlier. When she used to have herself bled, I would say to her 'if I were you, I would prefer to have Chopin.' She could have spared herself many lancet pricks. Because I know them so well, I think they will get on each other's nerves after a month of living together; they are two 'antipodic' natures, but I am quite happy about it".

Appalled at Marie's treacherous words, Countess Marliani wrote to George in Majorca and advised her to break off the friendship. Having consulted the Abbe de Lamennais who considered that the letters reflected a nasty, jealous irony, Marliani sent them on to George, who, from that time, gave Marie a wide berth, only occasionally going along to the soirees she held in her exotic Moorish salon on the rue Neuve des Mathurins, not far from George's apartment in the rue Pigalle. Pauline, who had first met George in the Countess's salon, was well aware of the animosity and also gave Marie a wide berth.

Liszt's final London performance of the season took place on June 29th at 4, Ecclestone Street, Victoria, the home of Harriet Grote, the Swedish writer, and biographer of Ary Scheffer, and her husband, George Grote, historian, radical MP, and one of the founders of London University. It was arranged by the English soprano and authoress, Adelaide Kemble, a member of the famous theatrical family, who was now known as Mme Sartoris, a leading society hostess. On first hearing Pauline, she had been impressed by the girl's obvious vocal talent, charisma and first rate musicianship, and had introduced her to people of influence, as Lady Blessington had done, and procured prestigious concert engagements for her. On this occasion, Pauline's colleagues were the tenor Rubini, with whom she had sung in 'Otello' and 'Semiramide', and the baritone Michael Balfe, the composer of 'The Bohemian Girl' and 'The Maid of Artois', with both of whom she sang duets.

Louis returned to London after three weeks in Paris, and to his delight, learned that Pauline was pregnant. Like many first-time mothers, however, Pauline, despite being pleased, was nevertheless apprehensive at the thought of the responsibility involved in rearing a child, and trusted that it would not affect her career adversely. In addition, there were very real fears about the process itself because many women died giving birth, and infant mortality was high in all classes of society. However, she was a cheerful young woman with a supportive husband, and if thoughts of a negative nature arose, she soon dismissed them, and endeavoured to look forward to the event with optimism.

In June, Louis wrote some articles about English life for 'Le Siecle', describing the countryside, and changes taking place in the large industrial towns such as Manchester, Leeds and Birmingham. He was extremely impressed by the burgeoning railway system that was run with maximum efficiency, and told his readers that "one leaves London at ten o'clock in the morning, travels at thirty miles an hour, and arrives at Manchester at seven o'clock in the evening, fresh, relaxed, as if one has just left one's house, not counting the thirty minutes spent at Birmingham where it is possible, for two shillings, to eat a good meal of steaming roast beef, lamb, poultry or ham, and partake of puddings and pies."

However, twenty years later, the rot had already set in, according to Charles Dickens, because with larger numbers of people travelling, culinary standards dropped considerably: "The training of the young ladies behind the counter who are to restore me, has been from their infancy directed to the assumption of a defiant dramatic show that I am 'not' expected. It is in vain for me to represent to them by my humble and conciliatory manners, that I wish to be liberal. It is in vain for me to represent to myself, for the encouragement of my sinking soul, that the young ladies have a pecuniary interest in my arrival... Chilling fast, in the deadly tornadoes to which my upper and lower extremities are exposed, and subdued by the moral disadvantage at which I stand, I turn my disconsolate eyes on the refreshments that are to restore me. I find that I must either scald my throat by insanely ladling into it, against time and for no wager, brown hot water stiffened with flour (Windsor Soup); or I must make myself flaky and sick with Banbury cake; or, I must stuff into my delicate organisation, a currant pincushion which I know will swell into immeasurable dimensions when it has got there; or, I must extort from an iron-bound quarry with a fork, as if I were farming an inhospitable soil, some glutinous lumps of gristle and grease, called pork-pie".

The first commercial railway in England opened in 1825, to transport coal between Darlington and Stockton, and the Post Office began sending mail on the Liverpool and Manchester line in 1830. It soon became apparent that there was a commercial opportunity in transporting people by train, though at first many travellers were reluctant to exchange coaches for rolling stock, because it was considered dangerous, accidents being quite frequent, and it was uncomfortable. There were three classes of passengers, and for those who could only afford second or third class fares, conditions were pretty unpleasant and primitive, as they travelled in open wagons, not all of which had seats, and the passengers suffered from the smoke and cinders spewed from the engine, in addition to the noise and the rigours of the British climate. They must have arrived at their destination looking as if they were trying to impersonate chimney sweeps.

For first class passengers, however, conditions were more comfortable, as they rode in covered carriages that had upholstered seats and some even had oil or candle lamps in sconces. These carriages were based upon the design of stage-coaches. Sometimes travellers actually arrived at the railway station in their private carriage and the vehicle was hoisted bodily onto flat railway wagons to continue the journey at a greater speed.

When Prince Albert returned by train to London from Windsor in 1839, on the Great Western Railway line between Slough and Paddington, the train was seen as something modern and desirable, but it was three years before Queen Victoria tried this form of travel herself, although in 1840, the Dowager Queen Adelaide, widow of William 1V, became the first Queen to make a train journey, and by 1842, many people were trying out the new system for themselves. The most dramatic period of railway construction and speculation was opening up, with branches eventually covering the length and breadth of the British Isles.

Thanks to people such as Louis Viardot who had the foresight to see the immense potential of rail travel, and the publicity they gave to the new invention, the French began to catch up with the British and soon there was a link between Paris and Rouen, and Paris and Le Havre, which was a godsend for Pauline on her journeys to and from England. In fact, railways revolutionised life, and between 1841 and 1848 there was a veritable burgeoning of construction not only in the British Isles and France but throughout the Continent, with many miles of railroad laid, making concert and opera tours more easily negotiable and thus more frequent.

On July 6th, Pauline gave her last operatic performance of the season, playing the role of Angiolina in 'La Cenerentola' opposite Rubini, as Prince Ramiro. The critics agreed that she was gaining in confidence with every appearance, and developing into an artist of the first rank whom they looked forward to welcoming in future seasons. A 'tongue in cheek' review by the critic of the

'Morning Post' appeared in 'Punch' declaring: "The only decided nouveautes that made their appearance were 'Fausta' and 'Roberto Devereux', both of them jejune, as regards their libretti and the composita musicale. The latter opera, however, serving as it did to introduce a pleasing rifacciamento of the lamented Malibran in her talented sister Pauline (Mme Viardot) may, on that account be remembered as a pleasing reminiscence of the past season."

Rubini had finally decided to retire, and on Saturday, 21st August he appeared before a fashionable audience 'amidst an abundance of tears – shed in the choicest Italian and showers of bouquets'. A wry review stated: "Signor Rubini is in stature what might be denominated 'juste milieu' his taille is graceful, his figure pleasing, his eyes full of expression, his hair bushy; his comport upon the stage, when not excited by passion is full of verve and brusquerie, but in passages marked 'con passione' nothing can exceed the elegance of his attitudes, and the pleasing dignity of his gestures. His pantomime in the allegri was no less captivating; but it was in the stretta that his beauty of action was most exquisitely apparent; there worked up by an elaborate crescendo, the furor with which this cantatrice hurried his hands into the thick clumps of his picturesque perruque, and seemed to tear its cheveux out by the roots – the vigour with which he beat his breast – his final expansion of arms, elevation of toes and the impressive frappe of his right foot upon the stage immediately before disappearing behind the coulisses – must be fresh in the souvenir of our dilettante readers. But how shall we parle concerning his voix? That exquisite organ, whose falsetto emulated the sweetness of flutes, and reached A flat altissimo, the voce media of which possesses an unequalled aplomb, whose deep double G must still find a well-in-tune echo in the tympanum of every amateur of taste. Who that heard it on Saturday last, has yet recovered the ravishing sensation produced by the thrilling tremour with which Rubini gave the 'Notte d'Orrore' in Rossini's 'Marino Faliero'? Who can forget the recitative con andante et allegro in the last scene of 'La Sonnambula', or the burst of anguish when accused of treason, while personating his favourite role in 'Lucia'? Never will his sotto voce be equalled."

With the waning of Rubini's star, a change came about in the style of tenor singing. His art derived from the Italian bel canto, which originated with the polyphonic music of the 16th century and expressed the truth of the text. This required a huge variety of expression and gradually a method was cultivated which allowed singers to produce volume, and develop the ability to create remarkable varieties of tone colour. This skill, known as messa di voce, was built up on a single note by the intensity of vocal tone, increased or diminished at will by varying the intensity, which was increased or decreased according to the air pressure on the glottal lips, but not by enlarging the oral chamber, which merely resulted in more volume.

Rubini was highly skilled in this method, which resulted in beauty of tone and quality of voice. It was based on the principle that the voice possesses two tones – a diapason, which is produced when the larynx is in a relatively low position and a flute tone when the larynx is in a higher position. The physical aspects of producing bel canto requires a posture in which the chest is raised and stomach drawn in, a loose jaw by which the soft palate is raised and lowers the larynx, and the drawing back of the chin to open the throat. Allied to this the correct method of breathing is crucial, and is achieved by a contraction of the upper abdominal muscles, so that control is maintained over the diaphragm, ensuring that the flow of air pressure is kept steady throughout the process of singing. The Italian method guarantees that "he who knows how to breathe can sing".

Manuel Garcia stated that "the lungs are for tone emission, the glottis is for pitch, the oral cavity is for vowel and timbre, and the front of the mouth is for consonants". The diaphragm regulates the pressure of air, and the larynx, as a nozzle in a water spray, directs the nature of the flow.

The elder Garcia had trained Adolphe Nourrit, who sang with enormous success at the Paris Opera for thirteen seasons. However, Gilbert Duprez was a tenor of the future having developed a chest method necessitated by the works of Verdi, Berlioz and Wagner, and to a certain extent, Meyerbeer, who were writing for larger orchestral forces that required powerful voices to surmount the massive sound. Nourrit realised that his style of singing would shortly become obsolete, and made determined efforts to acquire the new style. Duprez created the part of Arnold in Rossini's 'William Tell', a role that required more volume and muscular strength. Nourrit resigned from the Paris Opera and went to study the new Italian system with Donizetti in Naples. The acquisition of the modern method presented him with great difficulties because he could not muster the physical strength and stamina that it needed. He became confused and lost the ability to sing in his old, familiar way, while totally unable to encompass the new technique. He lamented that he could no longer colour his voice, and felt that the more he pushed for volume the less flexibility he had.

Duprez had sung the title role in the premiere of Berlioz's ' Benvenuto Cellini', and many people mourned the fact that he was sacrificing tonal quality for power, as he pushed his chest voice up unto the head register, limiting his true range. Yet, the genie was out of the bottle and the trend continued unchecked. In addition, pitch was constantly rising, and tenors, perhaps more than other voices, were over-stretched, and range and quality suffered.

To a certain extent this requirement for more power also affected women, and the lower female voices began to be pushed up, as they sought to develop strong high notes that would tell over the body of the orchestra. Contraltos and mezzos, having to compete with the lower strings and brass decided that they would have less chance of being drowned by larger instrumental forces if they sang in a higher tessitura. Of course, not all voices could function in this way, and many were damaged or actually destroyed.

Nourrit became clinically depressed because he found himself in a vocal 'no man's land'. Although he did not know it, his physical powers were diminishing due to a terminal liver disease, and he found it impossible to sing in a more virile, energetic way. He was only thirty-six, had six young children and a wife who was pregnant with a seventh, but his despair was so great that he committed suicide by throwing himself off the roof of his hotel. His wife duly gave birth, but the child died, and the mother followed the baby and her husband shortly afterwards.

Despite their best efforts, singers found it impossible to be forceful and elegant at the same time. Alfred de Musset said that Duprez sang like a lion, and Rubini like a nightingale. Pushed voices lost their agility and range, and the older operas that required lightness of touch in fioriture and embellishment from all types of voices, deep basses to the highest sopranos, gradually fell by the wayside, to be superseded by the music dramas of Wagner, Verdi, and later Richard Strauss, Puccini and other Verismo composers.

For decades, the old training was in abeyance and it was not until the coming of the Greek soprano, Maria Callas, who was born in 1923, and appeared 'as a reincarnation of Maria Malibran,' that the trend was reversed, and past methods of teaching rediscovered, bringing about a renaissance of the old operas. Callas was born in America of Greek parents, but returned to Greece at the age of thirteen and began her vocal studies with the Spanish coloratura soprano, Elvira de Hidalgo, who remained her sole teacher. Almost single-handedly, Callas effected the resurgence of the old repertoire, opening the door to other singers such as Joan Sutherland, Marilyn Horne, Beverley Sills and Montserat Caballe. She was a superb dramatic actress with a phenomenal coloratura technique and sang an enormous variety of roles. Her recordings are legion and cover the widest possible gamut of vocal styles.

Pauline told one of her students that she had spoiled her voice by wanting to sing everything: Callas did much the same and also damaged her voice. Although Pauline's career was over by the time recording techniques became available, by analysing descriptions of her singing, it is possible to make a calculated guess that hers was a very similar instrument to that of Callas, who, like Pauline, was basically a mezzo soprano who extended her higher range artificially. She died suddenly in 1977, at the age of 52, with two pictures beside her bed, one of Hidalgo and one of Malibran.

When the English season ended, the Viardots took a short break in Boulogne-sur-Mer, where Pauline and her mother had spent a holiday in 1839. It was a popular resort enjoyed by both the English and the French, and the Viardots looked forward to some sea bathing.

The town was bright and airy with many attractive buildings, three well-paved main streets, and several good hotels, all usually full of visitors in the summer months. At five o'clock each day, they would sit down to dinner at beautifully laid tables with napkins folded like fans, gleaming silver cutlery, and fine porcelain services, and delicious smells of sumptuous food being served to guests made hungry by the fresh sea air wafted through the windows.

The town, surrounded by a wall, was set upon a hill; it had a tall old belfry that could be seen from miles around, and was blessed with several good wells, providing fresh drinking water. Many of the houses had pretty courtyards, decked with pots of geraniums and summer plants. The Viardots were fond of walking, and soon discovered a charming area, arched and shaded by old trees, with a path running along the thirteenth century walls that formed the four sides of the town, that allowed splendid views of the river, surrounding hills and the sea.

There were large crowds of holiday-makers, and lots of English children, whose nursemaids and governesses gossiped together, enjoying the sunshine as they kept a watchful eye on their young charges. The French boys wore straw hats shaped like beehives or work baskets, and were accompanied by their pretty, snow white-capped bonnes.

In the Place d'Armes there was a market each morning, snaking its way up the hill, providing a plentiful supply of fresh vegetables, fruit, eggs, haberdashery, wine, kitchen equipment, and old chairs needing renovation. After lunch, the people and the bustle disappeared like magic, stalls, stands and umbrellas were folded away, the square was swept, and hackney carriages awaited visitors desirous to be driven out of town to enjoy the splendid countryside, passing neatly dressed peasant women riding home with their empty panniers, clean milk pails, and bright butter kegs, 'on the sweetest little donkeys in the world.'

There were many reasonably priced public amusements, but it was sea bathing, astoundingly cheap, that was the main reason for the Viardots being in the town. Each day, they were picked up by a horse drawn omnibus from the door of their hotel and taken to the beach, where they had a clean, comfortable bathing machine, a bathing dress and clean linen for the princely price of half a franc. Most people spent at least an hour in the sea, or even longer, when the weather was hot and fine.

After drying and dressing themselves, Pauline and Louis would saunter along the pier where there was usually a guitar player strumming popular melodies and a boy or woman singing 'without any voice, little songs without any tune'. It didn't matter, they were enjoying themselves, happy to be free for a little while from commitments. Louis was a quiet man who didn't waste words, but Pauline loved to talk and he delighted in listening to her, appreciating the way her eyes flashed and sparkled when she was animated. She seemed to have been spared most of the ills experienced by pregnant women; she was young, fit and healthy, and felt wonderfully well, now that she was able to rest whenever she wished. In the afternoons, she and Louis would sit on the beach or in the hotel garden reading, or perhaps take a gentle stroll up the hill, and lie on the grass looking out over the sea.

In the evenings they visited the commodious, attractive theatre, where a vaudeville preceded an opera. The standard of performance was pretty mixed, but Pauline found that, for a change, she quite enjoyed being on the other side of the footlights, free from nervous tension and fractious colleagues. When there was a fete in one of the surrounding villages, they took a hackney carriage and watched the villagers, dressed in their traditional costumes, and surrounded by flags and streamers, dancing on the green to the strains of a little orchestra.

Sometimes, they met acquaintances from Paris or London, and enjoyed games of whist or billiards with them. It was all very pleasant, but soon it was time to return to Paris. Much to the chagrin of Louis' sisters, who had hoped to enjoy their brother's company while he was in the capital, his work for the Revue took up all his time and he was not often at home.

Pauline resumed her trips to the rue Chaptal, where she amused Ary and Cornelie with stories of her London exploits, and the whims and vagaries of her operatic colleagues. When she was alone with Ary, she told him her news, and was relieved to be able to talk frankly, explaining how ambivalent she felt about the coming baby. He was remarkably understanding, and told her that he had felt the same when, a decade ago, the woman he loved, but to whom he was not married, had told him that she was expecting his child. He could not now imagine life without the daughter whom he adored, the sole link with his dead love, and he encouraged Pauline to see that she would not be alone in bringing up her baby; she would have a nursemaid, and her own and Louis' relatives who, he was sure, would be only too delighted to care for the little one, while Pauline was pursuing her career.

George Sand and Chopin were at Nohant for the summer months and invited the Viardots to join them but as Pauline was due back in England for the Three Choirs Festival in September, they could only stay for two weeks. However, they thought the long journey worthwhile because Pauline longed to see George's beloved chateau, and looked forward to making music with Chopin.

George adored having friends to stay at her country house, which was usually full to bursting point during the summer months. Franz Liszt and Marie d'Agoult had stayed there, as had Honore de Balzac. George's hospitality was legendary, and intangibly, her warmth generated a pleasing ambience in the chateau. She did not appear to make any special efforts; everything was very informal, and everyone was free to do as they pleased, without any restrictions or impositions. In his article on Chopin, written in 1852, Liszt reminisced about life at Nohant with George, saying: 'Like her, he manages racket and chatter, fright and delight".

The writer prided herself on her culinary skills, and made sure that her guests were well fed. Food was fresh and plentiful, grown in her own extensive kitchen garden and prepared in an enormous but rather chaotic kitchen by her devoted cook, Suzanne. In a letter written in 1839, on the occasion of Chopin's first visit, she observed: 'We dine alfresco, friends arrive, first one, then another; we chatter and smoke, and in the evening, when everyone has left, Chopin goes to the piano and, between dog and wolf, plays for me, after which he goes to bed, and is soon sleeping like a baby, at the same time as Maurice and Solange. In the meantime, I read the Encyclopedie, and prepare the childrens' lesson for tomorrow'. As this letter clearly shows, the lovers did not keep the same hours, or share a bedroom, although they were next door to each other.

George's eighteen-year-old son Maurice studied in the atelier of Eugene Delacroix in Paris, together with his friend Eugene Lambert, who was also staying at Nohant, but Solange, George's difficult, spoiled, thirteen-year-old daughter, was still at her boarding school in Paris, sulking and feeling left out of things and did not arrive until August 23rd.

Nohant was good for Chopin, who did much of his creative work there during the summer months. George, ever sensitive to his needs, had procured a

Pleyel piano from Paris, and she said that while he composed, he paced up and down his music room on the first floor, singing, breaking his pens, and altering every bar a hundred times. Some of his compositions written at Nohant included the Sonata in B minor; the third and fourth Ballades, the Sonata in B flat minor (the 'Funeral'), fifteen Mazurkas, the third and fourth Scherzos, and the Fantasie Polonaise in A flat major,

He was not by nature a country man; he preferred the sophisticated life of the city, but his months in Berry gave him the opportunity to work undisturbed. In the summer of 1841, the weather was often inclement, with a good deal of rain, so he didn't need much persuasion to stay indoors and compose, and his friends were able to enjoy the delicious sounds that drifted through the house as he worked. George enjoyed her visitors during the day, but as she didn't need much sleep, once they had gone to bed she worked hard, writing into the early hours of the morning, then she slipped into her bed where she stayed till lunch time.

The journey from Paris to Nohant is over a hundred and fifty miles, and Louis decided that they should travel in their own vehicle, the interior made into a bed, so that Pauline could sleep whenever she wished, and they would only need to make brief stops to change horses. On Sunday, August 1st, they left Paris at seven o'clock in the morning, stopped for lunch at mid-day and dinner in the evening, and made changes at Vierzon, Issoudun, Orleans and Chateauroux. Keeping on the move they made speedy progress during the night, and arrived at the hamlet of Nohant Vic in time for breakfast.

They turned into a narrow lane off the main La Chatre road, along which ran an ancient stone wall with a turret, a reminder of the medieval building that had once occupied the site of the chateau. At the end of the track was a small square with a handful of picturesque old cottages, and a tiny, Romanesque church of golden hued stone, with a shingle roof. The door was open, revealing an interior resembling a dark cavern, the gloom broken only by a red votary light burning steadily within. On the right, at the uppermost corner of the square, behind ancient stone walls broken by two tall stone pillars with a large, wrought iron gate, stood the chateau. The extensive stone-paved courtyard was broken by a large circular lawn on which stood a grand old fir tree, and either side of the gate were two garden pavilions. Hearing the sound of hoof beats and the rattle of the carriage, the inhabitants of the house rushed into the entrance hall, the double doors were flung open, and George, Chopin, Maurice, George's son, Countess Charlotte Marliani,Eugene Lambert, Maurice's artist friend, and half a dozen servants stood ready to receive the visitors.

There was great excitement and much chatter, as George swept the Viardots into the house, up the curving staircase, flanked by stone walls. Pauline was much moved to see a bust of Malibran in a niche cut into the wall, and let out a little cry of delight, as George led her into a beautiful, spacious, lofty room, still furnished in charming eighteenth century style. This had been her grandmother's room. Its walls were lined in soft, grey/green painted boiseries, festooned with slender floral garlands, with panels of a soft creamy colour, decorated with Pompeian motifs. Elegant Louis XV1 furniture stood upon a parquet floor; there were two beds, a smaller one, close to which stood a pretty rococco screen, and one with a canopy of striped, floral chinz 'a la Polonaise'. Large windows and double doors overlooked the garden. Pauline knew that she was going to enjoy her visit immensely because Nohant was already exercising its magical charm upon her. The servants brought in the luggage and warm water for her and Louis to freshen up after their long journey, then they joined the family and guests in the dining room for a welcome breakfast.

The expansive room in which they found themselves was most attractive, with long windows along the garden wall, a high ceiling, and pale, oyster coloured panelling inset into which were several wide, double doors. A glass fronted cabinet containing a collection of china stood in a rounded niche at the far end of the room; over it stood a terracotta bust of the young Solange, and the centre of the room was occupied by a large, oval table around which were placed several grey painted dining chairs, upholstered in amber velvet. Above the table hung an intricate, many-hued Venetian glass chandelier. Although Nohant was not a huge, rambling house, it was spacious and elegant with beautifully proportioned rooms.

French windows opened onto shallow, semi-circular steps, that led down to a gravelled terrace opening onto an informal patchwork of bushes, hedges, trees, a small circular pool, and lawns stretching to the old moat running along the road to La Chatre. George had planted two Cypress trees on the birth of each of her children, and they were now tall and mature. On fine summer evenings, she loved to stroll in her garden, smoking a cigar, cogitating over her current novel, or chatting to her friends.

After breakfast, George took the Viardots on a tour of the house and related its history. Although it stood on older foundations, the chateau was relatively recent, having been built in the latter part of the seventeenth century, and acquired in the late eighteenth century by George's paternal grandmother, Aurore Dupin de Francueil. She was the daughter of the famous soldier, Maurice de Saxe, the victor of Fontenoy, and illegimate son of Augustus the Strong of Saxony and Poland and Aurore de Koenigsmark. Mme Dupin was also illegitimate but due to her noble lineage she was related to the Kings of France and was imprisoned for a short time during the French Revolution.

Her son, Maurice, George's father, was an officer in Napoleon's army. Although his mother wished for him to make an advantageous marriage, he tied the knot with Antoinette Sophie-Victoire Delabord, whose family were in no way distinguished. She was five years older than himself and already had a daughter from a previous relationship. When George, who was then known as Aurore, was four years old her mother took her to join her father on active service in Spain. As a pregnant camp follower, Sophie found conditions very harsh, and her baby son did not survive for very long, but little Aurore grew strong and developed a highly individual and adventurous personality.

Her father returned to France unscathed by battle, but died as the result of a fall from a horse on his way home one night after a convivial evening with friends at La Chatre. He was only thirty-six years old. For some years, Aurore lived with her mother and half sister, Caroline, in Paris. However, Mme Dupin disapproved of the life lived by her daughter-in-law. She would not receive Caroline, although Aurore was very fond of her, and sent her granddaughter to board at the English Convent in Paris. In future years, George looked back notalgically on her school days. She loved the nuns, learned to speak English well, and even considered becoming a nun herself for a while. Mme Dupin did not approve of this plan, and when she died, she left the mansion to the eighteen- year-old George who adored the place, and was ready to make any sacrifice in order to maintain it.

Pauline enjoyed listening to George's family history, and was enchanted with everything she saw. She felt immediately at home in the mellow, old house with its warm, creamy pink walls, long windows with soft grey shutters, and blue/grey high-pitched Mansard roof. In the late afternoon, as the sun set, the whole area was bathed in glorious colour, bringing a blush to the walls, enhancing the natural beauty of the place, and illuminating everything with a golden, rose coloured light, imprinting an eternal picture upon Pauline's memory. All her life, her recollections of Nohant were very special to her; a bond was formed, making it a truly enchanted place, and whenever she felt depressed or burdened by the trials of everyday life, she would lighten her mood by re-living her first, perfect visit to Nohant.

In the evenings everyone gathered in the large, elegant salon with its pretty blue floral wallpaper, where masses of family portraits in gilded frames covered each wall, one of the most prominent being that of George's great-grandfather, the Marechal de Saxe. Chopin's upright piano was placed to one side, and the room was graced with all the usual kind of impedimenta collected by a family over many decades, while in the centre stood a large oval table, the work of the estate carpenter, surrounded by chairs of white painted wood, upholstered in blue and white striped silk in Empire style.

George's half brother, Hippolyte Chatiron, owned the chateau of Montgivray, on the edge of La Chatre, and often rode over to see her. He was an unsophisticated country man, full of humour, whom Marie de Rozieres, one of Chopin's pupils, who often stayed at Nohant, considered positively coarse. Although he kept an apartment in Paris, he went there very infrequently, as he had no interest in city life, preferring his country pursuits. He was an enthusiastic sportsman, which endeared him to Louis and they soon found a great deal to talk about. Although in no way artistic or literary himself, he was interested in his sister's artistic, aristocratic friends and relished convivial evenings with them. He was a bluff, unpretentious man, with no airs or graces, devoted to Chopin, despite being rather in awe of him. His wife was Emilie Devilleneuve, and they had one daughter, Leontine. Being an inveterate drinker and always in debt, there is little doubt that George had to bail him out financially on more than one occasion.

George had many good friends in the neighbourhood, most notably her doctor, the wealthy Gustave Papet, who lived at the nearby Chateau d'Ars, and Charles Duvernet, the owner of the chateau of Coudrey, Verneuil-sur-Igneraie, about six kilometres from Nohant. Papet, because of his substantial wealth, was able to treat the inhabitants of the hamlet free of charge. As he was an enthusiastic and skilled hunter, he and Hippolyte were great chums. Duvernet, on the other hand, was a passionate music lover, who on first hearing Pauline sing, became a devoted admirer for the rest of his life.

After dinner, Chopin sat at the piano, playing dreamily, as if in his own world; Pauline began to embroider a night-gown for her baby's layette, Louis, Hippolyte, Duvernet and Papet were recounting stories about their numerous hunting adventures; Maurice sketched Pauline, while Lambert, Charlotte Marliani and George argued some obscure point about a painting near the fireplace. Maurice was very attached to his mother, and there was a deep and abiding affinity between them that made up for the increasingly stormy relationship between George and Solange, her headstrong adolescent daughter. Her son was an impressionable youth, who, up to that time, as far as she knew, had never fallen deeply in love with anyone, but from the time of Pauline's first visit to Nohant, became strongly infatuated by her. Like many men, he found her fascinating, and when Charlotte and George prevailed on her to sing that evening to Chopin's accompaniment, he was emotionally overwhelmed. Chopin adored the human voice, and in Pauline he discovered a musician of a rare order. He told George that he loved the singer's company because however dark his mood, she could lighten it, and renew his creative gift when it failed.

Now, for the sheer fun of making music, they embarked on piano duets together. During the holiday, they also explored some of the works of Bach, Handel, and manuscripts of other old masters that Chopin had discovered. Both musicians were deeply interested in music of the seventeenth and eighteenth centuries, which had fallen out of fashion with modern audiences. Mendelssohn had talked to Pauline about Bach and played her some of his music, as well as showing her autographed copies of his work when she visited Leipzig, and these had whetted her appetite, and encouraged her to wish to hear more. George told a friend that the two musicians had poured over a host of manuscripts together, but in one of Chopin's letters he said that there hadn't been enough time for music because there had been so many other distractions.

When they finished playing, the pianist joined the men over a glass of wine, while Pauline and George took advantage of the fine evening, and walked around the garden, arm in arm, chatting. Pauline coaxed George to tell her about their trip to Majorca in 1838, which had raised the ire of Marie d'Agoult, and been the subject of much speculation in Paris at the time. It was common knowledge that the holiday had been a disastrous failure, but now that the awful experience was over, George could laugh about their exploits and she kept Pauline amused as she recounted them. Initially, she, Chopin and her children, had travelled south in the hope that the pianist's health would improve in a warmer climate, but ironically, that year, Majorca had its worst winter for decades, with severe storms and heavy rainfall. To make matters worse, they stayed on a high hill, some distance from the village, in the old, uninhabited monastery of Valdamosa, which in summer would have been idyllic but in winter, with its vast, unheated rooms, was terribly cold and damp, and Chopin was soon running a fever. The children were bored, and the superstitious villagers kept away from the unconventional group, terrified that they might catch Chopin's malady. Fortunately, George was an amazingly fit and energetic woman, and despite everything, she wrote prolifically. When the fever abated, and Chopin recovered, he also began to work and composed several pieces, including the one that has become known as the 'Raindrop Prelude'.

Eventually, as the bad weather had shown no signs of abating, the lovers packed up and left, although the only boat immediately available was one carrying a load of pigs to Marseilles. As there was no other boat leaving the island for another week, they gritted their teeth and joined the animals. The voyage was desperately uncomfortable, not only because of the overpowering smell of the pigs, but due to the horrendously high seas: by the time Marseilles came into sight it was like a glimpse of heaven after all they had suffered.

During the summer of 1841, the weather at Nohant also left much to be desired, but whenever a fine day dawned, the guests seized the opportunity to explore the surrounding countryside. Pauline was fascinated by the music she heard among the peasants of Berry, played on a kind of bagpipe, and their songs and dances, such as the bourree, delighted her. The traditional costumes were distinctive, both men and women wearing clothes of a kind of blue denim, the women with white headdresses and pretty aprons, and the men with black hats, white stockings and buckled shoes. Maurice enjoyed painting the people who lived around his mother's chateau when they celebrated their festive days, and Pauline was so taken with their lovely old melodies that she copied some of them out of a volume of 'La Chanson populairs'.

George kept her guests amused and well fed, and when the weather was too inclement for outdoor pursuits, they enjoyed card games, sketching, billiards, and wrote copious letters. Pauline was an enthusiastic billiard player, and with practice, her skill developedquickly, which pleased Chopin and Francois Rollinat, a lawyer from Chateauroux whom George nicknamed 'Pylade', who were also keen players. The Viardots had brought a bitch, Jessy, from England as a mate for George's dog Pistolet, and the writer looked forward to the little 'bride' producing a litter of puppies in due course.

Louis and his new hunting friends did not often let the damp conditions deter them, but went off happily across the fields in squelching mud to see what sport they could bag, often returning home with something for the pot, even if it was only a couple of rabbits or a hare.

Pauline and Chopin were in their element making music together, and Maurice drew an amusing sketch of Pauline at the piano, looking up with a surprised expression, as Chopin stood over her, wagging his finger. As a teacher, he was strict and hard to please, because he had a sacred zeal for his art and endeavoured to raise his students to his own standard. Yet, his aim was always to encourage and Pauline was only too happy to place herself in his hands. She gained much skill from the exercises he gave her that developed suppleness and independence of individual fingers, and he paid great attention to different kinds of touch, and the development of a melodious legato. He made her play scales with full, even tone, slowly at first, then gathering speed. With his own students, he advocated working on Clementi's Preludes and Exercises and Cramer's Etudes, and Pauline willingly applied herself to these pieces, finding them invaluable in developing flexiblity and strength in the wrists, and stretching the fingers.

Pauline began to understand how much Chopin had been influenced by the great singers, such as Henrietta Sontag, Giuditta Pasta and Malibran in the development of a beautiful singing tone, true legato, and perfectly even trills. He also emulated their use of gruppetti and appoggiature and emphasized the importance of shapely phrasing. Famous for his use of rubato, Pauline was surprised to discover that he always kept a metronome on his piano. In his accompanying hand he kept strict time, but used his right hand, either with an undecided hesitation, or more rapidly, with a certain impatient excitement while keeping the musical expression free from all rhythmic restrictions.

When the weather was really bad nobody ventured out of doors, instead they entertained themselves with charades and theatricals. The pianist often surprised people by his talent for mimicry and acting, and had once impressed the actor Piasecki, who had seen him in a play when he was a schoolboy at the Lyceum in Warsaw, and suggested that the lad should give up music and become a professional actor. Herve, another player who visited Poland with a French company, also sang his praises, having been astonished at Chopin's skilful imitation of a tailor at work.

As the pianist was preparing some of his works for publication, he and Pauline were not unduly put out by the unseasonal weather, and she was able to assist him in reading the proof copies that had arrived from Paris and included the Tarantelle in A flat major opus 43: the F sharp minor Polonaise opus 44: the Prelude in C sharp minor opus 45: the Allegro de Concert in A major opus 46: some Nocturnes opus 48: the Fantasie in F sharp minor, and the Mazurka in A minor.

The two weeks rushed by incredibly quickly and on August 13th, Charlotte Marliani left for Paris, followed on the 16th by the Viardots. Naturally, everybody was sad at the breaking up of such a lively party; even Chopin's delicate health had shown signs of improvement because he was musically fulfilled, and happy to be surrounded by congenial friends.

After Pauline left, Maurice was plunged into gloom because the house seemed suddenly empty and forlorn without her sunny personality. He confessed to his mother that he had fallen in love with her young friend, and although George admired his taste she was not slow to remind him that the singer was the wife of another man, whose child she was carrying. Of course, the fact that Pauline was unattainable only served to make her more attractive to Maurice, and she occupied his thoughts night and day.

Pauline's important concert at Arras in the north of France onAugust 24th was splendidly successful, and the local paper said that there had not been anything to match its quality in the city for at least a dozen years. There were three soloists, Pauline, Dorus the principal flautist of the Paris Opera, who was married to the famous singer, Julie Dorus Gras, and a local cellist.

The Viardots returned to Paris for a few days, then left for England. It was the turn of the city of Gloucester to host the Three Choirs Festival between the 7th and 10th of September, 1841, raising money from the revenue of concerts for the widows and orphans of the clergy. Pauline's colleagues included Mme Dorus Gras, Tamburini and the English singers, Miss Birch, Miss Harves, Mr. Bennett, Mr. Hobbs and Mr. Philips.

While taking part in the festival, Pauline and her husband stayed at the home of a rich gentleman farmer in Herefordshire. He was a typically English country squire, living for hunting, shooting and fishing, which should have recommended him to Louis, but his gamekeeper would not allow the Frenchman to shoot all the birds he desired, and this displeased him. Their host bred cattle and was famous for all the prizes he won at local agricultural shows, indeed, Pauline declared that the silver ewer for their ablutions must been won at such an event. Their bedroom was very grand, but bleak, with a huge four poster bed, which Louis said made him feel 'like a dead man on a catalfalque'.

The mansion was large and cold, and they found the company formal, the conversation stilted and boring. Meals were served at different times from those they were used to in France, and Louis was disgruntled because he was not able to have his breakfast until ten o'clock, by which time he was famished. He did not drink tea, which was considered very odd, and Pauline was not pleased when she found herself and the other ladies segregated from the men in the drawing room after dinner, ' like being in a mosque', as she told George. Apart from the writer, and one or two women friends, Pauline preferred men's company, as she soon tired of the usual things women talked of. She appreciated the exchange of ideas and delighted in the sort of weighty subjects that were more usually discussed by men rather than the generality of women at that time. Fortunately she, more than Louis, was able to suffer fools gladly, and joined in the small talk of her host's dour wife and two shy daughters, but she had difficulty stifling a yawn, as she found the trivia which occupied them very dreary, and longed to be back at home. How very different it was to life at Nohant!

Even the walks in the extensive park and gardens were regimented, taken at a certain pace, down stipulated paths, 'like prisoners exercising in a yard', and she longed to get on a horse and ride off to explore the area by herself, or with Louis, who was mystified by English country house customs, and resented being stopped by the gamekeeper from shooting too many birds.

It was torture sitting in the glacial drawing room after dinner, and the Viardots longed to curl up in bed in an endeavour to get warm. Pauline wore dresses with long sleeves and always had a shawl over her shoulders, but the daughters of the house wore flimsy white muslin evening dresses, their bare arms and shoulders blue with cold and pitted with goose pimples. Pauline thought that they adopted a formal style because they had visitors, and told them that it was not necessary, as she, for one, would be happy if they wore something warmer, but they assured her that it was nothing to do with her visit, as they always dressed formally for dinner because it was a family custom.

No doubt it was a relief for all concerned when the visit came to an end: it cannot have been easy for their hosts, accommodating foreigners whose ways they did not understand, and who, to compound matters, were from the bohemian world of the theatre, which was frowned upon in many upper class homes. Religious music in church was acceptable, but generally musicians and actors were considered very low down in the pecking order, and people were always surprised to discover that Pauline was very different from the stereotypical performer.

Unfortunately, she was able to learn little of what the gentlemen of the press thought of her performances, as there was hardly anything about the festival in the local papers, due to the fact that an immensely wealthy alderman had recently died, leaving all his money to the city, and there was much discussion in print, as to who or what should benefit from this largesse.

The Viardots returned to France by steamboat and Louis, who was never a good sailor, was sick. Back home in Paris, they received a letter from George who wanted them to pay another visit to Nohant but reluctantly, they had to decline, as Louis said he could not get away from his work and Pauline had several concert engagements.

George and Chopin returned to Paris at the end of October, and the pianist gave up his lodging in the rue Tronchet and moved into the ground floor apartment of George's home in the rue Pigalle. His contribution to the rent was welcome as George had a great need of money due to the high expenses incurred in a lawsuit in which she was involved. It was also more convenient for Chopin, as he was used to taking his dinner with her at 5 o'clock, then had to drive home in the cold evening air, which upset his weak chest. As he had a separate entrance for his aristocratic pupils and an elegant and comfortable salon in which to give his piano lessons, he was very pleased with the change of arrangements.

Louis, who appeared to have been the principal contributor of funds for 'La Revue Independente', wished that he had not become so heavily involved with the enterprise that was taking up too much of his time and eating into his finances. George was the 'godmother', Leroux, the editor, and with Louis's help, the three of them brought the new journal to birth in November 1841. It would appear that even before it appeared on the news stands, Leroux was having second thoughts about Louis, because he told George that he did not believe that Viardot was single-minded enough about the project on which they had all expended so much time and energy. Indeed this proved to be the case because, by the end of 1842, Louis had relinquished much of his responsibility, and two new directors were appointed, although he was perfectly content to submit articles, being happier in the role of journalist than that of accountant.

There was no difficulty in attracting notable contributors to the Revue, among them Louis Blanc, Etienne Arago and Victor de Laprade, and once the Revue hit the news stands, the founders were encouraged by the reception it received and the large number of advertisers who signed up for the available space. Nevertheless, the bulk of the articles were written by George, Viardot and Leroux themselves. The serialisation of the controversial 'Horace', which had caused the rift between George and the influential 'La Revue des Deux Mondes' was a cause celebre, generating gossip and pushing up the sales of the 'Revue Independente' enormously.

One of Pauline's most important concerts during the autumn was a performance of six excerpts from the Rossini 'Stabat Mater' on October 31st at Chez Herz.. She had already sung parts of this work informally at the house of the well known pianist and teacher, Pierre Zimmerman, but now she was to sing in a more formal setting, although this was still not the official public premiere, but for an invited audience of Rossini patrons, friends and colleagues who received the extracts with great enthusiasm. After this hearing, Troupenas bought the entire score for 6,000 francs, and within three months he had sold the performing rights in Paris to the Escudiers for Fr.8,000 and they disposed of it to the Theatre Italien for Fr.20,000. Thus, three people made a profit from a single work before it had been heard in its entirety.

Pauline's baby was due within six weeks, and after this concert, she concentrated on preparing for its arrival, sewing and knitting, embroidering the layette, and arranging the nursery. Sometimes as a welcome diversion, she would push domesticity aside and apply herself to composition. Naturally, Louis's sisters were very excited about the forthcoming event, as no baby had been born into their family for decades, and they busied themselves with needle and thread, preparing for the new arrival.

Pauline's mother now lived mainly in Brussels with her relatives, but she planned to be in Paris for the birth of her daughter's first baby. Manuel Garcia frequently visited the Viardots and kept an eye on his sister, informing his mother of her state of health and well-being. Louis, who was naturally concerned for his wife's welfare, and apprehensive about the birth of her first child, was not helped by his sisters, who fussed and talked about all the things that could go wrong. Pauline's mother was a breath of fresh air when she arrived, a sensible, practical woman who looked on the bright side, telling them that her daughter was young and fit, and all would be well. She kept Pauline calm, and ensured that she did not get bored during the waiting time. Often, they wrapped up warmly and went for short walks or drives together, visited the theatre or attended concerts, and in this way the time passed more quickly than it might have done.

When Pauline was safely delivered of a daughter onDecember 14th , there were sighs of relief all round, as the young mother came through her ordeal splendidly. Louis was delighted and proud of his first child and thought her the most perfect baby ever born. She was called Louise Pauline Marie, and soon all their friends came to visit, bringing presents for the new arrival and her mother. Ary Scheffer came with Cornelie, who was thrilled with this little living doll, and surprised and delighted at being allowed to hold her.

Ary was very relieved to see Pauline looking so well, aglow with health and happiness. Motherhood suited her, having rounded out some of the angularity of her features. He looked into her face and squeezed her hand, and she knew from his look, before he said anything, how relieved and happy he was for her. George, Maurice and Chopin came to visit, and George, who had a markedly maternal side to her nature, whooped with glee when she saw the little bundle in Pauline's arms, and prophesied that she would grow up to be a great woman, like her mama. Chopin was fascinated by the baby's tiny fingers, and took her hands in his own, declaring that he was sure that she would be a marvellous pianist, just like Pauline!

Many people, including Berlioz, left cards and their best wishes for the young mother, and she was humbled to know how many people cared about her for herself, and not just because she was a celebrated singer.

In a much shorter time than many new mothers took to recover from a lying in, she was up and about, keen to get back to work. Louise was a good baby, and there were lots of people willing to look after her, so Pauline had no need to worry about having to do everything herself. Having made the decision to not let motherhood stand in the way of her career, on December 29th, she gave a concert at the Paris Conservatoire.

When she learned that the first official public performance of the Rossini 'Stabat Mater' on January 7th, 1842 at the Salle Ventadour was to take place without her, she was deeply upset, especially when she learned that Grisi, Mario, Albertazzi and Tamburini (the Italian League) were the soloists. She did not know whether it was because she had not been expected to perform again so quickly after the birth of her baby, or if, once more, it was a case of being kept away by rival factions. She considered that at least she could have been asked, especially as she had already performed extracts from the work.

The concert that Chopin had given the previous year had been an outstanding success from which he made 5,000 francs, and he was now tempted to give another one. George complained that it would have taken her many weeks of writing to earn so much, and he had done it in one evening! For what Chopin had suffered before his ordeal, it was cheap at the price, but he was now optimistically planning another one on February 21st at the Salle Pleyel, and this time his dear Pauline would be taking part. Although the seats were expensive, fifteen and twenty francs – the hall was soon sold out. Knowing how nerves lacerated the pianist, Camille Pleyel, herself a pianist and the wife of the piano manufacturer and owner of the Salle, had arranged for several of his friends, including George, Heinrich Heine, Franz Liszt, Delacroix, the cellist Auguste Franchomme, the musicologist Ernest Legouve, and the Polish poets Mickiewicz and Witwicki, to sit on the platform, so that he could imagine he was playing to them in his drawing room.

The evening before the concert, Pauline sang again at the Paris Conservatoire, and included the Marcello Psalm, scenes from Gluck's 'Orfeo' and an extract from 'La Cenerentola' in her programme.

Chopin's recital was, as might have been expected, one of the musical highlights of Parisian life, and attracted the fashionable world. He played three of his Etudes, the Ballade in A flat major, the Impromptu in F sharp, several Mazurkas, and accompanied Pauline in her own setting of La Fontaine's 'Le Chene et le Roseau,' much to George's delight because she thought very highly of Pauline's songs. This one was included in a group of eight that she published in 1841 with lithographs by Ary Scheffer and Soltau. She also sang several pieces by Handel and a Melodie by Joseph Dessauer. The evening was a triumph for Chopin and herself, not only artistically but financially. In a letter to Pauline, George declared that she was a great woman and complained that her hands were swollen with so much clapping. This was all very gratifying, but concerts did not further Pauline's operatic career, so Louis decided to take matters into his own hands. If France wasn't prepared to offer her the work she deserved, he would take her to Spain.

Night-time ablutions at Courtavenel, the Viardots' country home

Louis Viardot to
whom Pauline
was married for
forty years

Sketch by Pauline Viardot as Zerlina in 'Don Giovanni' from a letter she sent
to Julius Rietz in 1859

Pauline in her costume as Gluck's 'Orfeo' (1859)

Pauline and Marini in a scene from the 1848 Covent Garden production of 'Les Huguenots'

The Coronation scene from the London premiere of Meyerbeer's 'Le Prophete' in 1849

Chapter Twelve

1842

At the beginning of March, the Viardots visited Brussels to show off their new baby to relatives, and stayed at Ixelles with Joaquina, Charles de Beriot, his second wife, Marie Huber, whom he had married in 1840, and Pauline's nine-year-old nephew Charles Wilfred, who was studying the piano and showing signs of the extraordinary musicianship for which the Garcias were famed. It had taken Charles a long time to get over Maria's death, and although he was universally recognised as one of the most eminent of living violinists, he had made few public appearances since his German tour with Pauline in 1838. He had recently been offered a professorship at the Paris Conservatoire, but turned it down, as he preferred to stay in Belgium. However, in 1843 he became a professor of the Brussels Conservatoire and laid the foundation of the Franco-Belgian school of violin-playing, as distinct from the classical Parisian school represented by Viotti, by whom he had been influenced in his youth. Paganini had been a great inspiration and de Beriot adopted many of the brilliant effects, such as pizzicatos, harmonics and arpeggios, epitomised by the Italian. The Belgian was noted for the purity of his intonation, and the grace and elegance of his bowing technique, attributes that he passed on to the next generation of string players.

Singers can learn a lot from violinists about elegance of tone and the shaping of phrases, and Pauline learned much from her brother-in-law who had been an important mentor to her, but it is probable that he also learned from the brilliance of her execution, passionate commitment and emotional freedom, which she demonstrated every time she sang. If so, he was in good company, because Chopin maintained that he had a learned a great deal from the way singers used their voices and incorporated elements into his piano compositions.

The Viardots returned to Paris early in April and on the 16th, Pauline gave a concert at Chez Erard with her good friends, the pianist, George Alexander Osborne, the singer Michael Balfe and his wife, the Hungarian singer, Lina Rosa, who had recently settled in Paris. The men were natives of the 'Emerald Isle', and Pauline loved their repartee and banter, both of them having the proverbial wit and humour of their race. Osborne played a selection of his own compositions, and Michael Balfe, as well as singing some of his own songs, gave a spirited rendering of the 'Largo Al Factotum'. He was a noted Figaro, a role in which he had first enjoyed a major success in Italy, and had often sung with Malibran in that country, notably at 'La Scala'.

The other singers taking part were W. H. Weiss, a pupil of Balfe, and Henriette Nissen, who had studied with Manuel Garcia. One of Pauline's pieces was the rondo-finale from 'The Maid of Artois' which Balfe had originally composed for Malibran.

A few days later, leaving baby Louise with her aunts and nursemaid, the Viardots set off for Spain. Louis was overjoyed to be returning to a country he loved, and naturally Pauline was full of excitement at the prospect of seeing her parents' homeland for the first time. Like all exiles, the Garcias had always remembered their country nostalgically, conveniently forgetting the less pleasant aspects of life there.

In Bordeaux on April 21st, Pauline sang Rosina in 'Il Barbiere' in French, and was thrilled by her great success with an audience usually considered 'so severe, so difficult, and so indomitable'. Apparently, she had obtained a 'rare success' in the theatrical annals of the city, and was pleased because she felt that she had been in wonderful voice. Writing to George Sand, she said that it had been a marvellous evening, and she had been gladdened by the tremendously enthusiastic applause. She had sung numerous encores, and the floral tributes had overwhelmed her.

Her health was already benefiting from the southern climate and she was feeling more alive and vital than she did in Paris. On the 23rd she gave her second performance of Rosina, and the press commented on the extraordinary flexibility and range of her voice. The following day, the critic of the 'Memorial bordelais' praised the charm and power of her singing, adding that the timbre of her voice was 'unctuous'. The writer even forgave the director of the Grand Theatre of Bordeaux for the way he had mutilated Rossini's score with cuts and alterations.

On April 27th the Viardots were in Bayonne in the Basque Country, where Pauline sang Rosina again. Their stay in the town was short, and they soon pressed on toward the Spanish border. When they reached the Custom Post at Irun, Louis was gratified to find that his name was known to the officials, and they even allowed him to keep his French gun. He was acknowledged as someone who had played a significant part in bringing the present regime into power. He still believed that the revolution had been successful, and that the Catholic Church had lost its power. He abhorred clerics who foisted their narrow brand

of religion on the populace and brought about great harm through the imposition of their bigoted concepts. During the revolution they had been expelled, as
had Don Carlos from Navarre, and the Queen-mother from the seat of power.
Louis had not visited the country for some years, and was unaware that the
Catholic Church was stealthily increasing its hold on Spain once more.

He intended to introduce 'La Revue Independente' into the country and
prepared to send back articles on Spanish affairs to Pierre Leroux. However, he
did not intend to spend all his time working, and looked forward to the pursuit
of the chase. In England, he had been disgruntled by the petty-fogging rules
regarding slaughter and hoped that he would have a freer hand in Spain where
regulations were less stringent.

When the Viardots arrived in Madrid, Pauline was dismayed to discover that
the Italian opera company had been disbanded, and she had to set about recruiting a new one, drawing mostly on amateur talent, as there was a paucity of
professional singers. It was an enormous task, but she was young and keen
and threw herself into it with a will, proving herself to be her father's daughter.
Soon, another blow fell when a relative of the tenor died, and rehearsals had to
be postponed for nine days so that he could observe the obligatory time of
mourning. When he returned, Pauline became almost a one-woman band, acting as repetiteur and chorus master, teaching the group the music of 'Il Barbiere,
and then doing the same for 'Otello'.

Despite the difficulties, she was in her element, and capable of tackling all
aspects of an opera production, as her father had done. She loved the climate
and felt well and happy in this sunny, bright land, and rather than being cast
down by the problems with which she was beset, found it stimulating, challenging and rewarding, the result being that she was transformed into a different person from the frustrated, disappointed singer she had been in Paris. At
least here, she was appreciated and respected as a true artist, and welcomed
everywhere as the daughter of the famous Manuel Garcia, who had brought
honour to his native land.

The twelve-year-old Queen Isabella II, and her little sister, the Infanta Marie-
Ferdinande-Louise, came to one of the rehearsals, and Pauline sat at the piano
and played and sang for them. The little Queen and her young sister were
delighted, and complimented her charmingly.

Pauline appeared at least twice before the Regent, the Duke of Vittoria, and
his wife, who opened their salon on Sundays to the elite of Madrid society, and
on May 23rd, a great crowd of notables were invited to hear Pauline sing the
'Semiramide' duet with Mme Garostiza, two arias, and some Spanish songs,
including 'Bajelito' and 'Jales' by her father. She was congratulated on her

superb Spanish pronunciation, so true and clear, and a commentator observed: 'she is, as usual, ravishing, admirable and a great artiste'. The following day, she received a bracelet ornamented with opals and rubies and an ornate silver chain from the Regent.

The 'Iberia musicale' of May 20th announced that she had 'a soul full of passion, a pure voice, and her acting was elegant, animated and dramatic'. On one occasion, in the second act of 'Il Barbiere' she sang an Andalusian air in a supremely original way, with masses of ornamental embroidery, improvised in an entirely new mode 'with a brio and a superior precision'. It brought the house down, and on May 24th, a report appeared in the 'Courrier' stating that Pauline's medium and low notes made her voice the most beautiful contralto, but added that her soprano notes were in no way remarkable.

A few days later, the Viardots were installed as members of the Lycee in a splendid ceremony where the President made a fine speech praising them, and Pauline responded in excellent Spanish, much to everyone's delight. Thanks to Louis's influential connections, the Viardots were received by the highest in the land, but they found the society of Madrid insular, and the city a hot-bed of gossip and rumour. Pauline told George Sand that Louis was despondent because Spain was falling back into the reactionary place it had been prior to the revolution. Year by year, the Catholic Church was growing in strength, and in supporting the Regent, had allowed him to become a despot who limited the freedom of the individual. Spain was still split by conflicts between the monarchists and the Liberals, and in May the government was dissolved, and it was not until July that a new one was installed.

Pauline received honours, flowers and jewellery everywhere she sang, but fell foul of some members of the British Embassy because it was alleged that she had snubbed an Englishwoman when she walked out before the end of a performance of 'La Sonnambula', which was scheduled to finish at 1 am. Mrs Scott, the individual concerned, who was singing Amina, was highly incensed, but Pauline was tired, bored to tears, and feared that she would fall asleep in her chair. She had to rehearse early the next morning, and through no fault of her own, she made an enemy of a vindictive woman, who strove to discredit her in Madrid, bribing a journalist of the important 'El Corresponsal' to cast aspersions and belittle her talent, insinuating that she had been jealous of the English woman, who declared that it was not enough for a prima donna to have a good voice, she should also have a good heart and know how to behave in society! Of course, Pauline thought this hilarious, and made light of it to George Sand, observing that it was merely a storm in a teacup. George was indignant on her protégé's behalf, and used the incident to show rivalry between an ambitious Englishwoman and a young singer in her next novel.

In a letter to George from Madrid, dated the 14th of May, Pauline apologised for the delay in writing but said that she had not had a moment to herself, what with the preparations for the opera, and the amount of visiting she and Louis were required to do. It was in Spain that she first tackled that 'Everest' of soprano roles, Bellini's 'Norma' that he had written for the great Giuditta Pasta, with whom every other soprano in the role was compared.

The heroine is a Druidic priestess, who, despite her vows of chastity, falls in love with the Roman Proconsul, Pollione, by whom she has two children. When she discovers that he is in love with her fellow priestess, Adalgisa, she is distraught and plans to kill her children, whom she loves, but is prepared to sacrifice, in order to punish their father. After many machinations, and Norma's declared plan to send the childrens' bodies to Pollione and then kill herself, Pollione is arrested by her Gallic warriors and brought in judgement before her. She offers him his freedom if he will leave Gaul without Adalgisa, but he refuses, although she tells him that he and Adalgisa will be burned alive. He begs her to have mercy on Adalgisa, and says he will kill himself. Norma then calls the Druids to her side and reveals that the temple has been defiled by one of its priestesses, and the miscreant must die for having betrayed her God and her country. When they demand the name of the fallen one, she cries 'It is I', then implores her father, Oraveso, to forgive her, and asks him to protect her children. Pollione, his love re-born through her courage, asks her pardon, and together they go to their death in the flames.

The role of Norma is written for a powerful dramatic soprano but also requires a phenomenal coloratura technique. It is on a par with the heroic tenor role of Verdi's 'Otello' that requires a powerful voice and great stamina, but unlike Norma, the male singer is not required to sing florid passages. Unsurprisingly, singers who excel in these roles are very rare. Lili Lehmann, who was a famous Norma and Brunnhilde in Wagner's 'Ring' cycle, maintained that Norma was the more taxing of the two.

All her life, the Bellini heroine held a great attraction for Pauline because she considered herself to be a priestess of music, and felt empathy for a woman who was as prepared to give up everything for love, as Pauline was for music. Vocally, it was not an ideal vehicle for her, although she would have been an excellent Adalgisa.

The role of Norma requires the voice to be constantly exposed over the whole range, and different styles are demanded of the singer. An ability to spin a seamless legato line, to sustain over the soprano passaggio, and to have great flexibility in fioriture are essential. The role is long and extremely demanding and needs tremendous stamina because the voice must soar effortlessly without the advantage of the orchestral covering that sustains the singer in the operas of Verdi and Wagner.

Pauline was a superb singer, highly trained in the vocal methods of the eighteenth century, but it was a matter of tessitura, (an Italian vocal term that means texture or 'to weave' and signifies the prevailing or average position of the notes in relation to the compass of the voice for which it is written, whether high, low, or medium). A mezzo soprano may have an extensive range with available notes up to high C, or even up to F or G in alt in the flute register, but if a role is written in a consistently high soprano register, particularly over the soprano passagio, the laryngeal muscles will become stressed and quality and tuning will suffer. The part of Adalgisa also demands high notes and a coloratura technique, but the tessitura is mainly in the medium register.

While Pauline was preparing Norma, she received several letters from George telling her how 'Louisette' was faring. The writer often popped in to see the baby, whom she found 'gay, pink and charming'. Pauline also received copies of the 'Revue Independente' in which George's new novel 'Consuelo', was being serialised, the heroine being based on Pauline herself.

On July 18th , the singer celebrated her twenty-first birthday at the home of friends of Louis, who gave a dinner party for her. She wore a dress of deep green silk, with a full skirt, and tight bodice, and her chain with the gold cross, and pearl earrings. Her hair was parted in the middle, smoothed over the crown and caught up into a knot at the back of her head, secured with a large pearl hair comb.

After dinner, the guests adjourned to the large conservatory, which was full of exotic plants from the New World. It was reminiscent of an Amazonian rainforest, everything was so lush and verdant. Outside, the night was hot and oppressive, and midges and mosquitos swarmed mercilessly, but in the conservatory, with its pools and fountains, it was cool and comfortable, and Pauline enjoyed conversing in Spanish with her hosts and their friends. Although she missed 'Louisette' and her family and friends, it was nevertheless a charming birthday.

On July 29th, she wrote to George telling her how much she was enjoying the episodes of 'Consuelo': "I am so proud to have been one of the fragments that have served to create this admirable character. This will, no doubt, be one of the best things I have done in this world." George had written to her in June praising her incredible goodness of heart, her charity, her absurd modesty, and like a cat protecting her kitten, had berated the baseness of Pauline's rivals.

Years later, Pauline told a friend that if he wanted to understand her, he should read the first part of 'Consuelo', and it is apparent that George delineated Pauline's personality and appearance in portraying Consuelo. She wrote that Consuelo was sublime in simplicity, pathos or grandeur and said that when Pauline sang she made everyone forget her plain features. One of the characters in the book says: "I never saw a creature so strangely beautiful as Consuelo; she is like a lamp that pales from time to time, but which, at the moment when it is apparently about to expire, sheds so bright a light that the very stars are eclipsed", and another sighs: "that little black dress and white collar, that slender and half devout toilette, that pale, calm face, at first so little remarkable, that frank address and astonishing absence of coquetry – all are transformed, and, as it were, become divine when inspired by her own mighty genius of song."

In a further section, George is obviously thinking of Pauline: "At first glance, Consuelo neither impressed nor dazzled any one; she was always pale, and her modest, studious approach precluded that brilliant glance that is seen in the eyes of women whose only thought is to shine. She had a reflective seriousness, and one might observe her eat and talk, and bother herself with trivial everyday concerns, without even beginning to consider that she was pretty; but when a smile of enjoyment, so easily linked to serenity of soul, came to light up her features, how charming she became! And when she was animated, when she was really interested in something – she displayed tenderness, exaltation of mind, and the manifestation of her inward life and occult power shone resplendently with all the fire of love and genius, and she became another being. She buoyed her audience up by passion, annihilated them at pleasure, but could not explain the mystery of her power. In addition, she was so different to other women of the theatre, who were all too easily corrupted by seductions and offers of riches".

The novel begins at a school of singing in eighteenth century Venice where the young Consuelo, who has a superb, natural voice, is the favourite student of the famous teacher, Niccolo Porpora. He is aware that she has a deep, intuitive, artistic understanding, and he instils into her a profound dedication to her chosen art. She is an orphan from a nomadic gypsy family, said to be of 'good Spanish blood,' and descended from the Moors who overran the country in the 8th century. She is known as Consuelo, and has no surname.

The author states frankly that as a fourteen-year-old Consuelo is ugly, 'black and thin as a grasshopper,' but by the time she is seventeen, she has blossomed and is transformed and totally unrecognisable from what she had been, having magnificent black hair, a handsome figure with a tiny waist, and truly small, Andalusian feet. The essence of her beauty, however, is not physical, but spiritual, and is most apparent when she sings, for then a divine fire rises and bursts into flame so that her large black eyes sparkle and shine. However, she does not live on an exalted plane, she is a human being, with a sense of humour, who works hard. Her general demeanour is calm, but at the same time, she is an active person.

George Sand had seen a great development in Pauline between 1840 and 1842, and this is reflected in the character of Consuelo, who is not only a singer but an actress, able to portray profound emotions, reducing her audience to tears one minute and into fits of laughter the next. The writer acknowledged that Pauline was versatile, with an extraordinary memory that enabled her to learn roles with amazing facility. George recalled how when Fanny Persianni was suddenly taken ill, Pauline had taken over the role of Zerlina in Mozart's 'Don Giovanni' at short notice, and sang it 'in a style to gladden the composer's heart'. Like her, Consuelo is skilful at disguising her voice in such a way as to completely deceive her audience when she sings a travesti role, and it illustrates the phenomenal range that Pauline possessed, shown in a duet with Tamburini in Gnecco's 'La Prova' in which she was required to sing the baritone role and he that of the female in falsetto.

In her novel, George praised traditional music, for she loved to hear Pauline sing authentic Spanish folk songs, and she was, of course, influenced by both Chopin and Liszt, who drew largely on the folk music of their native lands. In the novel, Consuelo says that these old songs have the qualities of rough diamonds combined with pure genius, and one wonders if this is the voice of George or Pauline speaking.

In the course of the story, Consuelo is loved by two men, Anzoleto, who is a Venetian, the same age as herself, half gondolier, half singer, and as poor as she is, whose love she innocently returns, and Albert, the Count of Rudolstadt, thirty years old, serious, often lost in dreams and reverie. He is prone to depression, and his family indulge his fancies because they believe that he is mentally ill. However, he is not ill, but is a natural psychic, who lives in an active inner world, and remembers a series of past lives, spanning several centuries, which he has lived within the same family in Bohemia.

When Consuelo first arrives at the Castle of the Giants, Albert takes little notice of her, but he soon realises that she has the ability to raise his spirits and still his feverish imaginings. Anzoleto, on the other hand is a hedonist, rooted in the physical world; he loves the good life, is vain, and easily inveigled into theatrical intrigues.

In her debut, Consuelo is rapturously received by her audience, but she is scared by all the corruption she discovers in the theatre, particularly around

Anzoleto. She leaves Venice and has many amazing and exciting adventures, through all of which she remains chaste. The Count of Rudolstadt wants to marry her, but his family disapprove, and Consuelo has no desire to give up her career. She escapes from the Castle in the middle of the night and sets out for Vienna where she knows she will find Porpora, her old teacher. On the journey, she meets the young composer, Joseph Haydn, and a deep, though pure friendship, develops between them.

Some time later, she hears that Albert is on his death bed, and returns to the castle. He believes that he was once the Hussite chief, Ziska, and that she was his sister Wando. Ziska was responsible for atrocities during a religious war, and Albert knows that he still has to make reparation for that life, and for subsequent ones. He tells Consuelo: "I leave you for a time, but I shall soon return to earth under a new form. I shall be distraught when I come back if you abandon me now. You know that the crimes of Ziska still remain unexpurgated, and you alone, my sister, can purify me in the new phase of my eternal existence. We are brethren: to become lovers, death must cast his shadow between us. But we must, by a solemn betrothal, become man and wife, so that in my new birth I shall regain my serenity and strength, and become, like other men, freed from the dreary memories of the past. Only consent to this engagement; it will not bind you in this life, which I shall shortly leave, but it will unite us in eternity. It will be a pledge whereby we can recognize each other, should death affect the clearness of our recollections. Consent!. It is a mere church ceremony, but necessary in the eyes of society, and indissoluble in our hearts, as it is sacred in intention."

Consuelo agrees to marry him; a priest is called, but once the ceremony is over, Albert expires. Looking at him, Consuelo queries the process of death: "yielding up his last breath, had he ceased to exist, or did he live on in a cloudless existence, or was he conducted to a place of temporary repose. Perhaps he was drawn into a realm of pure consciousness and state of heavenly being?" Consuelo, already initiated by Albert into the Hussite doctrines, and other mysterious sects of bygone ages, who had all tried to interpret the teachings of Christ, was convinced, more by her own gentle and affectionate nature than by strong reasoning, that Albert's soul was not suddenly removed from her forever, and carried into inaccessible regions. She retained superstitions from her gypsy childhood and believed in spirits as common people believe in them, having more than once dreamed that she saw her dead mother approaching, protecting her from danger. It was a belief in the unending communion of the souls of the living and the dead – a simple, childlike faith, which has always existed to overcome the creed that seeks to separate the spirits of the departed from those of the lower world. 'No' she thought, 'the Divine spark still lingers, and hesitates to return to the hand who gave it, and who is about to resume his gift in order to send it forth under a renewed form into some loftier sphere. There is, maybe, a mysterious life existing in the still warm body; and besides, wherever the soul of Albert is, it sees, understands, and knows all that is happening here. It seeks, possibly, some comfort from my love – an impulsive power to aid it in a new and heavenly career'… briefly, in feeling and idea to treat him, not as a deceased spirit for whom one weeps without hope, but as a friend who is sleeping and whose awakening smiles we joyfully await."

The book eventually ran to three volumes, but through all the trials, tribulations and mystical, extraordinary happenings, Consuelo remained pure The criticism levelled at the novel is that it is over long, and that George was intent on expressing certain musical, artistic, and social ideas and mystical philosophies dear to her heart besides simply telling a story.

Musically, of course, she was most influenced by Chopin, Liszt and Pauline, as well as by the memory of her grandmother who had educated her in the music of the early eighteenth century masters. Chopin and Pauline often played works from the classical repertoire during the summer at Nohant, while George was planning the book, and she was always profoundly moved by Pauline's singing of the Psalms of Marcello, and the arias of Bach, Handel, Gluck and Mozart.

The mystical and occult aspects in 'Consuelo' are very strong, and result from a variety of sources, such as a belief in life after death and re-incarnation. The philosophical ideas of Pierre Leroux feature strongly, as well as the influence of Slavonic thought with its emphasis on political messianism that Chopin's Polish friends frequently discussed. In addition, George drew on the climate of the eighteenth century and the rise of interest in occultism, as a counter-balance to the Age of Reason. The word occult simply means 'hidden', and refers to the 'etheric blueprint' lying beyond the material world, as expressed by the Hussites, Rosicrucians and Freemasons, the last of which had a great influence on Mozart.

The writer, Victor Hugo, kept a journal about the happenings during the seances he held during his exile in Jersey, and many of the writers with whom Pauline became acquainted, such as Robert Browning, Alfred Tennyson, Bulwer Lytton and Dante Gabriel Rossetti, among others, were all curious about other realms of reality, things 'unseen and unheard' by the normal senses. In April 1842, Chopin was devastated by the news of his great friend, Dr. Jan Matuszinski's death, and when his father died, Chopin had waking dreams of the two men, seeing them clearly and feeling the coldness of their hands.

Whether Louis ever experienced such highly imaginative fantasies is doubtful; he shared George's concerns about political and social reform, but it is
unlikely that he ever entered into her mystical world, and although he sent
Pierre Leroux enthusiastic letters about 'Consuelo' from Spain, Leroux commented, 'how little he understands it. What delights him most is that 'mothers
will be able to allow their daughters to read it'!

Was it of Louis or her brother Hippolyte and their enthusiam for sport of
whom George was thinking, when she wrote of Baron Frederick: "His only
passion was love of the chase, to which he devoted most of his time, going out
each morning and returning each evening, ruddy with exercise, out of breath
and hungry."

At one point in the story, an incident occurs in Berlin when Consuelo is
singing at the opera, sees what she believes to be her husband's ghost sitting
in one of the boxes, and faints in the middle of an aria. No doubt Pauline told
George about a similiar incident that happened to her when she was performing
in Andalusia. At a performance, as she came on-stage, she thought she saw her
dead father in the orchestra, collapsed, and the curtain had to be lowered and
the opera postponed until she recovered.

Strangely, many of the things that Consuelo experienced in her career, and
with Anzoleto, foretold events in Pauline's own life. George touched on the
theme of 'art for the people', an ideal that Pauline espoused. About her public
in Spain, the singer told George: "Though it may not be knowledgeable, this
audience is neither surfeited nor sycophantic, but is naively carried away by its
enthusiasm. I love this public, it makes me improve. It is the one which Nourrit
– who was wonderful – adored and with which he was happy to sing for nothing on the king's birthday. An unsophisticated public, but attractive and intelligent, in a word – the people!"

George had decided opinions on the role of the artist in society, and was
deeply influenced by the views of Liszt, and the teachings of Saint-Simon and
Lammenais, to which he introduced her. As dedicated artists, Chopin and Pauline
lived by these tenets, believing that they had a divine mission to serve humanity and raise its consciousness.

The profession of music is a modern phenomenon as, for centuries, music
was made either by the people in their folk traditions, singing at their work,
celebrating special occasions, and church services, or by the leisured classes,
who were taught by masters, and used their skills to entertain themselves, their
friends and families. To make money from music was considered vulgar and
was only gradually accepted by polite society. Composers had patrons who
commissioned works and even minor princelings kept orchestras, but music as

a profession was relatively new, and it was never easy to make a living, however gifted the performer or composer.

The Viardots were avid for each new instalment of 'Consuelo', and Pauline wrote to George from Madrid, 'Chere Ninoune, This month's 'Revue' has not yet arrived, but in the last number I made the acquaintance of a strange family (the Rudolstadts) and wish to know more about them'. In July she wrote from Granada: "'Consuelo' makes us laugh, cry, shudder and think. Oh! My dear Ninoune, how admirable you are, and how wonderful for you to be able to give so much pleasure to your readers. I cannot express how I feel within me since I began reading 'Consuelo,' I only know that I love you ten thousand times more and I am so proud to have been one of the fragments, which you have used to create that admirable figure. Without doubt, this will be one of the best things I have done in this world....." That Pauline thought George's portrait of her was true to life is confirmed by what she told Julius Rietz nearly twenty years later: 'If you wish to really know me, read the first part of 'Consuelo'. While George was writing, Chopin was working on a new Scherzo, Ballade and Polonaise and they saw little of each other, but they looked forward to the return of the Viardots and to hearing Pauline's news at first hand.

It is interesting to see how Solange Sand reacted to her mother's work, because the following year she wrote: "Edmonde (heroine of 'Mauprat') is the most beautiful of all your daughters. Me, I am the worst. She is how I would like to be, but not like Consuelo". Of course, she knew that Consuelo was Pauline Viardot, and she resented the fact that her mother adored the singer.

Felix Mendelssohn's sister Rebecca, wrote to Fanny Hensel: "Have you heard Viardot-Consuelo? This damned Sand woman, I think of her every time I pass a vegetable garden", to which Fanny replied: "I can quite believe that you see 'Consuelo' in every vegetable garden, but it's really too bad you can't see and hear the original model on the stage. What a unique personality! And many of her characteristics have been portrayed very well: I recognise Consuelo when I hear her talk".

Pauline's last performance in Madrid was as Desdemona and, as usual, she received tumultuous applause, calls for encore after encore, and enough flowers to stock a market. Eventually things quietened down, but the audience did not want to let their favourite go and she was prevailed upon to sing the Rondo from the finale of 'La Cenerentola' and some Spanish airs. Their enthusiasm knew no bounds, and far from feeling fatigued, Pauline was exhilarated and full of energy, her reception making up for all the worry, boredom and difficulty she had experienced in her parents' homeland during the rehearsal period.

From Madrid, the Viardots travelled south to Granada in Andalusia, a city famed for its inspired Moorish architecture and gardens, set against a backdrop of towering, white tipped mountains. Pauline was particularly captivated by the ancient splendour of the Alhambra, a wedding cake confection of a palace, its stonework a riot of intricate, delicately interwoven filigree. Sadly, in the sixteenth century, the Emperor, Charles V, had vandalised the work of the Moors by ripping away a portion of the palace, imposing a classical edifice in its midst. The latter building was abandoned unfinished and its ugly, roofless walls still disturbed the tranquil rhythm of the earlier architecture, which had long been neglected, and the mournful gardens were choked with weeds.

Here, Pauline sang, and her presence created great excitement in the city of the Albaicin, a gypsy race living in nearby caves, who spent their time dancing, singing, wildly clapping hands, playing castanets and guitars, bombarding the air with the wild rhythm of flamenco. To them, Pauline was one of their own, and she drew an estimated crowd of ten thousand to her performance at the Alhambra, where scores of people, unable to pass through the gates, climbed over the walls in order to hear her sing vitos and peteneras of Andalusia in a scene reminiscent of the 'Arabian Nights' of Harun al Rashid.

The visit to Granada was the grand climax of the trip, and then the Viardots left for France, taking the waters en route at Biaritz. Pauline sang again in Bordeaux and was even more wildly acclaimed than on her previous visit.

Louis was very happy to be returning home because, although he hated to admit it, things were not going well in his beloved Spain. Despite all the sufferings of the people over the past decades of war and revolution, little had improved for them, and despotism, corruption and distress were commonplace. To his surprise, when he returned to France, everything appeared positively rosy in contrast.

Pauline had not been so keen to leave a place where she had been truly appreciated and where the sun shone constantly. The climate suited her because she was a child of the south, whose olive skin, dark eyes and hair fitted her ideally for a hot country. Yet, home they must go, and the thought of seeing their baby again was a consolation. But what would Pauline's professional fate be in France? Only time would tell, but she had to admit that she didn't feel optimistic. The success of 'Consuelo' was spreading her fame near and far, of course, and it certainly brought her name to a wide public, but it also linked her with George Sand, a writer who, in the eyes of the Establishment was highly suspect.

The Viardots planned to stay with George at Nohant for a few days on their way to Paris, and Pauline wrote saying how much they were looking forward to their visit, and told George to give her love to Chopin, Maurice, Hippolyte and his wife, Emilie, Dr. Papet, and 'all those who have not forgotten me'.

As expected, the visit to Nohant was delightful, if too short, and on their return to Paris, the fond parents were overjoyed to be reunited with 'Louisette', although alarmed at first because she didn't seem to remember them; however, young children are adaptable and they soon became familiar to her. She had been looked after by her nursemaid, grandmother and aunts since her birth, and must have been confused, as to who was really responsible for her welfare. At that time, it was quite common for children to be brought up by nursemaids and governesses, and Louise was no exception in not receiving constant attention from her mother, but later in life, she said that she believed she had been harmed by Pauline's frequent absences during her childhood.

In September, the Viardots set out for another trip to Nohant, but this time they took Louise and her nursemaid with them, arriving at the chateau on Solange's birthday. A party was in full swing, with George and Chopin surrounded by guests and neighbours. Maurice was thrilled to see Pauline again, claimed her for several dances, and it was not until 1 am that the party broke up.

The weather, in contrast to the previous summer, was fine and warm, despite the advent of autumn, and the members of the Nohant house party, which this year included the painter Eugene Delacroix, indulged in many excursions and picnics in the open countryside in the valley of the River Indre. Chopin rode a donkey, while George, her children and guests rambled through woods and meadows on foot, calling at farmhouses to buy bread, eggs, milk, cheese, butter, and fruit, getting dishevelled and dirty, sleeping in barns amongst the hay, and having a marvellous time. Louis was in his element, as he and his cronies had some splendid sport, and everybody agreed that to be carefree on an open road, with no deadlines to meet was heaven, and a wonderful antidote to the stresses and strains of living in Paris, for the time being at least.

Solange, who was on holiday from her boarding school in the capital, was less disagreeable than usual, and joined in the fun; George, Delacroix, Pauline and Maurice sketched and painted in water colours, while Louis, Papet, and Hippolyte pursued their quarry. Chopin, happy and relaxed, thoroughly enjoyed himself and kept everybody entertained with his dry wit and clever impersonations.

Delacroix was in his element at Nohant because George had installed a studio for him in an outbuilding close to the main house, where he was able to work undisturbed, whenever he wished. Chopin appreciated the painter's friendship and thought him the best of men, but did not profess to like or understand his work, finding it bizarre, crude in colouring and too avant garde for his taste. The artist told a friend "when we are not gathered for dinner, breakfast or billiards, or out on a walk, each of us stays in his room reading or lolling on his couch. At times, through the window opening on to the garden there would waft in gusts of Chopin's music, for he too is working; they mingle with the singing of the nightingales and the scent of the rose bushes". Of the pianist himself, he observed: "He has an infinite amount of wit, finesse, and malice, but he is unable to understand anything of painting and statuary. Michaelangelo frightens him, Rubens repels him. Everything that seems eccentric scandalizes him". In spite of this, he enjoyed his conversations with Chopin – "whom I like very much and who is a man of rare distinction; indeed, the truest artist I have met".

The artist was most impressed by Pauline's talent for drawing and painting, and amazed at her rare ability to capture her sitters' true likeness. He discerned that she had an excellent eye, as well as ear, and exquisite taste. She was not afraid of contemporary art, in contrast to Louis, who was very conservative in his tastes, although Delacroix acknowledged his erudition and expertise as an art historian. The two men had little natural affinity, and the painter began to refer to Louis as 'poor Viardot'. Despite this, he became a valued friend of the Viardots and a regular dinner guest at their Paris home.

When the time came to leave for Paris, everybody was sad to go, and it was with reluctance that they said goodbye to the dear old chateau, as it was being closed up for the winter. Chopin had at last agreed to defy convention and move lock, stock and barrel into George's new apartment in the smart Square d'Orleans, where their friend, the Countess Charlotte Marliani, had already taken up residence in a newly built apartment block. Chopin was allocated rooms on the ground floor, with a courtyard and a small, attractive garden, all for 600 francs a year. George's section of the apartment was on the first floor, with several large rooms and a studio in the attic for Maurice, which cost her the princely sum of 3,000 francs a year.

Their neighbours were an illustrious assortment of musicians, dancers and artists, and included the pianists Valentin Alkan, Pierre Zimmerman and Friedrich Wilhelm Kalkbrenner, the dancer Marie Taglioni, the painters Claude and Edouard Dubufe, and the sculptor Jean-Pierre Dantan. To cut costs, George, her children and Chopin took their five o'clock dinner with Charlotte Marliani, using her cook and contributing to the house-keeping. The Viardots were very impressed with George's new abode, and shortly afterwards, found themselves an attractive apartment in the fashionable square.

Sadly, Pauline's career was going nowhere, and hoped for engagements in Italy had failed to materialise. When the Viardots married, George had taken it for granted that Louis would become Pauline's impressario, and selflessly promote her career, but he had relinquished his post at the Theatre Italien, which George considered an unwise move, and now he seemed only too pleased to relax into a peaceful, domestic routine, writing articles, hunting on friends' estates, and enjoying a social life. The arrangements for the Spanish tour had tired him; the political situation had depressed him, and he was happy to be back in his own home, surrounded by his family and intimate friends.

George, Chopin and Delacroix put their heads together, and wrote a frank letter to the Viardots. All three of them were convinced that Pauline had genius of a rare kind, and that nothing should obstruct her path. The three friends tried to stimulate Louis into activity on his wife's behalf, but it was difficult because he was in no hurry to be uprooted again so quickly, whereas Pauline, young, enthusiastic, vital and ambitious, was champing at the bit, full of energy and longing to be presented with new challenges.

As the autumn months passed into winter, life itself took a hand. First of all, Pauline was invited to sing some performances at the Theatre Italien, not in her own right, but stepping in as Arsace in 'Semiramide' for an indisposed singer. In London, she had received splendid reviews for this role, but in Paris, she, Louis and their friends, were devastated by the vitriolic reports of her performances that appeared in the French press. It was claimed that in the last year she had not only lost her voice, but had forgotten how to sing! Louis was furious, and vented his spleen in a letter to the editor of 'Le Siecle' complaining about the deplorable critique in 'La Revue des Deux Mondes'. He declared that this venom had nothing to do with music, but everything to do with politics, and that Mme Viardot had been used as a target in order to get at her left-wing friends. He alleged that the root cause of the animosity came from the fact that he, George Sand and Pierre Leroux were the founders of a rival periodical, which was unashamedly socialist in its aims, and was in direct opposition to the right wing, ultra conservative organ of the Establishment.

In the face of this hostility, Louis found the necessary energy to push him into action, and in consultation with George and the others, it was decided that Pauline should seek her career in pastures new. Negotiations were opened with the composer Gaetano Donizetti, the director of the Karnthnerthortheatre in

Vienna, who had been a dear friend and colleague of Malibran. He engaged
Pauline to sing Rosina in 'Il Barbiere' and she took the theatre by storm. Her aria
and the duet with Figaro in the first act, and the comic trio with Almaviva and
Figaro, where the men are trying to help the girl escape from the clutches of her
mercenary guardian, Dr. Bartolo, only to discover that someone (actually Bartolo
himself) has removed the ladder and they are marooned in Rosina's room, were
all enthusiastically encored. Pauline sang in six performances, and on April
17th, 1843, Donizetti wrote to Leon Pillet, the director of the Paris Opera, telling
him that Mme Viardot had made her debut, and that she and Giorgio Ronconi,
the Figaro, were excellent.

While in Vienna, Pauline was fortunate enough to catch up with her friend
Fanny Elssler who was dancing the role of Giselle. The singer found Fanny's
performance a very moving experience, and from that time counted this collaboration by her friends Adolphe Adam and Theophile Gautier, as one of her
favourite ballets. Even many years later, the thought of the scene in the cemetery could bring tears to her eyes. Donizetti reported to Pillet that Elssler had
been a great success in the role.

Soon reports of Pauline's 'colossal' triumph were printed in the Parisian
press, and in the first letter from Vienna, which she wrote to George Sand early
in May she said that she had been invited to the Hofburg by the Empress
Marie-Anna Caroline to sing to the sick and ailing old Emperor Ferdinand. She
was impressed by the sumptuous apartments through which she was led, and
found the Austrian Rococco style infinitely appealing, quite over the top, of
course, with its flamboyant, intricate carvings, gildings, and multitude of flying
cupids, vast painted ceilings, and delicate pastel colours. Some of the elaborately decorated rooms reminded her of enormous wedding cakes, with swirls
of white stucco embellishments reminiscent of moulded icing sugar.

In contrast to the splendour of his surroundings, the poor old emperor was
in a decrepit, sorry state. He was epileptic and senile, and was probably suffering from what in modern parlance is known as Alzheimer's disease, however, he
had seen 'Il Barbiere', and said that it had made him laugh. He was pleased that
Pauline had come to see him, but was worried that she might catch cold, and
asked her if she had a warm cloak.

After this visit, invitations came thick and fast from the haute monde. Life
was mimicking art, and Pauline was echoing her alter ego, Consuelo, who had
found fame in Vienna. There are, of course, always people who are jealous of
successful individuals, and Princess Metternich, the wife of the Austrian Foreign Minister, the previous Ambassador to France, was no exception. She said
that the singer must be talented indeed, if her ugliness could be overlooked. As

for Pauline, she declared, 'one cannot have everything all the time, and I'm happy with my lot at present'.

Not everything went smoothly though, as one can judge from a letter written by Donizetti to Giacomo Pedroni: "I have to tell you about the fiasco of 'Alina' with Mme (Pauline Viardot) Garcia, (Agostino) Rovere, (Felice) Varesi and Severi. The protagonist (Pauline) interpolated at the end of the work a rondeau by Beriot (based on an aria in L'Elisir d'Amore). Nevertheless, the opera made no effect'. It is interesting that Donizetti should have allowed Pauline to interpolate an aria by another composer based on one of his own, but it had become a very popular item, as arranged and extended by the Belgian composer, and it is significant that Donizetti thought that even with the inclusion of this crowd pleaser, his opera had fallen flat.

Although 'Alina' did not have much success in Vienna, Pauline was engaged to sing three complete performances, and one in a truncated version, at La Scala, Milan, between May 23rd, 1843 and June 4th, 1846. At that time, it was most essential for an ambitious singer to have a great success in Italy, as well as in London and Paris, to set the seal on an international career. Maria Malibran had triumphed in Italy, but it was unfortunate that Pauline did not have a better vehicle than 'Alina' in which to show off her own unique talent. In an ideal world, a singer's abilities should speak for themselves and guarantee engagements, but the operatic world is an intricate web of politics, intrigue, cabals, and vested interests. Composers have also suffered from the machinations of rival factions that set out to destroy the premiere of a new work, turning it into a fiasco. But time usually has the last word and many works that were originally greeted with derision and scorn are now the staple fare of the operatic repertoire across the globe.

Although Pauline did not know it at the time, her star was in the ascendant, despite present difficulties. She had been contracted to sing Amina in 'La Sonnambula' in Vienna, but her conductor and accompanist, Carl von Banier, begged her not to do so, as he had heard that there was trouble brewing. The Italian singers in the company who considered that this work was their property were outraged that a French prima donna should be given preference over their own favourite, Eugenia Tadolini.

Mme Tadolini was the wife of the composer Giovanni Tadolini, a woman of charm and taste who was well loved in Vienna, where she sang for several seasons. However, the Court authorities, that had jurisdiction over the Opera, insisted that Pauline should sing Amina, although the public was divided in its loyalties to the two singers. Naturally enough, Pauline was extremely nervous before her entrance, but with her first aria, she silenced her enemies and left her fans triumphant. Nevertheless, the Italians wanted blood, and craved a scape-goat, which they found in the bass Prosper Derivis, who was singing the part of the Count. He had a most beautiful voice, but unlike other male members of the cast, he was not an Italian, and he received a barrage of boos, and whistling from certain sections of the audience, while, at the same time, receiving cheers and enthusiastic applause from the other side. The tenor role was sung by Lorenzo Salvi, whose style was elegant and pure, but whose voice lacked power, and when he missed a high C, another storm broke out, and for some minutes, the performance was held up due to the excessive noise and commotion.

Naturally, Pauline was very upset on behalf of her colleagues who were being treated so unjustly, and although she did her utmost to keep calm, she knew that she had not sung as well at the end of the opera, as she had at the beginning. In the second act, the bass, thoroughly unnerved and distraught really did sing badly due to his overwrought state, and brought even further disapprobation upon himself.

At the end of the opera Pauline was well received, but the evening had been an ordeal and had upset her concentration, due to her concern for her fellow artists. Even at the next performance, the audience were ill disposed, cold and indifferent at first, however, forewarned is forearmed, and she rose splendidly to the challenge, giving an animated performance that gradually triumphed over their recalcitrance. At the end of the opera, she received an enthusiastic ovation, and was pleased by the fact that her colleagues had been treated with the respect they deserved.

On June 14th, 1843, Pauline wrote to George Sand, thanking her for a letter in which her friend had given her news of little Louise, who was staying at Nohant, and Pauline said that she and Louis talked all the time of Nohant, which was the dearest place on earth to them both, and admitted that although they were living their physical lives in Vienna, intellectually they were with them all in Berry.

Pauline apologised that she had so little time to write, and told George that she had sung in Donizetti's 'Maria di Rohan', but that the opera had not enjoyed the success as had the same composer's highly acclaimed 'Linda di Chamonix' the year before.

The season ended with Pauline singing at a benefit concert for Herr Strampfer, an actor who had fallen on hard times. In this she emulated her sister, as Malibran had often given her services in order to raise money for needy colleagues. The occasion was a terrific success, artistically and financially, causing the poor actor and his family to weep and kiss the singer's hands in gratitude. Pauline sang a piece in the Viennese patois, was re-called ten times, and deluiged with floral tributes.

After leaving Vienna, she gave three performances of 'Il Barbiere' on three successive evenings in the magnificent baroque city of Prague in Bohemia, and was impressed by the quality of the audiences who were musically knowledgeable and intelligent. The day after the final performance, she travelled to Berlin with Louis and stayed for three weeks. They were invited everywhere, visiting the Mendelssohn family, and Felix's sister Fanny Hensel and her painter husband, Wilhelm. Much to Louis' gratification, he discovered that his work was known in Berlin and he was consulted on artistic and literary matters, as someone in his own right, and not just the husband of a prima donna.

On July 30th, Pauline sang excerpts from Rossini's 'Otello'at a concert arranged by Meyerbeer. The composer had recently been appointed to the highly influential post of Generalmusikdirector by the King of Prussia. His duties at the opera were very taxing, and his position was not made any easier by the fact that as a conductor he lacked personal charisma, and as he had a great propensity to please all the people all the time, he was not firm enough with his players. He was always beset by nervous anxiety, which spoiled his enjoyment of music making, and as soon as he was able, he relinquished his general conducting commitments and concentrated largely on producing and conducting his own works.

From the time he had first heard Pauline in Wiesbaden, he had been impressed by her deep, innate musical understanding, and the fact that she did not obscure the meaning of a work with her own 'interpretation', but manifested the thoughts and feelings of the composer and librettist through her skilful reading of the score and text,and more than ever he was determined to create a role for her in one of his own operas.

The Berlin correspondent of the RGM observed: "All talk of the presence of Pauline Viardot Garcia in our city. The Court and persons of high society all flock to the theatre for her performances. It is the same enthusiasm that Liszt excites. We have never heard a more beautiful voice united with a more superb technique. Thanks to this exceptional combination, she sings Rosina with the same perfection as she does Desdemona, and she is no less brilliant in concert in the great arias of Meyerbeer, Rossini, Donizetti, and Beriot than in those of Handel and Pergolesi". On August 13th, the same paper stated that Meyerbeer had refused to work on his new opera 'Le Prophete' unless he was assured that Pauline Viardot would be engaged to perform in it, and added that both he and Liszt dreamed of writing an opera based on George Sand's novel 'Consuelo'. Unfortunately, neither composer's dream evermaterialised.

The Viardots returned to Paris on August 25th, but soon left for Nohant, taking Joaquina with them. Louise was already there, having travelled with George, Chopin and Maurice on the new railway line to Orleans, which reduced the time of the journey considerably, and was more comfortable, except that Chopin suffered a fierce headache caused by the sound of the wheels on the iron rail. From Orleans they took a coach to Nohant, where the weather was very wet again. However, this did not deter Chopin, and he did a great deal of work, because he preferred the cooler weather to the oppressive heat of the previous summer.

George, as usual, loved being at Nohant where, asalways, she was amazingly industrious, as well as being a wonderful hostess. Everybody adored Louise, and enjoyed playing with her; she was particularly fond of 'Morice', and thrived tremendously in such a happy, affectionate atmosphere and secure surroundings, where she was accepted as one of the family.

She was growing into a bonny toddler with a mind of her own, and, like most babies, she had some amusing and pretty ways; Chopin thought her adorable and willingly entered into her childish games and chatter, but George was very perturbed when she discovered that the nursemaid, Jeannette, who was pretty and outwardly charming, was nothing but a coquette. She neglected Louise, and had pulled the wool over the eyes of Mlle Berthe, Louis's sister, who had originally been left in Paris to oversee the baby's welfare. George said she had no doubt that Berthe was a well meaning woman, but as a spinster who knew nothing about babies, she had been easy to fool, and during Jeanette's amorous escapades, Louise must have witnessed such scenes, as would have made her aunt faint clean away. Fortunately, when the Viardots arrived, they dismissed the brazen Jeannette, and sent her back to Paris.

Louise was now running about, getting into all kinds of mischief, and chattering away like a little monkey. Pauline thought her 'as good as an angel', and enjoyed spending time with her baby, who was becoming quite a little personality in her own right. Pauline taught her some Spanish songs, and some of the old folk songs of Berry, which she had first learned at Nohant. She told her daughter magical stories, and the child blossomed in her mother's company. Louis was proud of Louise and was delighted to see her again, playing with her in a relaxed and happy fashion, as Chopin and George also did. He and Pauline had thought about her constantly when they were travelling, and had even chatted together in baby language in memory of their little daughter's burgeoning speech. In old age, when Louise wrote her autobiography, she described her father as strict and firm, but her main grudge against him seemed to be that he would not allow her to talk at meals and refused her second helpings! No doubt he was ensuring that she wouldn't get indigestion or put on too much weight!

For the past year, George had been experiencing trouble with her eyes, finding it increasingly painful to read. Delacroix had sent down some medicine from Paris, which, she said, had helped, but she thought that her sight had changed. It is not surprising, considering the weight of work she undertook, and the fact that she did so much writing through the night when she had to rely on oil lamps or candles. Her output as a writer was colossal, with a great many novels and endless articles to her credit, but her personal correspondence was also enormous, and by the time she died, it is estimated that she had written at least 40,000 letters.

After two wonderful weeks, the Viardots returned to Paris, re-packed their bags and set out once more for Berlin. Pauline gave a concert in the old town palace, where she was greeted very warmly by Princess Augusta and Prince William, who were becoming increasingly fond of her. Each time they saw her, they found her more assured and confident, and they considered that her voice had grown in size and become even more sumptuous, dark and vibrant. The Princess spoke excellent French, and Louis and the prince were on friendly terms, discussing hunting, dogs, horses, and guns. With Pauline's quiet prompting, Louis exercised discretion, and great self control keeping off the vexed subject of politics, much to her relief. Social issues and the political climate were so much a part of his everyday thought that it was very difficult for him to avoid speaking his mind, but he had promised Pauline that he would keep his thoughts to himself, and he did.

Unfortunately, the Opera House had burned down in August, so no performances could take place there, however Pauline sang several concerts in other venues. She enjoyed her visits to Schloss Charlottenburg, the summer palace of the Prussian royal family, on the outskirts of the city. Here, Prince William and his sister, Princess Charlotte, now the Tsarina of Russia, had a small, two storey, Italian style garden pavilion, where in their youth they had enjoyed relaxing away from the formality of the court.

With such a busy schedule, Pauline had not had time to visit the Mendelssohns, and felt very guilty when one day, leaving the Berlin Museum, she bumped into Fanny Hensel. Fanny was always delighted to see the singer, and she and the Viardots expressed surprise that their paths had not crossed in Italy in 1840, when they had all been in Rome at the same time, and had been guests at the Villa Medici, where both women had met and impressed the young Charles Gounod. Fanny invited the Viardots to dinner at her home before they left for Leipzig, and Pauline promised to carry messages to her beloved brother Felix.

A few days later, they were back in the dear old city again, working with Mendelssohn at the splendid Gewandhaus, Pauline's favourite concert hall. She gave him news of his family, and told him about her two seasons in England, and they had many laughs about the awful climate, the oddity of the people, and their somewhat 'philistine' attitude to art and artists. Mendelssohn had visited the country several times, and had made a terrific impression on his first visit in 1829. He said that he had been taken for a 'gentleman' because he did not accept fees for playing at soirees!

He told Pauline that most of the English singers at that time left a lot to be desired, and said that he had almost fallen off his chair, laughing at some of them, although he had not liked the Italians much either, and considered that the much vaunted tenor Donzelli roared dreadfully and sang sharp all the time. But of Pauline's sister he had nothing but praise, and declared that she had had one of those voices whose very timbre moves one to tears. He said she sang passionately and earnestly but was also capable of great tenderness, and had been an excellent actress.

Of course, the Viardots also met the Schumanns and it was good to see them looking so happy after all their trials and tribulations, and to know that Robert's music was at last finding favour with the public, particularly in Leipzig. Earlier in the year, on January 8th, his Quintet for Piano and Strings, dedicated to Clara, had received its first performance in the Gewandhaus, with Clara as pianist and had been enthusiastically received. The pianist took part in a concert with Pauline at the Gewandhaus, under the baton of Felix Mendelssohn. His protégé, the twelve-year-old violinist Joseph Joachim made his debut in a sonata accompanied by his mentor, and Pauline sang a bravura aria from 'Ines de Castro' by Persiani, the rondo finale from 'La Cenerentola,' an unpublished aria by de Beriot, 'Lascio ch'io pianga' from 'Rinaldo' by Handel and a collection of French, German and Spanish songs, for which she played her own piano accompaniments. Clara Schumann was highly complimentary, (and, if the truth be told, not a little jealous of her friend's pianistic skill).

The Viardots thoroughly enjoyed their time in Leipzig, despite the fact that Louis did not speak German, but as several of their friends spoke reasonable French, he was not at a loss for conversation. The journey to Paris took them five days and nights, and although it was sad to leave their Leipzig friends, they were pleased to be going home and looked forward to seeing Louise, their family and friends again, although they had little expectation of anything significant awaiting them regarding Pauline's career.

It is quite amazing how life can suddenly throw up extraordinary and unexpected opportunities, and this now happened to Pauline. On September 20th, 1843, she wrote to George to say that she had, an hour before, signed a contract for the 1843/44 season at the Imperial Opera in St. Petersburg and was very happy about it. Although it was not certain if this would be the turning point she needed, she was excited at the prospect of singing in that strange, far away land. The invitation came from her old friend and colleague Giovanni Rubini, who, although he had officially retired, was only forty-eight, and his public still clamoured to hear him, despite the fact that his voice had lost much of its youthful bloom. He was a great favourite in Russia, and the Imperial authorities prevailed upon him to form an Italian opera company for them. He was to sing the principal tenor roles, and he engaged Pauline as his prima donna, and Antonio Tamburini as his principal baritone.

There was great excitement amongst Pauline's family and friends when they heard the news, but for poor little Louise, it was yet another separation from her mother, who had only just returned home. Pauline viewed it as the beginning of a terrific adventure that might have great advantages, and she had accepted the offer with alacrity. Even her sisters-in-law were beginning to accept a fait accompli regarding her career, and hoped that their brother would continue to find the health and strength to exist in such a ramshackle way, living the Bohemian life, imposed upon him by his young and headstrong wife. Everybody wished her well, and considered that if she was successful in Russia, it could be the making of her international career, and maybe, even open the doors of the Paris Opera to her, despite the powerful presence of Mme Stolz.

The Viardots had a long and arduous journey ahead of them. Autumn had commenced and it would be late October when they arrived in St. Petersburg. Louis, of course, was hoping to indulge in an orgy of hunting and killing wolves in that semi-civilised land, before the severity of winter closed in.

He and George took pains to work out how they could continue to correspond with each other without drawing the undue attention of the Russian authorities. Naturally enough, George whose socialist works encouraged young aristocratic intellectuals to harbour thoughts of political dissension, was viewed with great suspicion by the absolutist state, and Louis, who, with his Republican sympathies and connections, was known to be her close friend, would have to tread carefully.

They playfully discussed how he should address George in order to allay suspicion on the part of the censors, and thought that it would be fun for him to call the writer 'aunt', though she was four years his junior! It was finally decided that all the Viardots' correspondence to her should be posted to

Maurice, using his father's name of Dudevant, in order to deceive the authorities. They would also ask Louis's sisters and 'Mamita' (Joaquina) to pass on news they received from the Viardots. Of course, they had to assume that all their mail would be read because censorship was all pervasive.

Louise would initially be left with Joaquina , but would later go to George. Maurice, being very fond of the little girl, assured them that he was ready to accompany her and her nursemaid to Nohant when the time came. The Viardots were happy with this arrangement, and considered that it would be the best thing for their 'treasure'. There was so much to do before they left, and on October 3rd, Pauline wrote to George saying that she could not leave without sending her a few lines. Louis had called at her apartment several times but, having failed to find her at home, had hoped at least to discover a servant there to whom he could give a message, but without success. The reason the Viardots could not get in touch with George was that she and Chopin had taken a trip to Crozant, and George's letter, telling them of this arrangement, had not arrived in time.

Pauline was upset to go away for such a long time without seeing them, and wrote to say how much she looked forward to receiving George's letters. She asked Chopin and Maurice (Bouli) to drop her a few lines, and for Solange to add a few words as postscript. In fact, she wanted to receive letters from all the family, and promised that she would write throughout the journey, so that they would receive 'fresh news' regularly. She closed her note by telling them that she loved them with all her life and soul.

CHAPTER FOURTEEN

1843

OnOctober 5th, the Viardots left Paris for the long overland journey to Lubeck, the Hanseatic port on the Baltic Sea, where they spent some time sight-seeing, enjoying the local cuisine, and delighting in the wonderful marzipan confectioneries for which the city is famous. From there they took a ship bound for Stettin, eighty-four miles north of Berlin.

It was cold and the sea and sky were grey and heavy, but the crossing was not as rough as Louis had feared. Where he was concerned, the shorter the time spent at sea, the better. Pauline took it all in her stride and spent much of her time on deck, enjoying the seascape, and observing the day-to-day life of the busy ports at which they called.

Leaving the ship at Stettin, they set off for Berlin where they arrived on the 20th of October. Pauline was beginning to feel very much at home in the Prussian capital, having discovered that the traditionally 'cold Germans' provided warmer audiences than those of Vienna. From the Prussian capital they travelled east three hundred and twenty-five miles to Warsaw where they visited Chopin's family, as they had promised.

The pianist's parents, Nicolas and Justina Chopin were most welcoming: Nicolas was now seventy-two years old, but alert and intelligent as ever. Fritz was the couple's only son, and they had had three daughters, Ludwiga, Isabelle and Emilia, but the youngest had died from tuberculosis in 1827. Ludwiga and Chopin were particularly close and corresponded frequently. Everybody wanted to know about Chopin's health, which had always caused them anxiety, and they were curious to hear about Mme Sand to whom they were all so grateful 'for the care she gave him'.

Justina Chopin always held a salon on Thursdays, and she played the piano while her guests sang or danced. The family were excited at the prospect of hearing Pauline sing, as Chopin had whetted their appetite. She did not disappoint them, and they were simply amazed at the range and quality of her voice and her marvellous musicianship. First she performed a song of her own composition, in the Spanish idiom, which she had sung to the pianist when they were at Nohant, and he had told his family that he hoped she would sing it to them, because they would not hear a better example of its type. This piece was probably the 'Cana Espagna' (L'Absence'), which she had published in 1841, with a dedication to Giacomo Meyerbeer.

Nicholas Chopin was born in a village in Lorraine when it was governed by Louis XV's father-in-law, the Polish King Stanislas Leszcynski. He was a self-taught, self-made man, who played the violin well, and in 1788 he had settled in Poland where he became tutor to the children of Count Skarbek at Zelazowa Wola. Here he met Justina; they married in 1806, and the pianist was born in a villa on the Skarbek estate, four years later. When Nicholas was appointed professor of French at the prestigious Lyceum where the sons of the aristocracy were educated, the family moved to Warsaw. Chopin was educated at this school, and made several lifelong friends among the sons of the nobility.

The Chopins were tremendously proud of their son and his success in the great French capital, but they mourned the fact that they saw him so rarely and never on Polish soil. Apart from the long journey, there were complications because Poland was under the Russia yoke, and Chopin, who considered himself an exile, thought it prudent that they should only meet on neutral ground, usually in Germany, although his sister Ludwika and her husband, Kolosanty visited him in Paris.

Chopin took French nationality and never returned to his native land, but he carried the spirit of Poland in his heart, and was moved by the plight of his compatriots under Russian occupation. The failure of a national uprising caused him such distress that in his despair for his people he wrote the stirring Revolutionary Prelude. In Paris, he often met Polish exiles and contributed to the cause of Polish freedom, but as an artist he believed that his function was to produce music, leaving political activity to others, many of whom saw him as a figure-head for their cause, perceiving his compositions, filled as they were with folk melodies, as a yearning for their native land.

The Viardots found Warsaw an attractive city, terraced high above the River Vistula, with wide thoroughfares, handsome Baroque buildings in the main part of the town, and a fine National Theatre. They learned that Chopin's special pianistic gifts had been apparent from an early age, and with his father's connections, he was soon giving performances in aristocratichomes. The melancholic Grand Duke Constantine, brother of the Tzar, and Commander-in-Chief of the Army of Occupation, doted on the boy, and often sent his carriage to fetch him to the elegant Bruhl Palace to play for him. The youth was also noted for his great sense of humour and amused everybody with his gift for mimicry and talent for caricatures.

From his childhood, Chopin was acquainted with the Czartoryski Princes, the Sapiehas, Radziwills and Count Potocki, and this stood him in good stead when he settled in Paris, as they all gave him letters of introduction that eased his path in his adopted city, and won him invitations to elite social gatherings.

The next part of the Viardots' journey took them to Riga, a town situated on the Gulf of Finland, from where they travelled to St. Petersburg, arriving in the Russian capital at the end of October, to be welcomed by a long wait for customs clearance, which made them nervous. The Russian authorities were notorious for keeping travellers waiting, as they were assiduous in their searches, not only for contraband, but for any seditious literature. Unknown to the Viardots, they had been under the surveillance of a Russian spy in Paris, who had reported that Louis Viardot was a friend and colleague of George Sand and Pierre Leroux, and was believed to be a dangerous, liberal, free thinker.

Oblivious to all this, when at last they reached the centre of the city, the Viardots were amazed at the scale of St. Petersburg and the beauty of its architecture, as well as its sophisticated western atmosphere. At that time it was the capital of the Empire, and very different in tone from the more Slavic Moscow, several hundred miles away. Peter the Great had founded his capital in 1703 at the head of the Gulf of Finland, which is split up by the mouths of the River Neva and the Lake of Ladoga. It gave his Navy excellent access into the Baltic Sea, although for part of the year it is blocked by ice, and did not actually become a sea-port until a ship canal was begun in 1875. The site is not a healthy one, being full of low lying swamps, and built on piles set in drained marshes. When great numbers of peasants perished during its construction, it became known as 'the city built on bones'.

As Pauline observed the sweep of the superb Winter Palace set along the banks of the great, broad expanse of the beautiful, limpid and tremulous water of the River Neva, filtered and purified by the Ladoga Lake, she thought that the rhythms and perfect symmetry of the Italianate architecture, with its purity of line, and classical harmonies, equated with the eighteenth century music of Bach, Gluck or Mozart. The whole city staggered the Viardots by its spaciousness and the magnificence of its buildings, although nothing now remained of the original palace in Dutch style, which Peter the Great had erected in 1711, occupying the site of the present Hermitage Theatre. That had been a modest building, that gave way to the vast edifice designed by Domenico Tressini.

The Viardots' apartment was in the elegant, Demidov House on the fashionable Nevski Prospekt, a wide, tree-lined boulevard, near the Bolshoi Theatre. This great avenue originated from Tzar Peter's wish to link the Admiralty with the Monastery, making it one of the most famous and prestigious routes in

Russia. The theatre stands in a huge square, around which are other splendid buildings of classical mien, each separated by wide spaces. It was a fashionable area where aristocrats and members of the highest society lived, and was light years away from the hovels where many of the poorer classes and peasants eked out their miserable lives on the fringes of the city. For the most part, the Viardots were spared such unpleasant sights because Pauline's work was principally here, but when Louis set out on hunting trips to outlying estates, he was made perfectly aware of the true inequities of Russian life.

The Viardots had seen poor quarters in many of the major European cities, and London had enormous problems, but they were dwarfed by the conditions prevailing in Russia. There was a vast chasm between the highest and the lowest classes in material terms, as the result of the evils perpetrated through the feudal serf system that ran through the whole of society. Great landowners bought and sold serfs like so much merchandise, and even the doctor, school teacher and lawyer were properties of these magnates, who held enormous tracts of land, comprising many villages and towns and their inhabitants.

Nicolas I was a tyrannical ruler who held total sway in matters large and small in his gigantic realm that comprised a sixth of the world's land mass. Censorship was widespread, and writers lived in constant fear of the authorities. The Decembrist Uprising of 1825 was still fresh in the minds of many people, and there was a deep, underlying fear of social upheaval, due to the anarchic and revolutionary resentments smouldering just under the surface. The Russian people were not encouraged to develop initiative, and were certainly not encouraged to think for themselves. They were expected to do as they were told, and be grateful. The Tsar was not called 'the little father' for nothing. He ruled with a strict paternal hand, and everyone was expected to agree that 'father knows best'. Imprisonment was imposed for the merest trifles and many people were sent to the wastes of Siberia never to return. Even members of the aristocracy and upper classes could be sentenced to house arrest for several years for a mere peccadillo.

Bureaucracy was ubiquitous, and most young men from noble families joined the Civil Service when their education was completed, or became officers in the military. Everywhere uniforms were predominant, and few men wore civilian clothes. In order to stop people thinking for themselves and causing political trouble, Nicolas used the same tactics employed by Louis X1V in seventeenth century France, keeping the intelligentsia occupied with frivolity, pleasure, fashion, matters of etiquette, placement and all kinds of trivia. Music and the arts were encouraged, not for their intrinsic worth, but because they kept people occupied. The theatre was favoured, but reading and writing were viewed with suspicion. As in all authoritarian regimes the intelligentsia, because they are independent minded, were perceived as dangerous, subversive, ready to foment trouble, and writers were considered the most menacing of all because it is the nature of their craft to influence the conciousness of the populace.

Poetry was extremely popular with the literati because meanings could be well hidden within that form, and, hopefully, evade the eyes of the censors, while speaking to the initiated. Writers such as the lowly born young Vissarion Grigorevich Belinski concentrated on literary criticism as a means of promulgating their philosophical and political ideas. For a long period, French was the language of the educated classes and many people spoke it in preference to Russian, which was associated with the peasantry.

However, things were changing, and Russia was becoming a breeding ground for new writing and music, based on a Slav heritage which, although in its infancy, would eventually come to fruition in the works of Gogol, Tourgueniev, Dostoyevsky and Tolstoy, and the music of Glinka, Rimski-Korsakov, Moussorsky, Tchaikovsky, and Borodin. All of these were rooted in a true Slav culture, which was influenced more by the east than the west, based on native values, and largely independent of Europe with its origins in the classical worlds of Greece and Rome. To some extent, Tourgueniev was the exception to this Slavic cult as he was truly cosmopolitan, and although he cared deeply about his native land, he was very much at home in Europe, where he was destined to spend a great deal of his life.

Russian newspapers were dull, with no political news, merely announcements and theatrical and literary criticisms, but already an underground movement was rippling the surface and would bring forth some very fine periodicals later in the century. French newspapers were on sale, but were so truncated that there was little left to read in them.

Summing up this situation, Louis was gratified to discover in what esteem George Sand was held in literary circles, and was delighted that 'Consuelo' had become a great favourite with the reading public. It was a surprise, however, to find his own publication of 'Les Musees d'Espagne, d'Angleterre et de Belgique' on sale in French and caused him to wonder at the eccentricity of the censors in allowing these works to go unhindered since both he and George were termed 'dangerous radicals'.

When the announcement of the advent of the Italian Opera was published, there was a flurry of excitement and a great rush for tickets. Although in the eighteenth century, Italian musicians and singers had flocked to St. Petersburg, in recent years there had been a paucity of opera in the city.

Rubini was remembered as a great artist, a singer with the charisma to profoundly move audiences, and music lovers were avid to hear him again. There was also a great deal of curiosity about the young prima donna, who was known to be 'Consuelo's' model.

The Bolshoi theatre was a grand and impressive edifice with sweeping staircases, great marble columns, powerful arches, huge sparkling chandeliers, boxes lined with crimson velvet, masses of gilding and ornate decoration, and floors comprising the finest woods, highly polished, inlaid with striking geometric patterns, and an auditorium holding three thousand people, which, despite its size was already sold out for all performances.

Because the Italian Opera was such a highly fashionable affair, it set the seal on the season, ensuring that it would be more brilliant than ever, and nobody who valued their status dared be left out. For weeks, nothing was talked about or thought of but 'the opera', and all society anticipated something splendid beyond measure. The ladies chattered about their toilettes and rushed to dressmakers to procure something new and fine in which to be seen and admired. Tiaras were sent to jewellers to have stones cleaned, reset and polished, yards of silks and satins were inspected and purchased, new fur cloaks were sought, and shoemakers could barely keep up with the demand for pretty evening footwear. Glove-makers stood to make fortunes, and white silk stockings were in high demand, as were attractive beaded reticules in which to keep handkerchiefs, perfumes and sundry indispensable items that no fashionable lady could do without.

The men were not to be outdone either; new uniforms were ordered, as were splendid, tall black boots, dark coloured evening suits, highly polished shoes, and white kid gloves. Jewelled orders and medals were cleaned and buffed as never before, and placed upon new sashes of deep blue, emerald green or vibrant red silk or satin.

When the season opened, there was no disappointment either in the splendour of the theatre itself, or in the elegance and magnificence of the brilliant audience, and they were certainly not let down by the performers from France. The three principal singers, Rubini, Viardot and Tamburini, in addition to having first rate voices, were well trained and capable of all manner of expression. They had something even more significant and special, which cannot be taught or learned: charisma, magnetism, timing, and an ability to electrify and light up the stage. It is called 'star quality'; something no one can define or produce at will, yet when it is present, everybody is aware of it, and though intangible, it is extremely powerful. Naturally, it is a rare attribute, and to have three performers on the stage at any one time who all possessed this quality in such measure was truly remarkable, and left an extraordinarily strong impression on audiences.

In a letter to George via Maurice, Pauline told her how prophetic she had been when she wrote of Consuelo's success; life echoed art once more and Pauline was experiencing immense success in Russia. Her first performance was on November 3rd, and she told George that her voice had doubled in strength in the past few months, and although she had been dreadfully indisposed by a severe cold and not been able to sing for eight days, when she returned as Rosina, she was welcomed so enthusiastically and with such prolonged applause that the proceedings were held up for several minutes. It moved her so completely that she could hardly sing from emotion.

At a later performance of 'Il Barbiere', on November 27th, the audience responded even more frantically when, in the lesson scene in the second act, where it was then usual to insert music by a composer other than Rossini, she sang the well known song 'O My Ratmir' from Glinka's 'Russland and Ludmilla' in Russian, and brought the house down. The emperor was beside himself with enthusiasm, and clapped like a madman. After the opera, she, Rubini, who had sung Count Almaviva, and Tamburini, who had played Figaro, had to take twelve curtain calls. Next day, the newspapers were full of Pauline's feat, and said that her pronunciation was that of a true Moscovite.

George had certainly written of Consuelo's success, but Pauline told her friend she had not mentioned what she herself was discovering at each performance, that her success grew and grew.

The premiere of 'La Sonnambula', in which she sang Amina, was received even more wildly, with tears and applause such as never before and everybody declared that its reception had no precedent. The young singer was observed to surmount all vocal difficulties with ease, and surprised her audiences even more with her great gift as an actress of tremendous versatility.

The composer Michael Ivanovitch Glinka, who was then forty, was introduced to Pauline, and they struck up a friendship based on mutual respect for each other's work. Pauline was immensely impressed by his songs, which she studied with great enjoyment, and he was full of admiration for her performances, becoming one of her most fervent supporters. Through him, she developed an interest in Russian music, of which, until her visit to St. Petersburg she had known little; she began to sing Glinka's songs at concerts, and when she returned home, she introduced his work to French audiences.

He wrote: "Rubini, Tamburini and Viardot Garcia arrived in St. Petersburg and an Italian Theatre is established. Viardot was outstanding, and Tamburini is still relatively good." Rubini's voice he considered 'a ruin', and said: "Rubini sometimes sang so-so, but sometimes his voice betrayed him to the point that he even cried". Being a stern critic, he was hard on the cast of 'Don Giovanni', which was a benefit for Tamburini on December 12th: "All the important parts were murdered. Only Zerlina (Viardot) and Masetto (Artemovsky) went excellently. I cried from irritation and from that moment conceived a hatred for Italian songsters and fashionable Italian music".

However, when he visited Paris in 1844, he wrote to Elizaveta Fleury: "The Italian Theatre here, in my opinion, is the best opera theatre in the world. The ensemble is marvellous, orchestra, chorus and the singing of the principals is outstanding. The hall is a marvellous sight. Persiani sings distinctly, with feeling and rare grace and reminds one of Rossi (Sontag) though in my opinion her voice is stronger, and she sings with greater passion than Rossi. I will not attempt to compare her with Viardot, you know I am her zealous admirer, which, however, does not prevent me being fair to Persiani. Brambilla, the contralto, brought tears, with unusual delicacy and charm. Mario is simply bad and extremely ignoble".

All the slights and insults that Pauline had suffered in Paris were now relegated to the past. The Russians literally adored her and turned her into a 'superstar' overnight. They appreciated the 'heart' she brought to her singing; they were not afraid of emotion and were only too happy to be moved to tears. Speedily, news of her triumphs spread across Europe to Berlin, Paris and London, and Yakhontov said that in St. Petersburg there was not a single salon where opera was not the principle subject of conversation. Everyone agreed that it was the strength of the performers that ensured the tremendous success of the operas presented. Many of these works had been heard before, but they had never been performed with such excellence.

P. M. Zotov wrote: "We knew about all the difficulties involved but had never before had our hearts touched in this way. Rubini had such an affect on the audience that sometimes they completely forgot themselves, and full of emotion they jumped up, cheered and applauded this famous singer. Even his fellow performers were impressed and once, when Rubini and Viardot were called before the curtain after 'La Sonnambula' amidst all the clamour of shouts and applause, Viardot went down on her knees and kissed Rubini's hand, causing even more excitement".

In December, during an interval in a performance of 'Il Barbiere', Pauline, Rubini and Tamburini were revealed on-stage at the head of a Russian choir singing the Tzarist Hymn in Russian, which brought forth waves of enthusiasm, and had to be repeated, so great was the delight of the audience. Again, the press complimented Pauline on her excellent diction, declaring that she sounded like a 'born Russian'. Her acute musical ear enabled her to pick up languages with an accurate accent and true intonation to an extraordinary degree. Rubini and Tamburini also had fine musical hearing, but apparently, could not match Pauline in the purity of Russian diction. However, the prima donna had the advantage of receiving regular lessons from a devoted teacher, a budding young Russian writer and poet.

Besides singing Amina, Rosina, and Lucia di Lammermoor, Pauline portrayed Desdemona, which was a revelation to her audience, who applauded her not just as Rossini's heroine, but as Shakespeare's own creation, and marvelled that she reduced men, as well as women to tears. One daring Russian even went so far as to say that the poetry of Pushkin could hardly express all the magic that resonated in her voice.

After a performance, admirers flocked to Pauline's dressing room, which always had the appearance of an overstocked florist's shop. Many of them were young, and some were more mature men from noble families who were infatuated with the youthful prima donna, such as the Wielhorski brothers, Counts Matthew and Michael, and General Alexei Lvov, who corresponded frequently with Pauline after she left Russia. Louis took their adulation of his wife in his stride, and welcomed them generously. Pauline found it all very amusing, but it was good for her morale and built her confidence that had been so badly dented by the ferocity of the press at home during the last couple of years. However, she was without vanity, and did not take the gushing enthusiasm too seriously, although she flirted with her admirers, and answered their effusions with banter.

One of them stood head and shoulders above the others. This was Ivan Sergeyevitch Tourgueniev, who taught her Russian, a handsome twenty-five year old, broad-shouldered giant, with a mop of chestnut hair, a fair moustache, and deep set, hooded eyes of an amazing blue. From the moment he set eyes on Pauline as Rosina, he became completely obsessed by her, and persuaded a friend to introduce him to her husband, so that he could meet her. As well as being besotted with literature and opera, he was a keen hunter and a very good shot, which immediately endeared him to Louis, and the two men were soon on common ground, making plans to go hunting together.

OnNovember 13th, the young Russian was formally introduced to Pauline in the Demidov apartment, and became her most fervent admirer and one of the most frequent visitors to her dressing room. He was the second son of a wealthy, aristocratic family from the province of Oryol who had vast estates, the principal one being at Spasskoye. His father, a charming, but weak cavalry officer, had died in 1836, and his dominating mother, Varvara, ruled her two sons,

Nicolai and Ivan, her estates and hundreds of serfs, with an autocracy bordering on insanity and sadism. To Pauline, Tourgueniev was introduced as a good conversationalist and a bad poet.

He told her that he had studied philosophy in Berlin, and had travelled widely in Germany and Italy, returning to Russia in 1841, where he had recently taken up a post in the Ministry of the Interior, but he found it utterly boring. He said that his greatest interest was literature, but admitted that he was very lazy. Recently, his story in verse entitled 'Parasha' had been published, and had met with the approbation of the influential critic Vissarion Belinsky, who had stated that he discerned something of value in the young writer's embryonic talent.

To Pauline he was simply one of her brood of admirers, very charming, but rather a poseur, determined to be noticed and priding himself on being different from everybody else. It took time and patience to break through this façade, in order to discover the real man behind the mask, but he was good, kind, tender, deeply intelligent, highly cultured and above all, a humane being. As he grew older, his social gifts developed so that he was welcomed into the most fashionable salons, but when he first met Pauline, he was affected and dandified. In strange contrast to his masculine figure, his voice was high pitched and not particularly attractive, also, he lisped slightly, and there was something rather feminine in his general demeanour.

The prima donna was besieged with invitations; her celebrity alone ensured that, but when it was discovered that off-stage she possessed all the charm, wit, and intelligence that she brought to her performances, she was doubly welcome for her own sake. Louis, as a sophisticated man of the world, was at home in any society, interested in literature, music, art and the chase, he was supremely at ease with the men he met, although he trod carefully on the vexed subject of politics. He was inundated with invitations to hunt on estates around St. Petersburg, and thoroughly enjoyed his excursions, where he was much admired for his skill with a gun, and the quantity of animals he bagged, often comprising over a thousand birds. On one occasion he even succeeded in killing a wolf, which made him quite a celebrity in the hunting fraternity.

Pauline was occupied with rehearsals, which could be very chaotic affairs, attended by principal singers, chorus, ballet principals and corps de ballet, as well as instrumentalists, the conductor, and three stage directors, one responsible for the principals, one for the chorus, and another for the dancers and supernumararies. She also had at least three or four performances of opera a week, and gave concerts in the grand houses of the rich. With all her social commitments in addition, it is hardly surprising that she had so little time to write to George Sand, who was, nevertheless, avid for news.

Tourgueniev took every opportunity to pursue the diva, although at this time his mother kept him very short of money, and in order to attend her performances, he had to beg a place in the boxes of friends, as he could not afford to buy a ticket for himself. Many of his acquaintances became clearly irritated with him because he took up so much room, and was not averse to pushing himself to the front of the box in order to get a good view of his goddess.

He made no secret of his adoration, and bored his friends by constantly subjecting them to his love-sick confessions. When he discovered that Pauline was serious about wishing to learn Russian, he had offered his services immediately, considering this a god-sent opportunity to be with her in private and get to know her more intimately. He also spent a good deal of time with Louis when Pauline was engaged elsewhere, and an easy, relaxed friendship developed between the three of them.

The Emperor and Empress were frequent visitors to Pauline's performances and on at least one occasion, she was summoned to their box during an intermission, complimented and presented with a gift of expensive jewellery. The Empress had been born Princess Charlotte of Prussia, but on her marriage to Nicolas I, in the traditional custom, she took the Russian name of Alexandra Feodorovna. She was the sister of Prince William of Prussia, and she had already heard about Pauline's great talent from her sister-in-law, the Princess Augusta, who was one of Pauline's staunchest fans. The Empress was very musical herself and was a good pianist, but her health was poor, and she often travelled abroad seeking cures at German spas, notably at Baden Baden where she was sometimes joined by her brother and his wife.

The Russians treated Pauline as a great celebrity and her success in their country was confirmed by her contract being renewed in the spring of 1844 for the following autumn. Tourgueniev was thrilled when it was announced that she would be returning to St. Petersburg because he was sure that he could no longer live without her, and was already dreaming on how he could become a part of her life.

His passion for Pauline never waned, and it is possible that he suffered from a malady which has, in recent times, been codified as 'erotomania', an obsessive complaint that can lead to 'stalking'. If victims of this condition are frustrated by not being with the object of their desire, they can become vindictive and sometimes downright dangerous. It never went this far with Tourgueniev, but he suffered throughout his life because of his over riding infatuation with Mme Viardot. Several of his stories have plots involving an ineffectual man who cannot overcome his fixation with an unattainable, married woman, reflecting the grief that ensues from never having a 'nest' of one's own.

Even as a young man he was hyper-sensitive and neurosthenic, with a tendency to hypochondria, which became progressively worse as he got older, especially when he was particularly unhappy and depressed. When Pauline first met him, he had recently become the father of an illegitimate baby girl. The child's mother was a seamstress who worked for Varvara Tourgueniev, and having been at a loose end during a stay at Spasskoye he had rather half-heartedly started the affair with the young woman. He made no pretence of being in love, and to be charitable, he was doing nothing more than many other careless young men of noble families have done before,simply because they have too much leisure at their disposal. Amazingly, his strange mother actively encouraged him in this escapade.

Varvara Tourguenieva was a psychotic character and emotionally damaged her younger son from his earliest years by her oddities and perverse thinking, sending very conflicting signals to the young child. He was a sensitive boy and was appalled and upset by his inability to help when his mother behaved sadistically towards her serfs, ordering them to be whipped for the most minor misdemeanours. All his life, he needed a strong woman, and Pauline was such a woman, but very different from his cruel mother, for she was kind and loving and he clove to her as if his life depended on it.

Because their friendship lasted for forty years, it has always been assumed that it was simply a straightforward love affair, but it was far more complex. For one thing, there is an ambiguity about Tourgueniev's sexuality, and many people remarked that there was something feminine about him, despite his physique, so it is perfectly possible that there was a latent homosexuality, which he strove to overcome by having liaisons with women of the lower orders, or by courting young women from good families in the hope that it might lead to marriage, but it never did.

Just as the word 'effeminate' was applied to Tourgueniev, some saw Pauline as having masculine traits, her gait being like that of 'a little hussar', and gossip insinuated that she and George Sand were lesbians. Certainly, the relationship that developed between Pauline and Tourgueniev over many years was far from a simple love affair, and it would appear that her hold on him was more spiritual than sexual, which could explain why it continued until his death. A sexual affair can be very short-lived if it does not work out satisfactorily, leading to disappointment and recriminations, but a spiritual passion that is idealistic, existing more on the mental than the physical plane can be very powerful indeed, and last indefinitely. Tourgueniev always had great respect for Pauline, and even when he became one of her closest, most intimate friends, he continued to call her 'Mme Viardot'. Many years after they first met, he declared that their friendship was absolutely unique, because there had never been another like it in the history of the world.

When he was in his thirties he came close to getting engaged to his pretty, eighteen-year-old cousin Olga Tourguenieva, as he desperately wanted a normal family life, but he broke her heart because when it came to the moment of decision, he could not face marriage. At that time, homosexuality was a capital offence in most countries, or could lead to imprisonment. Many men such as Piotr Tchaikovsky and his brother, Modeste, struggled to overcome their natural proclivities, usually without success. Some young men did not consciously recognise the depth of their problems, and they married because their families and society expected it of them, which subjected them and their wives to great unhappiness, although they may not have truly understood the seriousness of the underlying cause of their distress before the advent of Freud.

The French have always recognised the reality of a loving, non-sexual relationship between a man and a woman, which they term an 'amitie amoureuse'. Sometimes it commences with a sensual affair, such as that of Mme Jaubert and Alfred de Musset, but after a short time sexual activity is abandoned and the couple develop a deep and lasting friendship, or perhaps it is, from the beginning, a real friendship without the complications imposed by a sexual liaison.

There was little in the way of a musical profession in Russia at that time, many musicians being talented aristocratic amateurs, or serfs who were employed in orchestras in the houses of their rich owners. However, Pauline was delighted by the standard and quality of the music making she heard, particularly among gifted amateurs such as the Wielhorski brothers, Count Matthew, a cellist, and Count Michael, a composer, who became life long friends. Indeed, she and Count Matthew continued a regular correspondence until his death.

The director of the Imperial Chapel, General Alexei Lvov, was a composer, and it was he who introduced Pauline to Russian liturgical music, which impressed her by its strange and colourful harmonies, and the unique vocal qualities of the Russian singers, particularly the heavy, deep, dark-toned basses for which the country is famous. She dedicated her song 'Villanelle' to Lvov, and 'Un jour du printemps' to Matthew Wielhorski.

It was a very different kind of music from that of the gypsies she heard at a private house. This exotic music touched a deep vein within Pauline, fascinating her with echoes of the familiar Spanish gypsy songs she had heard her exuberant father sing many years ago. When the group of Russians had completed their performance, they clustered around her, begging her to sing to them. At first she sang her customary French and Italian songs and arias, and the gypsies listened attentively, but although they marvelled at the quality and range of her voice, she quickly realised that music from her regular repertoire was unintelligible to them, so she began to sing her Spanish songs instead. These were received rapturously, and the gypsies demanded that she repeat them several times so that they could learn them by ear. Who knows what Spanish idioms found their way into the traditional Russian gypsy music after this encounter with the prima donna from France, whose roots were in the soil of Spain, and whose father, she believed, had been a gypsy himself.?

Lent was approaching, which signalled the end of the opera season, but first there was a week of Shrovetide celebrations and carnival. Pauline sang the 18th Psalm of Marcello when she took part in the Philharmonic Society's concert, but, of course, most people wanted to see her on the stage, and it was only the real music lovers who attended concerts. But when she sang for the students of St. Petersburg University, she had a truly popular success, and was besieged by them when she had to leave before the end of the concert as she was due to sing at the palace of the Grand Duchess Elena Pavlovna, the sister-in-law of the Emperor, that same evening. In the rumpus caused by dozens of young men dashing from their seats, yelling 'Vivat' and 'Adieu',when they followed the prima donna to her carriage, one old lady fainted because she thought a riot had broken out, and Pauline admitted that she had been nervous in the middle of such ascrimmage.

Shortly before the singer left Russia, Robert and Clara Schumann arrived. It was wonderful to see them again, and Pauline introduced them to her influential friends who, she hoped, might further their careers. At a soiree given by the Wielhorski brothers, Schumann conducted his B flat symphony to an audience of connoiseurs, and dedicated his Quartet Op. 47 to a Count Wielhorski. Clara, who was still the rather introverted creature she had always been, rather brusque in her Germanic way, had been engaged to give concerts in Riga, Mitau, Moscow and St. Petersburg. She had always envied Pauline's joie de vivre, and was now even more impressed by the way she had grown in confidence, at home in any society, and at ease with the Royal Family.

Despite their friendship, Clara found it difficult not to be overwhelmed and intimidated by Pauline's success. The singer, ever ready to help a friend, told the press that Clara's 'singing on the piano is better than mine', and although the pianist and Robert's music were well received by the music lovers of St. Petersburg, they showed no signs of repeating the hysteria generated by the prima donna they had taken to their hearts. The way Pauline had moved the Russians so deeply was truly extraordinary. Few others, however famous or talented, had been greeted with quite such hysterical enthusiasm and called 'our own'.

Of course, the extent of Pauline's success stirred envy in the hearts of several of her colleagues, and resentment on the part of the Russian prime donne who were passed over in her favour. The only female singer who mattered to St. Petersburg audiences was Pauline Viardot Garcia, and the seeds of enmity were sown at that time, and subsequently grew. But for now, Pauline was above such worries; she was delighted to be returning for the next season and was merely saying 'Au Revoir' to her devotees. Ivan Tourgueniev, although sad to see her go and wondering how he would face the lonely months till her return, wished her happiness from the depths of his heart, and prayed that the months would pass quickly.

The Viardots bade farewell to their Russian friends and set off for Vienna, where Pauline's newly found fame had preceeded her, but everything was an anti-climax after the stunning Russian season, not only in the theatre, but in the palatial houses, with their great banquets. On first being invited to dine at a grand house in Russia, she had assumed that the sumptuous buffet was the meal, with its lashings of caviar, delicacies of every kind, both savoury and sweet, and having partaken of a great variety of food, including slices of a delicious pie filled with a mixture of rice and salmon, she was dismayed to find that when the great double doors were opened they led to an enormous and splendid dining room where the extensive table was laid for dinner. She and Louis, who had also tucked into the aperitifs heartily, were rather embarrassed to have to refuse several dishes, as they were already full. The menu included numerous kinds of meat and a great variety of fish, accompanied by dumplings, vegetables and borsch, and wondrous sweets of marzipan, chocolate, cherries soaked in liqueur and cream, sweet confections, decorated like works of art, too beautiful to eat. All this was washed down with fine wines, of which their fellow guests partook lavishly, and by the time they left the table, Louis was feeling distinctly weak-kneed. Fortunately, Pauline had drunk a lot of water with her food, so she was firmer on her feet. Neither of the Viardots drank very much, usually just a little wine with a meal, but they found that many of their Russian friends had a great capacity for their liquor.

After the splendours of Russia, Pauline found Vienna dull, particularly as she was not occupied sufficiently at the opera house because she did not have as many performances as she would have liked. Louis soon departed for Paris, leaving her alone; she felt homesick, and longed to rejoin her 'Loulou,' her little daughter and her friends and family.

Tourgueniev wrote to tell her that he had now returned to St. Petersburg from Moscow where he had been ill with a chest complaint for two months, having been confined to his room, but he was now feeling much better. He had read in the 'Allegemeine Theater Zeitung' that she had arrived in Vienna in good health. He hoped that she would have a well-earned rest in France, and waited impatiently for her return to Russia, where everybody was looking forward to hearing her again, judging by the comments of her intimates, 'the faithful and the old guard'. He and the Italian singer Eugene Pizzolato (who sang frequently in St. Petersburg during the 1840's) often chatted about her. He said that 'Pizzo' was very much attached to her, and called him ' a good fellow'. Tourgueniev had just made him sing so many things, including the last scene of Vaccai's 'Romeo and Juliet' that the poor chap was rendered almost voiceless. Obviously he soon regained his voice because on May 27th he left for Vienna to fulfil operatic engagements.

The writer was downcast due to lack of money, and he could not contemplate travelling abroad. He reminded himself that in six weeks Pauline would be in France, even further away from him, and he told her what profound memories she had left behind – 'people speak of you with love, all that is, except Mlle Volkoff, who is your sworn enemy.' This lady was the sister of one of Pauline's most fervent admirers, Sergei Sergeievitch Volkov, who was a relative of the Wielhorski brothers. Turgueniev did not say what Pauline had done to incur the displeasure of the young lady, but told his idol that he would be in and around St. Petersburg all summer, hunting from morning to night each day, as he loved nothing more than being out in the fields where he could 'dream at ease', and added – 'You know that I am naturally a little dreamy', then he closed his letter by sending his 'best wishes to Viardot.'

Since 1842, the Viardots had been discussing the possibility of acquiring a country house of their own. Having enjoyed their visits to Nohant so much, the seeds had been sown, and they began to long for such a place, surrounded by large gardens and parks where Louise could enjoy a pleasant, country childhood. At first they had asked George to keep an eye open for any likely property on the market in the Berry area, and for a short time, Louis had toyed with the idea of a house in the Sologne region because the hunting was first rate, but it was one of the most unhealthy places in France with thousands of Etangs (small pools) frequented by malarial mosquitos.

Even so, as late as 23rd September, 1843, he had contemplated buying a property twenty miles south of Orleans, which would have been within a convenient distance of Nohant. However, common sense prevailed and that idea was given up, as it was more sensible for the Viardots to look for somewhere in the country closer to Paris, and they began to think about the Brie region, south east of the city.

Pauline had earned enormous sums in Russia and received expensive presents of jewellery, so they decided that it was a good time to buy themselves a chateau, which is why Louis had gone on ahead of Pauline. Now it remained to be seen what he would find.

CHAPTER FIFTEEN

1844

Louis discovered a suitable house in the Seine et Marne department, about sixty kilometres east-south-east of Paris at Rozay-en-Brie. The region lay in a gently rolling landscape, on a largely unpopulated plain, with isolated woods and tiny villages. The building to be auctioned was the Chateau of Courtavenel which was close to the tiny hamlet of Vaudoy. It was a large, solidly built mansion, with six turreted towers, a moat fed by a natural spring, and a drawbridge. A large dovecot graced the well designed park of expansive lawns and flower gardens stocked with masses of roses, dahlias and geraniums, together with a large quantity of old trees that formed a veritable curtain of greenery. In addition there was a farmyard, various farm buildings, a vegetable garden, canals, avenues, orchards, woods, quincunxes, arable land, meadows, fallow land and pastures, all of which comprised 39 hectares 40 ares and 13 centiares.

Louis was delighted with all he saw, and as the area abounded in birds and wild life, he knew the hunting would be good. He wrote to Pauline immediately, and on receiving his letter, she was swept along by his enthusiasm. On April 26th, Louis and her mother signed a deed before a M. Huet, which enabled Joaquina to act as proxy for the purchase of the estate that was due to be auctioned in Paris on May 7th. Mme Garcia was obliged to obtain Pauline's ratification of the bill of sale within a period of two months, but if she did not, Louis would be liable for the payment. At the auction, which was held in the office of M. Fourchy on the quai Malaquais, there were two bids at a starting price of 100,000 francs. M. Huet proposed a sum of 100,200 francs on behalf of his client, Joaquina Garcia, and this was accepted.

In the meantime, Louis returned to Vienna to join his wife, who was burning with curiosity about the property that was to cost her more than the large fees she had earned in Russia. Louis's enthusiasm was infectious, but she knew him well enough to realise that his delight with the estate was linked with his anticipation of superb hunting. Nevertheless, it was fashionable to have a country chateau and would do her social standing a great deal of good.

On their return to Paris in July, 1844, the Viardots lost no time in visiting their new purchase. Before the railway was built, the journey to Courtavenel was a long one. There was a choice of a slow coach from Paris to Mormant or Nangisthat took between seven and eight hours, and a faster one to Rozay-en-Brie, which took five to five and a half hours. As there was no local coach service available, visitors to the chateau had to be met by carriage. On Pauline's first visit, the Viardots caught the coach to Mormant from the rue Petit-Saint-Martin (now the rue Berger) at 9.30 in the morning, and after a noisy journey with a great many stops, reached Courtavenel by early evening.

When Pauline caught sight of the south front of the chateau she was stunned by the size of the old stone building with its stout towers and high turrets peeping through a curtain of trees. The forecourt was reached via a little bridge over the moat, and a shallow flight of steps led up to the lofty entrance hall. No one knew exactly when the chateau had originally been built but the present building with its massive stone walls, and deeply set windows, possibly dated from the reign of Francois I in the early sixteenth century.

As the Viardots crossed the footbridge, Louis noted that the moat would need a great deal of labour to clear all the weeds and rushes that clogged it. At the top of the steps leading into the house, they entered a high, imposing hallthat reached from the front to the back of the building. There was an impressive staircase, and an ante-room to the left, and a massive grand salon to the right. It was two storeys high, reaching from light to light, and surrounded by a balcony. Pauline rushed from room to room, gasping at the size of it all and wondering how she was going to find enough furniture to fill such a spacious house.

The vast dining room was at the back of the building over-looking the park, with the kitchen, scullery, several store rooms and domestic offices in close proximity. There was a smaller salon and a breakfast or morning room, and two other rooms, which she thought could be used as studies. Upstairs, a large space was occupied by the second storey of the grand salon, and there were several bedrooms and two tower rooms, as well as rooms for staff. The attics had bedrooms and storage areas, and Pauline realised that the very large area sited over the grand salon could be converted into a theatre.

As she explored her house, she declared that it was ' true, ancient, and noble' and thought it could have been built during the reign of Henri IV who succeeded to the throne in 1589. She added that in her opinion the south façade was 'rather philistine….but very nice'.

It may well be that the original massive foundations with their arrow slits were from a much older building, and that the chateau as it appeared when the

Viardots bought it was mainly from around 1600, as it was in the French Renaissance style, although a low annex on the western side was obviously more modern. Actually, the history of Courtavenel was far more ancient than the Viardots were aware, and, like Nohant, was built on the site of an ancient fortified manor. The earliest references are in thirteenth century chronicles; different spellings of the name are given, but by 1398, it appears to have become fixed as Courtavenel, and between the sixteenth to the eighteenth centuries it was frequently mentioned in public and private records.

By the beginning of the nineteenth century, the whole estate was in decline due to neglect in the aftermath of the French Revolution, having been divided up between various heirs. Several hundred trees had been cut down to supply Napoleon's navy, and in the census return for 1836, it was stated that a Count Arsene-Rene Demarchais, who was ninety-eight at the time, lived there alone. In 1839, it was sold to the Viardots' immediate predecessor, Francois-Ursule-Adolphe, Baron d'Astanieres.

This gentleman had not paid his local taxes, or the premiums on his fire insurance and policy 'for the upkeep of the roofs'. By the terms of his lease of the farm and vineyards, he was allowed two annual trips to Paris at the farmer's expense, and he persuaded M. Fourchy who had handled the auction, to incorporate a clause into the bill of sale so that he could use one of these journeys to remove his furniture and effects – even 'the stove in the so-called summer room, and the bath-tubs in the bathroom'!

Very soon the Viardots realised that they would need to spend substantial sums on their estate, in addition to the cost of the purchase, which had to be paid in full within four months of signing the contract to avoid crippling interest charges. In a letter to George Sand on August 14th, Louis said that another 30,000 francs were required immediately for furnishing and repairs, and Pauline would be giving everything she had earned so far, almost to the last farthing. Not all her Russian roubles would be enough to make the house really habitable, and Courtavenel would always be a tremendous drain on the Viardot's finances, despite giving them standing, position and influence in the region of Seine-et-Marne.

There was always a great deal to do, and never enough time. Joaquina's help was enlisted in supervising the workmen who swarmed over the house and grounds, and she and little Louise settled into the chateau while the workers banged and scraped around them, repairing roofs, altering rooms and putting in new locks, but she declined to make decisions regarding furnishings, colour schemes and décor, as she knew that Pauline had a good eye for period style and decor, and her mother did not want to upset her by choosing the wrong things.

Joaquina, who could remain calm in a real crisis, often tormented herself over trifles, and Pauline said that she loved to make herself suffer over nothing in particular. By 1844, there were so many styles from which to choose, including Empire, Biedermeir, or the fashionable neo-Gothic, and Pauline was unsure if the chateau should be furnished in its own grand Renaissance period or if it should simply be adapted to a more modern, comfortable style. Joaquina was pleased that she didn't have to make the decision, but was sure that Pauline would have plenty of ideas.

In July, the Viardots took up residence and Pauline began the serious business of choosing colour schemes for curtains, soft furnishings, wallpaper and paint, and deciding what furniture and accessories would be needed. Some things she bought in Paris, some she had shipped from England, and occasionally, she picked up interesting and useful items at brochante sales in the Seine et Marne region. Louis, who had collected paintings and objets d'art all his life, was delighted that his continually growing collection would now have a worthy home in which they could be shown to advantage. Since their marriage, Pauline had also been collecting beautiful pieces, such as Aubusson carpets, Meissen and Sevres china, statuettes and bronzes, crystal glass and silverware, which would find pride of place in their picturesque chateau.

The house was a hive of activity with workmen and helpers spread throughout the many rooms, as well as visitors, local worthies, such as the parish priest, the notary (touting for business), and Louis Chatriot, the old, blind Mayor of Vaudoy, as well as their illustrious neighbours from surrounding estates; Charles de Neuilly d'Eberstein of le Petit-Paris, the old Vicomte Davene de Fontaine, owner of the Chateau de Grangemenant, and five local farmers.

In addition to the frenetic activity of orchestrating the work on her house, Pauline was busily coaching her cousin Antonia, a correct, but not the most naturally gifted of singers, for whom she had obtained a contract to sing minor roles during her forthcoming engagement in St. Petersburg. It was absolute pandemonium in the house; Joaquina, thinking that her brother, Paolo and his wife Mariquita would be another welcome pair of hands, had asked them to come to Courtavenel, but far from assisting, Paolo, who smoked over a hundred cigarettes a day, became ill and had to be nursed for the rest of his stay.

Louisette, who was now a lively two and a half years old, chased all over the house in pursuit of Alphonse, the farmer's boy, and although Berthe, Louis' sister, tried to keep track of her, she was too fast for the poor woman. The babies brought along by their mothers who had come to clean and cook, added to the general turmoil, as did the barking dogs and screeching parrots. Sometimes, Louis escaped the chaos by going back and forth to Paris, winding up his tricycle firm and liquidating Pauline's bank account in order to pay d'Astanieres. In addition, he had to calculate how he could make the estate financially viable to replace some of the vast initial outlay. A first step was to increase the rent of his tenant farmer by 300 francs a year, although he did give him further amenities for this sum.

Despite the mayhem, Pauline decided that it was worth all the trouble, as she had fallen in love with Courtavenel on sight, although she had not contemplated owning anything quite so vast; it was even larger than Nohant. However, the great advantage was that they would be able to accommodate family and friends for weekends and holidays, and once things had settled down, Pauline would always be able to slip away in the large house and grounds and find solitude.

In the event, the style of furnishing proved eclectic; for the grand salon with its enormously high ceiling, Pauline acquired some English Regency furniture which was very much to her taste, as it was light and elegant and she liked its classical lines, and simplicity of style. The large armchairs, however, were Viennese and eminently comfortable. A splendid clock, topped by a man in armour, stood on the mantelpiece over the vast fireplace, making a fitting centre piece, and Louis was delighted to see his Rembrandt and other Dutch and Italian masters in pride on the ancient walls. The dining room was huge, and had originally been intended for large festive occasions, but the Viardots planned to use it as a concert hall.

Unfortunately, George Sand was disgruntled by the fact that the Viardots now had a country house of their own, and feared that they would no longer have time to visit Nohant. Nevertheless, she invited them to join her for a summer holiday, but didn't seem to understand the pressure under which Pauline was labouring to get her house into some sort of order before leaving for engagements in Germany and St. Petersburg. Pauline soon realized that it would be difficult to get away, but allowed George to believe that she would try to find time for a few days in Berry, although Louis stated outright that it would be impossible for him to get away. George felt that everything was going wrong, as other guests, apart from the Viardots, could not be counted on either.

Hyacinthe de Latouche, the cousin of her friend and neighbour, Charles Duvernet, had suffered an apoplectic stroke, and Albert Gryzmala, Chopin's dear old friend, on whom George was relying to keep his spirits up, had fallen down stairs and almost broken his back; in addition, Franz Liszt, now back in the fold after his separation from Marie d'Agoult, refused George's invitation as he had recently embarked on an adventure with the notorious Lola Montez, an Irish dancer who posed as a native of Andalusia. They soon tired of eachother and she took herself off to Munich, where King Ludwig I of Bavaria became besotted with her.Four years later, in 1848, his popularity had fallen so low through his shameless affaire with Lola, and the neglect of his long suffering wife, Queen Therese, that despite his reputation as an unusually liberal monarch, he was forced to abdicate.

Matters went from bad to worse at Nohant when Chopin received news from Poland that his father had died. He was prostrated with grief and locked himself in his room for forty-eight hours, seeing no one but George, who was beside herself with worry, and lost no time in sending for her doctor, Gustave Papet.

A few weeks later, Chopin's sister Ludwika and her husband Kolosanty Jedrzejewicz arrived in Paris, where they stayed in George's apartment in the Square d'Orleans. George invited them to Nohant, but was worried that they would see a marked change in Fritz who had grown thin and coughed constantly. He was finding each successive winter more difficult to bear and his delicate state of health gave cause for concern. His condition was further aggravated by the grief he suffered through the loss of his father, which he saw as yet another break in the chain that linked him with his Polish homeland. Despite being unwell, he insisted on going to Paris to meet his sister and her husband in mid-July. The stage-coach was crowded and his friend Manuel Marliani, who travelled with him, was forced to take a seat on the roof.

Chopin spent a whirlwind ten days with his relatives, meeting Polish friends, and spending his evenings at soirees, the theatre and the opera. When he returned to Nohant he was in an exhausted state, and accompanied only by his servant Jan, much to George's surprise. Unable to face any more sight-seeing or socialising, he had left Ludwika and Kolosanty with Charlotte Marliani and Albert Grzymala. They had agreed to stay on in the city until Pauline was ready to accompany them to Nohant. But she could not get away as she was completely involved in the thousand and one tasks that remained to be done before she left for Russia. So it was not until August 9th that Ludwika and her husband arrived at the chateau, albeit without Pauline, who had thoroughly upset their plans, as they had hung on for a week waiting for her. Of course, she was desperately sorry to let her friends down, but her vacillation had caused more upset than if she had been honest with George from the outset.

The writer was furious as Pauline had kept Ludwiga and her husband waiting needlessly, and Louis was forced to write George a long, explanatory letter on his wife's behalf. George suspected that her fears about the Viardots preferring to stay on their own estate rather than take the long journey to Nohant were justified, and realized that if the hunting around Courtavenel was better than she could offer, Louis would certainly prefer to remain at home, and she joked, half seriously, that she would like to put a match to 'Courtavenelle' (a pun meaning 'short alley'), and all its game. She insinuated that the Viardots would indulge in high living and become very grand, but Louis assured her that nothing could be further from the truth, stating: "We live far more simply here, dear Madame Sand, than you do over there, having no one but a cook and gardener to serve us all, and living very well off the milk of our cow, the eggs of our chickens and the vegetables from our kitchen-garden. Instead of dreaming of roubles, jewels and crowns, we go out in our heavy shoes to pick our plums and chat with the shepherds or the ploughmen that we meet. Pauline needs no urging to sing a song for them right there in the open fields. They say of us: 'these people give themselves no airs', and indeed we piously observe the cult – which you yourself profess – of 'sancta simplicitas'.

Pauline was upset by George's attitude to their new home, the first she and Louis had bought together, and she thought that her friend was tactless and unkind when she suggested that Courtavenel was not to be compared with Nohant, and that they would soon tire of it and sell up when they experienced the difficulties and expense of running such an estate. Pauline already knew well just how expensive it was turning out to be, but even so, she was delighted to be the mistress of such an establishment and intended to make it a worthy rival to Nohant. She was keen for George to visit her, but George was still smarting over Pauline's failure to turn up in Berry, and did not accept her invitation.

Basically, Pauline was a kind person who would do all in her power to avoid upsetting or letting down her friends, but sometimes, through vacillation or lack of complete honesty for fear of offending, she made things worse, for example, when she told Liszt that she was not intimate with Mme Sand because, knowing about the animosity between Marie and George at that time, she did not want him to think that she was being disloyal to him.

Pauline did send George a note saying that because of all the business in which she was involved at Courtavenel, she was not able to work on her voice and it was 'fallow' at present. That was a state of affairs that could not continue, of course, because she had important roles ahead of her, and no voice can be left unattended for long without losing its flexibility and strength, as muscles weaken if not regularly exercised.

Several friends and acquaintances of the Viardots had acquired large country properties around Paris, and all found them very expensive, including Eugene Scribe, the famous librettist and playwright who acquired a house in Seine et

Marne in 1835, putting himself in debt for many years. In contrast, Charles de Beriot sold his chateau at Roissy, near Tournan-en-Brie in 1838, and made the house at Ixelles his permanent residence when he married two years later. One of the reasons Malibran had continued to work even though extremely unwell, had been the necessity to keep earning large fees to finance two expensive houses.

By the end of August, the Viardots made the final payment on their property, and paid off the workmen. For a short time, life was more settled, and Louis was able to read the newspapers again, but with the Russian trip imminent, there was little time for leisure or to entertain guests.

At Nohant, as it happened, the fewer guests George had to deal with the better. She was very much occupied with her writing, having an urgent deadline to meet, as Louis Veron desperately needed her new novel 'Le Meunier d'Angibault'. This was a story inspired by an old mill near Nohant, for serialisation in his 'Constitutionnel' having been let down by an author who had succumbed to a nervous breakdown. Veron promised her a large fee if she would help him, and she gave up everything in order to do so, taking no exercise, not even riding, and staying up all night working at fever pitch. On August 12th she wrote to a friend in Paris, 'I have neither time to eat or sleep', but on August 26th she announced: 'I finished my novel yesterday – I'm dead!'

Despite working so hard, she went out of her way to ensure that Chopin's sister and her husband spent an enjoyable three weeks at Nohant. The pianist was working on his Sonata in B Minor, and he and Solange played duets together and kept their visitors entertained. When they left, George gave Ludwika a pencil sketch she had made of Chopin and sent his mother a rosary. Maurice offered to accompany them to Paris, and said he would return immediately with Chopin. However, as he was still under Pauline's spell, he took himself off to Courtavenel, and left poor Chopin to make his own way back to Nohant.

It seemed that Maurice's infatuation had developed into a real love for Pauline, although it is not known what happened at Courtavenel. George was aware of the seriousness of her twenty-one year old son's affections for the twenty-three year old singer, and knew that Pauline was not indifferent to him. Not only did he stay for several days at Courtavenel, but he even remained there after the Viardots left. His mother had given him instructions to bring Pauline back with him to Nohant, and was annoyed when he extended his stay, and she complained that he and Pauline obviously preferred their own company to hers.

In a letter to George, dated the 20th of September, written from Brussels on her way to Russia, Pauline asked: "How is Maurice after his journey? We promised one another to be brave... I cannot say more at present. I love him very seriously. Write to me soon – 'a double entente' (double meaning), if possible, and address your letters to the Imperial Management of St. Petersburg Theatres'. No doubt this was to spare Louis's feelings.

In the autumn of 1844, George was still stressed, as after the haste to finish her novel, Veron refused to publish it, declaring that it was too inflammatory. He had expected a country idyll, and instead received a 'stick of dynamite', a communistic diatribe. Much wrangling took place over the next few weeks, and George stated: 'It is not possible for creative artists not to be impressed by the advent of the future, and my novel is of today.' Eventually, Veron paid her an 'indemnity' of 5,000 francs, but this was a mere drop in the ocean compared to the 50,000 francs she had been promised.

Pierre Leroux, the editor of 'La Revue Independente' was always in financial difficulties and she often had to bail him out. She had promised to give him some of the money that was due to her from Veron,, but through being uncompromising she lost out, and was not able to do so.

Maurice's adolescent mooning over Pauline did not go down well at Nohant and Chopin was quite impatient with the love-sick young man. He considered this merely a passing fancy, and was annoyed with Maurice for having 'dumped' him in Paris. Chopin did not believe that it was the youth's first amorous adventure as, after all, he had been a student in Paris for some years, and many temptations must have come his way there. It was utter nonsense, in his opinion, for Maurice to settle his affections on Pauline, who, as far as Chopin was aware, had always behaved impeccably and who, up to now, appeared to have taken her marriage vows seriously. The sooner Maurice overcame these foolish feelings, the better. Naturally, Maurice, who considered himself to be truly in love for the first time, found Chopin's attitude unsympathetic.

The relationship between the pianist and George's children became more difficult as they grew older. George doted on Maurice and he adored her, but as he matured and understood the nature of the relationship between his mother and her lover, he instinctively resented Chopin's influence. He wanted to be the sole 'master of the house', and started to treat the pianist, as if he were merely a guest. Chopin, on the other hand, adored Solange. She was musically gifted and studied the piano with Marie de Rozieres, one of Chopin's former pupils. This woman was a well meaning busybody, who was by no means the most discreet person in the world. Solange's difficult personality had not been ameliorated over the past few years; she was still spoilt, unkind and often downright nasty. She and her mother had little affinity, though George bent over backwards to do her best for her recalcitrant daughter, and later impoverished herself in the process. The girl was extremely good looking, and as she grew up, began to use her charms seductively. Chopin could not see through this guile, and often, Solange acted as a wedge between him and George, who began to spend more time at Nohant and visited Paris less frequently.

She missed seeing the Viardots so often, although they wrote frequently, but as the years passed their meetings became fewer, due to their changed circumstances. Nevertheless, the friendship endured and their correspondence only ended with George's death. As ever, she was interested in Pauline's compositions and was delighted that some of her songs had appeared in a Russian publication in May 1844. This was an album of new works by various composers and included pieces by Pauline's St. Petersburg friends, Glinka, Lvov, Wielhorski, and Elkan. Tourgueniev was loud in his praise of Pauline's compositions and was particularly enamoured of several songs that she had published in Paris in 1843 with covers designed by Ary Scheffer. These included 'La Chapelle' to a text by Uhland, dedicated to Scheffer, 'L'Ombre et le jour' to a text by Turquety, and 'Adieux aux beaux jours' author unknown, dedicated to Auber, of which the Russian said: "It has a sad passion, sweet and sombre – with true expression," adding that it had made him weep.

In the autumn of 1844, the Viardots returned to St. Petersburg, where Pauline's first appearance was as Amina in 'La Sonnambula', a part in which she had enjoyed such notable success the previous season, and she added a new role to her repertoire, that of Adina in Donizetti's 'L'Elisir d'Amore'. This part, although it does not have any great dramatic moments, is a charming work that Pauline was to sing frequently during her career, and she always relished playing the mischievous young land-owner. The role lies beautifully for the female voice, requiring a good firm middle range, a skilful use of legato and a brilliance in coloratura, the vocal line being florid and the range extensive. Pauline had been trained on the old exercises of the bel canto school, and did not have any difficulty applying herself to Adina's music. The character of the girl is playful and teasing, at first seeming heartless in her desire to make fun of Nemorino, a poor lad who is desperately in love with her. However, underneath the banter and jollity there is a good heart, which is revealed at the end of the opera. The music is full of melody and invention and the Italian setting is picturesque and colourful. The audience loved Pauline's interpretation and once again, she was enthusiastically applauded, recalled time after time, and inundated with bouquets.

In addition to her opera performances, she was in great demand for concerts, and appeared at the home of Count Lavalle in the presence of the Emperor and Empress and members of their Court. One of the items she sang was Glinka's 'O

My Ratmir' from 'Russlan and Ludmilla' a piece that always went down well, especially as she sang it in the original language. This was the song she usually sang in the lesson scene in the second act of 'Il Barbiere' when she was in Russia.

Her greatest challenge came when she sang the role of Norma. Those who had a particular knowledge of the operatic repertoire thought that she was unwise to do so, because, great artist as she was, the part was not ideal for her type of voice. Her first performance as Bellini's heroine was on November 30th, and the public's curiosity meant that the theatre was full to overflowing, with all the panoply of wealth on show. At the end of the opera, the singer was given a great ovation and took numerous curtain calls. Next day, the 'Severnaya Pchela' declared that she had scaled the heights that only people of genius could reach.

To a great many Russians, everything that Pauline sang was beyond reproach, but there were others who were more realistic, and despite acknowledging her great gifts, considered that this particular role was not for her. It was obvious that the cost was unnecessarily great as the tessitura was really too high for her voice and her frame was too slight for the task.

Later, Giulia Grisi would sing the role to great acclaim in Russia, being judged the legitimate successor to its creator, Giuditta Pasta. Grisi was a 'soprano robusto' whose voice matched her physique and Pauline at that time was a high, coloratura mezzo soprano with a petite figure. Of course, all international singers have to possess a robust constitution to cope with the demands of the life-style, but there are certain types of soprano and tenor to whom the term is applied in a technical way, with specific roles written to exploit their prowess — Pauline was not one of them.

At that time she was considered without equal in opera buffa and in roles of the 'demi-character' kind, but was not and never would be a true dramatic soprano. Whenever she sang 'Norma' she allowed her friends to believe that it was very successful, and no doubt she thought that it was, after all the cheers, bravas and curtain calls, but in her quieter moments, when the applause had died away, she must have realized that it was a 'succes d'estime', and really beyond her natural capabilities, great as they were. With her magnetic stage presence, and consummate skill as a singer and actress, she was able to triumph over her limitations to such an extent that she convinced many people, but there were always those who knew better.

With her next roles she was on firmer ground, and no one could fault her. She sang her now customary Cenerentola and a new part, Norina in Donizetti's 'Don Pasquale', a delicious character, full of fun and good humour. Although it is not a heavy weight role, it is a demanding one, requiring stamina and ease in legato, as well as florid singing, she being the only female in the opera and having to soar over the voices of the three male protagonists in ensembles. However, it was well within herrepertoire, and she enjoyed a great success in the role.

Pauline's friend, General Lvov, the music director of the Court Chapel, had written a new opera to an Italian libretto, 'Bianca e Gualtierro' in which she was due to sing, but the premiere was postponed because all three principal singers, Tamburini, Rubini and Viardot were ill. It finally opened on December 11th, and although it was not a runaway success, with little mention of the music by the critics, the décor, ballet and singers were appreciated.

The opera season ended for Pauline with a performance of 'La Sonnambula'. Louis wrote to Ivan Tourgueniev on the 1st of March: 'You were present at the end of the season last year, so you will have an idea of the excitement that we experienced on this occasion. The theatre was packed with an enthusiastic audience, flowers, wreaths, shouts, calling without end, handkerchiefs and hats thrown in the air, and outside, the crowd milling around, pushing and gesticulating around our carriage and following us home to say their good-byes. This year, the farewell is even more poignant because Rubini is finally retiring and will never be heard as Elvino again. Pauline, already moved by her own reception, was in a flood of tears at the parting with her old friend and colleague. All this emotion is very singular, touching and beautiful.'

Pauline was presented with a gold flower holder, which had the signatures of the eighty-six subscribers on the handle, and bore the inscription: 'St. Petersburg, homage, admiration and recognition offered to Mme Viardot-Garcia, on February 25th, 1845.'Also inscribed, were the names of the dozen roles she had sung in Russia: Rosina, Desdemona, Amina, Romeo, Lucia, Zerlina, Tancredi, Adina, Norma, Cenerentola, Bianca, and Norina.

Louis also told Ivan of a visit to Pauline by three Russian merchants who came to tell her of a public subscription that had been opened in recognition of her wonderful performances. 'We want everyone to know that Russian moujiks also have ears to hear and hearts to feel', and saying this, one of them presented her with a beautiful and costly bracelet of diamonds and enamel work, made by a Russian jeweller, and worth, he said, 'an estimated two to three thousand roubles' – costlier than the bouquet holder!'

On the 9th of March, 1845, the season finally ended with a concert at the Bolshoi Theatre where Pauline was again inundated with bouquets. By April 5th, she had announced that she would return for a further season, and told a newspaper reporter how much she loved the warmth of the Russian people's response to her singing, adding that it even made up for the atrociously cold weather! She remained in St. Petersburg after the opera season ended and was deluged with concerts, to the extent that she became unwell due to the stress of so many performances in such a short time.

After she recovered, she and Louis travelled to Moscow for more concerts. There they were met by Tourgueniev who showed them around the city, which seemed very strange and foreign, far more so than cosmopolitan St. Petersburg. They were amazed by the scale of the Kremlin, with its brightly painted build-ings and enormous walled squares, containing several cathedrals, such as that of the Ascension, and churches with large round towers topped by tiered pinnacles, so different in style from those of France and Germany. At night, they stood on the Stone Bridge overlooking the mighty Moskva river and watched a firework display, a truly majestic sight in such an extraordinary set-ting. The sheer scale of everything was staggering, and the many buildings of different styles and periodsthat lay before them, including the squat-domed cathedral, dedicated to the Archangel Michael, where the pre-Romanov Tzars are buried, they found truly magnificent and unique.

The opulence of the palace took their breath away; several rooms were bar-rel-vaulted and richly decorated, with floors of the most costly marquetry, intri-cately decorated in many different types of wood. The craftsmen who created these wonderful floors were noted for their superb designs and workmanship, the inspiration for which came from old Russian designs and book illustrations. But much as the Viardots appreciated the superb works of art, testifying to the outstanding talents of Russian artists, sculptors and architects, they were amazed that so much money had been spent on unashamed luxury, when thou-sands of Russian lived in abject poverty.

The balance of society was desperately awry, with excessive wealth at one end of the scale, great need at the other, and only a small middle class in-between. Although Tourgueniev had been born into a wealthy aristocratic family, he was well aware of the iniquities in his beloved country, and dreamed of making a difference, as did many other politically aware young men, who hoped to bring about a state of affairs where every one would be treated equally, and poverty would be totally overcome.

One of his relatives, Alexander Tourgueniev, had been involved in the De-cember uprising of 1825, which was put down with vigour, resulting in the execution of many of the insurgents, but inspiring others to carry on where they had failed. Several of Ivan's friends were politically active, none more so than Michael Bakunin, who was a hot-headed anarchist. Tourgueniev didn't believe in extremes, his credo was that all must evolve step by step, because by destroying everything, you ran the risk of losing much that was beneficial. Reforms were tremendously necessary, but needed to be carefully thought through, and not overthrown willy nilly by revolution, which only brought grief and suffering to everyone, and usually simply transferred power, the underlying corruption going unchecked.

Pauline gave three concerts at the Bolshoi Theatre, and the reception she received at the end of each one was phenomenal even by the standards of St. Petersburg. She was recalled thirty times at one of them, and had to repeat the entire concert. Tourgueniev took his mother to hear her; he had made no secret of his devotion to the singer, and this had, naturally, not pleased Varvara at all. Later at supper, she fumed against Pauline as she ate her meal, but finally, in spite of herself, muttered, 'I have to admit it, that wretched gypsy can sing'.

Ivan was dreading Pauline's departure, knowing that it would be months before he would see her again; he could no longer envisage life without her because she had become the most important person in his sphere, and he decided to apply for permission to go abroad, telling Bakunin in a letter written on the 9th of January, 1845, that he needed to consult an occulist in Berlin as he was having trouble with his eyes. This was merely a pretext, the real reason being his need to be near Pauline Viardot, as he hinted when he told his friend that he had recently been living 'not in a fantasy as before, but in a more concrete way'.

A two month leave of absence was granted, but the fact that he resigned his post at the Ministry is significant, and proves that he intended to extend the period in order to travel further afield. Surprisingly out of character, his mother contributed funds for the journey.

Louis Viardot invited Tourgueniev to visit Courtavenel, and on April 30th, 1845, his mother wrote to a friend: "Ivan left here five days ago with some Italians: he plans to go abroad, with them or for them. I don't know". His initial visit to France was a brief one, but very successful. He loved the French countryside and the ease and freedom that the French appeared to enjoy. Everybody at the chateau considered him to be a charming and amusing guest, a brilliant conversationalist with a vivid imagination. He was given a bedroom situated between the grand salon and the billiard room, just off the main landing, and in the evenings after dinner, he read aloud and improvised tales. In June and July he spent some time in Paris, but returned to Courtavenel in the autumn for the shooting. He was warmly welcomed back and was soon regarded as one of the family. Joaquina took him to her heart and promised to teach him Spanish.

Finally, the Viardots prevailed on George Sand to visit them at Courtavenel, and she, Maurice and Solange stayed from the 7th to 9th of June. Her acceptance was on the strict understanding that Pauline would return with them to Nohant, which she did on the 12th of June. Presumably George spent a few days in Paris before leaving for her country home, and met Tourgueniev either at Courtavenel or at the Viardot's Paris salon on the 10th or 11th of June, as her name is noted in his memorandum.

Chopin, with his manservant Jan, conveyed George, her children and Pauline to Berry in a fashionable new caleche, which he had recently purchased. It was very cramped, but they arrived at the chateau safe and sound. Normally, George reckoned on being at her country home in the spring, but this year she had been very short of funds, in addition to which, a cholera epidemic had broken out in Berry, and it was thought wise to wait until it subsided. She had procured some money by writing a novelette, inspired by dear old Rossini, about a minstrel who brings joy and delight into the pedestrian life of an old Italian couple, and this enabled her to open up her house for the summer.

In addition to cholera, Berry suffered its worst storms and floods for several decades, and when Louis Viardot attempted to join Pauline, he had to turn back because the River Indre had broken its banks in many places, bridges had been swept away and there was widespread chaos. George's brother, Hippolyte was devastated when water swept through his chateau and gardens, but for Maurice, it was heaven sent as it meant that he could have Pauline to himself, as she had to stay on for another week. In all, she spent three weeks without Louis and had a wonderful time, resting, reading, playing and singing with Chopin, painting with Maurice, and generally enjoying herself in a place she dearly loved, where she was one of the family. Even Solange was slightly less objectionable.

Maurice painted a delightful picture of Pauline wearing a long pink dress, with low shoulder seams and a small white, pointed collar. Her expression is very thoughtful and she is holding a large straw sun hat decorated with ribbons. Today, this picture hangs in Ary Scheffer's house, which is now the 'Musee de la vie romantique', and includes a collection of Sand memorabilia.

During Pauline's stay at Nohant, the evenings were, naturally, taken up with music, charades, and billiards. George, however, was not her usual energetic self. Having turned night into day for so many years, she was now suffering from insomnia and was often subject to bouts of feverishness, but she endeavoured to keep this knowledge from the others, although she was also suffering badly with arthritis exacerbated by the wet weather. She was under a great deal of stress on several counts, but principally, through her growing awareness that Pierre Leroux was a liability, a charlatan and a sponger.

He had pocketed the 6,000 francs that was rightfully hers for a second edition of 'Consuelo' and 'La Comtesse de Rudolstadt', and had asked her to write a preface for a 'new' translation of 'Werther' by Goethe. This translation was really the work of a Frenchman who had died twelve years previously, and Leroux, who did not know German, had passed it off as his own. She put up with all this, even with his moving to the Auvergne, so that he could take over the printing of 'L'Eclaireur de l'Indre et du Cher', which up to that time had been published in Orleans, but it was his incessant demands for money that was really the last straw. In his defence, it must be said that he had nine children to support, as well as two indigent brothers and their mistresses!

George's novel, which had been refused publication by Louis Veron, was taken up by 'La Reforme'a new periodical that had been launched by Alexander Ledru-Rollin, Michel de Bourges, Etienne Arago, and a young social historian, Louis Blanc. The latter was seven years younger than George, and brought out her strong maternal instincts. He was a short man, slight and delicate looking, and she soon took to calling him her 'dear child' and 'my dear angel'. They probably became lovers at the beginning of 1845, but, of course, this was hidden from Chopin who remained ignorant of the true state of affairs. George admitted to Louis Blanc that she felt that she was fading fast, overworked and exhausted, but despite this, she said that she did not want to die for at least another ten years because she still had so much to achieve.

Her friendship with Blanc continued, despite the fact that its sexual aspect was short lived. Although George had a strong libido, at that time she was simply too drained of energy to indulge in amorous activity. She and Chopin had been sexually abstinent for some time because George said that she feared for his health, and didn't want to be responsible for over-taxing his physical strength. Chopin resented this enforcement, but it is quite likely that it was George herself who was too fatigued, although she made her lovers think that it was their welfare that concerned her most.

Chopin was miserable, the weather got him down, his piano was out of tune, and he lacked inspiration. Gustave Papet examined him and found nothing physically wrong, but he told George that Chopin was a hypochondriac who suffered through 'excessive sensibility'. If anyone could improve Chopin's moods it was Pauline, who was always able to lift his spirits just by her cheerful presence.

The pianist had admitted to his sister that the country bored him, and although he thrived on the fresh air, he longed to be in Paris again. George wrote to Marie de Rozieres: 'I would gladly sacrifice my love of being in the country for him, but Maurice disagrees, and if I took more notice of Chopin than of

Maurice, there would be an uproar. Even in the most close-knit families this kind of thing happens. We cannot have the same tastes and not everyone is happy at the same time."

To make matters worse, there was servant trouble with quarrels between Chopin's manservant, Jan, and George's cook, Suzanne, which led to Jan's dismissal when Maurice and Solange joined in the fray. George was also worried about Maurice and his continuing infatuation for Pauline, which showed no sign of abating. The writer had plans for him to marry, but, of course, he was not interested in any likely bride while still enchanted by Pauline.

The floods began to subside, and on July 4th, Pauline left Nohant, escorted part of the way by Maurice. He wanted to accompany her further, but she felt that it would be improper. She had been saddened to see how George and Chopin's relationship had deteriorated, and was aware of the friction in the air when Maurice and Solange were with them. Something was turning very sour at dear Nohant, and it distressed her greatly. The atmosphere had always been so warm and welcoming, and the house full of light and friendly warmth, but now a gloom hung over the chateau.

In Paris, she was met by a rather nervous Louis who, during her absence, had endured many sleepless nights, wondering about the true nature of her friendship with Maurice. He was no fool, and had been conscious for the last four years that George's son was in love with his wife. Although Pauline tried to hide her feelings from him, he was only too aware that she had become involved with a man half his age. When they married, Louis had taken it for granted that as he was so much older, she would sometimes be attracted to younger men, but he had determined not to allow jealousy or possessiveness to affect him. He loved Pauline so deeply that he was prepared to face unhappiness himself, rather than cause her to be unhappy.

On her return, Pauline wrote immediately to George to thank her for her hospitality, and told her that Maurice had been very 'nice'. She jocularly disguised her true feelings in the berrichon dialect, and soon after the receipt of this letter, George asked Maurice to go to Paris to deliver the first part of her new novel 'Le Peche de Monsieur Antoine' to the newspaper 'L'Epoque'. This was another communistic tract, and must have alarmed the editor of the ultra conservative newspaper, as he began to realise the full extent of the views propounded, as episode followed episode.

From Paris Maurice went to Courtavenel, where he spent three happy days with his 'beloved', walking, riding, painting and adoring her. Tourgueniev also visited the chateau during the summer, and together he and Pauline read George's 'Mauprat', a novel depicting ideal love, written in 1836. On the 27th of July,

Ivan left for Paris, from where, on the 29th, he set off on a tour of the South of France with Vasili Petrovich Botkin and another friend, travelling with them via Tours and Bordeaux to the Spanish border, where they split up, Tourgueniev spending time alone in the Pyrenees, supremely happy, thinking of Pauline and their readings of 'Mauprat'. Many years later, he admitted the deep and lasting impression this trip had made upon him.

After Maurice left Courtavenel, he stopped off in Paris, collected his third cousin, Augustine Brault, and took her back to Nohant with him. George had practically adopted this girl, and hoped that she would be a suitable wife for her son. She was a descendent of George's mother, and had been ill-treated by her own disreputable mother. Although she was poor, she was pretty and had a pleasant disposition, and George thought that in time Maurice might come to love her. It was not to be, and George was storing up trouble for herself in offering a home to Augustine, as it caused jealousy, rancour and bitterness. The girl, though not very talented, had a desire to sing, and Manuel Garcia gave her free musical instruction for a while. At first she and Solange were constant companions, but gradually the latter fell prey to the green-eyed monster once more, and did all she could to undermine Augustine, putting a wedge between her and Maurice.

Solange was now seventeen and a beauty, full-bosomed and nubile and George considered marrying her off to Louis Blanc. Chopin usually brought out the best in Solange and George was lulled into a false sense of security, believing that her daughter, who had been so difficult in her adolescence, was now, as she grew into womanhood, becoming calmer and more pleasant. This was not the case though, as there was always a nasty streak in Solange. Pauline told her friend Mme. Komarova: 'One day, the Sands came, at my invitation, to spend a little time with us on our estate in the Brie. Like any other lady of the manor I began to do them the honours of my domain, taking them around the yard to see the stables and the cattle-sheds, and giving them a tour of the garden; leading straight down from the house, there was a broad walk lined with lilies, irises, gladioli and narcissi. I went ahead with Mme Sand, and the young people followed after us. But all the time I was chatting with Mme Sand I could hear a swishing noise behind me. Turning round, I saw that as she walked along Solange was flicking at the heads of the flowers with her riding-whip, with the result that their stems were breaking and the heads snapping over. "My dear Solange," I said, "what on earth are you doing?" I was extremely annoyed with her; and what made me most indignant was the mean and nasty spitefulness of the girl, hateful because it seemed gratuitous, or rather purely sadistic in intent. And this was always the case; Solange did evil things for evil's sake, as if she were an artist creating art for the love of art....."

Professor Patrick Waddington makes an apology for Solange, stating that her jealousy of Pauline was provoked by the fact that in continually praising her young friend, George undermined her daughter's confidence, causing her to feel that her mother preferred the singer to herself. He says that the flowers at Courtavenel unconsciously reminded Solange of the regulated beauty of her rival's successful and harmonious existence. It was often Pauline's misfortune to invoke jealousy in people who envied her apparently charmed life.

All the family enjoyed the summer at Courtavenel, and Pauline found her country home a real blessing. Although she was light-hearted and sociable, she also had a deep need for solitude, and each morning she set off on her magnificent 'bleu' horse for a canter over her estate. In a letter to George Sand, which she wrote when Louis was away on business in Paris, she said: "I am alone with my Uncle, Mariquita and Louisette – you would not believe how happy I am in this solitude. I wish it could last for some time, not that my family inconvenience me, but it appears to me that I find myself and am better company to myself than when I am surrounded by people. Is this selfishness? No, it is too sweet a sensation to be wrongful. It is more a sense of clarity in the heart, and I feel more clearly, see more clearly and I breathe more clearly."

The Viardots treated their servants very well, and included them in many of the family activities. There was a housekeeper, a footman, a chambermaid and kitchen staff, and the valet de chambre who loved Moliere, Corneille and Racine, having memorised whole tracts by heart. Pauline had always wanted her own theatre, and she and Louis set one up in the largest section of the attic: it had a stage with curtains, and there were dressing rooms, as well as a prompt box, although it was expected that all the actors would know their roles by heart and make a prompter superfluous. It was called 'Le Theatre de Pommes de Terres' and the entrance fee was one potato. As well as friends and neighbours, the servants formed part of the audience, which sometimes included such luminaries as Eugene Vivier, Hector Berlioz, Henri Martin, Rose Cheri, and later, Camille Saint Saens. Works by Racine, Moliere and Beaumarchais were performed. Pauline always took part, but Louis did not consider himself an actor, and preferred to give moral support to the others from backstage, except, that is, in the case of Arnolphe in 'The Misanthrope' which, for some unknown reason he liked to play.

Tourgueniev loved acting and fooling about, as did Manuel Garcia, Louis Pomey, (who collaborated with Pauline on translations and texts for her songs), and Saint Saens. As they grew older, Louise, and Paulinette, (Tourgueniev's natural daughter), as well as several of Pauline's students joined the 'repertory company' and had great fun treading the boards.

Since their first meeting, Pauline had inspired Ivan, and he was now developing into an interesting, original writer. He had composed numerous poems, many of which had been published in 'Annals of the Fatherland', but when Alexander Herzen first met him, he had not been impressed, and considered him 'fatuous'. Yet the influential writer and critic, Belinsky saw something promising, and although Tourgueniev was perhaps a little too elegant, too immature and shallow, he divined that here was someone who would, perhaps, one day contribute to the glories of Russian literature. The young writer was deeply bound to his native land through upbringing and sentiment, but he was also inevitably drawn to the West, and did not see why he should choose one over the other, but rather intended to have a foot in both camps.

At first, he was influenced by the works of the Romantic poets with their emphasis on the natural world, as represented in the works of Goethe, Byron and Pushkin, but through Belinsky, he began to understand the need for social realism in literature. Russia was paralysed and terrorised by the regime of Nicolas I, and the critic taught his young followers that autocratic politics were an abomination, and that writers had a duty to represent life as they found it, in the hope of being able to improve conditions by making the landed gentry more aware of the evils around them. The Viardots were naturally interested in the ideas put forward by their young friend, especially as they had seen for themselves some of the dreadful conditions that prevailed in Russia.

On July 1st, 1845 Pauline received a letter from Giacomo Meyerbeer inviting her to take part in a grand Royal tournee in Germany, but he asked her not to tell anybody except Louis about his offer. The reason for this tour involved a ceremony for the unveiling of a monument to Beethoven in Bonn, and on the 14th Meyerbeer wrote to thank her for accepting, and asked her to be in Cologne by the 3rd of August at the latest.

For several years, Liszt had been the leading advocate for a Beethoven monument to be erected in the composer's birthplace, and had contributed large sums of his own money towards the fund that he had set up. Moreover, it was not simply financial aid that he gave, but his time, energy and enthusiasm. Now all was ready, and the great ceremony would be attended by the Queen of England, with her husband, Prince Albert; the King and Queen of the Belgians; the King and Queen of Prussia; their family and Court, and a vast crowd of dignitaries, musicians and artists from across Europe.

Queen Victoria set sail in the royal yacht on August 11th, 1845, crossing the Channel to Flushing on the first lap of her journey to Germany. On arrival in Belgium, she and Prince Albert were met by their Uncle Leopold, King of the Belgians, and his second wife, the former Princess Louise of Orleans, the daughter of King Louis Philippe, who had once been a pupil of Ary Scheffer. It was Victoria's first visit to the Continent, and everywhere crowds turned out in great profusion; she was beside herself with excitement, and was very moved that so many people had gathered to see her and the Prince. From Belgium, they travelled in King Leopold's private train, and entered Germany at Aachen where they stopped to see the famous chapel and relics of Charlemagne.

After this, they proceeded to Cologne, where they were met by King Frederick William IV of Prussia and several Prussian princes, to the sounds of the combined bands of the Fifteenth and Sixteenth Infantry Brigades. Choruses were sung; a quick march by Redern, the march from Mendelssohn's 'Midsummer Night's Dream' and another based on motifs from Meyerbeer's 'Feldlager in Schlesien' were played, then the royal party left immediately for Schloss Bruhl. By the time they arrived it was already 11pm, and as they had been up since 5.30 am, they were decidedly travel worn and tired. However, the festivities had only just begun.

The palace, a baroque masterpiece by the great architect, Balthasar Neumann, is situated half-way between Cologne and Bonn, and the energetic young Victoria, alert as ever, was entranced by the splendid yellow and grey building, lit with candles at all the windows, giving the impression of a giant birthday cake. The party had left the train at Bruhl, where a small railway station had recently been opened, and were met by carriages, which conveyed them into the huge palace courtyard, creating a deafening sound as the hooves of the horses beat a tatoo over the large cobbles.

On entering the palace, the Queen was stunned by the magnificence of the hall, comprising two storeys, with an enormous double staircase held up by massive caryatids The whole edifice was a concoction of riotous, yet tasteful decoration, with pale cream walls, panelled in faux green marble and cascades of putti and classical figures flying all over the walls. The exquisite oval ceiling was painted in sumptuous colours with gods and goddesses cavorting in a joyous pagan orgy . Victoria had never seen anything to match it and was amazed and delighted, although it made her own palaces fade into insignificance in comparison.

On meeting the Prussian King again, she wrote: 'he has grown fatter, but is as amusing as ever; his temper is violent, and he scolds his servants amazingly.' His consort, Queen Elizabeth, was now forty-four years old and had failed to produce an heir. Victoria observed: 'The Queen has no remains of good looks – her features were never regular – but she had beautiful eyes; her eyelids however are very red now, and she looks so haggard and suffering and pale. She is not very tall, and is lame, but she conceals it very gracefully ... she is very kind and natural but not very demonstrative, and she looks unhappy and suffering, but their Menage is as happy as possible'.

After a supper attended by royalty, ministers, ambassadors, and other dignitaries, a small concert was given under Meyerbeer's direction, in which Pauline and Jenny Lind sang.

The following day, August 12th, the Beethoven ceremony took place at Bonn in the middle of the market square. Much to the embarrassment of the organisers, when the statue of Germany's most famous composer was unveiled, the great man was found to have his back to the balcony where the royal guests were standing.

From Bonn the royals returned to Bruhl, and in the evening travelled by train to Cologne, where they boarded a boat and watched a firework display on the river. In her journal, the Queen observed: 'Anything more beautiful cannot be imagined ... blue and red lights – Rockets – salutes of every kind and sort. Houses, illuminated so as to appear red hot & finally the Cathedral glowing red – the most splendid thing possible, and all that reflected in that splendid river, the Rhine."

The next morning the royal party attended the first concert of the newly inaugurated Beethoven Festival , but Queen Victoria was disappointed because there was not enough of the composer's own music in the programme.

Pauline was pleased to see so many friends and colleagues again, especially Franz Liszt, who greeted her warmly. Despite his Festival responsibilities, he looked younger, more relaxed and cheerful than when she had last seen him, no doubt because he had finally separated from Marie d'Agoult and was enjoying his freedom.

He was not without female companionship, however, as he was still being pursued by the notorious Lola Montez, whom he had met in Dresden the previous year. Her uninhibited behaviour, about which he and Marie had laughed in their letters, was now becoming a nuisance, and he was trying to get rid of her, but she would not be put off and followed him around Germany. After the long and trying liaison with Marie, the last thing Liszt wanted was emotional involvement, preferring one night stands, usually with compliant married women; it was common knowledge that he never seduced young girls.

For years, Marie had been jealous of Liszt, suspecting him of infidelity when he was away from her. She was right, of course, and he had many minor affairs, although she was the titular mistress for eleven years. Other women in his life included the singer, Caroline Unger; Charlotte von Hagn; the insatiable Marie Pleyel, and Eva Hanska, Balzac's Polish mistress, who later became the writer's wife.

The King of Prussia had recently appointed Meyerbeer to the post of general music director in Berlin, and the responsibility for organising the music for the present royal tour fell to him. He had secured the services of the most eminent musicians in Europe, including Hector Berlioz, Felix Mendelssohn, the violinist, HenriVieuxtemps, who had been a pupil of Charles de Beriot, and Eugene Leon Vivier, the horn player, who kept everybody in fits of laughter with his practical jokes and hilarious stories. He was a phenomenally accomplished player and Meyerbeer wrote in his diary: ' he can play four notes at once, can produce a twenty-four-pedal note, possesses an unprecedented crescendo, and, moreover, has innate taste'. The singers taking part included Tichatschek, the tenor, who had created the role of Wagner's Rienzi in 1842, the basses Pischek and Staudigl, Mlle Tuzcek and Jenny Lind.

Of course, Pauline already knew Lind, but found her formal, cold and austere, with a strong Puritanical streak, and little sense of humour. Antipathy increased the rivalry between them and they never became real friends; however, Mendelssohn and Clara and Robert Schumann were devoted to Jenny, and seemed to bring out the best in her. She was a plain woman but when she sang, a transformation took place, and she produced a radiance that captured the hearts and minds of her listeners, and filled theatres to capacity. The German public was looking forward to a contest between these two young singers, who were reputed to be the most exciting of their generation.

After a 'family dinner' for twenty in the salon in Schloss Bruhl on the 13th, which included Pauline's admirers Crown Prince William and Princess Augusta of Prussia, a concert was given in the great 'Hall of Guards'. The programme was a full one: Jenny Lind sang an aria from Meyerbeer's opera 'The Camp in Silesia' in which she had recently enjoyed a stupendous success in Berlin; the duet from the third act of 'Les Huguenots', and the finale of Weber's

'Euryanthe'. Pauline sang an aria by de Beriot; the great scene from 'Orfeo' with choir, and an aria from 'Rinaldo' (Lascio ch'io pianga) by Handel, specially requested by the King of Prussia, who always asked Pauline to sing it for him. Meyerbeer acted as accompanist and Liszt played in his own inimitable style.

The next day the royal parties, together with the musicians, went by carriage to the banks of the Rhine from where a paddle-steamer took them along the most spectacular stretch of the river, passing the dramatic Drachenfels rock where the mythical figure of Siegfried slayed a dragon, bathed in its blood and became invincible. In her diary Victoria wrote: "At every turn of this most beautiful and unique river, the Rhine, you have another beautiful view – and so many villages with those curious wooden houses and little spiredchurches so indescribably picturesque – all the people out – and all the little schools drawn up – and the bells ringing – here and there a crucifix or a Madonna, in a vineyard and on the top of one of the mountains a cross."

Their destination was the medieval castle of Stolzenfels, which had been romanticised and gothicised in 1823 by Karl Friedrich Schinkel, a leading exponent of the Romantic style. Although Germany abounded in remarkable Baroque and Rococco structures, the fashion was now for everything Gothic, and even when inappropriate, attempts were made to impose the medieval style. Stolzenfels was originally built in the 13th century for the collection of tolls from the traffic, on the trading route below and hung on cliffs high above the Rhine with a magnificent, uninterrupted view of the majestic river and the numerous castles perched precariously on top of the steep cliffs that lined its banks. The schloss was burnt by the French in 1688, and used as a quarry by the local inhabitants, but had been restored by Frederick William when he was Crown Prince. Queen Victoria, (and Pauline) immediately fell in love with 'this bijou of a castle', and the Queen was so delighted with the place that she stayed an extra night there.

She and her ladies took tea with the Queen of Prussia in a pretty 'painted room', where below gothic archways there were scenes of idealised knightly chivalry. Victoria wrote that the repast was presented 'quite in the German way; we Princesses sat down to a table, where there was no cloth, and dicke Milch (soured milk) and excellent cakes and Kirschkuchen (cherry cakes) were served'. The Queen's ladies made the tea.

Close to the Painted Room stands the Great Hall, an enormous room with a splendid high-vaulted ceiling, formed over slender gothic pillars, which the Queen called 'the very pretty sort of Hall, ornamented with muskets, breastplates and crossbows'. Unfortunately, there were two inconvenient black pillars around which a specially constructed dining table stood, and it was not an ideal concert hall but here Pauline, Pischek, Meyerbeer and Jenny Lind performed for Frederick William and his guests.

On August 15th, a different concert was presented, but with the same artists as in Koblenz, and on the 16th, Jenny Lind sang Norma. The Parisian press was represented by Jules Janin, Louis Viardot and Eugene Guenot, who sent accounts of the festivities and concerts post haste to their editors in the French capital.

With the end of the festivities, Pauline and Louis returned to Courtavenel for a short rest, and were joined in the early part of September by Maurice Sand, who had delayed carrying his mother's manuscript to Paris until Pauline returned because he was banking on an invitation to spend a few days with her before she left for Berlin in the middle of September. The singer had written to George on the 26th of August assuring her that if Maurice wanted to come to Courtavenel he would be met 'with open arms'. She apologised for having no time to go into details of the German trip, but said that no doubt George had already read the review of the first concert at Schloss Bruhl in the 'RGM', which stated: 'a scene from 'Orfeo' and an aria from 'Rinaldo' by Handel were sung by Mme Viardot in an admirable manner, expansive and penetrating straight to the heart".

Tourgueniev returned to Courtavenel at the end of August, and Maurice arrived at the beginning of September. The writer appears to have liked the young artist, being unaware of anything clandestine in his friendship with Pauline. Maurice was rather subdued, and Pauline told George that he was quite unwell, and looked dreadful. George immediately ordered him home so that she could look after him. No doubt she had been uneasy about Maurice's continuing desire for Pauline, and was the last person in the world who wanted to see her son's illicit love causing disruption in the Viardot household. As far as George was aware, Tourgueniev was just a friend of the family.

In a letter written to Pauline in June, George had, to a certain extent, voiced her fears, perhaps in 'double entente': "Maurice is still good and well behaved. He did, however, have an impulse to enlist in the ranks at the time when we believed there would be a war, (perhaps a war Maurice was fighting within himself). I should not have stood in his way if there had indeed been war and duty; but I stopped him from doing this foolish thing in which there was no rhyme nor reason, and now that thoughts have turned to peace he thanks me for restraining his initial urge". George finished off by saying that Maurice sent 'greetings and fraternity' to Pauline, from the 'bottom of his heart'.

It is difficult to know just how deeply Pauline loved Maurice, although in the previous summer of 1844, she may have acquiesced in his youthful passion for her. It is certain that he always held a special place in her affections, and in letters, she addressed him as 'very dear friend,' or 'my good Maurice' and despatched 'fraternal kisses' or a 'most affectionate handshake'. What is patently clear is Pauline's infinite capacity for affection, and ability to love more than one man at a time. She was fortunate to be loved by men who saw her as a free spirit and did not expect to possess her exclusively.

In old age, Louise Viardot wrote her memoirs, and although they are not always reliable, because she gets events and experiences mixed up, they are useful for the picture she paints of life at Courtavenel. She says that Tourgueniev was always impeccably dressed and smelled delightfully of eau de Cologne, and admits that she was a terrific tomboy, who, as she grew older, delighted in pranks and practical jokes, in which she was aided and abetted by her mother, Tourgueniev often being the butt of their high spirits.

On one occasion, "he was awakened in the early morning by a concert of crowing cocks, cackling hens, and quacking ducks; greatly surprised to hear the sounds so close at hand, as the poultry-yard was down by the dairy farm, far away from the house, he finally discovered that the noise proceeded from a cupboard in his room. He took the birds in his arms and carried them back to their yard in a great rage, for it was only four o'clock in the morning". A couple of years later, the mischievous pair played the same trick on Eugene Vivier.

Meyerbeer called Louise 'Napoleon-Louise' because she was tough, uncompromising, climbed trees dressed in boys clothes, played with the hounds, rowed a boat across the moat, and shot hares with her father. Many years later, Saint Saens remarked that God had behaved very oddly in creating Louise a girl. In a letter dated 18th of June 1847, Louis Viardot told Meyerbeer that Louise delighted in the name he had given her, adding "she is pleased to send her Imperial regards to the princesses in your house".

Although we do not know what encouragement Pauline may or may not have given Tourgueniev during his visit, from his correspondence, it is clear that he was supremely happy at Courtavenel. He wrote hardly anything, but enjoyed the pastoral attractions around him, including shooting a plague of pigeons, authorised by the local mayor, before the official season opened. He was even asked to act as an official witness at a double baptism at the church of Vaudoy; Pauline was godmother to the girl, and Antonia to the boy.

When he looked out of the attic windows at Courtavenel, Tourgueniev probably thought of his own district of Oryol, where the surrounding trees are of wormwood and willow, and the gently rolling plain has woods, ponds, the occasional spire soaring above a village, expansive fields full of waving corn, barley, a little rye, a great deal of wheat, and several acres of oats, presenting a familiar, well-loved scene, reminiscent of his estate at Spasskoye.

In March, Pauline signed a contract for a third season at St. Petersburg, and in late September, she and Louis set off for Russia, taking the four-year-old Louisette with them. Tourgueniev followed on the 3rd of October. En route, the Viardots called on Chopin's family in Warsaw. Nicolas, Chopin's father, had died the previous year, but his widow and her family greeted the Viardots warmly, and made a great fuss over the little girl .

Chopin corresponded regularly with his mother and sisters and kept them up to date with Parisian gossip, and amused them and the Viardots with a story about the amorous activities of the writer Victor Hugo: "M. Billard, a historical painter (an ugly man), had a pretty wife, whom Victor Hugo seduced. M. Billard surprised his wife with the poet one day and it ended in a private separation; then Hugo took off on a trip of several months, and Mme Hugo gave protection to Mme Billard. In the meantime, Juliette Drouet (an actress who had been Hugo's mistress for several years), went with him'. What Chopin did not mention was the deepening rift between himself and George Sand. Pauline kept her own counsel, although even she was not yet fully aware of the seriousness of the situation.

After the heady, super-charged excitement of the previous season in St. Petersburg, everything seemed less colourful in comparison, despite Pauline's triumphant success as Norma and Amina. Not long after they arrived in Russia, the Viardots began to have health problems, starting with Louis, who contracted cholera, and was ill for several weeks. Even when the severity of the disease abated, he required time for recuperation. It was a harrowing time for · Pauline, but she continued to sing, although she restricted her performances to fewer than usual. She also noticed that the public was no longer so easy to please because there was now a plethora of opera, tastes were becoming jaded, and it was not so fashionable as in previous years. Her appearances were no longer fully subscribed because the directors had pushed up the price of tickets so greedily that fewer performances were sold out.

Even more worryingly, the critics began to notice faults in Pauline's voice and said that it showed signs of strain. This is not surprising in view of the stress caused by Louis's serious illness, the energy expended keeping Louise amused and occupied, and the need to fulfil her own commitments. Critics are rarely aware of such considerations, but stress has a deleterious effect upon the voice.

Fortunately for Pauline, her loyal public were still enthusiastic, and cheered her to the skies, especially when she sang Rosina, Norina and Amina. At her

Benefit on February 21st, she sang in 'La Sonnambula' for the first time that season, and as the opera was a great favourite, the theatre was soon sold out. A newspaper stated: "From the morning onwards one could guess what was going to happen in the theatre that evening. The price of flowers rose steeply from Friday evening to Saturday. Florists could not sleep for emotion, so much do they love music, particularly Madame Viardot-Garcia's benefices; in the morning the flower market opened and all the glass houses of the city and its suburbs were soon stripped".

In November, Ivan Tourgueniev arrived in St. Petersburg, full of joy at the prospect of seeing Pauline again, but he found her distracted with worry about Louis. The situation became even worse when Louise succumbed to a serious attack of whooping cough, then passed it on to her mother. It was impossible for Pauline to continue and she asked the Imperial authorities for permission to break her contract as she could not carry on, either vocally or physically. Being in such poor health, the Viardots couldn't wait to get back to France. The weather was appaling but they were determined to leave as soon as possible, and by the 24th of February were en route for France.

Tourgueniev was despondent because he could not accompany them, being very short of money. The French soprano, Jeanne Castellan very successfully took over Pauline's roles, but her fans and those of Pauline almost came to blows at a performance of 'La Sonnambula'. Nevertheless, her star was in the ascendant, and as far as audiences were concerned, the absent Pauline would soon become just a fond memory.

During the past few weeks, Pauline had seen Ivan frequently, and their friend-ship had become firmly established. While Louis was ill, he took on many of the everyday tasks with which his friend usually dealt, however, by the end of January Louis must have been feeling better because he wrote to Meyerbeer inviting him on behalf of the Grand Duchess Helena, the tsar's sister-in-law, to compose a Russian hymn in the hope that it would become the new national anthem. Meyerbeer accepted, but nothing more was heard of the matter.

On the 30th of March, 1846, Louis wrote from Paris to Ivan telling him that they had not been able to leave Berlin until March 24th, but had, thankfully, arrived home the previous evening at midnight. The return journey had been a nightmare due to shockingly severe weather, with gales, snow, blizzards and floods, impassable roads and damaged bridges, and by the time they reached Paris their carriage was a total wreck.

Although they looked forward to recuperating in the country, they did not go to Courtavenel immediately because the weather was bad. Louis said "The country air will finish off the cure, but we are not in a hurry to get to Courtavenel as we have been feeling the cold here for the past fortnight, and it has rained incessantly. The countryside (and especially the Brie) is still flooded, and it will be another fortnight yet before it is safe and agreeable to live in a house whose feet stand in water".

George Sand was in Paris, and Pauline visited her often, accompanied by Louisette. The women found the little girl very amusing, with her quaint ways and talk, and for a little while they forgot their problems. George was in the process of writing a new novel, 'Lucrezia Floriani', and in the first week of May, left Paris for Nohant in order to complete it in peaceful surroundings. Pauline was endeavouring to protect her health and build up her strength. She was usually as fit as a fiddle, and the severity of the bout of whooping cough had frightened her. Each day she exercised her horse, but was in bed by 8 or 9 pm. George was concerned about Louis because he looked so sad and his recuperation was taking longer than anticipated, although he acknowledged that he was lucky to be alive, having suffered a dangerous disease that was often fatal.

Manuel Garcia was also lucky to be alive after falling from a galloping horse and badly breaking his right arm while staying at Courtavenel in August. Pauline told George Sand: "He suffered horribly till the arrival of the doctor. Since his arm has been set, the pain has lessened somewhat, and he passed a relatively comfortable night, but will still suffer for a long time and will not be able to use his arm for a while. We have suffered with him and are more ill than he is, through emotion. How quickly a misfortune can occur. In the name of heaven – be careful, also Solange. Think of yourself and those you love. It is dreadful to see such suffering." Joaquina was very perturbed by this accident, which brought back all the trauma of Maria's death, and she implored Pauline to give up riding.

The accident was the result of 'sky-larking', to which Manuel was partial. He and Tourgueniev were like schoolboys when they were together, but naturally, the Russian was very concerned when he heard about his friend's severe accident. Since they had met the previous summer, he and Manuel had become the greatest of chums, egging each other on, indulging in fanatical games of chess, and horse-play.

The Viardots were very keen on seaside holidays, and during the summer spent a few days in Boulogne, their favourite resort, from where Pauline wrote to George giving her news of their activities and describing her recent meditations. She said that she had wasted time during the previous year, but had made up for her laziness during her holiday and would take the results of her musical labours back to Paris. She had spent some time alone sorting out her complex emotions, (regarding Maurice, Tourgueniev, or both?) and had re-dedicated herself to singing.

The diva possessed the ruthlessness of the dedicated artist, and although she experienced passionate moments in her life, she almost always sacrificed them to the demands of her vocation, her head ruling her heart. For her, music was a superior passion, a substitute for religion, or even love, as George had realized when she had written of Consuelo: "a divine fire rose to her cheeks, and the sacred flame burst forth from her great black eyes, when she filled the vaults with that unequalled voice of hers and those triumphant accents, pure and truly grand, which could not come from any but a great intelligence allied to a great heart."

A decade later, in a letter to Louis, dated 23rd of December, 1857, Pauline declared: "There is nothing more interesting, nothing more moving than to feel that you have an entire audience in the hollow of your hand, laughing when you laugh, weeping as you sob, and shaking with your anger. Believe me when I say that if one feels so happy at these moments, it is not simply that one's vanity is pleased, or that one experiences a sense of mastery over the audience, still less that one is simply in accord with them; no, it is rather that the power of creation, kinetic strength, is being openly revealed in the performer".

She had thought long and hard about whether to accept another season in St. Petersburg, and to Tourgueniev's disappointment she decided not to do so. Ivan told her that her audiences were missing her, and that rumours abounded about the fabulous sums of money the Tsar had promised her if she would return. He had written an anonymous article about music and musical taste in St. Petersburg, and of his dislike of the works of the fashionable composers, Verdi and Berlioz. Verdi's music, in particular, he considered unbelievably loud, and that of Berlioz heavy and discordant. Regarding the Russian audience, he said that when its curiosity was awakened, it would forget itself in fervent praise and furious discussion, but then sink back into its former blank indifference, or marvel at the Verdian vulgarities.

Pauline was realistic enough to know that the public fever had cooled, and it would be difficult to recapture the heady days of her amazing first season. Instead, she accepted Meyerbeer's offer to go to Berlin for the 1846/7 season. He continued to express his desire to collaborate with her, and as he was the most influential composer of the day, she hoped that he would open important doors for her, particularly those of the Paris Opera. In addition to St. Petersburg, she also turned down offers from Venice and Rome, as she said she would have been obliged to yawn through Verdian 'bellyaching' and to make a 'metier' of her art.

From Courtavenel she wrote to George reproaching her for her 'icy silence', which she found disturbing. She said that most of her family were in Paris, which left her time to read Voltaire, work at her songs, and 'make some awful translations of Dante and Byron'. At the same time, in Russia, Tourgueniev was translating Byron's poem, 'Darkness'). Pauline confided that she was having difficulty setting La Fontaine's 'Le Savetier et le financier', which tells of a cobbler who loses his natural enjoyment in life in the pursuit of money. Perhaps she was feeling guilty about her singing which for years had been her 'raison d'etre' but now success and property ownership made it more difficult for her to focus solely on her art for its own sake, and she cried: "Oh, give me back my songs, my sleep…Take back your hundred crowns". It is probable that she did not complete the song to her satisfaction, because it does not appear to have ever been published.

Louis was never truly happy away from his wife, but Pauline seemed little affected by his absence. She and Tourgueniev corresponded frequently now, whereas when they had first met, she had merely added footnotes to her husband's letters. The Russian implored her to give him every little detail of her life at Courtavenel so that he could re-live his time there. He asked if the new conservatory was finished and if she had written any more songs.

Strangely, although Pauline was alone at Courtavenel, Maurice Sand did not take the opportunity to visit her. Maybe he was not invited, was no longer infatuated, or was not allowed to go there, as his mother was very concerned about Louis, who still did not look well and was rather withdrawn, causing George to wonder at the true state of the Viardot marriage.

Pauline often questioned why men found her attractive; she had no illusions about her looks, as she knew she was considered ugly and said: "Perhaps the good Lord knew what he was doing when he made me ugly, for I am sure that I would otherwise have spent half my life admiring myself in the mirror. There's absolutely no danger of my doing that now!" However, as Patrick Waddington observes: 'certain kinds of 'ugliness' will fascinate where conventional beauty satiates and palls. The very irregularity of her features made her colouring more noticeable, her expressive eyes, her bewitching smile, all contributing to her appealing presence.'

As Pauline was the inspiration for the heroine of 'Consuelo', George Sand purposely portrayed her as ugly, telling her readers "the girl knew that she was ugly and that was her strength because her unusual, exotic looks drew attention, slowly revealing her elusive beauty – the lovely hair, well proportioned

bust and shoulders, and her charming hands and feet. When she laughed, she
warmed the heart; and when she sang, she seemed quite beautiful."
The advice the author gave to Anzoleto could equally have applied to
Tourgueniev: "She is ugly, I agree; but I also know that ugly women who please
men, ignite more furious passions and more violent infatuation in men than
earth's most perfect beauties. You cannot see that she is idolised, and that
wherever you may be present at her side you will be effaced, and pass unnoticed... When people see you they will ask: who is that handsome young man
standing behind her? He is nothing, will come the reply, nothing whatsoever:
he is the husband, or the lover, of the divine singer'.
On the 17th of September, 1846, the Viardots left for Berlin, arriving on the
23rd. The following day Pauline had lunch with Meyerbeer's mother, and Alexander von Humboldt, the eminent German scientist and diplomat, who had
explored the Orinoco and Amazon regions of South America, then spent the
next twenty-one years writing about his journeys, although the book for which
he is most famous is 'Cosmos', a treatise on the physical sciences.
Pauline made her debut at the Konigstadt Theatre as Amina in 'La Sonnambula',
on Monday, October 5th, and Meyerbeer said that she sang outstandingly and
created an extraordinaryfurore. With the memory of her Russian audiences,
Pauline considered those of Berlin very restrained, and told George Sand: 'when
they applaud, they do it in spite of themselves, and are embarrassed a moment
later. They say that I make them delirious, but when I hear that, it makes me want
to laugh in their faces. Yet they call me back many times during a performance,
and I read in the newspapers about my 'triumphs'. If it weren't for that, I should
not even suspect it. Of course, I am spoilt by the remembrance of the frenzy of
St. Petersburg..." What she found most difficult to cope with was that 'these
worthy Germans have such a ridiculous attachment to the importance of conventions." Despite her need for an orderly life, she was a free spirit and was
never bound to the status quo.
On October 11th, Chopin told his family that Pauline was in Berlin with her
husband and her mother, but he hoped to see her in Paris in November before
she returned to the Prussian capital for the rest of the season. From her return
from St. Petersburg in March 1846 until May 1848, the bulk of her performances
were almost exclusively on German soil.
The famous soprano, Henrietta Sontag, who had once been Malibran's rival,
was now married to Count di Rossi, an Italian nobleman and diplomat, and
resided in Berlin. With her new status, she had been commanded to give up the
stage by the King of Italy, although she sometimes sang in private concerts. In
his diary entry for the 9th of October, Meyerbeer writes that he took his noc-

turne, 'Mere-grand' to the Countess, and on the 13th, she and Viardot sang it together at the Italian embassy. The composer accompanied the whole concert and the Grand Duchess of Mecklenburg and members of the royal family were present.

On October the 19th, the King suddenly ordered a Court Concert at the summer palace of Sans Souci in Potsdam, a few miles from Berlin, and Meyerbeer engaged Pauline, Mme Tuczek and Herr Krause to take part. Pauline was utterly delighted by this jewel of a palace, built by Frederick the Great in 1745, during the Silesian War, as a place of relaxation where he could be 'without care'. It is a delicious edifice standing upon six vineyard terraces on the south side of a knoll in the woods above Potsdam, and has light, airy rooms splendidly decorated in shades of deep rose, yellow, and vermilion green, ornamented with masses of gilded carving, and attractive paintings. There is a small dome in the centre of the single-storied building, flanked by a curving Corinthian colonnade along the entrance front.

The concert hall, which is reached through an atrractive circular library, is elaborately decorated with gilding and has a ceiling adorned with a giant spider's web and golden hounds. The walls are of mirrored glass festooned with heavy gilded garlands, a regal setting for a court concert, where Mlle Tuczek and Pauline sang Meyerbeer's duet 'Mere-grand'.

Strangely, when Queen Victoria visited in 1858, she was not impressed by this gem of a palace, as she considered its rococco extravagance old-fashioned. She favoured the highly romanticised neo-Gothic style, but conceded that the circular marble hall at the centre of the structure was well lit by the central dome and windows, although she declared that otherwise, the place was 'very low, dark, damp and cheerless'.

Pauline, on the contrary, found everything at Sans Souci pleasing, and was interested in the fact that Voltaire, the famous French philosopher, whose works meant a good deal to her, had lived here for three years as an honoured guest of Frederick the Great, until they fell out. The philosopher had twice been imprisoned in France for his liberal views, and after leaving Sans Souci took refuge in Geneva.

On October 19th, Pauline wrote to George Sand to say how relieved she was to receive her long overdue letter, for which she had 'cried with joy'. She began to understand why George had not written, and said that she too had been inundated with work, which left her little time and energy for correspondence. It would not be until some time later, though, that Pauline would fully appreciate the trauma George was living through at that time. She wrote again onOctober 28th, asking why George hadn't replied to her last letter and said that she could not bear to think that her friend had forgotten her. She longed to have news of them all, and told George that Louisette was charming, and often spoke of 'Bouli' (Maurice).

She sang Norma for the first time in Berlin on November 2nd, and Tourgueniev, who had returned to Russia from Courtavenel, told her: "I was so pleased and happy to read of your triumph as Norma". He assured her that he was working hard and had signed a contract with the 'Contemporary', a review in which he was to become a regular contributor, penning short stories and articles, writing poetry and translating for his own enjoyment.

Pauline was tremendously occupied with rehearsals, concerts and operatic performances, and on November 18th she sang Norina in Donizetti's 'Don Pasquale'. Meyerbeer had been occupied all day with court business and an evening rehearsal, but arrived at the Konigstadt Theatre in time to see the third act.

The following morning, there was a rehearsal, that lasted until 3 pm, for the Court Concert at Schloss Charlottenburg that evening, to celebrate the Queen's name day. The schloss, on the outskirts of Berlin, was a summer residence of the Prussian royal family, a grand and elegant eighteenth century edifice, with an enormously tall dome. In Pauline's day it was in the country outside Berlin, but is now a suburb of the city. It stands in an extensive cobbled courtyard, in the centre of which is a large equestrian statue of the Great Elector by Andreas Schluter. In the grounds are other buildings, including the small, intimate Italian styled 'New Pavilion', and the large theatre block, built by Frederick William II, who loved and supported the theatre, and made Charlottenburg a cultural centre, in which the plays of Goethe and Lessing were staged. From 1795 onwards, the entertainments given there became accessible to all citizens.

The Court Concert was a splendid affair, attended by all the royal family and court dignitaries. Pauline sang the romance with obligato flute and harp from Morlacchi's 'Tebaldo e Isolina', the grand scena from 'Orfeo' with the Domchor. The evening ended with a brilliant display of horn playing by Vivier in a solo called 'Le Chasse', and an exotic selection of Spanish folk songs sung by Pauline and Antonia di Mendi.

When George finally replied, Pauline was relieved and assured her that she would always be devoted to their friendship, but said that a passage in George's letter could not pass without comment. It obviously concerned Chopin and the fact that the writer believed that he had sided with Solange, aiding and abetting her, opposing and denigrating George. Another complication was the involvement of the meddling Marie de Rozieres, by whom Solange was very much influenced.

George was quite paranoid and doubted all those around her, even such devoted friends as Pauline, imagining that everybody was 'ganging up' against her. Pauline risked her friend's wrath and told her that what she was saying about Chopin was untrue, that he had never said anything disloyal about her and that 'this dear and excellent friend' had only one concern, which was about the harm this business was doing to George herself. She added that she had not found the least change in Chopin's attitude towards his mistress – 'he is always good, always devoted and adores you as much as ever', and exclaimed: ' In the name of heaven, dear Mignounne, don't listen to officious friends who spread idle, malicious gossip, however close they may be to you.'

Years later, Pauline told Julius Rietz: "it is not true that the relationship between Chopin and George Sand was broken off suddenly, it decayed over a period. In my opinion 'Lucrezia Floriani' is a psychological and literary masterpiece, but is very cruel, and little by little, almost invisibly, brought about the end of the liaison, tormenting Chopin and subjecting Madame Sand to a slow death. It is a sad story. I think that in all those love-affairs there was no 'friendship' – that is a passion which cannot diminish, because it is the most beautiful of all".

Pauline's letter to George was interrupted, and it took several days for her to finish it, as the pressure of work was heavy. In addition to her engagements in Berlin, she had sung twice in Dresden, and was due to give four more performances, all in German, then she would go to Hamburg for six performances.

A drawing by Maurice Sand of Chopin giving Pauline a piano lesson at
Nohant in 1841

A sketch of Pauline at the age of 14 by Maria Malibran

William Hay on horseback outside Duns Castle

Crown Prince William and Princess Augusta of Prussia

Above left: A portrait of Gounod in middle age
Above right: A silver point drawing of Chopin by Winterhalter

Below left: Clara Wieck in 1838, the year she and Pauline first met
Below right: The French poet, critic and writer, Alfred de Musset

CHAPTER SEVENTEEN

1847/8

During the winter of 1847, Pauline sang at two theatres, The Konigstadt, where Italian opera was presented, and the Grand Royal German Theatre where works were performed in the vernacular. At the Konigstadt she appeared in 'La Sonnambula', 'Norma', 'Don Giovanni', 'L'Elisir d'Amore' and 'Otello', although she only gave a few performances of each role, and to less acclaim than those she sang at the Grand Theatre, alongside the veteran tenor, Tichatschek, who, through the subtlety of his art was able to disguise the passage of the years. The Berlin critics assured Pauline that her voice was more sonorous and fresh than ever, which must have been very reassuring after the comments of some of the Russian critics who said that her voice showed signs of strain. The operas she sang at the German Theatre, including three by Meyerbeer, suited her well, and allowed her to use all the fire and dramatic power which, as she matured, placed her beyond the range of the average opera singer.

Tourgueniev left Russia to join the Viardots in Berlin onJanuary 12th, enjoying the company of a pretty fellow traveller from Memel en route. This lady wrote under the pseudonym of Marko Vovchok, and she and Tourgueniev, were mutually attracted. Although they did not have the opportunity to meet very often, they correspondence regularly for several years. Women were charmed by Ivan, but he was too modest to believe that anyone could actually fall in love with him. Possibly, his peculiar mother had so deprived him of love when he was a young child, criticizing and making fun of him, that it undermined his confidence and caused him to believe that he was unlovable.

On January 22nd, Pauline wrote to George Sand telling her how hard she was working, singing 'Il Barbiere' and 'Otello' in German, 'with great success in this cold country'. The following day, she was to sing Valentine in 'Les Huguenots' in German for the first time, and said that her friend would not believe the work she was obliged to carry out on each role, because the language contained 'the cruellest, most difficult words, which distort the mouth'. To make matters worse, having worked on one translation, the text was then changed, and she had to forget what she had learned and start all over again. But her hard work paid off, and Tourgueniev said: You pronounce German well, but with a little too much exaggeration of accentuation. However, I am sure that with your usual application, you have already eliminated these light faults'.

Pauline was still unaware of what was really happening in George Sand's family, and of the gossip and rumours circulating around Paris, caused by Solange's erratic behaviour. The nubile girl had become engaged to the young Viscount Fernand de Preaulx, whom George had chosen for her, and mother and daughter set out for Paris to make arrangements for the wedding. However, nothing concerning Solange ever went smoothly, and just when George thought that her daughter's future was to be secured by marriage with a man of excellent family, the headstrong girl met the sculptor, Jean-Baptiste Clesinger in Paris. The previous year, he had written to George for permission to engrave on eternal marble the touching title of Consuelo'. Sand agreed, and when she and Solange arrived in the capital, he went out of his way to obtain an introduction to the writer.

On February 17th, Chopin and Franchomme, the cellist, played the Sonata in G minor for the first time to George and their friends, and the following day she and Solange went to Clesinger's studio to sit for him. He sculpted Solange, as a huntress with bare shoulders and hair flying in the wind; thrilled by his romantic depiction, she was soon madly in love with him, jilted de Preaulx and insisted on marrying Clesinger immediately, her excuse being that her former fiancé was plaster' and she preferred marble'.

Chopin wrote to his family: When they all arrived in Paris to sign the contract, she no longer wished to do so. I feel sorry for the young man who is very honest and very much in love'. George told Poncy, I believe that pride did not play a part in his life so much as tenderness and devotion. In six weeks, she broke off an engagement with a man whom she tried to love but could not, then accepted one to whom she submitted ardently. She married him and in place of a modest and sweet union, she submitted to one that is brilliant but fiery.'

It was the circumstances surrounding this marriage that effectively put an end to George and Chopin's relationship, causing them both a great deal of suffering and trying George's patience and finances for the rest of her life. Pauline was still unaware of the full facts when she wrote to George on the 27th of February: "I felicitate Solange for choosing the handsome devil you describe so well; the angel would soon have bored you to tears, Solange especially. It is all for the best, if one may say so."

It was certainly not for the best, and George felt that all the troubles of a lifetime had been stored up for her during 1847. Her unstable son-in-law was beset by debts and difficulties in Paris and within a few weeks of the wedding the couple dumped themselves on her at Nohant. Clesinger, a rough and brutal man, resented Augustine's presence in the house because George provided for her financially, and was very fond of her. He was jealous, because to him, she was receiving bounty that he believed rightfully belonged to his wife and himself. Augustine was engaged to the painter of the Barbizon School, Henri Rousseau, who was always known as Le Douanier' because he worked as a customs official, and George had agreed to supply the dowry.

Clesinger tackled her directly on this subject and demanded to know how much she was planning to give Augustine; George told him to mind his own business, he lost his temper and struck her, just as Maurice arrived unexpectedly. He intervened on his mother and cousin's behalf, a fight ensued, and George booted Clesinger out of Nohant immediately and unceremoniously. Solange took her husband's part, and the two of them retreated in a vindictive frame of mind, leaving George deeply distressed by the whole affair. She poured out her troubles in poignant letters to Delacroix and Dupont.

Immediately, Solange set about making trouble for Augustine, spreading false and malicious rumours that she and Maurice were having an affair. She was so successful in her evil scandal mongering that when Rousseau heard the gossip, he broke off his engagement at once.

England still beckoned Pauline, though she resisted the call for some time. With the advent of the new Italian Opera Company at Covent Garden in 1847, the London opera scene was changing, and the general view was that Mme Viardot would be a great acquisition. In September, a letter from her appeared in Le Siecle' refuting the rumour that she had refused work at the Academie Royale de Musique (the Opera) because the fee was not sufficient. She denied having been offered any such engagement, and added .... Allow me sir, this opportunity of contradicting a rumour that has appeared in the London and Paris journals, viz. I have signed an engagement for the ensuing winter with the management of the English Opera, Drury Lane, London. This report is equally without foundation."

The report stated: M. Jullien (a well-known impresario, conductor and composer of popular music), applied to the artiste we believe; that the artiste has refused M. Jullien's overtures it now appears, but wherefore, who can define? Perhaps we could, but we must not just now. It is for this, we presume that M. Jullien has journeyed to Milan to engage Miss Catherine Hayes (a pupil of Manuel Garcia) in Mme Viardot's place – if she can occupy Pauline Garcia's place, she must be an artiste indeed'.

Louis Jullien was a prominent figure in London musical life and Pauline did eventually sing for him. Although his tastes leaned towards the popular and sometimes downright vulgar, he was energetic in promoting music in England, and planned to stage Berlioz's 'The Damnation of Faust', in the 1848/9 season but before he could do so, he was declared bankrupt. Through him, cheap promenade concerts had become popular, and his famous quadrilles were played between serious items. His first piece in the genre was based on themes from 'Les Huguenots', which did not win Meyerbeer's approval. Jullien's musical taste was extremely suspect, for instance, when he added parts for four ophicleides and a saxophone in Beethoven's Fifth Symphony. However, he always engaged first-rate soloists, and Berlioz, especially, had cause to be grateful to Jullien who introduced his music to English audiences.

Like Meyerbeer, he was a great self-publicist, although somewhat more eccentric. In Edinburgh, on one occasion, he told the press that he had a machine in the orchestra with such a powerful sound that it would bring down the walls of the hall. Consequently, the box office was besieged, and the resulting queue went several times around the building. He was nothing if not astute and knew that above all, the general public loves novelty.

'Punch' satirised him as: "The Monsieur, with coat thrown widely open, white waistcoat, elaborately embroidered shirt-front, wrist bands of extravagant length turned back over his cuffs, a wealth of black hair, and a black moustache – itself a startling novelty – wielded his baton, encouraged his forces, repressed the turbulence of his audience with indescribable gravity and magnificence, went through all the pantomime of the British Army or Navy Quadrille, seized a violin or piccolo at the moment of climax, and at last sank exhausted into his gorgeous velvet chair.'

This was the kind of thing the public liked and was one of the reasons why Pauline denigrated the musical taste of the English so much. It must have been galling for serious artists such as herself and Berlioz, who considered music to be the highest form of art, to tolerate such goings on.

Pauline had her German engagements to fulfil, and was not free to sing in England until the Berlin season was over. Louis and Louise were with her, and her itinerary included Dresden and Hamburg. In Berlin, she disappointed Clara Schumann because she turned down the opportunity to sing in Robert's opera 'Das Paradies und die Peri,' as she had no time to learn a new role, although she offered to take part in a concert of his songs. Schumann's opera had received its first performance in December 1843 in Leipzig and had been enthusiastically received and favourably reviewed. It was set to a libretto adapted from Moore's 'Lalla Rookh'. Schumann conducted two performances in Leipzig, and at the Opera House in Dresden, where he and Clara were now living on the 23rd of December.

Jenny Lind, who since 1846 had been a great friend of the Schumanns, heard that they had been slighted in Vienna , and their livelihood endangered. She travelled immediately to the Austrian capital, and gave a benefit concert for them, which changed public taste and improved their fortunes. She also proved very valuable to them in the production of Robert's opera in Berlin.

Clara disapproved of Pauline singing so much French and Italian music, and told her so. Both she and Robert were dismayed by her association with Meyerbeer, who was absolute anathema to them. Liszt, another of Pauline's champions, was also becoming one of Clara's 'bete noir', despite the fact that she had initially admired his playing and compositions. Disgruntled, she complained that Pauline was not capable of understanding Schumann's 'tender, German music'.

It was now a decade since the two women had become friends, and they had long used the informal 'tu' and 'du' to each other, but in January 1848, the even tenor of their relationship was threatened by the frankness of their letters. Pauline wrote: 'My good Clara, I hope that you are all better than when we last met in Dresden. Think of your own health, dear little Clara, because the complete happiness and livelihood of your family depends on it. These days, one gains little financial reward from composition, except for musical works for the stage. Even the greatest talents die of hunger if they have insufficient recompense for their labour. Literature is almost as bad, because serious works don't pay; only that which is frivolous and amusing finds favour with editors. I don't know why I am saying this, because you know it better than I do, certainly Robert does. But he does not fully appreciate a woman's position, and the enormous responsibility you bear, looking after your home, and taking on far more than is good for you. He worries about your health, and fears for the future, but cannot see that he adds to your burdens. Even if you are cross with me, I feel that I would not be your friend, if I did not tell you this. You will never be able to get enough rest, because your husband does not do enough to spare your efforts.' She ends the letter by asking Clara to write soon, and let her know that she is well. She sends her best wishes to Robert, and asks Clara to give a thousand kisses to the pretty children, signing herself 'faithful Pauline'.

During her sixteen years of marriage, Clara was to bear eight children and suffer two miscarriages, and the letter obviously touched a raw nerve, because she reacted with indignation, telling Pauline that although she was welcome to criticize her, Robert was 'out of bounds' and she would not hear a word against him. She wrote in French: "I know that you love me and wish me well, but you criticize my husband, and that is the easiest way to wound me. You do not know him at all, either as man, or artist, so do not attack him, unless you wish to upset me. See, dear Pauline, I intend to speak frankly to you because the depth of our friendship gives that freedom. You have the blood of a Spaniard, and love men full of fire and brilliance, and the same applies to music. I have Teutonic blood, and Robert is a true German, a profound artist, who carries his universe within himself. How can you understand and value such a man, when you have declared that Meyerbeer is the premier composer of our time? How can you appreciate my husband's music when our tastes are so far apart? It is not possible, and I know very well, that you do not even appreciate the music of Mendelssohn as it deserves, and it pains me to admit that our musical ideas are not in harmony. You value the outer covering of virtuosity, I the artistic creator. I can see that in your position, it is natural to do so, to receive the approbation of the crowd, but sometimes it appears exaggerated, because to me, the most important thing is inner satisfaction. As you misunderstand my husband, so you misunderstand the Germans".

This illustrates the stereotypical aspect of nineteenth century life, when it was taken for granted that woman was subservient to man, and the different cultures in which Pauline and Clara grew up. Here were friends, who represented two distinct realms of music, Italian and French opera on one side, and purely instrumental music on the other. Clara's attitude to her private life also shows why Pauline and George Sand were usually considered alien to their sex, early feminists, one might say, who would never have allowed themselves to become the slave of any man, however much they cared for him.

The attitude to child bearing is also highlighted: Pauline was well aware that constant pregnancies and the responsibility of caring for a brood of children was not conducive to an artistic career, and although she had her first child in 1841 just over a year after her marriage, it was not until eleven years later, when she had made her international reputation, that she had another baby. George Sand had realised from the beginning of her friendship with Pauline that her head would always rule her heart where her work was concerned, but Clara saw herself primarily as Robert's wife and the mother of his children, and despite the demands of her career, she always put them first. Her husband had a strong libido, as his intimate, sexual diary records, and she felt it her duty to respond to his needs, regardless of any suffering it caused her.

Despite this hiccup in their friendship, Pauline was not one to bear a grudge, and her next letter was as friendly and chatty as ever, telling Clara how busy she was and explaining the amount of detailed work involved in creating a believable, fully rounded operatic character on-stage. She then went on to explain that she venerated the creative artist just as much as the interpreter, because to her they were inseparable; each on their own remained dumb, but together they elevated man's most noble pleasure into art.

Another of Pauline's friends whom she usually visited when she was in Berlin was Amalia Wichmann, the wife of the sculptor, Hermann Wichmann, who was a great friend of Meyerbeer. Amalia was also very fond of Jenny Lind, with whom she corresonded for over thirty years, and despite Pauline's lack of affinity with the Swede, and her reservations about her 'peculiar temperament', Lind was truly loved by the Mendelssohns, the Schumanns and the Wichmanns. From one of Jenny's letters to Amalia, written from Sweden in December 1847, it would appear that Pauline may have felt herself slighted by something Jenny had said, because Lind asks her friend to: 'Give my warm greetings to Viardot. Tell her that I have never doubted that she is a splendid and magnificent woman, and that it never occurred to me to compare her with the vast majority of ordinary artists, that is, with most of the women singers of today. I am delighted that we shall see each other in London".

At the beginning of February, Meyerbeer was still in Vienna for the production of his 'Feldlager' with Jenny Lind as Vielka. His diary entry for the 3rd of February states that he had received news from Berlin of the performance of 'Les Huguenots' in which Pauline sang Valentine for the first time in German. She had a huge ovation and was called out five times. However, the raised prices had angered the public, and they stayed away from Viardot's and the dancer Cerrito's performances in protest. Nevertheless, when the second performance was announced, all seats were sold

The 'Journal francais de Berlin' stated: 'The great singer has again surpassed herself. How can one describe this admirable musical feeling, this sweet poignancy, these cries of love and desperation so real, so pathetic, and so harrowing? And particularly, the grace, the nobility and dignity which she brings to the beautiful and difficult role of Valentine. She is far superior to Mlle Jenny Lind, who, as a dramatic actress, has always left a lot to be desired'. Pauline would have been less than human not to have appreciated that remark, but it would not have helped her relationship with Jenny.

She was now beginning to perform more dramatic roles, and when little Louise was taken to the opera, she had to watch her mother meeting such horrible deaths as that of Rachel, who is boiled alive at the end of 'La Juive'. The little girl would cry aloud with terror, and it is likely that psychological damage was caused to the delicate psyche of the small, impressionable child, as she saw her mother suffering on-stage, and it probably caused her nightmares.

Meyerbeer prized Pauline's work, not only because she was a consummate singer, but because she was a highly gifted actress. Like him, she was an indefatigable worker and she never stopped learning. Now, more than ever, he was determined to create a role that would display her manifold talents.

The celebrated composer, Adolph Adam was another of Pauline's admirers, and in a letter from Berlin, dated March 26th, he wrote: "To hear her, especially in 'Robert' or 'Huguenots' one would believe that the music of Meyerbeer had never until now been understood in Berlin. The trio from 'Robert' sung by Mlle Viardot, Tichatschek and Dollcher, drew transports of enthusiasm and I cannot recall having heard singing, even in Paris, of such verve, such expressive colours, and such ensemble, which made it seem almost new to us".

Rellstab added his voice to the general appreciation, when on the 30th March, he wrote in the 'Gazette Musicale': "At the second performance of 'Robert le Diable', Mme Viardot obtained a triumph most rare in the annals of the theatre; she sang, at the same time, two principal roles in the opera, Alice and Isabella, not merely to shine, but because of the indisposition of Mlle Tuczek who could not be replaced by anyone else at such short notice, but in two days, and despite being in a language not her own, Mme Viardot, took on this task. As Isabella she was perfect, as was her conception of Alice. How is it possible for an artiste to switch from two such different characters, one dramatic, the other gentle, as in the aria 'Grace'! From the tender surprise of love, to the first impressions of fear, the artiste rose to the most complete expression of terror and put into her singing all the stages of emotion leading to fright".

In April, when Pauline sang Donna Anna in 'Don Giovanni', Meyerbeer suspected that she was unwell because he found her performance less than satisfying, but by the 13th she had recovered sufficiently to sing Rachel in 'La Juive', however, Meyerbeer was only able to hear the second act, as he had to attend a ball given by the Prince of Prussia for 'at least fifteen hundred people'. On the 20th he saw a complete performance of the work, with Pauline and Herr Kraus as Eleazar. The composer of the opera, Jacques Halevy, was so thrilled with Pauline's performance in the Berlin production that he wrote her a flattering letter, which was printed in all the German newspapers.

Her next role was as Iphigenie in Gluck's 'Iphigenie in Tauris' in a matinee musicale at the home of Countess Rossi, (Henriette Sontag), attended by Meyerbeer. A further performance was given the following day, but at that time all the talk was of the riots that had broken out in Berlin due to the scarcity of food, and a day or so later, there was rioting in Stettin for the same reason.

On the 24th, Pauline sang at a concert given by Karl Eckert, and Meyerbeer was in the audience once more. Excerpts from Eckert's opera 'Wilhelm von Oranien', which had already been produced in Berlin, were presented, and Pauline sang the aria from Handel's 'Rinaldo' that Meyerbeer had orchestrated specially for her.

The Princess of Prussia asked Meyerbeer to prepare a Court Concert for the following Monday and requested that Pauline be one of the soloists. On the morning of the day, he rehearsed the singers, chorus and orchestra in the Opera House, then they all travelled to the Neue Palais, the Princess' Postsdam residence. This is an enormous, square palace of red brick and grey stonework with a huge bronze dome. It is the largest building of all the palaces in the extensive grounds of Sans souci, and far from cosy. There are three hundred and twenty two windows, set within stone pilasters, and four hundred and twenty eight statues lined along the edge of the parapet, but it was an ideal place for formal entertaining, as the rooms are so vast, and the Prince and Princess were easily able to receive a thousand guests.

Pauline sang the letter duet from the 'Marriage of Figaro' with Mlle Tuczek, the 'Inflammatus' from Rossini's 'Stabat Mater', the 'Rinaldo' aria and the act 1 finale from Weber's 'Euryanthe'. As may be imagined, Meyerbeer who was responsible for the proceedings, was vastly relieved that everything passed off with great precision.

The following evening, Pauline sang Iphigenie again, after which there was a great soiree at the house of Minister von Savigny. Two days later, Meyerbeer paid her a social call, to discuss his romance, 'Parmi mes pleurs mon reve se ranime', as she wanted to sing it in the fourth act of 'Les Hugenots' at her benefit. They rehearsed on the 3rd, and also worked on the fourth act of 'Robert' because she intended to sing it with Herr Kraus on the same occasion.

This charitable affair took place on May 4th, and although Meyerbeer was suffering from a stomach chill and a bad headache, he went to hear her. She sang acts three and four of 'Les Huguenots', including the romance, which had never been heard in Berlin before, the role of Isabella in act four of 'Robert', and brought the house down with the final scene of 'La Sonnambula'. The King and Queen stayed until the end of the 'Robert' extract, and Pauline was warmly applauded all evening, receiving several bouquets.

A further Court Concert was announced, and Meyerbeer held the rehearsal at Pauline's rented house on the morning of May 8th. In the evening at Potsdam, she performed a duet from 'I Marinari' by Rossini with Herr Ronzi, an aria from Handel's 'Susanna', and the finale from 'La Sonnambula'. The two young Neruda sisters, who came from a famous family of violinists going back to 1732, performed a duo for piano and violin by Jansa, seven-year-old Wilma's violin teacher. The child had played the violin almost from babyhood, and made her debut in Vienna in 1846. Despite the smallness of her hands, she excited astonishment by the power of her bow, her sensitive cantilena and great execution. She was later to become famous as Mme Norman Neruda, whose second husband was the Viardot's friend Charles Halle.

While in Berlin, Pauline sang the role of Romeo in Bellini's 'I Capuletti e I Montecchi', and that of Vielka in 'Feldlager'. Meyerbeer had called at her home on May 15th, in order to persuade her to take on the role, but found her curiously resistant. He said that she explained 'with a great many circumlocutions, that she does not find the role of Vielka suitable for herself.' Possibly, her lack of enthusiasm came from the fact that Jenny Lind was strongly identified with the part. However, Meyerbeer used all his famous persuasion, and she agreed to sing the role.

When the sudden death of Fanny Hensel, Mendelssohn's sister, was announced, everyone was greatly shocked and upset by the dreadful news. She was only forty-two and apparently in good health when she suffered a fatal stroke, as she was getting ready to go to a choir rehearsal. Pauline found it difficult to concern herself with professional matters at such a time, thinking more of the grief of the Mendelssohn family, particularly that of Felix.

Apparently, when he heard the news, the composer let out a piercing shriek and collapsed, losing consciousness for several minutes, and when he recovered, he cried distractedly for several hours. Everyone in the musical world was aghast at Fanny's death, and Chopin, himself far from well, was devastated that a woman who had shown no signs of illness, could die so suddenly, and he sent his heartfelt condolences to Felix and his family.

The season in the Prussian capital had been a very fulfilling one for Pauline, and on April 4th, the Berlin correspondent of 'France Musicale' had written: 'Mme Viardot is very pleased with Berlin where she obtains an immense success, and she is not disposed to come to Paris'. He also said that she was a great favourite with the Prussian royal family. When, as an adult, Louise wrote her memoirs, she told of her mother's almost intimate relationship with the Prussian Court, and mentioned how often she was invited to visit the Crown Princess.

Even as a young child, Louise was often included in these visits to the great town palace, situated at the upper end of Unter den Linden, where she would be stood upon a table and encouraged to sing Spanish duets with her mother for their hostess and her friends, and would charm the company with a solo, such as the fiendishly difficult cabaletta 'Ah, non giunge' from 'La Sonnambula'. After she had finished, she would be handed down from her improvised stage, and play 'hide and seek' with thirteen-year-old Prince Frederick, the future emperor. They would dash up and down the main staircase, which led to the royal apartments, where two sumptuous parakeets sat upon their perches, emitting piercing shrieks.

On May 16th, Pauline sang Donna Anna for her last guest appearance of the season. The following day, she, Louis, Meyerbeer and many other friends and colleagues attended Fanny Hensel's funeral, a sad and dismal occasion with which to conclude her Berlin season. She then left for performances in Dresden, followed by Tourgueniev, who was accompanied by the young but ailing critic Belinsky, who complained that Ivan kept him running around, in his effort to pursue the Viardots everywhere.

They met Pauline and her husband twice in the Art Gallery, but the first time the Viardots merely bowed and passed on. The second time, Pauline spoke to them; Belinsky, who spoke little French, held back, but Pauline addressed him in her fluent, but rather inaccurate Russian, and he was completely charmed by her. Tourgueniev's obsession with his prima donna perplexed all his friends, but once they met her, they too fell under her spell.

With the Viardot's departure imminent, Tourgueniev left for Salzbrunn with Pavel Annenkov and Belinsky, who was hoping that the medicinal waters of the spa town would halt his advancing tuberculosis. However, within a very short time, Ivan became tired of such a sedentary life, and told them that he was going to take leave of some friends. Although he had promised to return, he failed to do so, and Annenkov and Belinksy had to take his luggage, as well as their own, to Paris. The Viardots were due in England in July, to negotiate a contract for Pauline with the new Italian Opera Company at Covent Garden for the 1848 season, and Tourgueniev went with them to London and spent an enjoyable few days, seeing friends, and making new acquaintances. On their return to France they all went to Courtavenel for a summer holiday.

CHAPTER EIGHTEEN

1848

By the beginning of 1848, Meyerbeer was already in Paris, negotiating terms with the director of the Opera, Nestor Roqueplan, for the production of his new opera 'Le Prophete', and discussing the drawing up of the contract with Armand Bertin, an eminent journalist, and the lawyer and politician, Isaac-Adolphe Cremieux. He also sought the opinion of Germain Delavigne, on Eugene Scribe's libretto.

He heard Gustave Roger in Auber's new opera 'Haydee' on January 1st and stated: Roger plays his very serious role so outstandingly that he shows himself more than appropriate for 'Le Prophete'. But whether his singing will suit the style of this big opera, or if his voice will be strong enough for the huge auditorium and large orchestra of the Grand Opera, is still an open question.

Negotiations for the production of a gigantic stage work are never simple and Meyerbeer's main concern was to avoid being cheated. He said that if he could not obtain the terms he sought, he would prefer to withdraw the work. At the same time, the two new directors of the Italian Opera at Covent Garden, Delafield and Webster, offered him £1,000 for the sole right to produce and publish 'Le Prophete' in London.

Meyerbeer had already made an offer to Louis Viardot, who acted as his wife's impressario, and on January 5th, he received his reply, which he communicated to the directors of the Paris Opera. The composer had a wealth of commitments to fulfil; he was still writing the opera, having discussions about the text with Scribe, occupied with his men of business, and examining the students of the Paris Conservatoire. He was also auditioning singers, one of whom, Mlle Zelmer, a pupil of Manuel Garcia, the composer turned down, because she was not yet schooled enough. With all this activity, it is not surprising that his health was troubling him, and in fact, all his life he suffered with nervous headaches, and frequently caught severe colds and coughs that laid him low, yet with supreme will power, he fulfilled his commitments.

When he received a letter from Louis Viardot on January 17th saying that he could not allow Pauline to sing beyond April 15th, he was dismayed, to say the least. If the period of stage rehearsals, starting onJanuary 15th, 1849, should over-run, which might easily happen, she would then sing in 'Le Prophete' for only two months. Meyerbeer complained that if Pauline could not commit herself for a longer period, it would be better if she did not sing in the opera at all.

He showed Louis Viardot's letter to the directors of the Opera, and received a reply from them, which he sent to Viardot on January 22nd. Eight days later, he received Viardot's reply, after which letters and copies of letters passed to and fro for several days. On February 19th, he received a letter from Pauline, which he took to Nestor Roqueplan.

While these negotiations were going on, serious social unrest had begun in Paris, due to the governments' refusal to grant permission for a debate on electoral reform. On 23rd February, Meyerbeer spent most of the day on the streets watching events unfold. The National Guard, (a voluntary body) had declared itself for electoral reform and sought to prevent lines of troops from attacking the people.

At mid-day, news arrived that the prime minister, Guizot, and his cabinet had been dismissed by the king, who had agreed to grant the desired reforms. There was great rejoicing and it appeared that everything had been resolved peacefully. However, in the evening, the racket began all over again, and the troops fired on the crowd, killing several people in front of the Ministry of Foreign Affairs.

The next day, Meyerbeer again spent time on the streets watching the riots, as they quickly developed into full scale revolution. At two o'clock, the king abdicated, and the Tuileries Palace was over-run by a violent crowd, that destroyed and burned valuable furniture and books in a bonfire in the courtyard. They did the same at the Royal Palace, where the royal carriage was set alight and dragged through the streets, finally ending up on another bonfire. It seemed that a republic would be proclaimed, and everyone was told to illuminate their houses, but most people closed their shutters and the city became a silent, eerie place. Barricades had been constructed across many streets, and there were few carriages to be seen.

The expected republic was proclaimed that evening and a provisional government was sworn in.

Two of the ministers, Cremieux, Meyerbeer's man of business, who became Minister of Justice, and Godchaux, the Finance Minister, were Jews, like himself.

The next day, Meyerbeer, foreseeing further trouble, visited Scribe and asked him to make the agreed alterations to the libretto as soon as possible, since he intended to leave Paris. He called on the German ambassador to get his passport renewed, and saw that the shutters of most of the houses were still closed, and gangs of armed National Guardsmen were singing and swaggering along the streets.

Pauline was still in Berlin, unaware of the mayhem taking place in Paris. Etienne Arago, a friend of the Viardots, George Sand, and Meyerbeer, had been appointed general director of the post, and the new government lifted the death sentence for political crimes. Money was collected for the wounded, and Meyerbeer contributed 500 francs.

The new Minister of the Interior, Alexandre Ledru-Rollin, was also a friend of Louis Viardot and George Sand, and praised Meyerbeer in one of his speeches, declaring that he looked forward to seeing the production of 'Le Prophete'. Negotiations with the Opera were still going on, the first contract having been torn up. On April 12th, Meyerbeer worked on the recitative of Fides' aria in act 5, and bythe 24th, Pauline was back in Paris. The composer asked her to sing several pieces to him, so that he could recall her vocal characteristics, then he worked laboriously on her role, changing, re-arranging and altering the vocal line for several months, to take advantage of Pauline's individual vocal and dramatic capabilities.

For a while it seemed as if, with the formation of the provisional government, the situation in Paris had calmed down, and the Viardots bought a town house in the rue de Douai near the Place de Clichy. At the end of April, they arrived in London. Since her previous visit in 1841, there had been changes in the operatic firmament, and she was to perform with the new Italian Opera Company at the Covent Garden Theatre, although the personnel were practically the same as at Her Majesty's.

The lawyer, Benjamin Lumley, had succeeded Pierre Laporte, but he was very different from his predecessor, firm and commanding, who brooked no nonsense from his singers. Nordid he tolerate the conditions that Laporte had suffered, and was determined to avoid being held to ransom by the 'old guard', led by Guilia Grisi, forced to change and re-change the operas billed, simply because singers took umbrage at the least thing and threatened to go on strike. Lumley put his foot down, with the result that most of his disgruntled singers decamped to the Covent Garden Theatre in 1847. Fanny Persiani's husband put up money for the lease and formed a new company, 'The Royal Italian Opera'.

Lumley now found himself virtually without a company, as only the veteran bass, Luigi Lablache remained loyal to him. However, he was a resourceful man, went to the Continent to audition new singers and returned with his trump card – Jenny Lind.

Pauline accepted a contract with the new company and Grisi now had even more reason to be jealous of her because she had become an internationally celebrated prima donna. Reports of her phenomenal success in Russia and Germany had been published in all the English newspapers, and consolidated her reputation not only as a singer, but as an actress of genius.

In the intervening seven years since Pauline's last season in England, she had honed her art and developed into a confident, sophisticated woman, very soignee, always elegantly but simply dressed, presenting achic appearance, able to express herself in any company, and fluent in English, Spanish, German, Italian, besides, of course, French, the language of the countryof her birth. It is interesting that Tourgueniev considered that she pronounced German better than French, probably because she had spoken Spanish from babyhood and had acquired French as a second language, also, thanks to him, she had a working knowledge of Russian.

Grisi was now in her thirty-seventh year, and fifteenth London season. Intellectually, she knew that she was no match for Pauline, yet she had a truly fine voice and was a keen worker who practiced and vocalised every day, regardless of whether she had performances or not, which is why her voice had lasted so well. Mario only worked on his voice when he had performances to prepare; despite this, he had developed both as a singer and actor in the past few years, becoming a great favourite in the capital.

Pauline told George Sand that she was expecting a battle in London, due to the 'old guard' and the supremacy of Grisi, who was still in fine vocal form and whose beauty was as remarkable as her voice. She had the ego and ruthlessness required to ascend the ladder of success and stay at the top through force of will, and her personality. Many considered her to be a good actress and she excelled in certain roles that fitted her like a glove, namely, Semiramide, Norma, Anna Bolena, and Lucrezia Borgia.

Discerning critics such as Theophile Gautier, who saw most of her appearances in Paris, admired her hugely. In 1841 he wrote: 'For Grisi's benefit 'Norma' was given, and the moment this beautiful woman appeared, armed with her golden sickle, her brow crowned with vervain, her gaze as if lost in the light of the moon, we know she alone can do this part and make it impossible for others, for Grisi and Norma are one: it is the ideal realised. Few can sit in the golden throne left vacant by Malibran, but if you love the real Italian voice, simple, large, with a happy facility of being true on every note, with equal ease for scales (or runs) like a flute, go and listen to Giulia Grisi!'

Few singers are equally admired by everyone, and the American prose writer N. P. Willis, who heard Grisi in London in 1834 declared in his 'Pencillings by the Way', that he did not care for her. On the other hand, the German poet Heinrich Heine, who heard her in Paris in 1840, stated in his 'Lutetia' that he liked her very much.

Mrs. Pearse, who wrote a biography of her parents, Mario and Grisi, said that her mother's voice had the most superb soprano quality and was just over two octaves in compass, rising effortlessly to top C. With all her gifts, it was irrational for her to fear Pauline, but humans are irrational beings, and Grisi placed obstacles in the younger singer's path at every opportunity.

It is difficult to understand why Pauline, who was usually so astute, chose to make her debut as Amina in 'La Sonnambula'. Of course, she had sung the role to great acclaim in Germany and Russia, but Jenny Lind had enjoyed an unprecedented success as Amina at Her Majesty's Theatre during the previous season and this should have made Pauline wary of taking on her mantle. There were plenty of other operas in which Pauline could excel without courting direct comparison with the Swedish soprano.

Since her advent on the London scene, Lind had created a veritable 'fever' in the popular press, and there were articles about her, prints, statues and busts were on sale, and her name had become a household word. Louis Jullien rated Pauline Viardot the better singer, but the impressario, Alfred Bunn, had created an image of Jenny Lind as a freak of nature whom everyone must hear, and he generated an insatiable curiosity about her. Practically everyday, stories about her appeared in the popular press, and 'Punch' frequently featured cartoons, such as one of a young man tearing out his hair in despair, who, when his friend asked him the cause of his trouble, answered that he had no money and could not go to hear Lind. Another picture showed an audience entering the theatre beautifully dressed, and then coming out tattered and torn because there was always such an almighty crush on a Jenny Lind night.

The soprano had been sent by the Queen of Sweden in 1841, to sing to Manuel Garcia in Paris because, notwithstanding her obvious talent, her vocal technique was faulty and her voice was deteriorating badly, although she was only twenty years old. From the age of nine she had been under contract to the Royal Theatre in Stockholm, where she had regularly taken part in plays and operas, with the result that at an age when most singers are just beginning, her voice was badly impaired.

This type of breakdown is not uncommon in adults whose voices have been over-worked in childhood, and Jenny was extremely lucky to find Manuel Garcia before irreparable damage was done. The voice is not a machine, and can be harmed by injudicious treatment. At first, Garcia thought that Jenny's voice was already too badly damaged, but Lind implored him to help her. He sent her away for a six-week rest, but said he would see her again after that. He demanded that she remain totally silent, not even speaking, but writing everything down. After six weeks, he felt that the voice still needed more time to recover, but after a further period of silence, he agreed to teach her. Lind wrote to a friend: "I have already had five lessons from Malibran's brother. I have to start again from the beginning; to sing scales up and down, slowly and with great care; then to practise the shake – very, very slowly; and to try and get rid of the hoarseness, if possible. His method is the best of our time, and one that all here are striving to follow. I am well satisfied with my singing-master. With regard to weak points, especially, he is excellent. I think it very fortunate for me that there exists a Garcia, and I believe him also to be a very good man. I am very much pleased – nay, enchanted with his instruction."

Clara Novello considered that several notes in Jenny Lind's middle voice that had always had a veiled quality showed that the early damage was never entirely eradicated, and the American diva, Clara Louise Kellogg said that she was told by Sir Julius Benedict, Lind's accompanist on her American tour in 1850, that the Swede had a 'hole' in the middle of her voice due to which he had to arrange his accompaniments skilfully to cover up her deficiencies.

Although Meyerbeer had wanted Lind to sing in London in 1842, Garcia had advised her to wait, telling her to be patient and to continue to develop her skills elsewhere before she set herself up in direct competition to Grisi, and it was not until 1847 that Jenny made her London debut, but by then she was mistress of her art, and had a phenomenal success.

Garcia said that she had such a wonderful ear, she never sang even a hair's breadth out of tune, and whenever she made a mistake, he only had to mention it once and explain the cause, showing her how to correct it, and she never repeated the same mistake. He declared that the supremacy of the ear was even more important than the voice, because without a fine ear, there was no hope of making a singer.

Pauline was aware of her brother's pride in his pupil, and often had to bear comparison with the Swede, much to her chagrin. She, of course, knew that she and Jenny were as different as chalk from cheese, not only vocally, but culturally. Jenny originated from the cold north, she from the south, and she resented being compared with her rival.

Chopin was another of Lind's admirers and on a visit to London, he wrote to his friend, Gryzmala: "I have just come back from the Italian Theatre: I saw Jenny Lind and the Queen. Both made a great impression. So did old Wellington. He was sitting under the royal box like a 'royal' old dog in his kennel. Then

I met Jenny Lind, who had saved a place for me: this Swedish lady does not glow with ordinary light, there is something of the aurora borealis about her".

It is interesting to read two different reports of Jenny's singing, one from Charles Halle, the founder of the Halle Orchestra and one from the well-known English baritone Henry Phillips. Charles Halle wrote: "Never had I been moved by any singer as by her, and never again shall be, I feel certain. Her first air was the grand scena from 'Der Freischutz', and I will never forget the impression it made upon me. Her singing of the long high note (F sharp – the note which Mendelssohn also thought superb in Lind's voice), with the descent that follows, upon the words 'Welche stille Nacht', nearly suffocated me. I was sobbing audibly, and yet this extraordinary effect was produced by the simplest means. It was indeed true art coupled with enthusiasm and unconscious inspiration. Added to this, was a perfection of execution, which itself was a marvel, and I can say without fear of contradiction that we shall never hear her like again".

In his memoirs, Phillips says: "Jenny Lind was announced from all the musical points of the compass – her singing, her acting, and her benevolence. Such a pitch of enthusiasm did the people in one continental city reach, that, the morning after her concert, when she had left the hotel, the public rushed in by force, entered her bedroom, tore up the sheets, blankets, and curtains to ribbons, and wore them in their coats as trophies of the astounding vocalist, and not before twenty-four hours had elapsed did they discover they had entered the wrong room, as Jenny Lind slept in an opposite wing.' In London, there was a fever of anxiety to hear her, and, on her arrival in England, the enthusiasm nearly equalled that on the Continent – for people rushed in thousands to Her Majesty's Theatre.

Phillips goes on to say that she was undoubtedly great as a sustained singer, with a lovely voice, over which she had supreme command, but added "As early as 1845, the approach of Jenny Lind had been heralded in England,(courtesy of Alfred Bunn) – the London papers continually giving extracts from the foreign journals, of her wonderfully surprising execution, and above all, her unsurpassedportrayal of Norma.

In 1847, she was engaged by Mr. Lumley for a season at Her Majesty's, though under a contract previously made with Mr. Bunn, for Drury Lane. No singer since Catalani had excited the public mind so much as Jenny Lind – and she was certainly a great artist. However, she was not always fairly represented by the Continental papers that were carried away by their enthusiasm and advertised her as a wonderfully florid singer, which she really was not. The power of her genius lay in the surprising command she had over her voice in sustaining passages, and her beautiful, prolonged shake, while the simplicity with which she sang, and the way she presented the characters, was extremely natural.

However, her appearance in 'Norma' did not produce quite the effect that it was reported to have done abroad. English audiences had been accustomed to two great representatives of that character, Madame Pasta, and Grisi – who, great as they were, could not have surpassed Jenny Lind as Amina in 'La Sonnambula'.

Pauline, in addition to her rivalry with Grisi, now had to contend with comparisons with Lind, who was fast becoming a goddess in the eyes of the British public, not only through her singing, but due to her good works, her piety, and the vast sums of money she gave to charity.

In a letter to her mother written from London, Pauline complained that Manuel was always comparing her to Lind, and she stated firmly that she had no wish to emulate the Swedish singer, as their voices and personalities were very different. Pauline admitted that she did not give away riches, nor did she read the bible much, but she said that whenever she had the opportunity to do good, she did so, privately and without fuss, as she had no wish to pass herself off as a saint.

This makes it harder to understand why she courted direct competition with Lind in the case of 'La Sonnambula'. It is a true soprano role, and she was a mezzo-soprano, so she must have made transpositions, as she did all her life, in common with many singers of the period, the practice being universally accepted.

Her first performance of the season took place on May 9th, and at the eleventh hour, Mario, who was to have sung Elvino, announced that he was too ill to sing. On the following day, the 10th, Pauline wrote to her Russian friend, Count Matthius Wielhorski: "Good day to you, my very dear friend. Why have you not replied to a letter of mine that you should have received a month ago...? But, I don't want to waste time reproaching you, because if the postman brings the much desired letter from you tomorrow, I shall feel guilty of those reproaches, and I want to invite you to join in the happy success of my debut in 'La Sonnambula', which took place last evening. The Cavatina and the last aria were received rapturously, but the rest was a shambles. Mario, who should have sung, was suddenly struck down with a chest cold, and found it impossible even to rehearse. Laloi was called upon to replace him, but declined to do so. The directors declared they would sue, and threatened him with loss of further work. At this late hour, the house was sold out; the Queen, the Queen Dowager, and all the Royal Family were due to attend the performance. It was unthinkable to cancel it, but they were still searching for a tenor. Clovis had arrived the previous evening, and it was with this gentleman that I sang, but, of course, without a rehearsal. The poor man sings quite well, but his acting is tiresomely stiff. In addition, he is over six feet tall, though handsome. All this makes him difficult (she was small). In the finale (to the first act) he dragged the tempo of the andante 'un pentiro' so shamefully that everyone was dozing off. He retrieved himself somewhat from this fiasco by singing his second act aria quite well, but from his entrance, he had thrown a barrel of cold water over the audience. Happily, in the last scene my 'Ah, non giunge' was encored, amid cries, tears and applause. I hope that Mario will be recovered for the second performance, which will take place on Saturday, and that the opera will go well from beginning to end."

She added that she had been annoyed since her arrival at the theatre as, although she was shortly to appear in 'Les Huguenots' the Italian translation had not been completed; this would be followed by 'I Capuletti e Montecchi' in which she was to sing Romeo, but there was no music. (The copying out of parts for principals, chorus and orchestra was a laborious and time consuming business). She went on – "'Fidelio' is to be given immediately, but the recitatives have not been written, and 'Iphigenie' is likewise on the programme – I discovered a translation in the library in Berlin and sent it whilst I was singing there, but it has fallen through the hands of four directors and is lost. Despite being English, the directors are hopeless, they cannot even advertise their productions properly."

Covent Garden was enjoying better business than Her Majesty's, except for Jenny Lind nights, but despite this, finances were in a bad way because of mismanagement during the previous season, and it was feared that the Company might not survive.

Despite professional worries, the Viardots were lucky to be in England because in Europe, all hell had broken loose, with revolutions springing up in most of the major cities. A year or so earlier, a liberal movement had begun in the Grand Duchy of Baden and had spread rapidly throughout southern Germany, with a public outcry for liberal leaders to be brought to power, and for a Federal Government to be set up in Frankfurt.

In Italy and Hungary, there were uprisings against Austrian domination. Louis Philippe and his family fled to England, where they were welcomed by Queen Victoria, whose beloved Aunt Louise, wife of her Uncle Leopold, was a daughter of the former king. At the same time, Prince Louis Napoleon Bonaparte, who had been living in exile in England since his escape from Ham, had gambled everything on a return to his own country, despite the fact that he faced instant imprisonment in France.

Violence stalked the Parisian streets and hundreds of people left the city, including Chopin and many other musicians, who, finding themselves without pupils, set sail for the safety of the United Kingdom, and soon the English capital was brimming over with French emigres. This fact was not lost on the satirists of 'Punch' who wrote: "The French have changed their sovereign (Louis Phillipe) and all they have got for it as yet, has been the suspension of cash payments. Never did a sovereign fetch so little on 'Change'".

The Viardots were, naturally enough, anxious for Ary Scheffer, who was a member of the National Guard. He stayed loyal to the Orleans family, although he deplored the weakness and corruption that had developed within the Orleans Party. Many people believed that with the removal of the royal regime, the way would be clear for true Republicanism and the establishment of a fairer, more democratic government.

Hector Berlioz was one of the first to be disillusioned with the new state of affairs, and a year later was calling it a 'confounded Republic', despite the fact that he had no reason to regret Louis Philippe, who had taken scant interest in his music, not even attending a performance of the 'Damnation of Faust' when it was performed at court. He said he had written to the King three times requesting an audience but had received no reply. With the coming of the new administration he approached Ledru-Rollin with the same result. He complained: "There's only one opera house in Paris, the Opera, and it's run by a cretin and its doors are closed to me." He was pessimistic about a possible change for the better, declaring that even if Duponchel were dismissed 'there would be twenty such as him to take his place'.

The composer compared the cold indifference experienced in his own country to the warmth of emotion inspired by his music in Germany and Russia and of the interest shown in his work by the Princess of Prussia, (Pauline's dear Augusta), who had got up at eight o'clock one morning in order to attend a rehearsal of his music in a cold, dark hall in Berlin.

Berlioz was in London from November 1847 until July 13th, 1848, while the Parisian excesses were taking place. The English capital was filled with French actors and musicians, one of whom was Pierre Bocage, the friend and sometime lover of George Sand. The Viardots allowed themselves a wry smile when they read a report of one of his performances where he was taken to task by the critic of 'Punch' "for the reality of his theatrical effect in dragging poor Antigone across the stage by the hair of her head," and it was suggested that a dummy should be substituted to save the actress a good deal of discomfort (and loss of hair!).

A report about French equestrian artistes performing at Drury Lane declared that "they are no doubt glad enough to be 'from Paris' in the present fraternising times, when a state of 'universal brotherhood' seems likely to lead to 'universal botherhood' if not something worse". And.... "Mlle Caroline's is the triumph of equestrianism. Mounted on a charger that is constantly 'kicking up behind and before' she keeps her seat as tenaciously as M. Ledru-Rollin would keep his seat at the Council Table of the Provisional Government. Like him, she overrides the spirit exerted for throwing her off, and like him, she turns towards the multitude, and plunges on as if she would stop at nothing. Like him, she leaps over every barrier with surprising audacity, but unlike him, she gains admiration and applause for her achievements".

There was carping about the behaviour of some of the Frenchmen who had descended on London in an article entitled: "Paris Clubs in London." The clubs may have been abolished in Paris, but there was no shutting one's ears to the fact that they existed with equal fury in London, having taken refuge in the coffee-shops and restaurants around Leicester Square. In any of the cafes, where the long beards met, it was impossible to get through a newspaper. A hundred voices, each shouting the loudest, made nonsense of the very best Leader, and completely ruined all attempt at reading – a real Babel de Paris, and gave a faint idea of what the National Assembly must be like, with every Frenchman talking at once. The arguments were so heated that every minute it seemed they could only be settled by blows, and ideally, such wild denizens of the Parisian clubs should have had a room to themselves.

Louis Viardot had been in Paris for three weeks, but returned to London unharmed, bringing Manuel with him. Pauline was naturally relieved to see them safe and well, and thankful that her mother and Louise were with her. Their friend Charles Halle and his family were in Paris when matters began to get out of hand, and experienced the realities of the unfolding events. On the eve of the Revolution, when nothing serious was expected, he had gone with a friend to look at the crowds on the Boulevards. He found that the Foreign Office on the Boulevard des Capucines was guarded by a group of militia, which made it necessary for them to pass through the Rue Basse des Remparts, soldiers being about ten or twelve feet above their heads. The street was densely crowded and they had to advance slowly, but suddenly, without any warning, they were fired upon with devastating effect; a woman and child close to Halle were both shot dead. The surprise was dreadful and the Boulevard and the street were cleared in an instant. Thankfully, Halle reached his house without accident, meeting only flying people, and intensely enjoyed the feeling of safety. At that time, he lived at the corner of the Place St. George and awoke one morning to the sound of his own and surrounding streets being barricaded. He saw Mme Thiers, the wife of the Opposition leader, Louis-Adolphe Thiers, come out of her house in her dressing gown and hand rifles to gangs of insurgents. Halle was aquainted with the Thiers, who lived two doors away, and put himself and his family under their protection. As the Nouvelle Athenes area is a little way from the centre of the city, it was difficult to get news of what was happening there. The barricades made prisoners of the inhabitants of the streets around the Place St. George, and some ruffians turned up asking Halle for arms and wine. He had no guns to give them but offered wine that they drank, though not to excess.

On the first day, the flags on the barricades bore the inscription "Vive la Reforme', but the next day, this was changed to 'Vive la Republique'. During the day a group of soldiers passed through the rue St. Lazare at the end of the street with their guns reversed, from which Halle concluded that part of the army must have fraternised with the people. The men on the barricades cheered them noisily, but they had no news for them.

Tourgueniev was in Paris in May and kept the Viardots informed. The purchase of their town house in the rue de Douai was going forward at that time. It was in the fashionable ninth arrondissement, the Nouvelles Athenes area, within five minutes walking distance from Ary Scheffer's house, and conditions in the capital must have caused the Viardots anxiety about the safety of their property during the disturbances.

When Halle was given permission to pass through the barricade to visit his friend, the pianist, Stephen Heller, he heard of the flight of Louis Philippe and the formation of a provisional government. He returned home with this weighty news and 'approaching the lower barricade of our street, I was challenged by a most ferocious-looking individual in the gruffest of voices with 'Qui vive?'" I drew as near to him as I could and said that I really did not know the proper answer to give under the circumstances, but that I only wanted to return to my family in the Place St. Georges, which I had left only an hour before. Apparently satisfied, he screamed out, looking more grim than before, 'Eh bien, passez! Mais prenez garde la'bas!' Alarmed, and thinking of a possible ambush, I asked him what danger threatened me 'below'. 'C'est qu'il y a de l'eau' was the answer. It had been raining, and the pavement having been partially taken up, there were pools of water here and there, and my formidable-looking challenger was anxious that I should not wet my feet! A rose-coloured revolution, indeed!"

Not for everyone though. Halle was lucky, but a great many people were not, and as the situation deteriorated through spring and summer, thousands lost their lives, including the Archbishop of Paris. With the situation worsening daily, all Halle's chances of making a living in the city were destroyed, and in March, he set off for England, followed shortly by his family.

From London, on July 11th, Berlioz wrote to tell his sister, Nanci, that his wife Harriet, who lived in the rue Blanche, near Ary Scheffer's house, was walking in the garden around seven o'clock one evening when someone fired at her and one of the bullets lodged in a tree a few inches from her left side. He said he didn't know what was to become of them, but would be returning in two days time to the 'hell of Paris', not knowing where he would stay, as he felt he could not return to Montmartre, because he and Harriet had separated, and Marie Recio, with whom he now had a liaison, had moved from her apartment in the Rue de Provence.

Pauline was sensible enough to realise that compared with the enormous events taking place in Europe, her worries about professional incompetence and rivalries were trivial, and she soon put the unpleasant experiences of the first night of the season behind her. Her fears were for her friends who were still in Paris.

Tourgueniev's compatriot, the anarchist Michael Bakunin, had been expelled from France as a revolutionary agitator. Like Tourgueniev, he was from an aristocratic family and had once served in the Imperial Guard, but he had become disgusted by the Tsarist treatment of the Poles, resigned his commission, and devoted the rest of his life to revolutionary causes. His ways were far too extreme for Tourgueniev, who, much as he desired change, was convinced that revolutions were not the answer, but that change should evolve steadily, if permanent improvements for the masses were to be realized.

Despite the momentous events happening at home, Pauline's career continued on its way and the critic of 'The Illustrated London News', George Hogarth, the father-in-law of Charles Dickens, said of her first performance: "It may be conceived that the natural trepidation of Mme Viardot was considerably increased by this untoward event (Mario's sudden absence), and in fact, she never completely recovered from her fright until the sleep walking scene of the last act. Had we not, from Continental experience, been well acquainted with her musical and histrionic genius, we should not have recognised Viardot until her finale. We must defer criticism as to the earlier scenes for her future appearance, which will be this evening (Saturday), and as we are glad to learn, with

Mario as the lover. Like Malibran, Viardot is a singer of impulse, and her successes are greatly dependent on external or physical causes."

Another report stated that instead of the audience showing sympathy for Viardot's plight, it appeared to feel insulted and vented its disappointment on her, almost causing an abject failure. But she rose to the occasion and moved the cold house to something like warmth. When the finale came, she produced a furore that had not been witnessed before in the new Covent Garden theatre, entirely defeating her opponents, (the old guard) but not thereby rendering them less malicious or vindictive.

Chorley wrote that she passed through her ordeal so well that it was a cause for wonder. She was nervous and her rebellious voice more than once refused to obey her and because of lack of rehearsal with a new tenor, her acting was not all it could have been, but those who had eyes to see and ears to hear, must have recognised a great artist, and he observed: "I have never seen a somnambulist heroine whose sleep was so dead as Mme Viardot's. The warmth and flexibility of her execution, throughout marked by new touches, told in her first and her last air (though the rondo, to be just, has been sung by no one so well as by Mme Persiani). What she was next to do, and where she was to be, in a theatre where every throne seemed to be occupied by those who sat firm, it was hard to divine". Chorley was referring to the London scene, but Alfred de Musset had already voiced the same concern regarding that of Paris.

The critic declared that Grisi was not happy until she had acquired nearly all of Pauline's roles, and there is a certain irony in her daughter, Mrs. Pearse's statement that: 'there was not a shade of jealousy in my parents towards other singers'. No doubt Pauline would have disagreed with this assertion.

The 'Illustrated London News' for May 20th, gave a report of the second performance of 'La Sonnambula' and said that Mme Viardot's triumph as Amina was complete. "Having overcome the stage fright she had experienced on her first performance, and with Mario as Elvino, her vocal and histrionic powers were fully developed, and it was difficult to recognise in the Amina of Saturday night, the one from the preceding Tuesday. In her opening cavatina, she was quite another being, taking the most difficult divisions with a volume of voice and a certainty that drew forth immense applause. In the finale of the bedroom scene she exhibited all the intensity of Malibran without the exaggeration, encouraging Mario to sing with extraordinary fervour – the effect was electric, and there were loud cheers and calling for the singers at the end of the act."

The report continued: "Mme Viardot, by this second performance of Amina, has proved that her dramatic genius is of the highest order, and that she possesses originality of musical conception to a remarkable degree. Her fioriture are thoroughly artistic, andentirely her own. In respect to the quality of her organ, it is beautiful in the medium notes and soul stirring in the lower tones, but in the upper octave there is a want of timbre, as if this portion of the register had been fatigued by over-exertion or by forcing them in her early studies".

George Hogarth alluded to this 'want of timbre' in the upper register of Viardot's voice on more than one occasion. If she was truly a mezzo soprano, or even a mezzo-contralto, it is possible that in the higher range (up to F in alt) she was using the equivalent of the bass or baritone falsetto, which the late Walther Gruner, Professor of Singing at the Guildhall School of Music and Drama in London, and an advocate of the 'Garcia method', called the 'flute' register in the female voice. The deeper the voice, the more likely it is that this register exists, although many singers never discover it. It is a sound completely divorced from the true timbre of the middle voice and is rarely used today because it is so different from the warmer, richer sound of the lower female voice. For sopranos who sing up to F in alt or even higher, the quality remains that of a soprano throughout the range, it is only the lower voices to which the term' flute' register really applies.

The critic and writer, Julien Budden observes that: "The real explanation lies in the nineteenth-century attitude to vocal registers, a subject that has not so far received the attention it deserves. Musicologists who are eager at all costs to revive the performing traditions of a past age would do well to remember that some of them might prove unacceptable today, as for instance, the alternative method of portamento that Niccolo Vaccai advocates for fast movements in his singing method of 1833 and which now exists only in pop and folk music. The ideal of an even vocal quality from top to bottom of a singer's compass was unknown to Verdi's contemporaries. A sharp break, like a change of gear, between registers, so objectionable today, was tolerated then and indeed this yodelling effect can still be heard in certain pre-electric recordings, such as those made by the contralto Clara Butt."

In Italy, vocal categories hardly existed, at least until the middle of the nineteenth century, and singers described themselves as they chose. The term mezzo-soprano suggested a seconda donna, and for this reason, many singers desiring the title of prima donna called themselves sopranos even when they were not. A careful examination of the music that was specially written for them, reveals the true state of affairs, as in the case of Malibran and Viardot. When music was not tailor-made for them, they had no compunction about using transposition if a role did not sit comfortably in their voice, but some singers, in order to be classed as prima donna, sang roles that were too high for them, and as Donizetti said: 'It is the old story of the right way to ruin your voice'.

In Bentley's Miscellany, an anonymous English critic wrote of Pauline: "Her voice is Spanish, having that touch of bitter orange (some will understand the phantasy) analogous to that characteristic beauty, partly sullen, partly piquant, which distinguishes the women of Murillo from those of Titian – a rich, guttural tone, entirely distinct from the timbre of Italy or those of Germany, France or England... Out of a few skeleton situations and insipid airs, she works up a complete and completer character".

Pauline told George Sand that she had an 'Italian League' against her. This was the group of singers led by Grisi that included Fanny Persiani, Antonio Tamburini, Emma Albertazzi, Mario and Marietta Alboni. The latter was an easygoing woman, with a velvet voice but, like many of her kind, had a large ego. Possibly through want of a quiet life, she allowed herself to be carried along by the powerful Grisi, although as Pauline dedicated a song to her in 1850, it would appear that she had no personal axe to grind with Marietta.

Despite the daily unpleasantness that Pauline faced, she was not without friends in London, the dearest of whom was Chopin, who had arrived in April. He had many acquaintances in the city and was very much occupied paying and returning calls, playing, and giving lessons for which he charged enormously high fees. His health was a daily cause for concern and the months he spent in England did nothing to improve it. He found the smoky air of London positively stifling, and had great difficulty in breathing. By now, he was regularly coughing up blood, and it was apparent to those around him that his lungs were in a perilous state. Over the years, doctors had misled him, telling him that he was not consumptive, merely suffering from 'nerves' and a weak chest.

George Sand and he had finally parted and this made meetings between himself and Pauline painful and embarrassing, as he knew that she still corresponded with his former lover. She was dreadfully upset for both of them because it was for all of them the end of an era, and she was reminded of her youth, the early days of marriage, and of wonderful times together at Nohant, that could never be repeated in the same way. When she thought of the part the wretched Solange had played in this unhappy affair, she could cheerfully have wrung her neck. Chopin, however, placed all the blame on George, and on November 17th, 1848, he wrote to Grzymala: 'I have never cursed anyone, but now I am so weary of life, that I am near cursing Lucrezia (George). But she suffers too, and suffers more because she grows older in wickedness. What a pity about Soli. Alas! Everything goes wrong with the world!'

In the decade he had spent with George, Chopin had put down roots and accepted her family as his own. He was a creature of habit who loathed change, and missing the everyday routine that life with George had provided, he was like a fish out of water. George, already suffering emotional turmoil, now had to mourn the death of her half brother, Hippolyte Chatiron, who had died suddenly, at the early age of forty-nine. Although, on the face of it, he and George had little in common, there was a strong family bond between them, and she had enjoyed his cheerful company, and devil may care attitude to life. As his chateau was nearby, he was always a frequent visitor, who brought warmth and humour into her house, joining in with whatever was going on, and making her friends his own. Her family circle had never been large, which is why friendship was so important to her, and with Hippolyte's death, she was conscious of the loss of the last remaining link with the handsome father she had lost at such an early age.

Chopin was also moved by news of Hippolyte's death, a man who had been strong, virile and full of life, while he, neurasthenic and tubercular was still hanging on to life. He saw most of Pauline's London performances, and on June 2nd he wrote enigmatically to his old friend Grzymala: "Mme Viardot has not had a great success here because she is singing with Grisi and Alboni, who are, as you know, very much liked, but her genius made itself felt". Chorley in his column mentioned an intrigue relating to the 'indisposition' of Mario, but praised Pauline and said that she had an absolutely original genius; he appreciated the quality of her voice and of her powerful, unequalled dramatic gifts, which enabled her to surmount all obstacles.

In early July, Chopin wrote again to Gryzmala: "Tell (Marie) de Rozieres that Mme Viardot was very kind to me, for the news will get back here. Mme Sand, I know, wrote to Mme Viardot, asking for news of me with much solicitude!!! How well she must play the role of a mother full ofequanimity". He added that he and Mme Viardot had performed in a concert together and she had sung her own vocal arrangements of his mazurkas. Pauline made diplomatic and determined efforts to heal the rift between Chopin and George, but without avail. The composer was already too embittered through the influence of Solange and Marie de Rozieres, who did all they could to blacken George's character, and by what he considered to be George's own betrayal of him through the writing of her vituperative novel 'Lucrezia Floriani'.

Some months later, Pauline replied to two letters from George saying, 'You ask me for news of Chopin – his health is declining slowly, and he has some fairly good days when he is able to go out in his carriage, but others when he is overcome by choking fits and the coughing of blood. He doesn't go out at night, but he does still give a few lessons and when he is feeling better he can be cheerful....But it has been a while since I last saw him....He always speaks of you with the highest respect, and I affirm that he never speaks of you otherwise'. Here we must acknowledge that Pauline was playing the peacemaker by telling 'white lies'.

The letters make sorrowful reading, particularly with regard to George, who only wished her former lover well. 'Did you see Chopin in London, and have you news of him?' she asked Pauline, in a letter dated early December, 1848. 'I ask everyone but receive no news'. He had only returned to Paris on the 23rd of November and was already very ill. 'I love him as my son, even though he was most ungrateful toward his mother, but I must get used to not being made happy by my children. There remain Maurice, you and Augustine'.

The concert to which Chopin referred had taken place at Covent Garden on May 12th, when Pauline sang two of his mazurkas that were received with great enthusiasm and encored. There are two sets of these arrangements, each comprising six songs. They are virtuoso pieces that require a superb technique, a vocal range from low B flat to high C sharp, facility in long chromatic scales, and consummate ease in legato and coloratura singing. A press notice for this concert read: "Mme Viardot was rapturously encored in Handel's 'Lascio ch'io pianga' from 'Rinaldo', beautifully scored by Meyerbeer expressly for her, and in one (sic) of Chopin's quaint pianoforte Mazurkas, arranged by herself for the voice, a marvellous exhibition of skill in fioriture".

In addition to her operatic performances, Pauline sang in many prestigious concerts, particularly those of the Philharmonic Society, held in the Hanover Square Rooms. She also sang for the Society of Ancient Music at Exeter Hall in the Strand. The 'Illustrated London News' of May 20th stated: "The great attraction at the fifth concert on Wednesday night under the direction of the Duke of Wellington, was the appearance of Mme Viardot Garcia. She sang first in a motteto 'I cielo immense narrano' by Marcello, with chorus, next in a quaint Sicilienne 'Ogni pena piu spietata' by Pergolesi and finally in the scene from Mozart's 'Cosi fan Tutte', 'Per pieta', a scene of such exceeding difficulty, and exacting varied dramatic declamatory and musical powers – that she electrified the audience. We have heard her gifted sister and Sontag in this same air, but whilst yielding to these artistes the palm of superiority in quality of voice in the upper notes, we must award to Mme Viardot Garcia the palm of genius".

She was engaged for the sixth concert and on May 27th, the same newspaper reported: "There was a duo by Nasolini – 'Il tuo destino' sung by Mme Viardot and Mr. Sims Reeves, composed in 1790, and sung with such spirit as to secure the usual honour of an encore. Mme Viardot electrified the company by her superb delivery of Gluck's 'Che faro' and of the 'Ombra adorata' from Zingarelli's 'Romeo and Giulietta'".

In June, Pauline sang Donna Anna in 'Don Giovanni', but at that time, Zerlina, the peasant girl, was considered the leading female role. A report of June 10th stated: "The fame acquired by Mme Viardot in Germany, by her performance of Donna Anna in Mozart's 'Don Giovanni', rendered her first performance in that character in this country, on Saturday night, a matter of considerable interest, further increased by the general persuasion that her predecessor Grisi had made the part her own, by her powerful and brilliant voice, and vehement declamation. It was thus no ordinary ordeal for Mme Viardot, but she achieved a decided triumph."

After the Mozart opera, Viardot and Antonio Tamburini (who had played the Don) joined forces again for a scene from Gnecco's amusing one-act opera 'La Prova d'un Opera Seria' in which Pauline played a capricious prima donna and Tamburini, her manager. She performed this popular piece many times, with Ronconi and Lablache, as well as Tamburini. On this occasion, the comic piece followed Grisi in 'Lucrezia Borgia' and 'was received with shouts of laughter and thunders of applause, and both artists were called for after their imitations of each other's voice and style".

Ronconi and Lablache were two colleagues with whom Pauline sang throughout her operatic career. Ronconi was a practical joker, and Clara Novello tells of time in Italy when she was in the audience and Ronconi was on-stage. Clara's party were in a stage-box, and when the baritone caught sight of her, he did all in his power to reduce her to helpless giggles by making animal noises and saucy comments under cover of the orchestra. At one point, he approached her box, loudly imitating a cat, while at the same time looking fixedly at the audience, taking delight in Clara's hilarity. It is one thing to cause merriment to one's colleagues off-stage, but to fool around self-indulgently in performance is not fair to the paying public and one wonders how Pauline reacted to such antics when he sang with her.

Hector Berlioz had been working for Louis Jullien at Drury Lane and Pauline was saddened to learn of his financial difficulties due to Jullien's recent bankruptcy. This meant that Berlioz never received his full fee and was robbed of three benefits at Drury Lane. He had to leave his apartment at 76 Harley Street, as creditors were pressing and, in an effort to raise some much needed revenue, he decided to mount a concert at his own expense. He invited all the best musicians in London to take part, including Pauline, and when he explained his financial position, most of them agreed to play without a fee. This event took place on June 29th at the Hanover Square Rooms, and drew a large audience to hear a fine orchestra assembled from members of the Royal Italian Opera, Her

Majesty's and other theatres. However, Berlioz was not able to recruit enough instruments for the Marche Hongroise.

The composer, who was held in high esteem in England, was applauded on his entrance to conduct his Roman Carnival Overture. Several of his vocal pieces were sung by Mme Sabatir, Pauline and M. Bonchi. A press report stated: "A Spanish jota, sung by Mme Viardot and Mlle di Mendi, was demanded a second time with fervour, it was admirably sung and the quaintness of the subject produced unusual interest".

Berlioz made a new orchestral arrangement of his cantata 'La Captive' specially for Pauline, transposing the original version down a tone. The text for this piece has an exotic, middle eastern flavour, and tells of a girl who has been captured by pirates and placed in a harem. The composer was thrilled by Pauline's interpretation of the piece, and from this time, he became one of her most ardent admirers, devoted to her as a musician and a woman, declaring that she was one of the greatest singers of all time.

Unfortunately for Berlioz, despite all the good will of his friends and colleagues, and the artistic value of the concert, little profit was made. Gustave Roger was in the audience and considered that it had been very successful, despite some of the instrumentalists having to rush away before the end of the performance, as they were playing in evening performances at various theatres, but he bemoaned the fact that enthusiasm and excellence did not fill empty pockets.

In March, Berlioz had written to his friend d'Ortigue that life in London was even more absorbing than that of Paris and he wished to stay as long as possible. Giving a report of how he spent his days, he informed him that he got up at mid-day, and began receiving visitors at l o'clock, 'friends, new acquaintances and musicians who've come to introduce themselves, whether I like it or not; that's three hours lost.' He said that he actually worked from four until six o'clock, and that if he didn't have any invitations he would go out for dinner some way away from his Harley Street apartment, read the papers and then go to a theatre or concert, staying until about 11.30 pm, then going off with fellow musicians to supper in a tavern and smoking until two in the morning. Presumably, this was the regime he followed when he did not have rehearsals or performances.

Despairing of France, he saw his future as being either in England or Russia, and admitted that if he only depended on his native land he would starve. "Under the old government I had to combat the hatred engendered by my articles against the ineptitude of those who governed our theatres and against the public's indifference. Now, I should have to deal with the mass of great composers recently discovered by the new republic, with music termed popular, philanthropic, national and economic. The arts in France are dead and music in particular is beginning to putrefy'. He added that he always felt a compulsion to return to France whenever he had some musical success, but that it was a habit he would grow out of. "From the musical point of view, France is merely a land of cretins and ne'er-do-wells, you have to be an outright chauvinist not to recognise the fact." No doubt Pauline agreed with him.

In April, Berlioz wrote to his sister Nanci about the disturbing news from Paris, regretting that "it gets more and more upsetting every day. He was also perturbed because trouble was brewing in London, due to the expected appearance of "a hundred and fifty thousand Chartists roaming the streets. The clubs are busy making long lances to arm those who haven't got guns, and the Irish are raging in their corner, but the arrogant English aristocracy won't give an inch because they think that they should have everything and the poor nothing."

The London disturbances were soon quelled, being less violent than those in Paris, and the Chartist demonstration on April 10th ended in a fiasco. In a post script, Berlioz concluded: "The riots here are over; they don't know how to go about these things. They know how to steal jewellery, though. In Trafalgar Square, during the disturbances, I lost an attractive tie-pin that someone snatched off my cravat. That's how things are".

The Viardots had rented a house for the 1848 season at 27 Clifton Villas, in Maida Vale, about four miles north-west of the city. (This house still exists near Warwick Avenue Underground Station). The property was quite newly built, in an elegant terrace of cream stuccoed town houses, close to the Regent's Park Canal, the district now known as 'Little Venice', and the area was then surrounded by verdant countryside and small villages. Pauline enjoyed open air pursuits; she was fond of walking, and riding, and on a sunny day, if she had the opportunity, she loved to sit under a tree with a good book. Louis, of course, was always on the look-out for likely places where he could indulge his passion for hunting.

One of the first visitors to their temporary home was Gustave Roger, who had dinner with them. He was in England to take part in a provincial tour with Jenny Lind, and came to London particularly to hear Pauline at Covent Garden ,as he knew that they would be performing in Meyerbeer's new opera in the following year. At first Pauline did not impress him, and he noted in his diary that her performance was studied and rather artificial. He thought that her Romeo was 'lifeless,' and described her as "a magnificent inner thought, with no expansion, a camelia condemned to dream of perfume... A young feuilleton by old Madame Sand, the skeleton of beauty, without the flesh and velveti-ness, and I do not think she will do for Meyerbeer and 'Le Prophete'". How-ever, off-stage, he was won over by her personality, musicianship, expansive knowledge, and lack of pedantry.

Histrionically, Pauline was ahead of her time in being more subtle on-stage than the majority of her colleagues, whose acting, by modern standards, was grossly exaggerated . Tourgueniev stated that to a public that preferred nov-elty and showmanship, Pauline would always be something of an enigma, and only really appreciated by those who recognised the true artist, dedicated to the music and text rather than to self-glorification.

Another friend of the Viardots was in London. This was the horn-player of the Paris Opera, Eugene Vivier ,with whom Pauline had taken part in concerts in the Rhineland during August, 1845. The Viardots always had a great deal of fun when he was around, and as usual, he was up to his tricks, causing great consternation on one famous occasion, when he made a noise on his horn that sounded like a fire alarm, and sent everybody running in all directions, believ-ing that a fire had really broken out.

Roger and Vivier were old friends, and in his memoirs, the tenor writes: 'on June 30th, Vivier came to take me to dine with Mme Viardot at Clifton Villa, St. John's Wood, Maida Vale.. (It is like sleeping in the open, an address such as this!) Ah, well, she is a decidedly charming woman, as I thought. She has won me over by the real prestige she exercises over those with whom she wishes to be intimate. This is science without pedantry, and the most complete musician-ship. It is intended this year or another for us to appear in 'Le Prophete' to-gether and I believe that we will make something fine of it. She says that I will make my debut here (at Covent Garden) in a most fitting manner, but nothing in which I am to appear is ready, and Mario holds the rest. The directors (Delafield and Webster) are charming and enable us to live like princes, but they do not busy themselves with their theatre'.

On the 1st of July, he wrote: "After dinner, I went to look at the music that I shall rehearse with Mme Viardot", and his entry for the next day states: "This evening I went to Fulham with Vivier, to whom I lent a shirt; I sang 'Adelaide'. Webster sang with Tamburini in the duet from 'Guillaume Tell', Tamburini sang in Italian and Webster in French – it was the most curious thing in the world. Vivier had a great success. Corbari, Castellan and Viardot sang. De Glimes arrived completely drunk. He is in love with Corbari, and in his agitated state, he cut his hand quite badly with a table knife".

Like many foreign visitors to England, including Pauline, Roger deplored the dullness and boredom of Sundays, whether in London or the provinces. His diary entry for July 23rd noted: "One of the most sad Sundays in London. Rain, wind. At 2 o'clock, I went to Mme Viardot's house. I took the omnibus 'Atlas', which took me to Alpha Street, instead of Clifton Villa like the others. I believed myself to be lost in London. I asked for Maida Hilt (sic) and an Englishman told me that I was there. At the same time, I heard someone whistling 'Ah, what pleasure to be a soldier' in the distance'! Just then, a carriage stopped, and who should be in it but Osborne (the pianist) who was the whistler. He was with his brother-in-law, Hampton, and his sister, Mme Hampton, to rehearse with Mme Viardot. Lady Essex was also there, and Mme Balfe, who was of the opinion that the only place for Italian Opera was Covent Garden, due to the excellence of its chorus, execution and orchestra. When the others left, I stayed with Mme Viardot, to go over the Italian version of the libretto of the 'Huguenots' with her, comparing it with the original text, then I returned home".

Pauline wrote to Count Wielhorsky on July 4th, telling him of her activities: " Rehearsals for 'Les Huguenots' take up all my days and in the evenings I have the theatre and concerts, then my carriage comes to take me to my 'sweet home'. My brother has been in London for fifteen days. My husband and he returned from Paris before the worst bloodshed. My mother, my cousin, and Louisette are also in London with me, the whole family, in fact, is re-united, and contributes not a little to making my stay in 'perfidious Albion' supportable. One absolutely essential thing for men and women and for me in particular, is the sun. We live under a cold shower, it just never stops raining. I prefer the winter in St. Petersburg a thousand times to the summer in London, besides my affection for the inhabitants of the first city, and my antipathy for those of the latter. I have nothing very extraordinary to tell you about myself – do you know that 'Capuletti' has been played, that the music has not been a great success, but that Romeo has been a real triumph? I would like you to hear me now. The Romeo that you saw in St. Petersburg was a boy, but now he has become a man. I sang the role on Thursday for the fourth time. Berlioz has given a very interesting concert. All the musicians of London were in the audience. It had a great success, but applause doesn't fill pockets. Oh, goodness, I've come to the bottom of my paper, so it's necessary to be brief and to tell you that I love you from my heart".

Chopin was still in London, and when Pauline heard that Henry Broadwood, a prominent member of the family of piano makers, was arranging a concert on July 12th at the home of Lord Falmouth in St. James' Square, she volunteered her services. His lordship, who was the epitome of the eccentric Englishman, was an amateur violinist: Chopin said that if you heard him playing in the street, you might give him three pence, and declared " his house is full of servants, all of whom are better dressed than their employer."

The pianist accompanied Pauline in his mazurkas, and they enjoyed all the old exhilaration of making music together. He had always considered her a brilliant musician of extraordinary refinement and intelligence, and when he was bored or depressed, he longed for her company, and said that she could inspire him and 'restore his musical faculty'. Now, his failing health often made him taciturn, and he suffered greatly from the malady that was rapidly taking over his body and draining his physical strength, but from time to time, flashes of the wittily sardonic Chopin returned, and he became an amusing mimic.

Pauline sometimes met him at the homes of her friends Mme Sartoris and Henry Chorley, where he played to select gatherings. He was in great demand in aristocratic circles, despite the fact that he charged a fee of twenty-five guineas, which was amazingly expensive at that time. He told Albert Gryzmala: "They don't talk while I play, and apparently they all speak well of my music, but it is above all the hopelessness of my local colleagues, who are in the habit of being pushed around, which is the reason why they consider me a sort of amateur. I shall soon become a grand seigneur, because I have clean shoes and don't carry about cards, saying, 'Will give lessons at home, available for evening parties, etc.'

His wealthy friend and pupil, Jane Stirling, invited him to Scotland, where she and her sister lionised him. It was obvious that he was sorely in need of rest, but the two women, proud of their prize, kept him on the move, visiting their aristocratic friends and acquaintances. He complained to Grzymala: "One day longer here and I won't just die – I'll go mad. My Scottish ladies are such bores that god save me – they've latched on so hard that I cannot get away".

In London, in the meantime, Pauline was preparing for her next challenge, the role of Valentine in Meyerbeer's 'Les Hugenots', which she was to sing in Italian for the first time.

CHAPTER NINETEEN

Of course, Pauline had recently sung the role in German, but she was only given the opportunity to sing it in England, because La Grisi was not interested in doing so. Few of the Italian singers had any desire to take part in this work because it seemed like 'Chinese' to them. Pauline knew that it could achieve the same success in England as it had elsewhere, and it was due to her tenacity and perseverance that the opera was actually produced during the 1848 season. She persuaded the other singers that it would be in their interests to take part, and so began her rise in England, as a unique artist of the first order in roles outside the usual soprano territory.

This was, to date, Meyerbeer's most successful work: its premiere had taken place at the Paris Opera on February 29th, 1836, and the first German performance was given at Cologne on the 21st March 1837. The action takes place in sixteenth century France, and tells the story of the massacre of Protestants by Catholics on St. Bartholomew's Eve. In many countries, due to Catholic sensitivities, the title was changed to 'Margarethe von Navarra', 'Die Anglicaner und Puritaner' or 'Die Gibellinen in Pisa'.

The basis of Meyerbeer's extraordinary success was his belief that opera should be a synthesis of all the arts. He emphasised the importance of décor and spectacle and cannot only be judged on his music. His operatic plots were carefully designed to take advantage of stage effects, which were sometimes added as after thoughts, as, for instance, the skating scene in 'Le Prophete', inspired by a roller skating virtuoso, and incorporated at the last minute, much to the disgust of Berlioz, who considered that it held up the dramatic flow.

Chorley believed that credit had to be given to the great tenor, Adolphe Nourrit, the elder Manuel Garcia's most famous pupil, for his suggestion that Meyerbeer should create a duet for Raoul and Valentine in the fourth act of 'Les Huguenots'. The composer did so and it became one of the most effective pieces, both musically and dramatically, in the entire work. 'Certainly, never was suggestion acted on with more power and felicity'.

Meyerbeer's operas were altered and re-orchestrated during the rehearsal period in what Chorley calls 'the extreme fidgettiness (sic) of his notation', putting in half bars ' so as to reduce the singer into a condition of an obsequious automaton', but his piano scores give little idea of the orchestral colour and effects so essential to the entire work.

The composer had many enemies among his distinguished contemporaries: Mendelssohn once dismissed him with the phrase 'something for everybody': Schumann pulled him to pieces in a priggish article, and Wagner talked of 'effects without causes', and said that Meyerbeer did disservice to Eugene Scribe's clever libretti, devised to provide for every kind of musical effect. With such abuse, one can only suspect that there were many positive and active forces in the music to arouse such unwarranted dislike and envy.

It is usually assumed that Richard Wagner invented the leit-motif in opera (a different musical theme for each character that occurs throughout the work in various guises), but Meyerbeer predated him in the use of this device, and even such a work as 'Gotterdammerung' owes a great deal to the example of 'Les Huguenots'. All his life Wagner was antagonistic to his rival, and no doubt spoke with his tongue in his cheek when he said that Meyerbeer was; 'beyond cavil, one of the most imposing phenomena of the music-dramatic world.'

When it was announced that Queen Victoria and Prince Albert were to pay their first state visit to the newly inaugurated Royal Italian Opera Company at Covent Garden to see 'Les Huguenots', there was an immediate demand for tickets and soon the theatre was completely sold out. Then, a few hours before the performance was due to begin, Mario suddenly announced that he was indisposed and could not sing. Perhaps it would be charitable to give him the benefit of the doubt and assume that this was just an unfortunate co-incidence with 'La Sonnambula', but it smacks of an audacious plot to unseat Pauline Viardot on a tremendously important occasion.

The theatre directors were beside themselves, and did all they could to persuade Mario, but he was adamant that he could not sing. Pauline remembered that Gustave Roger was still in the city, and he agreed to take part, although there was no time to rehearse. He had sung the role in French at the Paris Opera, and had already begun to study the Italian translation, but he was not assured enough to risk singing it in Italian that evening.

The Frenchman was of smaller stature than Mario, but compactly built, with a remarkably handsome face, fine eyes, and a wide variety of facial expression. A costume was hastily assembled for him, and with people pouring into the auditorium, and a buzz of excitement in the air, he and Pauline quickly went through the score, marking important points, particularly in the crucial duet they would sing in the fourth act. She assured the tenor that when she was off-stage she would learn as much of the French text as possible. The performance was rescued, and Pauline was forever in his debt. He was an extremely competent singer, a pure chest tenor with a voice of extensive compass, beautiful quality and average power. His unerring intonation and excellent technique found favour with the cognoscenti, while his passionate expression and dramatic power brought him the applause of the general public.

From back-stage the orchestra was heard striking up the National Anthem as the Royal Party arrived, and in the wings everybody felt the tension in the air. Soon the performance was under way, the very situation adding to the flow of adrenaline, but there was no time for Pauline or Roger to be nervous; they needed the utmost concentration, and had to keep their wits about them, as they had never appeared on stage together before, and were completely unrehearsed.

That they made a superlative success is a matter of history, and when the public realized that Pauline had learned her role in French as she went along, they were truly amazed at her feat. She and Roger had a tremendous triumph, particularly in the vocally and dramatically difficult duet. Henry Chorley was full of praise, but insinuated that Mario's defection smelled of intrigue.

The name of Viardot was on all lips; she had scaled the summit of her role, despite all the obstacles in her path, and there were many. The Marcel, with whom Valentine has an important scene was sung by the bass, Ignazio Marini, of whom the press said: "Signor Marini is a great artist in every sense of the word. He has one of the most superb organs ever heard, but his intonation is exceedingly uncertain. Sublime in his 'beaux moments' he is intolerable when his voice gets flat'. Singing with him must have been torture for Pauline whose own tuning was accurate and true, but to be kind, the tense atmosphere and his state of nerves may have played their part in causing his faulty intonation.

'The Illustrated London News' of July 29th stated: "Great was the sensation created on its first representation on the command night on Thursday week, and it has increased tenfold on every performance. Although the opera lasts nearly four hours, the amateurs remain to hear the last notes, spellbound by the dramatic interest of the story, by the exquisite beauty of the music and by the powerful execution of the singers and instrumentalists'.

On August 5th another review reported: 'On Saturday night, Mario having recovered from his indisposition, he re-appeared as Raoul in Meyerbeer's 'Huguenots'. Excited, probably by the great success of the French tenor, M. Roger on the previous Thursday, who assumed his part at a few hours notice, Mario exerted himself strenuously, and on no previous occasion did he sing with such sweetness and power. The grand duo between Viardot and Mario in the third act, was received with rapturous plaudits'. It need hardly be added that Roger never sang Raoul at Covent Garden again.

With Viardot's outstanding success, Grisi regretted her lack of interest in Valentine, and assumed the role herself in future seasons. Mario was born to sing Raoul both vocally and physically; he was tall, with a remarkably handsome physique, so necessary for a dramatic hero and admitted 'I live to sing and to love'. Chorley asserted: 'Mario is the best opera lover the world has ever seen', and Davison of the 'Times' declared: 'To see and hear Mario in the 'Huguenots' was to hear singing like Rubini's, and to see acting like Edmund Kean's'.

On August 8th, the Viardots entertained three of their political friends at Clifton Villas, Louis Blanc, Alexandre Ledru-Rollin and Etienne Arago, who, since the fall of the provisional government in France, had lost their cabinet posts, and taken refuge in England. Manuel Garcia joined them for dinner, and although not actively involved in politics himself, he was an interested observer. As the lamps burned low, and the cigar smoke grew thicker, they discussed the complexities of the situation, not only in France but in all the other European countries, where revolutionary fervour had been unleashed.

The poet Alphonse Prat de Lamartine's moderate government was now in power, and had stood its ground, despite George Sand and her fellow conspirators' efforts to inspire 30,000 union members to march on the Hotel de Ville to overthrow the new administration. Word had reached the Mayor of Paris informing him of the plan, and he mobilised one hundred thousand National Guardsmen to protect the approaches to the building.

At the sight of so many armed men, revolutionary ardour was soon dampened and the chance of change was lost. The National Guard had been formed in such a way as to limit the movement of the crowd, they broke up factions, and ensured that the demonstration lost its central solidity. Soon, men were dispersing and disappearing into side streets. That night, George Sand wrote to Maurice: "I disappeared at the same moment so as not to have the signal honour of also being passed in review, (Lamertine had reviewed the National Guard after the crowds had dispersed) and I came back to dine at Pinsons, very sad and realising that the 'republican republic' was down and out for a long time perhaps'.

Soon, students and shop-keepers were roaming the streets shouting, 'down with all Communists', and the fact that George and her friends were known for their radical views did not endear them to the new administration. Sensibly, they made themselves scare, George returning to Nohant, and her fellow revolutionaries to London.

For a long time, Manuel Garcia had been unhappy with the life he was leading in Paris, and decided to settle permanently in England. He formally separated from his wife, resigned his post at the Paris Conservatoire and made his home in London, where he became a professor of voice at the Royal Academy of Music. As Jenny Lind's teacher and brother of Pauline Viardot, Manuel was soon in demand and set up a private teaching practice, in addition to his work at the Academy. Pauline told George: "the poor boy dies of antipathy for the English, and could not get enough of the Frenchmen's company." But in order to make a living, Manuel had to overcome his dislike of England, where apart from the occasional holiday in France or Germany, he remained for the rest of his life.

Pauline said he was stupid to stay if he was so miserable, but he replied that as his wife was in Paris, he preferred to be as far away as possible. He was perfectly at home with the Viardots' political friends, as he loved discussing politics, and having little time to read the newspapers, he was delighted to hear the news at first hand. Unfortunately, matters in France did not turn out as Blanc and Arrago wished, Louis Napoleon was elected Prince President by a massive vote, and by 1855, they were both living in exile in Piedmont in Italy.

After the London season ended, the Viardots enjoyed a short holiday as guests of William Hay at Duns Castle in Berwickshire. Pauline's next engagement was at the Norwich Music Festival, so it seemed pointless to return to France for such a short time. The festival, held in St. Andrew's Hall was one of the great events of the English musical calendar, the others being the 'Three Choirs Festival' based in turn on the cathedral towns of Hereford, Gloucester and Worcester, and the trienniel Birmingham Music Festival in the industrial heartland of the Midlands.

The ancient cathedral city of Norwich is situated in wind-swept East Anglia, in a verdant but rather flat landscape. Agriculture had long been the mainstay of the region, but throughout the land, the countryside was giving way to the development of urban areas, and many villages were losing inhabitants due to the forward momentum of the industrial revolution with its need for a massive labour force. In addition, a new middle class was emerging, of merchants, bankers and entrepreneurial industrialists, who took a pride in their cities and their music festivals.

There was supreme confidence amongst these people, many of whom were becoming seriously rich and powerful; great civic buildings were erected, industry boomed and British exports supplied the world. Despite this wealth, however, there was a vast underclass of poor and distressed people, as the novels of the Viardots' friend, Charles Dickens testify, and 'Oliver Twist' left no one in any doubt of the enormous injustices in society, especially in the case of children, and gradually helped to bring about much needed reform.

Louis Viardot was an interested observer of the English scene, and contributed articles to Parisian publications on his experiences in Great Britain. He was a man of erudition who put his knowledge at the service of others, and could easily have become a politician or university professor. Modest and disinterested, he preferred to be 'outside of politics and financial affairs, of employment and business, in the noble and difficult career where I have introduced my tastes and my preferences.' He had an encyclopaedic knowledge of many subjects and played the role of catalyst and wise counsellor, happy to allow others to make their voices heard.

In Norwich, Pauline was joined by Jeanne Castellan, Marietta Alboni, Luigi Lablache, and several British singers, including Martha Williams, contralto, Sims Reeves, and Charles Lockey, tenors, and Henry Phillips, baritone. The 'Illustrated London News' for the 16th of September states: "On Wednesday, Viardot sang 'Ah, non credea' – the exquisite beauty of her delivery of the adagio did not excite her hearers so much as her fine vocalisation merited; but when she poured forth the 'Ah, non giunge' (the vivacious cavatina from 'La Sonnambula'), she produced an electrical effect. Her deep contralto notes in the passage 'Ah, m'abbraccia' recalled the voice of Malibran and when she took the highest notes in the upper octave of the soprano register, finishing with a marvellously executed shake, there was no end to the plaudits and she was obliged to repeat the finale. Her debut at the Festival was thus triumphant".

In the second half of the concert, there were scenes from 'The Marriage of Figaro' in which Pauline sang Susanna, Castellan was the Countess, and the page, Cherubino, was sung by Alboni. The duet, 'Sull aria' in which the Countess dictates a letter to Susanna, to play a trick on her husband, the Count Almaviva, was encored, and 'all sang with great spirit'! "The genius of Viardot then asserted its supremacy by the splendid interpretation of 'Farewell ye limpid streams' (from Jephtha by Handel). The fervour with which she poured forth the movement 'Brighter scenes', her exquisite musical accent and her refined and intellectual conception of the sublime composition, created an altogether prodigious sensation; and although applause at these occasions is strictly refrained from, there was that indescribable murmur of delight at the close of her sympathetic singing, which showed how deeply it was felt and appreciated".

There was also a performance of Haydn's 'The Creation', in which the arias were shared out among the soloists. Pauline's contribution was 'On Mighty Pens', and on the following Thursday, she and Lablache gave the comic scene 'Ah, guardate' from 'La Prova d'un Opera Seria', a hilarious performance, which had the audience chuckling, and Pauline was then joined by Alboni for the duet from 'Semiramide'. In addition, 'there was grand vocalisation from Viardot in Weber's 'Der Freischutz' scena, sung in German, and finally, Viardot and Alboni were joined by Miss Martha Williams for the trio 'Lift thine eyes'.

Pauline was a supremely fortunate woman, not only because of her talent, but through her marriage to Louis Viardot. He was a man of principle who adored her and could very adequately provide for her and their family, even if she had not been capable of earning her own living, but he understood her independent spirit and need to express herself artistically. Through him, she met a wide range of the most interesting people in the fields of journalism, literature, politics and art, and despite his own gifts and abilities he was happy to promote his wife's career rather than his own, to see her shine, while he remained behind the scenes, quietly writing his articles, translations and books. Tourgueniev and Louis were content to live a quiet life not craving the limelight for themselves, only desiring acclamation and worldly honours for their ' beloved Pauline.' Most women would feel supremely privileged to be loved devotedly by one man, but Pauline was adored by three men who never let her down, her husband, Tourgueniev and Ary Scheffer.

The year of revolution saw the stirrings of female emancipation and some of the more courageous women became involved in the Chartist Movement. This was a radical, democratic organisation founded by members of the working classes between 1838 and 1850, but the power of the people frightened the Establishment, and the movement was held down by repressive measures.

When women began to join the Chartists, the Establishment was alerted to the dangers that could ensue, and a tongue in cheek article appeared in 'Punch' headed: "How to treat the female Chartists". 'London is threatened with an eruption of female Chartists and every man of experience is naturally alarmed, for he knows that the vox femine is the vox diaboli when it is set going. The women must be put down, as any unfortunate victim to female dominance can testify. How then, are we to deal with the female Chartist? We have something to propose that will easily meet the emergency. A heroine who would never run away from a man would fly in dismay before an industrious flea or a burly black beetle. We have only to collect together a good supply of cockroaches with a fair sprinkling of rats and a muster of mice, in order to disperse the largest and most ferocious crowd of females that ever was collected, in order to allay their turbulence.'

After the Norwich Festival, the Viardots returned to Paris where Pauline was engaged to sing Valentine in 'Les Huguenots' in French at the Paris Opera, called the Theatre de la Nation since the recent revolution. She was also involved in acquiring furniture, carpets and curtains, and over-seeing the re-decoration of their new town house, purchased for 100,000 francs.

Politically, life was still far from normal. Everyone was amazed at how quickly the disturbances had developed into what was really a revolution of the working classes that vented their hatred on those who controlled them. Initially, the government had installed National Workshops to overcome large scale unemployment, and this had drawn many workers to Paris, where they received a daily payment. Unfortunately, there was not enough work to go round, and apart from joining the army, or cleaning the infested swamps in the Sologne, the labouring classes had little occupation. The government, which was heavily in debt, could not justify paying workers to be idle, and although there had been no basis or plan for an uprising, by late June the lower classes were in revolt, and a mere spark turned into a raging fire, bringing great cruelty and suffering in its wake.

Alphonse de Lamartine, whose 'History of the Girondins', published in 1847, had influenced the political dissidents, imposed some order, but George Sand, Louis Viardot and their friends were not satisfied, as they considered more should be done to right old wrongs.

Due to her friendships with well-known socialists and political activists, Pauline was viewed suspiciously in establishment circles, and it is alleged that a police file was kept on her, and no doubt, on Louis too. In blissful ignorance, she was very busy and had no time to rest, but she enjoyed getting her large, new house in order, as a welcome respite from the alarms and excursions of revolution, and the stresses and strains of her London season.

It is interesting, that eight years after moving into the rue de Douai, Charles Dickens mentioned in a letter to a friend that he had visited the Viardots' Paris home and was surprised to see so little evidence of a musical life; indeed, the piano was not even open. He declared that it looked as if the family had moved in last week, and intended to move out again very shortly.

In a letter dated 29th October, 1849, Berlioz wrote to his sister Nanci: "I think my Elegie on the English poem 'When he who adores thee' would move your heart and soul....Mme Viardot played it on the piano for me the other evening (without singing it)." And a decade later, he wrote to his other sister, Adele: "This evening I'm having dinner with my neighbours M. and Mme Viardot, a charming family with whom I can breathe freely. Both of them are so intelligent and so good, and their children are so graceful and well brought up! Added to which, the flower of art fills the house with its scent. There they love what I love, they admire what I admire in music, in literature and in all matters of the spirit."

CHAPTER TWENTY

Pauline was impatient to begin working on 'Le Prophete' Meyerbeer's new opera, which would open the doors of the Paris Opera to her at last, and she told George Sand, "I need work, a great deal of work, that is what has saved me up till now, and it will, I hope, be my safeguard for as long as I have a voice." Despite her enjoyment of family life, it was never enough for her, because she found the greatest fulfilment in her work.

In her biography, 'The Price of Genius', April Fitzlyon speculates on the nature of Pauline's emotional needs, postulating that the singer longed for Tourgueniev, who was the most important man in her life. Fitzlyon assumes that her statement implies that work was the anodine she needed in order to tolerate her situation, but it is more likely that she simply revealed the need of the dedicated artist to express herself through her art.

Pauline analysed herself very succinctly, in a letter to Julius Rietz a decade later, when she told him that there appeared to be contradictions between her intellectual and moral character. She confessed that her Bohemian blood, inherited from her father, caused a kind of instability, a restless need for change and abhorrence of the rigidity of $2 + 2$ making 4. She admitted that she totally lacked mathematical ability, but that she needed and appreciated order, and had a great love of beauty and well being, preferring the countryside to the town. Of her will power, she stated: 'When I have to do a thing, I will, despite water, fire or society. How many bad things I might have done without this sister conscience'.

Meyerbeer and the Viardots finally agreed terms with the directors of the Opera, and contracts were signed, but in June, because of continuing political unrest, a codicil was added as an insurance policy in the event of war. Rehearsals for the Paris production were scheduled to begin on 1st October, 1848, when Meyerbeer arrived from Berlin, and Pauline from England.

The score was by no means complete at that time and Meyerbeer, added, subtracted, and changed all aspects of the work constantly. He said that on the 1st of October he worked on the last tempo of Fides's aria, with good results, and in the evening he copied out almost the entire piece, continuing until breakfast the next morning.

Jeanne Castellan was engaged to sing the soprano role of Berthe, the fiancee of the hero, Jean de Leyden, and Meyerbeer observed that she had a wide-ranging voice, the low register being the best, as the higher range was artificial, with no genuine silver tones. Although he admitted that she sang with spirit, taste and method, and had an outstanding trill and fioriture, she left him cold, unlike Pauline, whose singing 'electrified' him.

The rehearsal period for 'Le Prophete' was an unusually long and arduous one , continuing until April, 1849 when the premiere took place. Because of commitments in England, Gustave Roger was not available until November. Usually, he kept a daily journal, but from December until April, it was discontinued because of the frequent demands made upon him by Meyerbeer. He said that this colossal opera needed ceaseless work, study and research by its interpreters, himself, Viardot, Castellan, Gueymard, Prevost, Genibrel and Nicolas-Prosper Levasseur.

Meyerbeer was the most meticulous and demanding of task masters, to whom no detail was too small, and even before rehearsals began, he insisted that Pauline had a protruding front tooth removed; she agreed, although she knew it would be painful. In the event, she was pleased with the result because it improved her appearance tremendously.

In Paris, there was great anticipation about the new opera, and the composer used all kinds of ploys to whet the appetite of the public. Every day, tit-bits appeared in the newspapers about the prestigious event, and it was alleged that the mise en scene alone would cost 150,000 francs. However, details of the music and production were kept secret, so much so, that a cartoon appeared in 'L'Illustration' showing the musicians rehearsing in blindfolds and ear-muffs. Of course, this only generated more public curiosity, which was Meyerbeer's intention.

The Viardots returned to Paris, after a short holiday at Courtavenel, and visited the composer on October 22nd. He also received a visit from Michael Costa, who invited him, on behalf of the Birmingham Festival Committee, to compose a cantata for the 1849 music festival, the first such offer Meyerbeer had ever received from England.

As usual, he was keen to please everyone, and Blaze de Bury relates how he cut an original and expressive aria for the tenor in the third act because Mme Roger thought it might strain her husband's voice. Mme Castellan asked for an entrance aria and Meyerbeer, although he really considered that a solo at this point was unnecessary, obliged by writing two; the first more suited to the overall style of the work, the second, vocally brilliant. Naturally, Mme Castellan chose the more showy of the two.

In her subtle way, Pauline used her influence with Meyerbeer, both musically and dramatically in the creation of her role, and Chorley considered that Mme Viardot's contribution to the writing of 'Le Prophete' was as great as that of Nourrit in the creation of 'Les Huguenots'.

Pauline later told her Irish friend, the composer Charles Villiers Stanford, that Meyerbeer would mingle backstage with the stage-hands, listening to their comments and noting which snatches of melody they whistled or sang. He personally directed the chef de claque at the Opera, 'Pere' David, and showed him in the score where he wanted the applause or cheering to take place. If David disagreed and recommended other places, Meyerbeer would willingly comply with his suggestions.

Berlioz commented that: "The claqueurs in our theatres have become experts in a profession that they have raised to the level of an art. People have often admired, but never sufficiently to my mind, the wonderful talent with which Augustus used to direct the great works of our modern repertory, and the soundness of the advice that he gave to the actors on many occasions. Hidden in a ground-floor box, he attended all the artists' rehearsals before starting his own military rehearsals. Then, when the maestro came and told him, 'Here, you must give three rounds of applause, there, shout encore,' he replied with un-shakeable self-assurance, depending on the case: 'Sir, that's risky,' or 'I must think about it, I haven't yet reached a decision. Lay on a few amateurs for a trial assault and if it catches on, I'll follow up.' Because of the claque, managers were able to manipulate their performers and the public alike, and Berlioz main-tained that if the claqueurs were banned from certain performances, the house would be completely empty. 'Heaven and earth may pass away, but Rome is eternal, and the claque will endure!'

Despite the carping of many of Meyerbeer's critics, such as Robert Schumann who said: 'I place him with Franconi's circus people', he had a real dramatic gift, and although his flamboyance was not to everyone's taste, his compositional style was original and individual, enormously colourful and exciting.

'Le Prophete' is based on the Anabaptist wars in Holland, and the action centres around the figure of Jean de Leyden, who is hailed as the Messiah. The role of his mother, Fides, (Pauline Viardot) was totally new as a central character in opera. John is betrothed to Berthe, played by Jeanne Castellan, but the romantic interest is minimal, and Fides emerges as the important female role.

As well as dealing with the musical aspect of his new work, Meyerbeer was, naturally, involved with the visual side of the production, and on November

15th, there was a conference with the directors of the Opera, and Scribe read the libretto to the scenic designers. The following day, the composer played the entire role of Fides to Pauline, although he continued to make changes to his score for several months, but despite his enormously taxing schedule, Meyerbeer still found time to go to opera and ballet performances at least twice a week.

He started coaching the chorus and comprimario singers at the theatre in October, but Viardot, Roger and Castellan received him in their own homes for their coaching sessions, and only went to the theatre when stage rehearsals were scheduled in the new year. On Sunday, December 3rd, Meyerbeer played Pauline the act 5 duet, and the Chanson de la Mendiante for the second time. In the evening, he revised the overture and made preparations for the orchestration. Pauline had previously only sung in established works, and found it a rich and rewarding experience to observe Meyerbeer, as he created his complex musical and dramatic tapestry.

On December 7th, the composer bemoaned the fact that the rehearsal with the singers had been less than satisfactory because Gueynard, who appeared in most of the scenes in 'Le Prophete', was so exhausted by rehearsals for 'Les Huguenots' and 'Robert' that he could not sing, and the following day, Meyerbeer was held up by visits from Gruneisen, the English critic, and discussions regarding the London contract with Beale, the music dealer.

The press, in the form of 'La Patrie' was already making waves about the high cost of staging 'Le Prophete', and Meyerbeer blamed the directors of the Opera for these comments. He retaliated by writing an article refuting such exaggerated statements, which he gave to Edouard Monnais for publication in 'Revue musicale', but Monnais advised against it. There had already been an article by Leon Escudier in 'La France musicale (20th February, 1848) alluding to Meyerbeer's Jewish origins, which pointed to an already discernable anti-Semitism in the French press. As early as 1839, Meyerbeer had warned his mother in advance that this could happen.

Besides working with his principal singers for 'Le Prophete', he was also coaching Mme Lagrange in the role of Isabella, which she was shortly due to sing. Pauline had performances of 'Les Hugenots' while she prepared Fides, and Christmas came and went with little respite, as Meyerbeer rehearsed her on the 25th, 27th and 31st of December.

Coaching sessions continued throughout January, and the first orchestral rehearsal took place on February 15th. Meyerbeer declared that the orchestra treated him with icy coldness and showed no enthusiasm for the work, but Pauline was applauded a little, after her arioso in act 2, but at a rehearsal on

March 13th, Pauline's aria and her duet with Roger were greeted enthusiastically.

By April 8th, Meyerbeer was still completing abridgements, scoring various items, including Castellan's cavatina, and he and Pauline discussed the conclusion of the act 4 duet and the first 'Couplet de la Mendiante.'

The premiere was scheduled for April 16th, and as the date drew near, tickets were at a premium, with touts making small fortunes in their transactions. Those for orchestral stalls changed hands at a hundred francs, and people travelled to Paris from far and near. In his diary, Meyerbeer wrote: "the first performance was very brilliant. Roger was called out after act 2, and Viardot and Roger after act 4, and I after act 5, when I appeared with all the singers. Flowers and garlands were thrown on my entry. Among the performers, Madame Viardot deserves the palm, and I have her to thank in large measure for my success. Madame Viardot, Madame Castellan, and Herr Roger all made their debuts at the Opera in 'Le Prophete'. Almost all the important papers, with the exception of 'La Reforme (Castil-Blaze) and 'La Musique' (the brothers Escudier) expressed themselves in favor of the opera, and on May 4th, 'Le Moniteur' published my nomination as Commandeur de la Legion d'Honneur at the request of the Minister of the Interior.

After the performance, Meyerbeer greeted Pauline with the words: "What can I say to you? There were the tears of thousands to prove the effect of your singing and I totally forgot that I was the composer of the opera, in sharing the emotions of your audience". Then he presented her with a broach made from her tooth that had been covered in enamel and set with diamonds!

At the end of the first act of the opera, Richard Wagner ostentatiously left his seat with ill disguised contempt. In Paris, politics were never far from the surface, and although the story tells of the plight of the poor against the power of the nobility, and the ideal of evangelistic brotherhood, it roused the ire of certain left-wing factions, while, surprisingly, those of the right judged it more favourably.

Some journalists were less than complimentary to Meyerbeer, but Berlioz, in accord with less reactionary musicians, found more to praise than to criticize, despite the traces of the 'bravura' that he disliked so much. All his professional life, Meyerbeer was badly treated by certain elements of the press, and as a sensitive man, it hurt him deeply, damaging his health and destroying his creativity for several days, after a particularly vicious assault.

He desired no better Fides than Viardot, but during rehearsals he had confided to his friend Johannes Weber, that he wanted to make his prophet 'great, energetic, convinced of his divine mission, not merely pleasant, courteous and a good child'. In his diary, Roger expressed his satisfaction and pride in the achievements of Viardot and himself, particularly in the great cathedral scene, and said that from the first rehearsal to the last performance, all went wonderfully well between them, and that all the work and conscientious study resulted in a tremendous triumph for them both.

The premiere was attended by Louis Napoleon Bonaparte, the nephew of Napoleon I, who, since the recent revolution had been elected Prince President of France by five and a half million votes. To many people, the name Bonaparte signified order, and Ledru-Rollin, the representative of the left wing faction merely polled 400,000 votes. Most of the populace were still preoccupied with the parlous political situation, and were endeavouring to overcome the results of the disastrous events of 1848, with its class hatred and bloodshed, not only in Paris, but throughout Europe, and the presence of the Prince and his entourage lent a certain eclat to the occasion.

To add to the general misery caused by revolution, a severe cholera epidemic had broken out and people began to avoid public places for fear of contracting the deadly disease. In the latter part of May, Tourgueniev was one of those who succumbed, collapsing at the home of his friends, the Russian anarchist Alexander Herzen and his wife, Natalie. Alexandre was away at the time, in Ville d'Avray, but Natalie nursed Tourgueniev devotedly for two weeks, before going to join her husband. Ivan took himself to the hospital, but it was overflowing with the seriously ill, and the streets were strewn with rotting corpses. To make matters worse, the weather was extremely hot, and there were severe storms, one of which devastated Louis Viardot's fields at Courtavenel: since he was not insured against hail, he suffered a substantial financial loss.

The Viardots and Maurice Sand arrived at the chateau on June 9th, and Tourgueniev, now recuperating, but still weak, followed them shortly afterwards. It was generally accepted that the country was a safe refuge from cholera, but there were several deaths in the neighbourhood, which greatly alarmed the Russian, and for the rest of his life, even to hear the word 'cholera' disturbed him immensely .

Maurice feared that he was no longer special to Pauline, and was distressed because she paid more attention to Tourgueniev than himself. Thackeray's latest novel, 'Vanity Fair', had arrived and she and Ivan read it together, thoroughly enjoying its 'originality, vigour, and fine portrayal of character'. It may be, that by this time, Pauline and Ivan had physically consumated their relationship, although there is no actual evidence, except that Tourgueniev was spectacularly happy that summer at Courtavenel, even after Pauline left on

June 18th. Maurice remained for a few days after the Viardot's departure, but Tourgueniev stayed on for several weeks, often alone, but perfectly content.

London was avid for its own premiere of 'Le Prophete', although changes would inevitably have to be made. Meyerbeer knew that London audiences would not find it easy to sit through four hours of serious opera, and gave Michael Costa, who was to conduct, carte blanche to make his own excisions. The part of Berthe was reduced, and Catherine Hayes, a Manuel Garcia pupil, took over the role from Castellan. Although the opera had been sung in French in Paris, the cast now had to relearn it in Italian for Covent Garden.

On July 8th, 1849, Louis Viardot wrote to George Sand from London, saying that they regretted leaving Paris, as the Covent Garden Company was in disarray – 'the rule more and more in the hands of the Italians, with bribery for appointments'. He considered the direction of the theatre weak, and thought it possible that the season would be curtailed. However, the company survived, thanks to the success of 'Le Prophete' and the financial situation was further improved when, in September, Frederick Gye obtained the lease of the Covent Garden theatre for seven years as sole director, paying himself £1500 per annum. A committee of artistic directors was set up, comprising – Grisi, Viardot, Castellan, Mario, Tamberlik, Tamburini, Formes and Costa. This group became known as 'The Commonwealth', and many were the strains and stresses experienced during the following season as a result of this organisation. The artists were always quarrelling amongst themselves about casting, and often disagreed with Costa over musical discipline. Despite this, there were some marvellous performances.

Matters were even worse at Her Majesty's Theatre, where Benjamin Lumley was again in difficulties because his star singer, the pious, puritanical Jenny Lind, had decided to give up the 'wicked stage' and concentrate on concert performances. She had been a tremendous draw at his theatre, and it seemed that there was no one who could replace her, until Lumley had a brainwave and remembered Henrietta Sontag whom he had heard singing with Pauline in Berlin in 1846. She had been one of the most celebrated singers of her day, and was still a good-looking woman, who had kept her figure, despite having given birth to several children. As a very young woman, she was chosen by Beethoven as soprano soloist in the premiere of his Ninth Symphony, and by Weber for the title role in the premiere of 'Euryanthe'.

Goethe called her 'the girl with the angel's head'; Berlioz likened her voice to a silver altar bell, and Gautier said that never before had a human soul been endowed with such exquisite musical organisation, or a voice in which heart and melody were so beautifully and intimately blended. Chopin first saw her in

Warsaw in 1830, and told his friend Titus Woyciechowski: "She seems to exude from the stage a scent of fresh flowers, which caresses her voluptuously. Her diminishing notes could not be more exquisite, her rising chromatic scales are superb." He added: "She has infinitely more grace off stage than on, although her conversation remains impersonal".

Benjamin Lumley took a great risk in engaging her because she was already forty-five years old and had not appeared on the-stage for eighteen years. However, she had continued to sing at private gatherings, and her voice was well preserved. One journalist said that he believed she had substituted her daughter, as she could not possibly look so young at her age.

While Pauline was preparing for the London premiere of 'Le Prophete', Henrietta sang in 'Linda di Chamonix' at Her Majesty's, and the first night audience included such luminaries as the Duke of Wellington and the Duchess of Mecklenburg Strelitz in their boxes. Michael Balfe conducted, and on her entry, Sontag, looking young and lovely in her pretty peasant costume, was not given a chance to sing a note, because the audience stood up and applauded until their hands ached. She was overcome with emotion, and Balfe took the orchestra back to the introduction, so that she could compose herself. The critics were very kind, although some people, who had known her in her prime, naturally thought that the voice had lost some of its youthful bloom.

The operatic world was now in need of more operas because Rossini had virtually retired, and in April 1848, Donizetti died from syphilis at the age of fifty-one. Consquently, an opera by Meyerbeer, the first for thirteen years, was most welcome, and on July 24th, the long awaited premiere of 'Le Prophete' took place at Covent Garden.

'The Illustrated London News' for July 28th, reported: "The excitement was prodigious – an event like a European musical congress – Royalty, rank, fashion, literature, music and art. Between the acts, the lobbies and saloons were crowded with dilettanti of all nations, and the house was packed. The interest was increased by the opera being the first in which the gifted Viardot would appear this season. The first act was of an exquisitely painted Dutch landscape. Miss Catherine Hayes played Berthe, and on Viardot's entrance she was hailed with continuous bursts of cheering. Jean was sung by Mario and in the 'pastoral' in 9/8 he sang deliciously. Viardot sang an impassioned air in F sharp with such intensity of feeling and acted with such simple and unaffected grace that the house rang with the plaudits. In the third act set in Munster, the wail of the mendicant in E minor in 3/4 time, so touchingly sung by Viardot is a lovely melody. Costa conducted".

Berlioz commented: "People will long remember the first performance of 'Le Prophete' at Covent Garden, when Mario broke down more than once because he had not had time to learn his part". Berlioz puts this down to "the English having raised the art of high-speed musical studies to a pitch of glory unsuspected by other nations". He observes that they congratulate themselves for putting on an opera in ten days, regardless of the final result, but adds that the French give themselves months of preparation, but fail to turn up for rehearsals. Obviously, he thinks that Mario is a victim of the system, but with the exacting Meyerbeer overseeing the production, plenty of time would have been allowed for the tenor to learn his role. In addition, Mario was fortunate to be singing in his own language, while Pauline had to learn a new translation. The tenor admitted that he did not like the role of Jean de Leyden and although he was to sing it forty-five times, he gave it up as soon as possible. He was not a skilled musician and learned slowly, finding the new idiom difficult to assimilate and memorise.

However, like Pauline, he was extremely particular about his stage costumes, and took the trouble to find the correct period styles from books and paintings. In 'Le Prophete' his appearance was said to be 'Christ-like'. As he had a high forehead he painted it with grease-paint to make his hairline appear lower, and his daughter relates that: 'on one occasion he was acting with Mme Viardot, who created the part of the Prophet's mother, Fides, and was a great actress. After her famous song 'Oh, my son!' she took his head in her two hands and pressed a kiss upon his forehead. Mario, looking up, saw to his horror, two large moustaches on Mme Viardot's upper lip. In kissing him she had taken a most lifelike impression of his grease-paint! Scarcely able to control his laughter, 'sotto voce' Mario told her not to turn round, and she had to get off stage, as best she could with her back to the audience".

Charles Dickens wrote to a friend: "I am engaged to dine with Miss Coutts, (Angela Burdett Coutts of the banking family), and go with her to the 'Prophete', otherwise I should have been really delighted to dine with you". In later years, he recalled Pauline's wonderful personification and her ability to move him to tears.

For her last performance of the season, she sang Fides once more and was as enthusiastically received as ever, although George Hogarth stated: 'Mme Viardot claimed the audience's indulgence due to a severe cold and sore throat, the great tragedian sang and acted with prodigious power, frequently electrifying the house by her magnificent burst of histrionic genius. Being the last night of her appearance, there was no end to the ovations, and the floral shower at the close was most abundant".

Wilhelm Kuhe observed that 'Le Prophete' was no love story in the accepted sense, but a tale of a mother's love for her son and "Viardot Garcia invested the part she created with a living interest, which made it quite as attractive as that of the ordinary youthful heroine. How beautifully she sang her two arias 'Ah, mon fils' and 'Pieta, pieta' and how transcendentally she acted in the Coronation scene; none who heard and saw her will ever forget". He also remembered her in other roles: 'Excellent as she was as Valentine in 'Les Huguenots' and many other dramatic roles, I remember her particularly as Rosina in 'Il Barbiere' and as Adina in 'L'Elisir d'Amore. In these characters, her manner was full of grace and charm, although it seemed to me rather artificial than natural'.

Her great admirer, Henry Chorley, wrote that the composer had first intended the soprano role of Berthe to be that of the heroine... but that character was effaced from the moment Mme Viardot became associated with the production of the tragedy, since it was felt that she was admirably fitted by nature to add to the gallery of portraits a figure, which as yet did not exist there, and her power of identification with the character was remarkably aided by her person and voice. The mature burgher woman, in her quaint costume, the pale, tear-worn devotee, going from city to city searching for her lost son, and her horror at finding him a victim of hypocritical blasphemy. Viardot's Fides was a being entirely beyond the pale of the ordinary prima donna's comprehension; with subtle art she conveyed the woman's simplicity, her tenderness, as well as her force, a renunciation of woman's ordinary coquetries and a skill to impress all hearts by the picture of homely love, desolate grief, and religious enthusiasm. Chorley declared that 'there can be no reading of Fides save hers; and thus the opera, compared with 'Les Huguenots', has languished, when others have attempted her part.'

In August, Joaquina Garcia travelled to Brussels for the marriage of her niece, Antonia, to the violinist, Hubert Leonard, a former pupil of Charles de Beriot, but the Viardots were unable to attend, as Pauline was engaged to sing a performance of 'Elijah' in Liverpool with Karl Formes, the foremost interpreter of the title role at that time. In the chorus was a boy, who later became a pupil of Manuel Garcia and was himself destined to become a fine interpreter of Elijah. This was the English baritone, Charles Santley, who would one day be knighted by Queen Victoria. He wrote in his memoirs: "Of the singers, the one who impressed me most was Mme Viardot Garcia, signally in the scene of Queen Jezebel in the 'Elijah'; the song, 'If guiltless blood' from 'Susannah'; and the great air 'Leise, leise, fromme weise', from 'Der Freischutz'. No woman in my day has ever approached Mme Viardot as a dramatic singer, she was perfect, as far as it is possible to attain perfection, both as singer and actress'. Chorley echoes Santley in the matter of 'Elijah' – 'It was proved by her bringing out in the same oratorio world, the recitative of Jezebel, in 'Elijah', which, till Mme Viardot declaimed it, had passed unnoticed."

After Liverpool, Pauline packed her bags and returned to Paris, where on the October 17th, her dear friend, Frederick Chopin breathed his last, but neither George nor Pauline were called to his bedside. He was in the hands of other women, notably his one time student, the Polish aristocrat, Countess Delphine Potocka, who ministered to him devotedly. She was an extremely beautiful woman, despite having borne five children, none of whom survived into adulthood, and she possessed a wonderful voice. Her libido was strong and she had had many lovers since settling in Paris in 1831, but by 1849 she was Krasinski's mistress. It is possible that Chopin had been aesthetically, secretly and platonically in love with her for several years and he dedicated the Waltz in D-flat major Opus 64 to her. This is an amazingly light-hearted work considering the state of his mental and physical health when he wrote it. In her album, he inscribed the words 'Nella Miseria' (In Misery). This is a line from Dante's 'Inferno' where the poet expresses the belief that there is no pain greater than remembering, in times of misery, the happiness of the past.

It was tragic that the rupture between George and Chopin never healed. There had been so much misunderstanding, super-charged emotions, mis-placed pride, but no explanation, and the depth of their grief was not alleviated. George couldn't forgive him for siding with Solange and Clesinger, and believed that he must secretly be in love with Solange, as he declared that he would never abandon her. When he had called George a bad mother, it devastated her, and convinced her that it was the proverbial last straw. She was beside herself with injured pride, anger, jealousy, and resentment, amazed that after all she had meant to him he could be so ungrateful and vindictive. She appeared unaware of the harm and hurt that she had caused him by her unkind and obvious portrayal of his character in her recent novel 'Lucrezia Floriani'. It was as if she had written the book as a therapy, allowing all her pent up, unspoken, festering resentments against him to focus on the person of Prince Karol, the aesthetic lover of Lucrezia, who drained her so emotionally that he caused her death.

Their last meeting had been on March 4th the previous year, when Chopin and his friend Edmond Combes had been visiting Charlotte Marliani at her new lodgings in the rue de la Ville-Eveque, near the boulevard Malesherbes. As the two men were leaving her apartment, they met George in the foyer of the building; she was on her way to visit Charlotte, and was accompanied by Eugene Lambert, Maurice's friend, who was very probably her current lover, as he lived permanently at Nohant. Chopin acknowledged her and asked if she had received a letter from Solange. She replied that she had not, and he told her that she was now a grandmother, as Solange had given birth to a daughter a couple of days before. Without waiting for her comments, he bowed and left. Regretting his haste, but not wanting to climb the stairs, he sent Combes to tell George that her daughter was well. When his friend returned, he was accompanied by George, who asked if Solange's husband was with her, and enquired about his own health. He said that he was well, then asked the porter to open the door – bowed and walked toward the Square d'Orleans. The former lovers never met again, although Chopin was well acquainted with George's movements, and knew that she had given up her apartment and stayed with Maurice at 8, rue Conde, whenever she returned to Paris.

The pianist had moved to the rue Chaillot, a quiet area, almost in the country, where his most devoted friends, knowing how seriously ill he was, visited him frequently; though Delacroix, one of his dearest and oldest friends was away from Paris. In June, he wrote: "I left Paris, very sad to see the condition of my poor Chopin, it was most unpleasant for me to have to leave him in such a state". Another devoted friend, Gavard, kept him company when he was alone, and often read aloud to him from one of his favourite works, Voltaire's 'Dictionnaire philosophique'.

Berlioz called on him, but said that visits tired him dreadfully: "His weakness and his sufferings had become so great that it was not possible for him to play or compose, and even the merest conversation fatigued him." In June, his old friends, the Czartoryskis, engaged a Polish nurse for him, and she kept the family at the Hotel Lambert informed of his condition. He was having frequent haemorrhages, so they sent their own doctor to see him, but the physician declared that Chopin was in the last stages of consumption and nothing further could be done for him.

He hung on for a further four months, declining daily, until the final agony, which began on the 14th of October. His sister Ludwika had come from Poland to be at his bedside, and he accepted Extreme Unction and told Father Jelowicki that he believed in God. His sufferings were dreadful and he implored his physician not to try to save him, but to allow him to die. After four days and nights of prolonged torment, on October 17th, his emaciated body gave up its long struggle, and he died at peace with God, himself and the world.

After his death, Jane Stirling took charge of his affairs, affronting some of his friends by acting as though she were his widow. But his true 'widow' was at Nohant engrossed in writing her autobiography, which only began to be published in 1854. She was deeply distressed when she heard the news of Chopin's death, deploring to her dying day the fact that they had not been able to settle their differences and make their peace while he was still alive. Even if there was no possibility of returning to their former relationship, at least they should have parted friends. Sadly, after Chopin's death, George retrieved all her letters to him, and burned them.

The pianist was buried in the Cemetery of Pere Lachaise, but his sister carried his heart back to Poland, the land where he chose not to live, but which was an ideal he carried in his heart thoughout his short life. Meyerbeer caught cold by walkingbareheaded on a chilly windy day, and Pauline and Jeanne Castellan sang in the 'Mozart Requiem' at the funeral service. Pauline was criticized for insisting on a fee of 2,000 francs, but, in her defence, she viewed it as a professional engagement, and had always insisted that singers should receive a fee, as it was easy to be exploited.

Berlioz complained to his sister Nanci: "I'm no more cheerful today; I have just been to the church of the Madeleine for the funeral service of poor Chopin who has died at the age of thirty-nine. This time, at least, the service was a seemly one; the whole of artistic and aristocratic Paris was there. The pallbearers were Meyerbeer, Paul de Laroche, Eugene Delacroix and Prince Czartoriski (sic). They performed Mozart's 'Requiem' accurately but to no effect, and a few notes on the organ and the 'De profundis' sung in fauxbourdon touched the congregation more deeply than that great composer's famous but unfinished score. Luckily, I completed my article on Chopin last Saturday and shan't have to rewrite it; it would be too embarrassing to have to mention Mozart's 'Requiem'. I no longer have the courage to go on as I should, with this everlasting play-acting, producing admiration to order."

Pauline continued with her performances, notably in 'Le Prophete' at the Paris Opera, however, she fell foul of the gentlemen of the press and on October 24th, Meyerbeer spent the whole day full of anxiety because an article had appeared in several newspapers saying that Viardot had held a dinner for the fugitive Socialist deputies in London, where Socialist toasts were proposed and Madame Viardot sang Socialist songs. Consequently, several members of the clubs declared that they intended to hiss Madame Viardot on her appearance in 'Le Prophete', which naturally would have ruined the performance. Fortunately, this was a threat and they simply failed to applaud, but this was hardly noticed because the majority of the public, ignorant of the facts, cheered Madame Viardot with enthusiasm, and even threw her bouquets.

This unwarranted unpleasantness, coupled with the sadness of Chopin's death, upset Pauline greatly, and reminded her of the sudden deaths of friends who had died too young, like Fanny Mendelssohn, and her brother Felix, who only survived her by a matter of months, and of dear Gaetano Donizetti, whose

'L'Elisir d'Amore' she so enjoyed singing. These deaths over the past two years, gave both Pauline and Louis pause for thought regarding their own mortality. Louis was now forty-nine, only two years younger than Donizetti had been. However, life flows on, and Pauline was only twenty-eight and at the height of her powers. Within a matter of weeks, another young composer would appear on the horizon who would have a powerful significance in her life.

One evening, the Viardots were at a concert arranged by the Belgian violinist, Francois Seghers, director of the Societe Sainte-Cecile, and heard some pieces by Charles Gounod. The Viardots had first met the composer while on honeymoon in Rome in 1840. At that time he was a twenty-two-year old student, at the Villa Medici, and Pauline was a nineteen-year-old, budding opera singer. Now Charles was thirty-one years old, still struggling to make his mark, and she was a celebrated prima donna of twenty-eight.

Pauline congratulated Gounod on the music she had just heard and asked if he would care to visit her at home and play some of his other compositions to her. He was flattered, said that he would be very happy to do so, and a time was arranged.

Charles duly presented himself in the rue de Douai, and stayed for several hours, playing the piano and conversing with Pauline. She was deeply impressed by his melodic gift, and was immediately aware of his sensitivity and tremendous sense of beauty. Immensely impressed, she exclaimed, 'but Monsieur Gounod, why don't you write an opera'? 'Dear Madame, I would like nothing better', he responded 'but I don't have a libretto'. 'Surely you must know someone who could supply one'? she retorted.

'Well' answered Gounod, 'I used to know Emile Augier when we were boys, but he is now very well known, and as I am not, I am hesitant to approach him'. On the strength of the quality of the music he had just played to her, she persuaded him to go at once to Augier and tell him that if he would provide a libretto, she would guarantee to sing the principal female role in the opera, and would ask Nestor Roqueplan, the director of the Paris Opera, to stage it . Gounod lost no time in seeking an interview with Augier, who welcomed Pauline's proposal with open arms. 'Madame Viardot'! he exclaimed, 'wonderful, but who will produce it?'. Gounod replied that Pauline intended to approach Roqueplan, and Augier, fully aware of the immense success she was then enjoying in 'Le Prophete' at the Opera, thought it unlikely that the director would refuse her proposal, and despite the fact that he was then busily engaged in writing a play,

'Diane' for Rachel, he agreed to begin work on a libretto, as soon as a subject had been agreed upon.

Having always been drawn to the church, Gounod had originally toyed with the idea of becoming a priest and in October 1847, had been given permission to attend lectures at the Carmelite Seminary of Saint Sulpice in the rue Vaugirard. He wore a cassock and submitted willingly to the strict rules of the seminary, but despite his religious fervour, he was a sensualist, drawn to the colourful world of the theatre, and gradually, clerical austerity became too much for him . By the time he was thirty, he regretted that he had wasted so much of his time, although he had written several pieces of church music.

In February 1848, with the collapse of the monarchy, there had been much talk of freedom and brotherhood, but as in 1789, these ideals soon gave way to murder, mayhem and riot. About 20,000 people were put down with savage fury, and Gounod left Saint Sulpice as the barricades were being set up in the street. With a sense of futility, he questioned where his true course lay.

Pauline was pleased to observe that the intervening years since they had met in Italy had only served to enhance Gounod's appearance and personable charm. He was a little over medium height, with a good figure, a high forehead with a broad brow, a finely shaped nose, and soft, light-brown hair. His neatly trimmed beard and moustache gave him a distinguished air, but it was his deep, mesmerising blue eyes, which were his most arresting feature. Intelligent and well read, quoting Sir Francis Bacon or St. Augustine with equal fluency, he was a fascinating conversationalist, who delighted in all that was beautiful. In him, Pauline recognized a kindred spirit, and could easily believe that he was a great favourite with the ladies, his vivacity and manly appeal acting as a magnet for them.

As a pianist, he had an individual style and technique, and delighted his listeners by singing to his own accompaniment, in a tenor voice full of expression, if lacking in power. Men did not see him in quite the same light as did his female admirers, and many of them agreed with the comic actor, Edmond Got, that he was 'exuberant, shamelessly pushy and much given to kissing – both males and females!" Some years later, Charles Halle told his daughter that "Gounod was very nice and kissed me, 'a la francaise', which I thought unnecessary."

The composer was ecstatic at having acquired a patroness who was enjoying a measure of celebrity second to none, knew everyone in the musical world, and who, despite her 'picturesque weirdness' and lack of conventional beauty, fascinated him. He knew that people described her as plain, ugly even, but he was so impressed by her personality and charm that he failed to see the plainness of her features, which, when she was interested and enthusiastic were animated and suffused with a radiance that totally captivated him. He considered her one of the most attractive women he had ever met and looked forward to their next meeting with impatience.

Augier, a pipe smoking member of the Academy de France, was famous for his bourgeois comedies, and was a frequent and popular guest at fashionable dinner parties. He was a hedonist with a jolly laugh, 'as lusty and substantial as the prose of Rabelais', a plump, balding rake, whose fringe of curly hair gave him a seraphic look, very pleasing to theatrical ladies, such as Rachel and her sister, who were not averse to indulging in a little light dalliance with him.

Both Pauline and Gounod, who were fascinated by the classical world, favoured an ancient Greek theme as a subject for the opera, and after much discussion, finally settled on the life of the poetess Sapho, of Lesbos. Although her namewas well known, hardly any of her work had survived, and little was known about her personal life, but that did not deter Augier, who allowed his imagination full rein.

Nestor Roqueplan, an eccentric dandy and womaniser, took more interest in his own pleasures than in the running of his opera house, but Pauline was riding high in public esteem, and with an eye to commercial interests, he stated that as long as she sang the title role, he was willing to sponsor Gounod's first dramatic work. He made three stipulations, first, that it should be short, second, it must be serious, and third, that the female character should be the principal role. In a separate contract, signed by Louis Viardot, confirming his approval, Pauline agreed to sing two winter seasons at the Opera, running in each case from October 15th to May 31st, for a minimum of fifty performances in various operas, at 1000 francs each. She also had to pledge to 'turn up regularly and punctually for rehearsals,' and if she absented herself, she had to produce a medical certificate or pay a fine equivalent to 10% of her salary.

When she told Gounod the news, he was ecstatic and called her his wonderful angel, which indeed she was, as without her active influence he might have had to wait several years for a performance of his work at such a prestigious establishment. Gounod signed his contract on April 3rd, Augier completed the libretto by the end of the month, and the composer promised to deliver the score by 30th September, 1850, or earlier if possible. That only gave him six months to write an opera in three acts for his theatrical debut, but fortunately the work was not scheduled to be staged until 1851.

Pauline left for a tour of Germany, which included several performances of 'Le Prophete' in Berlin, and Gounod threw himself into the composition of his first opera. All was going smoothly until, on 6th April, his beloved brother

Urbain died suddenly. He was only forty-three, and left a distraught, pregnant wife, and a two-year-old son. This tragic event naturally threw Charles into despair, and he recalled how, most uncannily, on the evening before Urbain's death, he and Tourgueniev, had discussed the immortality of the soul.

Gounod's mother was prostrate with grief, and Charles was catapulted into the depressing business of funeral arrangements, and dealing with Urbain's business and family affairs. There was no question of continuing with composition at such a time and with great reluctance, he put his work aside in order to minister to his family in their hour of need. Urbain had owned an architectural practice, and it fell to Gounod to wind up the firm, which delayed the writing of his opera for a month.

When the Viardots received the news they were shocked, and heartily pitied poor Gounod. Louis, always the kindest of men, told Tourgueniev that he believed Urbain had been the main provider for the family and asked him to discreetly enquire if Gounod was in need of money, as he would be happy to be of assistance. Tourgueniev told Pauline that Gounod was well but had a pile of formalities with which to deal and would be very relieved when he was able to get back to work again. When informed of Viardot's offer of financial help, the composer was moved by such a mark of friendship, but asked Tourgueniev to assure Louis that it would not be necessary.

Pauline made Tourgueniev promise that he would befriend Gounod and give him moral support. The Russian had intended to go to Courtavenel but remained in Paris for eight further days to be of assistance to Charles.

The Viardots first suggested that the composer should stay with Tourgueniev in their house in the rue de Douai, but then had the happy thought of sending both men to Courtavenel and invited Charles's mother to join them. The invitation was gratefully accepted and, as soon as they were free to leave the city, the three of them went into the country, where, by the beginning of May, the composer had resumed work on his opera.

Almost fifty years later, when Gounod published his memoirs, he wrote of this visit: "I accepted (Pauline Viardot's) advice, and we left, my mother and I, for this residence. Mme Viardot's mother was there, in company with a sister of M. Viardot's (Berthe) and a little girl (Louise), today Mme Heritte, a remarkable lady musician and composer. Ivan Tourgueniev, the eminent Russian writer, an excellent and intimate friend of the Viardot family, was staying in the house. I began to work as soon as I arrived, but here is a curious thing, my soul, so recently disturbed by cruel emotion, rather than inspiring pathetic accents, brought forth the opposite effect and I was seized by scenes full of light, as if my spirit, bowed down by grief and sorrow, had felt the need to react more

positively, after those hours of agony and days of tears and sobbing. Thanks
to the calm which reigned about me, my work progressed more rapidly than I
had hoped".

Mme Gounod was comforted by the presence of Joaquina who fully understood the depth of her grief, having herself lost a dearly loved child. She was
given a pleasant room overlooking the park, and the extensive grounds of the
chateau afforded her solitary walks in delightful surroundings.

Joaquina and Tourgueniev were old friends who enjoyed each other's company immensely, and she resumed the Spanish lessons she usually gave him
when he was at Courtavenel. Charles was gradually recovering his spirits and
was pleased with the way 'Sapho' was taking shape. Although Pauline was far
away, she corresponded frequently, and the memory of her voice haunted him,
as he composed the music that she would sing. He relished being able to talk to
Tourgueniev about her, and Ivan was only too happy to chat endlessly about
his goddess, as he could never get her out of his mind. In a letter to Pauline,
Tourgueniev related how, on the evenings when she was performing, he and
Gounod would mentally follow her progress through the opera, willing her to
do well, praying that she would receive a great ovation with masses of floral
tributes, cheers and bravas at the end of the evening, and said that they searched
avidly for news of her whereabouts and reviews of her performances in all the
available newspapers and periodicals.

Ivan felt very much at home at Courtavenel, and did not want to leave a place
where there was so much to remind him of Pauline; he even felt affection for her
poor likeness painted before her marriage by Pierrre-Asthasie-Theodore Senties,
that hung beside that of her mother, and the bust of her colleague Tamburini,
which Jean, the servant, admired so much. There was also the big brown porcelain dog with a curly tail; the lame and earless little stuffed boar, and the great,
grey marble fireplace, around which they all gathered on dismal evenings, warm-
ing themselves at the log fire, chatting, reading or listening to Ivan's stories.

Both young men were working hard, Charles on his opera, and Tourgueniev
on his play 'A Month in the Country'. For relaxation they read Spanish classics
aloud with Joaquina, and strove to improve their Spanish conversation. All
wrote letters to Pauline and she to them, but Tourgueniev noted sadly that hers
to Gounod were always longer than the ones she sent him. Gounod showed
him one that ran to eight pages, and said that Pauline was an angel.

Tourgueniev had begun his play in 1848 and had already written the first act
before his stay at Courtavenel, admitting that he had set himself a 'psychological problem'. Perhaps it is unwise to read too much autobiography into any
writer's work, but in Ivan's case, his own feelings and experiences were always

near the surface in his writing, and there is a great deal in this play, which suggests that he was describing situations and feelings he experienced in the spring and early summer of 1850. Some years later, he admitted to the actress Maria Savina, who had taken the part of Vera in a Russian production of the play, that in many respects it was autobiographical, and based on some real people-: 'Natalia Petrovna really existed', he said, and added 'and Rakitin is me. In my works, I always present myself as the unsuccessful lover'.

The character of Natalia Petrovna, long presumed to be a portrait of Pauline, is hardly an attractive one, but anyone can behave out of character when in the grip of a strong passion. There is a scene in the play where Natalia, unhappy over her love for the student, Belyaev, who is tutoring her son during the summer holidays, breaks down and cries on Rakitin's shoulder. He comforts her, and they are disturbed by Islaev, Natalia's middle-aged husband and his mother coming into the room. They misunderstand the situation, and Islayev jumps to the conclusion that it is Rakitin with whom Natalia is in love. He likes the younger man and has turned a blind eye to the semi-amorous friendship between him and his wife, but he cannot disregard impropriety, and advises Rakitin to leave, still unaware that it is the student with whom Natalia is really in love. Islaev, who has no illusions about himself, acknowledges that he is much older than his wife, is preoccupied with his work, yet he loves her dearly and desires her happiness above all things, understanding that she needs younger company and more excitement than he can give her, but at the same time, he insists that she should not contravene accepted conventions.

Louis Viardot trusted Pauline and Tourgueniev, although he knew how much his wife meant to the younger man, because he never made any secret of his devotion, and both men were firm friends, with a great deal in common, apart from their feelings for Pauline. Louis was now middle-aged and occupied with his own writing and interests, accepting that as a lively, active young woman, she needed younger companionship, which reflects the situation in the play, and the conversations between Rakitin and Natalia in Act I, where Rakitin says that although he loves her, he knows he bores her, and she answers that their relationship is like making lace: "In stuffy rooms, always sitting still…lace is a fine thing, but a draught of cool water on a hot day is much better". Maybe Gounod was the 'cool water', and possibly this attitude illustrates the stage that Pauline and Ivan's friendship had reached by 1850. They had known each other since 1843, and maybe they had hit a kind of 'seven year itch', and all had become too familiar and predictable.

Pauline admitted that she "craved change", and liked meeting new, interest-ing, talented people, particularly men. When Camille Saint Saens mentioned her 'numerous infidelities' in his memoirs, he was probably over-stating the case, but, undoubtedly there had been talk over the years, and she knew how to flirt. She loved variety and excitement, and although she was not a naturally promiscuous woman, she found many men very attractive, although it is likely that most of her infatuations were largely of the imagination. Four years previously, on December 19th, 1846, after she had given a performance of Nikolai's 'Il Templario' in St. Petersburg, Ivan made a note in his memorandum that he had received his first real kiss from her. It is not known whether this was as significant for her as it appeared to be for him, or just a casual kiss during the celebrations for the French New Year, but Ivan was blissful. However, if he thought that there were more such kisses to follow, he was disappointed because Pauline contracted whooping cough shortly afterwards and had to leave Russia.

It is probable that if she did occasionally commit sexual indiscretions, she regretted them immediately afterwards. With her strong moral conscience, she would have felt guilty at betraying her devoted husband, and in a kind of panic, would push the other man away, causing misunderstandings. It is apparent that Tourgueniev, having experienced great happiness, could be cast down into the depths, by Pauline treating him in such a way. When a woman gives herself to a man, that man, especially if he is deeply in love with her, assumes that she will continue to do so, but if he finds her rejecting him after expressing her love, or allowing him to make love to her, he is confused, and distressed.

There is every likelihood that Pauline's kind heart sometimes led her into compromising situations, and it does appear that she was sexually naïve, unconsciously teasing the men who attracted her, without realizing how easily they could be aroused. In 1840, George Sand had been very perceptive when she prophesied that Pauline's love would always be chaste and pure, without passion or suffering, and that she would not even be able to understand the passion of others, whereas George was ruled by her passions and lived a deeply emotional life.

In Russia, as in France, there was speculation regarding the true relationship between Pauline and Tourgueniev; Boborykin said that Berg told him that Pauline had never had any sexual relations with Tourgueniev, but Nedrasov said that she had at one time, but then refused him; Dumas believed that she might have done, but said that as she was a lesbian, it hardly mattered.

Many writers at that time were fascinated by the image of the androgyne, a person possessing both masculine and feminine organs, and Gautier, who considered it possible that George Sand and Pauline belonged in this category, expanded on the theme in 'Mademoiselle de Maupin', and 'Contralto from Emaux et camees'. It is said that there was some mention of sexual matters in the file that the Police are alleged to have held on Pauline. Some men are titilated at the thought of two women making love, but also suspicious of strong, talented women in a masculine world, believing them freakish, and alien to the majority of their sex. However, at that time women had to be strong to hold their ground with men, and clung together from self interest, paying a psychological price.

Pauline tended to express her natural affections for men and women in an equally passionate way. This may have been a cover for a basic lack of eroticism in her nature, and could explain why Tourgueniev often felt so ambivalent towards her. In his story 'Punin and Baburin', his heroine Muza Pavlovna speaks 'daring and dangerous things' to the narrator in the presence of her elderly protector, going 'just as far as possible without arousing his suspicions'. Tourgueniev said: 'a woman's favourite pastime is to go to the extreme, and walk along the very edge of the abyss', but later in the story he showed the girl's single-minded devotion to her benefactor-husband.

What George had underestimated was her friend's overwhelming capacity for compassion and self-sacrifice. Almost a decade later, Pauline told Julius Rietz that from her earliest years, she had only known wounded hearts, but loved caring for them, as a sister of mercy would. This is borne out by the kind of men with whom she fell in love, and there is no doubt that Maurice Sand, Tourgueniev, Gounod, Julius Rietz, and Berlioz were all emotionally needy. Her affection for them remained constant, but was expressed in the language of 'amitie amoureuse' that she used for her other friends, both male and female. Occasionally, however, her feelings became those of conventional love, and the question is – did she give herself entirely to these men, or did other equally strong aspects of her make-up hold her back from the brink?

Gustave Dulong, her first biographer, who had access to the whole of Tourgueniev's correspondence with her, did not believe that she had betrayed Louis, and said that it would have been psychologically impossible for Ivan to write such friendly and noble letters to Louis and Joaquina had he been cohabiting with Pauline. There is no doubt that Tourgueniev loved Pauline passionately, and sought to draw her into the depths of his being, but perhaps his actual relationship with her served to confirm his life-long destiny: 'never to possess the women he loved, and frequently to possess women whom he hardly loved at all'. Dulong was not entirely frank, because when Halperine-Kaminsky was preparing to publish Tourgueniev's letters during Pauline's lifetime, she censored many of them, not only because Ivan made rude or unkind remarks about people still living, but because there were many details of 'a private nature' that embarrassed her, and she did not want them made public.

Many of the letters have sentences scored in black ink by Pauline, and it is tempting to speculate as to what Tourgueniev might have written, to cause her to do this.

Summing up these letters collectively, it is apparent that Pauline's feelings for Ivan waxed and waned, died and were reborn. There was also a certain amount of vacillation in Louis' friendship with Tourgueniev, and their letters illustrate the shifting nature of the three-sided relationship. Louis must often have felt neglected, and as late as the 26th of November, 1865, when they and the Russian were living side by side in Baden-Baden, Louis wrote a touching letter to his wife, complaining that she often seemed to esteem the writer more than himself, and he asked her how she would feel if he placed another woman higher than her, making her redundant: "I desire with all my being to fall mentally ill, for my heart is well and full of you, it loves you and reveres you. Let us then work together, as you say, to chase away these wicked, multicoloured devils, to restore my peace and gaiety, to make me fully enjoy the happiness and pride at having you for my wife and friend.'

Usually, Tourgueniev discussed work in progress with Pauline, but it is significant that in the summer of 1850, when he was deeply immersed in 'A Month in the Country' he did not do so, although it is very possible that he had little opportunity because she was totally involved with Gounod and his opera. Ivan acknowledged a debt of gratitude to the Viardots for introducing him into theatrical circles, which enabled him to make useful contacts, and his five most important plays were all written in France between 1847 and 1851 when he was staying at Courtavenel. Some years later he told a friend: "Courtavenel is, one may say, in somewhat flowery language, the cradle of my literary reputation". Although his plays were not particularly successful during his life-time, posterity has elevated them to an important place in Russian and European drama, and maybe without Tourgueniev, there would not have been a Chekhov.

Every time Pauline returned to France, she rushed to Courtavenel to see how her opera was progressing, spending very little time in the rue de Douai. Gounod was amazed at her grasp of a new musical style and idiom, and of her prodigious facility for committing music to memory. She told George Sand that she had been very happy since she had known Charles, because his music was as divine as his person was noble and distinguished, and she 'plugged' into it from morning till night, and night till morning. She also sang the praises of her 'man of genius' to Count Wielhorski telling him that although Gounod was at present unknown, he was destined for greatness. She said the same to Liszt when she replied to his letter inviting her to sing in Weimar.

Despite Gounod's high-mindedness, some of his fellow musicians called him 'the flirtatious monk', and the general concensus was that he was very unpredictable, and highly emotional. He could fool about climbing trees, then retreat into a religious trance, or kiss the husband one day, and make love to the wife the next. Wagner was not taken in by him at all and dismissed him as 'amiable-looking, upright-endeavouring, but it seems, not a highly gifted artist'.

In Ivan's play, the student Belyaev, with whom Natalia is in love, is hardly a true portrayal of Gounod. The student is frank and straightforward, but Gounod was nothing of the kind. His character was a complex one, prone to hypocrisy, and throughout his life, he enjoyed sexual flirtations, mingled with a kind of adolescent ecstasy, despite the fact that he posed as a man of high morals and ideals.

Although Tourgueniev had already written part of his play in Paris, the coincidence of the situation at Courtavenel was remarkable, considering that the last two acts were written while he and Gounod were living under the same roof. There is no doubt that Tourgueniev liked and admired the composer, but he adored Pauline, and was not blind to the way she responded to his companion. He believed that Charles was a serious rival for her affections, and being highly sensitive, perceived the difference in her attitude between himself and her protégé, aware that there was more than friendship between them. When Pauline was at Courtavenel, she could not hide her pleasure at being with Charles, and made excuses to be alone with him, walking in the garden and woods, causing Ivan to feel pushed aside, left to keep Louis company. Of course, the opera dictated that they should collaborate, but Ivan feared that matters had gone further than a mere professional partnership demanded.

The writer had frequently received summons from his mother to return to Russia, but he usually ignored her commands, despite the fact that she held the purse strings. Now, it appeared that she was gravely ill, and fearing she was dying, wanted him at her bedside. It is possible, of course, that the situation at Courtavenel had become so untenable that it was this, rather than concern for his mother, that finally made him decide to leave France. He was deeply unhappy and had no wish to return home, yet it was from this time that his greatness as a writer began to reveal itself, even though he believed that his youth had gone and that he had reached the end of an era. Perhaps his despair released his creativity, because he rarely wrote anything when he was happy, and in 'Spring Waters' he declared: "weak people never cause things to end by themselves, they always wait for the end to come".

He obviously didn't take news of his mother's illness seriously because after leaving Courtavenel, he went to Paris and stayed at the Hotel Port-Mahon in the second arrondissement. In a letter to Pauline he confided; "I have been too happy, now I see the unpleasant side of life's coin. If I have your affection, I will be supported in all the imagined disagreeable events." He said that he had thoroughly enjoyed the hunting at Courtavenel, and encouraged the Viardots to buy "The White House", which lay close to their estate, to conserve the game. Louis took his advice and two years later, he purchased it.

Ivan said that the garden had been neglected in their absence, and hoped that they would instruct Berthe and Joaquina to employ an assistant for the gardener. He told them that the weather was bad, and that they were sadly missed, and on the eve of his departure, he declared that Courtavenel was the most beautiful place on earth.

Charles had recently completed the ode for Alcee, and Tourgueniev had re-read George Sand's novel 'Jeanne' that he found beautiful but too pedantic, as were so many of her heroines, he concluded, such as Fadette and Consuelo in 'La Comtess de Rudolstadt". Remembering happy times, he reminded Pauline of how they had read 'Mauprat', and 'Hermann and Dorothea' together at the table where he was writing his letter, and he found it hard to believe that five years had already passed.

He said that Charles was angry with himself because he lacked inspiration and was lying on a bear skin, "like a bad tempered child, obstinate and tenacious, but he has my admiration." He admitted that he found it hard to refrain from laughing at Gounod's despair and desolation, but instead put his fingers over his stomach and said 'it is atrocious'. Of course, he knew the desperation caused by the absence of the muse, and he was flattered that Gounod confided these 'little sorrows of creation' to him.

While in Paris, he had a bad cold, but news of Pauline's London success cheered him and told her that he believed 'Sapho' would be truly beautiful and find favour with musicians. Yet he wondered how the public would react, used as they were to vulgar talents: despite this reservation, he had great confidence in Gounod's immense creative gift, which he said was 'rare and spiritual', and he declared that he was taking a paternal interest in the birth of 'Sapho.' Pauline had given both men a daguerreotype of herself, and Ivan was delighted with the image because he felt that the eyes were looking deeply into his own.

It is possible that the command to return to Russia was timely for Ivan, and may have had as much to do with the authorities as with his mother, as he said that if he did not return soon, he risked being exiled. On a personal level, it is very probable that a scene such as that in the play between Islaev, Natalia's husband and Rakitin, which results in the younger man leaving the house, had actually taken place between Louis Viardot and Tourgueniev before the Viardots left for England. Louis was a most sensitive, civilised man and it is easy to imagine him behaving just as Islaev did, because he was aware of the hopelessness of Ivan's situation.

Louis, unaware of the Gounod complication, was prepared to play a waiting game even if, as he thought, Pauline was in love with Ivan. She was a woman of principal and integrity, who, he believed, would not throw aside her marriage, any more than she had done at the height of her infatuation for Maurice Sand. It is quite possible that they had actually been lovers, and certainly George Sand believed so, as Maurice discussed everything with her, and Georges Lubin, the noted authority on the writer, is persuaded that there was a passing affair, and that George was very proud and happy about it. Whether or not Pauline and Maurice actually made love cannot, of course, be proved, but over the years he became a valued friend, and any romantic feelings there might once have been matured and evolved into a fraternal friendship.

A letter from Gounod, dated 9th May, shows that 'neuralgia of the bladder' was causing Tourgueniev great pain at this time: "Courtavenel can really do nothing at all this year, it seems, for poor Tourgueniev's affliction: it is giving him more trouble now than it has done for a long time, and I am most apprehensive that it may prove to be a very stubborn companion that he will have to drag around with him for the rest of his days. He was all right yesterday, and felt quite relaxed and in excellent spirits at the holiday that it had so unexpectedly granted him; but today the wind has changed, and not, unfortunately, for the better. The permanence of Tourgueniev's illness, and his approaching departure, distress me very much'.

When the Russian eventually left France on June 25th, Pauline was enjoying her 'star' status in the English capital. On June 22nd, the 'Illustrated London News' stated: "The great musical event of the season was the revival on Thursday night of Meyerbeer's 'Le Prophete' with the return of the gifted Viardot, in her celebrated character of Fides'.

In a letter to Pauline, Gounod asked her to be kind to Tourgueniev, and comfort him because he knew how much Ivan was suffering at being parted from her. The composer sent his 'tender kisses', and three little violets that he had picked while walking in Blandureau Wood, and gently reproached her for not writing to him often enough: "My own dear one! Can it be that you are ill? Oh, wicked, wicked distances, how I do resent you!"

Yet, at the same time that the composer was penning this missive, Tourgueniev was having a violent dispute with Paolo, Joaquina and Berthe over their fanatical, regular evening game of whist. Ivan left Courtavenel a few days later, weeping all the way from Rozay to Fontenay-Tresigny, but on the 14th of May, he told Pauline that thanks to an influential Russian whom he met in Paris, he had learned that the Tsar was in a war-like mood and persecution was rampant; the man advised him to put off his journey for a while, so that the situation would have time to improve. The following day, Ivan returned to Courtavenel and laughed all the way to Rozay, where he was met by Gounod with the tilbury. He was given a new bedroom, which was next door to cousin Theodore (the privy), and he slept wonderfully well. The 16th dawned bright and fair and Gounod spent the whole day walking in Blandureau Wood seeking musical ideas, but inspiration, capricious as a woman, would not come.

In her memoires, Louise states that during the time Gounod was at Courtavenel, they performed Beaumarchais' comedy, 'The Marriage of Figaro' in the Theatre des pommes de terre, with Gounod as Figaro, herself as a nine-year-old Cherubin, her mother as Suzanne, Tourgueniev as Count Almaviva, and, surprisingly, Joaquina, who was usually wardrobe mistress, as 'the sly, malicious, hypocritical, amusing Jesuit, Don Bazile'; Louis, as usual, preferred to be a member of the audience. Louise says it was very successful, but did she invent this performance? It seems strange that when they were all so busy with their individual pursuits, they should have found time to learn and perform such a long play just for fun.

Psychologically, however, it is interesting that Louise mentions this particular drama, as it echoes the situation at Courtavenel, when Tourgueniev's pursuit of Pauline and her apparent preference for Gounod were so aptly illustrated on the stage. Beaumarchais described Suzanne, as a 'clever and witty young person, fond of laughter but devoid of that almost wanton gaiety of our debased soubrettes'. He said that Almaviva, who for most of the play is dressed in hunting attire, should be played 'very nobly...the corruption of his heart should not detract in the least from his air of good breeding'; and the role of Figaro needed an actor with 'subtlety and lightness of touch, able to steep himself in the spirit of the character.'

These roles could have been written for Pauline and her two suitors because after some initial business about the size of beds and the choice of an appropriate marriage chamber for Suzanne and Figaro in Count Almaviva's chateau, the couple outwit the Count's amorous designs, cheating him out of his 'droit du seigneur' (the right of the master to make love to the bride before the wedding night). Spectators who understood the true nature of affairs at Courtavenel would have found Figaro-Gounod's lines very pertinent: "This young lady does me the honour of her personal services... I know that a nobleman took an interest in her for a time; but whether it is that he neglected her, or whether she likes me more than better-bred men, it is on me that she has now fixed her choice".

On June 17th, Tourgueniev accompanied the Viardots to the Gare du Nord to see them off to England. The parting was emotional, but Ivan said nothing of his plans, although Pauline thought that he intended to leave France as he had brought his luggage, money and dogs with him. He promised to write to her the next day, but his heart was so heavy that he found it difficult to put pen to paper. On the 21st, not knowing when he would see her again, he wrote: 'Farewell, may the good Lord guard and keep you every moment of the day. Be happy, blessed, gay, contented, well. I am for ever yours..."

He also wrote to Gounod, who replied at length, assuring him of his undying friendship, adding 'in our case God has been pleased to guarantee our feeling for one another with the highest of assets, for we are bound together not only by ourselves, but also by excellent friends whom we both love very deeply. Whatever place, therefore, my heart may hold in yours, you may believe that I shall be true to it, and that I shall try to keep it generous towards you: this is my very great desire', he goes on to say 'as for this nest that you feel so sorry to leave, it will not leave you. Do you remember that touching word of Mendelssohn's which made me weep so much: "Fear not, abide in peace, For He never sleeps!" He begged Tourgueniev not to forget him, but added, "I will allow you to inform me only indirectly, i.e. through Mme Viardot, of anything in your life, which you know will be dear to me – which will not prevent anything addressed to me personally from affording me very great pleasure. As for myself, God grant that, as you say, my letters bring you joy. This is the only good thing that can happen to them, for there is nothing really good in this world except being good to other people..."

Patrick Waddington observes that this letter 'seems to show the confidence and sporting condescension of the favourite candidate, the insolent piety of the evangelist who offers to pray for your soul and sends you a bill for his services', adding that 'the stage on which the Viardots' dramatic collision with Gounod would ultimately be played out could hardly have a better setting than this verbose, unnatural letter, which reminds one inevitably of the treatment given to poor Volyntsev by his buoyant rival Rudin, in Tourgueniev's novel of that name."

In contrast, the letter that Tourgueniev wrote to Louis Viardot, against the background of his extraordinary, painful love for Pauline, is noble and sincere: "I do not want to leave France, my dear good friend, without expressing my affection and esteem for you, or saying how sorry I am that we must part. I take with me the friendliest remembrance of you; I have come to appreciate the excellence and nobility of your character, and you must believe me when I say that I shall never feel truly happy until I shall again be able, gun in hand and by your side, to tread the beloved plains of the Brie. I accept your prophecy and will try to believe in it. One's homeland has its rights; but is not the true home-land that place where one has found the most affection for it, where one's heart and spirit feel the most at ease? There is nowhere on earth that I love so much as Courtavenel. I could never tell you how touched I have been by all the proofs of friendship that I have received in the last few days; I really do not know in what way I have deserved them, but I know that as long as I live I shall preserve the memory of them in my heart. You have in me, my dear Viardot, a staunch and loyal friend. Be happy, then; I wish you the best that the world can offer. We shall meet again one day, and this will be a happy day for me, one that will amply compensate for all the sorrows that await me. I thank you for your kind advice, and give you my most heartfelt good wishes."

So ended Tourgueniev's visit of three and a half years, the longest period he had ever spent away from Russia. As Herzen said, his impossible love for Pauline drove him back to the only other roots he knew, and it would be six long years before he returned to his beloved Courtavenel again.

In the event, Tourgueniev's visit to Oryol was timely because his mother did actually die, leaving him a considerable fortune. His elder brother Nicolai had inherited a substantial estate, but that still left Ivan with Spasskoye and a great deal of other property to administer, making it more difficult for him to pursue his former itinerant life.

In London, Pauline was as busy as ever, and on June 29th, she wrote to Ivan saying that she had given a concert at Court, and amused him by commenting on the evening dresses worn by her colleagues; "Grisi was as resplendent as a reliquary, and Castellan was literally covered in flowers of every kind over a pink robe." She herself wore a simple, white dress, the same one that she had worn at the Berlioz concert (where she considered she had sung the Iphigenie aria badly!). She wore roses in her hair and corsage, but no jewels, other than two beautiful bracelets. She presents an example of real French restraint, as opposed to the English tendency to "over-gild the lily", a trap many women fall into on special occasions. Queen Victoria, she related, "was dressed in bad taste, in a gown that made her look like a stick of 'Rouen rock'". Nor was Pauline impressed by the comments made to her by the Queen, because they were obviously stock phrases she used to all the singers with only a little variation. In Pauline's case she said "I have admired your recent performance in the 'Prophete' very much. It must have tired you, but it was very beautiful". Despite the lack of imagination behind these comments, the Queen was genuinely enthusiastic about music and the theatre, particularly opera, and many were the musicians, singers and actors invited to provide entertainment for her royal or noble guests at Buckingham Palace or Windsor.

As Louis had returned to Courtavenel to attend to estate matters, Pauline was alone in London. While there, on the 31st of July, Louis celebrated his fiftieth birthday, and wrote to tell her of his intense activity. Tourgueniev had advised him about the farms on the estate but he ignored his friend's suggestions, and decided instead to demolish the farm of la Vicomte, to benefit Courtavenel. He was dashing hither and thither, sometimes accompanied by Louise, and said that utter chaos reigned at Courtavenel, where the two farms 'were like forts taken by assault, nothing but ruins and debris'. On August 2nd, he wrote to his wife again, telling her that he had concluded all the business to his satisfaction and would soon be able to go to Paris, leaving Gounod and his architect friend to sort out the various problems.

He joined Pauline in London on August 12th, but regretted having to leave Courtavenel. In a letter to Tourgueniev, he said that he envisaged a rather grandiose and very expensive scheme, raising a wall to incorporate more windows and intended to split the level of the bedrooms, making the little guest rooms bigger and more attractive. He said that his project for the following year was to give the grand salon a new ceiling and a parquetry floor 'so that it will no longer be envious of the room that always bears your name and awaits your return'.

During the Viardots' absence, the work did not progress as smoothly as they had hoped, and when they returned to the Brie, Louis's spirits were low due to the conditions in which they were living, and by October 1st, he admitted that whatever was achieved, a great deal more remained to be done. He was further perturbed when a stone bridge that led to the farm, dubbed by Tourgueniev 'the Devil's Bridge', fell down while workmen were attempting to repair it and had to be completely replaced. Louis was aware that the workmen would not be finished by winter, and realized that another 20,000 francs would be required, with nothing to show in the way of increased revenue. 'Oh the charms of ownership,' he groaned, aware that in Paris a similar situation awaited him in the rue de Douai. However, in spite of his despondency, by the spring of 1851, the work on the farm was completed.

Whether it was due to the Viardots' politics, or rumours about Pauline and Gounod, who often walked together in Blandureau Wood, it seems that there was some difficulty with their tenants, and despite the recent improvements to his farm, Monsieur Negros left, and the Camus family soon followed him, 'apparently frightened off by certain charming neighbours', observed Pauline.

Several of their servants left, and there was domestic chaos, which must have been a real trial to Pauline, who freely admitted that she was not good at giving orders, and no doubt her good nature was often abused. Despite all the trials, however, the Viardots were determined to retain Courtavenel, and they envisaged extending their property even further, buying more land as it became available.

During her 1850 season, Pauline brought a new character to life for the first time in England, that of Rachel in 'La Juive' by Halevy. She had already sung it several times in Germany and Paris, where the production was very splendid. London, not to be out-done, created a fine version of its own, which was extremely well received but Chorley, while appreciating the merits of the staging and the excellence of the performances did not think that the tunes were memorable enough to ensure a permanent place in the operatic repertoire. The cast included Mario, Enrico Tamberlik, Karl Formes and Mlle Vera, and the conductor was Michael Costa. Chorley wrote: "As sung by Viardot and Mario on Saturday, the house rang with the furore of the audience". The Queen and Prince Albert attended the tenth performance, and a press notice read: "Viardot's success in the highly dramatic role of Rachel was all the more amazing after her girlish Zerlina and innocent Desdemona". Chorley said ' her voice had become sweeter and more flexible by practice, her declamation was what it had always been, and her acting was incomparable'. He relates how in the last act of 'La Juive', at the Royal Italian Opera, she was supported on the stage, hardly conscious of time, place, or the frightful fate so near. Raising her languid eyes, she saw the tremendous cauldron in the distance. Disengaging herself from the executioners she staggered towards her father, fascinated by that hideous machine of torture. She had her back to the audience, but there have been few such impressions of mortal terror received in any theatre, as that conveyed to the audience by the countenances of every one on the stage, whom the gestures of the actress, and the expression of her features, obviously terrified".

On June 25th, as Tourgueniev left Paris for Berlin, Pauline was scheduled to sing with Mario, but that morning he cancelled his performance, once more causing gossip and consternation. He wrote to Frederick Gye, the manager, saying "I waited in case, but no use, 'La Juive' will have to be postponed till Saturday, for this evening don't think of it, it's quite impossible for me to sing, it is the evil eye!" Grisi suggested that 'Norma' should be substituted for 'La Juive' with herself in the title role. Pauline thanked her profusely, but said that if 'Norma' was presented, she, and not Grisi, would sing it.

In the event, 'La Juive' went ahead as planned with the tenor Enrico Maralti, who had sung Eleazar in Brussels, in place of the sick Mario. He did not know the role in Italian, having only sung it in French, and as usual, in the case of sudden indisposition, there was no time to rehearse, but thanks to his and Viardot's professionalism, all went splendidly. There were rumours aplenty, of course, and much blame was put on Grisi and her obsessive jealousy of Pauline, but this time, Mario's illness appeared to be genuine, although a critic remarked that he was hoarse due to singing at a concert at Lord Lansdowne's!

The Illustrated London News of August 3rd remarked: "At the second performance, Castellan sang instead of Vera. Mario was back on form. The triumph of 'La Juive' is now beyond doubt. The Rachel of Viardot is the very character she assumes, as in Fides, as Valentine, she has stamped the part of 'La Juive' with her marked individuality. The denunciation of Leopoldo was withering in passionate scorn – the whole frame of Viardot was convulsed with powerful emotions; but the triumph of her histrionic genius is in the march to the place of execution." Chorley, although admitting that Pauline sang sublimely, considered that the part was really too high for her.

In great contrast, her next role was that of the delicious Adina in 'L'Elisir d'Amore' with Mario as Nemorino, Tamburini as Belcore and Ronconi as Dr. Dulcamara. Pauline loved playing, this light-hearted part which was full of fun, in pleasant contrast to all the suffering and dying in her more dramatic roles. Adina is a minx, and teases Nemorino, the village lad who is in love with her, mercilessly, but at the end of the opera she takes pity on him and shows that underneath the mischief there is a good heart. In 'Prendi per me', she repents her cruelty, and Pauline moved her audience to tears with the sincerity of her love for him; she packs off the arrogant military man, Belcore, who has been wooing her and agrees to marry Nemorino. In this role Viardot showed her versatility, proving that she could be amusing, mischievous and tender, as well as dramatic. She loved this kind of singing where she could use the whole range of her voice, leaping over large intervals, but always returning to the comfortable middle and lower part of the register after scaling the heights.

A press notice remarked: 'L'Elisir' was revived, Mme Viardot making her first Covent Garden appearance as Adina. It was one of the great hits of the season. Her Adina was a piece of genuine, refined comedy and her vocalisation was distinguished by the most brilliant cadenzas. In 'Prendi per me' she was immensely applauded, as also in the two duets. Jeanne Castellan took over as Adina when Mme Viardot left, although her vocalisation could not compete with Mme Viardot's brilliant style".

The singer Blanche Marchesi made some pertinent comments about style and ornamentation at that period. She was the daughter of the famous teacher Mathilde Marchesi, who had studied with both Viardot and Manuel Garcia, and said how important ornaments were considered at that time, indeed the only thing worthwhile listening to, and the artists jealously guarded their 'points d'orgue', which they composed privately with the greatest care. They made them as long as possible, spicing them with every conceivable difficulty, and were so jealous that they only sang minor ornaments in rehearsals, keeping their real efforts for the first night, so that it was impossible for their colleagues to steal their effects. 'How long this fashion of exaggerated, senseless, even unmusical heaping up of difficulties and culmination points, clad in ornamental figures, lasted, how they maintained this taste in the public, is proved by the fact, incredible as it sounds that even Mme Viardot, who was not only a great singer but a great musical genius, and one of the most remarkable women of the time, had to make her success, keep her public well in hand and stamp every evening with a triumph (even at the end of her career) by introducing in 'Orfeo' of Gluck, a point d'orgue which fitted in that opera like a monkey's head on the figure of the Queen of Sheba'. Blanche was mistaken in thinking this style was an imposition on Pauline; quite the contrary, she relished it as it was an important part of the Italian tradition in which she had been trained, but she was no mere canary. To her these additions were necessary to the dramatic expression of the role.

The season ended on the 24th of August with Pauline as Zerlina in 'Don Giovanni', the first time she had sung it in England, having previously appeared as Donna Anna in that opera. Chorley said it was a "delicious blending of peasant wonderment and girlish complacency". Writing nine years later to Julius Rietz, Pauline described the character of the young peasant girl: "Zerlina, to my mind, is not at all a doll prinking as a shepherdess, a soubrette assuming a naïve role, a coquette who lures Don Giovanni under a mien of pretended innocence. She is confidently naïve, much of a child, but a child of the South in flesh and blood – she yields involuntarily to the influence of the demonic nature of Don Giovanni – she is fascinated by him as a bird by a serpent. During their duo, I make Don Giovanni play in a different manner from the ordinary. If Don Giovanni assumes the attitude of an ordinary seducer, this scene becomes heartrending. But if the man is capable of assuming a certain resemblance to a serpent (especially like the one in Eden), if he can put himself in the serpent's skin for a few minutes, then the demonic power with which one has always liked to set off Don Giovanni is no mere invention of Hoffman's and, before him, of the Spaniard's; this power, I repeat, is admirably reflected in the music. Mozart divined it and depicted it, in spite of words that are simply shocking. To sum up, Zerlina is good, gay, impressionable and weak but innocent, although having an ardent temperament".

Pauline was now ready to go home for a short, well earned rest, and returned to Paris in September, but soon left for the country. She had been counting the hours until she could see Gounod again, and hear what he had written in her absence. Courtavenel was full of family, friends and servants, so the two musicians had little time alone when she first arrived. One of the guests was Gounod's student, a musically gifted boy of fifteen, Camille Saint-Saens, who worked as his copyist. The youth soon fell under Pauline's spell, becoming quite fascinated by her, and so began their life-long friendship. Young as he was, he already had many fine compositions to his credit, and soon became a regular visitor to the Viardot's home.

Charles had written to Pauline frequently while she was away, and she lived in happy anticipation of his letters, which were always very affectionate and revealed his true feelings for her. Tourgueniev wrote frequently, but he complained that she did not write to him often enough.

Louis, as always, was his own reserved, sage, dear and kind self, but now, after many years of marriage, Pauline was apt to take him for granted, and she did not consciously realise how much she still needed him. She knew him so well, and almost accepted him as part of the furnishings. His extraordinary kindness was illustrated once more when he allowed her to receive Tourgueniev's eight- year-old daughter into their home so that she could be brought up with Louise, who was a year older than the Russian girl.

On his return home, Ivan had been distressed to discover that his illegitimate daughter, who had been accidentally conceived in 1842, was being ill-treated and mocked by the servants, and had previously been taunted by his own mother. As the unwanted child of the son of the house, her position was untenable, and he was determined to send her away from Russia. Her mother, Avdotia, had married a Moscovite and abandoned the child to her fate, but Ivan, full of pity for the little girl, turned to his best friends and begged them to help. They did not disappoint him and it was agreed that Pelagaya should go to France. The child only spoke Russian, and up to that time had lived exclusively among the serfs on the Spasskoye estate. Being uprooted and sent to live with strangers in a distant country must have been truly traumatic for her, and could not have been easy for the Viardots either, but they resolved to do their best for the little girl. As might be imagined, Louise was not happy about this state of affairs; she was an intelligent and observant child and resented Tourgueniev's place in her mother's life. Now, to add insult to injury, she was expected to share her mother with his daughter, and, as could have been foreseen, the Viardot's noble intentions did not work out as well as they had hoped.

Above left:
George Sand,
Pauline's life-
long friend in
male attire

Above right:
woodcut of
George Sand
and de Musset
on their
'honeymoon' in
Venice

Right: Franz
Liszt with
whom Pauline
studied piano,
and on whom
she had a girlish
infatuation

Behind the Scenes: A dressing room in an English theatre

Interior of Her Majesty's Theatre, Haymarket where Pauline made her debut
in 1839 two months before her eighteenth birthday

Gounod was due to complete his score of 'Sapho' by September 30th, 1850, but there were still several unfinished items and others needing revision, so he was obliged to stay on at Courtavenel for another two weeks. Louis had intended that they should all be back in Paris by the first week of October, but as the weather was bad, they delayed their departure until the 25th, although Pauline had to be in Paris on the 18th for a rehearsed of 'Le Prophete'. The season opened quietly, until the revival of 'Les Huguenots' on the 18th of November, after which Pauline returned to Courtavenel several times.

She appreciated the benefits of the timeless, tranquil atmosphere of the autumn in the Brie, and she told George Sand what an invaluable period her holiday at Courtavenel had been. She said that her musical taste had been distinctly purified by her friendship with Gounod, and vowed in future to eschew everything that was mediocre. In all, she and Charles spent seven weeks together at the chateau in the summer and early autumn, and their relationship developed more quickly and deeply than that of herself and Ivan in the whole seven years they had known each other.

Now that he was back in Russia, Tourgueniev felt that Pauline was slipping away from him, and he told her of a profoundly disturbing dream he had had about her: "I seemed to be walking back to Courtavenel during a flood. The grass in the forecourt was covered with water, in which there swam enormous fish. I went into the hall, saw you, and held out my hand; but you began to laugh. The laughter hurt me". The dream is interesting because the fish symbol relates to both sexual and spiritual love. In his story 'Asya', which he wrote in 1857, he used this nightmare theme at a time when he was separated from Pauline: "The last of the dying lanterns that the students had set out in the hotel garden were lighting up the leaves of the trees from below, giving them a festive and fantastic air. We found Asya by the shore: she was chatting with the boatman. I jumped into the boat and said goodbye to my new friends. Gagin promised to visit me on the following day; I shook his hand, then offered mine to Asya – but she only looked at me and shook her head. The boat cast off and was carried down the swift river. The boatman, a hale old man, plied his oars with effort in the dark water. 'You've entered the column of light, and broken it up', shouted Asya. I looked down. Around the boat the rocking waves were black. 'Farewell!' – her voice was heard again."

In the draft version of this story, the manuscript reads: ' Asya started to sing a loud song…..' As the narrator goes home he muses about this song and its mysterious singer, and laments her refusal to shake his hand.

On 1st February Pauline wrote to Count Wielhorski telling him that she had been resting for a while after her performances of 'Les Huguenots', but was now beginning to work very hard on her beloved 'Sapho'. No doubt Tourgueniev had told the Count about Gounod's opera, for he was also tremendously enthusiastic about Pauline's 'man of genius', whom, they both believed, was destined to become another Mozart. She told Wielhorski that everyone was mad about him and that he possessed a fine and noble talent, a heart to match, and refined and unaffected manners, and added: "He has become a member of the family, and we all adore him".

In his memoires, Gounod remembered how delighted Pauline had been on her return from England when he played and sang the whole of his opera to her. Nevertheless, her letters to Tourgueniev reveal that she had suggested a number of changes, notably asking Gounod to include his earlier 'Chanson du pecheur' for Sapho's last soliloquy, 'O ma lyre immortelle'. Louis also made suggestions of his own to ensure the predominance of his wife's role. Pauline quickly learned her part and was soon so familiar with the score that she began to accompany herself from memory and Gounod declared that it was the most extraordinary musical feat he had witnessed.

Earlier in the year, she had introduced Charles to George Sand and soon the writer and the composer were corresponding regularly. When Pauline enthused about Gounod, George wanted to know if he was a good man, observing: "There are so few artists who are great men"! However, when she met Charles she, like the rest of her sex, succumbed to his good looks and charm, and soon they were the best of friends.

Despite her busy schedule, Pauline always found time to compose songs, and in 1850, she brought out an album of ten of them dedicated to several of her colleagues. For Berlioz there was 'En Mer', a setting of a poem recalling the ancient world, with references to Carthage; for Meyerbeer, 'En Cana' (L'Absence), the song in the Spanish idiom which had appealed to Chopin so much; for Roger 'Marie et Julie', which served to show off the tenor's exquisite legato, and for Marietta Alboni, 'La Chanson de Loic'.

Life at Courtavenel became more relaxed, and several guests visited, including Henry Chorley and Gustave Roger. The tenor had been expected to sing the part of Phaon, but had declined it, as he did not think the character was of sufficient importance to the story. Emile Augier was invited to the chateau to make changes to the libretto, but Berlioz reluctantly refused the Viardots' invitation, due to 'a host of anxieties, of unpostponable tasks, of idiocies, and of occupation that absolutely prevent me from accepting." He wanted to know when Pauline was returning to Paris, and jokingly said that he hoped she would be beset by 'hail, cold, wind, neighbours and games of whist', which would make her long for the capital, adding: "May local poets come to read you their verses! May the priest try to convert you! May you be invited on daunting picnics! In short, may the provinces unleash themselves upon you, those are my wishes on your behalf. Perhaps then you might return to the civilized world." He said that he failed to understand why M. Viardot preferred staying in the country when he had no wolves or bears to hunt, declaring that he was sure there was nothing in their woods but titmice, and was amazed that they were content to stay away from the metropolis for so long – asking: "what could be the attraction"?

Manuel and his children came to stay, and on September 10th, Pauline wrote to Tourgueniev telling him that each day they all looked for the postman in the hope of receiving a letter from him. She said that the weather was pleasant at the moment, with a light breeze animating the trees in the court, and three cockerels striding about, crowing, and sometimes fighting with each other. It was eleven o'clock in the morning, Manuel was sitting at her side copying some Mexican songs, Joaquina was sitting next to him doing her needlework; a little further away, Berthe was rather slowly writing a letter, using very small lettering, and Pauline said that if she carried on at that rate it would take her about four hours to finish it. Her nephew Manuel was reading some Moliere, and near the window to the left of the little tower, Charles Gounod was working on his manuscript. Louise was having a Spanish lesson from her great-uncle Paolo, and Mariquita, his wife, was sitting by his side.

Mme Gounod was in her own room, taking her medicine, and Louis, accompanied by Pauline's nephew Gustave, and Sultan, the dog, had gone to do some business in Villars, a nearby hamlet of some thirty inhabitants. She told Ivan; "Your absence and the pain we feel in our hearts replaces your dear presence, I assure you, each moment of the day. Your memory is with us, in all our actions, from morning till night. For seven years you have known all our habits; they are always the same, so that at each hour of the day, as you think of us, you know where we will be. But we cannot follow you, so please describe to me one of your days, then I can imagine your activities. In your solitude, there cannot be much variety." To her dismay, she discovered that some of her letters had failed to reach him, which was why he complained that she did not write often enough.

She assured him that she had thought about him a great deal, having been as lazy as a lizard in the sun, and that she was eating very heartily. She asked him about his daughter Pelagaya, who was on her way to France, and said that Augier had arrived the previous evening and that Gounod had pounced on him immediately, insisting that he alter parts of the text. Each day Charles walked in Blandureau Wood in the hope of finding inspiration, but it did not always come, and Pauline told Ivan: "The poor boy is all of a fever. He will not be able to rest until the entire opera is finished. Roqueplan has only given him until the end of the month. I have not made a sound since my return from London, but I shall start again today because I want to sing my role to Charles before the end of the holidays."

While Pauline was awaiting her return to the Opera, Marietta Alboni was enjoying a great success in Donizetti's 'La Favorita', but as she was leaving for Madrid on October 1st, Pauline said that she would not have the pleasure of her company.

At Courtavenel, the harvest had taken place and the Viardots had given the annual dinner for the farmers, who got drunk and thoroughly enjoyed themselves. Manuel and his children had left, and although Pauline missed her brother, she was not sorry to see the boys go, because they had been a disruptive force in the house: "Three years has not made them less destructive and Manuel is tormented by them, at his wit's end to know what to do with them. They don't work and are all disobedient, yet their hearts are good. Such children must be a great worry to their parents. My Louisette is much as always, excessively intelligent, but horribly opinionated. No one is severe with her, and I hope she will not become spoiled through indulgence."

Tourgueniev's daughter arrived from Russia, disorientated by the long journey and bemused by her new surroundings. As she did not speak French, she was at a loss when Pauline was not around to translate for her, but Mme Garcia was a good hearted woman and took to the girl immediately, endeavouring to help her fit into her new family. Louise was jealous and resented another distraction for her mother.

Pelagaya, who was re-named Paulinette on her father's orders, had been told by him to treat Pauline as her real mother. This did not go down well with the girl and she disliked the hold the singer had on her father. She never approved of Pauline, and as she grew older, she positively rejected her. There was never an affinity between them, and in future years, Paulinette sought to put a wedge between Tourgueniev and Pauline. When it was obvious that things were not going to work out, her father removed her from the Viardots' home, found her a governess, and rented an apartment in the nearby rue Montmartre for them.

For the time being, however, all was done to welcome her. Pauline, of course, had more to contend with than purely family and domestic matters, and was soon on the move again. She and Gounod continued to correspond in the most affectionate fashion, and rumours circulated that they were more than just good friends and colleagues. For many years it had been assumed that Tourgueniev was Pauline's lover, and that Louis was a complaisant, cuckolded husband. Now, it seemed to the gossip mongers that she had thrown over Tourgueniev for Gounod, and the Russian was believed to have returned to his homeland in chagrin. When it became known that his illegitimate daughter had become the Viardots' ward, tongues wagged more energetically than ever, and nobody quite knew what to make of this bizarre situation.

Of course, it is easy for people to think the worst, particularly when they do not know the full facts, and there is no doubt that the friendship between Tourgueniev and Pauline was of a rare kind. The writer made no secret of his absolute devotion to her, but even to this day, their relationship remains ambiguous and there is no proof that she ever regarded him as anything more than a dear friend, as she did Ary Scheffer, although gossips inferred that her relationship with even him, was not so innocent.

As the rehearsals for 'Sapho' commenced at the Opera in the first week of February, 1851, the singer and the composer were thrown together continually, and they could not disguise their personal feelings for each other, nor their kinship as musicians. In 1846, Gounod had declared: 'Today, art is a means rather than a real end in itself and people work to make a fortune or a name, rather than to create a beautiful thing; everyone is enlisted under the flag of self-interest and with this multitude of individual proclivities it is hard to know where things are going'.

Pauline fascinated Gounod, and he loved to watch her when she did not know that she was being observed. Her eyes would flash brilliantly as she sang or talked, although sometimes she was very grave, and totally concentrated. In another moment, her wonderful smile would flash across her face, and her attractive laugh would ring out. As she created her role she showed such stature, such intensity and such a command of her voice, manoeuvring it skilfully even in the most difficult passages, that Gounod was more amazed than ever by her vocal, dramatic and musical skills.

The responsibility on Pauline was great, because the rest of the cast were not equal to her either in quality or experience, and she had to dominate the production. As rehearsals progressed it became apparent that there were deficiencies in the cast, and that the work itself had flaws. This was to be expected, of course, as a first work for the stage by a composer without theatrical experience was hardly likely to be a masterpiece. Gounod, despite being a talented composer, was untried in stage-craft and had not yet developed a dramatic sense, even with Pauline to advise him. Sections of the music were splendid, but as a whole, the opera lacked cohesion, although the seeds of Gounod's later, successful works, were already there for those who were prescient enough to perceive them.

In Paris the political situation was once again giving cause for alarm, although few people had any idea that the Prince President, Louis Napoleon was secretly planning a coup d'etat. Sometime previously, he had declared his intentions to the English Foreign Secretary, Lord Palmerston, to see how Great Britain would react, and Palmerston had taken it upon himself to inform the President that the English had no interest in the affair and would not interfere. This very individualistic statesman, with whom Tourgueniev was later to be acquainted, was a thorn in the flesh of Queen Victoria and the Prince Consort, because he frequently' forgot' to inform them of what he was up to at the Foreign Office, and they only learned about his actions when it was too late to stop him. The royal couple were totally unaware of what was afoot on the other side of the Channel, and when the news broke, and Palmerston's collusion was discovered, he was forced to resign.

Despite political turmoil, domestic life goes on, and Pauline's cousin, Antonia, was about to give birth to her first child, and her parents, Paolo and Mariquita Sitches, had joined her and her husband in Brussels. Louis was busy looking after his investments in a somewhat unstable Market, but found time to write to Tourgueniev telling him that his book about the Arabs in Spain was going well at the printers.

Rehearsals for 'Sapho' progressed, and Gounod and Pauline were full of optimism, despite the usual hold ups and chaos that occur in putting a work onto the stage. Sometimes these were due to incompetence, but not always, as there were many factors involved: it was like assembling a large jigsaw puzzle, and difficult to get all the pieces in place at the same time. In the company, this caused anger, brought on by tiredness, frustration or irritation, and temperamental displays, due to dented egos, harsh words and wounded amour propre. The complexity of technical matters caused things to go awry at the first dress rehearsal, with scenery still not finished, wet paint, carpenters hammering, many props still to be provided, the performers complaining about their wigs or shoes, alterations being made to costumes, due to singers having put on or lost weight since the last fitting, and a myriad other things that go to make up an opera production. Pauline had experienced this many times, of course, and she was used to the dread feeling that nothing would be ready in time for the first night, but to Gounod it was all new, his nerves were stretched to breaking point, and he felt out of control, now that his opera was in the hands of strangers who knew a great deal more about the staging of a work than he did. He had been in his element while he only had to cope with music rehearsals, and could answer the queries of the players who could not read the notes in front of them, due to the incompetence of the copyists, but once the rehearsals moved on to the stage of this mad house called a theatre, he felt side-lined, disorientated and alien.

Despite her own nerves and concerns, Pauline, seeing Charles in a distraught state, attempted to calm him, took him into the privacy of her dressing room, and quietly told him that it would literally be 'all right on the night'. She put her arms around the hypersensitive man and embraced him lovingly, stroking his hair and murmuring soothing sounds, as if he were a distressed child. He responded to her caresses immediately, and held her close, but she, aware that they could be disturbed at any moment, firmly, though gently, put him away from her, and said that they must return to the rehearsal.

All too soon, the great evening arrived, and on April 16th, 'Sapho' took place at the Paris Opera. Pauline's performance as the heroine was generally admired, but Augier's libretto was harshly criticized, as were some aspects of Gounod's music, and it was generally regretted that the opera contained no ballet.

What was worse, some members of the audience thought it was 'political, dangerous and subversive' because the sub-plot concerned the assassination of a political tyrant, and many suspected that it reflected the uncertain political situation in Paris, and the ominous figure of Louis Napoleon. According to Gounod, Berlioz came up to him on the first night weeping from emotion, but this was wishful thinking, because the older composer actually thought it 'too fierce', and said, rather enigmatically, that: 'before all else, a musician must write music.' He was damning in his praise as, even though he used the adjectives 'grand' and 'beautiful' he also said that it was 'repulsive, hideous and horrible'.

On the other hand, Theophile Gautier did not see it as polemic, and wrote: "'Sapho' was cleanly and firmly written and genuinely dramatic; the characters were alive, even if they were sentimentally conceived". He said that the work was wholly French, but declared that the lack of a ballet was a distinct disadvantage. Adolphe Adam, wrote that he considered it a fine work, and was particularly pleased because 'above all, there was no hint of Rossini or Meyerbeer. It was Gluck who appeared to have been Gounod's ideal'.

This succes d'estime was hard for Gounod and Pauline to accept as they had put their faith in a triumph. When Pauline read the report by the critic Escudier in 'La France Musicale', she was dumbstruck at finding herself the victim of a most vituperative attack, and was at a loss to understand what had brought on this tirade: "Mme Viardot no longer sings. Every note that emerges from her intelligent voice is an ear-splitting shout. This singer, whom I once admired so much, is more or less dead to art. Her shattered vocal powers have lost their charm. They are but the shadow of a once beautiful picture". Pauline was not quite thirty, but as far as this report was concerned she might have been ready for retirement. As a result of this onslaught, many other critics followed suit and 'Sapho' was taken off after a dozen performances, although the cause of its removal was more political than artistic. Pauline appeared seven times, then left for London, and another singer took her place in the remaining performances.

As in 1842, when she had been a victim of appalling press notices, causing Louis to write to 'Le Siecle' complaining that his wife was being targeted in a cowardly fashion, which had nothing to do with her standing as an artist, but due to her friends' political affiliations, she was once more receiving ill treatment for the same reason.

Although in a letter to Tourgueniev dated April 29th, Pauline described her costume, and ended 'yours affectionately, constant in heart and mind', her enchantment with Gounod had soured her relationship with Ivan. It even affected her logic, because the critical attacks merely served to increase her championship of Gounod, seeing their mixed reactions as proof of the opera's controversial modernity. George Sand was alarmed by Charles' apparently proprietorial attitude to Pauline, as he told the writer that she could address her letters to him, or to Pauline, it was all the same.

The fact that the opera was now in performance did not mean that the couple saw less of each other, and Gounod suggested that he and Pauline should spend a weekend together at Courtavenel. As she was not intending to go back to Paris until the Monday, Charles proposed to stay on the Saturday night and the whole of Sunday with her, and suggested that they return together. He wrote on Tuesday the 20th, and again next day, saying that he would catch the coach to Rozay at midday on Saturday, and from there set off to Courtavenel on foot. She would then be able to meet him after dinner on the route du Poteau, which intersected the road through the forest of Blandurea. He rejoiced at the prospect of seeing her again, and expected to spend a pleasant time at the chateau, despite the cloudy weather. He sent her some flowers, and his best wishes to Louis and 'the rest of Spain', and said that he had a libretto to discuss with him. On the Thursday, in a very loving mood, he wrote again:

'Rest assured that your letters will not remove my appetite for seeing you, and I promise to look at you and our dear countryside with famished eyes'.

There is little doubt that during 1850 and most of 1851, Gounod was as besotted with Pauline, as she was with him. At first he had welcomed her into his life for her influence on his career. Her celebrity and fame as a prima donna, as well as her social standing as the mistress of a substantial Parisian house, and a country estate, added to her attraction, and he was not averse to the fact that she was obviously very infatuated with him, and he soon fancied himself in love with her.

Pauline sent him frequent letters and bunches of wild flowers, and had little time to think either of Louis or Tourgueniev, because Charles occupied all her thoughts. She went ahead of him to London, and on June 27th, just a few days before he left to join her he wrote: 'My God, how time drags at not being able to see your two good dear faces again! How round and wide my eyes will open on the first occasion I shall have to do so! You know that the good Tourgueniev says that when I am happy my eyes are round, and it is true; I am quite astonished not to see you now, for you are so much a function of my eyes that your absence has the same effect on me, as an enormous man-made clearing in a wood that I had once known, dense and in excellent condition".

In advance of the Parisian premiere, Pauline had persuaded Frederick Gye at Covent Garden that 'Sapho' should be included in her 1851 contract. Now its creators put their faith in its English premiere, hoping that it would receive a better reception in London, where Parisian politics counted little, and where the English were en fete for the Great Exhibition. Immediately, Gounod set about making changes to his work, composed a new aria for Glycere, and wrote some ballet music.

In London, he and Pauline indulged in a number of secret trysts and amorous exchanges, and when apart, Gounod wrote her loving letters, such as: "London, Tuesday, a quarter past midnight.....I love you tenderly....I embrace you with all the strength of my love for you".

In the summer of 1851, thousands of people descended on the capital from all corners of the globe, to visit the Crystal Palace in Hyde Park. This vast edifice, made of glass, was the design of the gardener, Joseph Paxton, which he had based on the glass houses where exotic plants were reared at the Duke of Devonshire's great estate of Chatsworth in Derbyshire. But the Exhibition itself was the brain child of the Prince Consort, and was intended to house artifacts brought together from all over the far flung British Empire, the exotic mixing with the mundane. As Britain was the seat of the industrial revolution, manufacturing naturally played a major role in this great public event.

It was a gigantic undertaking, but the Prince's vision paid off handsomely and it was an enormous success, much to the Queen's delight. She opened the proceedings, and was beside herself with joy at her 'dear Albert's' triumph over all the odds, and she made many further visits before the Exhibition finally closed, having made a profit of over £150,000 that was used for the building of the Victoria and Albert, the National History and Science museums in South Kensington, and, as a permanent memorial to her beloved husband, the Albert Hall was constructed as a temple of music for the masses.

London was full of visitors, among whom were a great number of foreign musicians and performers, including Rachel, the French actress, who was appearing at the St. James' Theatre, and living at 15, Half Moon Street. It was one of the most brilliant seasons in living memory, and Rachel was taken to the exhibition by her good friend, Lord Granville who, at the end of the year, was to become Foreign Secretary in place of the disgraced Lord Palmerston.

Despite the glamour of the Great Exhibition, in 1851 London was not a healthy place because the air was noxious due to the enormous number of coal fires and the smoke from the railways, which, when mixed with Thames mists, created dreadful fogs, known as 'pea-soupers', causing serious and often fatal lung ailments, and in the winter, so many people suffered from bronchitis that it was known as the 'English disease'. In addition to the pollution, problems were caused by the weight of traffic, which was even heavier than on Pauline's first visit to England, a seething, chaotic mass of carriages, horses and pedestrians, causing frequent road accidents.

On February 10th, Charles Dickens wrote to his friend, the writer Edward Bulwer Lytton, then living in Italy: "London is a vile place, I sincerely believe. I have never taken kindly to it since I lived abroad. Whenever I come back from the country now, and see that great heavy canopy lowering over the house-tops, I wonder what on earth I do there, except on obligation. You will have read in the papers that the Thames is most horrible. I have to cross Waterloo or London Bridge to get to the Railroad when I come down there, and I can certify that the offensive smells, even in that short whiff, have been of a most head and stomach distracting nature'.

Pauline's first role in the 1851 season was that of Fides, the part she was now most strongly identified with, and on July 5th, the 'Illustrated London News' reported: "On Tuesday night, 'Le Prophete', adjourned through the illness of Mario, was presented for the second time. The sublime picture of the devoted and pious mother, the simple and dignified Fides, is still as perfect as ever, in the hands of the gifted child of genius, Mme Viardot. Whether she be in more or less voice, she never fails to excite her hearers to an extraordinary degree;

nothing but exalted genius could accomplish such thrilling effects, for physically, Viardot has everything against her. A vocalist who cannot boast of personal attractions, nor of a naturally fine organ, should indeed be endowed with the divine spark, to cause the most exciting emotions. The eye is never tired of following every graceful movement, of watching her statuesque attitudes, nor the ear fatigued by listening to those soul stirring tones, in which the trials and griefs of the lofty minded mother of the false prophet are so powerfully developed and expressed."

Mario had obviously been genuinely unwell on this occasion. Singers are often thought to be superhuman, untouched by all the things that affect ordinary mortals, and although the tenor cried 'wolf' on several occasions, presumably egged on by Grisi, he was a human being, just as prone to illness, as anyone else. The life of a singer is a difficult one because the body is his instrument, and all the things that affect it will affect the voice. The bulk of the roles in the tenor repertory at Covent Garden fell on Mario, and it is not surprising that he sometimes became over tired, or that with his constant smoking and the pollution in the city, he developed chest infections, which affected his voice, making it impossible for him to sing.

The Times critic, J. W. Davison, was still unsure of the merits of Meyerbeer, and wrote a dismissive critique that displeased his editor, Mowbray Morris, who told him to re-write it. He said there was a diversity of opinion regarding the merits of 'Le Prophete' as a work, but "the orchestra is perfect, the mise en scene has never been surpassed, and that of the two principal characters, Viardot and Mario, has never been equalled. Costa is entitled to great praise for having organised so admirable a band, and the managers of the theatre deserve the public gratitude for their selection of music, which has tended to elevate the public taste and to make us acquainted with music that was hardly known except through the imperfect performance of drawing rooms. Try your hand again and give due praise to the admirable acting of Viardot and Mario, especially the former".

As light relief for Pauline after the drama of Fides, she played the small but significant role of Papagena in 'The Magic Flute' by Mozart. On July 11th, the Queen, the Prince Consort and members of the Royal Family made a State visit to Covent Garden; as usual, it was a very fashionable event, but perhaps the Queen was feeling out of sorts because the performance did not meet with her customary approval. She wrote in her journal : "...the opera being performed in a slovenly manner. The three black ladies (sic) sang very badly, the scenery etc., very inferior and Mario really only walked through his part. The performance was only saved by Ronconi with his inimitable drollery, keeping one in fits of laughter with his tricks".

Chorley thought differently and observed: "The music was most carefully rendered by Mme Grisi, (Pamina), Signor Mario (Tamino) and excellently by Herr Formes, who was heard and seen to his best advantage in Sarastro. Every conceivable quaintness and unpremeditated freak was thrown into the part of Papageno by Signor Ronconi; and the smaller part of Papagena was taken with zeal and relish by Mme Viardot". George Hogarth, always a supporter of Pauline, said: "The prominence given to the trifling part of Papagena by the genius of Viardot is one of the most attractive features of the ensemble."

On July 14th, a 'morning' concert at Covent Garden in which Viardot took part turned out to be a fiasco. This event had been billed as the final one of the season, and the last in London in which Grisi would ever appear as her farewell had been announced. The doors opened at one o'clock, and 'the first thing that disturbed the proverbial equanimity of the British Lion was a horrible placard posted at the doors and putting forth in large and wet, but painfully clear type, that the great star of the morning, Mme Grisi could not sing, the cause being sudden indisposition. There were sounds of disappointment, but the audience took their seats, and the concert began with the overture 'Oberon' conducted by Julius Benedict, and a chorus from Verdi's 'I Masnadieri'. These items should have been followed by the whole of Rossini's 'Stabat Mater', but due to Grisi's absence, only excerpts could be given. However, the audience soon became aware of another absentee when the 'Cujus animam' was also omitted. Where was Mario? A babble of voices broke out calling his name. Luigi Lablache sang 'Videt suum dulcem natum' in respectful silence, but when he'd finished, the disturbance broke out again. The quartet 'Sancta Mater' was sung amidst the fury of the audience and the stage manager, Augustus Harris, announced that 'Signor Mario had not yet arrived but that he was expected momentarily and would, of course, sing the aria set down for him.' The tenor arrived soon after, and sang the 'Cujus animam' but the audience was not to be placated and Mario retired, probably for the first time in his life, to a chorus of hisses.

Viardot sang 'Fac ut portem' and the final chorus of the oratorio was followed by a piano concerto and a French horn solo, but the storm started up again, even more violently, for Mario should have sung twice more. There followed furious demands for Mario, and another tenor, Enrico Tamberlik, obviously very angry, rushed onto the stage followed by his perplexed colleagues to sing the finale of 'Mose'. Before they could begin, Mr. Harris made another announcement to the effect that Mario was no longer in the building, having departed indisposed. There were shouts of 'humbug' and 'this won't do', which led to a general uproar. Mr. Harris promised money back to those who wished to leave, and several took the opportunity to do so. Many people remained in their seats, but soon there was more dissatisfaction when it was realised that Giorgio Ronconi, whose name was on the programme, had failed to put in an appearance. Eventually order was restored by the fine singing of Mme Bosio who performed the great scena 'Ernani involami' from Verdi's 'Ernani', which was vociferously encored".

Strangely enough, the errant singers overcame their sudden indispositions pretty swiftly, and appeared at a reception and concert given by Lady Manners at her fashionable house in Upper Brook Street that evening. It was a splendid occasion attended by over three hundred guests, including the Duchess of Cambridge and her daughter Princess Mary Adelaide. Pauline and Angiolina Bosio were two of the singers, accompanied by the indispensable Julius Benedict, but in the 'Morning Post' the following day, it was noted that although not well enough to attend the concert earlier in the day, Mario and Ronconi had recovered sufficiently to take part in Lady Manner's concert!

During the rehearsal period of 'Sapho', on August 2nd, Pauline repeated the role of Adina. This time she had a new tenor, Ciaffa, as Nemorino, but he was summarily dismissed, as his voice was not big enough for the opera house. The rest of the cast were highly praised, Viardot being hailed as a captivating Adina, Tamburini as a vivacious sergeant, and Ronconi, as an intensely droll Dulcamara.

The premiere of Gounod's opera took place on the 9th of August, but disappointingly, it fared little better in London than it had in Paris, and was condemned out of hand by several critics, the most dismissive being J. W. Davison, who wrote that he found it "wanting in melody, had indecision of style, ineffective treatment of voices, inexperience in use of instruments, accentuated by an affectation of originality disclosed in strange, unsuccessful experiments, excess of modulation, established forms, and general absence of continuity, vexing the ear with beginnings that rarely arrive at consummation". Again Davison was taken to task by his editor, Mowbray, and chastised for 'being hostile to young Gounod'.

Chorley, realised that Gounod had potential as an operatic composer, and stated that he considered 'Sapho' to be one of the best first operas ever written and chided his fellow critics and the public for their attitude towards new music. He found it interesting that Gounod did not follow the modern fashion of his contemporaries by imitating successful composers such as Meyerbeer, but frequently set his music to a ground bass, as the older composers had done. The critic considered that it had rarely been used in the theatre to a more happy effect than in Sapho's song, and the chorus in the second act.

He wrote: "although 'Sapho' was well received by the audience, in spite of our habitual timidity in approval of the work of one hitherto unknown, the wrath and ridicule outpoured by most of the censors of the press were too vehement and curious not to be put on record. The event has not justified the sagacity of those who jeered at and assailed the music, and who declared that any expectation invested in its writer was only so much sheer hallucination. There is dispraise of a quality which defeats its own object".

George Hogarth mixed his praise for the singers and much of the music with criticism of the libretto.

Augier's original French had been translated into Italian by Fontana (for the Covent Garden production). Hogarth wrote that 'Sapho' had been mounted with great splendour and praised the mise en scene by Grieve and Telbin. He thought that the casting of the principal roles was first rate and said that the chorus and orchestra were beyond praise and that the music in the first and last acts was superb. Yet, he added the caveat that despite all these positive elements it would prove a failure, due to the 'dull, wearisome, and repulsive libretto.' He declared Gounod to be a gifted composer, but said that the opera would perish because of the weakness of the poem. Of the singers he wrote: "Tamberlik, as Phaon, sang a lovely romance in A flat, encored rapturously – an exquisite melody. Viardot sang 'Grecia a voti' on her entrance, and in the third act, Sapho awakening from her swoon, sings for the last time, despairingly to her lyre 'O ma lyre immortelle' bidding adieu to the world, and finally ascending a rock to throw herself into the sea". He added that Viardot's acting and singing of this scene were sublime, worthy of her greatest moments as Fides.

Despite the approbation of such men as Chorley and Hogarth, Charles and Pauline were downcast because their beloved work had been denied the triumphant success for which they had striven. Gounod was aware that he had much for which to thank Pauline, not least the fact that she had introduced him to English concert organisers, who had presented some of his sacred works before his opera appeared in England, and these had been warmly received, particularly the 'Solemn Mass'. However, soon the old maxim 'biting the hand that feeds' would be very relevant where Charles and his benefactress were concerned.

As a man, Gounod was a mixture of two diverse personalities, the priest and the sensualist; he yearned desperately for mysticism, which was probably one of the things that appealed to Pauline about him as she had a deeply mystical nature herself. Yet Charles was hungry for fame in the material world and desperate to make a name for himself as a composer of the first rank.

The romantic attachment between him and Pauline had been much remarked upon, and rumours circulated in London, just as they had in Paris. The composer was full of high phrases, and lofty feelings 'mingled with a sort of adolescent ecstasy', but it is not known if this ecstasy was translated into sexual activity during his bachelorhood, although he spent a lifetime in sexual flirtation, and as he grew older he developed a penchant for young girls.

From circumstantial evidence, it appears that between 1851 and 1852 Pauline suffered some kind of emotional crisis, possibly concerning Gounod. She and the composer were together in London in the early part of August 1851, and it is highly probable that there was physical intimacy between them at that time and possibly earlier, although with the failure of his opera, Gounod gradually experienced mixed feelings regarding Pauline, who he increasingly used as a scapegoat for its lack of success. His main grudge was that she had chosen Augier as librettist, and it was the libretto that had received the strongest criticism.

When the season concluded at the end of August, instead of returning to France, the Viardots went to stay with their friends the Hays at Duns Castle in Scotland for three weeks. Gounod continued to write to Pauline and kept in touch through Berthe, with whom he had a somewhat uneasy relationship. He said that he was frequently at the theatre, which had become his staple 'diet', and casually mentioned that he was seeing a great deal of the Zimmerman family. He apologised to Pauline for not writing as frequently as usual, but said that with his many activities he had little time to spare.

While she was in London Pauline had learned from a piece in the 'Revue Musicale' that her contract at the Paris Opera had been cancelled. The official reason was that she needed a rest, but the reality was that her politics and that of her friends were not acceptable to those in authority. It was known that during 1848, the year of revolutions, the Viardots had entertained Alexandre Ledru-Rollin, Louis Blanc and Etienne Arago at their London home, and it harmed the Viardots to be linked with them. The reactionary 'La Patrie' accused them and their friends publicly of being traitors to France. Pauline herself was declared a dangerous, subversive republican, the intimate friend of the 'sulphurous' George Sand, who had encouraged Alexandre Ledru Rollin, when he was temporarily in charge of the Provisional Government, to commission Pauline to compose a piece for tenor and womens' chorus, 'La Jeune Republique'. It had been performed at the Theatre de la Republique by Gustave Roger and fifty girls from the Paris Conservatoire, wearing white dresses with tricolour sashes,

and had caused great offence in certain quarters because it had been intended
to replace the 'Marseillaise.' George had hoped that Pauline would perform the
solo part, but at that time she was suffering greatly from migraines and was not
at all well.

She was very shaken by her treatment at the hands of the Parisian press, and
was in no hurry to return to France for more of the same treatment. William Hay,
their host at Duns Castle, was a well known figure amongst the aristocratic
families of the lowland hills of Scotland, and an enthusiastic, sportsman with
whom Louis had much in common, despite their differing political affiliations.
Some members of the Hay family had originally met the Viardots in Paris and
they had struck up a friendship. Lady Monson was a mutual friend who often
stayed with the Hays in Scotland, and it may have been at her suggestion that
William Hay had originally invited them to visit his home. Pauline looked forward to being out of the public eye for a while, and decided to let matters die
down before returning to Paris.

For more than a year her emotions had been played upon like a stringed
instrument, and her normally strong will power had been weakened. Now, although she missed Charles, she longed to have time to herself, to rest, read,
sketch, embroider, and go for long walks in the beautiful grounds of the castle,
against the magnificent backcloth of the Lammermuir hills, in a countryside
more lovely because of the magnificent red/gold of the autumn leaves. With the
ever faithful Louis by her side, Pauline hoped that her over-taxed emotions
would find some peace. Tourgueniev was far away and she was free from his
constant adoration which, while she was under Gounod's spell, had been the
last thing she desired, although she still valued his friendship.

In September, Pauline discovered that she was pregnant, conception having
taken place at the beginning of August, when she and Charles had been together in London. Perhaps it is significant that Louise was almost ten years old
and there had been no sign of another child during that time. Of course, Louis
could have been the father, but there is every possiblity that Gounod was
responsible for Pauline's condition. Unfortunately, short of DNA testing the
truth will never be revealed.

At the end of the month, the Viardots returned to Paris, and in October,
Gounod joined them at Courtavenel. He had been looking forward to his visit,
and expressed his delight in breathing "'our' good Courtavenel air once more".
He recalled 'the round table in the sitting-room...at which we have lived so
often and so well, reading, writing, chatting, and posing for sketches... Work is
probably going on there at this moment, but it is very short of people.' When he
arrived, Pauline was already awaiting him, and all seemed much as before,

except that she was now pregnant, and pregnancy affects women in strange ways. Whether Gounod was the father or not, he must have been disconcerted when he heard the news. Writers have taken the fact that Pauline now turned to Louis for support and comfort as proof that he was the father of her child, but psychologically, nothing was so simple where Pauline was concerned, and it may well have signified quite the opposite. Often, when she had apparently gone too far with men, she upset and confused them by withdrawing, just when they thought she had declared herself. She became frightened of her own feelings, and regretted arousing their desires. In each case, both figuratively and literally, she rushed home to the protective arms of Louis, her father figure, who would kiss her better and make everything come right. Deep down, she knew that he would never desert her, and even when she strayed, he would always be there for her.

Gounod had been warmly accepted into the Viardot circle, but he was an ambitious man, morally weak, lacking in loyalty, and conveniently overlooked how much he owed to Pauline, Louis and their friends, not only professionally, but in the generous hospitality they had extended to him for over a year. In his own way, he had loved Pauline, but he now began to repudiate her because, in his innermost heart, he blamed her for arousing his emotions and the sensuality that was such a prominant part of his nature, but which he sought to control. When that control gave way, and he was swept along on the tide of passion, the 'priest' could not forgive the 'temptress'.

He began to discover the extent of the rumours and gossip about himself and Pauline, which had been circulating for over a year, and far from abating, had become more titillating, with the news of her pregnancy; naturally he was appalled, and thought it prudent to put some distance between them. This proved to be his last stay at Courtavenel, and over the following months, he and Pauline grew further apart. It may well have been her intention to keep Charles at arms length, particularly if she suspected that he was the father of the child she was carrying. As there was something of the priest about Charles, there was something of the nun about Pauline. Her Mediterranean blood was strong, but all her life she strove to keep her sensual nature at bay. She could let her passion loose upon the stage, but in her personal life she did her best to subdue it, and if Charles had really been the father of her unborn baby, there is every possibility that she would have resented him on poor, cuckolded, Louis's behalf.

In addition, the Viardots were viewed with suspicion by the political estab-lishment, and this alarmed Gounod, and he decided that it would be sensible for the sake of his career to see less of them, as he had no wish to offend those with the power to elevate him. Pauline had served her purpose as a patroness and now that he was becoming known, he could afford to turn his back on her, as other influential people came into his life. To exonerate himself, he began to run her down behind her back, saying that as a singer she was past her best, and singing out of tune all the time. In this way, he provided further tinder to the onslaughts of the press, and presented her enemies with additional fuel. It was not the behaviour of a grateful friend, least of all of a gentleman, and demonstrated the hypocritical side of this charismatic charmer.

It is also perfectly possible that Gounod thought the child was his own, and in keeping with his lifelong practice of running away from difficult or unpleasant situations, decided to remove himself from the Viardots, to put a stop to the rumours. He was now a frequent visitor to the home of his former teacher at the Paris Conservatoire, the highly influential pianist Pierre Zimmerman. Pauline had known the Zimmerman family all her life and considered herself to be on good terms with them.

The pianist was married to a dominating woman with a propensity for jealousy, and they had four very plain daughters. One of them, Anna, set her cap at Gounod – after all, he was still young, handsome, personable, and she found him decidedly attractive. He was also beginning to be talked about as an up and coming composer, and her father thought that he had a fine career ahead of him, despite 'Sapho's' lack of success, which had, nevertheless, brought him to public notice. Pauline had always imagined herself to be a welcome guest at the Zimmerman home, but unknown to her, she was disliked by Mme Zimmerman and Anna because they were both deeply jealous of her.

Before he realised it, Gounod, whose own mother was of a dominant disposition, was more deeply enmeshed in the Zimmerman net than he intended. Mme Zimmerman had decided that he would be a suitable husband for Anna, and never noted for her subtlety, she put the matter fairly and squarely to him, then sent him away to consider the advantages of the match. He thought it over, and decided that he was not ready for marriage. Unfortunately, when he returned to the Zimmerman home, he was not able to summon the courage to speak plainly, and Mme Zimmerman mistakenly assumed that he had come to propose. Before he could speak, she spoke for him, telling him how thrilled she was to accept him as a son-in-law. Gounod, not daring to contradict her, allowed himself to be swept along by her powerful personality, submitted to a fait accompli and proposed to Anna, who eagerly accepted him.

Despite such dramas in the private lives of individuals, in Paris, political events were gathering momentum and the news of the coup d'etat by Louis Napoleon on December 2nd, came as a shock, especially to the Viardots and their friends. They had long despised and blamed the Prince President for the terrible massacres and excesses of 1848, during which time, he had given his ministers a free hand to curb the violence taking place, not only in Paris but throughout the country. In addition to the brutal severity meted out to the actual insurgents, twenty-seven thousand of their alleged supporters were arrested on suspicion or tried in their absence, with no witnesses and no right of appeal. Many were innocent of any atrocities, merely holding 'dangerous' opinions, but this was enough to condemn them and they were imprisoned, transported or executed.

To be fair to Louis Napoleon, when he realised what was taking place, he commuted many of the sentences, and after a time, some 3,500 people were set free. However, it was not until an amnesty in 1859 that the last 1,800 prisoners were released.

To the Viardots and their politically committed friends, the coup d'etat of 1851 was a savage blow, and it is certain that Ary Scheffer, for one, never really recovered from it. In March 1850, he had married Sophie, the widow of his friend General Baudrand. He was now fifty-six, and suffered from heart trouble which made him rather reclusive, but he and Sophie seemed happy together, despite the fact that she was rather possessive. His fame and reputation continued to grow, but with the triumphal progress of Louis Napoleon, he gave up exhibiting at the State sponsored Salon, and took no more official commissions.

On the day of the coup, barricades were set up at Rochechouart, and the rue Blanche, very close to the rue de Douai and the rue Chaptal. Tourgueniev wrote to his daughter from St. Petersburg, and advised them all to avoid standing near the windows, in case of stray bullets.

George Sand, who had been a supporter of Louis Napoleon during his imprisonment at the Chateau of Ham, was appalled at the actions being carried out in his name. She wrote to him, begging for clemency for his political opponents, and he invited her to visit him. He was moved by her plea and shed a tear, which she believed was genuine, telling her that it was not his fault. Through her eloquence, she persuaded him to commute some orders of execution to imprisonment, and even to free a number of prisoners. Many years later, seeing Louis Napoleon in a gloomy mood, his wife, Eugenie, declared: "You wear the memory of December 2nd like a hair shirt," and he replied: "I think of it constantly", but in 1870, he told one of his ministers: "You did your duty then, as I did. I could have done nothing else".

There is no doubt that George Sand was a truly courageous and generous woman, and she worked indefatigably to earn money to sustain the families of imprisoned friends. She was still in personal danger at Nohant, due to those who did not share her political ideals in the surrounding region and factions at Le Chatre.

Shortly after the coup, a group of friends gathered at the house in the rue de Douai to discuss the crisis, and it is possible that this event caused the Viardots' home to be searched soon afterwards. On the evening in question, Louis was out and Pauline was practising in her music room when a friend, the writer and historian, Henri Martin, a man of whom she was very fond, was shown in. He was in a frantic state and implored her to help him, telling her that he had learned that the authorities were about to search his house. With no time to lose, he had fled precipitately, bringing his two young sons with him.

Pauline showed him where they could hide, but she had only just returned from leading them across the inner courtyard when the front doorbell rang noisily in the still night air. Too late, she discovered that it was not Martin's, but her own house that the authorities had a warrant to search. Taking her time, she proceeded to the entrance and opened the door to a group of militia, who demanded to be admitted. Always rising to her best in times of crises, she calmly let them in, then returned to her room and continued to sing, all the time watching what was happening out of the corner of her eye.

No stone was left unturned and the ruffians ransacked drawers and cupboards; in rifling Louis's desk, they struck gold when they found letters from Daniel Manin, who had striven to restore the Republic of Venice, by freeing the city from Austrian occupation, and from the freedom fighter, Lajos Kossuth, who had led the fight to overthrow the Imperial Austrian domination of Hungary. In 1848, he had proclaimed independence from the House of Hapsburg, but the Austrians, supported by the Russians, put down the insurrection with ferocious cruelty and Kossuth fled to Turkey. He risked his life again in 1851, when he travelled to London, where he was greeted by the populace as a hero, the English always being on the side of the oppressed, and he was lavishly entertained at the Guildhall by the City Fathers. As an asylum seeker, he was welcomed by the English, and made his home in the capital.

Louis's correspondence was confiscated, but little else was found, despite the stripping of Pauline's desk, which, dangerously, contained several letters from that 'notorious libertarian' George Sand. Fortunately for the two ladies, only nicknames were used and the soldiers, not realising the true origin of the letters, let them pass, and after turning the house upside down, left without making any arrests.

As soon as Louis learned what had happened, he realized that the time had come to remove his family from Paris, and hurried to make arrangements to return to stay with William Hay and his family at Duns Castle.

The Viardots were preoccupied with the political situation, and Pauline had no idea of the seriousness of the developments between Gounod and the Zimmermans, when on the 21st of December, they set out for Scotland, taking Louise with them. During the Channel crossing, Pauline spent most of her time on deck, leaning against the rail, deep in thought, meditating on the past year and all that had happened. They boarded the train at Dover, and on their arrival in London, found Manuel waiting for them. When he heard about their house being searched, he was naturally apprehensive for them, and believed they were doing the right thing to get away from Paris for a while.

Very early the next morning, the Viardots caught a train for Scotland. London was shrouded in a pall of mist, its grey, grimy buildings and naked trees forlorn in the cold, gloomy weather as the train pulled out of the station, but after Grantham the weather improved; the sun broke through, and gradually the flat landscape of Lincolnshire gave way to the beautiful, rolling Yorkshire country-side, with its verdant, dales, and dark, sullen moors, spectrally dramatic under the wintry sky. By the time they arrived at the shipbuilding centre of Newcastle upon Tyne, night had descended, and the ancient walls, a remnant of the Roman city of Pons Aelii, loomed solidly in the gloom.

The present city takes its name from the 'new castle' built in 1080 AD, by Robert, the son of William the Conqueror, who is the title character in Meyerbeer's opera 'Robert the Devil', in which Pauline had sung the roles of Alice and Isabella, in the same performance on one famous occasion!

Here, the Viardots broke their journey, staying at the Railway Hotel, from where they could make out the dark shape of the massive cast iron bridge, the enormous span of which was considered one of the wonders of the modern world, completed just two years before. They spent a comfortable night, and breakfasted early, Louis and Louise tucking into a substantial English break-fast, while Pauline merely drank a cup of black coffee, and then they set off on the last lap of their journey.

In contrast to the previous day, the morning dawned bright and fair, with a clear, blue sky and only a light breeze. The temperature was mild for the time of year and the landscape was bathed in a soft, silvery light. As the train headed northwards, the scenery became starkly beautiful, and the horizon opened out into the wide expansive Northumbrian scene, with small villages and picturesque churches dotted over the wide landscape. The train stopped at Morpeth and took on water, and farming folk with baskets and boxes of produce for the market at Berwick-upon-Tweed, came on board. The train chugged along to Alnmouth, then along the coastal road, allowing a fine view of Holy Island and the Farnes, those lonely bastions of the early Christian age.

Belford was the next stop in the gentle countryside of the Tweed valley, looking towards the Cheviot Hills, and the Viardots left the train at the attractive border citadel of Berwick, with its Elizabethan, grass covered earthworks. Looking towards the sea, they could not miss the church with its tall steeple, around which clustered houses, shops and inns. Here, the Viardots changed onto a branch line, and at the little country station that served the village of Duns, William Hay met them with his carriage.

After all the anxieties of the past month, they were only too happy to be back with the delightful Hays family. William was keen to hear about present conditions in Paris, and sympathised with their difficulties. He had been horrified to learn of the coup d'etat and of their personal danger, and was very willing to extend his hospitality and the safety of his castle to them, for whatever length of time they needed.

Passing through the village street of Duns, the carriage then drove through the archway of an attractive, turreted lodge, and swept up the long drive, lined with ancient lime trees. The castle was built over a fourteenth century stronghold, one tower of which remains, but the rest of the building had been fashionably styled in 'Regency Gothic' during the 1820's, presenting a neat, picturesque appearance of warm, pink stone walls and crenellated walls and towers that Pauline, always conscious of her architectural surroundings, found absolutely charming. The central portion predominates, standing proud of the rest of the castle, with a Tudor style porch and massive double doors, set under a Tudor drip stone, over which are set three long Gothic windows, with an oriel window on the upper floor. Hays had lived at the castle for almost five hundred years, and although not a titled family, they were proud of their ancient lineage. William Hay was a respected landowner, known for his fair treatment of his servants, workers and tenants, a man who, as one of the leading members of the community, took his responsibilities seriously.

As the carriage came to a halt, the front doors were flung open, and Mr. Hay's wife, Mary, and other members of the family rushed out to greet them. Servants appeared to carry the luggage and the guests were led up the impressive stone staircase, and along wide corridors to their light, high-ceiling rooms with long windows over-looking the landscaped park. Hot water was poured for them, and they were left to freshen up from their journey before joining the family in the dining room for lunch.

The estate was large by the standards of the British Isles, but Louis Viardot, who had hunted over the extensive lands of his Russian and Continental friends, considered it far from vast. He told Tourgueniev that he spent his time as best he could, and hunted with his 'good host' M. Hay, but the laird's estate was neither large nor well stocked with game, and he envied the splendid sport enjoyed by his Russian friend. Nevertheless, he was having a pleasant vacation in a delightful spot, wandering over the countryside, his gun at the ready, should game appear, and this was sufficient for him, as he preferred the fatigue and trouble of the chase, to a large amount of carnage.

He had Cid, a favourite hound with him, and a very funny little black pointer called Kit, who was full of vigour and courage, and he gave Ivan a list of the creatures he had 'assassinated' since arriving at Duns, which amounted to: 19 hares, 16 rabbits, 3 pheasants, 4 woodcocks, 11 partridges, 4 snipe, and 2 ringdoves. He said it was little enough, yet sufficient for him, and added that the weather had been very mild when they arrived, and was still fair, like November in France. The recently fallen snow reminded him of Russia., although the temperature was an insignificant 2 or 3 degrees.

Each day, between the chase and dinner, Louis became a professor of French and taught spelling and reading to a class of five young people, including Louise, who were receptive and good at their studies. When not teaching or hunting, he worked on his own researches, and had recently been reading Pausanias, which had given him an idea for an excellent opera plot based on the legend of the ashes of Orpheus, which he had sent to Gounod, advising him to ask Augier for a libretto. However, there is no evidence that Gounod ever approached Augier on this subject, or that he contemplated writing any music for it. Considering that Augier's libretto for 'Sapho' had been less than successful, it appears that Louis was somewhat ingenuous in making such a suggestion to the composer.

Duns Castle is about half a mile from the village of Duns, close to the Whiteadder and Blackadder Waters in the Border Country, an area with a bloody history going back to the Romans and beyond. Here, many a savage battle took place between rival clans, and between the English against the Scots. There are several old castles, some ruined, and large country houses in the vicinity, but by the beginning of the nineteenth century, the terrible feuds, which had once been so prevalent, were a far memory; peace reigned and there was a good deal of visiting between the neighbouring families. William Hay was a very keen fox hunter, and would travel many miles to enjoy a good day's hunting on the estates of his fellow land owners, and no doubt Louis welcomed the opportunity to accompany him.

The life of the ladies was necessarily more sedentary than that of their menfolk, and after breakfast when the men set off with their guns and dogs, they would sit in the large, airy morning room on the first floor, with its great windows overlooking the park and the distant hills, write their letters and answer invitations, take up their needlework, or dip into a book from the glazed Gothic book-case that occupied the whole of one wall. Mrs. Hay inspected the menus for the day, and gave instructions to her staff, but the daily routine of the castle was not rigid, and life was very comfortable, even cosy, for such a grand establishment. Log fires roared in the huge fireplaces, and the winter sun, made more brilliant by the light covering of snow, streamed through the windows.

Sometimes, the ladies wrapped up warmly, put on their galoshes, and went out to the park to play with their children, making snowmen and tossing snowballs at each other. Then, when they got too cold and wet, they would go indoors, and warm themselves by the fire with a hot, spiced drink. Luncheon was a light meal, after which some of them would retire to their rooms for a nap, while the children attended to their lessons. Pauline was grateful for the chance to be alone, and if the weather was fine, would go out for a walk, taking one of the family dogs with her. If it was inclement, she enjoyed sitting quietly in front of the fire reading, or would play the piano, compose, or sing.

There was no question of riding, now that she was pregnant; sometimes her condition made her feel unwell, and contrary to her usual cheerful self, gloomy thoughts would intrude, making her fearful for the safety of herself and her baby. Charles was often in her thoughts, but the early excitement and rapture of their love affaire had passed, and she now experienced a more painful emotion. She was haunted by visions of him in Paris, surrounded by attractive women, and was well aware that he might succumb to their charms. It would have been too distressing for her to have seen him flirting, while she felt heavy and unattractive, and she was thankful to be spared the experience. She had a very real fear that he would tire of her and become infatuated with someone else, and her concerns were not assuaged by the fact that Manuel always jokingly referred to the composer as 'Don Juan', and had written a satirical poem about him. Gounod no longer wrote as often as he had in 1850, nor as affectionately as during the first half of 1851, when he had written 'Je vous aime tendrement ...Je vous embrasse comme je vous aime'.

In the previous April, on the very evening of the Paris premiere of 'Sapho', Gounod had been asked by the well known writer Francois Ponsard, the author of 'Lucrece', to compose the incidental music for a tragedy in five acts entitled 'Ulysse', which he accepted. In June 1851, he began work on the piece, but despite the quality of the verses, he lacked inspiration. He now realized that 'Sapho' had come to him comparatively easily because Pauline had been his muse, but by the end of the summer, the score for Ponsard was still not complete. Despondently he told Pauline: "I am stressed over my 'Ulysse', it is still arduous, difficult work, and I don't think that I will write incidental music again for a very long time."

In correspondence with George Sand, he spoke of his difficulties, adding that the ancient musical colour he sought eluded him and exhausted his spirit. Since Charles and George first met, they had talked of collaborating on Sand's play 'Moliere', with incidental music by Gounod, but it fell by the wayside due to the attitude of the theatre's conductor, who did not wish to give up his rights as musical arranger. George then suggested that Gounod should write the music for an opera with a libretto by herself on a Berrichon subject, (probably her 'La Mare au diable') with a part for Pauline, but as she was busy writing her memoirs at the time, she said that she could not supply him with anything for another three months at least.

Pauline missed George and her own home, but life at the castle was seductive, and she soon settled into its tranquil routine. At four o'clock each day, everyone would appear in the large, homely drawing room on the first floor, one wall of which contains the largest single mirror in Scotland, facing long, triple Gothic windows. When a servant closed the curtains and lit the lamps, the silvery glass reflected the lights, and the dancing, darting golden/orange flames in the elegant fireplace gave the room a mellow cosiness. The butler would bring in the large silver salver laden with a heavy silver teapot and milk and sugar basin; then a footman would deposit an urn, fill it with water, and light a spirit stove beneath it. Mrs Hay made the tea herself, and the footman handed it to her guests and family. Beautifully decorated porcelain plates laden with Scottish shortbread, fruit cake topped with preserved cherries and nuts, fresh scones, eaten with delicious home made butter and jams, and delicate sandwiches filled with fish or meat paste, stood on occasional tables placed around the room.

The men talked of their experiences in the hunting field, regretting the ones that got away, and congratulating themselves on anything they had caught, and the ladies chattered among themselves or played board games with the children, until it was time for them to go to their nursery supper, and the adults repaired to their rooms to dress for dinner.

Louis was very attentive to Pauline, and encouraged her to rest as much as possible. If she was on her feet too long, her ankles swelled; often she breakfasted in bed, not hurrying to get up. She thought long and hard about her relationship with her husband, appreciating how much he loved and cared for her, and she comforted herself with the knowledge that despite caring deeply for Gounod, Tourgueniev and Scheffer, she did not neglect him. During her long life, those she loved appealed to her for different reasons, and one did not cancel out another, although she felt guilty when she allowed her thoughts to stray towards Gounod too often.

Totally devoid of jealousy and ego, Louis always put Pauline's welfare before his own: he was tolerant to a fault, but he was no fool, and could almost read her mind, fully aware that she was suffering because of her love for another man. He never taunted or upbraided her, and he was prepared to wait patiently until the forbidden passion faded.

The ambience at Duns was a balm for Pauline's troubled spirit, and she was thankful that Louis never questioned her. If she wished to be quiet, he left her alone, but was ready to listen when she wanted to talk. Often, they strolled together down the great avenue of lime trees for which Duns Castle was famous, and revelled in the exquisite beauty and undisturbed peace of the surrounding countryside, set against the panorama of the distant, mauve hills with their light dusting of snow. Despite her emotional pain, Pauline realised what a great treasure she had in her husband, and was thankful for his moral support, yet, because of her guilty conscience, his presence troubled her, and she preferred to be alone with her thoughts.

Despite her great capacity for love and kindness, Pauline was not a truly maternal woman and, although she liked children, she did not wish to devote herself totally to motherly pursuits. She appreciated women's company in small doses, but she was an intellectual who became bored by too much small talk. Her interests lay in ideas, philosophies and the creative projects that were her life-blood, rather than the things that entertained most women of her class, and she soon tired of gossip, talk of the latest fashions, shopping, parties, or of children and families, and would switch off and retreat into her own fascinating, inner world.

However, she was woman enough to be attracted to men, flirtatious, but wary of the way infatuation is likely to develop into something stronger, bringing emotional suffering or disillusionment when it is over. She had always endeavoured to safeguard and protect her emotions, and until she met Gounod she had been pretty successful at doing so, but now she was confused and annoyed with herself because she suffered from feelings she found difficult to control.

The news from Paris when it came was not reassuring. Despite the new regime paying lip service to democracy, France was now a police state, and continued to be so for the whole of the eighteen-year reign of the despotic Louis Napoleon. On the 21st and 22nd of December, he called for a plebiscite and on the 31st, the final figures were counted. Eight million males voted on the proposal that: 'The French people wish to maintain the authority of Louis Napoleon Bonaparte and delegates to him the powers necessary to establish a Constitution on the basis set out in the Proclamation of 2nd December." The Prince received a landslide victory with 7,145,000 for, and only 592,000 against, which gave him unlimited power and carte blanche to do anything he wished.

On the 17th of February 1852, he brought out a Press Decree that effectively curbed freedom of speech and political debate. Anyone who stepped out of line was subject to stringent measures, and editors who ignored government warnings were punished, as if they were naughty schoolboys. Three warnings were given, first, to be more careful in future as to what appeared in their newspapers, second, suspension of publications for a given period, and third, the complete closing down of their presses.

In addition to press censorship, authors were muzzled, and many books were banned. Writers had to tread very warily, but Victor Hugo, who had once supported Louis Napoleon, but now decried his methods, was safe in exile in Brussels and wrote a vitriolic criticism "Napoleon le Petit". Naturally, the book was banned in France, but it was published in London and found its way over the Channel by ingenious means, including balloon, and in plaster busts of Louis Napoleon that arrived at the Gare du Nord in Paris.

When Pauline received a letter from Charles Gounod announcing his engagement to Anna Zimmerman, she was so devastated that the political situation faded into insignificance. Deep in her heart, she had always known that the time would come when Charles would want to settle down, but she trusted that it would be a long time in the future. Emotionally, she was in turmoil, and the trauma of pregnancy compounded her problems. Although she struggled to hide her feelings, she could not fool Louis who, once he heard the news, felt great compassion for the wife he loved so devotedly. It was a relief to be away from Paris at this time, as Pauline felt that she could not publicly face the situation until she had had time to get over the rawness of her feelings.

At Duns, a welcome distraction from all the political upheaval and emotional upset occurred when Lady Monson, who was a great friend of William Hay, came to stay. She was a no-nonsense woman, whose company the Viardots enjoyed enormously, seeing her as a quintessentially eccentric English female, who cared not a jot for anybody. She was a large lady in every sense of the word, with a long horse-like face and a brusque manner, under which she concealed a generous and tender heart. Her way of talking amused her friends tremendously and gave them scope for impersonations. She was a dear friend of Charles Dickens, and had been the inspiration for the character of Betsy Trotwood in 'David Copperfield'. Pauline was very fond of her ladyship and had dedicated her song 'Solitude' to her, when it was published in 1850. This is an attractive but simple setting in G minor with a rhythm in 6/8, in Schubertian vein, set to two verses by Turquety, depicting dreams of love.

It is quite amazing that Louis Viardot, a committed Republican, should have become such a good friend of William Hay, the staunch Tory. This gentleman was still bitter about the repeal of the Corn Laws in 1846 by Sir Robert Peel, the Conservative Prime Minister, whom Hay branded 'a traitor to the cause.' Politics apart, William Hay had an affectionate nature, and was a most loving father to his daughters. Everybody knew, however, that the real apple of his eye was his elder daughter, who had married into the neighbouring Home Drummond family. In his own family circle, William was known as 'Lord Ross' and his daughters' letters all prove how devoted they were to him. Lady Monson, who was the widow of the fifth Lord Monson, used to stay at Duns for long periods, and was loved by all the family, who nick-named her 'Ydal' which is 'Lady' backwards. However, she had some strange tastes and one of these put an end to her friendship with William.

Her inordinate fondness was for chickens, which she bred, and she used to have them brought to her bedroom, sometimes taking them to bed with her. The Hay family indulged her peculiarity in this matter, and she would have been welcome at Duns Castle for the rest of her life, but once, when the laird was away, she had his favourite peacock shot, because it had savaged one of her birds. When William returned and was told what had happened, he was heartily incensed, and his language was so ripe that her ladyship, feeling highly insulted, packed her bags and left.

Her absence was regretted, but there were always other, if less colourful guests to be entertained. Dinner at Duns was a lengthy affair in the great, wood panelled dining room with its lofty ceiling, full-length windows, set in spacious alcoves along the wall opposite the gigantic carved wooden fireplace. Like the other reception rooms, the dining room was on the first floor and overlooked the avenue of limes. It led from the wide landing, hung with gaily coloured banners at the head of the main staircase, and its enormous table comfortably seated at least two dozen guests.

The kitchen was on the ground floor, which made it difficult to keep the food sufficiently warm in winter, but chafing dishes and spirit stoves were set upon sideboards in the dining room, to ensure that the food was as hot as possible when brought to table. The food, even by French standards, was delicious - fresh and natural, well-cooked in native Scottish fashion, and the Viardots particularly enjoyed the fish, sometimes fresh, sometimes cured, served poached with a butter sauce, or coated in oatmeal and crisply fried.

Naturally, the family and guests wore evening dress for dinner, but the ladies' gowns took the Scottish climate into account, and were stylish but not over modishly skimpy, or cut too low over the bosom, with arms bared. To help off-set the winter temperature, tartan and cashmere shawls were worn. Often neighbours joined the family for dinner, brought to the castle by carriage, especially on moonlit nights, when travelling on the dark country roads was safer. If the journey was a long one, guests stayed the night in one of the numerous bedrooms, and returned home the next day. Fortunately, Louis and Pauline spoke English, and there was never any lack of interesting conversation, which sometimes got a little heated when politics was discussed, but nobody took offence.

With dinner over, the company would retire to the drawing room for music or cards, and if they felt particularly energetic they would play charades, or even push back the furniture, roll up the carpet and dance until the tea tray was brought in. Another activity that Pauline enjoyed, of course, was billiards, and Duns possessed a large room set aside specially for the game.

In March, the Viardots decided to risk a return to Paris, hoping that the tenor of life had improved sufficiently to enable them to settle down safely either in their house in the rue de Douai or at Courtavenel. Pauline was now seven months pregnant and becoming broody, wanting to be in her own home once more. The nesting instinct was upon her, and she and Louis had always intended that the child should be born in France. Before Pauline left, however, she gave a concert for the Hays, their neighbours and friends, choosing a programme from her regular concert repertoire. For several days before the event, she practised assiduously and because she had had no professional performances for several months, her voice was beautifully rested. She was in splendid form; invitations were sent out, and the drawing room was prepared as a recital hall.

For many in her audience, it was the first time they had heard a professional singer of such eminence at close range, being more used to the warblings of talented amateurs in drawing rooms, and they were amazed at the size, opulence, and quality of her voice, and the sense of drama she conveyed by her amazing ability to heighten the emotions of her listeners. She sang many of her favourite items, such as Schubert's 'The Erl King', 'O rest in the Lord', from 'Elijah' by Mendelssohn, Handel's 'Lascia ch'io pianga', Spanish folksongs, and some of her own songs, including 'L'Hirondelle et le prisonnier' and 'Solitude'. It was thrilling to hear and see such a superlative artist, and at the end of the evening, they were so enthusiastic that they did not want to let her go, nor did the Hays, when a few days later, the carriage drew up outside the castle entrance to take the Viardots to the railway station. Pauline gave the Hays photographs of herself, Louis and Louise, and these are still to be seen in a photograph album, kept in the glazed bookcase in the morning room.

After the lengthy journey south and a hasty visit to Manuel in London, the Viardots were back in Paris by Easter of 1852. They had hardly unpacked when Charles Gounod paid them a visit, anxious to explain the facts of his engagement to Pauline. Later she declared that it had come like a bolt from the blue, but Gounod always maintained that he had prepared her for the event.

Whether Gounod was telling the truth or not, Pauline had been stunned by the suddeness of his engagement, and even more surprised by the fact that Charles was planning to marry the plain, small-minded, Anna Zimmerman, because there had been many times when she had laughingly chided Charles for calling the Zimmerman girls 'horrible dwarfs'. Now, merciful heaven, he was to marry one of them! If he had fallen in love with a ravishing beauty with a fortune it would have been understandable, but Anna, of all people. Pauline had known her all her life, and found her very dull and uninteresting. Fortunately, the singer was a consummate actress, and she congratulated Charles on his engagement without allowing him to realise the punishing blow he had delivered.

Despite the unpromising start, the way in which Gounod talked about Anna to his friends was in no way insulting, and he told George Sand that she was "of excellent disposition – seemly, affectionate, loyal, full of reason and good sense, of firm and simple piety". However, once they were married, and he got to know her better, he began to repent his choice, and despite the birth of two children, he finally ran away from her, taking up residence in London with the eccentric amateur singer Georgina Weldon and her husband Harry.

Pauline was quite aware that it was the end of their idyll, but worse still, she was beginning to perceive Charles in his true light, and did not like what she saw. As the weeks passed, she found even more reason to resent him, realising that her idol had feet of clay, and that for all his elevated talk, he was just a weak, immature man.

The Viardots accepted a dinner invitation from the Zimmermans and found Madame virtually crowing with pride at her daughter's fine catch. When the ladies retired to the drawing room, leaving the men to their brandy and cigars, there was much talk of wedding finery and the possible date for the marriage. When the men joined them, Louis was asked to be a witness at the wedding ceremony, to which he agreed, but Gounod said that they couldn't fix an early date, as Pauline was to be an honoured guest and they had to wait until her confinement was over.

The influential Pierre Zimmerman was a pleasant, easy going man who let his wife rule the roost, quietly smiling at her idiosyncrasies, and leaving her to deal with the household and their daughters' welfare. He was highly respected in the world of music, an experienced pianist and teacher, who was convinced of Gounod's talent, believed that he would have a great career, and welcomed him as a prospective son-in-law..

Shortly after the evening with the Zimmermans, Pauline invited them and Gounod to dinner in the rue de Douai, but her invitation was refused, with the excuse that they had another engagement. Three times she proffered invitations, all of which were turned down with flimsy excuses. She then asked them to set a date, but again she was fobbed off, and finally she had to accept that they were doing their best to avoid her. She had no idea why they wished to do so, and their behaviour puzzled her, but she was unaware that they had received an anonymous letter alleging sexual misconduct between herself and Gounod.

On May 20th, the composer paid Pauline a visit, but she was already experiencing the first pangs of labour, and could not see him. He had come to tell her that the wedding was to be in a few days time, but without any guests, quite overlooking the fact that Louis had already been asked to be a witness. Despite this rudeness, the Viardots gave the couple a handsome inkstand as a wedding present, and as a personal gift, Pauline sent the bride a gold bracelet.

Much to Louis' distress, his wife had a very difficult labour, but finally gave birth to a healthy girl on the 21st of May. They named her Claudine, as Claude was Louis's second name, and in choosing its female equivalent, it served to emphasise his paternity. Perhaps this was a psychological move on Pauline's part, either because Louis was not the father, or because neither of them could be certain that he was. There is also the fact that George Sand had written a play called 'Claudine' and this could have influenced their choice of name.

Fortunately, Pauline soon recovered from the birth, and a few weeks later wrote to Count Wielhorski, saying: "I have no need to tell you how happy I am to have a new baby. I had wanted one for a long time, and this one came as a real blessing from heaven." The ten and a half year gap between the birth of her two children begs the question if Louis was likely to have fathered the child, or if Gounod had provided the 'blessing'!

In acknowledging the Viardot's gift of an inkstand, Charles wrote: "Believe me when I say how sincerely grateful I am to you for everything you have done for me, and for your kind wishes in my regard". In the light of these words, they were totally perplexed when he returned the bracelet that Pauline had sent to Anna, saying that he was giving a bracelet to his bride, and she did not care to wear any other. Louis's violent reaction to the offence is interesting, and implies something even deeper than the slight to his wife. Of course, the Viardots being unaware of the anonymous letter received by the Zimmermans were deeply hurt.

Louis tackled Charles about his slight to Pauline, and was finally told about the letter. At last, the whole wretched business was out in the open, and made the attitude of the Zimmermans explicable. Louis demanded that Gounod call on Pauline to apologize and reveal the full facts. However, no visit was made and no apology was forthcoming, and although Charles strenuously denied any impropriety between himself and Pauline to his future in-laws, neither Mme Zimmerman nor Anna believed him, and were adamant that he must relinquish his friendship with the Viardots immediately. Reluctantly, Gounod did as he was told.

If Louis believed that Pauline had been Charles's mistress, he kept his thoughts to himself, but when he realised that it was the subject of slanderous gossip in Parisian salons, and that many people were insinuating that Gounod had fathered Pauline's baby, it was the last straw, and would explain why the normally calm, disciplined Louis became so angry over the affair of the bracelet, which could have been regarded as a storm in a teacup. Ironically, after Claudine's birth, Pauline wrote to George Sand saying that the advent of another daughter had done Louis a great deal of good, but it may have been quite otherwise, as he was inevitably confronted with the question of her paternity.

Ary Scheffer was told about the anonymous letter, and of Gounod's ignoble conduct, and Louis asked his advice on what action to take. Ary was naturally incensed on Pauline's behalf, and together they drafted a letter to Gounod telling him that if he did not comply with their wishes, he would no longer be welcome in their homes. Charles panicked, rushed to the rue Chaptal, and poured out his misery to Ary, agreeing to the older man's insistence that he should

write to Louis and apologize, which, to his credit, he did. Scheffer also demanded that Gounod and Anna should call on Pauline and apologize to her
personally. Charles promised to do this once they were married, but said that
for the present he could not go against the dictates of the Zimmermans. He was
most worried by the fact that he stood to lose the good will of the Viardots'
influential friends, and repeated his promise to Scheffer that he and Anna would
make a bridal call on Pauline. Ary threatened that if they did not, he would send
a copy of his letter to Pierre Zimmerman.

The marriage duly took place, but no visit was made, so Ary sent the letter to
Gounod's in-laws, as he had threatened to do. In return, he received a charming
letter from Pierre Zimmerman stating that he had never believed the rumours
and had been surprised when the Viardots had not been at the wedding. Pauline
and Louis were deeply wounded when they heard this, and shocked at
Gounod's duplicity. Naturally, their friends soon learned of the unpleasant
situation, and in disgust, George Sand, Ary Scheffer and Tourgueniev broke off
all contacts with Gounod.

Due to the good offices of his influential father-in-law, Charles soon received the prestigious and lucrative post of Director of the Orpheon de la Ville
de Paris, so, obviously, his 'arranged' marriage was already bearing fruit with
regard to his career.

There is little doubt that Pauline's relationship with Gounod brought about
the greatest emotional crisis of her life, and it is certain that secrets must have
been buried. Supposing she had given birth to Gounod's child, those who
dearly loved her, Louis, Ary Scheffer and Tourgueniev, despite their hurt and
disappointment, would not only have forgiven her lapse, but would have closed
ranks and done all in their power to shield her from scandal and further distress.

When the weather improved, the Viardots left for Courtavenel, where after a
prolonged silence, during which Louis fumed, Gounod wrote to them in a vain
attempt to resurrect their friendship, which according to Pauline, this 'weak,
cowardly, stupid and ungrateful man' could not do without. On July17[th], Louis
answered in a long, pedantic letter, refuting Gounod's pathetic attempts to
explain himself, saying: "When you swore upon your honour to the family of
which you were about to become a member that the disgraceful reports that
they had obtained were nothing but slander, either you were believed, or you
were not. If you were not believed, but had nevertheless gone through with the
engagement in spite of being more insulted in this matter than ourselves, then
I have nothing to say to you, and leave you to judge for yourself what complexion should be put upon your abominable behaviour. But if, as I like to suppose,
your oath was believed, why is it that all the Zimmermans, father, mother and

daughters, a family that has known Pauline since her childhood and has always shown her affection and esteem, did not immediately come running to my wife to ask her forgiveness for having lent their ears to such despicable gossip...? No reparation, meanwhile, has been made, and the slander is becoming still more poisonous."

It is maybe significant that Louis did not ask Gounod plainly what he had told the Zimmermans, and the only explanation of his attack upon Charles was that he was still unsure of the truth himself, and wanted to hear Gounod's assertion that Pauline was innocent. Could it be that the injured party was ashamed of her ambiguous behaviour, and could not reveal to her husband the actual – and delicate – truth even if she knew it?

In later years, Pauline told Julius Rietz that if he wished to know her better he should read the first part of 'Consuelo'. Rietz did so and wanted to know her 'Anzoleto'. In the novel, this character is the man Consuelo loves, but does not marry because her master, Porpora, convinces her that he is unworthy of her, and that she must put her art before all else. In answer to Rietz's question, Pauline replied: "As to an Anzoleto, let me just tell you something; it is that without Ary Scheffer I would have committed a great sin – for I had lost my will-power – I recovered it in time to *break my heart* and do my duty. I had my reward later – oh! I had my gypsy instincts to fight – to kill passion – I almost died of it – I wanted to kill myself …..that was from cowardice. Scheffer, who watched over me like a father, stopped me. He brought me home, half senseless – and little by little my reason returned – and with it my will-power. As soon as I *could exercise my will,* I had the upper hand. I did not commit a sin, I thank God for that – and my poor, dearly loved Scheffer suffered a great deal, believe me, in seeing my sufferings…"

In a footnote in her biography, *The Price of Genius,* April Fitzlyon states that Pauline's child must have been conceived at the beginning of August 1851, and that it is most unlikely that Tourgueniev could have been the father as he was in Russia at the time, and it would have been impossible for him to leave the country without anyone knowing about it. However, according to Professor Patrick Waddington, there is written evidence that Gounod was definitely with Pauline on August 5th and 6th in the English capital. With regard to the letter quoted above, Fitzlyon equates Anzoleto with Tourgueniev, but Pauline never considered Ivan an unworthy man, although she came to regard Gounod in that light.

If a scenario is projected in which Pauline is overtaken by a passion for Gounod (Anzoleto) that is so strong that her will power is negated, and she then becomes pregnant by him, it can be imagined that her conscience would be wracked with guilt by her betrayal of her devoted husband. She says that without Scheffer's wise counsel, she would have died. (Scheffer taking the place of Porpora in the novel). Maybe the intention to commit suicide was the 'great sin' from which he brought her to her senses.

Scheffer was a man of great probity, and he believed that the artist has a duty to society as well as to himself and his art. Pauline was like a daughter to him, and in one of his letters to his own child, Cornelie, he gives moral advice, which is also applicable to Pauline, saying: "It is, in a way, easier to make a sacrifice on great occasions than in the daily things of life". There is no doubt that he would have encouraged her to make a 'great sacrifice' stamp out her passion for Gounod and live for her art, and for those to whom she meant so much.

Pauline told George Sand: "From the moment the question of his marriage came up, Gounod behaved most ungratefully towards us. With all his show of having a heart, that heart which he talks about so incessantly and in such fine phrases, he is nothing but a bag of egotism, vanity and scheming – in a word, he is a Tartuffe…he is a great musician, the foremost, perhaps, of our time. How is it possible for such genius to exist where there is no true heart? Yet in spite of the pain, in spite of how much this has hurt me, I do not regret the good I was able to do for this ungrateful man. There he is, launched on his career, and if his family and his own character do not destroy his genius, which is very much to be feared, he will compose masterpieces that will do honour to the art and bring happiness to those who hear them".

Pauline's real sorrow was in discovering that the man for whom she had risked all, perhaps even her life, was 'a Tartuffe', and that was the hardest part to bear, producing deep scars that were never to be forgotten. She had revered him and placed him on a pedestal, and her heartbreak was in discovering him to be a mere, flawed mortal, despite his ability to write 'divine' music. Not able to forgive herself for her stupidity and cupidity, she buried her emotions deeply; however, they did not go away, they echoed through her psyche for a lifetime. We will never know whether Claudie, as the family called her, was Gounod's child or not, but maybe he suspected that she was, because in 1874, on hearing that she was to marry, he told a friend that he considered himself a member of the family!

In her studied, but sympathetic reply to Pauline's letter, George expressed the opinion that she considered Gounod's greatest failing to be that he talked too much, always wanting to explain things, but actually causing more confusion in the process. She observed that genius often went hand in hand with vanity, but in spite of this, the heart could still be in the right place, and she delicately suggested to her friend that jealousy and slander might be blinding her to Charles's true virtues.

Tourgueniev agreed that Gounod's behaviour towards the Viardots had been disgraceful, and blamed it on his Jesuit training. He struck Charles's name from his list of friends but, no more than Pauline or George, could he hate the man's music. As far as Manuel Garcia was concerned, he was less surprised than anybody at the recent turn of events as he had, from the start, eyed Gounod's manners and behaviour with more than a little irony, and shortly before the unpleasantness of May, 1852, had written derisively to Pauline: 'Tell Gounod that I would like a moral share in his future physical bliss".

CHAPTER TWENTY-FOUR

In June 1852, the Viardots received the alarming news from Russia that Ivan Tourgueniev had been arrested for writing an article entitled 'Letters on Gogol'. Nicolai Vasilyevich Gogol, an eminent Russian writer, had recently died, and Tourgueniev's article had been a commemoration of his life and work. Gogol had fulminated against Russian bureaucracy and was deeply resented by the autocratic regime because of the liberal spirit encapsulated in his writing. In praising him, Tourgueniev had incurred the wrath of the Tsar and his government, and had been imprisoned for a month, and then released a week after Claudie's birth. This was not the end of the affair, however, as he was immediately sentenced to house arrest at Spasskoye for an indefinite period. The irony of the situation must have struck him keenly because he was now a rich man, thanks to the fortune he had inherited from his mother, and was wealthy enough to travel anywhere he wished, but was deprived of the liberty to do so.

Contrary to Louis' hopes, Ivan had not overcome his obsession with Pauline, and was as deeply in love with her as ever. Of course, the Viardots were concerned for his welfare, and prayed for his early release, but maybe, subconsciously, they were relieved to know that they would not be seeing him for a while. The last thing either of them wanted, was further emotional upset after the difficult year they had just passed through. Pauline needed time and space to recover from the Gounod affair, and the last thing she needed was another 'wounded heart' to deal with. She was occupied with her work, family responsibilities and the running of two large households, and was finding it increasingly difficult to be away for long periods.

In a letter to George Sand, Pauline described how busy she was domestically and George replied: 'Come now, breathe more freely on your great estate, and rest your voice, your brain, and your heart as well. For all one's energies are drained in those great driving ecstasies on the stage – and don't go to foggy England too soon, either, especially if you are to exercise your trade there. Have you not reached the point where you can simply exercise your art?"

Ever since her great success in 'Le Prophete', Pauline had longed to create other new roles. She had looked to Gounod to fulfil her hopes, but he had let her down, and she could not 'make art' unless there was art to be made. Nor was she helped by the fact that her husband's known political sympathies, and her friendships with George Sand, and other 'undesirables', excluded her from state-subsidised theatres. Art apart, she needed to ply her trade, in order to help produce the income necessary to maintain their life style. As France did not present her with opportunities, she looked to England, where she had a fine reputation, in order to earn large fees.

Her responsibilities weighed heavily on her and as she left her youth behind, she became less exuberant, less prone to practical jokes, and transformed herself into the ideal wife, mother, and chatelaine of a large town house and grand chateau. She told Count Wielhorski how much she hoped that a rest in the country would enable her to feel fit enough to fulfil her engagements in England, and in September she resumed her career, appearing at the Norwich and Birmingham Music Festivals, and with the Sacred Harmonic Society at Exeter Hall in London.

Religious music had many fervent admirers in England, and Viardot excelled in this style. She had the requisite seriousness, profundity and ability to convey the drama with her voice, and had explored the older styles of music with Chopin, Berlioz, Mendelssohn and Gounod, whose own sacred music was becoming very popular in England. She continued to interest herself in the works of the classical composers, and on the oratorio and concert platform she always met with approval, causing Chorley to state: "Nothing of our age has been seen to compare with her execution of sacred music. In religious music, this woman has never been surpassed".

Upto the middle of the nineteenth century, English musical taste left much to be desired because the majority of people preferred ballads and frivolous fare, but from 1850 onwards, improvements began to appear, thanks to such musicians as Pauline Viardot, Sterndale Bennett, Berlioz, Gounod, Clara Novello, and Jenny Lind, who introduced the public to more elevated works.

As Pauline put her unhappy experiences with Charles behind her, the old ruthlessness of the dedicated artist re-asserted itself and she began to concentrate on her career with single-minded determination. Her head ruled her heart and she would brook no deflection from her chosen path, saying; "if you want to be an artist, try to be indifferent to everything except your art." She worked at her vocal technique assiduously and found new delight in her technical mastery. Some years before, she had advised Maurice Sand to concentrate on acquiring technical expertise in his painting, because: 'the technical part is indispensable in all the arts: the comparison is striking between painting and music. A singer gifted with a beautiful voice and intelligence will achieve nothing unless he possesses the foundation of technique and the mechanism of singing".

While Pauline was busy in England, Tourgueniev found his imposed imprisonment at Spasskoye a severe trial; it was just bearable during the spring and summer, but in winter, a deep depression overcame him. With no hope of travelling abroad, he could only dream of Pauline, and was gratified when she resumed her correspondence with him. He clutched at her letters, as a drowning man grasps a lifeline, relishing the much needed light they brought into his gloomy world: his only complaint was that she didn't write often enough. In his deep loneliness, he sought the comfort of a young serf woman, Feoktista Petrovna Volkova, whom he had bought from his cousin, granted her freedom, then taken her into his 'service' at Spasskoye.

Ever since they had first met, Ivan had planned his life around Pauline, but now it was impossible, and truth to tell, she was relieved. Although she valued his friendship, she experienced more peace of mind when he was in another country. Writing letters was a therapy for her and she enjoyed corresponding with him, able to be more open and affectionate on paper, because she knew that he could not take advantage and expect more from her than she was willing to give.

Ivan's deep, obsessive love made Pauline feel claustrophobic, and she had always been the one to attempt to put distance between them, but he was like a limpet and would not be shaken off. Circumstances now decreed that they be kept apart, but by an ironic stroke of fate, after several years absence from Russia, Pauline received an invitation to return to St. Petersburg for the 1852/3 season. Tourgueniev was ecstatic when he heard that she had accepted, although there was little chance that he would be able to see her. He dreamed of her coming to him at Spasskoye, but Louis did not deem it wise, and no plans were made for them to meet there.

When first arrested, Ivan had written to Pauline from his prison in St. Petersburg: "I knew very well on leaving you that it would be for a long time, if not for ever... My health is good, but I have grown ridiculously old: I could send you a lock of grey hair... Your letters, and my memories of days at Courtavenel, are everything to me now... My life is finished, all its charm is gone. I have eaten all my white bread, and must chew the whole-meal that remains... I send you all my love, and bless you a thousand times over."

News of Pauline's great success in 'Le Prophete' had reached Russia, as well as rumours that her voice was deteriorating, and there was a great deal of public curiosity since she had not been heard in Russia for several years. In the autumn, she, Louis and Antonia, her cousin, returned to St. Petersburg, and when she gave her first performance, she received as enthusiastic a reception from her dear Russians as she had always done, but she was now thirty-two years old, had been singing professionally for sixteen years, and one critic had the effrontery to suggest that she was no longer 'une gamine', a comment which, naturally, incensed Tourgueniev and he told Pauline that as far as he was concerned, she would always be like a seventeen-year-old.

He reminisced about their first meeting in 1843, nine years earlier, and vowed that for two more nine-year periods he would still be hers in heart and soul. In the spring of 1848, he had written to her recalling their wonderful, idyllic summer at Courtavenel the previous year: "I am always moved by the sight of a branch with young green leaves outlined against a clear blue sky. Why is this, I wonder? Is it because of the contrast between this little living shoot, which sways at the command of the slightest breath of wind, which I can snap, which has to die, and yet is given life and colour by its bountiful sap – and that immense and everlasting vacuum, that sky which is bright and blue only because the earth makes it so?"

This imagery appeared several times in Tourgueniev's novels, and he had recently sent Pauline a copy of his 'Notes from my shooting expeditions' where, in the story 'Kasyan', written in 1851, he had penned the lines: "I lay on my back and admired the peaceful play of tangled leaves against the brightness of the distant sky. What a marvellously pleasant occupation it is to lie on one's back in a wood!" In the story, the writer comments indirectly on the beauty of the Brie, and perhaps when he wrote it, he was re-living a bright, sunny day, lying under the trees with Pauline in the Wood of Blandureau?

During the 1853 Russian season, the singer performed many of her established roles, adding that of Fides in 'Le Prophete', which was new to St. Petersburg. In January she sang Rosina, and Mario should have been the Almaviva, but, true to form, he cancelled at short notice. Without rehearsal, Pauline substituted 'La Cenerentola', which she had not sung for eight years. The performance was a truly brilliant success, and her public clamoured for more.

As in Europe, her Fides was considered a tour de force, and although in some quarters it was said that the voice was not what it had once been, her portrayals of the roles that had made her famous were still very popular. However, no voice stays the same forever, because like the rest of the human body, it evolves and ages, and no doubt, by 1853, Pauline's voice had lost many of its higher harmonics and some of its youthful bloom. Nevertheless, it must have developed an even richer, heavier, more mature middle and lower register, which meant that gradually, some of her earlier roles would have to be abandoned.

This happens to all singers, but as former roles are cast aside, others that were not previously possible, take their place. For some years, Pauline had delayed the inevitability of change by means of transposition, but it was never a truly satisfactory solution.

As on his last disastrous trip to St. Petersburg, Louis became very ill. He had been out shooting in bitterly cold weather, caught influenza and took to his bed. When he recovered, he agreed with Pauline that it would be better if he returned home straight away. Pauline and her cousin, Antonia had been engaged to sing in Moscow, and in March, they made the long journey by themselves.

Tourgueniev was overjoyed that Pauline was to sing in Moscow, and determined that somehow or other, he would slip his leash at Spasskoye and travel to the Metropolis. She was only engaged for concert performances because the Bolshoi Theatre had recently burned down, so she would not be able to sing any of her operatic roles in the city. Although this was unfortunate, on a personal level, it gave her more time to enjoy her visit, as she was spared exhausting stage rehearsals and opera performances.

When the Viardots had arrived in St. Petersburg, it had been Louis, not Pauline, who had endeavoured to gain permission for Tourgueniev to visit them. This was not granted, but after Louis returned to France alone, Ivan and Pauline had a clandestine meeting in Moscow at the end of March, the writer having risked further penalties by defying his order of house arrest; strangely, his absence went undetected. It is not known what transpired between him and the woman he adored, but he appeared to be very happy at the outcome of the unexpected reunion, and Alexander Herzen remarked that Pauline returned to Europe a decided Russophile, which meant, perhaps, that she talked a great deal about Tourgueniev.

On the other hand, in a letter to Count Wielhorski, written before she left Paris, she had said that she was looking forward to renewing contact with her 'dear Russian public' note 'public' not 'friends', and she stated that despite having to give up her 'comfortable fireside' and her 'tenderly-loved little family' for her 'dream' she was willing to make the sacrifice. Writing to Louis from Moscow, during March and April, 1853, she intimated that her twin and only concerns were for her art and her family. She begged him not to be anxious about her as, if she fell ill she would be able to let him know, and if she died, the authorities would inform him!

Her concerts were going splendidly and she declared that she loved the Russian audiences because they made her sing better than any other. Antonia was singing pleasantly enough, though as usual, rather mechanically. Pauline had done her best to inculcate a sound vocal technique into her cousin, but she could not turn her into an artist. She also compared the girl's 'sad' and 'ceremonious' marriage with her own dear union with Louis, and on March 27th, she wrote to him: "How good you are, how kind, and how I love you!"

By the middle of April, Ivan was complaining of the laconic nature of Pauline's letters, and said they were different from those she had formerly written. It appears that yet again, he had misread her warm regard and admiration for love. On May 24th, he wrote: "Do not abandon your plan to come and give concerts in Russia next year. Your last triumph, particularly in Moscow, must encourage you. If you come with Viardot to Moscow, I very much hope that you will make it a point to visit me. My garden is splendid at this time... if I can imagine you walking there one day! This is not impossible, but is hardly probable." As it happened, no visit ever took place, because this was the last time Pauline visited Russia, the country where she had enjoyed some of her greatest successes.

In his unhappiness, Tourgueniev again suffered psychosomatic illnesses, and was convinced that he had cancer of the pylorus. Yet, despite his inner fears, he did not quite lose his sense of humour, and when his dog, Diane produced a litter, he named one of her pups Pylore. Over the next three years, although he regained his freedom, he virtually lost contact with the Viardots and France, and feared that he would never see them or Courtavenel again. In the meantime, he found consolation in the friendship of a neighbour, the unhappily married Marya, the sister of the writer Leo Tolstoy. Although Pauline always remained his divinity, there were several other ladies who would have been happy to receive a proposal of marriage from the charming writer. Ironically, it was during this time, when he was deeply unhappy and far away from Pauline that his stature as a writer truly revealed itself.

On leaving Russia, other places and other challenges awaited Pauline, but for the time being, England called her again, and on April 1st, the 'Musical Times' of London announced: "It is reported on good authority that Mr. Gye has come to terms with Mme Viardot and also to have engaged Mlle Donzelli and Signor Luchesi. There are rumours that Her Majesty's is to close. Singers are scarce, and composers scarcer".

By June 13th, Pauline was back in London, taking part in a concert for the Philharmonic Society with the English soprano, Louisa Pyne, who later took over the successful management of the Covent Garden Theatre. The male soloists were the tenor, Italo Gardoni (son in law of Antonio Tamburini), and the bass, Karl Formes. The ubiquitous Michael Costa conducted. The programme consisted of Mendelssohn's 'Ye spotted snakes' from 'A Midsummer Night's

Dream' with chorus and Viardot and Pyne as soloists. Pauline sang the duet
'Nella notte' from 'Les Huguenots' with Karl Formes, the aria 'Lascio ch'io
pianga', (a great favourite with English audiences), and the programme finished with the quartet 'Gran Nume, in Ogni Evento' from 'Gerusalem Liberata'
by Righini.

On the 25th and 27th of June she appeared again with the Philharmonic
Society, singing the great scena from 'Der Freischutz', the duet 'Ah facciamo'
from 'Jessonda' by Spohr and 'Ah guarda sorella' from 'Cosi fan Tutte' by
Mozart, with Castellan. On July 4th, the Queen and Prince Albert were present
at another Philharmonic concert when Louisa Pyne and Pauline again per-
formed 'Ye spotted snakes' and Pauline sang 'Return O God of Hosts' from
'Samson' by Handel, and took part in the trio 'Pria di Partir' from 'Idomeneo' by
Mozart, with Pyne and Gardoni.

Hector Berlioz was in London, separated from his wife, the Irish actress,
Harriet Smithson, having arrived in the spring of 1852, while Pauline was in
Paris, awaiting Claudie's birth.

For the past few years, he had been living with Marie Recio, a third-rate
singer, who had accompanied him to London. Despite being a handsome woman,
Marie had an unpleasant, difficult character, and when Wagner asked Berlioz
why he tolerated her abominable treatment, he replied lamely, 'because I love
her'.

The composer was conductor of the New Philharmonic Society, and he and
Pauline saw each other from time to time both as colleagues, and socially. He
and Marie were staying at 17 Old Cavendish Street, where he was in the process of writing his witty 'Evenings in the Orchestra', which he was planning to
publish in Paris, complete with illustrations.

Pauline's last performance of the 1853 season was at Liverpool, where she
sang in Handel's 'Samson' and then returned to Paris, where it seemed that her
career had reached a lull. Her enemies' spite ensured that she had no work
there, and her successes in other places did not make up for the neglect of her
compatriots; she felt unappreciated and purposeless. Gounod was no longer a
friend and Tourgueniev, who was a good morale booster, even when he irritated
her, was far away.

Fortunately, she had the friendship of her dear old mentor, Ary Scheffer, who
was always ready to listen and advise her, and she was able to confess her
innermost thoughts to him, but he was married now, and she had to tread more
warily so as not to monopolise him, since his wife, Sophie, could be jealous.
Occasionally, Pauline gave concerts in the larger of Ary's two studios, where
he had a grand piano, to an audience made up of their closest friends and

British fleet sailed into the Black Sea. Once more, Palmerston was taking matters into his own hands and using gun-boat diplomacy, having persuaded Lord Aberdeen to make a pro-Turkish demonstration.

Tensions escalated and on the 23rd of October, 1854 Turkey declared war on Russia, and Palmerston, as head of the war party, called for the Sultan to be supported through joint action with France, threatening to resign if he was opposed. When the Russian fleet sank that of the Turks at Sinope on November 30th, England was set upon an irrevocable course, and war was declared. Suddenly, xenophobia reared its ugly head, and the Prince Consort was accused of treachery by the populace and press who used him as a scapegoat, declaring that he was pro-Russian and had plotted for Palmerston's resignation. The Queen blamed Palmerston for these calumnies, but he did little to refute them.

The war lasted for a further two years, bringing great suffering in its wake, and the Queen was beside herself with worry and grief, due to the disasters her troops were experiencing. When she visited wounded soldiers, she was visibly moved to tears. Conditions in the Crimea were atrocious; the men were ill-equipped, hygiene was unknown, food was scarce, and most often rancid, and until the advent of Florence Nightingale, there were few medical facilities.

Miss Nightingale was an aristocrat, who defied her family, recruited women of good character as nurses, and took up residence at Scutari, where she organised a hospital, which served as the model for the future. Tourgueniev was on good terms with her family, and stayed at their country estate on one of his visits to England. His and Pauline's old friend, Richard Monckton Milnes, had been in love with Florence and had repeatedly proposed to her, but she always refused him and remained a spinster.

After the opera season, Pauline returned to France for a short holiday, but in September, she returned to England and sang at the Three Choirs Festival in Gloucester. In the meantime, in Russia, Tourgueniev was making a real effort to put his life in order, and was contemplating marriage with his cousin, eighteen year old Olga Alexandrovna Tourgueniev, the daughter of a retired general. However, when Pauline learned this news, far from being relieved, she was annoyed and not a little jealous.

Despite all his good intentions, finally, Ivan's love for Pauline got the better of him, and he could not bring himself to propose to Olga. On a purely sensual level, he had always had casual encounters with women of the lower orders, but there was some flaw in him that stopped him from seriously committing to an unattached woman of his own class. He wrote to Pauline in October,1854, telling her that: "All this has passed and I can tell you between selves us that the young person in question bears the same family name as mine". He infers that whatever originally attracted him to the girl soon waned.

At the same time that Tourgueniev was contemplating marriage with Olga, he began a relationship in St. Petersburg with the Countess Elizabeth Lambert, a married woman from a distinguished family, who was the same age as himself. She was not particularly pretty, but was intelligent, cultivated, and socially agreeable, and the hostess of one of the most prestigious salons in the city. In a short time, she and the writer were seeing a great deal of each other, and when apart, developed a voluminous and very intimate correspondence, which became extremely important to both of them, and continued until 1866. The Countess soon learned about his long relationship with Pauline Viardot and of his total, ill-fated obsession with her, and was human enough to resent the iron-hold the French woman had over her compatriot.

For those who believe that Tourgueniev was actually Pauline's lover, it is worth looking at the kinds of men he portrayed in his books. Firstly, there is the man of the world, brave and successful with women, and secondly, the losers and failures, the men who love unattainable women who dominate them, those who cannot find the courage to defy convention, and merely trail around after the object of desire, or perch on the edge of someone else's nest because they are too weak or lazy to do otherwise.

When the Viardots had first met Ivan in Russia, he was only one of Pauline's many male admirers, but he was the most persistent, and he courted the Viardots to such an extent that he became a constant member of their inner circle. They probably mentioned casually, 'you must come and visit us when you are in France', and were subsequently surprised when, without further ado, he took them up on their invitation, obtained leave of absence from his Ministry and set off for Europe. Generous to a fault, they offered him hospitality, and saved him a great deal of expense during the years when he was financially in straitened circumstances.

Yet, even the best of friends can outstay their welcome and, as far as the Viardot marriage was concerned, in many ways he was decidedly 'de trop', but they were courteous and kind-hearted, so it didn't bother them for him to stay at their home occasionally or even to leave him there when they went away. Mme Garcia enjoyed his company; he was treated like one of the family, and habit set in. Louis was extremely long suffering, but because he shared hunting and intellectual pursuits with Ivan, he allowed the situation to continue, so the years rolled on, and a pattern of familiarity developed.

In her memoirs, Louise Viardot is quite scathing about Tourgueniev sponging on her parents: she obviously resented the part he played in the household and, of course, the fact that his daughter had been foisted on her family. She was also embarrassed, as she grew to adulthood, by the enigmatic nature of her mother's relationship with the writer, knowing that it had long been the cause of gossip and speculation. It would appear that the Viardots were rather lazy and let matters drift, despite any resentment on their part, because they were too sensitive to risk hurting their friend's feelings by being honest, and letting him see that he was taking advantage of their good nature. Then, in 1850, it seems that Louis did actually advise Ivan to go home and try to overcome his love for Pauline, and to make a fresh start. Unfortunately, the whole affair lacked balance – it was all or nothing, and not the give and take of a normal friendship, seeing each other occasionally and corresponding from time to time. Ivan only felt really well when he was with Pauline; without her, he fell prey to hypochondria and lacked a focus in life.

With regard to money, Louise was too severe in her condemnation of Ivan's willingness to let the Viardots pay his way, although he did persuade Louis to lend money to his friend Botkin and, perhaps others. Once he had money of his own, he contributed, and even made provision for a dowry for Claudie, a child he absolutely adored, whom he saw as a miniature Pauline, and for whom nothing was too good or too much trouble. He loved her far more than he was ever able to love his own daughter, which is one of the reasons why people suspected that he was Claudie's father, but he could not have been. He simply loved her for her own sake. Patrick Waddington makes the point that Tourgueniev may have believed that she was Gounod's daughter, in which case her illegitimacy would help to explain the writer's preference for her, if she was not Louis's child.

Ivan was now thirty-five, and, despite his tall, handsome figure, he was prematurely grey and ageing fast. The Countess, however, found him attractive, and gave him sound and sage advice regarding his personal life, but when the crunch came two years later, it was obvious that her homilies had made not a jot of difference to Ivan's obsession with Pauline. He had long accepted that he would never find his 'nest' in Russia, nor could his own country cure him of his desire to fly to Pauline's side. In a letter to Elizabeth Lambert, he said: "At my age, going abroad implies a final dedication to a gypsy-style existence and the abandonment of every thought of family life. But what is to be done? It seems that such is my fate. There is, of course, another way of putting this: people without strength of character love to build themselves a 'fate' – it saves them from the need to have a will of their own or to feel a sense of personal responsibility."

Psychologically, the Countess was good for Tourgueniev, as she allowed him to unburden himself at a difficult time in his life, and he used her as a kind of psychoanalyst. Pauline also had her therapist – Ary Scheffer. In a letter to Count Wielhorski, she said: "I think I can hear the bell of our country postman's little dog. He is still some way off, which gives me time to send you my tender greetings.....Does your Academy of Arts still exist? If I were at St. Petersburg I would love to ask your permission to go to it, but being in Paris, I shall go and work in Scheffer's studio. I shall paint, while my little Louise draws. At the present moment Louise is playing Bach preludes – from which you will gather that she has been making progress as a musician. Since my arrival at Courtavenel, I have done nothing but look after her. It wasn't the postman's dog whose bell I heard – it must have been a stray sheep…"

Pauline was still a frequent performer at Scheffer's impromptu concerts in his 'spiritualistic' studio, where 'no smoking was allowed, there were no signs of disorder, and people chatted as they would in a drawing room, without loud laughter, though not without gaiety'.

On Tourgueniev's return to France, he did not go to Courtavenel, but left immediately for England, as Pauline was singing there, and he stayed in London for just over a week, seeing her and visiting his exiled friends. He had written to Pauline from St. Petersburg on the 15th of April, 1856: "And we shall make music at Courtavenel, God willing. If only you knew how often I think – or rather, dream – of Courtavenel. Does the stuffed peacock in the billiards room still exist? Have my rosebushes grown? I expect that my grey jacket (which he had left hanging on a hook there in 1850) is in rags now."

By September 10th, Ivan and the Viardot family were in the Brie, where, on the 14th, they were joined by Paulinette. The weeks passed by very pleasantly and the writer told Botkin: "How splendidly we spent our time at Courtavenel: Each day seemed like a gift; our lives were shot through with a kind of natural iridescence, wholly independent of ourselves… In short, we were as happy as trout in a sparkling stream with sunlight bouncing up and down upon its waters." Pauline must have provided the sunshine, however, because the weather was cold and the shooting was abominable.

In January 1855, Pauline was at home in Paris when she received a visit from the distinguished Italian composer, Giuseppe Verdi, whose new opera 'Il Trovatore' was being staged at the Paris Opera. He had come to beg Pauline to sing the role of Azucena as Madame Alboni was unwell, and would not be able to sing in the next performance. With a surprised look, Pauline laughed aloud, and said that she could not possibly oblige him, as she was very busy herself and, even if she had not been, she had never even seen a copy of the music.

Verdi said that was soon remedied, produced a manuscript score, and took Pauline through the role. She liked what she saw, thought that it was within her capabilities and agreed to help him. Without further loss of time, she settled down to learn the music, attended a rehearsal the following day, and sang at the next performance.

Like Gounod before him, Verdi was amazed at Pauline's astonishing grasp of a musical idiom new to her, and of her ability to commit it to memory almost instantaneously. Of this wonderful feat, the Italian said: "I can never forget it – she's a woman of great talent and altogether remarkable". Pauline sang several performances in Paris, and was cast for the London premiere of 'Il Trovatore', at Verdi's insistence.

The first performance took place on May 19th, and Hogarth in the 'Illustrated London News' reported: "The production of 'Il Trovatore' at the Royal Italian Opera, has been attended with complete success. (This occasion was a State Visit by the Queen and Prince Albert, accompanied by their Imperial guests, the Emperor Napoleon III and Empress Eugenie and members of their court). It was received with warm applause; and on the Saturday following and on Tuesday last, its reception was more and more enthusiastic. It has probably never been better performed than by the company of the Royal Italian Opera. Azucena, the Gypsy woman, on whose terrible revenge the whole piece turns, is represented by Mme Viardot in a manner worthy of her original genius. Like Fides in the 'Prophete', it is a creation entirely her own; full of individuality and truthfulness. She is a true Gypsy, exhibiting the peculiar features and violent passions of her race. Nothing can be more artistic than her singing, though the extraordinary power of her acting throws it into the shade. The opera has been put onto the stage with even more than usual splendour".

Chorley said: "Viardot's Azucena was one of the most remarkable performances of its time. Such spirit as could be thrown into the opera was contributed by Mme Viardot in the dismal character of the Spanish gypsy mother. Her few bars of cantabile in the last scene, where sleep overcomes her while she sings, were among the most exquisitely beautiful and pathetic things heard on any stage".

Verdi was in London for the production, accompanied by his mistress Giuseppina Strepponi, his publisher Giulio Riccordi, and the composer's great supporter Leon Escudier, a man who had previously been one of Pauline's detractors; but now everybody was full of praise for her portrayal of Azucena. Verdi had seen Pauline as Fides in 'Le Prophete' and perhaps her wonderful performance inspired him to base the character of Azucena on Fides.

On June 23rd, Pauline showed her versatility once more when she sang the role of Rosina in 'Il Barbiere' at Covent Garden, and a critic remarked: "Its most remarkable feature was Mme Viardot in the character of Rosina, a fine display of drama and vocal art, but too much elaborated (Pauline over-doing the ornamentation again!!), and less pleasing than the simple and unpretending performance of Mme Bosio".

Julius Benedict's grand annual concert on July 1st was presented with the "usual aggregation of all the musical talent to be obtained in London. Covent Garden Theatre was crowded in every part of the house. Some part songs for female voices by Mr. Benedict, were performed for the first time on this occasion, and had every justice done to their remarkable beauty, by Mesdames Clara Novello, (Charlotte) Dolby (an English contralto) and Viardot to whom they were entrusted". Pauline, of course, was based in France and Clara in Italy, but they corresponded regularly, and it is amusing to read the comments of the proud mamas, each vying with the other, boasting about the musical talents of their children.

When the singers were in London together they often met and enjoyed singing duets, usually accompanied on the piano by the elderly Edward Holmes. When Clara had first suggested that he should play for them, he was delighted and asked the soprano to tell Mme Viardot that "he was the friend of Berlioz who introduced him into England – also of our infantile connection. She will probably remember me. I was in a box at the opera with her and M. Viardot, on the night of the British premiere of 'Benvenuto Cellini' at Covent Garden in 1853, when she said to me 'Don't you think, sir, it is very wrong to hiss an opera like this"? I could hardly reply to her from vexation. To see the generous work of Berlioz so crushed – the labour of months and years destroyed in a few hours quite overpowered me."

Berlioz's estranged wife, Harriet, who had suffered minor strokes for several years, finally died in 1854. Despite all the torment she had caused him, she was the mother of his beloved son Louis, who had always kept in touch with her, although as a sailor, he was away most of the time. The composer often recalled how wonderful Harriet had been, when he first saw her as Ophelia in 'Hamlet'so many years ago, when they were both young and full of optimism. But his tragedy, and hers too, was that he had not fallen in love with a mortal woman of flesh and blood but with an ideal, and no woman, least of all poor Harriet, could live up to his fantasies. With her death, he was now free to marry Marie Recio, who had been his mistress for the past few years, and lost no time in doing so.

Tourgueniev's friend, the anarchist, Alexander Herzen, whom the Viardots had known for several years, was now living in exile in England, having been granted political asylum. Grateful to the English he said "They invented personal liberty, and did it without having any theories about it. The English value liberty for its own sake". He moved house frequently and during 1855 lived in Twickenham, Richmond and Finchley. The Viardots often visited him, as they enjoyed his company and appreciated the opportunity to talk about Russian music and literature. Pauline believed that she had a mission to make Russian music known in the West, but in St. Petersburg, many people resented what they saw as the audacity of a foreigner promoting their music, which they themselves were too lazy or uninterested to do, because it made them feel guilty. After one of the Viardots' visits, Herzen told a friend that between the three of them they constituted the whole of Russian publicity, Louis translating, Pauline singing, and himself writing.

Over the years the Viardots had made several good friends in England, such as George Grove the compiler of the dictionary of musicians; William Sterndale Bennett; the tall, stout, self-assured, but eccentric Swede, Harriet Grote, and her husband George, one of the founders of London University, at whose house in Eccleston Street, Pauline had first performed in 1841,and Richard Monckton Milnes, the former suitor of Florence Nightingale, who was now married to the Honorable Annabel Crewe. Pauline had first met him in 1839, and introduced him to Tourgueniev when the Russian was in London in 1857. The two men were soon on friendly terms, and Milnes introduced him into English literary circles, where he met such men as Sir Alfred Tennyson, Robert Browning, William Makepeace Thackeray and George Eliot, as well as enabling him to become a temporary member of the prestigious Athenaeneum Club.

Richard Monckton Milnes was one of the most kaleidoscopic of Victorian figures, famous for his 'breakfasts' at which he invited very diverse personalities, frequently dining with such opposites as King Louis Philippe and Louis Blanc. Famously, in Paris in 1848, he had unwittingly invited both George Sand and her ex-lover Prosper Merimee, the author of 'Carmen', to dinner, but the embarrassment occasioned by their ill-fated love affair and their diametrically opposed political views made it a disaster. Although Tourgueniev was later to collaborate with Merimee, he considered him 'cold, like his works, intellectual and elegant, with a highly developed sense of beauty and measure, but completely lacking in any sort of faith or even enthusiasm', which probably explains why George tired of him so quickly.

Monckton Milnes lived at 16 Upper Brook Street in fashionable Mayfair, and among his many interests was an enthusiasm for pornographic prints, which he collected assiduously. He was MP for Pontefract, and a great chum of that incorrigible old statesman, Lord Palmerston.

In 1855, Charles Dickens visited the Paris Exhibition, and the Viardots saw him socially on several occasions. At that time he was working on the proofs of 'Little Dorrit', and relished being away from the constant interruptions he experienced at home. While he was in France, Ary Scheffer painted his portrait, but the writer didn't really have the patience for this, and found it irksome to sit still for so long. Although he admired Scheffer as a man, calling him a 'frank and noble fellow', he was not an admirer of his painting, nor, incidentally, was Tourgueniev, whose favourite contemporary artist was Delacroix. Scheffer's brother Henri took the opportunity to paint Dicken's portrait while he sat for Ary, and when she was able to find time, Pauline sang to them while they worked!

On November 23rd, from his apartment at 49, Avenue des Champs Elysee, Dickens wrote: "My dear Scheffer, I hope I shall not inconvenience you by proposing to resume our seances on Monday at a quarter before three, instead of today. The approach of Christmas brings so many proof sheets from England and involves me in so much correspondence (in addition to my regular occupation with my new book), that I am compelled to ask this favour of you. Unless I hear from you to the contrary, I will reappear on Monday; and our appointment for Wednesday I shall, of course, punctually keep. With cordial remembrances to Mme Scheffer and all your house".

Ary Scheffer introduced Dickens to Daniel Manin, the Italian patriot, and last Doge of Venice, who had fled from the Austrian occupation of the former republic after an unsuccessful uprising against them. He was living in exile in Scheffer's house, which is how he came to know the Viardots, with whom he was soon on very friendly terms. His wife had died in 1849, and he had recently lost his epileptic daughter, on whom he had doted. Ary was kindness itself to Manin, and encouraged Dickens to engage him to give Italian lessons to his daughters while they were in Paris.

One evening, Ary gathered a group of some sixty friends into his large studio, to hear the great writer give one of his dramatic readings. As some of Ary's friends did not speak English, Dickens was sceptical about the wisdom of this event, but Ary insisted and 'The Cricket on the Hearth' written in 1845, was requested. This is a Christmas tale that deals with a misunderstanding on the part of a husband who believes that his wife is being unfaithful to him. In reality, she is helping her friend's fiance who fears that the woman he loves is planning to marry a rich man, but after much unhappiness, everything is resolved and all ends happily. At the conclusion of the evening, Pauline was in a flood of tears, and Dickens playfully told her that he now had his own back, as her singing had often had the same effect on him.

The author was still in the city after Christmas, and Pauline invited him to meet George Sand. He replied in French on January 7th: "My dear Mme Viardot, Next Saturday will suit me perfectly. I will be charmed to see you again and to make the acquaintance of that illustrious lady at your house. Mrs. Dickens will be pleased to accompany me. Believe me always, one of the most sincere admirers of your genius, and one of the most constant".

As it happened, the date had to be changed to fit in with George's plans, and the dinner took place on 10th January. In a letter to his friend, the novelist Wilkie Collins, Dickens wrote: "I met Mme George Sand the other day at a dinner got up by Mme Viardot for that great purpose. The human mind cannot conceive anyone more astonishingly opposed to all my preconceptions. If I had been shown her in a state of repose and asked what I thought her to be, I should have said 'the Queen's monthly nurse'. Au reste, she has nothing of the Bas bleu about her, and is very quiet and agreeable."

Over the years, the hospitable Dickens gave numerous parties at his various homes in London. In 1848, he lived in Devonshire Terrace, then moved to York Gate, Regents Park. His last address in the metropolis, before he settled at Gad's Hill Place in Kent, was Tavistock House in Bloomsbury, where strangely enough, Gounod was later to live when it was owned by his lady friend, Georgina Weldon and her husband.

Clara Novello said that Dicken's parties were great fun and all the writer's friends enjoyed themselves immensely, but as soon as music was played or sung, he insisted that all chatter must stop, and every one was required to give their full attention to the performance. One of his prime delights on those occasions was to hear Pauline and Clara sing duets together.

On the 3rd of December, 1855, Dickens wrote to Pauline in English: "Dear Mme Viardot, Mrs Dickens tells me that you have only borrowed the first number of 'Little Dorrit' and are going to send it back. Pray do nothing of the sort, and allow me to have the great pleasure of sending you the succeeding numbers as they reach me. I have had such delight in your great genius, and have so high an interest in it and admiration of it, that I am proud of the honour of giving you a moment's intellectual pleasure".

Ary Scheffer's portrait of Dickens did not please either the painter or the sitter. Scheffer was not satisfied because he did not think that he had caught a sufficient likeness and the author was sure that he had not. Ary told Mrs. Dickens that he would see what he could do to improve it. Although he was technically skilled, and experienced in the painting of portraits, he was not adept at catching a true likeness of his sitters, except in the case of his oil painting of Pauline, which now hangs in the Dordrecht Art Gallery, which captured her character beautifully. Dickens' portrait was hung in the Royal Academy in London in May 1856, but many English artists considered that there was something lacking.

Although the Viardots, George Sand and Ary Scheffer had broken off their friendship with Gounod in 1852, Scheffer painted his portrait in 1855. The sittings must have been initially embarrassing, but, of course, from time to time it was inevitable that the composer's path and theirs would cross as they moved in the same circles.

Pauline's career was now rather pedestrian, and she was repeating the same roles that she had played for years. She still had many concert engagements in distinguished salons, and sang in her own house in Paris, before noted connoisseurs who truly appreciated her genius. In England she was a stalwart of the opera season, and she frequently toured Germany, where it was always a pleasure to perform under the direction of Julius Rietz, who had relinquished his post with the Opera at Dusseldorf a year before, in order to conduct more often in Leipzig and Dresden.

Just as Tourgueniev had assiduously sought Pauline's friendship, so she sought that of Rietz. He was not an easy man to get to know, as he was very reserved and had a rather taciturn disposition. His bearing was dignified and he was very serious and intellectual, with little sense of humour. What attracted Pauline to him is a mystery, but attracted she was. He was quite tall, broadly built, with a full head of hair that just touched his collar. He had begun his career as a cellist, and was a protégé of Mendelssohn, whom he assisted in the

holding small dinner parties, where simple, plain fare of good quality was served, as well as a Thursday salon, where such luminaries as Berlioz, Liszt, Wagner, Saint Saens, Delacroix, Corot, Scheffer, George Sand,,Cesar Franck, Rossini, Eugene Vivier, Gustave Dore, Flaubert, Renan, Ponsard, Henri Martin, and the violinists Henri Vieuxtemps and Joseph Joachim met from time to time. They also held a smaller, Sunday afternoon gathering for their most intimate friends.

Sometimes they received friends from abroad, like Charles Dickens, Lady Monson, the artist Sir Frederick Leighton, the baritone Julius Stockhausen, Clara Novello, Clara Schumann, Adelaide Sartoris; their Russian friends, the young Rubinstein brothers, Nicolai and Anton, and, occasionally dissidents such as Bakunin, Herzen, and another revolutionary, the German philologist and archaeologist, Hermann Muller-Strubing. This man had once been sentenced to death but had escaped to the safety of French soil, where Pauline introduced him to George Sand, who soon took him to Nohant and into her bed. On occasions, friends stayed at Courtavenel, where they enjoyed amateur theatrical performances in the little 'Theatre des pomme de terre', and Louis proudly took those who shared his taste for sport, shooting over his estate.

During the summer of 1856 Tourgueniev was once again at Courtavenel, so happy, relaxed and contented that he wrote very little, despite the fact that he had planned to work on an essay entitled 'Hamlet and Don Quixote'. Instead, he took part in family theatricals, and indulged himself reading and making music. A newcomer to Courtavenel that summer was the young soprano, Desiree Artot, who had come to study with Pauline. Apparently, her parents had sent her to Mme Viardot in the hope that she would persuade the girl to give up her desire to be a singer, but Pauline was so impressed with Desiree's voice and talent that she took charge of her musical education and gave her every encouragement. Considering that Pauline said she did not like teaching very much, she must have been convinced of Desiree's outstanding talent to take her as a student. It is ironic that Mme Viardot, who had a great gift for teaching and spent so much of the latter part of her life in that discipline, should have said in a letter to a Mr. Abel in 1848 or 1849: "There is nothing in the world I find more boring, and I always have something better to do". No doubt, she later changed her tune, especially when confronted with an exceptional student.

Contrary to what some writers and members of the Viardot family have implied, Courtavenel was not a luxurious place where a high standard of living was taken for granted. Despite its size, the Viardots lived simply, as Pauline's gentle irony shows in a letter dated 25th September, 1855, which she wrote to her friend, the actress, Rose Cheri, after she had declined an invitation. "What? Do you forsake this poor old Courtavenel that loves you so, and instead of taking possession of your inconvenient, narrow and uncomfortable little room overlooking the muddy park with its handful of wilting flowers, instead of coming to eat old Veronique's low-class, more or less Spanish concoctions, you rent a delightful place in the country, where you are up to your eyes in every imaginable comfort (and luxury, indeed), and before we know where we are you forget the old nest, full of hearts so truly yours".

One evening, Tourgueniev's friend, the Russian poet Afanasi Afanasevich Fet, a dark, handsome man, with a shapely moustache, arrived unannounced while the family was at dinner. He had once been an officer in the Russian army, as his bearing showed. Naturally, they were rather taken aback by the arrival of this uninvited guest, but they soon realised that Ivan, who was in Paris, had forgotten to tell them that he had invited the poet. Of course, the courteous Viardots behaved as if his visit was perfectly convenient, despite being annoyed with the absent-minded Tourgueniev for causing them and his friend embarrassment, but despite their efforts to make Fet feel at home, he was ill at ease at Courtavenel; his French was poor, and the Viardots were not exactly comfortable with him because, as a committed Slavophile who disliked Europe, he had little time for the French, and was politically very reactionary, so there was no common ground between them.

Fet was used to hearty Russian meals and didn't like the kind of food served in the Viardot household. As far as he could see, the French lived on starvation rations, although the meals were delicate, with the emphasis on quality rather than quantity, and served artistically in small portions. Poor Fet who was used to more lavish fare, still felt hungry after he had eaten, as a typical dinner menu at Courtavenel consisted of a clear Bouillon soup, pate, a main dish made from various types of beans, ham sliced so thinly that one could see through it, and a dessert of tiny pancakes, or omelette with jam. Fet was at a loss to understand how Ivan could be happy in such a place; to him it would have been a terrible penance because he lived in dread of being exiled from his beloved Russia.

Soon Pauline left Courtavenel for Germany, as Berlioz, who usually spent the summer months in Baden Baden, the famous spa town in the Black Forest, had invited her to take part in the town's music festival, which he was conducting at the beginning of August. The composer was now one of Pauline's most enthusiastic admirers and marvelled at the 'virginal purity' of her voice, the two and a half octave range that was quite remarkable because it comprised and united three different kinds of voices – contralto, mezzo-soprano and soprano, which was unusual to find in one singer, but accounts for the kind of vocal writing in her own songs, which require an extensive range, and a singer who is comfortable in the tessitura of all three voices.

Writing of Pauline's art, Berlioz stated: "Mme Viardot is a great musician and one sees this in the ease with which she overcomes the imperceptible difficulties of dealing with the great dramatic school", he added: "she unites an irrepressibly impetuous and imperious verve with a profound sensibility and with an almost deplorable faculty for expressing immense grief. Her gestures are sane, noble and true to life, and her power of facial expression is even more remarkable in dumb scenes than in those where she has to reinforce therewith the accents of song. She has that artful phrasing of the 'chant large', which has become so rare nowadays", and he concludes: "she is one of the greatest artists in the history of music".

Pauline was delighted when she heard that Berlioz had also asked Liszt to take part in the Baden festival; he was now forty-five years old, as thin as a post, and still retained his phenomenal charisma. Since 1842, he had been Director of Music to the Ducal Court of Weimar, and there, in 1847 he had set up home with a wealthy Polish aristocrat, the Princess Caroline Sayn-Wittgenstein, a blue stocking, who wrote voluminously about the Catholic Church. The lady was separated from her husband, and had a daughter, but she had not been able to obtain a divorce, as the Tsar decreed that if she did so, her extensive lands and riches would be confiscated.

Nevertheless, she was a determined woman, and spent years seeking an annulment from the Pope in order to over-rule the Tsar, but much to her chagrin her attempts were in vain, probably to Liszt's relief, because although he respected her greatly and lived quite happily with her, he feared marriage and did not appear to be in a hurry to tie the knot, preferring his freedom that enabled him to come and go as he pleased. However, if Caroline finally obtained her annulment, he was prepared to do the honourable thing and marry her, because she had, after all, been his intimate companion for nine years. Pauline observed that he did not have the air of a contented man and was often prey to melancholy moods. But she had always had the ability to lighten his gloom and he sought her out and enjoyed her company as she was able to amuse him, as well as talk on serious musical or philosophical matters. She had a more optimistic nature than he, but being a dedicated artist herself, she understood and was sympathetic to the feelings and frustrations that beset him. Both had deeply mystical natures, and knew intuitively many things hidden from others, and they did not find it easy living in a materialistic world, with its arrogant ignorance, its stresses and strains, jealousies and chicaneries.

Princess Caroline and Berlioz, it seemed, were also kindred spirits who corresponded frequently. Unable to communicate on the same level with his wife,

Marie, he confided in the Princess, whom he found sympathetic and understanding.

Pauline became very fond of the spa town, which is set in the hilly country of
the Black Forest, where all the elite of the beau monde gathered during the
summer months. The elegant, white, neo-classical casino, set in its own park in
the Tiergarten was the great draw, but both concerts and gambling took place
there. There were morning promenades, and the drinking of the waters in the
pump room, the exchange of gossip and the meeting of old friends and acquaintances. The Prince and Princess of Prussia usually paid an annual visit to
their daughter Louise, the Grand Duchess of Baden and her husband, and were
often joined by the Tsarina of Russia, the sister of Prince William. Her daughter
Olga was the Grand Duchess of Wurttemburg, and Baden was a convenient
meeting place for them all. The Tsarina was now a widow, her husband Nicolas
I having died the previous year, some said by his own hand, due to the disastrous outcome of the Crimean War, which had humiliated Russia. His politically
more moderate son Alexander II had succeeded him and Tourgueniev and friends
such as Herzen and Bakunin fervantly hoped that he would bring about the
reforms of which they dreamed.

The Grand Duchess, Louise, and her husband were highly cultured people
who made the duchy of Baden a centre for opera, music and theatre, as well as
a mecca for European royalty, aristocracy, nobility, celebrities of every sort,
gamblers, and adventurers of both sexes. There were many famous artists and
musicians who found rich pickings during the summer months, and it was here
that Pauline often bumped into friends and colleagues whom she had not seen
for a while.

Since the end of the Crimean War, those who had been constrained while it
raged, now began to move freely around Europe, but it was ironic that
Tourgueniev had left Russia just at a time when his first novel 'Rudin' had just
been published, and had received very favourable reviews, bringing his name
before a wider public. Countess Lambert could not understand him, and was
disappointed that he had not overcome his desire to go wandering in search of
his 'gypsy'.

Later in August, the Viardots were in England, and Tourgueniev saw them
several times before Pauline left to stay with Charles and Emma Trueman at
West Hill, Highgate, which is situated at the edge of Hampstead Heath, overlooking Highgate Ponds. Louis had accepted an invitation from Francis Baring
of the banking family, and his French wife, Hortense, to shoot over their estate
near Thetford in Norfolk. Pauline had no wish to spend time following the guns,
much preferring to stay with the Truemans, who happened to be friends of

Berthe Viardot, who always stayed with them on her visits to London. Pauline and George Sand thought Berthe an old bore, (she was three years younger than Louis) but she was not as straight-laced as they painted her, and while in London in 1857, she went to a pub with Muller-Strubing, and enjoyed a flutter on the horses at the Derby with him and Tourgueniev. She kept Ivan busy carrying out little errands for her while he was staying at the Sablouniere Hotel in Leicester Square.

No doubt, Tourgueniev was not over pleased when he learned that Pauline's arch rivals, Grisi and Jenny Lind were now celebrated in wax at Mme Tussauds. He saw her great admirer, Henry Chorley, freqently, going to the theatre with him and Manuel, and visiting him at his house at 13 Eaton Place West. Chorley, by this time, had become a confirmed alcoholic and was often the worse for wear, although occasionally they all spent an evening together when Chorley actually stayed sober.

Manuel Garcia was a member of the Garrick Club in Covent Garden, and introduced Tourgueniev to other members, one of whom was Charles Halle, who of course, Tourgueniev had known for several years. He and Manuel were close friends, who enjoyed making music, and playing chess together. The Russian liked Halle, but was puzzled by him, finding him too gentlemanlike and calm for an artist. Manuel, on the other hand, was impatient, impetuous and utterly delightful. His interests were wide-ranging and his intense conversation was highly stimulating. Although Tourgueniev read and wrote English well, like Manuel, he did not enjoy speaking the language very much and would always avoid it if he could. Fortunately, many of his English friends spoke good French which saved him the necessity of making the effort.

While in England, in 1856, Pauline sang at the Three Choirs Festival, staying with Sir James Buller East and his wife Caroline at Bourton House, Bourton-on-the-Hill, near Moreton-in-the-Marsh, in the beautiful Cotswold countryside of Gloucestershire. In September she was engaged at the Trienniel Music Festival in Birmingham, an event that had been taking place at three yearly intervals since its inception in 1768, in order to raise funds for the local hospital. The highest rate of admission was one guinea, a large sum in those days, equal to the weekly pay of an office worker. The concerts were given in the Town Hall, in the centre of the city, which is a fine example of Victorian Greek classicism, and she had a new premiere to sing – Michael Costa's oratorio 'Eli', with Jeanne Castellan, John Sims Reeves and Karl Formes, and local opinion had it that the soloists could not have been bettered. There had been a great deal of advanced publicity, and the chorus had undergone dozens of rehearsals, which accounted for their excellence. The work met with great acclaim and to a man, the critics considered it to be on a par with the music of Mendelssohn, which was praise indeed; however, posterity deemed otherwise, and the oratorio fell into obscurity.

Michael Costa was a first rate choral trainer and conductor, as Herman Klein acknowledges in his 'Music and Mummers': "The masterful Neapolitan exerted an extraordinary magnetic control over his singers; he had the power of infusing into them an irresistible rhythm and real dynamic energy. He had the reputation of being a severe taskmaster, a veritable martinet with his singers and orchestras; but the result afforded the best justification for his stern discipline. He used his baton decisively, with the requisite weight, and vigorous swing".

In England, a passion was growing for choral singing on a large scale, and many cities rivalled each other in building huge halls where vast musical forces could be assembled. Louis Jullien had set the fashion, assembling orchestras of over a hundred and choirs of up to a thousand. Clara Novello cornered the market in the opening of new town halls, where works on a modest scale were blown out of all proportion. Because of a severe puritanical attitude towards music making, oratorios were permitted, but the advent of bands in parks was met with opposition, and when 'La Traviata' was played in Birmingham, the theatre was almost empty, and the poor soprano, Marietta Piccolomini, who played the consumptive courtesan, was savagely attacked.

Although Pauline enjoyed her stay in the beautiful Cotswold countryside, she was not sorry to leave the smoke clogged streets of Birmingham, one of the busiest industrial centres in the country. The fresh air of Courtavenel, where Tourgueniev joined her, was balm to her soul, and she was delighted that Ivan found her little girls absolutely charming, although it was Claudie who stole his heart; she became one of the most special beings in his life and his devotion to her was absolute. Louis, despite some intial qualms about Tourgueniev's return, actually enjoyed having his old hunting partner with him once more, and the bonds of their friendship were soon re-established. Sometimes, Pauline would bring the children to meet the men as they returned from a day of sport; they would frolic and play in the autumn sunshine, and she would pick peaches from her trees, as they walked back to the house through the golden, pink glow of early evening.

Tourgueniev wrote letters in his little study, or fished in the moat, or in the ancient pond at Maisonfleur, which had once been a moat. This property now belonged to Louis Viardot who had bought it in 1852 for the sum of 12,000 francs. The Viardots experienced a lot of difficulty with drainage at Courtavenel over the years, and the moat at the chateau, which had three bridges to be maintained, was inclined to silt up and become choked with weeds and rushes, but Ivan took it upon himself to clear these, with the help of Jean, one of the servants, so that it would be navigable for their rowing boat.

Jean was a good worker who, Tourgueniev said, was on the go 'from morning till night, doing nothing but scrub, wash, clean, oil, dust, sweep, and polish. If only the gardener took after him". The Viardots were not lucky with their gardeners, who were all rather lazy, or perhaps there was just too much for them to do and more help should have been employed. The gardener's wife was a very industrious woman, but her husband enjoyed chatting and philosophising more than he did gardening. The Viardots put up with him for several years because of his Republican sympathies, but finally even the patient Louis had had enough and sacked him. He was replaced by Jean-Louis Dumoutier who remained at Courtavenel for a long time, but was also finally dismissed for inefficiency.

After dinner, if the evening was fine there would be further walks in the garden, then Pauline would sit at the piano and play or sing while the men, Berthe and other guests played whist, and Louis's eight dogs would arrive and settle down around them waiting to be fed by their master. Sometimes, he and Ivan would doze blissfully while Pauline's rich voice floated over them. It was quite, quite idyllic and the Russian wished that it could go on forever.

Pauline had her own study in one of the towers, where she was able to retreat and rehearse in private. Besides the work Tourgueniev did in the grounds, he also took pleasure rearranging the library, and discussed philosophical and political matters with his friends. In talking over the young nation of Hungary, downtrodden by authoritarian rule despite the efforts of their friend, Lajos Kossuth, while older nations simply looked on, he reminded them that Goethe had held the view that man was not born to be free, but then thanked God for individuals like Pauline: "If there were not still beings here and there on earth like you, one's very soul would spew out in disgust".

In his letters Tourgueniev told his friends, Herzen and Botkin how happy he was, in this place that he considered his home, his soul full of sweetness and light, and of how charmingly he and the family passed their days. He said that they had put on some comedies and tragedies in the little theatre in the attic and that his daughter had acted very well in Racine's 'Iphigenie', but he considered that he had performed extremely poorly in all the roles he had taken, although that hadn't spoiled his enjoyment. Beethoven sonatas were played by Louise, now a skilful pianist herself, who often accompanied her mother when she sang, and one of their favourite games was making caricatures of each other, having to guess who was who, but it was Pauline who contrived the best likenesses. Ivan stayed for several weeks, and the Viardots didn't leave until October 27th.

At the beginning of November, Tourgueniev went to Paris where he found an apartment, but it being too cold and uncomfortable, he found another one at 206, rue de Rivoli, where he installed his daughter and her governess. Paulinette had only been nine when he went away and they had been separated for five years. Resembling her father, at fourteen she was not particularly prepossessing; although he was considered a very handsome man, but his masculine looks were unsuitable for a woman, and Paulinette was very plain. She also lacked personality and vitality, and was slow and dull in her studies, nor had she inherited her father's charm. Tourgueniev must have been dreadfully disappointed in discovering how uninteresting and talentless she was, especially when compared to the delightful Claudie.

It was while Pauline was at her chateau, during the late autumn of 1856, that she conceived her last child, and as Tourgueniev was there at the relevant time, there have always been rumours that he was the father, but they have never been substantiated. When Ivan was happy he was well, and he was certainly happy that summer at Courtavenel because he was very well indeed.

One afternoon, Pauline went out riding alone; suddenly feeling dizzy, she fell from her horse, caught her foot in the stirrup and was dragged along. She lost consciousness, and when she regained it, the sun had set, and it was cold and dark. When she failed to appear for dinner, Joaquina went in search of her, found her, called for help and brought her home, nursing her until she recovered from the shock of the accident. The incident gave everyone a dreadful fright, resurrecting the awful spectre of Malibran's fate, but fortunately, Pauline had done herself little harm and was soon able to return to Paris, although her mother made her promise that she would give up riding.

The sunny mood Tourgueniev had enjoyed at Courtavenel changed quite rapidly when he returned to the capital, and in a letter to a friend on the 13th of January, 1857 he wrote: "If I had known what awaited me in Paris, I would not have left St. Petersburg." When Leo Tolstoy saw him, he thought he looked terrible, and said in a letter: "Tourgueniev is pitiable to see... I would not have thought him capable of such a love".

Afanasi Fet is another witness of Ivan's condition. He could never understand his friend's enthusiasm for Europe, and confronted him on this issue. Tourgueniev defending his position, said how kind the Viardots had been to him and how much he loved being at Courtavenel, acknowledging a debt of gratitude to Pauline as his daughter's guardian, but then his mood suddenly changed and he became belligerent, exclaiming : "and it is not only in this connection that I have to submit to that woman's will. No! Long ago, and forever, she blotted out everything else for me – and for me, that's just as it should be. I'm really only blissfully happy when a woman puts her heel on my neck and grinds my face in the dirt. Goodness! What luck for a woman to be hideous!" Could this outburst have unleashed something deeply buried in Ivan's psyche that might possibly be laid at the door of his dominating, domineering, sadistic mother, who had caused him to have a perverted, masochistic attitude to women, and a need to be dominated by them?

Is it possible that Tourgueniev said such a thing, or did Fet make it up when he wrote his memoirs many years later, after he and Ivan had quarrelled and gone their separate ways? There is no way of knowing, but Ivan did firmly believe that Pauline had cast a spell over him from which he could not escape. Blaming the woman is an age old masculine device for excusing their own shortcomings, of course, as seen in some Islamic cultures where men make their women keep their bodies and faces totally covered in case they inflame masculine passions.

Tourgueniev truly believed that Pauline had supernatural powers and although he was probably just indulging in Slavic superstition, there is little doubt that she did possess certain unusual gifts, and was probably a natural psychic (as are many artists and musicians) which accounted for her interest in mysticism, although she usually kept this fact very much to herself. In the middle of the nineteenth century there was a burgeoning interest in Spiritualism, a subject that was later to be investigated by some of the finest scientific minds in England, such as F. H. Myers, Sir Oliver Lodge and the author of 'Sherlock Holmes', Sir Arthur Conan Doyle who, after rigorous study came to the conclusion that the conciousness of the dead lived on in another dimension, after the demise of the physical body.

Mrs. Milner Gibson, a mutual friend of the Viardots, Tourgueniev, and Victor Hugo, whom they often saw in London, became very involved in Spiritualism, and they gradually gave her a wide berth, but this may not have been because they thought her activities cranky, but because they knew there was more to it than meets the eye. If Pauline possessed the knowledge that Tourgueniev believed she did, she would have known that the forces with which her friend and her associates were tampering in the seance room, or with the ouija board, should not be treated lightly, as they could prove dangerous to the uninitiated, and were better left alone.

Victor Hugo, had become a firm believer in Spiritualism, and when his daughter Adele fled from Guernsey where she had been forced to stay, due to her father's exile, Mrs. Milner Gibson welcomed her into her London home and looked after her until she left for America where she stayed for nine years. Hugo was a very possessive father, and his daughter, who was an imaginative and musical girl, resented the repressive way he treated her. She was in love and wanted to get married, but he wouldn't hear of it and his unsympathetic treatment caused her to become very neurotic. When the man she loved rejected her, she had a breakdown, returned to France, where her father was again living, was declared insane and committed to an asylum, where she died in 1920, at the age of ninety.

Patrick Waddington mentions Tourgueniev's own meditations of a metaphysical nature, and cites a remarkable passage in his letter of 28th July, 1849, in which he clearly elaborated a philosophy which, although already hinted at in his earlier works, was destined to play an important part in his mature writings. He considered that the universe was devoid of purpose or necessity, but appeared to be the product of an irresistible movement, which could be called Life, Nature, or God, and was often beautiful, and sometimes even positively beneficent, but should not be worshipped, as its essence was indifference. Like that of the English novelist, Thomas Hardy, his basic philosophy was one of deep pessimism, yet staying at Courtavenel at that time, he had expressed a more optimistic mood concerning life: "It is everything, it is in full flower and vigour; I don't know if this will last for long, but for the moment it is a fact, and it makes the blood course in my veins without any effort on my part..." He reflected that he was being fed and laundered in a fairy-tale castle, and said no man could desire anything more.

In Paris, in March 1857, Tourgueniev and Tolstoy attended a seance held by the medium, Daniel Dunglas Home. Tourgueniev was sceptical, but couldn't account for the three taps he experienced under the sole of his right foot. By 1860, Home was all the rage in England and his reputation became well established throughout Europe.

It is likely that Pauline heard a great deal of talk about Spiritualism when she was in England, as many people in the best circles were interested in such matters, visiting mediums out of curiosity. When the College of Psychic Studies was established in 1884, its founders were from the higher echelons of society, but for decades, the main interest was in phenomena which, unfortunately, are very easy to fake, and the whole area was dismissed by many intellectuals as fit only for cranks.

There is little actual evidence of Pauline's psychic facet, and if she was a true mystic, versed in gnosticism, she would not have wasted her time or been interested in such primitive aspects, yet Tourgueniev's confidences to Yakov Polonski are fascinating. He told his friend that Mme Viardot had 'some kind of special influence over him, keeping him at her feet as if by some type of sorcery, just like witchcraft', and that when he was with her, he was physically unable to do anything but submit to her, because it was beyond his strength to do otherwise, and that in her presence he felt as if in the grip of the most potent of hypnotic spells. Polonski said: "Once he seriously assured me that Mme Viardot was a witch, and said it with such conviction that I was surprised and astonished, and started to object, laughing at Tourgueniev's superstition." "You shouldn't laugh, Yakov Petrovich", he answered. "There have always been witches, and always will be. They have some sort of inner power over people, no matter what one says, and there's nothing to be done about it". He also told Polonski that Pauline was so gifted that she could see the back of the chair through the body of the person sitting upon it. If this is true, it would confirm that Pauline had clairvoyant sight.

Nekrasov, the nominal boss of the periodical 'Sovremennik', for which Tourgueniev contributed articles, complained that he demanded enormous advances in order to keep his 'insatiable old witch' Pauline Viardot happy, 'forever dragging from the unhappy chap his last old pair of trousers'.

With regard to Tourgueniev's medical history, there is no doubt that he suffered physically from various complaints over the years, but he was a confirmed hypochondriac, and one is tempted to believe that many of his ills were psychosomatic and exacerbated by unhappiness. There is also the fact that whenever he spent too much time alone or unoccupied, he had a tendency to become obsessed with his health. The question is, was Tourgueniev's bladder trouble, which flared up after his visit to Courtavenel a symptom or a cause? Pauline's attitude towards him certainly changed suddenly, and she became cold and distant, although the reason for this can only be surmised. Perhaps he was the father of the unborn child she was carrying, and with female contrariness she turned against him? Or was it that she simply did not have the time or energy to give him her undivided attention, as he wished, or perhaps he irritated her by his tendency to cling, and needing her own space, she held him at arms length because she wasn't able to cope with him. Whatever the cause, there is little doubt that during the early months of 1857 he went through a moral, physical, emotional, and spiritual crisis that alarmed his friends.

He was totally confused by Pauline's attitude after what he saw as a period of fulfilment, and wrote: "I really have been happy all this time – perhaps because 'late flowers' are fairer than the sumptuous firstlings of the fields". The writer Semenoff claims that Pauline continued to see Tourgueniev for a while when they returned to Paris, visiting him at his apartment and 'making herself at home' with him, but Semenoff admits that this could have been an invention by Paulinette who gave him the information. The relationship between the two Paulines continued to deteriorate, and Paulinette was disgusted by her father's liaison with her foster parent.

When the separations between Ivan and Pauline grew longer, the writer began to develop symptoms of urethritis and spermatorrhoeia, which would suggest that these illnesses were the result and not the cause of the change in his relations with Pauline. Later Ivan explained to Tolstoy: "I am already too old not to have a nest, to stay at home. I shall definitely come back to Russia in the spring, but when I leave here I must also say goodbye to my last dream of so-called happiness or – to speak more plainly – to the dream of joy which comes from a feeling of contentment in the way one's life is organised". It is difficult to know what Tourgueniev could have hoped – did he imagine that one day he would marry Pauline? His friends apparently had this impression, and ironically, as he was beginning to experience his 'neuralgia of the bladder', in Russia, there were persistent rumours that he and Pauline were to be married. Kolbasin told him that very slanderous things were being said about them in Russia, and in reply, Tourgueniev wrote that he did not know if he was being accused of kleptomania or sexual deviation. In a letter to Tolstoy written in January 1857, he angrily declared that Pauline's husband had never been in better health and there was absolutely no question of a marriage, yet told Leo, "But I love her more than ever, more than anything else on earth. And that is true!"

Ivan saw Pauline alternately as a saint to be worshipped and a woman to be desired, and he always thought of her as belonging to himself. Whether or not their love had been physically consummated, it is possible that he saw her pregnancy, after she had made him so supremely happy, as being tantamount to infidelity, if Louis was the father. His deepest fear was that she was two-faced, and gnawing claws of jealousy assailed him, turning him against the French and France, just at a time when his standing as a writer had never been higher in his adopted country. On December 7th, he told his friend Vasily Petrovich Botkin, the writer and critic: "I don't care whether I please the French or not, especially as Mme Viardot didn't like 'Faust.'" On a more personal note, he confessed that Botkin's venereal disease had frightened him into buying rubber condoms, then realized how useless they were to him in his present situation.

In May he spent a few days with Herzen in London, then went to Berlin for a while, moving on to Sinzig to take the waters. While there, he received news of the birth of Pauline's son, who had arrived at 4 pm on the 20th of July, and named Paul Louis Joaquim. He was born at Courtavenel because Pauline had

wanted to be delivered by her friend, Dr. Frisson, in whom she had more confidence than in Parisian doctors. At noon the next day, the birth was registered
before the mayor of Vaudoy, Alexis Blaque, whose signature was witnessed by
Louis-Desire Quillet, a local brick-layer, Jean-Louis Dumoutier, the gardener,
who now had the title of private warden, and Louis, as the child's legitimate
father, who soon despatched the news of Paul's birth to various friends, including Meyerbeer and Jules Michelet, the historian and professor of the College
de France, both of whom wrote charming letters of congratulation. Louis's
letter to Tourgueniev written on the 21st was formal, and Gustave Dulong
described it as 'laconic but very cordial'.

From Sinzig, Ivan replied to each parent separately, his letter to Louis being
sincere and friendly, but not overly expansive. In his letter of congratulation to
Pauline written on July 24th, he cried: "Hurrah! Ypa! Lebehoch! Vivat! Evviva!
Vive le petit Paul! Vive sa mere! Vive son pere! Vive toute la famille! So, you
have a boy, I felicitate and embrace you!" He asked for details of everything,
the health of the mother, and a description of Paul's looks, particularly the
colour of his eyes, (was this idle curiosity or more significant? Louis and Pauline
had brown eyes, but Ivan's were blue), and he prophesied (accurately) that
there would be an entry in the Lexicon of 1950 which would read: Viardot – Paul,
Louis, Joachim, famous... (I leave a blank space) born at Courtavenel (en Brie)
etc., etc., son of the famous Pauline Garcia, etc, and of the eminent writer and
translator of 'Don Quichotte'. He was right, as Groves Dictionary of Music
confirms with an entry in Paul's name, the blank space filled in as 'international
violinist, leader of the Paris Opera, and Director of the Conservatoire of Algiers.
The Viardots were prescient too as they had included the name Joachim in
honour of their friend the famous violinist Joseph Joachim, at whose debut
concert in Leipzig, in 1843, when he was twelve, Pauline and Clara Schumann
had performed.

Ivan told Pauline that he had tried to imagine how she must have felt when
she awoke refreshed by sleep on the morning of the 21st, seeing her sweet baby
and hearing his cry, which he said was 'comparable to music'. Some people
have taken this joyous letter as a confirmation that Tourgueniev was the father
of the child, but it could also have been the mark of his unselfishness and
supreme happiness for the couple he rated the best friends he had in the world.

Hector Berlioz (whom Viardot first met in 1839) in 1845

Below left: Charles Gounod in 1840 when Pauline Viardot first met him in
  Rome, drawn by Ingres
Below right: Richard Wagner whom Pauline met in 1839, for whom she
  sight-read the role of Isolde at a private audition in order to obtain
  funding for his work

Above: Mario di Candia, the celebrated Italian tenor, who was a source of unpleasant professional experiences for Pauline

Right: Pauline Viardot and Gustave Roger in the Parisian premiere of 'Le Prophete' by Meyerbeer

A charming study of Pauline in a pink dress by Maurice Sand which he
made in 1845 when he was in love with her (original in Musee de la vie
Romantique, Paris)

Pauline as Fides in 'Le Prophete,' one of her most notable roles

Pauline Garcia in her debut role in England as Desdemona in 'Otello' by Rossini, on May 9th, 1839, at Her Majesty's Theatre Haymarket.

S. ROGER.

Above: Gustave Hypolytte Roger, French tenor who created the role of John of Leyden in the Paris premiere of 'Le Prophete,' 1849. He also appeared in London with her in 'Les Huguenots' in 1848 when Mario cancelled at the last minute and Roger stepped in.

Right: Giacomo Meyerbeer (who wrote the role of Fides for Pauline), in 1843

Left: I.S. Tourgeniev, 1838-1839, by K. A. Gorbounov.

Below: A view of Unter den Linden in Berlin with the opera house and dome of the Royal Palace

CHAPTER TWENTY-SIX

1857/8

After leaving Sinzig, Tourgueniev journeyed to Rome with Botkin, from where he travelled throughout Italy for the whole of the winter. Is it, perhaps, significant that he didn't mention Paul's birth to any of his friends in his letters? Whether the child was his own or not, perhaps he saw Paul's entry into the world as the end of his own youthful hopes of making a life with the woman he loved so deeply. As the child grew older, many people observed that he resembled Tourgueniev more than he did his legal father, and they didn't understand why Pauline, rather than drawing closer to Ivan actually closed ranks with Louis. However, this makes perfect sense.If Tourgueniev was indeed the father, the last thing the Viardots wanted was gossip of the kind they had experienced during the Gounod affair, and they would have done all in their power to ensure that there was no speculation as to the true paternity of Pauline's son. There is also the distinct possibility that Pauline herself was not sure which of the two men was responsible for Paul's conception, and probably, neither did they. If Louis suspected that Tourgueniev was the father and Pauline knew of his suspicion, she would surely have done all in her power to make up for the wrong she had done him. Never was the proverb "it's a wise father who knows his own child' more true.

Tourgueniev's compatriot, Semenoff had no doubt that Paul was the writer's son, and he believed that Paul actually thought so. Pauline's first biographer, Gustave Dulong was of the opinion that Paul may have allowed people to think so, in order to be revenged upon Pauline, after a family quarrel in which he allied himself with Paulinette against his mother, then blamed her for repudiating both of them. However, Jacques-Paul Viardot, Paul's son from his second marriage, denied any such thing.

Some people, believing Ivan to be Paul's natural father, have expressed surprise that he did not seem especially fond of the lad, or wondered why he didn't take more interest in him. Perhaps this is explained by the fact that Tourgueniev was not sure if the child was his, or had not been given the opportunity to bond with him. However, it is surely significant that when the two-year-old child was desperately ill with pneumonia and there seemed every possibility that he would die, Pauline sent for Tourgueniev, who was then in Germany. Could it be that she did believe that he was Paul's father and gave him the opportunity to see the boy one last time?

Tourgueniev had no doubt that Paulinette was his own child and took his duties seriously, but it was out of a sense of responsibility, rather than a deep affection for her. His great love for Claudie caused gossip, and Alexandre Zviguilsky suggests that Ivan's devotion to the child was more sensual than paternal, and if this is true, he would not have been the first man to have a penchant for little girls.

In her youth, Pauline's character had been open, frank and uncomplicated, but as a woman coloured by life's experiences, she learned to keep her own counsel. Even her closest friends were unaware of her innermost thoughts and feelings, least of all Tourgueniev, which is what caused him such torment. With her celebrity, and the risk of unwanted journalistic prying, she became more cautious, but sometimes, as an emotional safety valve, she needed the therapy of the 'confessional', and in her correspondence with Julius Rietz, whose discretion she trusted implicitly, she said a lot more than she cared to reveal, even to such stalwart friends as George Sand.

For the time being, Pauline concentrated on her family and baby, and the recovery of her strength after his birth. Yet the family circle, however cosy and comforting, could never keep her indefinitely at home. She was now at the zenith of her powers, a great artist, who did not merely sing with her marvellous voice, but with her soul, which is why she moved so many people to tears, touching a deep well-spring of emotion in her listeners, releasing long held sorrows, tensions and stresses, bringing healing in her wake. All great artists have this ability to heal, and it is one of the reasons why art is not a luxury but a necessity.

Pauline, like Liszt, was always ready to help other musicians, and Camille Saint Saens was one of many who benefited from her friendship. He was ten years younger than Pauline, a fine musician who had been a prolific composer from his early youth, and a marvellous pianist who could read any music at sight. On Thursdays, he was a regular guest at the Viardots' salon, where he frequently acted as Pauline's accompanist, and it was not long before he was welcomed into her inner circle and invited to the intimate Sunday afternoons for family and close friends. Here there was a good deal of horse-play, with theatricals and dressing up, games and charades, when all the guests let down their hair and had a riotous time. Many years later, in 1913, in his collection of essays 'Ecole buissonniere', Saint Saens said of Pauline: "Mme Viardot was not beautiful: worse than that. Ary Scheffer's portrait of her is the only one that does justice to this unequalled woman. No other gives an adequate idea of her strange powers of fascination. Her personality rendered her even more captivating than her talent as a singer; without doubt her personality was one of the most astonishing I have encountered. Speaking and writing Spanish, French, Italian, English and German fluently, she was conversant with the literature of all countries and she corresponded with all Europe'.

This fascination inspired him to write the opera 'Samson and Delilah' for her, but unfortunately, by the time it reached the stage, Pauline was too old to sing the role of the Philistine seductress, although she did take part in a costumed, semi-staged version in 1870, at the Chateau of Croisset, near Rouen, the home of the writer Gustave Flaubert, who was, by that time, a great friend of Tourgueniev and George Sand with whom he correspondended regularly. Despite the fact that Pauline's voice was no longer that of a young woman, her power to fascinate was as strong as ever.

Because of Paul's birth Pauline missed the London opera season, but she returned to the capital to give concerts towards the end of the summer. At one of the performances of Ancient Music, she sang the arias 'Return O God of Hosts', and that of Lucifer from 'Resurrection'. Gounod's oratorio 'Redemption' was receiving a great success in England, but much as she admired his music, she chose to sing works by her beloved Gluck, including Clytemnestra's aria from 'Iphigenie en Aulide', and one from 'Iphigenie en Tauride', as well as three arias from 'Alceste', 'Ah malgre moi', 'Derobe-moi mes pleurs', 'Divinites du Styx', all of which she transposed down a tone; and, the 'Invocation' from 'Armide'.

In his memoirs, Chorley recalls: "One of the events of the year of 1856 which, though not presented on any opera stage, was not to be forgotten, was Mme Viardot's singing of a scene for Meduse – the music by Lulli. The music was stiff – bald (as modern critics might put it) – but true, as affording scope to the highest and the most free declamation, and having a grandeur of line (to adopt the artist's phrase), which can only come of grand imagination".

On the 21st of November, 1857, Pauline wrote to Tourgueniev saying: "Do you know where I am going? To Warsaw, on my own, that is to say, except for my maid. Is this not courageous for one who has never before relinquished the arm of her husband.? " Louis had been reluctant to allow her to travel alone with only a female companion, but had finally agreed that it would be better for him to stay at home to look after the family. Pauline wrote to him every day, and their letters show the warmest affection, as well as giving details of her artistic successes and the people she met. She had told Tourgueniev that she would again be staying with her friend Mme Kalergis, but for some unknown reason, she did not, although she visited her and another friend, Mme Laska, almost daily. These two ladies introduced Pauline to the highest circles of Polish society, and the Governor of Warsaw, Prince Michael Gortschakof, the illustrious commander of the Russian Army during the Crimean War, flattered the prima donna with his obvious admiration and assiduous attentions.

One of the roles she sang in Poland was Norma, which had always simultaneously fascinated and terrified her, and she admitted in a letter of December 15th, "I was frightened, absolutely and horribly frightened! I sang the opening recitative as badly as you can possibly imagine", but afterwards she declared that she would never be so scared again, as she had used up all her fear on that occasion! A few days later she was crowing with delight at the eleven calls she had received after her next performance of Norma, and told her husband: "Dear friend, I believe that you would have been very happy with me, you who are my best, most severe but benevolent judge, whose musical taste is so sure and precious to me...."

After Warsaw, Pauline sang in various towns and cities in northern Germany, and in February, 1858, she was in Berlin, at the reception for the young Prince Frederick William, the son of the Crown Prince and Princess of Prussia, and his bride, the seventeen-year-old Princess Victoria, the eldest child of Queen Victoria and Prince Albert, and Princess Royal of England, on their arrival in the Prussian capital after their wedding in the Chapel Royal at St. James' Palace in London on the 25th of January.

In Berlin, the Royal Family, the court and corps diplomatique were all lined up to receive the young couple, and even for a royal princess, it must have been a daunting experience, being the centre of attention and meeting so many new relations-in-law in this most formal of courts. Pauline thought that her old friend Prince William looked magnificent in his dashing white uniform that bore the order of the Black Eagle, but she was disappointed by his gauche-ness when he moved away to speak to his son, just as his new daughter-in-law swept him a deep curtsey. The girl looked up at him, as if expecting a fatherly kiss and was daunted when he moved away, but Elizabeth, the Queen of Prussia, his sister-in-law, moved forward to cover the awkwardness, and asked the girl if she was frozen. Vicky, with a radiant smile, answered diplomatically: 'I have only one warm place and that is my heart'.

From the Prussian capital, Pauline travelled to her beloved Leipzig, where she sang a scene from 'Orfeo' and was given a rapturous reception. She was inspired because she was under the direction of Julius Rietz once more, singing in concerts at the Gewandhaus on February 11th, March 7th, and April 10th.

She remained in the city after her performances, to give three guest appearances at the Opera House, moving the critic of the 'Neue Zeitschrift fur Musik' to call her 'the greatest singer of our time'.

It was while she was in Germany that she heard news of the death of the actress Rachel, which saddened her. They were contemporaries and their careers had begun at the same time, while still in their teens, and were both admired and loved by Alfred de Musset. Their professional lives had run parallel and they had both been credited with raising the standards of theatrical performance in France to renewed heights. The death of a close contemporary is always shocking, and emphasises one's own mortality, yet Pauline was destined to out-live Rachel by fifty-two years.

The thirty-seven-year old actress had died at her country home at Le Cannet in the south of France. In her relatively short life she had brought great honour to the French stage and paved the way for those who followed her. Her health had been failing for some time, but when she began to experience great pain, she knew it was time to put her affairs in order. During the night of January 2nd, she made a new will, although she was subjected to great paroxysms of coughing while this took place. In the morning, she called everyone to her bedside and gave each person a souvenir of herself, thanking them all for the love and care they had always shown her. She died later that day, and her body was transported to Paris, where she was buried at the cemetery of Pere Lachaise. Her funeral was attended by all the leading actors, actresses, society figures and celebrities of Paris, but many of her own intimate friends had already predeceased her. Shortly before she died, she said to Arsene Houssaye: "Do you remember the evening of the production of Victor Hugo's play 'Angelo'; how we all sat down to dinner at his house, 'thirteen of us'? Well, just see how many of those thirteen friends are alive today. Your wife is dead; Mme de Girardin is dead; my poor Rebecca is dead... Gerard de Nerval, Pradier, Musset, Perree and d'Orsay are all dead. Poor Victor Hugo and his wife are still alive but exiled in Jersey. There only remain you, Girardin and myself to be accounted for, and you know only too well what is happening to me. Don't laugh, I beg, at having thirteen to dinner".

With Rachel's death, a colourful, theatrical era came to an end in Paris. For some time previously, the press had been detecting a diminution in the actress's powers, no doubt due to the encroachment of the disease that killed her; but in London, she was appreciated right until the end, and her pioneering work in America prepared a ready-made audience for her gifted successor, Sarah Bernhardt. Rachel was dead, but Pauline Viardot was very much alive, and had yet to experience the apotheosis of her singular career.

It is clear that Pauline deliberately and purposefully set out to charm Julius Rietz, and despite his reserve, she won the friendship of the scholarly intellectual. He attracted her both as a man and a musician, and on Thursday, 22nd April, at 5 o'clock in the afternoon, she sent him a note, (delivered by hand), saying: "Dear Herr Rietz, If you are at liberty this evening bring your overtures, etc., and we will play them four-handed. Let me know if it is agreeable to you. From seven o'clock I shall expect you. Your friend, Pauline Viardot". Whether he accepted her invitation is not known, but Pauline did not forget him when she left Leipzig for Stettin and Dresden at the beginning of May.

After his Italian sojourn Tourgueniev, beset by worries about his health, went to Vienna to consult a specialist and while there, he learned that Pauline was in Germany. Immediately he travelled to Leipzig to hear her, but they did not spend much time together as she had her own commitments, and the rest of her tour to undertake.

By the end of May, Pauline was in London, and here the operatic scene was swiftly changing. Covent Garden had burned down in 1856, during a masked ball, and had been out of action for two years. In the meantime, performances had been given at the Lyceum Theatre just off the Strand, but now the newly constructed Royal Opera house was due to open, still under Frederick Gye's management. Despite Giulia Grisi's 'farewell' in 1855, she and Mario were still leading the company. The rival Italian Opera at Her Majesty's Theatre was in dire financial straits and there were rumours that the building was to be sold for re-development. In this climate, the impressario E. T. Smith, and his young assistant, Colonel Henry Mapleson, took the opportunity to set up a rival Italian opera company, advertised as 'for the people', at the Theatre Royal, Drury Lane. Here, they proposed that the prices should be much lower than those at the other two houses, to democratise opera. In his memoirs, Maplson declares: "I felt the great responsibility of the position I had undertaken and engaged the services of Salvini-Donatelli, Viardot, Persiani, Naudin, Badiali, Marini, Rovere, Charles Braham and other tried artists."

No doubt the 'opera for the people' appealed to the democratic Viardots. Pauline's colleague Fanny Persiani, with whom she had first worked in her debut season of 1839, was now vocally in decline, but as an experienced performer, she was a useful member of the new company. Pauline could cope with Persiani, but she was absolutely thrilled that she did not have to deal with the dreaded Grisi and Mario.

The Drury Lane season opened five days before the re-opening of Covent Garden with 'Don Giovanni'. Viardot sang Donna Anna, Persiani was Zerlina, Mme Rudersdorff sang Elvira, Badiali appeared as the Don, and Naudin was

Ottavio. Like Covent Garden, the Theatre Royal in Drury Lane was situated amongst a warren of mean, narrow streets, with decrepit housing, yet Grillparzer called it the most beautiful theatre imaginable, with an interior of imposing beauty, decorated in red and gold.

It was during this London season that Pauline acquired the autograph score of 'Don Giovanni' at auction. It cost the princely sum of £200, and to buy it, she had to sell some of her jewels, and Louis, one of his Rembrandts, but they thought it was worth the sacrifice. They were amazed that so little interest in the sale was shown by the British Museum and other libraries and museums. Many years later, Pauline presented this precious score to the Paris Conservatoire, on the grounds that it remained there in perpetuity, but it is now in the Bibliotheque National.

After 'Don Giovanni', Pauline sang Amina in 'La Sonnambula' and the 'Illustrated London News' stated on the 3rd July: "There was an immense house and the audience were enthusiastic in their applause. Amina is one of the fair prima donna's best parts. Her acting sparkles with genius, though it was too elaborate, too full of minute points. With less evident pains it would be still more effective. She sang with extraordinary brilliancy, embellishing Bellini's fioriture of the most original and fanciful kind.. She was well supported by Signor Naudin in the part of Elvino and Signor Manfredi's Count Rudolpho was gentlemanlike and pleasant".

Tourgueniev had been invited to attend a dinner of the Royal Literary Fund, in London, and while in the city, he visited Alexandre Herzen, who was now living in a menage a trois with Ogarev and his unstable wife, Natalie, who, as her husband was well aware, had become Herzen's mistress, and in all, bore him three children. The household was quite chaotic, full of visiting exiled Russian friends, the young children from Alexandre's liaison with Natalie, and those of his first marriage, all except nine-year-old Kolya who had been lost at sea some years before. The grief of this tragedy had led to the death of the other Natalie, Herzen's wife.

Occasionally, Ivan met Pauline, but she was rather distant, and to the sensitive writer, it appeared that she was trying to exclude him from her now well ordered life. Truth to tell, Pauline was enjoying her freedom and independence; Louis did not always accompany her on her travels, although he was with her in London. In her professional life, she was free of Mario and Grisi, for the time being at least, and she did not want to be constrained by the kind of friends who battened upon her. In addition to which, she enjoyed fantasising about her new found attraction, Julius Rietz, and relished having her own space, socialising with people she liked when she desired to do so, but without risking the loss of her precious liberty, and not having to bear Tourgueniev's melancholy, hypochondria and unhappiness, which, she felt, he frequently laid at her door.

Ivan was not left to his own devices, however, as he had many friends in London, by whom he was well respected, as author and man. Since the advent, in 1852, of his very successful 'Sportsman's Sketches' and the novels that followed, he had been acclaimed by many English men of letters. His circle in the capital included Carlyle, Disraeli, Thackeray, Dickens, Trollope, Browning, Swinburne, Tennyson, Henry James, George Henry Lewes and his long-time companion, Marian Evans, the author of 'Middlemarch' and 'Silas Marner' who was better known under her pseudonym of George Eliot. Tourgueniev and Lewes had been students together in Germany, and they occasionally met in Paris, where the Russian had introduced the two English writers to the Viardots.

During his stay in England, Ivan accompanied Lewes and George Elliot to Six Mile Bottom in Cambridgeshire, the former home of Byron's half-sister, Augusta Leigh, where they stayed with the Bullock-Hall family. The company included many writers and academics, but it was Tourgueniev who was the great attraction. Every one agreed that he was a delightful conversationalist and raconteur, and George Elliot relished his company; they sat together at the Newmarket Races and he explained the differences between English and Russian sport to her. At dinner, later that evening, when Lewes proposed a toast to the Russian as the greatest living novelist, Tourgueniev, charming as ever, modestly side-stepped the compliment by raising his glass to George Elliot.

Shortly after the Viardots had arrived in London, they received a visit from Ary Scheffer, and were shocked by his appearance. He was now sixty-three years old and his heart condition had become very serious. Against his better judgement, he had come to England to attend the funeral of the Duchess of Orleans at Weybridge. She was the widow of the late Prince Ferdinand, Ary's former pupil, who had been killed in a freak carriage accident in 1842. Ary should not have left France, but he insisted on doing his duty to a family he still held dear, but only stayed in London for a day and a night. He saw the Viardots in the afternoon, and dined with them at a restaurant in the evening. During the night he had a heart attack, and the Viardots were called to his bedside, where they did their best to make him comfortable and encouraged him to stay in London for a while so that he could recover, but despite their misgivings, he insisted on going home as soon as he was able to get back on his feet. He had never liked the city, where the heavy, smoky air impeded his breathing, and he longed to get away to his country house at Argenteuil. When he arrived in France, he was met by his daughter and her husband, Dr. Rene Marjolin, who nursed him devotedly. For a few days, he appeared to be making a good recovery, but died suddenly on the 15th of June.

Pauline was beside herself with grief when she received the news, and berated herself for not having forced him to stay in London for a longer period. Louis was deeply upset, and found it difficult to comfort Pauline when he was so badly affected by the death of his oldest friend. Ary had been one of the most important people in their lives, and for the past eighteen years, he had been like a father to Pauline, as well as her spiritual mentor, guide and counsel, who had never judged her, never criticised her, but who had always been there for her. She had been able to unburden herself and tell him things that she could never have told Louis, whose feelings she was always anxious to protect, but Ary, dear, loving Ary, had taken everything on his own shoulders, and had kept her confidences, continuing to love her absolutely unconditionally. How could he ever be replaced? In time, of course, the pain of her loss would become less intense, but through the passing years, he was never far from her thoughts, and was a deep and abiding influence on her whole life, right into old age.

Despite their mourning, the Viardots now had many friends in London, and life continued in much the same way as ever. Louise was with them and they stayed at the centrally placed York Hotel in Albemarle Street. The Crystal Palace, which had formerly been built in Hyde Park for the Great Exhibition in 1851, had been removed to the heights of Sydenham, south of London, and had become a tourist attraction, where concerts and entertainments were regularly held. The area was a natural beauty spot, and at weekends and holidays, Londoners made trips to the leafy suburb, where they picnicked and rambled to their hearts' content, often attending a concert before making their way back to the city.

The Viardots thought it would be enjoyable to do the same, and several of their friends agreed. According to seventeen-year-old Louise: "A large carriage pulled by four horses was ordered, called 'The Unique', because of its exceptional dimensions. The party consisted of Manuel Garcia, Joseph Joachim, 'young and beardless, but with his violin'; Anton Rubinstein, the young Russian pianist; Chorley, who had become one of the Viardot's most intimate friends whom Pauline described as "one of the ugliest men on earth but one of the most intelligent and knowledgeable". She added that he was a fine fellow... "sincere but English and judging the arts as an Englishman. Physically unsound, nervous, irritable and irritating. He can make himself thoroughly disagreeable to people who don't suit him. For the rest, I can depend on him like a brother – he likes me exceedingly and I return the liking". Chorley could be something of a pernickety old woman at times, but his sterling qualities made up for his deficiencies.

Another favourite was the young, handsome, and urbane artist, Sir Frederick Leighton, who had spent much of his life in Italy and France, and was courteous and charming, blessed with a rare talent for saying the right thing, at the right time. He often gave soirees at his home at which Pauline sang; he adored music and only invited real music lovers to these gatherings. The wine was always very good and plentiful and poor Chorley, who did not hold his drink well, sometimes became very drunk! Other members of the party were Frederick Gye, Charles Halle, John Ella, founder of the Musical Union; Scholcher, one of Louis's refugee friends; and the composers, Henry Leslie and Virginia Gabriel.

One can imagine what a merry group this must have been, wandering over Sydenham Hill, then tucking into a sumptuous picnic, comprising all kinds of goodies, such as smoked salmon, potted meats, gentleman's relish, pork pies, fresh bread, cheeses, and freshly baked fruit pies. After everybody had eaten their fill and cleared up, they went to visit the Crystal Palace, where various activities were taking place, and there were interesting exhibits to be seen. Louise says that they spent the whole day laughing, then with the onset of evening, they retraced their steps back to the gigantic carriage, which ambled along pleasantly to Greenwich, where they had a magnificent fish dinner. From the hotel window they could see the famous iron ship, "The Leviathan", later named the 'Great Eastern', the largest ship of its time, lying at anchor on the Thames.

Dinner was delicious: with fresh fish, nicely battered and crisply fried, served with potatoes in their jackets with lashings of fresh butter, and washed down with good old English cider, followed by a choice of bread and butter or summer pudding with cream. Some of the company even had room left over at the end of the meal for some Stilton. When the plates were cleared, the men sat back and smoked their cigars in a relaxed and convivial atmosphere, telling humorous stories and chatting idly, until suddenly Joachim realised that Chorley was no longer with them. They couldn't think what had happened to him, as no one had seen him leave the room, but he must have gone somewhere. The group set out to search the hotel, but he had simply disappeared into thin air. Everybody was very perplexed and, as they all contemplated what else they could do, they became aware of a muffled sound. Charles Halle drew up the table-cloth, and there, lying comfortably under the table, was Chorley, drunk as a lord and snoring very gently. The strong cider had been too much for him, and he had gently slipped from his seat, without anyone noticing, and settled onto the floor, where he had fallen into a deep sleep, probably thinking that he was in his own bed. With a quantity of black coffee, they sobered him enough to get him into the carriage, and then dropped him off at his own house in Eaton Place. In the morning, he was little the worse for wear, except that his head felt as if it had been kicked!

Three years had passed since the last Birmingham Festival when Pauline had sung in the premiere of 'Eli', and in September she took part in another premiere, this time in the title role of Henry Leslie's 'Judith', a piece specially written for contralto. The local paper said that "Judith was presented by Mme Viardot with that high dramatic genius for which she is pre-eminent among all the vocalists of the day."

Clara Novello sang the soprano solo in 'The Messiah' at the Festival. She was the possessor of a light, clear, silvery voice, not large, but well produced, with good carrying power. English audiences are fond of this vocal type, which has little vibrato, and suggests the sexlessness of a choirboy, but it is not ideal for opera, where a stronger, more substantial, rounder sound is necessary even in the lighter roles, and is the reason why Clara did not often perform in opera. In addition to Novello and Viardot there was a fine line-up of the most eminent singers of the day, including the tenor Belletti and Jeanne Castellan, but the local newspapers, with a touch of xenophobia, objected to there being so many foreigners, as they considered that the English singers had not been given their fair share of the musical items, due to the fact that the parts were divided between them and the foreigners: "Thus, Miss Dolby was deprived of two of her finest airs 'O Thou that tellest' and 'He shall feed his flock' so that they might be given to Mme Viardot, who, with all her talent, is less of a Handelian singer than our countrywomen. Miss Novello's 'I know that my Redeemer liveth' was divine!" Pauline, who was devoted to the music of Handel, and prided herself on her fine Handelian style, must have been most unpleasantly surprised and offended when she was made aware of this comment.

John Sims Reeves, the foremost British tenor was one of the soloists. He and Pauline often appeared in concerts together, although there is no mention of her in his memoirs, which are very pedestrian and dull. Although popular throughout the country, he caused consternation because he frequently cancelled performances. (There is a charming cartoon of Charles Halle pulling him out of bed in order to get him to a concert). Sims Reeves was of a nervous, sensitive temperament and would cancel at the drop of a hat if he thought he was not in vocal form. When engagements involved long journeys, he disregarded the expense and hired a private train: he also booked the rooms above his own when he stayed in hotels, to make sure that he was not disturbed by noise, and carried on a running battle with Michael Costa over the raising of pitch, refusing many engagements to the detriment of his pocket because he considered it disastrous for the voice. No wonder he had to continue singing into old age, because he was financially insecure!

His musical taste was often criticised, and Pauline's young friend, the Irish composer Charles Villiers Stanford, took him to task for his tendency to add high notes that were not written in the score: "Sims Reeves even changed the end of 'Thou shalt dash them' in 'Messiah' to a high note, to secure a round of applause. This was not for the sake of Handel, who knew what he was about when he put his high note climax on 'dash them', and not on the 'potter's vessel'," adding: "Now let us turn to those singers who had their music in mind rather than themselves, who used the voice which Divine nature had given them for the glory of Divine art, such as Pauline Viardot, queen of contraltos, who, with a voice less striking than that of Alboni, survives her contemporary in history, and surpasses her in mastery". He also praised Jenny Lind and added: "In this respect, she resembled the few great musicians of her day, such as Joachim and Viardot-Garcia, who rightly considered themselves "the priests, and not the servants of the public".

CHAPTER TWENTY-SEVEN

1858

During the summer of 1858, Pauline toured the English provinces with a company run by the impressario Willert Beale, and Louise accompanied her. The schedule was gruelling and the singers often travelled during the night to rehearse at 9.30 the following morning. In the larger cities, it was usual to give two or three performances, but in the smaller places, they only performed once before setting off for the next destination.

As they did not tour a chorus, and had only a nucleus of orchestral players with them, they had to augment their numbers at each new venue. This practice put an enormous strain upon the singers because they had to rehearse during the day, as well as perform in the evening, and there were many artistic difficulties, due to hurried rehearsals and the frequent lack of technical facilities. Louise said that the outcome was frequently farcical, such as the time the curtain rose on the graveyard scene of 'Don Giovanni' and instead of the statue of the Commendatore sitting astride his horse, he was dangling on a rope from the flies on the left side of the stage, while the horse was on the right.

The operatic repertoire consisted mainly of works in Italian, and the foreign singers were highly amused at the 'droll' pronunciation of the English choristers. Louise thoroughly enjoyed herself, and, being a good musician, she was enlisted to help the newcomers learn their parts, or acted as prompter. She said it was hard work and very fatiguing but she had a great deal of fun, and being young, she soon recharged her batteries.

In his memoirs, Willert Beale gives a lively account of the daily routine experienced on tour: "The company would travel by train and would always put up at the 'first hotels'. Dinner was at three o'clock, followed by a concert or an opera in the evening, and then supper". At meals, Beale sat at the head of the table with the conductor facing him and the singers sitting on his right and left. Everybody drank claret. However, "it must be vintage wine, for although each takes but a small quantity, we are very particular about the quality. We insist upon coffee immediately after dinner, and are not always pleased with the way in which it is made. It is not French, or even Italian coffee". Without exception, all the foreign artists found the monotony of the English food tiresome, as most of the hotels had practically the same bill of fare: macaroni soup with just a few sticks of pasta floating in each bowl, boiled turbot with pink sauce, saddles of mutton, boiled fowls, cabinet pudding and indigestible-looking apple tart; sometimes served, for variety, with Devonshire cream, which was a favourite with the rotund Mme Alboni.

Fortunately, some proprietors were willing to comply with Beale's requests for more varied fare if menus were sent on in advance, and at the Adelphi Hotel, Liverpool, the manager, Mr. Radley, was saluted by all, when he provided a dish of genuine Italian macaroni, which he called 'The Alboni', as a compliment to Madame, and it was such a success that he retained it on the menu for several years.

In the early autumn, the Viardots returned to France, from where the singer soon set off again, this time for a season in Budapest, accompanied by Louis. She was sorry to leave home quite so soon, as she felt she needed a longer interval to recover from the rigours of her English tour, and would have been happy to have spent more time with her children. Claudie was now six and Marianne four and at an interesting stage of development, while the baby, Paul, was feeling his feet, amusing his parents, as he lurched from side to side like a drunken sailor on deck in a storm, trying to keep up with his more mobile sisters.

During her short stay in Paris, Pauline took over a room for her own use in the house in the rue de Douai, telling Rietz: "I have made myself a present of a room in the second storey which was recently built – and have arranged it as a little study. Some day I shall send you a sketch of it. There all is as gay as gay can be. The paper has a very light green ground over which bouquets of roses and small bluebells are scattered in profusion. I have put my upright piano in it, as well as an etagere containing the works of Shakespeare, Goethe, Schiller, Byron, the four great Italian poets (Virgil, Dante, Petrarch, and Tasso): Don Quixote, Homer, Eschylus, Uhland, the Bible, Heine, 'Herman und Dorothea', and the two volumes of Goethe by Lewes. With the exception of Homer, of which I have the translations by Jacob and Monje (I prefer the former) all these works are, be it understood, in the original languages".

While they were staying at 13 Conduit Street, in London, the Viardots had signed a contract with the Hungarian National Theatre in Budapest, for Pauline to appear there in November, stipulating that she wished her debut role to be Rosina, with Amina as her second, and Norma, Fides, Rachel, Desdemona, Cenerentola, La Favorita, Azucena and Adina, to be available as required. On October 29th, the 'Pester Lloyd' announced that the Viardots were staying at the 'Queen of England' hotel. On their arrival, much to their amazement, no one from the theatre was there to greet them, nor did anyone visit them to tell Pauline when she would be required for rehearsals, what performances had been scheduled, when she would see the costumier, or receive the new cuts for the 'Barber' recitatives. She wrote to the intendant, Count Raday, asking for information, and told him that she was ready to sing any of the roles in her repertoire, whenever he wished.

In one of his letters to Tourgueniev, Louis mentioned that the director of the theatre was disgruntled, and not at all friendly, because he had wanted the roles that Pauline was to sing, to be given to his mistress, but he had been over- ruled by the opera board, and this had caused a good deal of ill feeling. Pauline's cause was not helped by the fact that the price of seats had been increased for her performances, and the theatre was only half full at her debut as Rosina. Consequently, the audience was frosty, there was little applause, except from the orchestral players, and no calls for encores. Louis observed that the Hungarians were only interested in opera seria, preferring to cry rather than laugh, which was borne out when Pauline sang her dramatic heroines, Rachel, Norma , Fides and Desdemona. 'Ten or twelve calls brought about a truce, and a quantity of tears fell, even over the grey moustaches.' Fides was a real victory, and Pauline was called out six times after the grand finale of act four, a rare thing as far as Hungarian audiences were concerned.

Despite the unpleasant atmosphere due to theatrical politics, Pauline received excellent notices in the Hungarian press; it was stated that nothing could be more beautiful, more grandiose, or more intense than her interpretation of Rachel, and the popular 'Holgyfutar' declared that the secret of her marvellous performance of the 'Casta Diva' in 'Norma' was that she began it pianissimo, then gradually rose to a wondrous crescendo! On the 11th and 16th she sang Fides, and the press, knowing that the role had been specially written for her, reported that she was 'the premiere dramatic soprano in the world, despite the fact that the highest register of her voice lacked brilliance'.

Liszt had given Pauline letters of introduction to two high ranking Hungarian officials, but these men reciprocated by assuming an air of utter indifference, which the Viardots found very wounding, and they considered that Magyar Society was aloof and unwelcoming. As Louis remarked: "We have never lived in a country less hospitable than Pest; we haven't set foot in a Hungarian house, and no Hungarian has entered our own". In a post script to Louis's letter, Pauline told Ivan that she was preparing to receive guests that evening, but of the twelve persons expected, not a single one was Hungarian. They were consoled, however, by the arrival of Clara Schumann, whom Liszt called 'The

Queen of the Piano', who was on a concert tour of Hungary. Pauline was in the audience for Clara's first concert in the city, and on November 28th, the musicians appeared together in a concert in the grand hall of the Hotel Europe. Up to that time the press had been unaware that they had been great friends for twenty years, and were amazed when they played a piece for two pianos by Robert Schumann. Pauline then sang an aria from Rossini's 'The Italian Girl in Algiers', and one of her own arrangements of a Chopin mazurka.

A day later, the Choral Society of Budapest gave a banquet in honour of Viardot and Schumann, and on December 2nd, they gave another concert together. Before they left the city, the 'Holgyfutar' reproached the sellers of prints because they had missed the opportunity of offering the public portraits of the two most celebrated musicians in the world.

Clara was now a widow, with seven children. Robert had died in 1856, after suffering from severe mental illness for many years, caused by tertiary syphilis. While living in Dusseldorf, where he was musical director between 1850 and 1853, he had experienced such mental and emotional torment that he had tried to drown himself in the Rhine, but had been rescued, and confined to a lunatic asylum. He was constantly beset by visions unseen and sounds unheard by others, which caused him unbearable distress, and he complained that sometimes he had a whole orchestra in his head that he could not turn off.

His young friend, the composer Johannes Brahms who, although several years younger than Clara, who had long been in love with her, befriended her and her children, and helped them through this difficult time. For years, Clara had been the breadwinner, undertaking tour after tour to provide for her family. Despite Robert's illness, his sexual appetite had always been strong, and Clara was frequently pregnant, which made touring even more taxing. Her father, who had fought for so long to stop her marriage to Robert, had been prophetic in his fears that as his wife, Clara would not have an easy life. One of their sons also became mentally ill at an early age, as did a daughter in adulthood, and both ended their long lives in asylums.

Julius Rietz knew Brahms, and must have asked Pauline if Clara had mentioned the young man, because Pauline replied: "Yes, I have often heard Clara Schumann speak of Brahms with the most profound conviction (on her part) of his *genius*. She has played me several things of his, which neither pleased nor interested me". Within a short time, however, she would change her opinion.

When she left Budapest in December, she went on to Weimar from where she wrote to Rietz on the 12th: "Liszt has taken supper with me. He has only just gone away, and I shall not go to bed until I have told you that 'Norma' went off quite well, and that your friend was very well received and appreciated, and that I felt tears welling in many 'furtive eyes'. Liszt has assured me that he was deeply moved and enthusiastic – if I were sure that he was telling the truth, I should be very glad. Yesterday he played for me – no one plays as well as he does, and he altogether enchanted me. I heard the Rhapsodies and the Funerailles from his Harmonies. Do you know the latter? It is really very interesting, and in my opinion very easy to understand.

Today I was at the Altenburg again (the Grand Ducal Palace where Liszt and Caroline had apartments), to give my voice some practice, and heard something that pleased me less; 'Orpheus' arranged for two pianos. Too inchoate for my taste – and yet it has form and there is a desire of melody in it. But one must admit that he is a most attractive person. It is quite impossible for anyone to be kinder than he is to me. He is very unaffected with me, which makes him doubly charming; he is even childlike, and I believe it comes naturally, for he has known me since my childhood... Perhaps he knows that he would be wasting his efforts, and so welcomes the opportunity to find rest and relaxation from his constant mental tension".

Pauline visited Liszt frequently, and in another letter to Rietz she said: "Here I am, back from the Altenburg once again. They are beginning to like me a little here – I go in and out without the least ceremony, as much as I please, and their faces look really delighted when I enter the Princess's rooms. Liszt is charming to me, but all our ideas are too different for there ever to be complete harmony between us. Now and then he comes to spend an hour or two quietly with me. It does him a lot of good, he says, and rejuvenates him. The life he is leading now is totally lacking in tranquillity and refreshment".

She was very moved when, in January, 1859, after her departure from Weimar, Liszt wrote a wonderfully glowing tribute to her in the German press, claiming that "there has never been a female composer of genius, but finally, here she is!". From England, she wrote to Rietz: "My good Louis has sent me the 'Neue Zeitscrift fur Musik', which contains a magnificent article – far too magnificent – on your friend, written by Liszt; perhaps you have read it. I have to admit that it gives me *very great* pleasure – although usually, I am indifferent to praise. I like severe and honest criticism. But in this case, my dear Liszt, besides offering a flattering artistic impression, shows a great deal of friendship for me. Do try to be a little bit less hard on him. I like him so much, despite his foibles, which upset me, but do not irritate me..."

She was beginning another extensive Willert Beale tour of the English provinces and Dublin, and on January 24th, she told Rietz about the opening concert: "The audience, this evening, for instance, knew that I am a 'celebrated singer' so it applauds everything I do with equal warmth. Had I sung not quite as well, it would have been no less satisfied, and had I sung better, it would not have been better satisfied! And that is what puts a damper on the artist's enthusiasm. Yes, decidedly, in matters of art, the English are great – 'speculators'.

The next day, she was in Brighton where violent winds and great waves swept over the quay with a mighty roar in front of her hotel and, for once she, who boasted 'sound sleep is one of my virtues' was kept awake by the elemental racket. "In the midst (of the storm) I seemed to hear cries, cannon shots, and fantastic symphonies in quite another sense from those by Berlioz and Co".

Again her schedule was punishing as on January 30th, she was in Bath, then followed Birmingham, Wolverhampton, Oxford, Sheffield, Leeds and Manchester where, on the 13th February, she sang the aria 'Parto, parto' from 'La Clemenza di Tito', which, she told Rietz "was greatly applauded, although I did not sing it nearly as well as I have sung it in 'my' Gewandhaus".

Of the concert in Oxford she writes: "I was greatly fatigued and I have the satisfaction of affording you the pleasure of learning that I sang frightfully and the stupid local newspaper tactfully observes that I sang well! Isn't that exasperating?" Despite the constant travelling, Pauline wrote frequently to Rietz. Many of the letters are of a deeply personal nature, and are very affectionate, as illustrated by the one she wrote from Birmingham on February 3rd: "O my friend, I love you with the most heartfelt, deepest, truest, warmest, sunshine-clearest love that ever woman felt as friend for friend. I know that our rare friendship is good and noble, and I love it inexpressibly. It is indispensable to me, our dear, sacred friendship. Build upon it as high as ever you will or can. I shall never disappoint you, nor you me, surely. So in this we have something for all our life. That, is a joy indeed".

She told him how much Louis missed her when she was away, which made her feel guilty, as she relished her freedom from his 'expression of love, which I cannot share', but added that absence served to fortify her friendship, esteem, 'and great respect for this man who is so noble and devoted, who would give his life to gratify the least of my caprices, if I had any", and, "Do not think that I am ridiculous when I say that Louis cannot live without me, but so it is. Are you smiling? It may seem hard to believe that after nineteen years of marriage a husband cannot get along without his wife. You are free to think that I am a *conceited wife,* but it is the simple truth. Louis and Scheffer have always been my dearest *friends*, but sadly, I have never been able to return the ardent and deep love of Louis, despite the best will in the world". She admitted that it felt wrong, a cruel irony of fate, but she knew that the human will, although it can force the heart to be silent, cannot compel it to speak.

In Dublin, the company stayed at Morrison's Hotel in the broad and elegant thoroughfare now known as O'Connell Street, and performed at the Theatre Royal. This playhouse had an excellent manager, John Harris, with whom Willert Beale was happy to do business. The frequenters of the gallery, however, were another matter entirely as they were unruly to a man. When they became too boisterously noisy, Harris would appear in front of the curtain and berate them as though they were naughty schoolboys. They loved this, and would harangue him in a good humoured way because, to them, it was all part of the fun of an evening out, and was enjoyed as a great pastime between the acts. They often brought sticks into the gallery and made a din banging them together, but the management took to confiscating them as they entered the theatre; in revenge, they brought bags of flour instead and sprinkled the contents over the unsuspecting heads of those in the pit below. When they weren't banging or sprinkling they would sing lustily, and some brave soul might launch into a solo which would be followed by cheers, cat-calls, hooting and cries of 'sing up – Mario's listening!

Dublin was a city of resplendence and squalor existing side by side, with elegant Adam buildings close to run-down old houses, sheltering families in rags and tatters in the derelict grandeur of former times. There were, however, gardens and spacious squares and views of the River Liffy, and the sea in Dublin Bay, and on the horizon, the beautiful Wicklow Mountains, sublime in the late afternoon glow of the setting sun. Pauline told Rietz that as soon as they arrived some of the other ladies went to bed, but she had a drive in 'a lovely park with my faithful cavalier (probably John Hatton, the composer of comic songs, whose light-hearted company she enjoyed). After an hour, we got out, sent away the funny, open omnibus-like vehicle – wobbling on two wheels in a most amusingly uncomfortable Irish fashion; and then we walked for nearly three hours at double-quick pace as if charging the enemy, so that now I haven't a leg to stand on".

On February 25th, her tone changed and she wrote: "I have scarcely time to breathe. Moreover, I am distressed – excessively fatigued, bored to death, disgusted to the last degree with the work I am doing, and ardently longing for my return to France. Ah, if I could meet you there with all my dear ones, I should be as happy as I can be without my dear, revered Ary Scheffer". But two days later she was saying 'I like Dublin very much – the audiences here are very enthusiastic and I am a great favourite. This is the third time I have come to Ireland, and I am to return at the end of March for three weeks with Mario and Grisi".

On March 3rd, back on the mainland, Pauline's maid was suddenly taken ill and she had to call a doctor in the middle of the night. For a while it looked serious and it was thought that the girl would have to stay behind when Pauline left for Northampton the next day. Fortunately, she was much improved the following morning, and they left as arranged. On 5th March the concert tour ended, and on the 9th Pauline returned to Paris, where she was met at the railway station by Louis and Louise: 'What joy was there! Poor things, they really find it hard to live without me". When she arrived home and looked in to see her two little girls, they awoke, and were delirious with happiness at seeing their mother again: "What an outcry of 'Mamma!' was there, and a wild dance in sheer night-gowns on small beds, and a jubilation, a kissing. Oh, that was delightful. After all, that is a lovelier reception than any success on the stage, but nevertheless, I have the courage to distress all these precious souls from time to time by absenting myself. Ah, this time I have made the unspoken resolution to try to arrange in future that my absences shall only be very short, or at least that any engagement shall be of definite duration, in which case, I shall take all my treasures with me."

The enjoyment of domesticity could not be prolonged, however, as she had to prepare for the role of Lady Macbeth for the British premiere of Verdi's opera, which was to be produced in Dublin in three weeks time.

CHAPTER TWENTY-EIGHT

1859

The young Italian composer, Luigi Arditi, was to conduct the performances of Verdi's 'Macbeth' in Dublin, and on March 15th, 1859, Pauline wrote to him regarding the changes to the score she felt were necessary, if the role of Lady Macbeth was to sit well in her voice, illustrating the kind of liberties that singers took in those days: "Caro maestro, Here are the transpositions I am making in the part of Lady Macbeth. The most difficult of all, which will necessitate certain changes in the instrumentation, will be that of the cavatina. The recitative in D flat, the andante, 'Vieni, t'affretta' in B flat, and the allegro in 'Or tutti sorgete' in D flat, consequently the whole scene must be a minor third lower. Not bad! All the rest of the act may be given as written. The cabaletta 'Trionfai' is not sung. In the banquet scene (Act II), there must be a transposition from the concluding phrase of the chorus finishing with the words 'Come', etc., to get into A flat, the key of the drinking song. The allegro as written in F. For the second verse of the brindisi it must be taken a whole tone lower, five beats before beginning the melody, by inserting A flat into the preceding chord of F; thus – in this way we approach the key of A flat. After the repeat of the brindisi, a transition must be introduced at the seventh beat of the allegro agitato, where we again find ourselves in the key of F major. Or we might take the beat of Macbeth's "Va!" excising the six previous beats. The sleep-walking scene must be a tone lower; that is, the melody and recitative in E flat minor, and the andante in B major. I fancy I see your orchestra making faces at the horrible aspect of the six double flats and five double sharps! Dear maestro, you must have the parts of these numbers copied, because the orchestra we shall have, only likes to transpose (transport) the public."

Pauline certainly added to the cost and time needed for the preparation of the score, with the many changes necessitated because her voice was not ideally suited to the tessitura of Lady Macbeth.

Yet, despite the extra burden imposed upon him, Arditi was full of admiration for her musicianship, acknowledging that she was more musically educated than the majority of singers.

On the 19th of March, four days after Pauline wrote her letter to Arditi, Gounod's new opera, 'Faust' was premiered at the Theatre Lyrique, in Paris, with Marie Miolan-Carvalho as Marguerite. Goethe's famous story of man's eternal struggle against the powers of evil was well known to Pauline, and had been an important theme for Ary Scheffer, whose paintings on the subject brought him early success at the Paris Salon. Despite Pauline's personal disillusionment with Gounod, she always believed in his music, and was probably present at the premiere. Did she allow herself to envy Mme Miolan-Carvalho, as Marguerite, singing the sublimely beautiful garden scene? It would not have been surprising if she had felt a pang of regret, but fortunately, she did not have time to dwell on such things, as she was in the process of creating a new and challenging role herself.

In a letter to Rietz, she said, "at the end of the month I am going to Dublin again – I place great dependence on 'Macbeth' for obtaining a good measure of success for me in London – in any event, the creation of the role of Lady Macbeth interests me extremely – it will be all the more a creation because, although I know Shakespeare's drama by heart, I have never seen it on the stage. In this opera, alongside trivia and dismally bad numbers, there are four very fine scenes – well declaimed – which add greatly to the dramatic action".

Of course, the version of the opera that Pauline sang was Verdi's original one, but some years later he re-wrote and re-arranged the whole score, leaving out some numbers and adding others, so that the two versions are entirely different.

In another letter to Rietz, Pauline described her rather unique manner of preparing a role: "Lady Macbeth is continually distracting my thoughts. Every time I have to learn an entirely new part, I lapse into a half dreamy condition. I feel as if there were a little theatrical stage in my forehead, on which my small actors move about. Even at night, and even whilst asleep, my private theatre haunts me – sometimes it grows unbearable. There is no remedy for it and so my roles learn themselves without my needing to sing aloud or to study before a mirror. Once in a while, though, when it strikes me that my Liliputian song-stress is behaving too boldly, I try to imitate her. This kind of work in which I participate, almost unconsciously, is strange. It costs me no exertion whatever, but continually demands my attention."

Once again she was working with Mario and Grisi, but life with them was easier because they had now matured and egos were not so dominant. On March 18th, she wrote to Rietz saying: "I had a rehearsal of Flotow's 'Martha' (she played the role of Nancy) to be sung in Dublin with Mario, Grisi and Graziani, the best of living baritones. It is dance music from one end to the other, and quite insignificant and unexciting, but at any rate, unpretentiously written. It is like homeopathy – if it does one no good – it does no harm".

In his memoirs, 'The Light of Other Days', Willert Beale admitted that he had been fortunate to secure the services of Mme Viardot for the role of Lady Macbeth when he presented the opera for the first time in Dublin, and on his autumn tour. "It was indeed a grand impersonation – grander if possible than 'Orfeo'. The outlines of the tragedy being very closely followed by Verdi, many of the 'points' made by Mme Viardot readily suggest themselves; but it is impossible to imagine or to describe the intensity and power of her Lady Macbeth as a whole. The impression it left upon the mind was that of a weird, imposing picture, the accessories of which were all in harmony with a highly dramatic and original conception carried out by the intuitive force of genius." He adds, "Graziani's Macbeth was excellent – his splendid voice making great effect. He showed discretion in not overacting the part, and in listening to Mme Viardot's advice at rehearsal, which contributed much to the success he won."

Arditi said that the final rehearsal of 'Macbeth' was so chaotic that everybody thought the performance would be a disaster, but great effort was made by all concerned and "at seven o'clock – when we all parted to rush in search of sandwiches and liquids wherewith to moisten our parched throats – that we stood a good chance, after all, of pulling the opera through safely, and we did!"

Pauline's wonderfully dramatic, yet artistic singing was alluded to enthusiastically in the press, though the singer who came in for most of the plaudits during the season was the young, pretty, petite soprano, Marietta Piccolomini.

There had been a slight hiatus towards the end of 'Macbeth' when Pauline was about to enter for the thrilling sleep walking scene. The waiting woman and the doctor were seated at the door of her ladyship's room with a small table between them on which stood a bottle of physic with the conventional long label of by-gone days attached to it. The capacity audience had already sat through three hours of unfamiliar music, and were tiring; the cellos and double basses groaned on and the spectators awaited Lady Macbeth... suddenly a voice from the gallery rang out, calling to the well-known leader of the band: "Ah, hurry now, Mr. Levey! Tell us, is it a boy or a girl"!. The raucous laughter which greeted this quip could have ruined the scene that was to follow, but Pauline was nothing if not experienced; she paused in the wings, giving time for the laughter to die down; her entrance music was repeated, and she appeared in her sleep walking trance, fixing the audience with a powerful stare, holding them in wrapt attention, creating a chillingly haunting atmosphere.

Afterwards, she told Rietz: "I have just achieved one of the most superb successes of my theatrical career through my creation of Lady Macbeth in

Verdi's opera – I had rehearsed it tremendously in my head and it appears that the result is very good – the entire evening has been one long cry of enthusiasm – they tell me that it much resembles a triumph".

On the 8th April, she revealed how much physical, emotional and mental stamina is required of an opera singer: "Terrible day. I got over-fatigued. A concert in the morning. In the evening a rehearsal of 'Martha' 7pm to midnight. I generally have to assume the part of the stage-manager for the operas in which I sing, being the only one who speaks English well, and have to serve as interpreter between all my comrades and the costumiers, machinists, choristers, supers, etc; it is far more fatiguing than singing – after four hours of work on the stage, I am worn out". The next day she wrote: A terrible week. Monday morning rehearsal of 'Don Giovanni' – ll am to 5 pm. Grisi singing Donna Anna with violence and without genuine dignity. Mario (Don Ottavio) not taking trouble in the ensembles but makes up for it by singing 'Il mio tessoro' deliciously. She declared that she sang Zerlina with "all the devotion that I bear in my heart for Mozart. 'Batti,batti', 'La ci darem' and 'Vedrai carino' were encored".

On Tuesday she spent the entire day studying the 'trouser' role of Orsini in 'Lucrezia Borgia' because the director had earnestly begged her to sing it, which she did that evening, and she had a superlative success. The Brindisi was so popular that she was obliged to sing it four times in succession! There was a second performance of 'Macbeth' on Tuesday, which came after a full day's rehearsal on 'Martha' that didn't end until 5 pm, but again, the Verdi was hugely successful.

She also revealed to Rietz how disgruntled she often felt with her colleagues: "Egoism, baseness, falsity are everywhere and nearly always the reverse of the coin in the life of a serious artist. It is true that the dedicated artist is an exception, whereas the sad defects mentioned above are often, too often the breadwinners of a great number of musicians, persons who are fit to blow or strum or pick or pound on some instrument or other – as long as they are pounding or picking or strumming or blowing they appear to be somebody, as soon as they stop their noise, they again become – nobody". One of the colleagues for whom she didn't have much time was the beautiful, popular French-born pianist, Arabella Goddard, whose husband, Davison, the Times critic, praised and publicised her excessively in print. Pauline called her 'a goose'.

For herself, she loved goodness, truth and beauty, and all her life she had endeavoured to convey these eternal verities to her audiences. On the other hand, Lady Macbeth was a complex character, with no apparently redeeming features, but even here, Pauline looked for even the merest glimmer of humanity. Her portrayal was an outstanding success and her reputation soared higher than ever in England, where it was now twenty years since she had first appeared at Her Majesty's Theatre, and all the years of hard work and dedication claimed their prize, because 1859 became the year of her apotheosis.

In the autumn, she returned to England for another tour, this time with Auguste Vianesi as conductor in place of Arditi, who had gone to America. Vianesi was only twenty-two, but he was a perfectionist, and was already making a reputation for himself. In 1857 he had arrived in Paris with a letter of introduction to Rossini from Giuditta Pasta, and in 1859 he was appointed conductor of the orchestra of the Theatre Royal, Drury Lane. He was young, enthusiastic and a fine musician whose intention was to make Beale's touring company second to none. Perhaps he was a little too idealistic, but at least he tried.

As previously, choristers were engaged in each different town, and during a rehearsal in Manchester, Vianesi was furious when the 'singers' who were playing the witches sang completely out of time and tune with the orchestra. The section was repeated but the result was the same. The conductor was beside himself with fury and demanded to know what they thought they were doing. The poor, frightened creatures looked at him in surprise, and said: "we are singing the witches in 'Macbeth', 'but' cried Vianesi, 'you are singing in English'. 'Yes', they answered 'it's the music we always sing in 'Macbeth'. They had assumed that they were appearing in the Shakespeare play with incidental music, as they had done before and, of course, didn't know a note of Verdi's music, so they had to be replaced by the prompter and two Italians from the orchestra who sang the trio as Verdi had written it, their heavy beards disguised by drapery.

However, troubles rarely come singly, and that was not the end of the problem. No one had thought to engage supernumeraries to play the part of the soldiers of King Duncan's army, so again the prompter and his two doughty helpers had to don costumes and come to the rescue. The music for the King's procession is very long, and usually there are at least two dozen soldiers, who exit from one side of the stage, rush round the back and enter from the opposite side, to keep the procession moving, and although the three 'helpers' did their best, by no stretch of the imagination could the audience believe in the reality of King Duncan's army. These inefficiencies must have have made a performer like Pauline weep, and it was a relief when the tour ended and she was able to return to France, where in her leisure hours, she played the superb organ that she had recently commissioned for the princely sum of 10,500 francs, and had installed in the rue de Douai house. The money was raised by the sale of a quantity of jewellery and gifts, which she had received on her Russian trips. Later the instrument was taken to Baden Baden, where she frequently gave recitals for family and friends, notably those of the Prussian royal house. Towards the end of her life, she sold it to a church in Melun for 7,000 francs.

On the 24th May a benefit was given for the soprano Marie Miolan-Carvalho, the wife of the theatre director, Leon Carvalho. Pauline sang 'Che faro' from Gluck's 'Orfeo', and Carvalho was overwhelmed by her performance. Courageously he decided to stage this largely forgotten work at the Theatre Lyrique with Pauline as Orfeo. Berlioz was engaged to revise the French version of the score. which Gluck had adapted in 1774 to suit the counter-tenor, Legros, but the original version had been sung by the castrato, Guadagni, and Berlioz now restored the music of the original score in order to accommodate Pauline's florid, mezzo soprano voice. Carvalho was taking a gamble as, at best it could only be a 'succes d'estime', but he, Pauline and Berlioz had enormous faith in this great work, and to everyone's surprise it turned out to be the most stupendous success of the season, and the crowning glory of Pauline's career.

On June 7th 1859, Pauline wrote to Julius Rietz asking him to procure a score of 'Orfeo' in Italian, to give her information about keys and the music of the main characters in that version. She said: "The reason is, that it is not impossible that I may sing 'Orfeo' at the Theatre Lyrique in September, but nothing has been decided yet – it all depends on the 'subvention' that is asked for this theatre. Should it be granted, then Orpheus will tune his lyre, and will charm the poor devils who come to hear him (if he can)."

Rietz must have told her that he had been unwell, for in her next letter to him on the 12th of June, she advised him, in a most motherly way, to take the homeopathic remedy 'Oleum Crotonense' which, she said, was wonderful for everything.

The prospect of singing the role of Orfeo excited her tremendously, and she signed a contract with Leon Carvalho on June 28th, 1859. Two of her great interests came together in this opera, Gluck's music, and the mythology of ancient Greece.

Strangely, in 1859, Berlioz, who had known Pauline for twenty years, now fell deeply in love with her. Naturally, she was sympathetic to him, prayed for his happiness, and gave him her friendship, but she was not able to return his adoration. He often visited her at home, and together they worked on his new opera 'The Trojans'. Berlioz also stayed for a few days at Courtavenel, but it tore Pauline apart to see him looking so ill and wretched, yet, there was little she could do other than be there for him.

On August 20th she wrote to Rietz from Baden Baden, inviting him to meet her there, but he did not arrive and she chided him roundly: "You faint-hearted man, irresolute friend, easy-going Bear, why, oh why, did you not come? All the reasons you give are nothing but bad excuses. You might have spent three days, three long, lovely days, with me, and you did not – out with the word! – 'dare to'! Can you have been afraid of your wife? If that was the case, why didn't you tell me so? I cannot think of any other 'intelligible' reason for your not coming. This time I have positively arrived at the point of being angry with you, if you do not 'instantly confess' the real truth. – How I was hoping to see you! How happy we should have been! O irresolute friend! A journey of twelve hours frightened you off"!

In Baden Baden on August 29th, Pauline and the baritone Lefort gave the first public performance of the scene between Cassandra and Choreb from Act I of Berlioz's monumental new work, which is based on Virgil's 'Aeneid'. Before the performance, Berlioz told Caroline von Sayn Wittgenstein that he hoped they would sing these litanies of love well.

Pauline and Berlioz had both studied harmony and counterpoint with Anton Reicha, but Berlioz did not play the piano, so Pauline helped him with the piano transcriptions of his orchestral score. Saint-Saens remembers calling at the house in the rue de Douai one day to discover Pauline, 'her eyes flashing fire' hard at work on a transcription of the Royal Hunt and Storm from the 'Trojans', and in a letter dated 30th October, Berlioz called her his 'dear critic' and thanked her for sending the score back, 'like a flag returning from the wars, more beautiful when it is mutilated!"

The work is in five acts of two unequal parts, and depicts the fall of Troy, which Berlioz first learned about as a very young boy in his Latin lessons with his father. His imagination was fired and it became his ambition to tell the story in music. His opera is epic, tempestuous, tragic, lyrical and above all atmospheric, and his use of the massive forces involved is riveting, with tumultuous climaxes, colours new to the orchestral palette, and vocal writing that is highly original, and calls for a vast chorus.

Even Berlioz's fellow composers found his music so far in advance of the time that they were puzzled by it and could not comprehend his vision. From his youth, his music had been greatly criticised and misunderstood, and Mendelssohn, usually so charitable about other composers, had declared that Berlioz was a freak, without a vestige of talent. Enigmatically, Wagner said that the Frenchman was 'devilishly smart'. Of his contemporaries, only Liszt appreciated the breadth of Berlioz's ideas, and the importance of his orchestral innovations.

Pauline gave Berlioz valuable musical assistance, and Louise maintained that her mother actually had the temerity to correct his harmonies, but her moral support was even more crucial. She told Rietz: "Poor man! I feel very badly on his account. He is so very sick, so embittered, so unhappy! I have a great affection for him – he loves me much, I know it – he loves me only too much! But that would be a long story – and it is all still so new – I feel too agitated to write about it. Perhaps I have already said too much. A word to the wise is sufficient. Who would ever have imagined such a thing! Just think: Berlioz, after a long, cordial friendship, has had the misfortune to fall in love with me all of a sudden. I assure you that I find myself in a very painful predicament, for I feel keenly that I, and I alone, am able to give comfort to this poor bleeding heart. It is a most difficult mission, and very delicate to perform, and at the same time highly embarrassing, for I know what pain is caused by a sore heart".

When Pauline returned from Baden she retreated to her tower room at Courtavenel, to prepare and practice 'Orfeo'. She went up every morning after breakfast to read, write, and sing, and as she sat at her desk she 'communed' with a portrait of Rietz. She told him that she was working hard on the recitatives, which had been transposed up a tone for her, as the original tessitura was too low. Other than that she made little mention of her preparations in her letters, although she must have been deeply immersed in her work.

Always interested in young composers, she informed Rietz: " Saint-Saens played me all manner of things; The Concerto, or rather the 'Symphonic Fantaisie', the Concerto for Violin, a duet for piano and violin, and a charming little 'Christmas Oratorio', which has been brought out in the Madeleine. You surely know that Saint Saens is organist there, do you not? Furthermore, several vocal pieces, songs, four-hand pieces. You see that he has been very industrious. The lad has a great resemblance to Weber in his physique".

In her next letter on the 22nd of September, she discussed Berlioz's state of health, having first admitted that she felt very melancholy, without knowing why: "You will understand it all when you learn that Berlioz has come to spend two days with us. What I have had to suffer cannot be told in words. The sight of this man, a prey to such mental and physical anguish, so unhappy in spirit, so touched by the kind reception we gave him, torn by horrible tortures of the heart, the violence of the efforts which he makes to hide them – this ardent soul bursting its bonds of clay; this life, which hangs only by a thread, so to speak, the vast tenderness that overflows in his gaze, in his least words – all this, I say, wrings my heart". She added that it seemed to be her destiny to minister to wounded hearts: "I have known no others since I have known myself, and so I feel myself peculiarly attached and drawn to them. It is something like the mission of a sister of charity, but I love it…"

Tourgueniev, that other 'wounded heart' had arrived in Paris and was also in a melancholy frame of mind, knowing that there was little hope of resuming his old relationship with Pauline. He was saddened by the fact that his daughter thoroughly disliked the woman he loved, but he wrote to Paulinette from Russia on June 22nd, telling her that he intended to go from Paris to Vichy and then to Courtavenel: "I hope I shall be invited,' he added despondently.

On July 18th, Pauline celebrated her 38th birthday, and in high good humour, she wrote to a friend: "Kind Louis blessed this day for the nineteenth time since we were married. Kind? At half past eight, the big bell gave the first signal for breakfast. It was rung again at a quarter to nine, and at five to nine we were called by the bright tinkle of a Russian handbell. I then went down into the dining-room, and found the children waiting for me, eager... for their food. After a hundred or more kisses given and received by the three girls, Mr. Paul, too, had to be embraced and kissed to suffocation point. My two sisters-in-law were there: the elder, (Nanine) an excellent woman of sixty-three, dull but kind-hearted, kissed me warmly, while the younger, (Berthe) an old maid, greeted me with a countenance, as comically woeful as could be. I know this look of hers, which puts in an annual appearance on this great day; for it was on this day of affliction (for her) that she, too, was born – only nineteen years earlier than me! Berthe still has pretensions though (she was pretty in her day), and I cannot endure her, nor she endure me – which is to say that we live together in the most cordial understanding. Sometimes she tries to provoke me, but on such occasions, I poke fun at her a bit and the harmony immediately returns."

The sun was already very hot and breakfast, which included grilled chops, was eaten with the windows and shutters almost closed. The adults talked about politics, and the 'Peace' of Villafranca, which stipulated that France took Lombardy and Parma for herself, forced Austria to restore Tuscany and Modena, but left her Venice. The Viardots had always supported the aspirations of Daniel Manin, and were so unhappy with this treaty that they were almost glad that he had not lived to see the awful spectacle of a people whose hopes were raised, then suddenly deceived in everything it held most sacred.

Yet, despicable as this state of affairs was, it was merely a prelude to further suffering for the Italian people who, Pauline said, "were like a drowning man to whom a plank of wood was proffered, and just as he was about to clutch it, he was thrown back into the sea with a blow dealt to his head."

Her sympathy with the Italian cause endeared her to Giuseppe Verdi who, with Garibaldi and Mazzini, strove for unity and freedom for their native land. Pauline's feelings on the matter were deep and sensible, and despite her commitment to her art, her egalitarian and democratic consciousness matched Louis's progressive philosophy. She had great empathy with downtrodden nations, and was uncompromising in her disgust of the monstrous imperialism of Napoleon III, often to the detriment of her own career, which made her sacrifice even greater than husband's.

After breakfast there were billiards, then Claudie and Marianne had lessons with their governess and Pauline withdrew to her tower, from where she wrote to Rietz, berating him for not writing to her, after which she settled down to read George Sand's 'Elle et lui', the novel based on her liaison with Alfred de Musset. When this book was first published, it had so upset Alfred's brother, Paul, that he immediately retaliated with one of his own entitled 'Lui et elle'. Pauline found both novels repugnant because she loathed public confession and considered, that to undress morally in front of the public was as vulgar as doing a strip-tease in a bar. She pushed George's book aside and began to concentrate on her music. Time flew by, and at half past four, the first bell rang for dinner, and she rushed to put on her evening gown.

At five o'clock, when she went downstairs, the little girls were already seated at the table, looking like spinning tops in their pretty crinolines; the family assembled, and as they were beginning the soup course, Tourgueniev casually walked in, unannounced.

Courtavenel had once been his favourite place in the whole world, but now it depressed him because the happy family life there only served to emphasise his own desolation of spirit. The fact that Pauline was so unpredictable, blowing hot and cold all the time, did nothing to raise his morale. During his stay, he wrote to a friend: "I am sitting at an open window, looking over the garden; everywhere is very quiet, except for the sound of children's voices in the distance (Mme Viardot has charming children); pigeons are cooing in the garden and a robin is singing; a soft breeze is touching my face; and in my heart there is almost the sadness of old age. There can be no happiness outside the family – and beyond one's own land; everyone should stay in his own nest and put down roots into his native soil. What is the point of clinging on to the edge of someone else's nest"? He read Homer aloud to Pauline, who treated him as an old, distant friend, and appeared to be oblivious of his sufferings.

In his misery, his work became his solace. He had recently published 'A Nest of Gentlefolk', and had begun to write 'On the Eve'. In the middle of September, he returned to Spasskoye, but continued to write to Pauline, although she did not often reply. He corresponded on business with Louis, and sometimes received a letter from Joaquina, but more than ever, he felt all the old familiar ties with the Viardots, although he believed that he had done the right thing in returning home.

On September 23rd, Berlioz told his son, Louis: "I went to spend two days with Mme Viardot at Courtavenel, where I felt dreadfully ill; they did not want to let me leave, but my distress at seeing that charming family looking after me, at grieving such friends, won the day…" While there, he went for a long walk with Pauline and told her: "My entire life has been a long and passionate aspiration towards an ideal that I created for myself. Alas, disillusionment has been my lot, but in you, my ideal has been re-created; let me spend my last days in blessing you, in thanking you for coming to prove to me that I am not mad'.

Another time, obviously in extreme anguish and needing her emotional support, he wrote: I desperately need to talk to you about a multitude of things; I am cruelly tortured by not being able to... I wish you would give me news of yourself, even in a few lines; frankly, it would be a kind deed. How unbearably tormenting slavery is!! To be a slave to everything!!I grind my teeth in anger at not being able to go and talk to you... O God, send me a few lines. My whole frame aches from the nervous anguish I am in." He said that he found it impossible to write the article on Ambroise Thomas' 'Le Roman d'Elvire': "that's another nightmare. I shall force myself to do it this evening, even if I have to sit beside the fire until one o'clock in the morning... alone... alone to fight against ghosts of ideas, to make strings of lies and nonsense. Just six lines from your hand to give me courage... Yours, yours, yours, always, in everything and everywhere and for everything. What torment!" He made Pauline promise that when he was dying she would be at his bedside, however difficult it might be.

However, his work on the score of 'Orfeo', appeared to have a calming effect on his nerves because it was a labour of love that he found conducive, as opposed to the journalistic hack-work, which he abhorred.

Although she was predominantly a musician, Pauline had a strong visual sense, and she wanted to know what kind of costume Orfeo would have worn. This was not easy to determine, because he was a mythical character, of no given historical period, and she turned for advice to Eugene Delacroix, who had become an increasingly dear friend since the death of Ary Scheffer, and he agreed to help her design a costume. In 1857, Delacroix had moved from Notre Dame de Lorette in Montmartre, where he had been a neighbour of the Viardots, to 6, rue de Furstenberg, so that he could be near the Church of St. Sulpice where he was decorating a chapel. He had a large, airy studio, and a year later, acquired a house at Champrosay, where, after completing the chapel, he spent most of his time, as his health had begun to deteriorate. Pauline was grateful for the trouble he took for her as 1859 was a very busy year for him, and the last in which he submitted works to the Salon, exhibiting eight large canvases, including 'The Abduction of Rebecca' and 'Hamlet'.

Delacroix wrote to tell George Sand that Pauline was to sing Orfeo at the Theatre Lyrique, and said that she must take the dilligence from Chateauroux and come to Paris. She obviously replied that she would do so, because he expressed delight at the thought of seeing the opera with her, and said that they would be able to weep together over the sad story.

In the event, the costume that Delacroix and Pauline contrived, although it looks quaint to modern eyes, was considered a masterpiece by George Sand, Gustave Flaubert, Dickens, Ingres, and Berlioz. It consisted of a white, sleeveless tunic, with rather a full skirt, the hem of which came down to just below the knee, covered by a white cloak, reaching to the ankles, fastened with gold brooches on the shoulder; a red cord belt, from which hung a sword in a golden sheath; white stockings and flat, white buskins, with red laces. Her shoulder length hair was loosely dressed, and bore a laurel wreath, while in her arms, she carried a lyre.

Although Pauline had sung Gluck's arias as concert items since the beginning of her career, she had never expected to take part in a fully staged work by the largely forgotten composer. Like her, Berlioz had revered Gluck all his life, and theirs was an ideal collaboration. The production of 'Orfeo' came like manna from heaven at a time when he was sorely in need of diversion. His second marriage had turned out to be a total disaster, which was why he spent as little time as possible in his own home. All the stress involved had a terrible effect on his health, and his friends were shocked to see how ill he looked.

Despite his general condition, Berlioz found the requisite energy to work on the score he loved: the string section of the orchestra was augmented, and a further twenty choristers were engaged from the Theatre Italien. He took charge of rehearsals, especially those concerning Pauline, although Deloffre was the official conductor who, if rumour is to be believed, directed from a first violin part. The designs and scene painting were carried out by the excellent team of Cambon and Thierry, and the ballet was in the capable hands of the distinguished dancer and choreographer, Lucien Petipa, who had created the role of Albrecht in Adolphe Adams's classical ballet, 'Giselle'. He was the brother of the even more famous Marius Petipa, who had founded the Russian school of dancing in St. Petersburg.

The premiere of 'Orfeo' took place on November 18th, 1859, and the opera presented a beautiful spectacle, thanks to its superb sets. All involved accepted that the production was a labour of love, but nobody dreamed that it would become a run-a-way success. At the same time, Offenbach's comic operetta 'Orpheus in the Underworld' was being staged in Paris, and maybe there was some confusion between the two productions, with members of the operetta audience finding themselves at 'Orfeo' by mistake However, once in their seats, they were captivated by Gluck's wonderfully evocative work, and Pauline's exquisitely moving performance. The production proved to be phenomenally successful, and seats were at a premium, because it appealed as much to the general public, who wished only to be entertained, as it did to the connoisseurs who expected to be transported to higher realms.

On the 21st November, thrilled at the reception her Orfeo had received, Pauline greeted her 'Bear' by exclaiming: "Good morning, mon cher, lieber, caro, dear, ljedegni, querido, and extremely lazy friend. I have not had time to write to you since Friday, the day of the great battle, of the great victory. Yes, my friend, 'Orfeo' has emerged victorious, triumphant, from the profound oblivion in which it was plunged. It was veritably an enormous success. Your friend was acclaimed, recalled with frenzy. My house has not been empty since 9 o'clock Saturday morning, I shall play this evening, then Wednesday, then Friday, then three times a week till the public and I can stand it no longer. The stage setting is very fine, without attempting, however, to outshine the music. My costume was thought to be very handsome.

"Every phrase, every word was understood by an intelligent audience composed of all that Paris contains in the way of musicians, amateurs, pedants, bald heads, the world of boredom, youthful lions, etc. Well, people embraced each other in the passage-ways during the intermissions, they wept, they laughed for delight, they tramped the floor – in a word, there was a turmoil, a jubilation, such as I never have seen in Paris. The role of Orfeo suits me as if it had been written for me".

Berlioz, in a letter to Pauline wrote: "I could talk with you until the Last Judgement. When I am in your fresh and poetic atmosphere, I feel like a fish in water; everywhere else, I continue to be a fish out of water', and on another occasion, he wrote: "How wonderful you were the day before yesterday, and how cold I must have appeared to you in what I said! (possibly at a rehearsal or after a performance of 'Orfeo') but, as you know, I refrain from going too far so as to control my nature, which is either too excessive or too violent. At one moment, I could have crushed your hand – and I stopped myself from attempting to shake it".

The day after the premiere, the Parisian press was almost unanimous in praise of Viardot's magnificent performance. Berlioz led the field, of course, writing in the 'Journal des Debats': "Her gifts are so complete, so varied, they touch art in so many areas, they unite so much learning with such seductive spontaneity, at the same time evoking astonishment and emotion". He eulogised the singer for several paragraphs, but took her to task for altering the text, and for the ornamentation she had interpolated, which he considered inappropriate. Yet, despite his reservations, his article is a splendid tribute by a great critic to a superb artist.

For as long as anyone could remember, Gluck had been judged 'heavy fare', but now that a contemporary audience had seen a staged work for themselves, especially with such a God-given interpreter as Mme Viardot, they found it tremendously appealing. Euridice was sung by the twenty-two year old soprano, Marie Sax, of whom Pauline said ' she had a lovely voice but it was untrained.' The youthful singer was not the most intelligent or musical of girls, yet Wagner chose her to create the role of Elizabeth for the Paris premiere of his 'Tannhauser' in 1861. The small, but important part of Amor, was sung by the twenty year old Marie Marimon, a pupil of Gilbert Duprez.

The effective staging of Gluck's opera is difficult because it is a work of great simplicity; the action of the plot is very limited, and it could easily become a 'concert in costume', but with the towering magnetism of Viardot, and the superb setting, the 1859 production came wondrously to life. Pauline was praised for the 'statuesque grace of her figure, which gave interest and meaning to every step and every attitude, yet there was not a single effect that might be called a pose or prepared gesture'. This was art concealing art because the great artist had studied and planned every movement, every gesture in advance, leaving nothing to chance.

Despite Pauline's serious approach to her art, she had a lively sense of humour and burst into fits of laughter at rehearsal one day when Marie Sax confided that she considered it the height of bad manners for Monsieur Gluck (he had died in 1787) to be absent from rehearsals, and for Monsieur Berlioz to have the effrontery to settle the tempi without his approval. Another time, during a performance, when Pauline had sung the "Che faro" so transcendently beautifully that her audience was in a rapturous trance, Marie whispered, as the last strains of the aria died away: "Phew, I thought that would never end'!

In a personal letter to Pauline, written on the 6th December, Berlioz said: "I have nothing to say to you. Nothing...but I must write to you. Yesterday's impression still remains with me. It is painful, obsessive. Anyhow, good morning! What kind of night did you have after that remarkable performance? Tell me. I have lost my bearings, like a compass needle after a hurricane."

The audience, of course, saw only the glamour of the production, Pauline's stunning portrayal of the title role, the wonderful sets, the first scene of which resembled Poussin's exquisite painting "Ego in Arcadia", and the beautiful ballet in the Elysian fields, but Berlioz knew just what Pauline's performance cost her. For a time she suffered the effects of a bad attack of bronchitis, and in a letter to Princess Caroline, he said: "Practically every evening, Mme Viardot arrives at her dressing room, with a cold, coughing, frightened; entreated to forget her cold, and fear nothing, she goes onto the stage like a lioness, more uplifted and uplifting than ever." He said that at the end of each performance, the stage was littered with floral tributes, each card bearing a message in a different language. Many were in Russian, but none of them were from Tourgueniev, who was far away in Spasskoye, and could only read about her triumphs in the newspapers.

For Pauline, the year ended in a blaze of glory, but for her dear Franz Liszt it brought tragedy, with the death of his twenty year old son, Daniel. From Paris on December 29th, Berlioz wrote: My dear Liszt, You have been struck a cruel blow; you must know how much I feel for you in your sorrow. You had, I think, for some time been expecting the loss of this poor child and I know that he died without pain. But Fate, until now, had spared you; you had never experienced heartache of this kind. You were very young when you lost your father, and since then you have not endured the death of a brother, sister, child or any other loved one, and it is this inexperience of sorrow that makes me apprehensive on your behalf".

The intense and frequent correspondence between Pauline and Rietz, which, in any case, had always been more fulsome on her side, appeared to have run its course, and on the 8th of January, 1860, she wrote to him saying: "Good morning, dear, naughty friend. I begin by asking you in all seriousness what has happened, that your correspondence should have slackened in a way so unexpected and so painful. You can have no idea of the veritable grief that it causes me – and I lose myself in conjectures, not one of which do I find agreeable. This beautiful, delightful and warm friendship – could it have been nothing but a mere straw-fire on your side? Have I deluded myself to the point of taking a butterfly… for a bear? Have you fallen into a decline? Are you sick? Are you dead???!"

Despite her annoyance, she was soon writing to him again, describing the staging of the scene in the Elysian Fields:" This is the way we put it together. After the air in F 'Cet asile aimable et tranquille', comes the entrée of ;Orfeo' in C. after this recitative, the chorus in F is sung in the wings, Orfeo remaining quite alone on the stage. Then, during the delicious instrumental number, the Shades come on in small, curious groups. Orfeo seeks for Euridice among them – by the end of the number, the entire chorus is on the stage. This scene in pantomime received two rounds of applause. The duo with Eurodice also made a great impression, but the number that marked the culminating point was the air 'J'ai perdu mon Euridice" (Che faro?") I think I have discovered three good ways of delivering the motif. The first time, sorrowful amazement, almost motionless. The second, choked with tears (the applause lasted two minutes, and they wanted an encore!!!) The third time, outbursts of despair".

Berlioz considered that her singing of this aria was matchless, but took her to task for including an extensive cadenza, which he considered unnecessary and out of style, but of which she was inordinately proud. The aria was taken from one of Gluck's earlier operas, 'Aristeo', but Berlioz erroneously thought it had been written and inserted into 'Orfeo' by Bertoni. "It's sublimely beautiful, and it's already moved me to tears on more than a score of occasions. Mme Viardot's beautiful performance is ideal for this role".

In the same letter he added: "Wagner has just given a concert which exasperated three quarters of the audience and enthused the rest... (on the 25th of January; the Prelude to 'Tristan and Isolde' was included). Personally, I found a lot of it painful, even though I admired the vehemence of his musical feelings in certain instances. But the diminished sevenths, the discords and the crude modulations made me feverish, and I have to say that I find this sort of music loathsome and revolting."

At that time, Wagner and his first wife Minna were living in Paris, in a small house in the rue Newton, near the Arc-de-Triomphe, because the composer was hoping that the Paris Opera would stage his 'Tannhauser'. Pauline told Rietz: "Wagner stirs up the same musical feuds here as in Germany. Unfortunately, I cannot hear his concerts, (at the Theatre Italien), for he gives all three of them on Wednesdays, and that is the 'Orfeo' day. The prelude to 'Lohengrin' has created a furore. Even his enemies have to admit it..."

It was true, the performances conducted by Wagner, with Hans von Bulow, the husband of Liszt's daughter Cosima, in charge of the choir, made a great sensation, and so impressed the influential Princess Metternich that she persuaded the Emperor to authorise the directors of the Opera.to stage 'Tannhauser'. Wagner lost a lot of money on his concerts, but was consoled by the fact that it seemed certain that the opera was to be staged in Paris at last.

In July, Pauline told Rietz that she knew how, the as yet un-staged 'Tristan und Isolde' sounded, "for I have had the honour of singing it with Wagner himself.!!!... But I shall say nothing about that because it would give you too much pleasure, and I am too greatly put out at you just now to treat you in any such agreeable fashion..." (He was still not writing frequently enough).

She was referring to an audition of the second act of 'Tristan' at her house in the rue de Douai. Wagner was always in need of rich patrons, and Mme Kalergis, for whom the run-through of 'Tristan' was arranged, was an immensely rich and highly cultured woman, a niece of Chancellor Nesselrode. She and Pauline had been friends for years, and the singer usually stayed at her house when she

visited Warsaw, so it is highly likely that it was Pauline who suggested performing a part of 'Tristan' for Mme Kalergis. Despite her barbed comments to Rietz
about Wagner, she had always been on friendly terms with him.

Pauline usually gave the impression that Wagner was delighted with her
rendition when she sight read parts of Isolde's music for him, but in his autobiography, written about 1870, he said: "I improvised a special audition for her
(Mme Kalergis) of the second act of 'Tristan' in which Mme Viardot, whose
friendship I succeeded in gaining on this occasion, was to share the singing
parts with myself; while for the pianoforte accompaniment I had summoned
Klindworth at my own expense from London. This very curious, intimate performance took place at Mme Viardot's home. (In February 1860). Besides Mme
Kalergis, in whose honour alone it was given, Berlioz was the only person
present. Mme Viardot had especially charged herself with securing his presence, apparently, with the avowed object of easing the strained relations between Berlioz and myself. I was never clear, as to the effect produced upon both
performers and listeners by the presentation under such circumstances, of this
eccentric fragment. Mme Kalergis remained dumb. Berlioz merely expressed
praise of the 'chaleur' (warmth) of my delivery, which may very well have afforded a strong contrast to that of my partner, who generally merely marked her
part with half voice. Klindworth seemed particularly stirred to anger at the
situation. His own share was admirably executed; but he declared that he had
been consumed with indignation at observing Viardot's lukewarm execution of
her part, in which she was probably determined by the presence of Berlioz".

This is interesting, and begs the question as to how comfortable Pauline was
sight-singing an avant garde work. There is no doubt that she was a brilliant
musician, and learned roles amazingly quickly, but there are several occasions
when composers wrote that although she played through their songs at the
piano, and expressed approval, she did not attempt to sing them at sight. To
sight-sing expertly is a particular skill that choristers are expected to have, but
Pauline had always been a soloist, and as long as she could read a score and
commit the music to memory, that was all that was necessary. She prepared her
music in her own practice room, knew it thoroughly by the first rehearsal, and it
is quite probable that she was not an expert sight-singer.

Isolde is one of the most demanding and arduous dramatic soprano roles in
the repertory, containing several exposed top C's and requiring great stamina in
sustained singing. Pauline, as a florid mezzo, would have found the tessitura
very daunting, and, quite naturally, marked the higher passages in half voice, or
down the octave. Isolde's role is also very difficult musically, and full of chro-

maticism. The complex score was new to Pauline and it is small wonder that she didn't come up to scratch at the audition.

Of course, she had sung roles in contemporary operas, and she tackled the role of Azucena at short notice, but she didn't have to sight-sing it to Verdi. It was in her range, and Verdi's score was more main-stream and easily accessible than that of Wagner. She simply had to sit at the piano, play her part and memorise it, which she did in an incredibly short time.

Pauline continued to sing the role of Orfeo at least twice a week or even more, and soon she had over a hundred and twenty performances to her credit. It was one of the ironies of fate that a few months after the death of Liszt's son, Daniel, Pauline was faced with a similar situation when Paul, who was not quite two years old, contracted bronchial pneumonia (an often fatal illness before the days of antibiotics), and nearly died. In spite of her anxieties and desperation over the state of her son's health, she continued to sing 'Orfeo', and the worry she experienced brought added poignancy to her singing of the famous 'Che faro'. The entire company was concerned for her and expressed their deepest sympathy, but Pauline was fortunate, and Paul made an excellent recovery.

During her period of despair and strain, Pauline turned to Tourgueniev who, devoted as ever, answered her call immediately: "I am going to Courtavenel at once, to Mme Viardot", he wrote from Soden, to his friend, Pavel Annenkov on the 8th of July, 1860. "I will stay there until the first of August because Mme Viardot wishes it, and for me her wishes are law. Her son almost died, and she suffered a great deal. She needs rest in peaceful, friendly company". Did Pauline call on him merely as a friend, or because he really was the boy's father, and she thought that if the child was dying, his 'natural' father should be with him at the end?

It is interesting that Jacques-Paul Viardot, Paul's son, said that his father once told him about an incident in his boyhood when, one evening, he was about to go to bed and his mother and Tourgueniev were sitting on either side of the fireplace in the salon; the boy kissed his mother goodnight, but ignored Tourgueniev. Pauline chided him for being so impolite to 'Tourguel', (as the family called the writer), and told Paul to shake hands and say goodnight properly, but the boy answered that he was not friends with 'Tourguel' who, that morning, had cuffed him around the ear for some misdemeanour, and the boy indignantly declared that he would not tolerate any chastisement except from his father. Paul recalled that a very meaningful look passed between his mother and her friend, which struck him, even young as he was, as rather odd.

In his teens, Paul once got into trouble gambling, and as he could not honour his debts, he was at his wit's end to know what to do: feeling particularly desperate, he confessed his plight to Tourgueniev, who scolded him, and said it should be a lesson to him, then made him promise never to gamble again. Paul readily agreed, having suffered through his folly, and Tourgueniev paid off the debt. It is also alleged that on another occasion, the writer presented Paul with a very expensive Stradivarius violin.

Pauline was now thirty-eight and had been singing professionally for twenty two years, which may have contributed to the obvious deterioration in her voice, although many opera singers have far longer careers and stay on fine form until they retire. Another factor that can have a bearing on a female voice is that of hormonal imbalance, particularly during menopause, which can happen early or late, depending on the individual. Modern singers now have the choice of hormone replacement therapy, which can remedy matters and prolong the health of the voice if the singer already has a reliable technique.

Most commentators have accepted the fact the Viardot's voice deteriorated prematurely because she made her debut at such an early age and over-stretched it by singing inappropriate roles, which is possible, yet all agree that she had a first rate technique that enabled her to overcome all degrees of difficulty, and she had no compunction in transposing a role if she thought the music would suit her better. There could have been a hormonal factor that later re-balanced itself, because Saint-Saens declared in 1870 that her voice was rejuvenated and, of course, at that time she was not singing as regularly as in earlier years.

However, whether on vocal form or not, Pauline's acting was always remarkable, and she played the part of Orfeo with such veracity, that one young girl, who saw the opera several times, became very infatuated with her, and although her parents tried to convince her that Pauline was a woman, she would not believe them. In desperation, they begged the singer to meet their daughter in order to disillusion her, which she did..

In July 1860, Pauline was engaged to sing a concert performance of Gluck's opera in England, and she told Rietz: 'On the 12th I travelled to London, to sing a concert performance of Orfeo at the home of Lord Dudley. It was a great success, and those who had seen the work at the Italian Opera at Covent Garden with Frau Csillag (from Vienna) could not believe it was the same opera. Although there were neither costumes nor scenery at Lord Dudley's, the chorus and small orchestra were excellent and the effect was tremendous. I stayed two days longer in London, so as to hear 'Orfeo' in the theatre. After that I felt no more surprise that people did not recognise the work. All the tempi were dragged so slowly, all went so one thing after another, so monotonously, without nuances, positively wearisome, so old-fogyish, that it seemed to me as if there were a mouldy smell in the theatre – no, I myself did not recognise the wondrously moving work... The public yawned heartily... isn't it dreadful? Even I had to yawn!!! Full of sorrow I came home again – my sole thought being the terrible responsibility resting on the interpreter of a great work! It is quite unutterable, we can slay a masterwork through our impotence! But then, how beautiful it is to be able to bear its weight!... and with such thought, I quietly fell asleep – the following day, at six o'clock, I was eating quietly at home in Paris'.

Chorley was ecstatic about Pauline's interpretation, despite the lack of staging, and in his memoirs he states: "Further, the peculiar quality of Mme. Viardot's voice – its unevenness, its occasional harshness and feebleness, consistent with tones of the gentlest sweetness – was turned by her to account with rare felicity, as giving the variety of light and shade to every word of solace, to every appeal of dialogue. A more perfect and honeyed voice might have recalled the woman too often, to fit with the idea of youth. Her musical handling of so peculiar an instrument will take place in the highest annals of art. After the mournful woefulness of the opening scenes, the kindling of hope and courage when Love points the way to the rescue were expressed by her, as by one whom reverence has tied fast, but who felt that the first act (the interpolation of which was sanctioned by Gluck, though the music is Bertoni's or Guadagni's – at all events not his own) showed the artist to be supreme in another light – in that grandeur of execution belonging to the old school, rapidly becoming a lost art. The torrents of roulades, the chains of notes, unmeaning in themselves, were flung out with such exactness, limitless volubility, and majesty as to convert what is essentially a commonplace piece of parade into one of those displays of passionate enthusiasm to which nothing less florid could give scope. As affording relief and contrast, they are not merely pardonable, they are defensible; and thus only to be despised by the indolence of the day, which, in obedience to false taste and narrow pedantry, has allowed on essential branch of art to fall into disuse". He added: "it would have been impossible to have spoken of Mme. Viardot's peculiar career – begun, carried through, and continued under difficulties – and to have omitted mention of her Orpheus, even though it has not be presented to the public in London".

Despite Chorley's enthusiastic comments, and the phenomenal success of her Orfeo in Paris, there is no doubt that Pauline's voice was in need of rest as, on one occasion, it cracked, which could have been a momentary aberration, or a sign that there was something really wrong. She had sung 'Orfeo' three times a week over a lengthy period, as well as giving other performances, and all voices show signs of fatigue if over worked. It is not only the time the singer spends in the theatre that causes tiredness, but the demands of everyday life.

Pauline was now a great celebrity and this meant more visitors, more talking, and more demands on her time and patience by aspiring singers and musicians who called on her in large numbers.

After the success of 'Orfeo', which she continued to sing regularly for the next two years, Leon Carvalho was anxious to find another vehicle for her, and Beethoven's 'Fidelio' was chosen, but this work had twice been produced in Paris without success, because it did not appeal to French audiences, although Malibran had been successful with it in England. It now remained to be seen what Pauline could make of its heroine, Leonora.

CHAPTER THIRTY

1860

The first performance of 'Fidelio' took place on the 5th of May, 1860, at the Theatre Lyrique in the Boulevard du Temple. The plot concerns the political imprisonment of Leonora's husband, Florestan, and her search to find the place where he is held. Although she is not sure if he is still alive, she dresses as a man, and finds employment as assistant to Rocco, the head gaoler of a prison with a large number of political captives.

The part of Rocco was sung by the distinguished bass, Charles Battaille, who was a year younger than Pauline, and a former student of her brother, Manuel Garcia. In 1848, he was engaged by the Opera Comique, but forced to retire from the stage in 1857, due to a serious laryngeal condition. After a period of recuperation, his voice returned to its former glory and he resumed his singing career. He was also a well respected teacher of singing; and trained Gustave Garcia, Manuel's son.

Pauline declared Battaille's portrayal of Rocco to be 'perfect', but she was not impressed by the rest of the cast, commenting: "they are not bad, neither are they good". She thought that the chorus sang passably, but were not numerous enough, and that the production was 'conventional'.

Her excellent reputation as a singing actress brought audiences into the theatre, and the opera made money, but 'Fidelio' was not a 'succes d'enthousiasme like 'Orfeo', because, as Pauline perceptively observed: "the elements of this work are altogether diverse, and it is too symphonic for the ears of the mass of the French public." There was still a measure of resistance on the part of the public to Beethoven's only operatic work, which eight years previously had been a fiasco at the Theatre Italien.

The new manager of the Theatre Lyrique, Charles Rety, and the producer of 'Fidelio', Leon Carvalho, decided to change its setting completely. Carre and Barbier were engaged to make a new French translation, placing the action at the court of the Sforza Family in Renaissance Milan. The names of the original characters were also changed so that Leonora became Isabella of Aragon: Florestan became Gian Galeazzo Sforza; Don Fernando became Charles VIII of

France, and Pizarro, the villain of the piece became Ludovico Sforza, the uncle of Isabella's husband Gian. Berlioz declared that Leon Carvalho made these changes, so that the opera could end with everyone in opulent costumes, which would not have been the case in the original setting.

The conductor, Leon Durocher, drily commented: "it is Beethoven's music for which people will go to the Theatre Lyrique, not merely to see opulent silks and velvets". The most stringent changes appeared in the story-line, although some of the music was also taken out of context, to accommodate the plot changes. A duet for Rocco and Pizarro was left out and one from the 1805 version was substituted for Leonora and Marzelline, Rocco's daughter, who falls in love with Leonora when she is dressed as a man!

After the great success of her Orfeo, Pauline's Leonora was a marked disappointment. Most critics had noticed that even in the Gluck, her voice was not without blemish, (not surprising, since she was singing with bronchitis!) but her deficiencies in the soprano range could not be hidden in Beethoven's demanding vocal writing. His music is extremely cruel because his vocal melodies are written in the same way as those he composed for orchestral instruments, without taking into account the capabilities of the voice, and it soon became clear that Pauline was not capable of sustaining the demanding tessitura of Leonora's music. She was predominantly a florid singer, and although Leonora is called upon to sing some coloratura passages, the music requires a true dramatic soprano with the strength to carry the high, sustained vocal line, which is closer to the vocal writing of Wagner than to that of Rossini or Meyerbeer, in which Pauline was so highly accomplished.

One reviewer stated: "The role is generally too high for her voice, and it imposes painful efforts...this new creation will add nothing to her glory, but to what heights of virtuosity did she raise the magnificent air in act two ('Abscheulicher'), ending it with an appoggiatura of unparalleled audacity on the final high B. Strangely, she appeared to have difficulty with the spoken dialogue, and many people felt that her obvious efforts caused embarrassment to her audience." Many opera singers find spoken dialogue difficult, even when they are experienced in recitative, and they struggle to memorise words when they are not linked to music. 'Fidelio' is a 'sing-spiel' – a 'sung-play'- rather than an opera, more like a modern musical, with dialogue between the set musical pieces, and Pauline had never undertaken such a work before.

Because of the poor reviews, audiences stayed away, and Rety's management experienced financial difficulties, making it necessary to cut back on expenditure. In June, it was announced that there would be no further performances of 'Fidelio', due to the necessary departure of Battaille and Viardot who had engagements elsewhere. This statement was merely a fortuitous excuse for discontinuing a production which was not bringing in sufficient revenue. Audiences had become used to a high standard of excellence during the previous management, and would not be content with anything less. Rety needed all his skill in encouraging them to return, but Viardot remained under contract at a salary of 3,000 francs a month.

On 14th May, Pauline and several other luminaries took part in Mme Delphine Ugalde's benefit held at the Theatre Lyrique. Charles Gounod played the organ in the finale, which featured his 'Ave Maria', based on a Bach prelude. This was sung by Mme Ugalde, with Felix Masse at the piano, and the sixteen-year-old Pablo de Sarasate playing the violin part. One wonders what went through Pauline's mind, finding herself in close proximity to Charles again, a decade after they had parted acrimoniously. Doubtless time had helped to heal the wound, but if Claudie was actually Gounod's child, Pauline would never have been able to dismiss him completely from her thoughts. Perhaps it is significant that after this concert, the two former lovers renewed their friendship.

It is tempting to see a likeness to Gounod in Claudie's early photographs, as they shared a refined shape of nose, whereas Pauline's was acquiline and Louis's was rather large. As Claudie grew older, she became a better looking version of her mother, the dark colouring of her Garcia genes being predominant. Like Gounod, she had a spontaneous charm, and was, as would be expected of a member of the Garcia family, a fine singer, but if her father as well as her mother was a musician, it is doubly to be expected, and it is also interesting that she became a painter of high distinction. Gounod's father was a professional painter and draughtsman, and Gounod was a highly competent artist himself, as Ingres had discovered when he was in Rome. Although Pauline drew and painted well, compared to her daughter, she was a talented amateur and never rose to the professional standard achieved by Claudie.

On July 25th, Pauline wrote to Julius Rietz from Courtavenel bemoaning the fact that she had not heard from him since May, and then only after a long silence. She asked him what was wrong, and enquired about his health and that of his family.

At the end of the summer of 1860, Willert Beale organised another tour of the principal cities in the United Kingdom, which included Birmingham, Liverpool, Manchester and Dublin. The performers were Viardot, Grisi, Gassier, the soprano for whom Luigi Arditi wrote his famous 'Il Baccio'; Mlle. Orwill, a pupil of Pauline's who had recently made her debut as Euridice in one of the Paris performances of 'Orfeo'; Mario; Graziani, and the bass Ciampi. Once again, Louise accompanied her mother, and made some pertinent remarks about

Pauline's colleagues. She considered that Grisi was ignorant, and had a fiery temperament; Gassier, who was very pretty and petite, she surprised one day in her dressing room where, dressed in a scanty costume, "she was sitting on the lap of a person whose blonde beard she was gently caressing".

She thought that Mario was a perfect, aristocratic gentleman, who had absolutely no monetary sense at all. This defect in Mario's character was to make his old age less comfortable than it might have been because, although he had earned substantial fees during his career, having been one of the highest paid opera singers in Europe, he had extravagant tastes and had squandered most of it.

With the end of her autumn tour, Pauline's steps turned towards the Continent, and it was a decade before she sang in England again. To all intents and purposes, her English career was over, but she left behind memories of countless superb performances.

Back in Paris, on October 19th, she told Rietz that she was at her wit's end wondering how to write to him. She called him 'ungrateful' and said that she ought not to write any longer, because she had sent him four or five letters, and her portrait, without receiving a single reply.

She stated: "You have taken no pity on the poor heart of a friend – you have not cared to answer with a word, a single word, to soothe and console me. You are a wicked man….whom I love with all my soul in spite of all. Tell me that despite this forgetfulness without explanation (without reason) you still cherish friendship for her whom you have often called your best friend…." Did she, perhaps spare a thought for Tourgueniev, to whom she had caused similar suffering over the years?

'Orfeo' continued to play to capacity audiences, and in a letter to his son Louis, Berlioz wrote: "I've been asked to put on *Alceste,* as I did *Orphee* at the Theatre-Lyrique, retaining full author's rights; for musical reasons that would take too long to explain, I have declined the offer. Those people think that money can persuade artists to do things directly against their conscience, but I have proved to them that this idea is false". He added "*Les Troyens* has definitely been accepted by the Opera. But works by Gounod and Gevaert will be staged before mine which will take two years. Gounod has climbed over the body of Gevaert, who was due to be performed first, and neither of them is ready, whereas I could go into rehearsal tomorrow. Gounod's work cannot be performed until March 1862 at the earliest, and my refusal to put on *Alceste* is upsetting a lot of people. They should not waste time and money insulting a masterpiece by Gluck but could put on *Les Troyens* right away. However, as that is the logical thing to do, it will not happen. Liszt played at court last week for the Emperor, and yesterday he was made a Commandeur de la Legion d'Honneur. Oh to be a pianist!"

In December, 1860, Pauline told Julius Rietz that she was having a little rest from her theatre and would probably not sing there again until March 1861, as they were performing new operas, and she asked him if it would be possible, if she had a fortnight's leave of absence, to give 'Orfeo' in Dresden. She longed to see him, and seized at the chance for them to work together again. In the early days of their friendship, she had written to him from Weimar: "Who would have thought, you say, that you would so soon address me as your friend? I felt from the very beginning of our acquaintance that we 'must' be friends, sooner or later. Do you not remember how friendly I was with you from the beginning? It is not always the case with me, but you were wonderfully congenial, and my warm affection drew me toward you – I think that initially you were astonished, mistrustful, and yet pleased were you not? Perhaps I seemed too familiar, too demonstrative, to feel deeply and seriously? Too 'southern' in my behaviour toward you to be sincere? Confess that you were a little afraid of me! The proud, self-absorbed man resented the invasion of his life, of his lonely, sacred 'ego', by a foreign element – and would not permit his repose to be disturbed by what might prove an illusion – am I not right? But I recognized the good, high-souled Man behind the diffident, stiff-necked 'Bear', and would not allow myself to be discouraged, and believe that you were rather glad of it."

At first they had written to each other at least every other day, and when she was in Weimar, she said she had a good excuse to visit Rietz in Leipzig as the Duke of Altenburg desired to hear her. However, she didn't go behind Louis's back, but sent him a telegram, saying that she intended to visit her colleague. There was, therefore, nothing clandestine about her friendship with the conductor, and she said that it gave Louis pleasure to know that she had loving friends. She told Rietz that Louis looked very cold, but had a warm heart, and a mind far superior to her own. She added that he worshipped art, and thoroughly appreciated the beautiful and the sublime. His sole fault was that he lacked the childlike element, the impressionable mood, but concluded " isn't that splendid – to have 'only one' fault?!"

Rietz did not take up Pauline's offer of a performance of 'Orfeo', and she decided to take a well earned holiday instead. By the time she wrote to him again on December 15th, she was comfortably settled in the attractive town of Bordeaux in south western France and told him: "In Paris, they are awaiting Wagner's 'Tannhauser' with ironical impatience. While waiting, the fellow does every thing possible to 'indispose the public'. She said that his book provoked indignation in all who read it, and that Berlioz was raving because Wagner had written a scene for Mme Tedesco, who was to sing the part of Venus, in his very latest style and the poor woman could not possibly commit it to memory. Wagner had been ill for a fortnight, and there were no rehearsals during that time, so the chorus had forgotten everything, and the whole thing had to be rehearsed from the beginning. Mme Tedesco was Italian, as was Morelli and he had chosen these singers, who understand his music the least, for leading roles.

In the early part of 1861, rehearsals for 'Tannhauser' began in earnest. No expense was spared and Wagner was told that he could have as many rehearsals as he liked and could choose his own cast. Edmond Roche and Charles Nuitter translated the German text into French, sumptuous scenery was designed and properties prepared. The number of rehearsals broke all records, amounting in all to something in the region of one hundred and sixty four, and Wagner entirely re-wrote the opening Venusberg scene and made a number of minor changes to the work itself.

On good advice, he printed a resume of his aims and opinions, but there were numerous upsets, quarrels and disputes, and finally a complete rupture with the conductor, Dietsch, whom Wagner considered incompetent, but could not get rid of. Finally, at a cost of around £8,000, the performances began on the 13th of March. In the event the whole thing was a disaster, due to cabals and enmities, and the disappointment and rage demonstrated by the audience because there was no ballet. At a time when fashion dictated that women wore a vast quantity of clothing, when crinolines hid their legs from view and the wearing of boots meant there was hardly even a glimpse of an ankle, a ballet with scantily dressed female dancers, showing a great deal of leg, was considered an absolutely essential part of the entertainment by the male members of the audience, even when it was inappropriate for the work.

Although it has been alleged that Pauline did not like Wagner's music, she was always willing to give it a fair hearing, despite the fact that she was often diametrically oposed to the views held by the composer himself. At a matinee given by Countess Lowenthal she sang excerpts from 'Tannhauser', and she enquired of Rietz: "How does it happen that you did not write to me when 'Tannhauser' was played here? Why did your curiosity to know the real truth not compel you to write me one word, one question? It was the man, above all, who was hissed, far more than the composition. Wagner made himself so detested in advance, by artists and public, that he was treated unjustly, in a revolting manner. They did not wish to hear the music; after that, if they had heard it, they might have hissed just the same! But for all that, Wagner will not have profited by the lesson, because he can always boast that he was the victim of a cabal".

A decade later, according to the singer, Sir George Henschel, Rietz was still performing Wagner's music under sufferance. Henschel had been engaged to sing in 'Die Meistersinger' at the Dresden Opera and Rietz was the conductor. The singer said that Rietz was an excellent musician of the old school, who was known for his ready and biting wit. One day Rietz was supervising a 'Correctur-Probe,'a rehearsal with the orchestra and singers in order to ascertain copyists' errors in the score of 'Die Meistersinger' which they were shortly to perform, and from time to time the whole orchestra would break into bursts of laughter at the 'awful dissonances' in Wagner's music, but one section was very concordant and Rietz told them: 'Gentlemen, this sounds so well – there must be something wrong in the parts!"

After all Wagner's efforts to obtain a production of 'Tannhauser' in Paris it was galling to witness such a debacle and he declared: "The less said the better as to the complicated causes of the disaster. But it was a blow to me; everybody concerned had been paid per month; my share was to consist in the usual honorarium after each performance, and this was now cut short. (He received about 750 francs for a years work). So I left Paris with a load of debt, not knowing where to turn. Apart from such things, however, my recollections of this distracting year are by no means unpleasant".

Thanks to the good offices of Princess Metternich, the widow of the Austrian statesman, Wagner, who had been exiled from Germany since 1849, received permission to 'to re-enter German states other than Saxony', and in

March 1862, this ban was lifted completely and he was allowed to return home without fear of imprisonment.

On May 2nd, Liszt who was in Paris to see his mother, joined Pauline and a group of friends at the composer Halevy's house in the rue de Douai, and heard Halevy's talented young pupil, (and later, son-in-law) Georges Bizet play the piano for the first time. Liszt, who could play anything at sight, fully appreciated Bizet's brilliant sight-reading and masterly playing. Pauline sang some of her Spanish songs, and it is interesting to speculate on how her own songs in this style, and those of her father, influenced such composers as Bizet, Chabrier and Lalo, who all introduced the Spanish idiom into French music. Indeed, there is more than a passing resemblance between Pauline's Iberian flavoured music in the 'Scena d'Hermione' and the card trio and Carmen's soliloquy in the third act of Bizet's 'Carmen', and poses the question, which came first? 'Carmen' was produced in 1875, and Pauline's scena was published in 1887, although, according to an American source, it was first published in 1850. Patrick Waddington considers this to have been unlikely, but the evidence of the music itself points to its authenticity. No doubt Pauline had been singing the scena for some time and Bizet had heard it, and either consciously or unconsciously incorporated it into his Spanish opera.

As Berlioz had cynically noted, Liszt had been invited to dinner at the Tuilleries Palace and feted by Napoleon III and his wife, Eugenie, and one wonders what the Viardots, who utterly despised the Emperor and his regime, thought about that. No doubt they would have considered Liszt a traitor to the democratic cause in accepting this invitation, and maybe Pauline was referring to his political leanings or willingness to compromise, rather than being ruled by his conscience, when she told Rietz about her differences of opinion with him.

Was Pauline a political hypocrite herself? There is no doubt that she sympathised with the republican principles of Louis, George Sand, and other friends, yet, she had long been on very friendly terms with Prince William and Princess Augusta, who became the King and Queen of Prussia in 1861, inheriting one of the most absolute monarchies in Europe. Their daughter, the Grand Duchess of Baden, welcomed the Viardots to court, and Pauline had been well acquainted with Tsar Nicolas I and Tsarina Alexandra Feodorovna, as well as being familiar with her daughter Olga, the Grand Duchess of Wurttemburg, and other members of the Russian and Prussian royal families.

From the mid 1850's, Pauline became a regular visitor to Baden Baden which, during the summer, was the European centre of social life, a meeting ground for royal relatives, where Queen Victoria's step-sister, Princess Feodora von

Leiningen had her permanent residence. It was not difficult to see why Tourgueniev teasingly referred to Pauline as a 'snob'.

Through house imprisonment and censorship, he had suffered at the hands of Tsar Nicolas, and knew just how venal authoritarian power can be. He endeavoured by his writings to inform and expand awareness regarding the evils of Russian society, in the hope of improving conditions for everyone, and it is generally acknowledged that he was a positive influence in bringing forward the emancipation of the serfs, particularly through his 'Sportsman's Sketches', and with the advent of the new tsar, Alexander II, this longed-for reform became reality. By this time, Tourgueniev had already freed his own serfs, but it is ironic that when the important event actually took place in Russia in 1861, he was in France. This fact did not go down well with his compatriots who considered that it was imperative for all Russians to return home for such an event. In answer to Herzen's reproach, he wrote: "What can I do, since I have a daughter I must marry off, and so I am sitting in Paris against my will. All my thoughts, all of myself is in Russia'. Herzen, who would have been only too glad to have been able to return to his own country, thought this a poor excuse.

Paulinette Tourgueniev lived in a comfortable apartment provided by her father, and was cared for by her chaperone and companion, Mrs. Innis, a pious English woman. Tourgueniev was generous with the funds he made readily available to them, and they were free to travel whenever they wished. He acknowledged his obligations to his daughter, but regretted that they had nothing in common, as she loved 'neither music, poetry, nature, or dogs'. Even worse, in his eyes, she did not love Pauline, and in a letter to Countess Lambert written from Courtavenel on the 3rd October, 1860, he said: 'My daughter and I have too little in common (this has to be admitted, although she is an excellent girl); and over the other relationship, which you know about, some sort of sad fog has descended'.

Although the Viardots disliked Louis Napoleon's regime, they admired the German administration. Tourgueniev had studied in Berlin and he appreciated the orderly regulation of Prussian life, in contrast to his own chaotic country, with its lack of proper organisation and distribution of wealth and goods, but that had long been ruled by the iron hand of the tsarist regime. The Viardots thought highly of the German appreciation of music, art and culture, but it is difficult to understand why they didn't look deeper into what it took to hold everything in place. So often, when a country is liberal and the citizens enjoy a large measure of freedom, chaos results, free speech and free thought are difficult to control, intellectuals and writers are suspect because they have the ability to change consciousness, crime soars, and when things get too far out of hand the citizens themselves call for more police and a strong leader. Insidiuously, democratic freedoms long taken for granted begin to diminish, more police are called in to restore law and order and in time, a police state is in place, politicians become more powerful; the strong leader is found and more legislation results, powers are removed from the people, and a dictator is born... chaos retreats and order is imposed, but usually at a terrible price. Next comes the building up of military force, expanionist ambitions leading to the control of other countries and the founding of an empire. However, if all individuals were educated from an early age to develop self discipline and take responsibility for their own lives, obeying laws created not for control but to ensure a willing concensus, then a calm, orderly society that everyone could enjoy would evolve, and a strong leader would not be necessary because true democracy and free-dom would no longer be such a dangerous thing in the eyes of the politicians. Unfortunately, humankind has still a long way to go before such a society is born.

In dwelling on the positive aspects of Prussian life, the Viardots failed to appreciate the measure of draconian control to which the Prussians were sub-ject under their militaristic, authoritarian regime, and the stealthy growth of Prussian power beyond its borders. In this, they were not alone, as many political thinkers were hoodwinked and lulled into a false sense of security, pretty much unaware of the sinister rise in Prussian nationalism.

In England, the Prince Consort had always looked to Prussia as the stabilis-ing force in Europe, and his views influenced the Queen. They were related to many German royal houses, by blood and marriage, and their daughter Vicki was married to the Crown Prince of Prussia, and would eventually become Empress. Despite her great belief in the principle of democracy, Pauline left the intricacies of political debate to others, because she, like Liszt, was an artist, and in a worldly sense, it did them no harm to be seen to be on good terms with crowned heads. However, Pauline was not cynical, she genuinely liked William and Augusta and valued their friendship.

On the 14th of December, 1861, which happened to be Louise Viardot's twen-tieth birthday, Albert, the Prince Consort of England, died of typhoid at the early age of forty-two, and the Queen went out of her mind with grief, shutting herself up at Windsor, away from everyone and everything. Unfortunately, Albert's Prussian sympathies became 'holy writ' to his widow, even when it was proved that Prussia, under the leadership of the excessively ambitious Otto, Prince von Bismarck, was hell-bent on European domination. The Prince Consort had been a highly intelligent and pragmatic man, and had he lived, there is no doubt that he would have perceived the danger and would have advised his wife and her ministers to take early steps to put a stop to Prussia's expansionist policies. It is not beyond the realms of possibility that had he lived longer, his wisdom and foresight might even have prevented the excesses that resulted in the First World War.

Pauline had a great fondness for Germany, the land of the lied, where she had been warmly received in the early days of her career, and where she had many friends. Every year, she spent several months there, and particularly looked forward to her trips to Weimar to see Liszt. Even his small, dark haired, dumpy, cigar smoking mistress, Princess Caroline, received her courteously, although Pauline did not think that this lady, with whom Liszt had now been linked for thirteen years, was the ideal woman for him. She described her as affected and lacking in sincerity in her relations with him, and told Rietz: "I think that what burns in his heart is little more than a straw fire – with a dreadful amount of ashes in his heart – poor devil, I believe him to be utterly unhappy. There is a great deal of bitter sadness which makes me terribly sorry for him, and increases my fondness."

Like Gounod, Liszt was also a perplexing mixture of the showman and the priest, two extremes which he never succeeded in integrating. From his earliest years he had been lionised and feted everywhere he went, but the two opposing forces in his nature gave him little peace, and as he aged he became, at heart, an unhappy man. He relished the glamour that surrounded him, most of it created by himself, and even in his old age, when he devoted the greater part of his time to teaching, his young female students worshipped him. After a time, the glamour would pall, and he would endeavour to live the life of a recluse, shutting himself away, disgusted with the worldliness of his professional life, and determined to write 'great works'. Then, just as suddenly, he would bounce back into the world, craving applause, and longing for fashionable society.

These extremes naturally led to a restless way of life, and in his latter years he travelled incessantly.

He bore a heavy weight of guilt, which he tried to assuage by giving lessons free of charge and donating the profits from his concerts to charitable causes, and in common with Pauline, who always craved work, he had a terrible fear of 'the idle uselessness that frets me'.

Pauline considered that Liszt, as a man of honour, would marry Caroline if her annulment was granted, but she believed that it would not add to the sum of his happiness if the marriage took place. She also thought that the Princess would prefer matters to remain as they were, as she had more power over him as his mistress than she would as his wife.

In Paris, a new Theatre Lyrique was being constructed, but work was behind schedule, so the existing theatre was used for the benefit concert of the bass, Charles Battaille. The programme consisted of act three of 'La Sonnambula' with Gilbert Duprez's daughter, Caroline Vandenheuvel-Duprez, as Amina, and the third act of Gluck's 'Armide' with Viardot, and her pupil, Julienne Orwil, as La Haine.

The critic of 'La France musicale' said that Pauline as Armide 'appeared transported into an ideal world,' but that the chorus was either too small, or under rehearsed, and Heugel commented: "If the Theatre Lyrique encouraged by this attempt, brings back 'Armide' to the stage as it has done with 'Orphee', nothing will be left undone to assist Mme Viardot, who remains sublime in Gluck. The three principal singers shared the honours of the evening, which would have been more profitable if the seat prices had not been increased so much".

It was not only inflated prices that deterred people of sensitivity from going to the theatre, as the upper levels of the auditorium were unpleasant: "Who would choose to enter a *salle* heated by hundreds of gas lights, (which were kept lit throughout the performance) without air, and infected by horrid smells of all kinds"... a reviewer of the old Theatre Lyrique asked, and apparently the remedies were little better than the affliction as witnessed by Pauline's Russian friend Mikhail Ivanovitch Glinka in 1852: 'I rarely went to the theatre because the Parisians use perfume so unsparingly that the air becomes unbearable'. The singers' voices, subjected to the heavy, stale atmosphere and general pollution, must have had to build up great resistance to such conditions in order to function satisfactorily.

Pauline's own benefit took place at the very end of the season, the first part of the concert being devoted to a new opera, 'Le Buisson vert' by Leon Gastinel, after which she sang extracts from Acts, 2, 3, and 4 of Gluck's 'Alceste'; and the third act of Rossini's 'Otello' with Gilbert Duprez.

She repeated the scenes from 'Alceste' at a concert at the Paris Conservatoire, and in a letter to Rietz dated 13th February, 1861she wrote: "I sang a large portion of Gluck's 'Alceste' at the fifth concert of the Conservatoire and everybody declared that such a success has never before been witnessed. We began with the Temple Scene (the march in G) in its entirety, with the choruses, the scene of the High Priest, the oracle as far as the air 'Non, ce n'est point un sacrifice', all inclusive, of course. Then we sang several fragments from the first and third acts of the Italian and French versions, which, combined, form a sublime ensemble. The audience went fairly wild with enthusiasm. As for me, I know that I have never witnessed one in such a state. I am well aware that it is the work that produced such an impression – but, all the same, I am very happy that I was able to sing it with integrity before an audience so worthy to hear it…"

Pauline's singing of the 'Alceste' excerpts whetted the public appetite, and despite Berlioz's misgivings, a production of the entire work was planned with Pauline in the title role.

Berlioz, having refused to work on 'Alceste' was putting all his hopes on a production of 'The Trojans', now that 'Tannhauser' had been taken out of the repertoire of the Paris Opera. But the management was still wary, and invited him to direct a revival of 'Der Freischutz' rather than mount a new opera. After a month, rehearsals of the Weber were terminated, and 'Alceste' replaced it, much to Berlioz's annoyance as his work was over-looked yet again.

On June 21st, 1861, Pauline wrote to tell Rietz the news: "Yes, my best friend, 'Alceste', but the entire part ranges too high for me, and is transposed, that is, only the arias. On the 26th, she wrote again: "Today I have no news to tell you, unless it be that the first act of 'Alceste' makes a great effect on the stage. If the two others do the same, all will go well. What beautiful music! What grandeur! What simplicity! What happiness to sing it!" She said that she had no compunction in transposing her arias down a tone because that was the pitch at which they would have been heard in the eighteenth century,

Pauline's difficulty was that as a famous prima donna she was expected to play leading roles, but at that time they were usually written for sopranos. She herself had created a precedent when she sang the mezzo role of Fides, making it the most important female character in 'Le Prophete', but parts written for mezzos were usually for 'seconde donne', either for young women in 'travesti', or older, character parts.

She arrived on the scene a little too early to take advantage of the plum mezzo roles that would shortly appear, such as Verdi's Amneris and the Princess Eboli, although she did sing Azucena, of course, and Lady Macbeth can be sung either by high mezzos or dramatic sopranos. Wagner created the high mezzo roles of Kundry, Venus, Ortrud, and Brangane, and from Berlioz came Dido and Cassandra in 'The Trojans' and Marguerite in 'The Damnation of Faust'. Saint Saens actually wrote the leading mezzo role of Delilah especially for Pauline, tailoring it to her individual voice and dramatic abilities. There is no doubt that she would have been formidable as Delilah, and it is regrettable that age had caught up with her by the time the work received its premiere.

At the beginning of rehearsals for 'Alceste' Berlioz wrote to his friend, Humbert Ferrand: "Although Count Walewski has been very gracious and well-disposed towards me, he is at the moment very displeased because I've refused to direct the rehearsals of 'Alceste' at the Opera. I've declined this honour because of the transpositions and alterations that have had to be made so that Mme Viardot can sing the role. (Alterations which included adding notes and altering cadences which she could not resist making – the equivalent of adding words and altering the rhymes in Corneille's verse – amounting to a desecration). Such practices are irreconcilable with the views I have held all my life. But ministers, and especially today's ministers, don't really understand such artistic scruples and won't accept for an instant that one of their wishes should be thwarted. So for the moment, I'm unpopular at court. Not that that prevents the whole musical world in Paris and Germany agreeing with me. I'll do no more than go to a few rehearsals and give instructions to the producer, to show the minister I'm not putting up any opposition. The director thinks this show of compliance will be enough to assuage Count Walewski's ill-humour."

From these comments it is seen that to safeguard 'The Trojans', Berlioz allowed himself to be pressured into attending rehearsals of the Gluck opera, despite his misgivings, and on the 21st of October, 1861, the premiere of 'Alceste' took place. Regardless of Berlioz's public refusal to arrange the music to accommodate Viardot's voice, he did in fact edit the score, and supervised the production. As the self-sacrificing wife, Pauline was an ideal interpreter. It was a character and story that appealed to her tremendously; she understood and was completely in accord with this woman who is willing to give up her life, to save the husband she loves.

Despite the fact that Pauline's voice was not ideally suited to the tessitura, she was still a great artist, and she convinced her audiences by the very power and dramatic sincerity of her portrayal. With her trim figure, she wore her Grecian costume well. It was simple, yet flattering, the draped bodice ending just below the waist, with short sleeves, a cloak falling down her back from the shoulders, and a long, full, delicately draped skirt with a deep, patterned border at the hem. She wore a gold head-dress and her hair was drawn back at the sides, and swept into a knot of curls on the back of her head. In later years, her Alceste was remembered with almost as much affection as her Orfeo, and her last performance took place on the 12th of May, 1862, after which she retired gracefully from the Paris Opera, although she continued to sing 'Orfeo' at the Theatre Lyrique until April 24th, 1863. Berlioz told a friend that after the performances of 'Alceste', Count Walewski wrote him a very gracious letter thanking him for producing and conducting rehearsals for 'Alceste', 'this wonderful masterpiece.'

For some time, the Viardots had been seriously thinking of leaving France, to settle permanently in Baden Baden, since Louis would never be reconciled to living under the yoke of Louis Napoleon, as he believed him to be the enemy of liberty, despite the public works he had undertaken that had given employment to the working classes, and his encouragement of agriculture, commerce and industry, in addition to the development of charity and credit organisations. Louis was depressed that there seemed to be no foreseeable end to this regime, yet surprisingly, considering his strong feelings, he and Pauline received the government minister, Count Walewski and his wife, at their Thursday salon. Knowing how disdainful Louis was in all matters concerning the Emperor and his family, Tourgueniev kept quiet about the fact that he accepted invitations to Princess Mathilde Bonaparte's fashionable salon, and even George Sand received Prince Jerome Bonaparte at Nohant.

Pauline had always thoroughly disliked the cabals, pettiness and intrigues of Parisian artistic life, but had learned to live with them, now, however, the Viardots finally decided that they had had enough and it was time to leave Paris and make their home in Germany. What probably pushed them into making the decision at that particular time, was the fact that when Berlioz's opera 'The Trojans' finally went into production at the Paris Opera, Pauline's name did not appear on the cast list. From a comment in one of his letters written earlier, Berlioz had said that it was her suggestion that she should sing either, or both of his heroines, but he was non-committal.

When she discovered that she had been passed over in favour of other singers, she was absolutely shattered and felt totally betrayed by Berlioz. She had been a true friend to him, both personally and professionally, at one of the darkest periods of his life, and had believed him when he protested his love and great need of her. Now, she felt cast aside like the proverbial glove, and it was galling in the extreme.

Maybe the Opera management had their own ideas about which singers they wanted in 'The Trojans', although with her success as Alceste, it is hard to believe that Pauline was not given consideration, and even if she was surplus to requirements, surely Berlioz, as the creator of the work, would have had a large say in the casting and could have fought for her? There seems to be little doubt that Pauline had compromised herself with Berlioz by her performing Alceste against his wishes, and by her lack of success as Leonora. The composer was a perfectionist, a committed, dedicated artist, who lived for and through his work, and would not compromise. To him, the music and its demands were paramount, and he might have had an easier artistic life, and would certainly have made more money, and friends, had he been less idealistic, but it was against his nature to allow even personal friendship to stand in his way, any more than Pauline herself would have done, if the truth were told. He did not think that she was suitable for either Dido or Cassandra, and he had suffered enough in the past by allowing Marie Recio to spoil his music, although, of course, there was no comparison between that untalented woman, and the 'divine' Pauline.

No doubt, it had long been accepted 'on the grapevine' that as Pauline was so close to Berlioz, he would offer her a part in his opera, and it must have been a great effort for her to put on a 'brave face', when her colleagues and friends showed their surprise that she had not been chosen. Rejection is always hard to bear, but stage performers experience it more than most people because theirs is such a fiercely competitive profession, and they become inured to it, but it is doubly hurtful to be rejected by a colleague who is also an intimate friend, and has professed undying love.

Pauline had her pride, and she knew that her enemies would be crowing, so she determined to make the first move and forestall speculation by announcing that she would retire from the Paris Opera after her last performance of 'Alceste'. The reason given was that she and her husband had chosen to live in Baden Baden, where she intended to concentrate on composition and teaching, although she would still sing in Germany.

Berlioz loved Baden Baden, and told two of his nieces in a letter of the 29th June, 1861: 'Once there you'll never want to leave. It's a garden, an oasis, a paradise, and staying there is no more expensive than anywhere else. If you're fond of flowers, that's the country, they're everywhere. And what mountains and ruins! What donkey rides! What lunches at the goat farm (where there are seventy white goats) and in addition a whole society of Parisians, Russians, Italians and Germans who will be asking me to introduce them to you. And sulphur baths, which restore one's health in five minutes!"

In the summer of 1861, Berlioz had been invited by an American impressario, probably Max Maretzek, to go to the United States, but he declined, the reasons being that the American Civil War had just begun, and he did not want to be away from Paris while 'The Trojans' was in production. In addition, he told Humbert Ferrand that he couldn't overcome his antipathies regarding that "great people and its 'utilitarian attitudes' because of a lack of keenness in my appreciation of money."

On June 13th, Berlioz's wife, Marie, died suddenly, and in a letter to Louis, Harriet's son, who was at sea at the time, he said that his nieces had offered to come to be with him, but he felt it was better to remain on his own. He added that he would appreciate it if Louis would join him in Baden Baden in early August, if he could get leave from his ship, although he was not sure how much money he would be able to spare him for the journey from Marseilles, he was also anxious that the young man might be tempted to gamble in that den of iniquity. Marie had been visiting friends in St. Germain en Laye when she died, and Berlioz had the expense of bringing her body home. He wrote: "Yesterday my mother-in-law came back from a visit to St. Germain. When I didn't arrive for dinner on Tuesday, she knew that something must be wrong. She arrived there soon after M. and Mme Delaroche and I had left, and saw her daughter's corpse... Half out of her mind, she remained there and has been looked after by one of her friends; you may imagine how distressing it was when we met again."

Despite the unhappy life he had lived with Marie, now that she was dead, he told a friend: "Yes, it has been a terrible blow. She was prepared for this death, but I was very far from being so. I'm not sure how I shall manage life on my own now. My friends are my only hope." It was his mother-in-law who came to his aid, taking over the reins of his household and looking after him until his own death, seven years later.

Princess Caroline's letters were a consolation to him, but he didn't have her religious convictions, and told her: "The insoluble enigma of the world, the existence of evil and pain, the furious madness of the human race, and its stupid ferocity, which it slakes by making scapegoats of the most inoffensive of mortals, and seeks to destroy itself, such things have reduced me to the glum, despairing resignation of the scorpion encompassed by fire. All I can do is resist wounding myself with my own sting."

He said that he suffered from physical ills, and was often beset by neuralgia, yet, one can imagine that after the initial shock of her death, he found life without Marie rather easier to cope with than it had been before. The light on the horizon was that at last 'The Trojans' would appear before the public, and he was finishing a one-act opera comique, entitled 'Beatrice and Benedict' based on scenes from Shakespeare's 'Much Ado About Nothing', which would open the new theatre recently built in Baden Baden. He told Ferrand " Benazet (the king of Baden Baden) is having it produced next year (if I think that's the right moment, which isn't certain). We shall have singers from Paris and Strasbourg. It needs a woman with so much spirit about her to play Beatrice! Will we find her in Paris…?"

To his friend, Princess Caroline had said that he believed all was going well, and that in addition to Shakespeare's characters, he had invented a silly ass of a choirmaster called Somarone 'whose asininities are ridiculous. I'd give a lot to be able to let you hear them." He added that he had despatched the score of 'The Trojans' to her the day before.

On the 4th of February 1862, he told his brother-in-law that he was too busy to leave the city, as he was occupied with preliminary rehearsals for his two act opera for the inauguration of the new theatre in Baden-Baden. "It'll be performed on the 5th or 8th of this coming August. Benazet, as always, has been the perfect gentleman; he asked me which actors I wanted, I gave him the list and he has engaged them all. The chorus will come from Strasbourg. God knows the money that involves, and for two performances!" Originally, Berlioz had envisaged 'Beatrice and Benedict' as a one-act opera, but as the writing progressed it grew into a two-act work.

In March, of the same year, 'La Reine de Saba' a new work by Gounod appeared at the Opera, and Berlioz told Auguste Morel: "I'm trying to give a little support to this wretched Gounod who has just had the worst fiasco ever seen. There's nothing in his score, absolutely nothing. How does one support something which has no bones or muscles? It's his third fiasco at the Opera; no doubt he'll go on to a fourth!"

In the summer the Viardots visited Baden Baden for the opening of the neo Baroque theatre, and heard the premiere of Berlioz's new opera. As Baden is such a small place, it would have been difficult for Pauline to avoid meeting Berlioz at this time, and although she would have wished his new opera to be successful, there is little doubt that their old intimacy was over. Berlioz had wounded Pauline deeply, and she would never forget what she saw as his betrayal. On August 10th the composer wrote to his son: "A great success! Beatrice was applauded from beginning to end and I was recalled I don't know how many times. All my friends are delighted.".

Tourgueniev left his daughter in Paris and joined the Viardots in Baden where he stayed for two months, 'reading, writing nothing, driving around, shooting, and seeing the Viardots frequently'.

Despite the fact that Louis was now sixty-two and not always in the best of health, one of the reasons for his new choice of abode was that he was assured of a grant deal of game in the surrounding mountainous, forested countryside.

During the next few months, the Viardots finally tied up loose ends in order to move permanently to Germany. Pauline continued to fulfil engagements in Paris, and in a concert in 1863 she performed the 'Nuit paisable' from Berlioz's 'Beatrice and Benedict'. Her portrayal of the heroine was hugely admired, and on the 24th of April 1863, by popular request she gave another performance of 'Orfeo'at the Theatre Lyrique. It was enormously successful and there was such a clamour for tickets, that a second performance had to be scheduled.

With her official French retirement, Pauline acknowledged that after all the heartache, and striving, she had triumphed in the one operatic firmament that had always mattered to her above all others. Paris was her own particular 'Mount Olympus', and despite her reservations about Parisian taste, and regardless of the success she had known in other great cities, to her this meant the fulfilment of a lifetime. She had reached the summit of her art, and it was time to go, although really it was only a semi-retirement, as she would continue to sing in Germany. The years of fame had reached their zenith, and she could leave while she was at the top of the musical profession. There was nothing further to hold her in Paris where, except for her successes in 'Le Prophete' and 'Orfeo', she had always felt unappreciated. But now she was vindicated and she turned her face optimistically towards Baden; loving change, she relished the thought of her new life and looked forward to the challenges and adventures awaiting her.

Around this time, Clara Schumann's daughter, Eugenie, wrote an appreciation of Pauline Viardot's art: "She once sang a duet with a tenor, and her part ended with a shake. She held on and on; the audience was breathless; her partner glanced at her in amazement, then he offered her a chair. She smiled and continued her shake. He drew out his watch and held it towards her. When at last she ended with a perfect appoggiatura, the audience broke into thunderous applause. An encore was insisted upon; she sat down at the piano and sang a Chopin mazurka to French words. Turning sideways to her audience, she gave a performance such as I have never seen or heard since. She sang, spoke, acted, smiled so that each individual felt she was singing, speaking, smiling for him alone. Not a muscle in her face remained inactive; vitality, fire, charm, animated every feature. Had it been done for mere effect by anyone who was not a genius, one would have thought it grotesque, but no-one could ever have felt this about Pauline Viardot. She studied effects in minutest detail; but is it not the highest art which, after having given the artist sleepless nights and many hours of strenuous work, appears perfectly simple and spontaneous? Pauline Viardot's art was like this. She gave of herself, and expressed her own personality to perfection."

The Viardots let the house in the rue de Douai where they had lived since 1848, then they closed Courtavenel, leaving the keys and instructions for its maintenance with their good friend, Dr. Frisson, who had brought Paul Viardot into the world. They left Paris with mixed feelings, glad to be away from all the petty politics, but knowing that they would miss their true friends, their enjoyable Thursday salons, and the happy, intimate Sunday 'at homes'.

Had they been able to look ahead they would have seen that seven of the happiest years of their lives lay ahead of them. They bought a charming, picturesque house in an idyllic setting with wonderful, mountain views, with a large expanse of land in which Pauline built a theatre. Here her children, students, and friends performed the operettas which she wrote to libretti by Tourgueniev, for whom a substantial villa was constructed next door to the Villa Viardot.

Pauline was probably more content now than at any time in her life. The tremendous urge to perform and conquer, which had driven her relentlessly since 1838 had weakened considerably, and the stresses of performing and the toll on her nervous and emotional energy were lessened because she only appeared when she chose and in roles that she still wanted to sing. She had the freedom to be creative and she composed prolifically. Students came to her from everywhere, and her international reputation as a teacher was formidable.

Everybody who was anybody visited Baden Baden in the summer months, and Pauline became a great musical hostess, highly influential, respected and courted by anyone with pretensions to a career in music. Clara Schumann also fell in love with Baden, and rented a house in the Lichtentaller Allee, where she and her children spent each summer for several years, and her friend, Johannes Brahms followed her there and settled into an apartment in the Maximilian Strasse. As Baden is small, there was a great deal of socialising and visiting because every body was within easy walking distance.

Louis and Tourgueniev had all the hunting they desired, and plenty of time in which to collaborate on literary projects and translations, happy because Pauline was happy. For once, they were able to live a more structured life, no longer gypsies rushing from place to place, although Pauline, after a life-time on the move, still felt the need to go to Paris, Weimar, and other familiar places from time to time, but generally, she was content to stay in Baden in the summer and in Karlsruhe in the winter.

The performances in her little theatre became part of the social scene, and people fell over themselves to obtain invitations. Here, a motley crowd rubbed shoulders with Pauline's old friends, the King and Queen of Prussia, and their son, Crown Prince Frederick, and his wife, Princess Victoria. The English Queen's half sister, Princess Feodora of Leiningen, and the reigning Duke and Duchess of Baden were frequent visitors to the Viardot home, as were the Grand Duke and Duchess of Wurttemburg, and the aristocratic statesmen, Prince von Bismarck and Count von Moltke. Pauline often saw old friends and colleagues such as Liszt, Berlioz, Saint Saens, Anton and Nicolai Rubenstein, Joseph Joachim, Johann Strauss II, and the Hungarian violinist, Leopold Auer, and even Grisi and Mario were no longer so awful when one didn't have to work with them. Tourgueniev had many Russians friends who came to see him, and there was a constant stream of writers, artists, musicians, and politicians at the Villa Viardot.

It was an idyllic life and the Viardots, their children and Tourgueniev enjoyed the happiest of times, until the dark, lowering clouds of 1870 erupted into war, and they became exiles, but that, as they say, is another story...

APPENDIX: THE ACCOMPANYING CD

SONGS BY PAULINE VIARDOT GARCIA

Barbara Kendall-Davies (soprano), Jillian Skerry (piano)

AU JARDIN DE MON PÈRE (16th Century poem, anonymous)

Au jardin de mon père il y croit un rousier
Trois jeunes demoiselles L'y si vont ombraiger.
Aymezmoy ma mignonne, Aymezmoy, sans danger,
Ma mignonne, Aymezmoy sans danger!
Mignonne, Aymezmoy!

Trois jeunes demoiselles L'y si vont ombraiger,
Trois jeunes gentilshommes L'y si vont regarder!
Aymezmoy, ma mignonne, Aymezmoy sans danger.
Ma mignonne, Aymezmoy sans danger.

Je choisy la plus belle Et la priay de m'aimer!
Mon père est dans sa chambre,
Allez luy demander!
Aymezmoy, ma mignonne, Aymezmoy sans danger.
Mon père est dans sa chambre, Allez luy demander..
Et s'il en est content, et s'il en est content,
Et s'il en est content, Je me veux accorder!

SOLITUDE (Turquety)

La primevère mourante
Aspirait la brise errante,
Et le printemps de retour
Berçait d'un souffle de rose
Le nid où l'oiseau repose,
Quand je vins rêver d'amour——

Et l'image accoutumée
De ma jeune bien aimée,
Aussi belle qu'un beau jour.
Glissait comme une ombre douce,
Parmi les fleurs et la mousse,
Quand je vins rêver d'amour.

Adieu, ville aux bruits sans nombre,
La campagne fraîche et sombre,
Voilà mon dernier séjour;
Pauvre oiseau de la vallée,
Je reviens chercher l'allée,
Qui me fait rêver d'amour.

IN DER FRÜHE (Mörike)

Kein Schlaf noch kühlt das Auge mir, dort gehet schon der Tag herfür an
    meinem kammerfenster.
Es wühlet mein verstörter Sinn noch zwischen Qualen her und hin,
Und schaffet Nacht gespenster, und schaffet Nacht gespenster.
Es wühlet mein verstörter Sinn und schaffet Nacht gespenster.

Aengste quäle dich nicht länger meine Seele!
Quäle dich nicht länger meine Seele!
Freu' dich, freu' dich, freu' dich! Schon sind da und dorten
Morgenglocken wach geworden,
Morgenglocken, Morgenglocken, Morgenglocken wach geworden.

BERCEUSE (de Chatillon)

Enfant, si tu dors, Les anges alors T'apporteront mille choses:
Des petits oiseaux, Des petits agneaux, Des lys, des lilas et des roses,
Puis, des lapins blancs, Avec des rubans
Pour traîner ta voiture; Ils te donneront Tout ce qu'ils auront,
Et des baisers, je t'assure!
Enfant, dors à mes accords, Dors, mon petit enfant, Dors! Dors! Petit enfant!

J'entends l'éléphant du grand Mogol, il s'avance, Portant sur son dos
Deux palanquins clos Que lentement il balance, lentement, lentement il
   balance!
Dans les palanquins sont les lapins blancs Qui vont traîner ta voiture....
Tu n'entends pas mon murmure, Enfant, dors à mes accords, Dors, mon petit
   enfant,
dors! dors! dors! dors!

INDECISION (Tuscan folk poem)

So innamorata di due giovinotti, Uno de due non so qual lasciare
Quel piccinino mi par il piu bello
Quello piu grande non posso lasciare
A quel piccino gl'ho dato la vita
A quel piu grande la palma fiorita
A quel piccino gli ho dato l'alma
A quel piu grande una fiorita palma.

Quello piu grande mi par tanto bello
Non so se l'e, o se'amore m'inganna
Ma quel piccino mi par anche bello
Perche l'ha fatto bello la sua mamma
Perche l'ha fatto bello e colorito,
Pare un rosajo quando gli e fiorito

So innamorata di due giovinotti,
Uno de due non so qual lasciare,
Quel piccinino mi par il piu bello,
Quello piu grande non posso lasciare
A quel piccino gli ho dato l'alma
A quel piu grande la palma fiorita
A quel piccino gli ho dato l'alma,
A quel piu grande una fiorita palma.

REPROCHES (Tuscan folk poem)

C'era una volta 'che con voi parlarva
Ora non son piu degna di vedervi
Alor se per la via v'in contrava

Bassava gl'occchi e il cor si rallegrava
Adesso' che son priva dell amore
Abbasso gli occhi, e convien chio mora! Adesso che son priva dal mio bene,
Abbasso gl'occhi E morir mi conviene!

Prendi colle tue mani un coltel d'oro
Ferisci l'alma mia con tuo diletto..
Cosi Vedrai se t'amo, se t'adoro, Cosi vedrai, s'e ver quel che t'ho detto
S'egli e la verita, caro amor mio,
Per un' che s'apre il petto e dice addio
S'eglie la verita, mio dolce amore,
Per lei che spira e chi ti dona il core.

1. AU JARDIN DE MON PÈRE: Three pretty girls are sitting in the shade of a rose bush in my father's garden, quietly observed by three handsome youths. Love me, my darling, love me without fear. My father is in his room, ask him for my hand, and if he consents, I will be yours.
2. BERCEUSE: Go to sleep, baby, and the angels will bring you many lovely things; little birds, little lambs, lilies, liac, roses, white rabbits with coloured ribbons to pull your little carriage, and lots of kisses. Sleep! I can hear the Great Mogul's elephant coming; it is carrying two closed palanquins in which the white rabbits ride. Now go to sleep....sleep!
3. IN DER FRÜHE: No light steals through my window, and sleep refuses to close my eyes. My thoughts toss and turn through my mind, tormenting me. My soul longs to be at peace, and I will greet the dawn with joy when the clocks chime the beginning of the new day.
4. INDECISION: I am in love with two young men, one is short, but very handsome, just as his mother made him; the other is tall and seductive, but I can't decide which one to accept.
5. REPROCHES: We used to talk happily together, but now you pass me by in the street without a word. Though you cause me suffering, my heart rejoices when I see you, and I would prefer to die than live without you. Take a knife and stab me, and you will find the words 'I adore you' inscribed on my heart.
6. SOLITUDE: The primroses are dying, but they will return next spring, and the breeze will carry the scent of the roses through the tranquil countryside, as I dream of love, far away from the noisy town.

Translations by Barbara Kendall-Davies

Abel, Mr., English acquaintance of
Pauline Viardot, 354
Aberdeen, George Hamilton Gordon, 4th
earl of, (1784-1860), statesman, 342
Adam, Adolphe Charles (1803-56)
French opera and ballet composer,
80, 103, 104, 158, 226, 303
Adelaide, dowager Queen of England,
(1792-1849) widow of William IV,
121
Agoult, Marie Comtesse de, (1805-76)
mistress of Franz Liszt wrote under
the pen name of Daniel Stern, 12, 38,
39, 85, 86, 111, 118, 119, 128, 132,
133, 188, 190, 192, 205, 206, 218
Aguado, Alexandre, Marquis de las
Marismas, Spanish banker and art
collector, 97
Albert, Prince Consort, (1819-61)
husband of Queen Victoria, 22, 65,
121, 203, 204, 255, 293, 339, 346,
370
Albertazzi Emma, (1814-47) (née
Howson) English operatic mezzo,
245
Alboni Marietta, ((1826-94) Italian
operatic contralto, 62, 71, 245, 259,
298, 300, 346, 378, 380
Alexandra Feodorova, (1797-1857),
Empress of Russia, formerly
Princess Charlotte of Prussia, wife of
Nicolas I, 177, 180, 193, 239, 357,
416
Alexander II of Russia, (1818-81), son
of the above, 357, 417

Alkan, Charles Henri Valentine
Morange, (1813-88), French pianist
and composer 156
Alt, Salome, mistress of Wolf-Dietrich
von Raintenau, Prince Archbishop of
Salzburg, 33, 36
Altenburg, Duke of, German aristocrat
and art patron, 413
Annenkov, Pavel Vasilevich, , (1812-
87), Russian literary critic, 229, 405
Arago, Etienne, Postmaster General,
Prov. Govt. 1848, 138, 199, 232,
257, 311
Arditi, Luigi, (1822-1903) Italian
composer and conductor, 387, 389,
391, 411
Artemovsky, Russian bass baritone, 174
Artot, Marguerite Josephine Desire
Montagney, (1835-1907), pupil of
Pauline Viardot, 356
Astanieres, Francois-Ursale-Adolphe,
Baron d', from whom the Viardots
purchased Courtavenel, 186, 187
Auer, Leopold, (1845-?) Hungarian
violinist, 429
Augier, Emile, (1820-89), French
dramatist and librettist, 276, 278,
298, 309, 310, 318
Augusta, Princess of Saxe-Weimar,
(1811-90), Crown Princess of
Prussia, Queen, 1861, Empress 1871;
19, 20, 163, 177, 206, 239, 370, 374,
416, 418
Augustine, (A.D.354-430) Christian
saint and theologian, 278
Austen, Jane, (1775-1817), English
novelist, 109

Beriot, Marie, née Huber, second wife
of Charles, 141
Beriot, Charles Wilfred, (1833-1913)
pianist, son of Charles de Beriot and
Maria Malibran, 10, 25
Berlioz, Louis, son of Hector Berlioz,
348, 397, 413, 417, 425, 426
Berlioz, Louis Hector, (1803-69) French
composer, 47, 48, 104, 123, 139,
202, 206, 213, 222, 239, 242, 248,
249, 250, 252, 254, 261, 267, 269,
271, 274, 275, 284, 291, 298, 299,
303, 334, 339, 348, 352, 354, 355,
356, 384, 392, 394, 395, 397, 399,
401, 403, 404, 412, 416, 421, 422,
423, 424, 425, 427
Berlioz, Marie, second wife of Hector
Berlioz, see Recio, Marie
Berlioz, Nanci, sister of Hector Berlioz,
242, 250, 261, 274
Berlioz, Adele, sister of Hector Berlioz,
261
Bernhardt, Sarah, celebrated French
actress, 371
Bernini, Giovanni Lorenzo, (1598-
1680), 93
Bertin, Armand, eminent journalist, 230
Bertoni, Ferdinando Giuseppe (1725-
1813) Italian composer, 403, 407
Billard, French historical painter, 210
Billard, Mme, wife of above, 210
Birch, Charlotte Ann, (1815-1901)
English soprano, 136
Bismarck, Prince Otto von, (1815-98),
German Chancellor, 418
Bizet, Georges, (1838-75) French
composer, 416
Blanc, Louis, (1811-82), French
politician, 138, 199, 201, 257, 311,
349
Blacque, Alexis, Mayor of Vaudoy, 187
Blessington, Marguerite, countess of,
(1789-1849) Irish writer, literary

hostess, friend of Prince Regent,
Lord Byron, mistress of Count
Alfred d'Orsay, 65-68, 92, 109, 119
Blessington, Earl of, husband of
Marguerite, wealthy art connoisseur,
67, 68
Boborykin, Piotr, Russian writer, friend
of Tourgueniev, 283
Bocage, Pierre, French actor, friend of
George Sand, 239
Bonaparte, Prince Jerome, (1784-1860)
brother of Napoleon I, 424,
Bonaparte, Prince Louis Napoleon,
(1803-1873) Prince President of
France, 1848, Emperor Napoleon III,
1852, 65, 68, 90, 238, 258, 268, 302,
303, 314, 315, 323, 417, 424
Bonaparte, Princess Matthilde, (1820-
1904) daughter of the above, 424
Bonaparte, Napoleon I, (1769-1821) 3,
17, 54, 102, 103, 131, 186, 209
Bonchi, Italian tenor, 249
Borodin, Alexander Porphyrievich
(1834-1887) illegitimate son of a
Prince of Imeretia, Professor of
Chemistry, Academy of Medicine,
St. Petersburg. Composer, 171
Bosio, Angiolina (1830-1859) Italian
soprano, 309, 347
Botkin, Vasily Petrovich, (1811-69)
Russian writer and critic, 3, 44345,
360, 365, 367,
Bourbonne, French perfume factory
owner, 55
Bourges, Michel de, French writer, 199
Braham, Charles, tenor and composer,
372
Brahms, Johannes (1833-97) German
composer, 382, 429
Brandenburg, Elector of, 16
Brault, Augustine, George Sand's niece,
201, 221, 247